D0226148

User Interface Design

A Software Engineering Perspective

We work with leading authors to develop the
strongest educational materials in computing,
bringing cutting-edge thinking and best
learning practice to a global market.

Under a range of well-known imprints, including
Addison Wesley, we craft high-quality print and
electronic publications that help readers to understand
and apply their content, whether studying or at work.

To find out more about the complete range of our
publishing, please visit us on the World Wide Web at:
www.pearsoned.co.uk

User Interface Design

A Software Engineering Perspective

Soren Lauesen

Harlow, England • London • New York • Boston • San Francisco • Toronto
Sydney • Tokyo • Singapore • Hong Kong • Seoul • Taipei • New Delhi
Cape Town • Madrid • Mexico City • Amsterdam • Munich • Paris • Milan

PEARSON EDUCATION LIMITED

Edinburgh Gate
Harlow
Essex CM20 2JE
England

and Associated Companies throughout the world

Visit us on the World Wide Web at:
www.pearsoned.co.uk

First published 2005

© Pearson Education Limited 2005

The right of Soren Lauesen to be identified as author
of this work has been asserted by him in accordance
with the Copyright, Designs and Patents Act 1988.

Cover Picture by Otto Frello (1995): The Road

All rights reserved. No part of this publication may be reproduced, stored
in a retrieval system, or transmitted in any form or by any means, electronic,
mechanical, photocopying, recording or otherwise, without either the prior
written permission of the publisher or a licence permitting restricted copying
in the United Kingdom issued by the Copyright Licensing Agency Ltd,
90 Tottenham Court Road, London W1T 4LP.

The programs in this book have been included for their instructional value.
They have been tested with care but are not guaranteed for any particular
purpose. The publisher does not offer any warranties or representations nor does
it accept any liabilities with respect to the programs.

All trademarks used herein are the property of their respective owners.
The use of any trademark in this text does not vest in the author or
publisher any trademark ownership rights in such trademarks, nor does
the use of such trademarks imply any affiliation with or endorsement
of this book by such owners.

ISBN 0 321 18143 3

British Library Cataloguing-in-Publication Data

A catalogue record for this book is available from the British Library

Library of Congress Cataloging-in-Publication Data

A catalog record for this book is available from the Library of Congress

ARP Impression 98

Typeset in Palatino 9.5/12 and Helvetica by 59

Printed in Great Britain by Clays Ltd, St Ives plc

The publisher's policy is to use paper manufactured from sustainable forests.

Contents

Preface

When you design the user interface to a computer system, you decide which screens the system will show, what exactly will be in each screen and how it will look. You also decide what the user can click on and what happens when he does so, plus all the other details of the user interface. It is the designer's responsibility that the system has adequate *usability* – it can do what is needed and is easy to use. It is the programmer's responsibility that the computer actually behaves as the designer prescribed.

If you are involved in designing user interfaces, this book is for you. You don't just learn about design and why it is important, you actually learn how to do it on a real-life scale.

Designing the user interface is only a small part of developing a computer system. Analysing and specifying the requirements to the system, programming the software and testing and installing the system usually require much more effort, and we will barely touch on it in this book.

Making the user interface

How do you design the user interface to a computer system? Ask a programmer and he may say:

The user interface? Oh, it is so boring. We add it when the important parts of the program have been made.

Ask a specialist in human–computer interaction (HCI) and he might say:

The user interface? Oh, you have to study the users and their tasks. To do this you must know a lot about psychology, ergonomics and sociology. Designing it? Well, you have to come up with a prototype of the user interface and review it with the users. Programming? Oh, that is what the programmers do when the user interface has been designed.

Is there a communication gap here? Yes, for sure. The truth is that it is easy to make a user interface – exactly as the programmer says – but it is hard to make a *good* user interface – and that is what the HCI specialist tries to do.

There are thousands of books on programming. Common to all those I have seen is that the user interface is rather unimportant – it is just a matter of input to and output from the program. Programming *is* very difficult and there is nothing wrong with dedicating thousands of books to it. The only problem is that the programmers don't learn to design the user interface, although typically more than half of a program deals with the user interface.

There are a few dozen books on HCI. They tell a lot about human psychology, how to study users and their tasks, how to test a prototype or a finished system for usability and many other good things. Amazingly, they say very little about the actual design of real-life user interfaces: how many screens are needed, what should they contain, how should we present data, how can we make sure that our first prototype is close to a good solution. To be fair, I have seen a few books that explain about design: Redmond-Pyle and Moore (1995), and to some extent Cox and Walker (1993) and Constantine and Lockwood (1999). However, even here most of the screen design pops out of the air.

Many programmers have looked into the books about HCI. They read and read, but find little they can use right away. And they don't get an answer on how to design a user interface. The books somehow assume that it is a trial and error process, but programmers don't trust this. They have learnt that trial and error doesn't work for programming. Why should it work for user interface design?

Bridging the two worlds

This book tries to bridge the gap. A crucial part of the book is how to design the user screens in a systematic way so that they are easy to understand and support the user efficiently. We call this approach the *virtual window method*. The virtual windows are an early graphical realization of the data presentation. Task analysis comes before the virtual windows and dialogue design after.

I have developed the virtual window method over many years with colleagues and students, and it has become a routine way to develop a user interface. We don't claim that the result is free of usability problems right from the beginning, just as a good program isn't free of bugs right from the beginning. But the large-scale structure of the interface becomes right and the problems can be corrected much better than trial and error.

The cover picture illustrates this. It was painted by the Danish artist Otto Frello in 1995. Imagine that it is the road to good user interfaces. It is a firm road, but it is not straight. However, there is support at every corner (notice the lady who appears repeatedly along the road).

In order to design in a systematic way, we have to draw on the programmer's world as well as the HCI specialist's world, but we pick only what it necessary and adapt it for our specific purpose. Here are some of the major things we draw on:

- How to measure usability

- Usability testing and heuristic evaluation

- Different kinds of prototypes

- Data presentation

- Psychological laws for how we perceive screens

- Task analysis and use cases

- Data modelling (programmer's world)

- State diagrams (programmer's world)

- Checking the design and keeping track of the problems (programmer's world)

To get from these classical issues to the systematic design, we add some novelties:

- Mental models for how users understand what they don't see

- Virtual windows: Presenting data in few screens that cover many tasks efficiently

- Function design of the interface: Adding buttons, menus, etc., to the screens in a structured and consistent fashion.

Programming the user interface

The book is about design of user interfaces down to the detail. Programming the user interface is closely related, so we need teaching material on how to do this too. Here is a pedagogical and even a political problem: which platform to use for the programming. There are many choices, Microsoft Windows, UNIX, HTML, Swing, etc. Ideally, we should have teaching material for each of these.

I have chosen to release a free companion to this book: a booklet on user interface programming with Microsoft Access. The main reason for this choice is that Microsoft Access is readily available to most students as part of Microsoft Office; the connection to a real database is easy; you can quite quickly systems that look real, and you can gradually add the full functionality. Access also exhibits the techniques found on other platforms, such as GUI objects, embedded SQL and event handling. My dream is to have additional booklets that cover other platforms.

The Access booklet is free for download from www.booksites.net/lauesen. It uses examples from this book and shows how to turn them into a functional system.

Design cases covered

The book illustrates most of the design techniques with a system for supporting a hotel reception. This is sufficiently complex to illustrate what happens in larger projects. However, it makes some people believe that this is the only kind of system you can design with the virtual window method. Fortunately, this is not true.

The book shows how to design different kinds of systems too with the same method. Chapter 10 shows how to design a Web system for course evaluation and management. Chapter 11 shows how to design an advanced e-mail system. In section 3.7 we show part of a complex planning system designed with the method. The design exercises in Chapter 17 deal with other kinds of systems, for instance a Web-based knowledge management system, a photocopier, a system for supporting small building contractors and an IT project management system.

Uncovered issues

In the book we pay little attention to aesthetics – how to make the screens look pretty and attractive – or to the entertainment value of the system. These issues are very important in some systems, but in this book we mainly look at systems that people use to carry out some tasks, and here aesthetics is not quite as important. And to be honest, I have not yet figured out how to deal with a esthetics in a systematic way.

The book focuses on systems with a visual interface where a lot of data has to be shown in some way. As a result, we don't discuss verbal interfaces (e.g. phone response systems) or user interfaces for the blind.

We also pay little attention to low-level aspects of the user interface, for instance how to display a button so that it appears in or out of the surface, how a scroll bar works, whether to use a mouse or a touch screen. We take these things for granted and determined by the platform our system has to run on. These issues are important in some projects, and they are excellently covered by, for instance, Preece *et al.* (1994, 2002), Cooper (1995) and Dix *et al.* (1998).

Why doesn't the author mention object orientation? Doesn't he know about it? Yes, he does, very well indeed, but the traditional object-oriented approaches don't really help us designing a user interface in a systematic way. However, we can describe the design results as objects, and this gives an interesting perspective on what the design produces and how it relates to traditional object-oriented approaches (see section 9.2.3).

How the book is organized

The book is organized as three parts that may be combined in various ways for different kinds of courses.

Part A: Best of the classics (Chapters 1–4)

Some classical usability topics: defining and measuring usability; using prototypes, usability tests and iterative design; data presentation and how users perceive what they see on the screen.

Part B: Systematic interface design (Chapters 5–9)

How to design the prototype in a systematic way so that it is close to being right early on. This includes task analysis, designing the virtual windows, defining the system functions and their graphical representation. Chapter 9 reflects on the virtual window approach and compares it with other design approaches.

Part C: Supplementary design issues (Chapters 10–16)

Optional topics that may be included depending on the audience. Examples are systems development in general, data modelling, user documentation and support, design cases for different kinds of systems.

Throughout parts A and B we present the topics in a learn-and-apply sequence: After each chapter you can do something that would be useful in a real development project. You then try it out in a design exercise. Here is a summary:

Chapter 1: Usability. Here you learn to identify the usability problems of an existing system through a usability test. You also learn how to specify and measure usability. In an exercise you specify and measure usability for an existing system, for instance an existing Web site.

Chapter 2: Prototyping and iterative design. You learn the classical design approach for usability: Make a prototype, test it for usability, revise the design, test again and so on. In an exercise you design a prototype of a small system with a few screens, and test it for usability.

Chapter 3: Data presentation. You learn about the many ways to present data on the screen, and the psychology behind them. You apply the rules on existing designs, and you try to design non-trivial data presentations.

Chapter 4: Mental models and interface design. You learn to use the psychological law of object permanence to explain why users often misunderstand what the system does, and how you can avoid it with a systematic way of designing the user interface. You also learn about the two extreme interface architectures: the database oriented and the step-by-step oriented.

Chapter 5: Analysis, visions and domain description. You learn how to model user tasks and data in a way suitable for user interface design. You apply it in a larger design project that continues over the next chapters. (Parts of task analysis and data modelling are explained in the supplementary part, since they are well-known topics needed only for some audiences.)

Chapter 6: Virtual windows design. You learn how to design *virtual windows*: the large-scale structure of the user interface – how many screens, which data they show, how they show it, how you make sure that they support user tasks efficiently and how you check the results. You try all of this in a larger design project.

Chapter 7: Function design. You learn how to convert the virtual windows into computer screens, and how to add system functions to the screens based on the task descriptions and state diagrams. You also learn how to decide whether a function is to be shown as a button, a menu, drag-and-drop, etc. Again you apply it in the large design project.

Chapter 8: Prototypes and defect correction. Based on the previous work products, it is rather easy to make a prototype – ready for usability testing. This chapter has a case study of how this worked in a real project, which problems were found, how they were removed and what happened when the final system was tested for usability. Your design exercise is to make a prototype for your design project, test it for usability and suggest ways to correct the problems.

Chapter 9: Reflections on user interface design. This chapter is theoretical. We review the virtual window method and compare it with other systematic design methods, for instance object-oriented design.

Courses

The book is based on material I have developed over many years and used at courses for many kinds of audiences.

IT beginner's course. The first semester for computer science and software engineering students is hard to fill in. Programming is mandatory in the first semester, and a prerequisite for most other IT courses. So what else can you teach? An introductory course in general computer technology and a database course are often the attempt. We have good experience with replacing either of these with user interface design based on this book. The course has a strong industrial flavour and students feel they learn to design real systems. And in fact, the course is readily useful. It is also a bit difficult, but in another way than programming.

Parts A and B of the book are aimed at this audience. Depending on what else they learn at the same time, we include data modelling from part C and constructing the user interface (the Access booklet). For some audiences, the full course is more suited for two semesters, and will then be an introductory systems development course at the same time.

When we include data modelling, the course replaces a large part of the traditional database course, and prepares students for an advanced database course. On our courses we often have students who have already followed a traditional database course, and to our surprise they follow our data model part enthusiastically. *Now we learn how to use it in practice*, they say.

We take the data model part concurrently with the soft parts about data presentation and mental models (part A). In this way we combine hard and soft topics and keep everyone on board.

We usually finish the course with a 4-hour written exam. This is not a multiple-choice or repeat-the-book exam. The students are, for instance, asked to specify usability requirements, make a data model and design screens for a real-life case. They may bring whatever books they like to the exam. Chapter 17 contains sample exam questions.

IT-convert course. In recent years we have had many students that come from humanities or social sciences and want to become IT professionals. This book has worked amazingly well with this audience. The students are mature and learn fast. They appreciate very much the real-life attitude of the whole thing, and they feel motivated to enter also the hard technical part of the course (the Access booklet).

Courses for mature IT-students. The book makes excellent courses for software engineering or information systems students who know about programming and the technical aspects of design. Parts A and B of the book are suited for such courses. If the students have followed a traditional HCI course already, we treat part A lightly.

In these courses the data model part need not be included, and the Access booklet might be replaced by programming the user interface for any other platform the students might know.

Professional courses. We have used parts A and B of the book for professional courses taking 2–3 days. The participants are systems developers and expert users participating in development. Data modelling is not essential here; the professional developers usually know it already, and the expert users don't have to learn it when they cooperate with developers. Actually, we invented the novel parts of the book through such courses. We observed that some professional design teams produced excellent user interfaces, while others ended up with a messy interface that users found hard to use and understand. By comparing their work, we learned the cause of these differences and used it to improve the systematic design approach.

Course material

Overheads corresponding to all the figures of the book, and solutions to most of the exercises, are available for teachers. See www.booksites.net/lauesen or e-mail the author at slauesen@itu.dk.

The Access booklet is free for download from www.booksites.net/lauesen. The package includes a handy reference card for Access and Visual Basic, plus the hotel system application in various stages of completeness corresponding to the exercises in the Access booklet.

The author's background

At the age of 19, I started to work in the software industry for the Danish computer manufacturer *Regnecentralen*. At that time user interfaces were extremely primitive. We fed data into the system through punched cards or paper tape, and output was printed reports. When we later began to talk about on-line computing, input/output was through typewriter-like equipment. Renting a computer for an hour cost the same as paying someone to work for 30 hours; and computers were 5000 times slower than they are today.

Nobody thought of usability. The customer paid until he had a program that printed results he could use with some effort. Everything to do with computers was a specialist's job.

My first project in 1962 was to develop a program that made the computer play a game invented by the Danish poet and designer Piet Hein. Neither he nor anybody else knew how to win the game. I had never programmed before, so I had to learn that too. And of course I didn't know that it was difficult to make such a program, so it took me a couple of weeks to solve the problem. Piet Hein wanted to have people play the game against the computer at exhibitions, but how could the user interact with the computer? Our hardware developers found a way to connect a bunch of buttons and lamps directly to the multiplier register of the CPU, and I made the program without multiplying anything. We then designed a nice user interface that people could use immediately. I didn't realize that this was the only good user interface I would make until 1973.

In the period until 1973, I developed many kinds of systems, for instance computation of molecule shapes based on X-ray diffraction, administration of pension contributions, optimization of tram schedules and rosters. Later I moved to another department in the company, where we developed compilers and operating systems. These systems became extremely fast, compact and reliable technical wonders. It took me many years to realize that we had made these miracles without understanding that the customers had other interests than speed and reliability. They also wanted usability – efficient task support – which we didn't provide and didn't understand.

In 1973, I moved to Brown Boveri, now part of ABB (Asea Brown Boveri). We were a new department and our first project was to develop a new line of process control systems with colour screens and special-purpose keyboards that could be operated by users with big, insulating gloves. Our first delivery was power distribution control for a part of Denmark. We knew how to make reliable, fast and compact code, but this was the first time I realized that ease of use was also important. If our system failed technically, 300,000 people wouldn't have power. But if the user couldn't figure out how to operate the system, the consequences might be the same. I had never been involved in anything as serious before. We made it, and usability became very good because we were inspired by the way users had controlled the power before.

In 1974–1975, I took temporary leave from Brown Boveri and worked for ILO in Ghana, helping with management consultancy in IT issues. This was the most fascinating year of my life. I learned how different other cultures and value systems could be, and that our own society had gained much in economic welfare and security, but lost a lot in other aspects of life quality. I also learned that I didn't know anything about management and that such knowledge was important. Returning home, I took a business diploma as fast as possible.

In 1979–1984, I moved to a new software division established by NCR in Copenhagen. For some reason I became a manager, but kept being involved in software development – even on the programming level. I soon got two management responsibilities: (1) developing experimental technology for the next generation of products, and (2) assuring that the rest of the division delivered adequate quality in the present products. My main lesson in these years was that there was a very, very long way from proving a new technology to having a multinational company accept it for new products.

Now, where did I learn about usability? Not in industry! In 1984, I became a full professor at the Copenhagen Business School. They had decided to establish a new degree program – Business and Software Engineering. I found it an excellent idea since I had seen so many bright IT people who didn't understand business; and I had seen so many excellent managers who didn't understand technology. There was a communication gap, and educating young people in both areas at the same time seemed a great idea. I was willing to take responsibility for the IT side of the new education.

Working here without the daily pressure of finishing new products gave me time to wonder why the users and customers of all the technical wonders we had made over the years didn't like our systems as much as we did ourselves. I started to study usability and wondered whether users tried to understand what the computer did, or whether they just thought of carrying out their tasks, as most researchers assumed. I ran several experiments and concluded that if the system has a certain complexity, users form a mental model of how it works. They do so unconsciously, and often their model doesn't match with what the system actually does. This is the source of many usability problems. (Norman, 1988, found similar results in the same period.)

At that time, user manuals was a big issue, and I used the mental-model insights to develop ways to write manuals that combined two things at the same time: learning how to carry out the tasks, and understanding – at a non-technical level – what happens in the system. The approach was quite successful, and I served as a consultant for many technical writers and gave courses on writing user documentation.

Later I became more interested in designing good user interfaces – where manuals weren't necessary. During a long cooperation with Morten Borup Harning and varying master's students, we developed the approach that is central to this book.

I had expected that I would return to industry after about five years, but found that the combination of IT and business was fascinating, and that working at a business school helped me open the doors to a wide range of companies. Gradually I became a researcher who worked closely with industry.

In 1999, I moved to the new IT University established in Copenhagen. Now my role seemed to be reversed. At the business school, I had been regarded as the technical guy who didn't quite understand that business was the most important thing, while technology had minor importance. Now my computer science colleagues regarded me as the business guy who thought that business and usability were more important than technology.

This taught me one more thing: balancing between the extremes is very hard but also very important. I have tried to strike such a balance in this book.

Acknowledgements

The ideas behind virtual windows (Chapter 6) were developed by Morten Borup Harning and I, with some input from Carsten Grønning.

I have also learned a lot from cooperation with many of my students, in particular Susanne Salbo and Ann Thomsen who planned and carried out a hit-rate comparison of mock-ups against the real system. I want to thank William Wong for reviewing part of the book and encouraging me to publish it, Jean-Guy Schneider and Lorraine Johnston for helping me develop terminology in some of the areas, Klaus Jul Jeppesen for many insights in the user support area, and Flemming Hedegaard and Jacob Winther Jespersen for trying the entire course material in their own courses and giving me much valuable feedback.

Finally, my colleagues Peter Carstensen, Jan C. Clausen, Anker Helms Jørgensen and Rolf Molich have for many years been my excellent sparring partners in the HCI area, and I am most grateful for the insights I have got from them in many matters.

Part A

Best of the classics

In part A of the book we look at some classical techniques in user interface design:

- How to detect what users find difficult or inconvenient when they use a system, and how to measure the goodness of the system (Chapter 1).

- How to use prototypes and iterative design to come up with a good user interface (Chapter 2).

- How users perceive the contents of a screen and how we can present data to them (Chapter 3).

- What users believe goes on in the system and how it relates to various kinds of user interfaces (Chapter 4).

The classical approaches to user interface design are to a large extent based on trial and error. The designers compose the user interface with their intuition and general understanding of users, and then measure how good the user interface is. If it isn't satisfactory – and they have time to improve it – they revise their design and measure once again how good it is. They will usually have to revise the design many times to get an adequate user interface.

There is one more important classical technique: How to study and describe the users, their tasks and the data they use. In part A of the book, we assume that this is part of an analysis and requirements phase that precedes the user interface design work. In part B of the book, we will expand our perspective and treat parts of the analysis phase together with a more systematic design approach.

The classical design approach works fine for small systems where design by trial and error is sufficient. You might compare it to building a small wooden bridge for bushwalkers. Trial and error is sufficient. However, when the system is larger and more demanding, a more systematic approach is necessary. You might compare it to building a long bridge for heavy traffic over troubled waters. It is much too expensive and dangerous to use trial and error here.

1

Usability

Highlights

- Usability is one of many quality factors.

- Usability has many sub-factors: Fit for use, easy to learn, efficient for daily use. . .

- Usability problems and how to find them with usability tests.

- How to measure and specify usability.

- Key exercises: Specify usability for an existing Web site. Run a usability test to measure it.

You have probably noticed that some computer systems are easy to use. They have high *usability*. Others are a nightmare. They have low usability.

As an example, old text-processing systems were hard to use, and they couldn't even do as much as modern text processors. Modern text processors are fairly easy to use. The main difference between old and new text processors is the user interface. The functionality inside the systems is much the same, yet one interface is easy, another hard.

With a low-usability system, you wonder whether the system is stupid or you are. The general rule in this book is that only the system is stupid. We can make the systems easier to use, but we cannot change human nature.

In this chapter we explain what user interfaces are, and how we can define and measure usability.

1.1   User interface

The user interface is the part of the system that you see, hear and feel. Other parts of the system are hidden to you, for instance the database where information is stored. Although users don't see the hidden parts, they imagine to some extent what is going on 'behind the screen'. This imagination or understanding of what goes on is often quite important, for instance when users have to deal with a system that doesn't work as usual.

When you use a computer, you give it orders, usually by means of the mouse and the keyboard. The computer replies, usually by showing something on the screen or making sounds. Sometimes the situation seems reversed the computer gives you instructions and you have to reply. In both cases we talk about *human–computer interaction*, and we call the system an *interactive* system. (There are also non-interactive systems. A cinema is one example – the customer doesn't interact with the movie. A smoke detector is another example – it patiently looks for smoke all the time, but only tells the user about it when it senses some.)

The interaction with the computer takes place through the *user interface*. In a standard PC, the user interface consists of the screen, keyboard, mouse and loudspeaker (Figure 1.1A). In more advanced systems, the interface may include voice input through a microphone; special buttons, lights and displays; electronic gloves that can feel the movements of your fingers; and eye sensors that can detect where you are looking at the screen.

We can also talk about the user interface to a photocopier, a television or even a car. These devices actually have a hidden computer inside. In principle, we can talk about the user interface to any device, also one without any computer, such as a door or a foldable table. However, in this book we focus on user interfaces to interactive computer systems.

The computer system will often have on-line help, paper manuals, training courses, hot-line support, etc. Some people say that these are parts of the user interface too, others that they are not. Whether you call them user interfaces or not, these things are an important part of the total system as experienced by the user. For this reason it can be important to plan them in connection with the user interface.

Technical interfaces

A computer system may have other interfaces than the user interface. It can have interfaces to other computer systems, for instance an account system. It can also have interfaces to physical processes, for instance temperature sensors, valves, etc. As an example, a chemical factory is computer controlled. The computer system measures the temperature, pressure, etc., and controls the chemical process by opening and closing valves, switching heaters on and off, etc.

Fig 1.1 A System interfaces

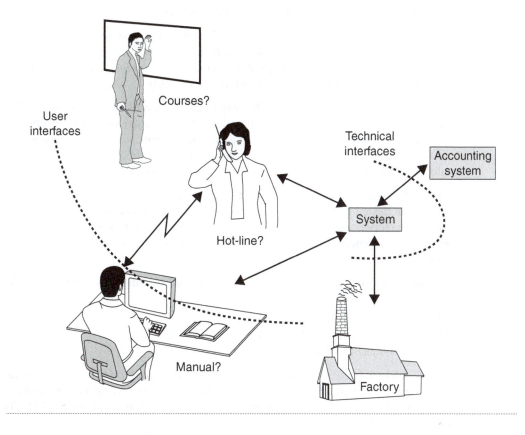

These technical interfaces are not user interfaces since the user doesn't interact directly across them. The user interacts *indirectly* with them through the user interface to the computer.

Design of user interfaces

In principle, it is easy to make a user interface. You just have to make it possible for the user to see and change all data in the system, and allow him to send any command across the technical interfaces.

As an example, assume that the system is dealing with sales and invoicing. It has a database of customers, products and invoices (Figure 1.1B). The user interface would just have to allow the user to create new records in the database, edit the records, print out invoices and delete old records. Modern database systems, such as Microsoft Access, have built-in screens for doing these things, and it is not necessary to program anything to make such a system. As a system developer, you just have to set up the necessary database tables and user windows.

Such a system has adequate functionality, but it will not be easy to use. The users don't get the necessary overview of data for their tasks, they will have to go through too many screens to do simple things and it is not easy to understand how to carry out the tasks. In other words, the system has low usability.

If we insist that the system shall also be easy to use, the problem becomes so hard that few IT-suppliers know how to deal with it. Often they get around the problem by claiming that nobody can define what ease of use means, and even if someone could, you cannot make the system easier to use than it is already. And even if you could make it easier to use, it would be much too expensive to do so.

Fortunately, these IT-suppliers are wrong. You can define what ease of use means, and you can design good user interfaces systematically. This book shows you how. Product developers using these techniques report that it is not more costly. On the contrary, development becomes much easier. Further, the product sells much better.

The professional area dealing with user interfaces and usability has many names, for instance:

HCI: Human–computer interaction
CHI: Computer–human interaction
MMI: Man–machine interface

Many countries have a SIGCHI group (Special Interest Group on Computer–Human Interaction). In the United States, we have ACM/SIGCHI (www.sigchi.org); in the United Kingdom, British HCI Group (www.bcs-hci.org.uk); in Denmark, SIGCHI.DK (www.sigchi.dk).

Quality factors in IT systems

From the system developer's point of view, ease of use is just one quality factor among others. Developers talk, for instance, about:

correctness (few errors in the system)
availability (e.g. access 23 hours a day)
performance (e.g. system responds within 20 seconds)
security (e.g. preventing hacker attacks)
ease of use (often called usability)
maintainability (easy to maintain the program)
. . .

The contrast to the quality factors is:

functionality (that the system has the necessary features)

Fig 1.1 B Quality factors

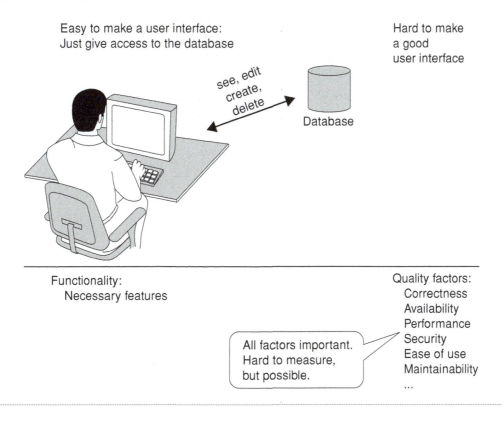

Easy to make a user interface:
Just give access to the database

Hard to make
a good
user interface

see, edit
create,
delete

Database

Functionality:
  Necessary features

Quality factors:
  Correctness
  Availability
  Performance
  Security
  Ease of use
  Maintainability
  ...

All factors important.
Hard to measure,
but possible.

Developers must deliver adequate functionality as well as adequate quality. They focus primarily on the functionality, and they are quite good at it, although they sometimes miss some features. They find it much more difficult to define and deliver the quality, so in this respect usability is not different from all the other quality factors.

Some HCI specialists claim that all quality factors are a matter of usability. Maintainability, for instance, is a matter of usability for those developers that have to correct and enhance the system.

In this book we limit ourselves to usability in daily operation of the system. We also assume that the system works correctly, is available when needed and responds fast enough. In other words, we assume that the correctness, availability and performance factors are okay. It is quite hard to obtain this, but it is not the topic of this book.

Usability. In the book we will focus on two factors that together form usability:

- Functionality. Providing the system features that allow the user to carry out his tasks.
- Ease of use. Providing the features in such a way that it is easy to learn the system and easy to carry out the tasks.

In the next section we go into detail with this definition.

1.2 Usability factors

If you ask programmers what *usability* means, many of them will give definitions such as the system must be menu-based with at most three menu levels; it must have on-line help; it must follow the Microsoft Windows style guide (Figure 1.2). Unfortunately, this doesn't guarantee usability. For instance, most of us know computer systems that look like other Microsoft Windows applications, yet are almost impossible to use.

These attempts at defining usability prescribe a technical solution, but don't catch the essentials: the user's experience when trying to use the system. Can he find out how to use it? Does it make his work easy?

The following definition better catches the essentials.

Usability factors

Usability consists of six factors:

a) **Fit for use** (or *functionality*). The system can support the tasks that the user has in real life.

b) **Ease of learning.** How easy is the system to learn for various groups of users?

c) **Task efficiency.** How efficient is it for the frequent user?

d) **Ease of remembering.** How easy is it to remember for the occasional user?

e) **Subjective satisfaction.** How satisfied is the user with the system?

f) **Understandability.** How easy is it to understand what the system does? This factor is particularly important in unusual situations, for instance error situations or system failures. Only an understanding of what the system does can help the user out.

Ease of use (or *user friendliness*) is a combination of factors b to f.

Developers often say that it is impossible to design a system that scores high on all factors. This may be true, and in practice it may be necessary to specify the level needed for each factor. As an example, a Web-based system for attracting new customers should have emphasis on ease of learning and subjective satisfaction, while a system for air-traffic control should have emphasis on task efficiency and understandability.

In the rest of the chapter we will look at ways to measure the usability factors and specify the level needed in the final system. It is easiest to measure usability in the final system. Unfortunately, it turns out to be much too costly to improve usability at that stage. For this reason it is crucial to find ways to measure usability much earlier, when it is still feasible to change the user interface. Fortunately, this is possible and quite cheap, as we will show throughout the book.

The usability factors above are based on Shneiderman's work (Shneiderman 1998). We have omitted his factor 'few errors', because it is covered by the factors b, c, d and f above. In return, we have added the factor 'understandability'. Traditionally, usability experts were reluctant to talk about the user's understanding. You couldn't readily measure it, and what really mattered was whether the user could perform his tasks. Today, understandability is more recognized. It is crucial for mastering complex systems with many functions, and we can measure understandability in the same way that we give marks at exams.

Game program usability

For some systems, the usability factors above are dubious. One example is game programs. They need not be easy to learn or task efficient – it is no fun if you too easily beat the opponent. So what are the important usability factors? The most relevant one is the subjective satisfaction – how much the users like the game program. But in order to improve a game program that users don't like, we need to dig deeper into the subjective satisfaction.

Rouse (2001) has identified some additional usability factors for games, for instance that games must be entertaining, challenging, fair, and for some, games allow socializing. These factors are important for games, but irrelevant for systems that support user tasks.

Importance of usability

Who is responsible for the usability of the final system? Programmers and other developers take responsibility for the technical correctness of the system and for the necessary functionality (fit for use). But who is responsible for the ease-of-use factors?

Traditionally, it was the user department's responsibility. They had to write user documentation and train users. That was the only way to compensate for poor usability in these traditional systems.

This is slowly changing. Mature development teams feel it is their joint responsibility that the system is easy to use. Although they feel a responsibility, they are still grappling with how to deal with it.

Why is usability more important now than earlier? Because the IT technology has become cheaper and cheaper, while users have become more and more precious. Usability pays in many ways: users save time, more people can use the system, people can handle many computer systems and don't have to specialize in a single system. Furthermore, the technology allows us to do it. The main barriers are that

Fig 1.2   What is usability?

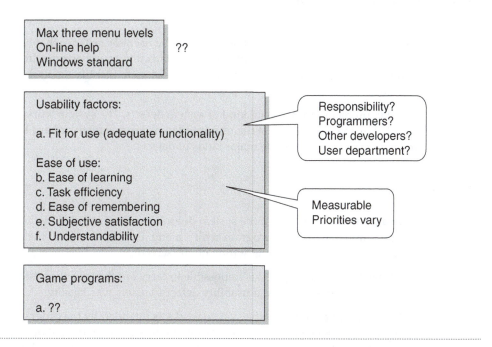

Max three menu levels
On-line help   ??
Windows standard

Usability factors:

a. Fit for use (adequate functionality)

Ease of use:
b. Ease of learning
c. Task efficiency
d. Ease of remembering
e. Subjective satisfaction
f. Understandability

Responsibility?
Programmers?
Other developers?
User department?

Measurable
Priorities vary

Game programs:

a. ??

developers don't know how to achieve usability and they fear it is too costly.
Fortunately, both barriers can be overcome.

1.3   Usability problems

A usability problem is anything that hampers the user, for instance that he cannot figure out how to carry out his task or finds it too cumbersome. In order to improve the usability of the system, it is important to identify the usability problems.

Usability problems are a special kind of system defects. The system works as intended by the developer, yet the user interface is inconvenient or hard to understand. Let us look at the major kinds of defects.

Defect types

- **Program error** (or *bug*). If the system doesn't work as intended by the programmer, we have a program error – a bug. Examples are that the system crashes or shows something wrong on the screen.

- **Missing functionality.** If it is impossible to carry out the task, the system is not fit for use. We classify this as a usability defect – *missing functionality*.

- **Ease-of-use problem.** If the system works as intended by the programmer and it can support the task, yet the user cannot figure out how to do it or doesn't like the system, the system is not easy to use. This is another kind of usability problem. We classify them according to their severity to the user, for instance a *task failure* or a *minor problem*. More on that below.

Here are a few examples of usability problems (Figure 1.3).

P1: The user cannot figure out how to start the search. The screen says that he should use F10, but for some reason he doesn't see it until he has tried several other ways.

P2: The user believes that he has completed the task and that the result is saved, but actually he should have pressed *Update* before closing the window.

P3: The user cannot figure out which discount code to give the customer, although he knows which field to use.

P4: The user says that it is completely crazy having to go through six screens in order to fill in ten fields.

P5: The user wants to print out the list of discount codes in order to put his own notes on it. After many attempts, he calls hot-line. They say that the system cannot do that.

Usually we classify usability problems according to their severity to the user. Here is a classification we often use.

Fig 1.3 Usability problems

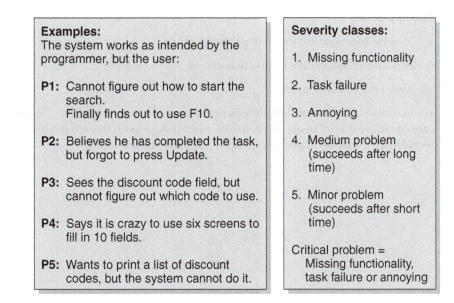

Examples:
The system works as intended by the programmer, but the user:

P1: Cannot figure out how to start the search.
Finally finds out to use F10.

P2: Believes he has completed the task, but forgot to press Update.

P3: Sees the discount code field, but cannot figure out which code to use.

P4: Says it is crazy to use six screens to fill in 10 fields.

P5: Wants to print a list of discount codes, but the system cannot do it.

Severity classes:

1. Missing functionality

2. Task failure

3. Annoying

4. Medium problem (succeeds after long time)

5. Minor problem (succeeds after short time)

Critical problem = Missing functionality, task failure or annoying

Problem classification

- **Missing functionality.** The system cannot support the user's task. Problem P5 is of this kind.

- **Task failure.** The user cannot complete the task on his own or he erroneously believes that it is completed. Problems P2 and P3 are of this kind.

- **Annoying.** The user complains that the system is annoying or cumbersome; or we observe that the user doesn't work in the optimal way. Problem P4 belongs here.

- **Medium problem.** The user finds the solution after lengthy attempts. P1 is this kind.

- **Minor problem.** The user finds the solution after a few short attempts. P1 would have been this kind if the user had found the solution fast.

Problems versus observations. It often happens that one user gets stuck on a certain problem, while another user soon finds the solution. Is the problem then a task failure? The answer is that severity is not a classification of the usability problems, but of the observations (occurrences) of the problems. Problem P1, for instance, might be observed twice. When user A encountered it, it was a task failure; when user B encountered it, it was a minor problem. If many users have task failures for P1, we might call P1 a task failure, but some judgement is involved to do this.

In practice we want to correct the most serious problems, the critical problems.

Critical problem

- Missing functionality for an important task, or

- Task failure that occurs for many users, or

- Annoying to many users.

We may also try to correct less serious problems if we can easily do so. Usually, we cannot ensure that *all* users succeed with everything – even though it would be wonderful. It may be impossible to do so, or it may be too costly.

1.4　Basics of usability testing

The most effective technique to find the usability problems is a usability test. There are many variants of usability tests. Below we outline our favoured, low-cost, high-effective technique. The description should be sufficient for your own first attempt at usability testing. When you have tried it once on your own, you will appreciate Chapter 13, which gives you more detail and practical advice.

Think-aloud test.　During a usability test, we let a user (the *test subject* or *test user*) try to carry out realistic tasks using the real system or a mock-up of it (Figure 1.4). There are several ways to do this. Our favoured technique is to ask the user to *think aloud* – explain what he is doing and why.

Real system.　You may want to find usability problems in a system that is finished or at least working to a large extent. The user will use the system to carry out various tasks.

Prototypes and mock-ups.　Early during the design process, there is no real system to test with. However, you can find usability problems with a prototype of the planned system. The simplest prototypes are mock-ups. They may consist entirely of screens on paper, and the user would fill in the fields by means of a pencil, 'click' on buttons with the pencil, etc. The leader of the test (the *facilitator*) would take paper windows away when they 'close' and bring them up when they open. Mock-ups are very useful early in development because they are fast to make and easy to throw away. More advanced prototypes run on the computer and look right, but have little functionality. (More on prototypes and testing in Chapter 2.)

Test team.　It is best to have two or three persons on the test team: The *facilitator* talks with the user, the *log keeper* notes down what happens, in particular the problems the user encounters. A possible third person can observe how the test proceeds and help the other two as the need arises.

Plan the test

Test users.　When you plan a usability test, you have to find *test users*. Choose people that might be typical users. If we are developing a Web site that will help people find public transportation from one point to another, the test users should be ordinary people with little IT knowledge. IT people will not be good test users since they know too much about what goes on behind the screen. They will not notice problems that would stop ordinary people.

If we are developing a system that will help hotel receptionists do their job, we should use test users with some reception background. Again IT specialists will not be good because they won't notice some problems that would stop non-IT people, while they may encounter problems relating to hotel terminology that wouldn't bother the receptionist.

Test tasks. You also have to choose some *test tasks* or situations where the user will use the system. As an example, if we want to test a system for hotel receptions, a good test task will be to book a room for a guest. There are many other tasks that should be tested too, of course. Choosing the right test tasks is a critical issue if we want to find all usability problems. A good test task should meet these criteria:

- Something the user would do in a *real work situation*. Booking a room for John Simpson is good, but booking one for *Donald Duck* is childish and suggests to the receptionist that the system is not for professional use. *Changing the system set-up* is not a realistic task for a receptionist.

- A full piece of meaningful work (a *closed task*). Booking is good – the receptionist handled the customer's call. *Logging in* is not a good task. The receptionist has not accomplished anything by logging in.

- Stated without *hidden help* – without hints on how to carry out the task.

Hidden help is a matter of how we explain the task to the user. If we are testing a Web site for finding public transportation, don't use a task stated like this:

> **Wrong:** Find a bus connection around 11 p.m. from route 6, stop 12 to route 8, stop 23.

This might be the way the Web site asks for start and end of the trip, but users would not state their problem in this way. You might try a more vivid scenario instead:

> **Better:** You are planning to go to a party tomorrow in 20 Brickwood Street, Brighton. You would like not driving home to 55 Westbank Terrace, Richmond. Is there any public transportation that could help you? How late? And what would it cost?

This also makes it possible for the test user to imagine the situation and draw on his intuition.

Study the system. Finally, you also have to learn how to use the system yourself. Otherwise you cannot understand what the user attempts and where he misunderstood something. If you are a member of the development team, this is easy. If not, you must experiment with the system on your own or have someone to guide you.

Carry out the test

When a test user arrives to the usability test, he is a bit nervous. He is scared of looking stupid. For this reason it is important to explain the *purpose* of the test:

> *We want to find out where the system is hard to understand or inconvenient. We know the system too well, so we cannot see it ourselves. We need your help. If you have problems with the system, it is the system's fault – not yours.*

Fig 1.4 Usability test – think aloud

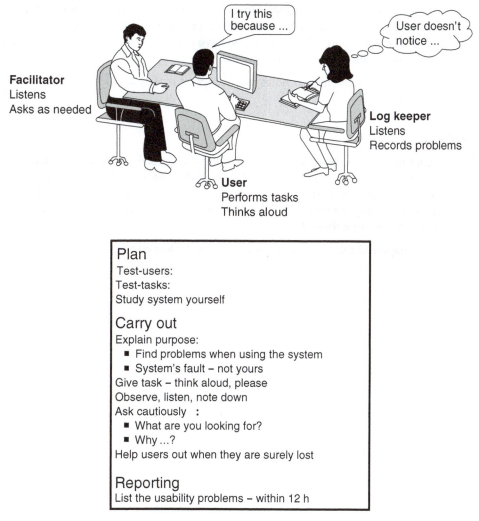

Purpose:
Find usability problems

Facilitator
Listens
Asks as needed

I try this because ...

User doesn't notice ...

Log keeper
Listens
Records problems

User
Performs tasks
Thinks aloud

Plan
Test-users:
Test-tasks:
Study system yourself

Carry out
Explain purpose:
  ▪ Find problems when using the system
  ▪ System's fault – not yours
Give task – think aloud, please
Observe, listen, note down
Ask cautiously :
  ▪ What are you looking for?
  ▪ Why ...?
Help users out when they are surely lost

Reporting
List the usability problems – within 12 h

Talking a bit about daily matters and the user's background also helps the user relax.

Next, you give the user the first test task and ask him to carry it out by means of the system. Invite him to *think aloud* by explaining what he does and why.

Then observe what the user does and listen to him. Write down brief notes on what happens, particularly when something caused problems.

When you cannot understand what the user is doing or why he gets stuck, ask him what he is looking for, and why he did as he did. Don't tell him how to do it until he has had lots of time to find out for himself.

When the user is truly lost and seems unable to succeed on his own, help him out with a hint. In this way he can help you observe areas in other parts of the system. However, when you help him out, you have to record it as a task failure – the user couldn't complete the task on his own.

If you cannot scribble your notes fast enough, it is okay to ask the user to wait a moment.

Reporting

After the test, you have to write a list of the problems the user encountered. They must be in such a form that people knowing the system understand what you write. You must write this list as soon as possible, preferably within 12 hours. Otherwise you cannot any longer understand your own scribbling and remember what happened during the test.

See Chapter 13 for how to write notes during the test and how to report the problems.

1.5   Heuristic evaluation and user reviews

Usability testing may sound cumbersome. Aren't there other ways to identify the usability problems? Maybe we could let a usability specialist look at the screens and point out the problems? This approach is called *heuristic evaluation*. We could also let an expert user look at the screens and discuss them with him. This approach is often called *user review.*

Heuristic evaluation

Heuristic evaluation can be made in many ways:

- We can let usability specialists look at the screens, or we can make fellow developers look at them.

- They can use their sound judgement and earlier experience, or they can use a list of *heuristic guidelines*. Guidelines may, for instance, say that the screens should not be too crowded, the error messages should tell the user what to do, there must be features for undoing, etc.

- Each evaluator may deliver his own list of defects, or we may ask all of them to reach agreement and come up with a common list.

Unfortunately, in many cases heuristic evaluation finds lots of problems, but about half of them are false in the sense that they don't cause problems to real users. It would be a waste of time trying to correct these false problems, but we don't know which of the problems are false. Furthermore, in these cases heuristic evaluation misses about half of the severe problems that real users encounter (Figure 1.5 illustrates this). I have jokingly called this the first law of usability:

> **First law of usability**
>
> Heuristic evaluation has only 50% hit-rate.

Would it help to have more usability specialists look at the screens? Yes, we get a few more hits, but a lot more false problems.

The first law is quite controversial, and many HCI specialists consider heuristic evaluation the best technique. My colleagues and I have often observed the low hit-rate, and several authors report similar results (e.g. Bailey *et al.* 1992; Desurvire *et al.* 1992; Cuomo and Bowen 1994). In section 2.3 we look at an example. It is a test of an early prototype, and the heuristic evaluators are fellow developers. In such cases the first law works well. If you carry out exercises 2.2 and 2.3, you will make an early prototype of a system, usability test it, and make a heuristic evaluation. You can then see whether the law worked in your specific case.

Although I have called it a *law of usability*, it doesn't work in all cases. Section 14.4 shows a precise comparison of usability testing and heuristic evaluation for a finished Web site. The evaluators were among the best HCI people in the world. In this case there were no statistically significant difference in hit-rates, but heuristic evaluators rated the problems as more serious than usability testers.

Although heuristic evaluation is quite popular, we strongly warn against it as the primary approach – particularly for early prototypes. It may supplement a usability test, but cannot replace it. If you get a heuristic evaluation of a system you design, there will be some problems that you immediately recognize as things you didn't think about. Work on them, but ignore for the time being problems that you feel are false. With a usability test it is different: you cannot reject problems as false. Some user actually encountered this problem. Chapter 14 explains much more about heuristic evaluation.

User review

A review is normally made with expert users who know the application area very well. Go through the screens with the expert user, show how they are to be used, and discuss how various tasks are carried out, what is missing, what is cumbersome, etc.

Such reviews are important for finding missing functionality. The expert user can point to many things the system cannot do. However, reviews are not good for finding ease-of-use problems. The expert user typically knows too much to encounter all the ease-of-use problems that would block typical users.

Would it be better to review with ordinary users? Unfortunately not. The way most designers conduct the review hides ease-of-use problems. The designer explains how it works and the user doesn't need to figure it out for himself. We have often seen designers present a new system to a group of users and managers. The designer shows how it works and everybody finds it great. But if you let the users try it on their own just a few minutes later, they may not be able to use the system at all.

Conclusion

- Review with expert users to find missing functionality.

- Use heuristic evaluation with caution. Correct the problems you feel are real, and let usability tests decide for the rest.

- Always make usability tests to find the true problems.

Fig 1.5 Heuristic evaluation

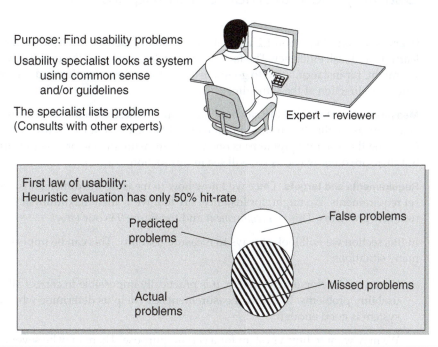

Purpose: Find usability problems

Usability specialist looks at system
using common sense
and/or guidelines

The specialist lists problems
(Consults with other experts)

Expert – reviewer

First law of usability:
Heuristic evaluation has only 50% hit-rate

Predicted
problems

False problems

Missed problems

Actual
problems

1.6 Usability measurements and requirements

Usability factors. In section 1.2 we looked at usability factors, for instance ease of learning and task efficiency. The factors are our dimensions in the usability world. We might, for instance, want to go in the ease-of-learning direction and the task efficiency direction at the same time.

Measurements. If we want to say how far we are in these directions, we must be able to measure the dimensions, but the usability factors don't say how to do this. Counting the usability problems is one way to measure the factor ease of learning, but there are other ways, as we will see in this section.

Requirements and targets. Once we know how to measure the dimensions, we may set requirements. We might, for instance, say that we want a maximum of 9 usability problems. This is a *requirement* and the figure 9 is our *target*.

In this section we will look at ways to measure usability. This can be important in many situations:

- When we develop a new system, it is practically impossible to correct all usability problems. Usability measurements can help us determine when the system is good enough.

- We may want to buy a system for a certain purpose. There may be several vendors of such systems, and as part of our comparison, it is useful to measure the usability of each system.

- We may want to expand an existing system that has been in service for some time. It is a good idea to measure its usability to see whether usability should be improved at the same time.

For each of the ways to measure usability, we will look at how useful it is during development and which usability factors we can measure with it. There are also standards in the area, see ISO 13407 (1989), ISO 9241 (1998) and ISO/IEC 9126 (2001–2002).

1.6.1 Task time (performance measurement)

The classical way to measure usability is to measure the time users take to carry out various tasks. This is also called *performance measurement*. Figure 1.6A shows two examples.

ATM example

The first example specifies usability measurement for an ATM (Automatic Teller Machine). Notice that the specification consists of three parts:

Fig 1.6 A Measuring usability – task time (performance)

ATM
Users:	20 bank customers, random selection.	*How to measure*
Task 1:	Withdraw $100 from ATM. No instructions.	
Measure:	How many succeed in 2 min?	*What to measure*
Task 2:	Withdraw as much as possible ($174)	
Measure:	How many succeed in 5 min?	
Reqs:	Task 1: 18 succeed.	*Requirement – target*
	Task 2: 12 succeed.	

Internal ordering system
Users:	5 secretaries in the company.	
	Have tried the internal ordering system.	
	Have not used it for a month.	*What to measure*
Task 1:	Order two boxes of letter paper + ...	*Risky!*
Measure:	Average time per user.	
Reqs:	Average time below 5 min.	

Pros:	Classic approach. Good when buying.
Cons:	Not good for development. Not possible early. Little feedback.

1 How to carry out the measurement

2 What to measure

3 The requirement or target

How to carry out the measurement. In the example we have specified that we at random select 20 customers visiting the bank, and ask them to participate in a usability test. They are given two tasks: to withdraw a standard amount of money, and to withdraw as much as possible from the account.

Sometimes it may be useful to specify a bit more on how to carry out the measurement, for instance that we hand the users a credit card, that we don't give them any instructions on how to use the ATM. We may also specify how to select the users at random.

What to measure. Basically, we measure how much time the users take to carry out the tasks. In order to end up with a single number, we then count the number of users doing the job in 2 minutes for the first task, and in 5 minutes for the second task. There are of course many other ways of ending up with a few numbers.

Requirement. Finally, we have specified what is good enough – the *requirement*. Our *target* is that 18 out of 20 users complete the first task within 2 minutes, and 12 out of 20 users complete the second within 5 minutes.

From where have we got all these figures – 18 out of 20, 5 minutes, and so on? A lot of judgement is involved, as we will discuss in section 1.6.2.

Order system example

The second example specifies usability for an internal ordering system in a large company. The secretaries use the system to order stationery for use in their department. This is something they do rarely, probably around once a month.

The specification follows the same pattern. Notice that we talk about test users who have not been using the system for some time.

In this example we try to reduce the number of measurements to a single result by taking the average of the task times. However, this would in practice turn out to be a bad idea. Why? Because some users may fail to complete the task. We cannot include them in the average, but excluding them would hide that many users had serious problems. One way to get around it is to use two measurements: the average of those users completing the task, and the number of users that failed.

Usability factors

Which usability factors can we cover with task time measurements? Let us look at them one by one:

a) **Fit for use.** We can, in principle, test that all user tasks can be supported. In practice this is hard for two reasons: we may not be aware of all tasks, and it may be overwhelming to include all of them in a usability test.

b) **Ease of learning.** Task time measurement is well suited for this. The ATM example shows how.

c) **Task efficiency.** This usability factor is about efficiency for experienced, daily users. Task time measurement is well suited for this too. We just have to specify that we will use experienced users for the test. However, when we develop a new system, we have a problem: we don't have experienced users yet.

d) **Ease of remembering.** Task time measurement is in principle suited for this too. The order system example shows how. When developing a new system, we have a problem because we have no suitable users yet. Some HCI specialists run another usability test with the same users a few days later. This will, to some extent, show how easy the system is to remember. In a typical stressed project, however, this is rarely done.

e) **Subjective satisfaction.** Task time measurement is not suited for this. Experience shows that there is little correlation between task time and the user's subjective satisfaction with the system.

f) **Understandability.** Task time is not suited for measuring ease of understanding. We might try things like asking users what they believe this error message means, and measure their time to produce a correct answer. But this is not a good way to measure understanding.

Task times: pros and cons

Task times can measure many usability factors. It is also the classical way of measuring usability.

When we want to buy a system, we can run usability tests with it to see how fast our users can learn to perform their tasks. Usually, the system is already used somewhere else, so we might even get access to experienced users and measure how fast they perform various tasks.

If we develop a new system, task time measurements are possible in principle, but less suited in practice. First of all, you need a working version of the system to measure task times. This is only possible late in development, and at that time it is very expensive to change the system to improve user performance. Second, we don't have access to experienced users, so we cannot measure task efficiency or ease of remembering.

The worst problem is probably that we get too little feedback for developers. We cannot see the usability problems after a task time measurement. If we know that only 10 out of 20 users completed the task, what is wrong? How can we improve?

Asking the test user to think aloud is an excellent way to identify and understand the usability problems. However, this slows the user down, so that the task times become too long.

Finally, selecting the right test tasks is a critical issue no matter whether we develop a new system or buy an existing one. For some systems it is hard to find meaningful test tasks at all. For instance, this is the case with entertainment products.

1.6.2   Choosing the numbers

We have more or less arbitrarily chosen the numbers in the examples. Why have we chosen 20 test users in the first example and 5 in the second? Why have we chosen 2 minutes as the *target* – the acceptable task time? Why do we insist on 18 out of 20?

The short answer is that it is a subjective assessment of cost versus benefit, combined with experience about what is possible (Figure 1.6B).

As an example, testing with 20 users takes more time than testing with 5. On the other hand, we have a good chance of finding rare usability problems also. The fact is that some problems in the user interface block almost every user, while other problems block only few of the users. We have a good chance of finding these rare problems if we test with 20 users, but not if we test with 5.

If the bank wants 90% of its customers to succeed with the ATM, it has to look also for the rare problems – those that block only 10% of the customers. So it should spend the cost of testing with around 20 users to have a good chance of including some of those 10% in the test. In contrast, the internal order system is not that crucial. The users can get help from their colleagues or the hot-line if they don't succeed, and so it is not so important to find also the rare problems. On the other hand, testing with just two users may let too many semi-frequent problems undetected. We return to this issue in section 13.4.

As another example, why have we chosen 18 out of 20? It doesn't make sense to ask for 20 out of 20. There will always be some users that for various reasons have troubles. On the other hand, asking for 10 out of 20 would mean that every second user had troubles. Most likely, that would harm our business because rumours would spread that our ATMs were hard to use. So, the 18 out of 20 matches a goal of 90% success. (Because of the randomness of our sample, we cannot be sure that 90% of the entire user population will succeed although 18 of the test persons succeeded. We will not discuss these statistical issues here.)

Finally, why have we chosen 2 minutes as the critical task time for the ATM? This might be based on observations of what people typically do with present ATMs. The new one should not be worse, but insisting on making it vastly better might be risky and costly. If the example was about the first ATM ever produced, we couldn't use this argument, but had to imagine an ideal way for the users to learn it – or observe users in similar situations elsewhere, for instance using a vending machine.

Actually, tests such as in the example were carried out with the first ATMs. Reaching the stated targets was very hard at that time. Today two things have changed: the ATM user interfaces have improved immensely and users have got more experience with such devices.

Open target. In practice, there is a way around choosing the targets early on. Leave the targets open and later see what is possible. It may turn out that we can get more than we expected or that we were too optimistic. However, we have specified what kind of thing we are after and how we want to measure it.

This approach is called *open target*. A good way is to combine it with our expectations. We could, for instance, state the ATM example with an open target:

18 out of 20 users must complete the task within __ minutes. (We expect around 2 minutes.)

See Lauesen (2002) for more about open targets and cost/benefit of quality in general.

1.6.3 Problem counts

Instead of measuring task times, we can use think-aloud tests and list the usability problems. This gives better feedback to developers, and can be done early in development with a prototype of the user interface.

Fig 1.6 B Choosing the numbers

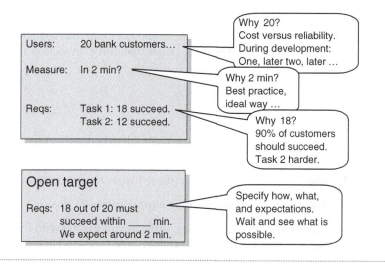

Figure 1.6C shows how we can specify usability in this way. The specification follows the same pattern as for task time measurements.

How to carry out the measurement. In the example we run usability tests with three potential users. They all carry out the same tasks – thinking aloud – and we record a list of all the problems they encounter. For each problem we also record the users who encountered it, and how severe it was to each user.

In principle, we could identify the usability problems in other ways, for instance through heuristic evaluation. Because of the first law of usability, we don't recommend this approach.

What to measure. In the example, we count the number of users encountering a critical problem (task failure, annoying, etc.). We also count the number of medium problems on the problem list. Now, what is a medium problem? Basically we record whether it was of medium severity to one or more users. We may choose to call the problem 'medium' if it was of medium severity to two or more users.

Requirement. The target is that at most one user will encounter a critical problem. In other words, two of the three users will be able to carry out all the tasks on their own. We also require that there are at most 5 medium problems on the list.

We can count the problems in many other ways. The figure is just an example.

Number of users. Are three users really enough? In principle, we should have more – about 10, but testing becomes more expensive. In practice, we measure usability several times during development, correcting usability problems after each round of testing. The first time, one user is enough – we will find many serious problems with a single user, and testing with more at this stage is largely a waste of time. In the next rounds of testing, we may use three users and get more detailed results. In this way the total number of users will become larger than three. In section 13.4 we look closer at the number of users.

Usability factors

Which usability factors can we cover with problem counts? Let us look at them one by one:

a) **Fit for use.** The choice of tasks is critical, just as for task time measurements.

b) **Ease of learning.** Problem counting easily deals with this.

c) **Task efficiency.** Problem counting deals only indirectly with this factor. If the user complains that the system is cumbersome (one kind of critical problem), we know that there is a task efficiency problem. Users with experience from similar systems are more likely to complain. Even if the user doesn't notice an efficiency problem, we may observe that he didn't follow the fast way through the system.

d) **Ease of remembering.** Problem counting is in principle suited for this. We simply specify how many problems second-time users may encounter. This works fine if we are buying a new system where we can find second-time users. When developing a new system, we have the same problem as for task time measurement: we have no second-time users. We can, however, run two usability tests with the same users a few days apart. Comparing the problem counts will give a good indication of the ease of remembering.

e) **Subjective satisfaction.** Problem counting may give some indication of this because user's comments during thinking aloud often reflect their opinion of the system as a whole. However, it is hard to get a real measurement of the satisfaction in this way.

f) **Understandability.** The thinking-aloud tests show a lot about the understandability, but cannot give a real measurement of it.

Some HCI specialists work with a further usability factor called *few errors*. Our problem counts would be a direct measurement of this factor.

Game programs. Measuring the usability for game programs is hard because there are no clear tasks. However, problem counts are useful for specifying that the users shall be able to operate the game as intended by the designers. In order to specify the entertainment value of the system and other usability factors specific for games, we cannot use problem counts of course. Opinion polls are better suited for this (see section 1.6.5).

Fig 1.6 C Measuring usability – problem counts

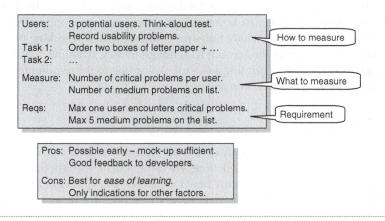

Users: 3 potential users. Think-aloud test.
          Record usability problems.   ◁── How to measure
Task 1:   Order two boxes of letter paper + ...
Task 2:   ...

Measure: Number of critical problems per user.   ◁── What to measure
          Number of medium problems on list.

Reqs: Max one user encounters critical problems.
          Max 5 medium problems on the list.   ◁── Requirement

Pros: Possible early – mock-up sufficient.
       Good feedback to developers.

Cons: Best for *ease of learning*.
       Only indications for other factors.

Problem counts: pros and cons

Problem counts are best for measuring ease of learning, but can give good indications for the other usability factors.

The great advantage is that usability can be measured early during system development. The usability tests can be done based on a paper prototype. No functional system is necessary. The usability test is at the same time a natural part of good development, and it gives excellent feedback to developers about what to correct.

Selecting the right test tasks is a critical issue, just as for task time measurements.

1.6.4   Keystroke counts

Keystroke counts can, to some extent, help us specify and measure task efficiency for experienced users. Figure 1.6D shows a way to do it in the ATM example.

How to carry out the measurement. We specify one or more user tasks. In practice, we specify only tasks where task efficiency is critical. In the example, we have specified the frequent case where the user just wants to withdraw a standard amount and has done it several times before. (Think of all the other customers waiting behind him in the queue at lunch time, and you can understand why this may be a critical task.)

What to measure. We count the number of keystrokes, mouse clicks, and other operations that the user would have to make to complete each task.

Requirement. We specify the maximum number of keystrokes, mouse clicks, etc., for the system to be good enough. In the example the requirement is at most 6 keystrokes including the PIN code.

To help us calculate the total task time, we have also specified the total response time for the system. The total response time is calculated in this way: the time the system takes to respond to the first keystroke, plus the time to respond to the second one, and so on. It will thus include times for reading the card, checking that the pin code is okay, checking that the account has enough money, counting the bills and dispensing them, and printing a receipt. According to the requirements, the total must be at most 8 seconds on average.

Calculating the task time

In principle, we may not really care about the number of keystrokes. The only thing of interest to us is the total task time. We can calculate the task time from the figures above. First we have to measure how long a time an experienced user on average takes for a keystroke. This figure is about 0.6 seconds for typical ATM keys because they are heavy to press. (For ordinary keyboard keys, the figure is around 0.2 seconds.) We can then calculate the total task time in this way:

6 keystrokes @ 0.6 seconds each	3.6 seconds
Total system response time	8.0 seconds
Total task time	11.6 seconds

This calculation is a bit too simple. First, since the user takes 0.6 seconds to push a key, any system response time needed during that period doesn't count.

Second, the user may have to read messages on the screen and understand them. We have assumed that the user is so experienced that he doesn't have to do this.

Finally, what is the task time really? Above we have assumed that the task starts when the user pushes the first key, and terminates when the system has dispensed the money and printed the receipt. The customers waiting behind in the queue don't consider this the true task time. They include the time the user fiddles with his card, getting it out of his wallet and inserting it into the machine, and the time he fiddles with receipt, money, and the card to get them back into the wallet.

Since many ATMs have no shelf to put all of these things, fiddling may take much longer than the computer transaction. It should be mentioned that many ATMs don't have a shelf in order to avoid users leaving their stuff there. The developers have made a design compromise between avoiding a disaster (forgetting the stuff) and reducing task time.

When we talk about PC systems for daily activities, the situation is somewhat different. The task time here is closely related to pushing keyboard keys, moving and clicking the mouse, waiting for the computer to respond, reading the screen, and sometimes talking to a customer meanwhile. Card *et al.* (1980) have shown how to compute task times for such systems based on keystroke counts (the *keystroke-level model*). They have also carefully measured times for pushing a key, moving the

Fig 1.6 D Measuring usability – keystroke counts

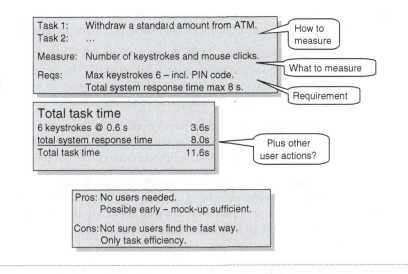

mouse, etc. Their model is also explained in Dix *et al.* (1998). Here are some of their figures:

Operation	Seconds
Keystroke or mouse click, depending on training	0.1–0.3
Keystrokes in codes, for instance product numbers	0.8
Pointing with mouse excluding the click, depending on length moved	0.8–1.5
Homing, i.e. moving hand from keyboard to mouse or vice versa	0.4
Next chunk – mental preparation to select a function or start entering a new chunk of data	1.4

Keystroke counts: pros and cons

Keystroke counts are a good way to specify task efficiency for short, simple tasks. The big advantage is that early in development we can see whether the requirement is met. We don't even need access to real users.

One disadvantage is that we cannot be sure that real users find out how to do it in this efficient way. We can, however, get some indication of it through usability tests.

Another disadvantage is that keystroke counts can give us a false understanding of what the task really comprises. It is usually much more than pushing keys, as shown in the ATM example above.

1.6.5　Opinion poll

Opinion polls are the classical way to measure the user's satisfaction. We ask a number of users to complete a questionnaire, such as the one outlined in Figure 1.6E.

How to carry out the measurement. With this technique, we ask users about their opinion, typically with questionnaires using a Likert scale. The example shows just three steps on the scale: agree, neutral, disagree. It is customary to have more steps, for instance agree, partly agree, neutral, partly disagree, disagree.

We can ask about the user's opinion on many matters, for instance the system is easy to use; the system was easy to learn; the system helps me do things faster; it is fun to use the system; it speeds up my tasks; I will recommend it to people I know.

Typically, we would ask many users to complete the questionnaire. This is of course possible only when the system has been used widely for some time. During system development, it is customary to let each test user fill in a questionnaire after the usability test. This doesn't give as much data, of course, because we have relatively few test users.

What to measure. Getting from the questionnaires to the measurement is easy. We just count the number of people that have marked each of the boxes.

Requirement. There are many ways to specify the target. On the figure, we have specified that 80% agree that the system is easy to learn, and 50% agree that they will recommend it to others. Instead of this, we could take averages, count worst cases, etc.

SUMI. Some usability specialists use the SUMI approach for the questionnaires. SUMI has 50 questions you can ask for any system. It also has a standard set of weights for these questions, so it ends up with one single number to characterize the usability. Furthermore, it has a database of how other systems fare on this scale so that you can compare your own system against others (see http://www.ucc.ie/hfrg/questionnaires/sumi/).

Usability factors

Which usability factors can we cover with opinion polls? It seems that they could cover all factors – we just have to ask the right questions. But let us have a closer look:

a) **Fit for use.** Opinion polls have a great advantage here. We don't have to specify the tasks; we can let the users state whether their tasks are well supported. We can even ask them to write on the form which tasks are not well supported. In that way we can learn what is missing. Of course, this works only for systems that have been used for some time. Even here, users are quite often unaware of the missing task support, so we cannot get complete data.

b) **Ease of learning.** At first sight it seems that opinion polls can give us reliable data on ease of learning, even if we use it after a usability test early during

Fig 1.6 E Measuring usability – opinion poll

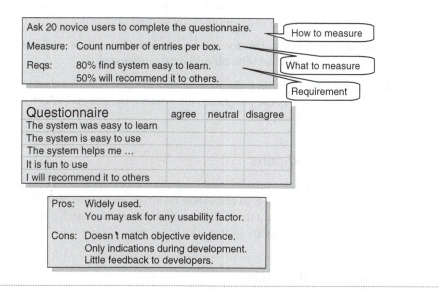

Ask 20 novice users to complete the questionnaire. — How to measure

Measure: Count number of entries per box. — What to measure

Reqs: 80% find system easy to learn. — Requirement
            50% will recommend it to others.

Questionnaire	agree	neutral	disagree
The system was easy to learn			
The system is easy to use			
The system helps me …			
It is fun to use			
I will recommend it to others			

Pros: Widely used.
        You may ask for any usability factor.

Cons: Doesn't match objective evidence.
        Only indications during development.
        Little feedback to developers.

development. Unfortunately, users often say that the system is easy to learn although they have spent a surprising amount of time learning the system. They even say so if they haven't learned to use it properly. So there is little correlation between the user's subjective opinion and more objective measurements.

c) **Task efficiency.** Here too, opinion polls seem a good measurement. And again, users often express satisfaction with their system in spite of evidence that the system is inconvenient and wastes a lot of user time. (If the boss knew about this, he would not be as satisfied as the users.)

d) **Ease of remembering.** Here too, opinion polls seem a good measurement. I must admit that I don't know to what extent the opinion matches objective measurements.

e) **Subjective satisfaction.** Opinion polls should be strong here. We simply ask the users whether they are satisfied. If they say yes, we trust them. It is their subjective opinion we are after, even if it has nothing to do with objective measures of task time, etc. Alas, people don't say what they really mean. Marketing people and psychologists have known this for many years. For that reason they ask the same thing in many ways to get down to the truth. We have a bit of it in the example in Figure 1.6E: 'Would you recommend the system to others?' In principle, it is the same as asking whether they like the system themselves. If they say they do, but don't mean it, they will usually not recommend it to others. Asking whether they think their colleague likes it, is a trick of the same kind.

Cultural differences are involved too. Asians typically say that things are good – feeling that if not, it is their fault. Europeans are different. They may complain about everything, and are more frank in their opinions.

f) **Understandability.** This too can be measured by opinion polls, but I don't know how well it correlates with objective measurements.

Game programs. Opinion polls are probably the best way to measure the special usability factors for game programs, for instance the entertainment value, the challenge, the fairness, etc.

Opinion polls: pros and cons

Many HCI specialists consider opinion polls the best measure of usability. They stress that opinion polls give consistent results from user to user. This may be true, but as explained above, it doesn't mean that the results match objective evidence. The second law of usability is at work:

Second law of usability

There is little correlation between subjective satisfaction and objective performance.

Subjective satisfaction is heavily influenced by organizational factors, for instance management style and good lunch breaks. Developers cannot control these factors.

Another problem with opinion polls is that they are hard to measure during development. We get more reliable results when we poll after delivering the system. If results show that users are satisfied, we cannot be sure that the system really is easy to use. If results show that users are dissatisfied, we don't know what the problem is, but it is a sign that developers should go and talk to the users to find out what the real problems are (see Henderson *et al.* 1995; Frøkjær *et al.* 2000).

1.6.6   Score for understanding

If we want to measure whether the system is easy to understand, a good approach is to ask users how they believe the system works. Figure 1.6F shows an example.

How to carry out the measurement. We ask users a number of questions about the system's behaviour. In the example we ask what various error messages mean when using an ATM.

We could also ask questions of the kind 'What do you think the system would do if . . . ' In the ATM case we could, for instance, ask 'What do you think the system would do if the wire connecting it to the bank was broken?' Or 'What do you think

Fig 1.6 F Measuring usability – score for understanding

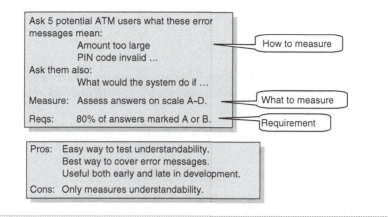

Ask 5 potential ATM users what these error messages mean:
>Amount too large
>PIN code invalid …

Ask them also:
>What would the system do if …

How to measure

Measure: Assess answers on scale A-D.

What to measure

Reqs: 80% of answers marked A or B.

Requirement

Pros: Easy way to test understandability.
Best way to cover error messages.
Useful both early and late in development.

Cons: Only measures understandability.

---

the system would do if you had just emptied your account from another ATM, and now tried to retrieve more?'

What to measure. We assess how correct the answers are, for instance as exam marks on the scale from A to D. This is a somewhat subjective assessment of the correctness, but gives a good indication anyway. (Remember that it is not the user we mark, but the system's understandability.)

Requirements. In the example, the target is that 80% of the answers (across all users) get marks A or B.

When I try the first ATM question with people, I get very few correct answers. Few people know that the message 'amount too large' may indicate that although they have ample money in their account, they have exceeded their daily cash allowance or their monthly limit. Both limits are there to prevent robberies and fraud, but most users are unaware of this.

Score for understanding: pros and cons

An understandability test can give us information that is hard to get with task time measurements or problem counts. It is particularly useful for finding usability problems in error messages. The reason is that today's systems have a huge number of error messages. Trying tasks where the user can encounter many of them is extremely time-consuming. Testing as shown in Figure 1.6F is an easy way out.

A further advantage is that we can test understandability early in development. When we test error messages, the test also helps us improve the message. This can even be done late in the project, where developers come up with most of the error messages. If we want to buy an existing system, we can carry out the test before we buy or sign the contract.

The main disadvantage of a score for understanding is that it measures only the understandability factor.

1.6.7 Guideline adherence

In many cases it is an advantage that the user interface follows some recommended guideline, for instance the style guide for Microsoft Windows applications. The guideline says things such as:

- Each window must have a cross in the top right corner. Clicking on the cross must close the window.

- The active window must have a blue title bar.

- Short-cut keys must be provided for all system functions in order to allow mouse-free operation.

- An example of a screen that follows the rules is shown in . . .

We can measure how well the system follows such a guideline. Figure 1.6G shows an example.

How to carry out the measurement. In the example, we ask an independent expert to scrutinize the user interface and identify the deviations from the guideline. Since there often is doubt about what a guideline actually means, it might be better to have two experts look at the interface and agree on the significant deviations from the guideline.

What to measure. Since we can expect more deviations in large systems than in smaller ones, we count the average number of deviations per screen. (A screen might be a window or a Web page.)

Requirement. In the example, the target is at most one deviation per screen. In practice, this is quite a strict requirement. In general, developers find it difficult to follow guidelines, even if they try hard.

Usability factors

Let us see how such a requirement contributes to the usability factors:

a) **Fit for use.** The guideline cannot say much about the specific user tasks to be supported. However, it may remind developers to support generic tasks, for instance printing, importing, and exporting data.

b) **Ease of learning.** Following a guideline definitely helps users learn a new system faster. Of course it works best if the users already are familiar with other software following the guideline. But even if they are not, the guideline may help

Fig 1.6 G Measuring usability – guideline adherence

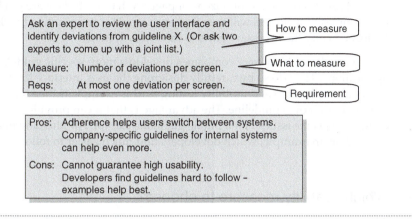

create consistency across various parts of the new system, thus making it easier for users to move between system screens.

Following a guideline does not *ensure* that the system is easy to learn. The guideline can only help learning the superficial aspects of the system.

c) **Task efficiency.** Following a guideline does not ensure that the system is efficient for daily use. The guideline may remind developers to provide short-cut keys, etc., but often this is not sufficient for effectiveness. In some cases a guideline may even prevent highly efficient solutions. As an example, the required use of message boxes and warnings in Microsoft Windows slows down experienced users. Designers are becoming aware of this, which is why you see more and more message boxes allowing you to click 'don't show this warning again'. Unfortunately, even experienced users hesitate to click this box, because they feel uncertain of the consequences.

d) **Ease of remembering.** A guideline can strongly help users remember how various things are to be done, because it is the same as in other parts of the system.

e) **Subjective satisfaction.** Following a guideline used in popular systems probably makes people more satisfied with the new system.

f) **Understandability.** A guideline helps users understand what the system does, but only on a superficial level. The guideline cannot help users understand the application-specific issues that relate to the world outside the computer system.

Guideline adherence: pros and cons

In general, it is an advantage to follow a guideline, particularly if it is also used in other systems that users know. Following a specific guideline cannot in itself guarantee high usability. In some cases, a guideline may hamper high task efficiency.

Experience shows that it is quite hard for developers to follow guidelines, particularly if they consist of dozens of pages. What works best are guidelines built on examples. Developers will then find an example corresponding to what they want to do, and copy the necessary parts to their own system.

Some consultants help large companies develop a more specific guideline for their applications. They do so by carefully designing the user interface for an existing company application and usability testing it. This example is then the core of the company's own guideline. The advantage is that it can provide guidelines in company-specific issues that a public guideline cannot. Another advantage is that it is based on an example, which developers find much easier to follow.

1.6.8   Which usability measure to choose?

Above we have looked at many ways of measuring usability. They all have their strengths and weaknesses. Which one should we use in practice? The short answer is that we have to combine several measures. Which ones depend on the kind of project and on the important usability factors for that system. Figure 1.6H summarizes what the different measurement techniques cover. The dark boxes show where the technique is particularly good.

If we talk about *developing* systems for non-critical daily use, ease of learning and understandability are the most important factors. My favourite choice in this case is

problem counts + score for understanding

Figure 1.6H shows that these techniques cover ease of learning and understandability, and that the techniques are also suited early during development. If we don't develop such a system, but buy it, we should use task time measurements instead of problem counts. In this way we better cover task efficiency.

If we talk about developing a Web system to attract customers, subjective satisfaction becomes important. I would add opinion polls and use many test subjects carefully selected to cover the many kinds of users we expect to attract. If we talk about developing a system that must support time-critical tasks, I would instead add keystroke counts for the critical tasks.

As far as I know, ease of remembering is rarely measured. We somehow assume that ease of learning also provides ease of remembering. Whether this is true, remains to be tested.

In conclusion, no two projects are alike – consider the proper choice of measurements for each project. In large industrial projects you may have to use different combinations of usability measures for different user groups. See Lauesen (2002, section 10.4) for an example.

Fig 1.6 H Which usability measure?

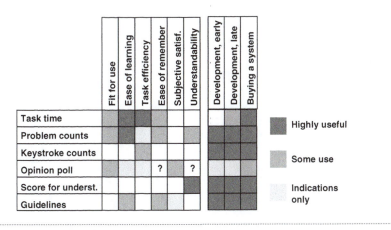

Test yourself

a) Mention some examples of quality factors.

b) Mention some examples of usability factors.

c) Mention some examples of usability requirements.

d) What is the difference between a factor and a requirement?

e) What is a usability problem?

f) What is a critical problem?

g) What is the difference between usability testing, heuristic evaluation, and user review?

h) Mention two good ways to measure ease of learning.

i) Which of them are good when you buy a finished system and when you are developing a new system?

j) What is an open target requirement?

k) What do the first and the second law of usability say?

Design exercises. See Chapter 17.

2

Prototyping and iterative design

Highlights

- Classical usability approach: Study users and tasks, make prototype, test for usability, revise the prototype.

- A hotel case: The prototype, what usability tests revealed, what heuristics revealed, how we cured the problems.

- A horror story: Faking the process and shipping a useless product.

- The costs and benefits of usability.

- Key exercise: Make a prototype for a small system and usability test it.

In this chapter we look at the development process – how new software systems are created. In particular, we look at how the user interface is designed, why it is hard to make it easy to use and what can be done about it.

A crucial part of making a good user interface is to make early prototypes of the user interface and test them for usability. This is called iterative design and we show how it worked out in a specific case – a hotel system with high usability requirements. Finally, we look at various forms of prototypes and their pros and cons.

2.1 Usability in the development process

Traditional systems development projects go through a number of phases, as outlined in Figure 2.1. The first phase is the analysis phase where the development team analyses the user's and customer's demands and considers various kinds of solutions. The results of this are used in the design phase, where the team plans the software parts to be developed. Next, the team programs the new software parts. In the test phase they try out the programs on the computer, correct errors and try again until the result is satisfactory. Finally, they deliver the system to the customer, who puts it into operation. During operation, the team corrects problems that were not detected earlier, and they expand the system to cover new demands.

In practice, developers don't complete one phase before starting on the next. Often they realize that something went wrong in an earlier phase, so part of it has to be redone. Sometimes they also carry out iterative analysis, design and even programming, thus intentionally repeating several phases. This is called *iterative development* and Chapter 15 explains more about it.

Good developers master the technical part of development very well, and usually there are few technical problems, such as bugs, in the final product. The reason they can do this is that they know how the computer and its software work, so they can foresee the serious problems early on. This doesn't mean that the programs are error free from the beginning. There are always many errors – mostly detected in the testing phase. The really important thing is that in good programs most errors are easy to correct. The difficult errors have been prevented through careful analysis and design.

Why usability is hard

The situation is quite different when we talk about usability. If we measure usability of the new system, for instance by counting the usability problems, we will find hundreds of critical problems in average systems. What is worse, they are not easy to correct. Many of them would require significant redesign of the system.

Why is this? The fact is that system developers don't know the users and their tasks as well as they know the computer. So the system will work fine on the computer, but not with the users. I have been a developer myself for more than 20 years, and we always believed we knew the users and their tasks, or that we could use reasoning and logic to find out. We never could.

Often developers don't design the user interface until late in programming. I often hear developers talk about the user interface as something boring to be added at the end of programming.

Fig 2.1   The development process

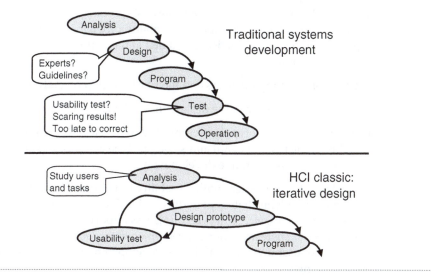

Since developers have troubles making the user interface, couldn't they ask some usability specialists to design it – or at least look at the developer's design and help them improve it? This would probably be better, but remember that even usability specialists are bad at predicting the usability problems early in development (the first law of usability). They probably understand users better than developers do, but not good enough. Furthermore, most usability specialists are good at finding usability problems, but not that good at removing them.

When a development team first becomes concerned about usability, they typically ask a usability specialist to help them improve the usability. At this stage the new system is almost finished, and the team just wants to have the usability problems removed – in the same way as they detect and remove bugs. The usability specialist helps them run a few usability tests. Results? Developers cannot believe the huge number of usability problems detected at this stage. Furthermore, for many of the errors nobody really knows what to do about them – except to correct some of the texts on the screens.

However, even when usability testing is tried very late, it can be worthwhile. Some critical problems can still be removed at that time. As an example, in one test we ran, we tested usability for a product that was to be shipped to sales offices all over the world in two days. We first tested the installation procedure, but the users couldn't figure out how to install the system. Why? The installation guide said: Run *install.exe* from the enclosed floppy. However, this file wasn't there – or rather it was called *create.exe*. This was easy to repair and saved thousands of hot-line hours – and probably the company's image.

Classical approach – iterative design

What is the solution? We have to attack the basic problem that developers don't know the users and their tasks, and that usability problems cannot be predicted. The best approach in common practice is outlined at the bottom of Figure 2.1. It consists of three core techniques:

1 Let developers study the users and their tasks as part of analysis (task analysis).

2 Make a prototype early in the design phase. Review it with expert users.

3 Usability test the prototype with typical users. Correct the prototype to remove usability problems, test again and so on until the result is satisfactory. This is *iterative design* – not iterative development.

It is a good idea to supplement with a usability test of the final system to remove small usability problems that crept in during development, make understandability tests of error messages, etc. However, this is less important than the three core techniques above. There are other good supplementary techniques, for instance various kinds of user involvement during development (sections 15.4 and 15.5 explain about this).

The study of users and their tasks give specific knowledge of the kind of users to select for the usability tests and the kind of tasks to be tried in the tests. The study also improves the developer's intuition for what the system should do. Usually developers become very surprised about what actually goes on in the user's world. Things happen there that developers didn't imagine at all – and these things have to be supported somehow by the new system.

There are many kinds of prototypes, for instance mock-ups made with paper and pencil, computer screens that look right but don't function, etc. We look at this in section 2.2. It is a good idea to review the prototype with expert users – people who know what goes on in the user's world, know the special cases to handle and so on. However, experience shows that they cannot see what the ordinary user finds difficult.

Usually the first prototype is wide of the mark when ordinary users try it out. When developers experience this, many of them make the mistake of trying to correct bits here and there – improve the title of fields, add warnings, etc. This helps only a bit. Often the right thing to do is to forget the first prototype and rethink it from a new perspective. Developers are not willing to do this if they have spent a long time developing the prototype. The third law of usability is at work:

Third law of usability

The more effort developers have spent making a prototype, the less they are willing to replace it.

How many rounds of prototyping are necessary? A rule of thumb is three rounds to get an acceptable result, more if it is critical to get high usability. This rule works for developers trained in user interface design. Other developers need more iterations and often give up.

A round of usability testing and prototype revision may take 2–5 days, so it is not a very costly process. As an example, when Bruel & Kjaer introduced this approach some years ago, developers tested their first prototype with three potential users at a major customer site. The result was very disappointing – lots of task failures. Over the weekend, the developers completely redesigned the prototype, and Monday morning they were ready for another usability test – this time very successful. There were still some problems, but they were easy to remove.

When the result is acceptable, there may still remain some serious usability problems that seem impossible to resolve. Instead, the development team has to train the users on these points, write a guide and maybe prepare hot-line staff to deal with the problems when users encounter them.

Weak points

However, the classical iterative design has some weak points:

1 There is no systematic way to design the screens. How many screens are needed? What should they contain? In the classical approach it is trial and error.

2 There is no systematic way to correct usability problems once they are detected.

3 It is hard to find test users with the right profile.

In the book we will also show ways to deal with these problems, thus improving the classical approach. For instance, Chapters 5 to 7 show a systematic design approach that can help you compose the screens. In Chapter 8 we show the results of such a design, the usability problems encountered and how they were removed. In section 13.3 we explain ways to find test users.

2.2   Case study: a hotel system

Throughout the book we will use a hotel system as the main example. We want to develop a computer system that can support the reception in a hotel. Figure 2.2 illustrates what the system must do. It must help the receptionist carry out a number of tasks.

User tasks

When a guest phones to book a room, the receptionist must record the name, address, etc., for the guest, the dates he is going to stay at the hotel and the room he will stay in. We call this the *booking task*.

When a guest arrives at the hotel, the receptionist must allocate a free room to him, give him the key and record that he now stays in this room and has to pay for it. The guest may or may not have booked the room in advance. This is the *check-in task*.

When the guest leaves the hotel, the receptionist must give him an invoice and collect the payment. The receptionist must also record that the room is now free and the guest has paid. This is the *checkout task*.

It may happen that the guest wants to change to another room. The system must also support this *change-room task*.

When the guest receives breakfast, makes phone calls or receives other services, the system must record it and put it on the bill. This is the *record-services task*.

Many hotels have a restaurant where the guests can get breakfast, and the staff use a special list for recording who got what. The list has one line per hotel room. Figure 2.2 shows a simple list where guests can have just two types of breakfast – breakfast served in the room and breakfast served buffet style in the restaurant. When served buffet style, the guests may have to show their room key as evidence that they are checked into that room. Later a waiter brings the list to the reception where a receptionist records the breakfasts on the bills. This is the *breakfast-list task*.

Simplifications

We have chosen the hotel example because most people have an idea what it is about, yet it is sufficiently complex to show typical solutions in larger systems. Some of the complexities are that a hotel has many types of rooms at different prices; a guest can book several rooms, maybe in overlapping periods; a room may need renovation or repair, making it unavailable for a period; the hotel keeps track of regular guests and their visits over time.

However, we have simplified the system in many other ways to shorten the discussion. For instance we ignore that in most hotels, rooms are not booked by room

Fig 2.2 Hotel system

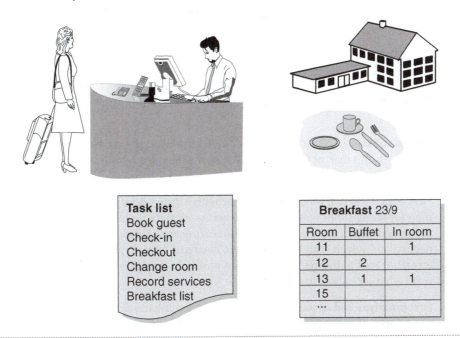

Task list
Book guest
Check-in
Checkout
Change room
Record services
Breakfast list

Breakfast 23/9		
Room	Buffet	In room
11		1
12	2	
13	1	1
15		
...		

number, but by room type; hotels usually overbook, i.e. book more rooms than they have, expecting that some customers will not turn up. We also ignore all the other aspects of operating a hotel, for instance keeping track of when rooms are cleaned and ready for the next guest, purchasing goods, planning who is to be on duty for the next weeks, payroll and general accounting. In spite of these simplifications, the example still shows the structure of larger systems.

Usability requirements

It is not realistic that we develop such a system for a single hotel. It would be much too expensive, and commercial hotel systems exist already. However, they are typically very complex and staff have to take a course before they are allowed to work in the reception. Hotel systems vary a lot in their ease of learning. Some can be learned in two days, others require more than a week.

To stress the usability aspect, we will develop part of a new hotel system targeted at smaller hotels, although it should be able to support large hotels too. Small hotels tend to use a lot of temporary staff, for instance students on vacation jobs, and this means that the receptionists cannot get several days of training. At best, a colleague will instruct them for half an hour. Our goal is that temporary staff will be able to handle the basic tasks on their own, and only ask the boss or experienced colleagues in more complex cases. In section 5.1.3 we describe the usability requirements more precisely.

Development history

The author, supported by varying colleagues, sets out to develop such a system. In the rest of the book I will show various snapshots of this process. The main steps are these:

Analysis phase. I had studied hotels while I travelled to many countries all over the world. I didn't look at the present IT systems they used, but I listened to the staff's comments on their system.

First design – virtual windows. Together with Morten Borup Harning, I developed a plan for screens that would show the necessary data for all the user tasks. We made a paper-and-pencil draft of them without caring about which buttons and menus were needed and which search screens were needed. (Actually, this was not just trial and error, but part of the systematic design method we explain in Chapter 6. The screens were what we call virtual windows.)

First prototype and usability tests. Later, I added the missing things to the screens and got a paper-and-pencil prototype (a *hand-drawn mock-up*). This was based on my intuition and done under time pressure, as it often happens in IT projects. I usability tested the prototype with three typical users. This revealed a lot of usability problems, as we will see in the next section.

Systematic design. The lesson I learned from these usability tests was that it would pay to make a more systematic design. Continuing in a trial-and-error fashion seemed unrealistic. So I followed the rest of the virtual window method, as explained in Chapters 6 and 7.

Next prototype and usability tests. The result of the systematic design process was rather easy to transform into a prototype. At this point I decided to use Microsoft Access, because it was widely available. (Previously I had imagined using Visual Basic or C++). I made a more advanced prototype – a *tool-based mock-up*. Screens were 'drawn' by means of Access and printed on paper. Data was added by pencil on these prints. Usability tests showed that a lot of the earlier problems had now disappeared – not so much because screens were more Access-like, but because of the first usability tests and the systematic design process. We explain about this in Chapter 8. However, a few of the problems persisted and didn't go away after several design changes.

These problems were not very serious, and with an hour of training, even novice users would be able to operate the system. However, the ambition was that novice users should be able to find out on their own – at least about basic tasks. Should I forget this goal?

Functional prototype. At this point in time, I was utterly frustrated about these stupid, persistent usability problems. The problems related to the important screen where the receptionist searched for guests. In a last attempt, I decided to try a live search where the search result changed each time the receptionist entered a single character, for instance in the name of the guest. However, you cannot test this with a paper mock-up. You need a system with some real functionality. So I had to develop one, but first I had to learn how Access really worked.

Although it is rather easy to make simple screens with Access, it is extremely hard to find out about advanced functionality, such as a live search. The documentation is very obscure and existing textbooks are either too basic or too advanced. Learning how Access really works took months of hard work. Many Access experts helped me on the way, but could not right away tell me how to make the user interface work as intended. When they developed Access applications, they based them on what was easy to do, not on usability observations. However, it turned out that the technical solutions were very simple, once you understood how things worked.

The result was worth it. The live search and a few other tricks made the system intuitively understandable. It was great to see the smile on the test user's face when the system responded immediately and they figured out how it worked.

The lesson. Some people conclude from this that I claim that live searches are the panacea. All wrong! The lesson is that some usability problems cannot be removed with paper-and-pencil prototypes. You need a partly functional prototype. Although a live search solved some hard usability problems in this case, it doesn't mean that other cases also need live searches.

The final system. Now there was no doubt about how the user interface should work, and the rest of the programming was fairly easy. We show pieces of it in the Access booklet available at www.booksites.net/lauesen At this point in time I started looking behind the desk in the hotel receptions to compare the existing systems with my own design. I found that the systems that receptionists found hard to learn, looked very different from mine.

I also found a hotel that had just changed to a new system that receptionists found very easy to use. It looked like my design in many ways, but also had a couple of clever things that surprised me. Some of them were easy to include in my own design, others would take much time.

2.3　The first hotel system prototype

In this section we will look at the first prototype of the hotel system, how it was usability tested and what usability problems we found. Figure 2.3A shows four screens of the prototype and three menus. As you can see it is a mock-up drawn by paper and pencil. The full prototype included two more screens and a couple of menus.

The design was based on some existing *virtual windows* – screen outlines without buttons and menus. It took me around two hours to transform these virtual windows into the six screens, including buttons and menus.

Screens. The receptionist will use the first screen to find guests, for instance when they have booked a room and now arrive. The receptionist can enter search criteria such as part of the guest's name or address, and then click *Find*. The system will now show a list of guests that match the criteria. The receptionist can then choose one of the guests and open his *Stay* screen, shown to the right. In case the guest is not in the system, the receptionist can use *New stay* to get a blank screen for entering guest data (the small screen *New stay*). In the start-up situation, the system shows the most frequent situation: the list of guests arriving today.

The *New stay* and *Stay* screens are used to record a stay for a guest, for instance when he books.

The receptionist will use the *Rooms* screen to find free rooms. It shows the state of the hotel rooms over a period of time. The dates run towards the right, the room numbers downward. B means that the room is Booked, O that it is Occupied (someone is checked into the room) and R that it is under repair. In a hotel with many rooms, the receptionist cannot get an overview of all the rooms, so the system must be able to find rooms according to criteria. The receptionist must, for instance, be able to look for all rooms free in a certain period (*From* and *To*). Once he has selected a room, he can use the menu to book it for the guest or check the guest into the room.

Menus and buttons. Harning and I had carefully planned the virtual windows, but not the buttons, menus and search screens. I had added them using intuition and official guidelines such as 'always have a File menu and an Edit menu'. In retrospect, this guideline was stupid in our case, but at the beginning you don't know any better.

Notice that each menu is on a separate piece of paper (stickers are good for this). When the test user, for instance, clicks *File* on *New stay*, the facilitator brings the menu out and puts it on the screen.

Operating the prototype. After a few minutes, test users find it quite natural to 'operate' such a prototype. They enter data in the empty fields with their pencil, and use it as a mouse to click buttons and menus.

Fig 2.3 A Hotel system prototype

The facilitator may soon be busy simulating the computer. He has to bring menus and lists out, close and open windows, fill in the computer's replies in the fields. He may have prepared a lot in advance, but often the user does something unexpected and the facilitator has to improvise a response, using eraser and pencil. As an example, he often has to improvise an error message. Keep these improvised error messages for later – they are useful for the programmers to remind them of things to check for in the program and how to phrase the error message.

Usability test of the prototype

In spite of its simple appearance, the prototype in Figure 2.3A revealed a lot of usability defects. Later, we ran tests of exactly the same version at many courses, with much the same result each time.

Test tasks. We used these test tasks during the usability tests:

Task 1:   Today is the 23rd of October. Andrew Bunting arrives. He says there should be two rooms waiting for him

If asked: He cannot remember his booking number or stay number. He lives 50 Buffalo Drive, Lalor, Vict 3075, Australia. His phone number is (03) 1533 1217. He will stay three nights.

Task 2:   Rodger A. Haynes phones to make a reservation of a single room from tomorrow and four nights.

If asked: He lives 12 Highland Court, Dandenong, Vict 3175, Australia. Home phone is 3455 8004, he is not too sure of the area code.

We had other tasks too, but few users ever got that far within the 30 minutes we ran the test.

Note that we have tried to avoid hidden help in the test tasks. We don't tell the test user whether this is a booking, a check-in, etc., and we don't use any of the words on the screen. For instance we don't use the words *booking number* or *stay number*.

Test users. The usability test was run with three potential users. Novice B and M were two secretaries with Microsoft Word experience. They had no experience from receptions. Their background corresponded to the difficult target group we aimed at. The third user had been a receptionist for about a year, but now worked as a secretary.

Before the usability test, we told the users that this was the draft version of a future hotel system that should support the receptionists when guests wanted rooms, paid the bill, etc. We also told them that we knew our draft too well, so we couldn't see the problems users might have with it. We needed the test user to help us make the system more intuitive to use. We didn't explain any of the screens or how they were used.

In real life, a new receptionist might get some instruction and help from other more experienced receptionists, but sometimes temporary staff are called in to help in busy periods, and there is little time to instruct them. We wanted to make the system very intuitive in order to deal with such situations.

The two novices completed the first task within the 30 minutes set off, but they got stuck several times on the way. When they got stuck, we recorded this as a task failure, and gave them a hint on what to do. In that way we could record many task failures for each user.

The receptionist completed both tasks and encountered only a single task failure. It was obvious that her hotel knowledge helped her overcome many problems that blocked the novices.

Figure 2.3B shows all the usability defects found during these three usability tests. We will comment on them below.

Heuristic evaluation results

The classical alternative to a usability test is a heuristic evaluation where you have other designers look at the user interface and identify the potential usability problems. There are many variants of this: you can have either usability specialists or fellow developers look at the interface; they can use either their sound judgement or check against design guidelines (see more variants in section 14.1).

At a course in user interface design, we had the 30 participants come up with as many problems in the hotel interface as possible. This was a heuristic evaluation with fellow developers using their sound judgement. The rightmost column of Figure 2.3B shows what they found. Before they were invited to come up with the problems, we briefly showed the screens and explained what they were supposed to do – with the same degree of detail as in the above introduction to section 2.3. We have made such evaluations many times at design courses. The results are much the same each time.

The defect list

The list shows 22 defects relating to the Find guest/stay window, 5 for the rooms window and 8 for the Stay and New stay windows. The columns to the right show who encountered each defect. Notice that many defects were encountered only during heuristic evaluation, e.g. D13 to D22. Let us look closer at some of the defects on the list and see who found what.

Terminology problem. Defect D1 was about the strange term 'stay' used on the Find guest/stay screen. Actually, the developers had been in doubt what to call it. People in the hotel business talk about a booking or a reservation, meaning a guest and the rooms he has booked. When asked about what a booking is called once the guest is checked in, receptionists become uneasy. They don't have a term for it and may say the *reservation* or the *guest*, but when asked, they can see it sounds strange. The designers had chosen the word *Stay*, which seemed to cover both bookings and check-ins.

What happened during the test? Novice B wondered what 'stay' was, and looked at other things on the screen before realizing what it was. Novice M never noticed any problem and completed the task without even caring about the Stay# appearing in several places. The receptionist user looked at the Stay# field for one second and then said, *Aha, this must be the booking number*. The usability specialists had predicted the stay concept to be a problem, and in the figure we have shown it as a *hit* – they correctly predicted it to be a problem, although only one out of three users encountered it.

Missed by usability specialists. Defect D7 was about the two novices not noting that the screen already showed the guest they were looking for. Andrew Bunting was there, and yet they didn't notice. Instead, they entered his name and address in the criteria fields at the top. The cause of the problem is a typical pattern: the novice reads from the top and stops at the first thing that seems relevant. The usability specialists had not predicted this problem.

Task not tried by all users. Defect D12 relates to task 2, book a guest. The receptionist couldn't guess that she first had to create a new stay with the button on the Find guest screen. Only the receptionist got that far, so we cannot know whether the other users would encounter the same problem, so they have a question mark for this defect. The usability specialists had not predicted the defect.

Likely but not encountered. D14 is about what to write in the search criterion *Address*. Should it be the zip code, the street name, or what? Actually, the system just looks for addresses that contain what the user entered. The usability specialists had predicted this to be a defect, but none of the users had encountered it. Novice B just entered part of the address, and the system found the right guest. Novice M found the guest by entering his name in the name field. The receptionist found him on the list shown at start-up. Is this a false defect predicted by the specialists? Well, although it didn't show up in the tests, the designers realized that it was likely to occur and decided to find a way to improve it. For this reason, it has a question mark after *false*.

Same defect? D18 is a usability specialist saying that the relation between the search criteria and the resulting list is obscure, but he didn't explain more. Does this statement predict D3 and D8, which users experienced? Maybe – it is hard to say, and sometimes judgement is needed to tell whether two reported defects are the same. (In the figure we have marked it as a potential problem.)

False problem. D19 is a usability specialist wanting the guest to be found by his passport number. None of the test users encountered this need, so it seems to be a false problem. The designers couldn't see a need for it either. Even if hotel staff found a lost passport, they wouldn't need to search for the number. The name in the passport would do.

Summary. Figure 2.3C summarizes the results. In total, the usability test revealed 20 usability defects – a good result of barely two hours testing. Only 6 (maybe 7) of these defects were predicted by the specialists. Heuristic evaluation predicted 15 other defects that were not encountered in the usability tests. Developers judged that 8 of these were likely to occur and should be repaired if not too hard to do.

We want to stress that we have not selected an example with an unusual large difference between heuristic evaluation and usability test. People more trained in

Fig 2.3 B Defect list for hotel system mock-up

ID	Defects in Find Guest/Stay window	Novice B	Novice M	Receptionist	Heur. eval.
D1	The *Stay* concept is not understood by ordinary users	Medium problem		Guesses immediately	Hit
D2	Doesn't notice the *Find* button		Task failure	Medium problem	Hit
D3	When you select a certain date, why does the list show earlier dates too?		Minor problem		Hit
D4	Not visible whether the guests have been checked in or not		Annoying		Hit
D5	How do you open the stay window from the Find guest/stay window?	Medium problem	Task failure	Medium problem	Hit
D6	Tries Enter to search, but it opens a Stay window. Then tries F2			Medium	
D7	Doesn't see that the guest is on the list already	Annoying	Annoying		
D8	Doesn't understand why the list becomes empty (made a spelling error)	Medium problem			
D9	Believes the task is complete when she sees the guest on the list	Task failure			
D10	Doesn't understand that the Stay screen must be opened	Task failure	Task failure		
D11	Fills in all search criteria, believing they are data fields	Minor problem	Task failure		
D12	Cannot figure out how to create a new booking	?	?	Task failure	
D13	Bad window title – avoid the slash				False ?
D14	What to write in the address field? Street name and zip?				False ?
D15	Where do you enter zip code or city?				False
D16	'Date' is insufficient, should be arrival date				False ?
D17	The #-sign is not understood by ordinary users				False ?
D18	Obscure what *Find* will give (may cover D3 and D8?)				False ?
D19	Search based on passport number is needed				False
D20	A guest number is needed in addition to the stay number				False
D21	Which of the guests are on the list?				False
D22	Not visible how the guest pays the bill?				False

ID	Defects in Rooms window	Novice B	Novice M	Receptionist	Heur. eval.
D23	Doesn't look for functions on the menu		Task failure		Hit
D24	Believes O means nobody there – room is free	Task failure			
D25	Doesn't understand the two room prices	Medium problem		Minor problem	
D26	Does *To* mean last night or departure date?			Medium problem	
D27	Why is there a File menu? *Tools* is better				False ?

ID	Defects in Stay and NewStay window	Novice B	Novice M	Receptionist	Heur. eval.
D28	Expects that the room can be marked *Occupied* on the Stay screen		Medium problem		
D29	Uncertain whether check-in has been recorded correctly		Medium problem		
D30	Cannot see how many rooms the guest has booked	Minor problem	Medium problem		
D31	Hard to find function for printing a booking confirmation	?	?	Minor problem	
D32	Are blank fields allowed?				False
D33	Why are date fields not editable?				False
D34	How to undo data entry?				False ?
D35	Where do you change the room prices or give discounts?				False ?
Critical problems per task (task failures + annoying)		4	7	0.5	

usability tend to find some more hits – about 50% of the observed problems, but also more misses.

Improving the prototype

The purpose of usability tests and heuristic evaluation is to improve the user interface. According to the classical iterative design approach, designers would look at the defect list and use their intuition to revise the screens – maybe restructure data into completely different screens.

In our case, we also revised the screens, but first we did the remaining part of the systematic design approach. Section 2.2 summarizes how we actually made the design. Section 8.3 gives details of what happened and how the usability problems disappeared.

A horror story

Here is a true story of another way to deal with usability problems. As a highly paid consultant, I helped a large mortgage company make usability tests of their new system. It was to be used by a lot of real-estate agents. The company had judged usability as a critical success factor for the product, and they had been designing and programming a functional prototype for more than a year. Although warned that early usability testing before programming was essential, they had delayed usability testing until now.

They really took a great effort with the usability tests. They had found just the right kind of potential users, they had planned the short course for future users and the test users got this course before the test. They paid me and a score of other consultants to help them, we spent time learning about the system and we used video cameras and advanced equipment for the tests.

What happened? Lots of task failures. The user interface consisted of many small windows for recording pieces of data, and in order to just record a property for sale, the user would have to go through about 10 screens in a surprising order. All the test users were completely bewildered. (The user interface was an example of a database-extreme interface, where users see the database details almost directly. See more in section 4.5.)

We tried to advise the developers on how to improve the user interface before the next round of usability tests, and they promised to do so. However, since they had programmed so much already, there was no money left to redo most of this. Their budget was running out, but what should they say to management who had funded the costly usability work?

They found a way out. They repaired some programming bugs that they had observed during usability testing, but didn't change the user interface. Then they ran the next round of usability tests, but this time they chose fellow developers as the test

Fig 2.3 C Hit-rate of hotel system evaluation

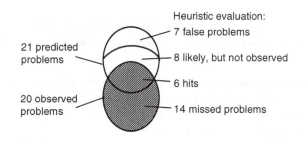

Heuristic evaluation:

21 predicted problems

7 false problems

8 likely, but not observed

6 hits

20 observed problems

14 missed problems

users. Not surprisingly, there were almost no usability problems any more. They could now report to management that usability testing was a great success and the huge amount of money well invested.

Needles to say, the product never became a success, and was soon called back from the market.

The story also illustrates the third law of usability. The developers had spent so much effort that they couldn't change the user interface.

2.4   Different kinds of prototypes

A prototype is a primitive version of a system. It is not intended for real use, but for experiments to resolve difficult issues. These issues can be of many kinds, for instance:

A) Is our idea technically feasible? Would it work with other systems? To answer this question our prototype must have program parts that try to cooperate with other systems to see that it works as expected. Some programming is needed, but the user interface is unimportant.

B) Is it fast enough? Can we obtain the response time we need? Here we also have to program critical parts of the system and simulate a lot of user requests. We can then measure the response time. Here too the user interface is unimportant.

C) Will the stakeholders like something of this kind? Here it is more important that the prototype has a user interface, and maybe some functionality that gives a hint of what the final system would do. The developers will demonstrate the prototype, so it is not important that it is easy to learn.

D) Can the users figure out how to use the system? In this case we have to make a fairly accurate prototype of the user interface, but it need not have any functionality at all. A paper mock-up will do in many cases.

A prototype is not intended for real use. In contrast, a *beta* version is a preliminary version for real use. Using it is often called a *pilot test*. The purpose is to find problems that could not be revealed with a prototype, for instance whether the user organization can deploy and support the system.

2.4.1   Prototypes of user interfaces

When we say 'prototype' in this book, we mean a prototype of the user interface. The central part of the prototype is screens (windows or Web pages) with data fields, menus, function keys, etc. We can make the screens in several ways, as outlined in Figure 2.4D. The four prototypes all show the same screen from the hotel system.

Hand-drawn mock-up. The designer draws the screens by hand using paper and pencil. During usability testing, he changes screens (or opens and closes windows) by putting screen pictures on the table or removing them. The user 'enters data' by writing in the fields with a pencil. He uses the pencil to 'click' on buttons and menus. The designer 'replies' on behalf of the computer by writing results on the screen. (This was the first hotel-system prototype.)

Tool-drawn mock-up. The designer draws the screens on the computer using the same tool that will be used in the final product. In the PC world, the tool might, for instance, be Microsoft Access or Visual Basic. All data fields are blank. The designer prints the screens and uses them in the same way as a hand-drawn mock-up. The

Fig 2.4   Various prototypes

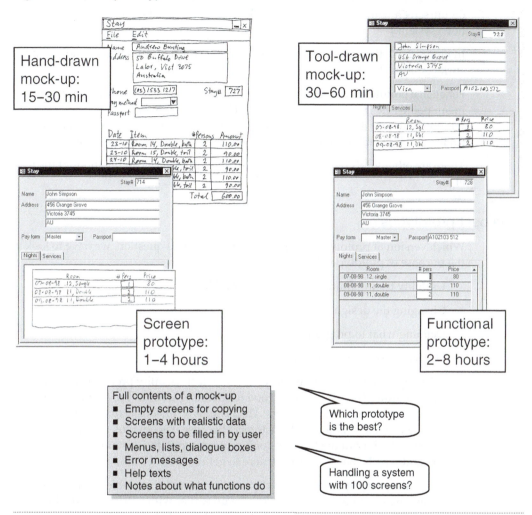

Hand-drawn mock-up: 15–30 min

Tool-drawn mock-up: 30–60 min

Screen prototype: 1–4 hours

Functional prototype: 2–8 hours

Full contents of a mock-up
- Empty screens for copying
- Screens with realistic data
- Screens to be filled in by user
- Menus, lists, dialogue boxes
- Error messages
- Help texts
- Notes about what functions do

Which prototype is the best?

Handling a system with 100 screens?

advantage is that the screens look more real than the hand-drawn ones. (This was the second hotel-system prototype.)

Screen prototype.   The screens are shown on the real computer screen, but they have little functionality. Typically, the user may enter data into some of the fields, but when he pushes a button or selects a menu point, nothing happens by itself. Instead, the designer has built a standard functionality into the system that allows him to use some 'secret' keys to open and close specific windows. Usually the designer needs to create several versions of each window with different data to reflect what the real system would show in various situations. A fast alternative is to put yellow stickers on the screen with the necessary data. (We didn't use this kind of prototype in the hotel system.)

In Figure 2.4D, the screen prototype has live data for the simple fields and yellow stickers for the harder ones.

Functional prototype. It is similar to a screen prototype, but many of the buttons, menu points, etc., actually do something. They may, for instance, open and close windows, update data on related screens and bring data forth from a real database. (In the hotel system we made a functional prototype for one of the screens.)

There are other kinds of prototypes than these, for instance combinations of the types above.

The best prototypes?

Which version of prototypes is the best? To answer this question, we have to look at the purpose of prototypes. They are used for:

- Usability testing (finding the usability problems)
- Changing the design – often radically
- Defining what to program
- Discussing solutions with users

Surprisingly, all four kinds of prototypes can detect usability problems with much the same hit-rate. They are equally good for defining what to program, and for discussing with users and customers. The primitive versions actually have an advantage when discussing with customers because it is obvious that the system is far from finished. With the finished-looking prototypes, the customer cannot understand why he has to pay a lot more to get the final system.

Although the prototypes can reveal the same problems, the problems appear more severe in the primitive versions. Users give up earlier with a primitive version, apparently because they don't want to trouble the facilitator and have him bring up more error messages and screens. As a result, a problem that looked like a task failure with the mock-up may become a medium or a minor problem with a functional prototype.

In special cases a partly functional prototype may be necessary, as we saw for the live search in the hotel system. If you are making virtual reality or multimedia systems, you also need a partly functional prototype.

However, the main difference between the prototypes is the time they take to make. If it takes a long time, developers are unwilling to change the prototype radically. The third law of usability is at work. Here the primitive prototypes have a big advantage.

Drawing a screen by hand, like the one shown, takes 15–30 minutes if you have a good idea what it will look like.

If you know the development tool very well, you will spend around twice that time to make a tool-drawn mock-up. A typical time is 30–60 minutes per screen. If you have little experience with the tool, it may take much longer.

Making a screen prototype will take much more time. With some tools, it is easy to add data to the screens, for others it means setting up a database. Notice that you typically have to make several versions of each screen with different data in them. In contrast, with a mock-up the testers can improvise a result by means of paper and pencil. With screen prototypes it also takes a lot of time setting up the navigation mechanism that allows the designer to switch between screens. A typical time is 1–4 hours per screen (including the time to make several versions of the screen).

When you make a functional prototype, an important issue is to limit the ambitions. You can go anywhere between a screen prototype and a fully functional system. How far to go depends on the system in question and the tool you use. The general rule is that it is more important to spend time on making several versions of the prototype, than providing a lot of functionality. A reasonable time is 2–8 hours per screen.

2.4.2   Contents of a mock-up

Figure 2.4D shows all screens filled in with realistic data, but we also need blank screens for copying. The user will fill in data in a blank screen. The test team will pre-fill others with data corresponding to the expected situations.

We may also need drop-down lists, error messages, etc. Here is a list of what we need for a complete mock-up:

a) Empty screens to be copied.

b) Screens filled out with realistic data (copies).

c) Screens that the user can fill in (copies).

d) Menus that can be brought up.

e) Lists that 'drop down' when the user clicks a combo box.

f) Dialogue boxes, for instance one asking whether to send a booking confirmation by letter, fax or e-mail.

g) Error messages, for instance one saying *You cannot book a room when you haven't selected the guest to book for.*

h) Help texts of various kinds, for instance pop-up help (control tips) coming up when the user lets the mouse 'rest' on a button.

i) Some notes for the facilitator to remind him of what the non-obvious functions and menu points are supposed to do.

Large data volumes

Many systems are dealing with large volumes of data, and it is important to give users a good overview of them. Search screens and specially designed graphical overviews are needed. However, this is not easy to handle in a mock-up. Are we going to manually write long lists of data – maybe ordered in many ways according to the search criteria chosen by the user? Another problem is live searches: As the user enters search criteria character by character, the system immediately updates the results – for instance in a graphical plot. This is hard to simulate with a paper mock-up.

As far as I know, little is written about how to deal with it. Here are the approaches I have seen in practice.

Mock-up samples of data lists. If the search results are to be shown as a list, restrict the display window so that only 10–20 items of the list are visible. Manually draw a couple of possible displays of the list. When the user tries something unexpected during the usability test (users always do so ☺), outline the result with paper and pencil.

Lists of existing large-volume data. Get some existing data files and transform them into a number of possible lists of data to be displayed. The lists may be quite long. Find the right list to show when the user does something.

Mock-ups of graphical displays. For complex, graphical presentations, draw a number of possible views and show the user the right one when he does something. Outline the result with paper and pencil when the user does something unexpected.

Partial, functional prototypes. Make a functional prototype of this specific part of the system. Don't try to include the rest of the system. Populate the system with data from an existing system. Let the user play with this prototype as part of a usability test. Quite often the graphical presentation is to be handled by some new piece of software, and experience shows that it is very beneficial for the programmers to try out this software at the same time with realistic data.

2.4.3 Lots of screens – accelerator effect

If you develop a large system with 100 screens, should you then develop prototypes for all of these? In principle yes, but our experience is that you don't have to usability test all screens to the same extent. Start with the central screens and get them right. Then design the other screens. One reason is that usability defects in the most important screens will cause users to misunderstand many other screens, thus giving a false impression of their usability. Furthermore, a major redesign of the central screens will influence the design of many other screens. We suggest this approach:

▪ Make mock-ups of the most important screens – those used much of the time or in critical situations.

- Usability test them carefully and revise them until they are easy to use.

- Now design the rest of the screens and make prototypes of them. It seems less critical whether these prototypes are mock-ups or more or less functional prototypes.

- Usability test these screens more or less carefully, depending on how important usability is in the project. In many projects a little will do. Revise and test in the same manner.

Bruel & Kjaer used this approach more or less intentionally in their first usability project. The final product had about 23 screens, but they made usability tests of only 8 of them. Yet the final product had 70% fewer usability problems per screen than comparable Bruel & Kjaer products (Lauesen and Vinter 2001).

We call this the *accelerator effect*. The careful testing of the eight key screens seemed to have two effects:

- When developers have the central screens right (including usability testing), they have learned how the users will understand the system. This helps them make good designs of the remaining screens.

- When users understand the central screens, they have formed a good mental model of the system and it helps them understand the rest. (We explain more about mental models in Chapter 4.)

2.5   Does usability pay?

All this trouble with mock-ups and usability tests – does it pay? For years HCI people tried to convince developers that although the usability stuff took some time, it paid in the long run. It was difficult to sell this message to busy and stressed developers.

Benefits of usability

Let us first look at the benefits of high usability:

Faster learning. When the system is easy to learn, users spend much less time learning to use the system, and they don't have to take expensive courses. All of this means cost savings.

Faster daily work. When the system is efficient for daily use, people work faster. More money is saved.

Fewer errors. When users don't make mistakes, they don't waste their own time, and they don't waste time for IT support or expert colleagues who have to sort out the mistakes.

Less demand for hot-line. When the system is easy to use, users call hot-line much less. The hot-line is expensive and needs highly skilled staff.

Better motivation and less stress. When users like the system, they feel motivated. This makes them work better and faster – also in areas that don't relate directly to the system.

More users. When the system is motivating and easy to learn, we can attract more users. This is particularly important when the system is optional – the users can choose to neglect the system. Most Web services are optional, and attracting users is a key concern.

Wider work areas. In traditional companies, users have highly specialized jobs. The consequence is that customers don't feel welcome. An example is a traditional insurance company where you have to call one number to get a health insurance, another number to insure the car and a third number to insure your dog. One reason is that each of these insurance systems has its own IT system, and this system is very difficult to master. As a result, nobody can handle several kinds of insurance. In modern insurance companies, the customer can call any service person and have all insurance questions sorted out there (almost).

Let the customer do the work. There is even more money to save if we can transfer the work to our customer. If the customer orders the goods electronically or sorts out technical problems with an on-line system, we save a lot of time among our own staff, and we can provide 24-hour on-line service. This is a major drive for the e-commerce wave. However, the systems must be far more easy to use than traditional business applications.

Some of these benefits relate to cost saving, some to quality improvement and some to strategic possibilities for the companies.

Cost of usability

Now, what is the cost of making user-friendly systems? There are few figures in this area. HCI people quote a few cases where the added cost was 5–10% of the entire development cost. Software houses that develop Web systems for their customers tell me that when they write a proposal, they specify usability testing as an optional deliverable. The price is 5–10% of the entire development contract. And how do their customers react? They always turn down the option. They are not willing to pay for usability – or the software house is not able to sell the usability issue to them.

My own experience is different. The cost of usability is negative! It is cheaper to develop a system with prototyping and usability testing. In addition, we get the benefits mentioned above.

We found this striking result in the Bruel & Kjaer project where we also learned about the accelerator effect. In their first usability project, the developers designed mock-ups of the user interface, usability tested them with potential customers, revised the design and tested it again. Then they programmed the system. At the end of development, these highly experienced developers reported:

> This is the first time we finished a project on schedule – and without stress. The reason? We knew exactly how the user interface should be – and that it was good. The rest was just programming according to the book.

The resulting product had 70% fewer usability problems than comparable products, it sold twice as many units – and at twice the usual price (Lauesen and Vinter 2001).

If Web houses knew about these results, they should not add 5–10% on the bill for mock-ups and usability tests. They should include them for free – and in that way save 20% on their own development costs.

Test yourself

a) What is the difference between traditional systems development, iterative development and iterative design?

b) How many design iterations are usually needed?

c) What are the main problems with the classical iterative design?

d) Did the first law of usability work in the hotel case?

e) What went wrong in the horror story?

f) How much should we add to the ordinary development costs to make the system user-friendly?

g) Mention the four basic kinds of user interface prototypes.

h) What is the accelerator effect?

i) What should a complete mock-up contain?

Design exercises. See Chapter 17.

3

Data presentation

Highlights

- Gestalt laws: What our vision considers an 'object' on the screen.

- Ways to show simple and complex data.

- Why some presentations mobilize several brain centres and improve usability.

- Key exercises: Explain existing designs with gestalt laws. Design non-trivial data presentations.

In this chapter we look at the psychological mechanisms in our visual perception that influence how we perceive computer screens and paper documents.

We also look at some of the many ways to present data, ranging from text form to 3-D graphs.

3.1 Gestalt laws

A *gestalt* is something we perceive as a unit or an object. The word *gestalt* is German and means a figure or a shape. The gestalt laws say what we intuitively perceive as a coherent unit or object – without any training or conscious effort. Many of the gestalt laws were developed by psychologists around 1900 (see Rock and Palmer 1990). The gestalt laws can, to some extent, be explained by the way the vision centres work in the brain (see Treisman 1986). (Notice that *gestalt laws* have nothing to do with *gestalt theory*, which tries to explain human thoughts and problem solving, or *gestalt therapy*, which tries to treat mental diseases.)

Figure 3.1A illustrates three important gestalt laws and their interaction.

Most of us will perceive example A as four columns of bubbles to the left and as four horizontal rows to the right. The reason is that the bubbles that are close together seem to form a shape. It is the *law of proximity* that is at work.

Law of proximity: Pieces that are close together are perceived as belonging together.

Example B also shows the law of proximity. If we know that these are mill wheels, we see mill wheels with narrow wings. The law of proximity makes us perceive the two lines that are close together as a unit – the borderlines of the wing. In principle, we might perceive the shapes as mill wheels with broad wings, but we don't do that intuitively.

Example C is clearly a mill wheel with broad wings. Here the *law of closure* is at work. The closed lines around the broad wings create strong gestalts. Notice that the law clearly suppresses the law of proximity, so that we no longer perceive the close lines as surrounding a unit.

Law of closure: The area inside a closed line is perceived as a shape.

Example D illustrates the *law of good continuation*. The pieces that appear to be on a curved line create a clear gestalt.

Law of good continuation: Pieces on a smooth line are perceived as belonging together.

Figure 3.1B shows how the law of closure and the law of proximity may interfere. Example E is ambiguous. We see it partly as three shapes (the law of closure), but even stronger we see the curved line that seems to cross through the three shapes (the law of good continuation). In this case the law of good continuation seems a bit stronger.

Example F shows what happens if we weaken the continuous line. The law of closure dominates and makes us see three gestalts.

Figure 3.1C, example G, illustrates the *law of similarity*. We perceive the small crosses as a single, weak gestalt. The gestalt is also supported by the law of proximity – the crosses are close together. In example H, the crosses are larger and the bubbles smaller. We perceive all the large crosses as belonging together, even though one cross is 'far away'. In this case the law of similarity defeats the law of proximity. It

Fig 3.1 A Three gestalt laws

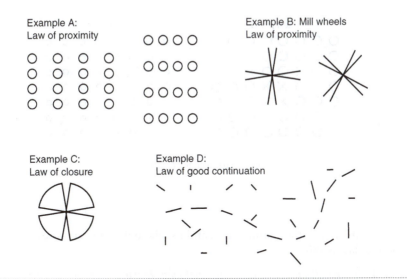

Example A:
Law of proximity

Example B: Mill wheels
Law of proximity

Example C:
Law of closure

Example D:
Law of good continuation

only works because now there is a large contrast between crosses and bubbles: shape as well as size.

Law of similarity: Things that look alike are perceived as belonging together.

We can also let colours signal the similarity. This is often useful on the screen, for instance if we have two things far apart on the screen and want the user to perceive them as related. We simply give them the same distinct colour. This only works if there aren't a lot of other colours on the same screen. In Chapter 10 we show an example (Figure 10.6). It is a complex overview screen where the user can apply two search criteria – one for one part of the data, another for the other part of the data. Users couldn't see the relationship between criteria and data until we gave them the same background colour. The law of similarity now made the connection obvious. See Treisman (1986) for how the brain finds out what is 'similar'.

Fig 3.1 B Closure versus continuation

Example E:
Law of good continuation

Example F:
Law of closure?

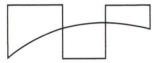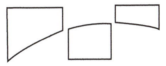

Fig 3.1 C Law of similarity and other gestalt laws

Example G

```
O O O O O O O O
O O O O O O O O
O O X O O X O O
O O O X X O O O
O O O X X O O O
O O O O O O O O
O O O O O O O O
```

Example H

```
o  o  o  o  o  o  o  o
o  o  o  X  o  o  o  o
o  o  X  X  o  o  o  o
o  o  o  o  o  o  o  o
o  o  o  o  o  o  o  o
o  o  o  o  o  o  X  o
o  o  o  o  o  o  o  o
```

Law of parallel movement

Law of . . .

There are many other gestalt laws, and psychologists detect more all the time. A very strong law is this:

> *Law of parallel movement: Things that move in parallel are perceived as belonging together.*

Although it is a very strong law, it rarely plays a role on user interfaces, which tend to be semi-static. One exception is of course game programs. Hearing about the law of parallel movement, a colleague said: 'This law *is* used on the screen; it makes the scroll bar work!' To his surprise, he was wrong. Scroll bar and document move in opposite directions.

Many of the laws are important for our perception of things in nature, where they often are partially hidden by trees and tall grass. 'Good continuation' and 'parallel movement' make the hunter able to perceive small glimpses of an animal as a single gestalt.

3.2   Screen gestalts

In this section we will apply the gestalt laws to simple screen layouts.

3.2.1   Line gestalts?

Figure 3.2A shows to the left a typical dialogue box for choosing the print format (from an older version of Microsoft Word). It consists of several clear gestalts formed by the laws of closure, proximity and similarity. We will try various other layouts of exactly the same information.

Some designers talk about a variant of the law of good continuation – the *law of lines*. It says that aligned items are perceived as belonging together, for instance aligned on a vertical line. This 'law' is not particularly outspoken in the original dialogue box (version A). Just for fun, I have made version B where the law of lines is heavily used since all items are left-aligned in one long column. I guess we all agree that this version is completely confusing, although it is strictly logical according to a well-known principle. The eye is good at seeing gestalts, but not good at seeing logic, and few people notice the logical principle.

What is wrong with this layout? There are lots of small gestalts, but no medium-sized gestalts, and as a result we lack some structure. There is a kind of line gestalt to the left (the line of alignment), but it consists of many different symbols (buttons, check boxes, radio buttons, etc.). As a result, the law of similarity tells us that these symbols don't belong together.

Now look at version C. You may notice a weak line gestalt consisting of the first letter of all the texts. They are on a vertical line. Once you have noticed this line, you may notice the logic: all the texts are ordered alphabetically.

Just to make sure: This is still an awful way to arrange the information. The alphabetical sequence doesn't help us at all, since most of the texts are unfamiliar anyway. On the other hand, the eye looks for some gestalts and may find, for instance, the four bottom lines that look similar and are aligned. But the logical part of our brain cannot see the logical relationship between these four lines. In other words, the eye cannot support the logic, and the logic is not even useful.

3.2.2   Proximity and closure

In Figure 3.2B we have made further experiments with the print set-up. Version D has four blocks of 'controls' that make four strong gestalts. The law of proximity is the major force here because the distance within each block is much smaller than the distance between the blocks. Inside each block gestalt, there are smaller gestalts that look alike, and the law of similarity further strengthens the block gestalts.

This version looks simpler and cleaner than the original one because there are fewer and stronger gestalts and the dominating box has disappeared.

Now have a look at version E. We have used a strong effect – the frame around the radio buttons – to make this gestalt even stronger. And just for fun, we have moved the OK button inside this frame. What would that imply in practice? Huge confusion!

The user thinks: *Why is the OK button here? Do you have to click OK after having chosen the print range? Why? And what should you click after having changed the other options?* Actually, it is the same OK button as before and with the same functionality. We have just moved it to another place.

The reason for the confusion is that the law of closure tells the user that everything inside the frame belongs together. In other words, the OK button works only on the print range. The example shows that the gestalts can have a huge influence on our mental model of how the system operates.

Frames have a strong effect, but they occupy much space on the screen. An alternative is to replace them with a light background colour. It has much the same effect, but takes no space. With old-fashioned computer terminals it was an easy solution. With Microsoft Windows it is a bit more difficult and against the guidelines. Various frames are used instead. On the Web it has again become easy and widely used.

Fig 3.2 A Law of lines?

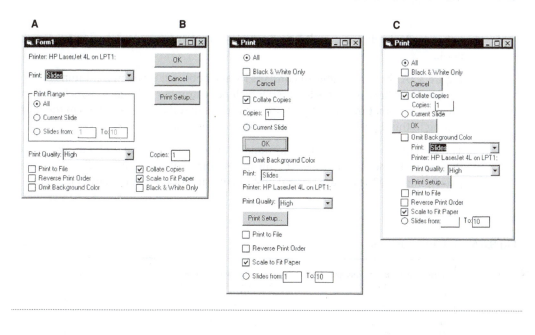

Fig 3.2 B Proximity and closure

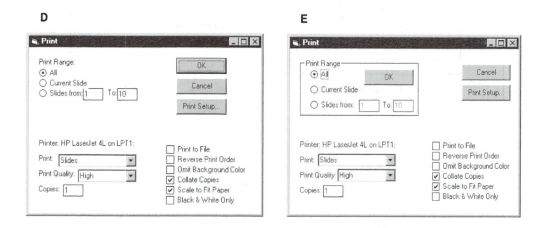

3.3 Text gestalts

Let us try to apply the gestalt laws to the layout of ordinary text, for instance in a book.

Figure 3.3A shows the table of contents from a book, set up as two columns of entries. Note how hard it is to grasp which page number belongs to which section. The reason is that the law of proximity suggests that the page numbers in the middle belong to the right-hand entries rather than the left-hand ones.

The second version shows the traditional way to overcome the problem. We connect the entries to the page numbers by means of dots. How does this work psychologically? There are several gestalt laws at work. First, the laws of good

Fig 3.3 A Column gestalts

Fig 3.3 B Heading proximity

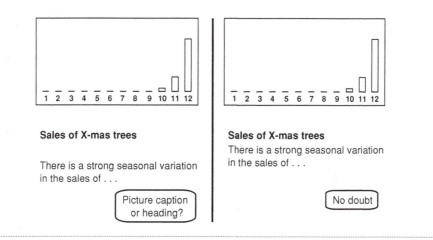

The layout should signal the right answer by means of proximity. The typographical rule is to put headings closer to the text below than to the text above. Isn't it amazing that the standard format on the Web (using HTML) uses headings that are exactly as bad as the version to the left?

continuation and proximity make the row of dots connect the entry with the page number. Second, the entire left-hand column is now a block of pieces with an imagined rectangular border. The law of closure makes the block into a single gestalt of related pieces. What should happen if we use dots only in the top and bottom line? Try it.

Figure 3.3B shows another example. At the left we have three gestalts: a figure, a line of bold text and some body text. But what is the bold text? A caption for the figure or a heading for the body text? If we move it up a bit, the eye will perceive it as a figure caption. If we move it down a bit it is a heading, as shown to the right.

The layout should signal the right answer by means of proximity. The typographical rule is to put headings closer to the text below than to the text above. Isn't it amazing that the standard format on the Web (using HTML) uses headings that are exactly as bad as the version to the left?

Paragraph gestalts

Figure 3.3C shows three layouts of body text. The difference is the way the paragraphs are separated.

In the first version, the paragraphs are separated by a slight indent of the first line of each paragraph. The lines are not right-aligned. The result is some weak gestalts at the left margin – the white areas of indentation, but no clear signal in the right margin. The paragraphs don't stand out as clear gestalts. You often see this layout when amateurs set up a text.

The second version is similar to the first except for the right margin, which now is aligned. There are now clear signals from the right margin too and they match the left-hand signals in most places. If you screw up your eyes, you can see each paragraph as a block of text. It is not a very strong gestalt, but clearly stronger than the first version. The effect is stronger when the text column is narrow. This layout requires careful hyphenation to avoid disturbing, white patches in the middle of the text. Newspapers normally use this layout to save space, and since the columns of text are very narrow, the paragraphs stand out well.

In the third version, blank lines separate the paragraphs. Now the law of proximity works fully, and we see each paragraph as a strong gestalt. The lines are not right-aligned, but still the gestalts are very clear. This layout is good for ordinary reports, and is often used in textbooks too. Some typesetters right-align the lines, taking also the trouble with the hyphenation. Does it have an effect on the gestalts? Yes a bit, because the blocks of text now have a smooth border all the way around, which allows the law of closure to work strongly too. Although this version has good gestalts, it is hard to read because the lines are too long.

Line length

The line length (column width) is very important for reading. There are two factors involved:

Retracing. When the eye has reached the end of a line, it has to retrace to the start of the next line. If the lines are long and densely packed, the eye easily hits a wrong line.

Saccades. The eye moves in jumps – saccades – along the line, but cannot see anything during the movement. It only sees the words while it stands still – the fixation periods. It has to stop around every 15 to 30 characters, depending on the complexity of the text, the reader's skill, etc. If it has to stop many times on each line, reading is harder and the eye may lose its way in the text. Skilled readers of newspapers don't move the eye along the line at all. The lines are so short that the reader can move the eye downwards only.

The lines in version 3 (Figure 3.3C) are too long, making reading harder than necessary. The problem would be much greater if versions 1 and 2 had similarly long lines. This is because the paragraph gestalts in version 3 are much stronger, thus giving more guidance to the eye. If the lines are spaced wider, for instance 1.1 or 1.2 times the letter size, they become somewhat easier to read.

An old typographical rule of thumb says:

- line length at most 12.5 cm (5 inches)
- lines at most 65 characters (average, excluding spaces)

Fig 3.3 C Body text

1

This report is intended to provide background information which will facilitate the development of procedures and tools to improve the tware producers to manage and control software quality and to demonstrate the achievement of software quality requirements.

The report surveys published work relating to the identification and specification of software quality characteristics, metrics relating to them, and inferences which can be drawn from the metrics. It does not attempt, however, to evaluate the published work to any great extent. It notes the ure, and identifies uality Management project. In summarising such large works it has not been possible to cover all the material, and the serious student may need to refer to the originals for further details.

Boehm et al's book entitled "Characteristics of Software Quality" reports on work done in the early seventies and is a precursor not only or McCall et al's work but also of Gilb's. The initial objectives of the study were to identify a set of characteristics of software quality, and for each characteristic to aimed at measuring the degree to which a program possesses the characteristic and hence provide an overall software quality assessment.

(Boehm et al soon abandoned the idea of an overall quality since they argued that the quality requirements for a given product will vary with the needs and priorities of the user, so there could be no single universally useful rating of software quality. They concluded that metrics would be best used as anomaly indicators - ie to note that an item of software differed from the normal pattern in a way that might be symptomatic of quality problems.)

2

This report is intended to provide background information which will facilitate the development of procedures and tools to improve the ability of software producers to manage and control software quality and to demonstrate the achievement of software quality requirements and improve the control software.

The report surveys published work relating to the identification and specification of software quality characteristics, metrics relating to them, and inferences which can be drawn from the metrics. It does not attempt, however, to evaluate the published work to any great summarising such large works it has not been possible to cover all the material, and the serious student may need to refer to the originals for further details defin place.

Boehm et al's book entitled "Characteristics of Software Quality" reports on work done in the early seventies and is a precursor not only or McCall et al's work but also of Gilb's. The initial objectives of the study were to identify a set of characteristics of software quality, and for each characteristic to identify one or more metrics aimed at measuring the degree to which a program possesses the characteristic and hence provide an overall

(Boehm et al soon abandoned the idea of an overall quality since they argued that the quality requirements for a given product will vary with the needs and priorities of the user, so there could be no single universally useful rating of software quality. They concluded that metrics would be best used as anomaly indicators - ie to note that an item of software differed from the normal pattern in a way that might be symptomatic of quality problems.)

3

This report is intended to provide background information which will facilitate the development of procedures and tools to improve the ability of software producers to manage and control software quality and to demonstrate the achievement of software quality requirements.

The report surveys published work relating to the identification and specification of software quality characteristics, metrics relating to them, and inferences which can be drawn from the metrics. It does not attempt, however, to evaluate the published work to any great extent. It notes the existence of relevant software tools referred to in the literature, and identifies areas of work which might be pursued further within Testing Specification and Quality Management project. In summarising such large works it has not been possible to cover all the material, and the serious student may need to refer to the originals for further details.

Boehm et al's book entitled "Characteristics of Software Quality" reports on work done in the early seventies and is a precursor not only or McCall et al's work but also of Gilb's. The initial objectives of the study were to identify a set of characteristics of software quality, and for each characteristic to identify one or more metrics aimed at measuring the degree to which a program possesses the characteristic and hence provide an overall software quality assessment.

(Boehm et al soon abandoned the idea of an overall quality since they argued that the quality requirements for a given product will vary with the needs and priorities of the user, so there could be no single universally useful rating of software quality. They concluded that metrics would be best used as anomaly indicators - ie to note that an item of software differed from the normal pattern in a way that might be symptomatic of quality problems.)

Clear gestalts
but lines too long.
Annoying to read.

For 10 point Times Roman, the 65 characters correspond to a line length of roughly 11 cm. For 12 point Times Roman, the 65 characters correspond to a line length of roughly 13 cm.

With standard paper size (A4 or Letter), the page is around 21 cm or 8.5 inches wide. The rules above are not easy to follow, but Figure 3.3D shows some possibilities:

- **Simple reports.** 12-point text and broad margins (3.5 cm or 1.5 inches). Not fully according to the rule of thumb, but an acceptable compromise for letters and simple reports.

- **Complex reports.** 10-point text and a very broad right margin (e.g. 3.5 cm left, 6 cm right). This is a nice layout for more complex reports, and it leaves good space for notes in the margin.

- **Technical documents.** 10-point text in two columns, narrow margins (2 cm or 3/4 inches). This uses the space of the page fully. It is a good format for documents where overview is important.

- **Books.** Smaller page size, like in professional books. This paper size is usually not available in offices.

Fig 3.3 D Line length, A4 or Letter paper

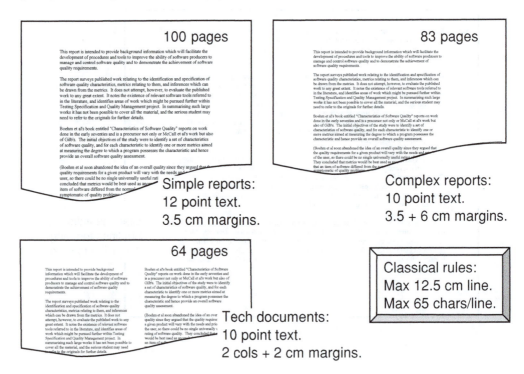

The same amount of text is shown in all the examples. Measured in number of pages, we have these document lengths:

Simple report format	100%
Complex report format	83%
Technical doc format	64%

In the academic world, I often see 10-point text on 16-cm lines. Each line has an average of 96 characters. This format saves another 10%, but it is horrible to read! Academic papers are hard to read anyway, and there is no reason to use a layout that makes it even harder.

Modern computer screens have space for very long lines, and designers are tempted to utilize the space by means of long lines. This is one of the reasons that texts are much harder to read on the screen than on paper.

3.4   Contrast

Sometimes we want to call attention to something on the screen or the page. Frames are one way to do it, but there are many others. Figure 3.4A shows various ways of creating contrast, that is make something stand out with the rest as background.

At the top we use shape differences as contrast. The pattern of bubbles creates a background where the crosses stand out. Since the crosses are far from each other, they don't create a single gestalt. If there were roughly the same number of crosses and bubbles, none of them would stand out.

The next example creates contrast by means of size or line thickness. The large text stands out from the rest. The thick-line rectangle stands out from the crowd.

The rectangles also use simple 3-D effects to show that something is in front of the background. One of the boxes is in front of the others by means of two 3-D effects: (1) the front box hides part of other boxes; (2) it is larger, suggesting that it is closer.

Deviating colour or darkness can also create a contrast, as shown in the next example. One of the words is light grey (red in the real document), and stands out. One of the boxes is darker than the rest. Notice that also the text that is smaller than the rest gives a contrast, but not so much as a large text does.

Finally, flashes and movements give an intense contrast, which attracts the eye to the extent that it may be hard to focus on other things – even see what the flashing text says. Many Web pages try to attract attention in this way, but fail to communicate a message. The flash effect touches on our instinctive fear of the approaching lion: don't look at the details, just run.

Process control systems usually signal alarms with something flashing, for instance a flashing message 'overheating'. It calls the operator's attention – even at a large distance. In disaster situations, there will be many flashing things that the operator has to read. This is fine for calling attention, but bad for reading the messages. For this reason there is an important feature on the interface: a button that stops the flashes so that the operator can think.

Use contrasts moderately

In order for the contrast to work, there must be a background for the contrast. If you emphasize too many things, the effect disappears. If everything is in vivid colours, nothing is emphasized. If many things are already emphasized, you need an even larger effect to emphasize one of those.

The general rule is to use contrasts and emphasis moderately. Otherwise the effect disappears.

Fig 3.4 A Contrast

Form

```
O O O O O O O O
O O O O O O O O
O O O O O X O O
O O O O O O O O
O O X O O O O O
O O O O O O O O
O O O O O O O O
```

Size, thickness, or 3-D

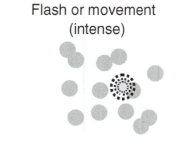

Colour or darkness

Flash or movement (intense)

Figure 3.4B shows an example. It is a Web page where frequent flyers can see their earned points and when they expire. Look at the list of points and find out how many points the person has earned.

Many people look at the list and expect to find the total at the bottom of the list. But it is not there. Then they start adding the points themselves. They don't notice that the total is somewhere above the list – in a very large font.

Why don't they notice? Maybe there are too many things shouting at them up there, and although the total tries to shout even louder, it doesn't always succeed. The gestalt laws tell a different story: the total doesn't seem to belong to the list of points, but to another gestalt. In this case, the gestalt laws overwrite the contrasts – at least to many users.

Vision centres for shape, colour and movement

Although a green shape on a red background gives contrast, it makes the shape details fainter. If you, for instance, show a green face on a red background with exactly the same darkness, you can see it is a face, but you cannot recognize the person.

Fig 3.4 B How many points earned?

Reproduced with permission from SAS EuroBonus

The reason for this is illustrated in Figure 3.4C. Our visual perception, positioned at the back of our brain, has three main centres, all of which see the entire field of vision, but with different emphasis:

■ The **shape vision** sees details, but is colour-blind. It sees sharply only in the central field of vision. It sends lots of data forward in the brain to consciousness and higher level centres (thoughts). The shape centre is crucial for reading.

■ The **colour vision** sees colours, but is not good at seeing shapes and details. It sends most of its data to the shape centre, and only some weak signals to higher level centres.

■ The **movement vision** sees things that move or flash, but is not good at seeing shapes or colour. It too sends data to the shape centre, but also sends strong

Fig 3.4 C Vision centres

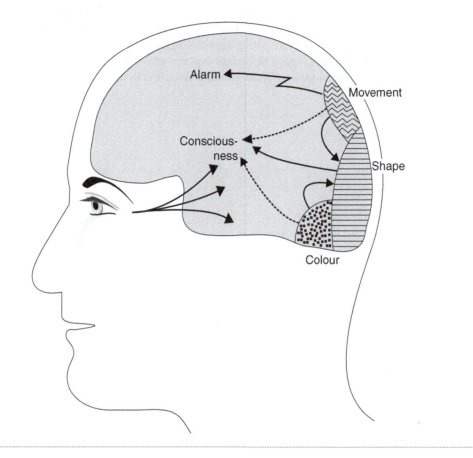

signals forward to the attention centre (alarm). The centre is also responsible for 3-D perception.

This explains why movement and flashing is so distracting. It also explains why we cannot clearly see green shapes on a red background. The shape centre is colour-blind and sees little if the two colours are equally dark. The colour centre tells the shape centre that there are red and green areas, but cannot provide the detailed shapes.

How do we know this? From many sources (Livingstone 1988; Zeki 1992). One source is studies of people with brain damage. A person with damaged shape vision appears blind, yet – if his movement vision is intact – he is able to catch a large ball thrown to him. He cannot understand himself how this happens, because he doesn't consciously see anything.

If the person has a damaged shape centre, but an intact colour centre, he claims he cannot see the colour of a sheet of coloured paper shown to him. He cannot even see the piece of paper. Yet, if we ask him to guess the colour, he has a very high hit-rate. The weak signals from the colour centre to higher level centres are probably responsible for this. Again he cannot explain why this happens since he doesn't consciously see anything. These phenomena are called *blind vision*.

3.5   Presentation formats

There are many ways to show data, and it is a good idea to experiment with the various forms. Presentation is particularly critical if we are to provide a good overview of complex data. Below we show many examples of data presentation, but there are many more. See primarily Spence (2001), but also Tufte (1983, 1990) for more presentations.

Example: room data

As the first example, we will look at data about rooms in a hotel system. The different presentation formats will be useful when we later design such a system.

Classical 'form'. Figure 3.5A shows data about a single room. This is the classical way of presenting data: a *form* with many *data fields* – similar to a paper form. We can see the various details of the room, the number of beds, whether there is sea view, the prices for different seasons and special prices if the room (a double room) is used as a single room. Forms are excellent for showing lots of detail. If we don't have enough space on one screen, we can use scroll bars or tab forms to conceptually extend the form.

A characteristic thing of a form is that it has a fixed number of fields, and all of these fields contain a single piece of data. However, if we want to show which dates the room has been occupied, we need a long list of dates. The example shows just the beginning of this list, starting the date after the room was last renovated. This is not a good way to show a long list of data. We get no overview, and cannot even see the date of current interest.

List format. The bottom of Figure 3.5A shows the list format, also called the table format. We have used the format to show the states of all the hotel rooms over time. To limit the list, there are search criteria where we can specify the dates of interest. We can scroll to see more list items. For each list element we can see only a few fields. We have, for instance, omitted the many prices.

Detail window. In user interfaces we often combine a list with a window that shows more detail of a selected element on the list. In the figure we have indicated that selecting a line will bring out the details of this room as a classical form. We have also shown a version where the details are in an adjoining frame, rather than a separate window.

The list format is the most common way of presenting bulk data on the screen, and from a programming point of view it is easy to make. Many programming tools also allow us to embed a list or table in a form. We could, for instance, replace the *occupied* field on the classical room form with a table of the occupied dates.

Fig 3.5 A Room data

Classical 'form' format

Room form

Room no.	011
Beds	2
Bath	full
Balcony	no
Seaview	no

Prices	high	med	low
Normal	88	80	58
As single	68	60	49

Last renovated 20-08-03

Occupied 21-08-03, 22-08-03, 31-08-03, 01-09

List or table format

Room states from 30-08-03 to 01-09-03

Room	Beds	Bath	State	Date
011	2	full	occ	30-08-03
011	2	full	occ	31-08-03
012	1	toil	book	30-08-03
012	1	toil	book	31-08-03
012	1	toil	book	01-09-03
013	2	toil	book	30-08-03
013	2	toil	repair	31-08-03

Prices	high	med	low
Normal	88	80	58
As single	68	60	49
Balcony	no		
Seaview	no		

Last renovated 20-08-03

Detail window
for selected item

Room states from 30-08-03 to 01-09-03

Room	Beds	Bath	State	Date
011	2	full	occ	30-08-03
011	2	full	occ	31-08-03
012	1	toil	book	30-08-03
012	1	toil	book	31-08-03
012	1	toil	book	01-09-03
013	2	toil	book	30-08-03
013	2	toil	repair	31-08-03

Prices	high	med	low
Normal	88	80	58
As single	68	60	49
Balcony	no		
Seaview	no		

Last renovated 20-08-03

Details shown in
adjoining frame

Fig 3.5 B Room status

Matrix format

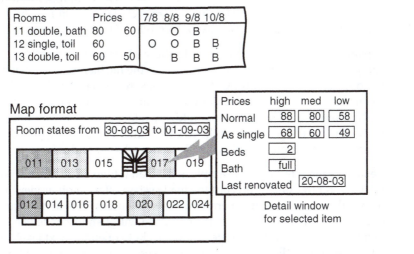

Rooms	Prices		7/8	8/8	9/8	10/8
11 double, bath	80	60		O	B	
12 single, toil	60		O	O	B	B
13 double, toil	60	50		B	B	B

Map format

Room states from 30-08-03 to 01-09-03

011	013	015		017	019

012	014	016	018	020	022	024

Prices	high	med	low
Normal	88	80	58
As single	68	60	49
Beds	2		
Bath	full		
Last renovated	20-08-03		

Detail window
for selected item

....

Matrix format. Unfortunately, the list form gives poor overview in many cases. For instance it is hard to see when a room is free. The matrix format shown in Figure 3.5B is a way to improve the overview. We have marked the dates horizontally and the rooms vertically. Whether a room is occupied or booked at a given date is marked by an O or a B. Now it is easy to get an overview of when each room is free. We might add scroll bars to allow the receptionist to look at many rooms and a wide range of dates.

In practice, we would provide search criteria that allow the user to look only at rooms free in a certain period, rooms of a particular kind, etc.

The matrix form can give an excellent overview, but it is hard to find space for all the details, for instance details of who occupies the room at a certain date. We might again combine it with a detail window.

Map format. The map format gives radically new possibilities. Here we have shown a floor map and colour-marked the rooms that are occupied or booked at a certain date. Now it is easy for the receptionist to see which rooms are quiet, which have a balcony, etc. We don't even have to code it into the database. The receptionist can also easily give the guest two neighbour rooms or two opposing rooms, for instance for parents with children.

It is more difficult to provide an overview of details such as the room prices, number of beds, etc. The form and list formats are better for this. Again we can combine formats, for instance with a detail window.

Maps, drawings, photos, etc., are becoming more widely used as the technical possibilities are improved.

Hierarchies. Sometimes we have to show a hierarchy of things, for instance a company divided into departments, where each department may be divided into sub-departments, etc. We also have a hierarchy of folders and files in the computer.

Explorer tree. There are many ways to show a hierarchy. Figure 3.5C shows two very compact forms. The first is a presentation of the file hierarchy, shown by the Explorer window. We can see that the C drive contains the folders Acrobat3, ATI, Compaq and so on. Acrobat3 contains a Reader folder, which in turn contains ActiveX, Browser, FONTS and so on. The user can unfold any folder and see its sub-folders. To the right we see the detailed contents of the Reader folder. This presentation gives an excellent overview of the hierarchy plus details of any selected folder.

Nested menus. The second example is the mail folders in an e-mail system. We see the Explorer tree once more, but the mail system offers another view too – nested menus that show the same hierarchy. When the user wants to move an e-mail from one folder to another, he selects the mail, and with a short-cut key he unfolds the first menu, selects the top-level folder, moves right to open the next level, and so on. The advantage is that the hierarchy only occupies screen space when it is used. (The user can also drag and drop the mail, using the Explorer tree to the left.)

If we only had the nested menus for the hierarchy, most users would feel they didn't have a good overview of the tree. The constant reinforcement of the hierarchy through the Explorer tree seems important to most users.

While most users find out to use the nested menus using the keyboard only, few of them find out that the Explorer tree can be operated exactly the same way. Although you can navigate the tree with the keyboard, it is not easy to move a mail with the keyboard in this way, but in principle it would be possible.

Example: business history

Figure 3.5D shows more ways of presenting data. The example is to visualize the history of a company over some years. We have chosen some key figures often used in TQM (Total Quality Management) : customer satisfaction, employee satisfaction, total sales and profit.

Matrix format. First we have the matrix format with a row for each of the three factors, and the years along the horizontal axis. It gives the exact details but little overview. Is there a message in all these numbers?

Line graph. Next we have the line graph format for the same numbers. We see a broken line or curve for each factor. The data are shown in two dimensions (two coordinates) – the years horizontally and the values vertically. This graph tells us a story of some turbulence in employee satisfaction. The problem has now been overcome, apparently at the cost of a dangerous drop in profits.

Fig 3.5 C Hierarchy presentations

Explorer tree

Detail window

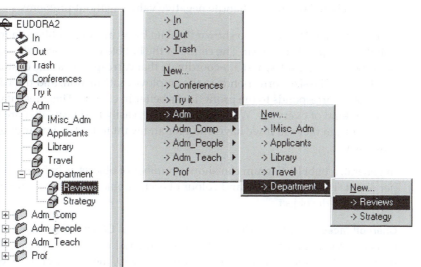

E-mail folders

Hierarchical menus

3-D surface. The 3-dimensional (3-D) graph uses three coordinate axes. We have put the years along the axis going into the paper, the values on the vertical axis and the factors along the horizontal axis. Imagine that you look at the 3-D block from its right-hand side. Then it would look very much like the line graph.

The 3-D surface doesn't give any better overview in this case, but for other kinds of data it can provide a splendid overview. There are many other kinds of 3-D data presentations.

Radar chart or spider web. Figure 3.5E shows a radar chart or spider web. It has a spoke for each of the factors, and a closed polygon for each of the years. It can easily accommodate a few more factors as suggested in the example. It cannot handle negative values, as the spokes have only one free end.

Radar charts are a popular way of presenting business data like this example, probably because progress in all areas shows up as a series of expanding circles. In our case, we can see that the 'circles' don't grow perfectly. There is some serious trouble with the profit and the employee satisfaction. If we give the years different colours, the troubles will stand out more clearly.

Parallel coordinate plot. The parallel coordinate plot is a cousin to the radar chart. We have simply taken the spokes apart and put all of them vertically side by side. The overview is much better, although steady progress doesn't look as impressive as in the radar chart. We can also handle negative values without problems.

Bubble diagram. We have also shown the data by means of a bubble diagram. Each bubble corresponds to a year. The centre of the bubble has an x-coordinate that corresponds to the sales, and a y-coordinate that corresponds to the customer satisfaction. The size corresponds to the employee satisfaction, and the whiteness of the bubble corresponds to the profit (looks better in colour). This presentation gives a different kind of overview. We can, for instance, easily find years that are very different from the rest. If we have one year and want to find a similar one, this is quite easy.

In general, a bubble diagram can show a number of objects as bubbles – one bubble per object. The position, size and colour of each bubble reflect four numerical attributes of the object.

Chernoff faces. Finally we show the same figures as *Chernoff faces*, named after their inventor. A Chernoff face is characterized by the radius of the forehead, the radius of the bottom face, the turn of the mouth (up or down), the height of the eyebrows and about 12 more factors. We now map the customer satisfaction to the radius of the forehead, the profit to the turn of the mouth, etc. The result is a face for each year.

Imagine that we have data for one year and want to find years that are similar, that is with similar key factors. The problem is now to find faces that are similar to one we have. Chernoff made experiments to show that faces are very efficient for this.

Fig 3.5 D Business history (1)

Matrix

	1996	1997	1998
Customer satisfact	7	8	9
Employee satisfact	6	4	8
Sales	12.5	14.5	15.8
Profit	2.7	1.9	0.8
. . .			

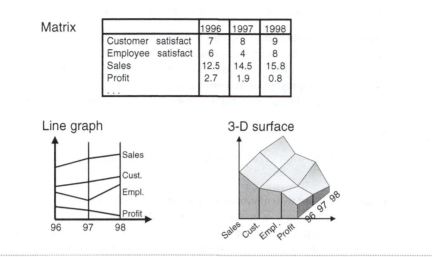

Line graph

3-D surface

Actually we have a large brain area in the temple that deals specifically with face recognition, and in this way we mobilize the centre for our task.

A Chernoff face is somewhat similar to a bubble diagram. It can show a number of objects as faces – one face per object. The shape of each face reflects up to

Fig 3.5 E Business history (2)

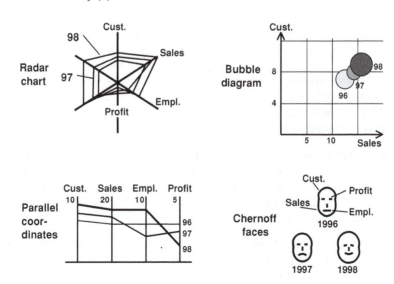

Radar chart

Bubble diagram

Parallel coor- dinates

Chernoff faces

16 numerical attributes for the object. In contrast to the bubble diagram, the Chernoff faces don't use position, size or colour to show the data.

Experiment on your own. You can experiment with some of these forms in Microsoft Excel. Enter the data matrix for the business history into a spreadsheet. Select the area that contains the matrix, and use the menu Insert -> Chart. You will see that Excel provides many presentation forms, but only some of the forms above. For instance, it provides a bubble diagram, but cannot colour the bubbles according to data values.

Analog numbers

Figure 3.5F shows several other ways to present numbers.

Electrical current with alarm limit. The first example is from a system that monitors power distribution in a geographical area. We must show a physical measurement (current in amperes) with an associated alarm limit. If the current exceeds 80 A, the system must raise an alarm and the operator has to do something to avoid overloading the power network. Currently the current is 62 A.

We have shown this in traditional digital form to the left, and as a circular meter to the right. The full circle corresponds to 100 A, and the alarm area, where the current is too large, is the grey part. The circular form is traditional in process control because it looks like the old meter instruments on the wall-size control panels.

On the much smaller computer screens, the circles occupy too much space. It is also clumsy to add a text label to the circle. The presentation form below the circle avoids these problems. This 'thermometer' display is as easy to read, occupies much less space and can easily be labelled with a text as shown in the figure.

Scroll bar. To the right in Figure 3.5F, you see scroll bars as they originally were used in IBM's OS/2, and later in many Microsoft products. The position of the scroll bar shows how far we are from the top and bottom of the document. The length of the scroll bar shows how much of the document we can see in the window. In the example on the top, we can see most of the document, and in the example below only a tiny part. This presentation form is not obvious from the beginning, but soon it becomes intuitive to the users.

High-speed trains. The last presentation shows part of the monitor screen for a high-speed train network. The stations are shown as dots and the trains as arrows. The direction and length of an arrow show where the train goes and with which speed. This is intuitive to most people. But it is not intuitive where the train is: at the tip of the arrow or at its base.

Actually, the train is at the base of the arrow and the tip of the arrow shows where the train will be in five minutes if it continues with its present speed. It takes a bit of training to learn this representation, but then it is easy to see that three trains are on

Fig 3.5 F Analog numbers

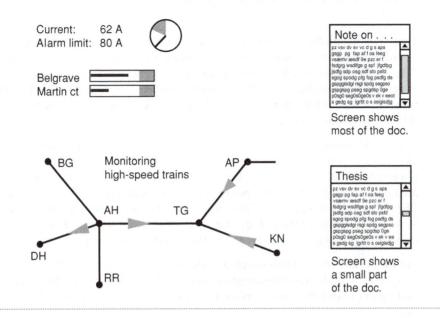

Current: 62 A
Alarm limit: 80 A

Belgrave
Martin ct

Note on . . .

pz vsv dv sv vc d g s aps
gsgp pg fap af f oa feeg
vsæmv æsdf 9e pzc er f
fsdgrg wsdtfgs g spf jfgdfpg
jsdfg sdp osg sdf sfo psfd
sgog spodg pfg fog psdfg ds
gspggisdgi rsgi spdg segpso
gspgspg pseg spgdsp 0ge
p0sg0 seg0s0ge0s v ek v eeot
s gsdg sg igrtit o s osigisdjg

Screen shows
most of the doc.

BG   Monitoring   AP
     high-speed trains

AH   TG

DH   KN

RR

Thesis

pz vsv dv sv vc d g s aps
gsgp pg fap af f oa feeg
vsæmv æsdf 9e pzc er f
fsdgrg wsdtfgs g spf jfgdfpg
jsdfg sdp osg sdf sfo psfd
sgog spodg pfg fog psdfg ds
gspggisdgi rsgi spdg segpso
gspgspg pseg spgdsp 0ge
p0sg0 seg0s0ge0s v ek v ee
s gsdg sg igrtit o s osigisdjg

Screen shows
a small part
of the doc.

their way to station TG, and the train from KN will arrive first although it currently is farther away from TG than the train from AP.

Analog display of complex data is still an art. Inspired by Danish research (Jens Rasmussen and his colleagues), an international group of researchers study these presentations. They call them *ecological user interfaces*.

3.6 Text form versus analog form

There is some profound difference between showing data in the traditional text form (words and decimal numbers) and in an analog form (as dials, curves, shapes, etc.). What is this difference? Well, we can see details in the text form, but we get a better overview in the analog form. We can see the analog form at a glance, while the text form requires our full attention. We will look at an example and then discuss the differences in more depth.

Figure 3.6A illustrates a case that Nygren *et al.* (1992) studied. The left side shows the old paper form that recorded lab tests for a patient at a hospital. Down the form there is a line for each type of lab test. To the right there is column for each date where tests are taken. The plan was to computerize the system, and the analysts asked the users (the doctors) what they looked at in the form. They answered that they of course looked at the name of the test, the date of the test and the result. The developers decided to present this on a screen like the one shown to the right.

But the system was not successful, and the doctors still preferred the paper form. Nygren now made the experiment to remove all details from the old paper form, so that numbers and texts were replaced by crosses. It looked like the left side of Figure 3.6A.

What do you see here, he asked, showing the form to a doctor. It turned out that the doctor could get a good overview of the patient's condition without any figures at all: This is a chronic disease, because they make tests all the time (the blocks of crosses in the right-hand part). They also suspected a liver disease, but there wasn't anything because they took the tests only once (the column of crosses at the bottom where the liver tests are).

The doctors perceived all of this automatically through the gestalts on the form. But the doctors were not conscious that this was what they did. In the IT system the gestalts had disappeared because the test results were shown as a uniform list.

3.6.1 Automatic and controlled activities

Let us first look at Nygren's own explanation of the observation. He and his colleagues noticed that some activities require our full attention. We have to focus on them. Others we can do while our attention is somewhere else. For instance, an experienced driver can conduct a conversation while he drives a car, but we cannot conduct a conversation while we read – no matter how much we practice.

Nygren used the concept of *automatic* activities, things we can do while doing something else. He didn't introduce a term for the other activities, but psychologists talk about *controlled* activities, things that require our full attention (Preece *et al.* 1994). Driving a car is an automatic activity, while reading a text and conducting a conversation are controlled activities.

Fig 3.6 A Automatic perception

Old paper lab form

Xxx	Xxxx									
Xxxx Xxxxxxxxxxxxxx	Xxxxx									
Xxxxx xxxx Xxxxxxx xxx x	Xxxxx									
xxx	Xxxxx xxxxxx	xx	x/x x/x x/x x/x x/x x/x x/x							
xxx	Xxxxx xxx	xxxx								
xxx	Xxxxxxx xxxxxx	xx								
xxx	Xxx xxx xxx	xxx	xx							
xxx	Xxxxxxxx xxxxx	xx	xx	xx			xx			
xxx	Xxxxx xxxxxx	xxxxx								
xxx	Xxxxx xxxxxxxxx	xxx								
xxx										
xxx	Xxx	xx								
xxx	Xxxxx xxxxxx	xxxx	xx	xx	xx	xx	xx	xx	xx	
xxx	Xxxxxxx xxxxx	xx	xx	xx	xx	xx	xx	xx	xx	
xxx	Xxx xxxxxxxxxx	xxx	xx	xx	xx	xx	xx	xx	xx	
xxx	Xxxx xxxxxx	xx								
xxx										
xxx	Xxxxx xxxxxx	xxx								
xxx	Xxxxx xxxxxx	xx								
xxx										
xxx	Xxxxx xxxxx xxxx	xxx								
xxx	Xxx xxxxxx xx	xx		xx						
xxx	Xxxxxxx xx xxxx	xxxx		xx						
xxx	Xxxxxxx xxxx	xx		xx						

Computer version

Test name	Date	Result
Xxxxx xxxxx	x/x	xxx
Xxx xxxx x	x/x	xxx
Xxxxxx xx	x/x	xxx
Xxxxx xxxxx	x/x	xxx
Xxx xxxx x	x/x	xxx
Xxxxxx xx	x/x	xxx
Xxxxx xxxxx	x/x	xxx
Xxx xxxx x	x/x	xxx
Xxxxxx xx	x/x	xxx
Xxxxx xxxxx	x/x	xxx
Xxx xxxx x	x/x	xxx
Xxxxxx xx	x/x	xxx

- **Controlled activity.** We can do only one controlled activity at a time, because our full attention can only be at one activity.

- **Automatic activity.** We can do automatic activities together with other activities, because the automatic activity doesn't require our attention.

The basic difference between the text form and the analog form is that the text form requires our full attention, while the analog form doesn't. We can see the analog form at a glance.

With the new system, perceiving the lab tests had become a controlled activity, while it used to be more of an automatic activity.

Notice that automatic activities may be quite complex, such as car driving or understanding a lab test form, but it takes time to learn doing them in an automatic way. Other automatic activities don't require much learning. Listening to music, for instance, is an automatic activity that requires little learning. Many people can listen to music while they read a book.

A doctor can learn to perceive the gestalts and patterns as an automatic activity, while extracting the same patterns from a text form will always remain a controlled activity.

What can we perceive automatically without focusing on it? Many things, for instance the spatial position of a thing (where was it on the screen?), its size, colour and shape; sound signals and smells.

What requires our focus so that we cannot focus on something else at the same time? Language sentences whether they are spoken or read; numbers in decimal form. These things require full attention no matter how much you practice.

So when we read a text, we cannot hear what someone says at the same time. For this reason it is a bad habit when a lecturer puts a text on the overhead while he talks. The audience must choose whether to listen or read.

We can to some extent perceive short sentences (*bullets*) while listening to a speech, probably because we can catch them through a brief change of focus.

While we read a book or talk with a colleague, we can easily see whether our e-mail icon says that there is new mail – or whether the amperes are up in the critical area. Here we mix a controlled activity with automatic activities, and this is possible.

Notice that the more creative data presentations in the previous sections allow us to perceive automatically. In general, automatic perception is great, but there is also a need for focusing on details. We can combine the things so that a survey screen supports the automatic part of the task, while a detail window gives the text form.

3.6.2   Multi-sensory association

This was Nygren's explanation. We get a somewhat different story if we use current knowledge of how the brain functions. Figure 3.6B is a much-simplified picture of the brain centres involved in sensation and memory.

Sensory memories.   Each sense has one or more centres in the brain. We have in section 3.4 seen how vision consists of three main centres, but other senses also have several centres. Hearing, for instance, has separate centres for language and music. The language centre even seems to have separate areas for nouns and verbs. All these centres not only process incoming sensations, but also keep a memory of them (actually a short-term memory as well as a long-term one). When we remember something, a neurologist can, in simple cases, measure that the sensory centres produce signals that somewhat look like the signals when we first experienced what we remember (see Finke 1986).

Association centres.   In addition to these sensory areas, there are several association centres. The figure outlines two of them: the Amygdala and the Hippocampus. (The words mean *almond* and *sea horse* in Greek. The ancient Greeks thought the centres looked that way.) An associative area somehow integrates the signals from several sensory areas. When you, for instance, hear the word *coffee*, you immediately get

Fig 3.6 B Multi-sensory association

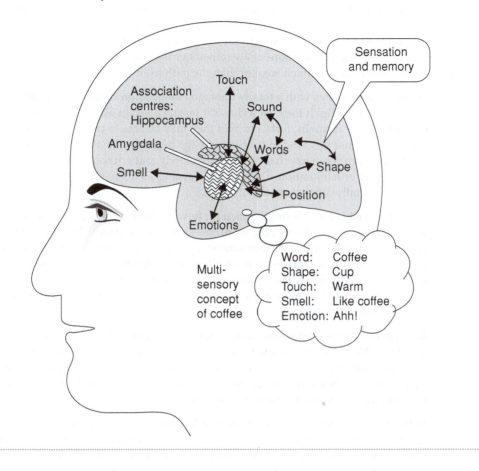

associations of the smell, the black colour, the warmth and maybe the shape of a cup. The association centres are responsible for waking up all of these sensory memories in the various centres.

The association centres are also long-term memories – memories of the association. Without them, a stimulus for one sensory area doesn't trigger long-term memories in other sensory areas.

This is not just theory. We have empirical evidence from studies of the working brain's blood flow, people with brain injuries and experiments with monkeys. As an example, a person with certain kinds of language-centre defects can recognize a cup of coffee and remember its smell, but not remember the word *coffee*. (See the evidence in Mishkin and Appenzeller 1987; Goldman-Rakic and Patricia 1992; Damasio and Damasio 1992.)

Some paths between the centres are stronger than others. Most of us find it difficult to remember, for instance, the name of smells we don't come across every day. We recognize it, but cannot find the word: *I know this smell, but what is it?* When told what it is, for instance rosemary, we will say, *Oh yes, why couldn't I remember*. However, if we talk about rosemary, we more easily remember the smell. Thus the path from smell to the word memory is much weaker than the path from word to the smell memory.

Humans or monkeys with a totally damaged association centre seem unable to remember anything. If they get a clue, for instance see an object, they cannot remember how it smells, feels, etc. Still they may be able to carry out old automatic activities because this kind of tacit knowledge bypasses the association centres. They may even learn some new habits, but very slowly and without understanding – as rote learning or habituation. This kind of learning seems to take place in developmentally older parts of the brain.

Concepts in memory. The mechanism for how we form a concept such as *coffee* is that we remember its 'attributes', the word, the shape, the warmth, the smell – even emotions about it – in the various sensory areas. The combination of all of these is the concept *coffee*. The association centres allow us to retrieve the various sensory attributes of the coffee concept from one or a few of the attributes, for instance the word or the smell. The more attributes we have, the stronger is the concept and the more can we use it in practice.

Concepts on the user interface. Maybe it is time to get back to the subject – user interfaces. How does this relate to Nygren's observations? In the old lab reports on paper, several sensory areas were involved when looking at a report: the large-scale shapes on the paper form (the gestalts), the position of data on the form (liver tests lower third), the words for the various tests.

In the computerized system, the user interface had lost a lot of these sensory attributes. First of all, the large-scale shapes had disappeared, but also the position attribute was gone. As a result, the computer version of a lab test report was a very impoverished concept. Getting an overview involved a strong focus on the word aspects, and it heavily loaded the language centre.

Focus aspects. This also explains why the old reports could be perceived as an automatic activity. The vision centres could do it much on their own without involving the word and language centres. For this reason, the doctor could conduct a conversation while glancing at the form. In the computer version, the language centre was always needed for perceiving the report, and it would be impossible to talk about something different at the same time.

3.7　Overview of complex data

Some tasks, for instance planning, require an overview of large amounts of complex data. It is difficult to provide this overview on a computer screen. Some professions have traditions for a specific kind of overview. As an example, production planners and project planners use Pert or Gantt diagrams. In other cases, there is no useful tradition for giving an overview.

Classroom allocation

Figure 3.7A shows two screens from a planning system where the user's traditional data presentation was insufficient, and the designer had to invent another form. The system supports booking and scheduling of classrooms in a university. Classrooms were the most critical resource at that time, and the existing system was entirely manual and an organizational disaster. A computer system had been attempted, but because of its heavy table-oriented data presentation, it was not successful.

The new system was developed by Morten Borup Harning by means of the virtual window method described later in this book. First, he tried to mirror the huge

Fig 3.7 A　Planning screens, room allocation

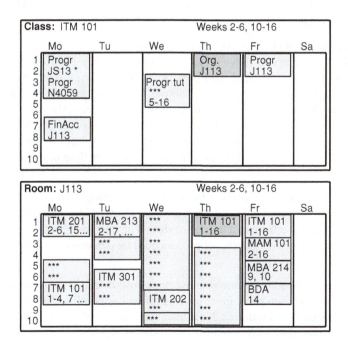

planning board the users currently used to represent room occupation, but during usability tests he found out that this presentation was not suited because it gave a false overview of the free rooms. A room seemed occupied if it was occupied just one single day during the semester. The planners had to dig into the details to find rooms that were free a particular day. As a result, it was largely impossible to book rooms, although a visit to the rooms often showed that there was nobody there.

Harning designed the new system by means of paper mock-ups and usability testing. The first three mock-ups had to be discarded because they built on the principles from the manual planning board. He redesigned the system completely and made further usability tests. The test report in section 13.7 is from the sixth mock-up, which was one of the last ones made.

Figure 3.7A shows the critical screens from the final mock-up. The base structure is a school timetable with the days of the week horizontally and the hours of the day vertically. (The hours were numbered from one and on, but all planners knew these numbers by heart.)

The screens exist in two versions: one for a class of students (at the top), and one for a single room (at the bottom). Notice the selected piece in the class timetable for Thursday. It shows that class ITM 101 has a lecture in Organization, room J113, Thursday hour 1–2. You find the matching piece in the timetable for room J113. It shows that class ITM 101 occupies the room these hours from week 1 to 16.

The timetable can cover one or more intervals of weeks, as shown at the top of each screen. In the example both timetables cover weeks 2–6 and 10–16. The user chooses which weeks he wants to cover.

A piece without stars represents a single booking. It covers one or more hours, and one or more intervals of weeks as shown on the piece. If different pieces ought to be shown in the same part of the timetable, only the common information is written, the rest is shown as stars. As an example, look at room J113, Wednesday. In the first seven hours, it is occupied by different bookings during the different weeks as shown by the stars. In hour 8–9 it is occupied by class ITM 202, but for more than one purpose, as shown by a single line of stars. The stars indicate to the planner that it will be harder to reschedule these hours, since more than one course must be rescheduled.

If there isn't space in the piece for all the information, for instance a long list of weeks, only the first part and three dots are shown. The user can see the full details for one piece at a time in a detail window. The designer chose the screen layout in such a way that the majority of pieces could be perceived without looking at the detail window.

Notice how the screens combine overview and detail. The matrix form gives the overview, and each piece gives as much detail as possible. The full details are visible in a separate detail window. Note also that some fields contain more than a single piece of data; they may contain a list of things separated by commas.

The system became a success and has, since 1995, been the way all room allocation is handled. It is the daily tool for the room managers. It requires a day of training, but then it gives excellent task support. (Later, teachers and secretaries got access to the system over the intranet for simple bookings, but they see simpler pictures than those shown here.)

We can characterize the system by these figures:

- Database: 20 types of records and 2 million records in total.

- Rooms: 150 rooms in 12 buildings.

- Bookings: 24 educations (*lines*) with a total of 7000 class activities.

- User screens: 2 highly complex (shown here), 10 with moderate complexity (like the *guest* or *rooms* windows for the hotel system) and 8 simple windows.

Behind the system is an ordinary database (Oracle). We have shown the data model in Figure 3.7B. The timetables on the complex screens combine data from the 10 tables shown on a grey background. It is quite common that screens for planning must show data from many tables at the same time to give the necessary overview.

Gantt diagram

Figure 3.7C shows a Gantt diagram as it is used in project planning. The tool used is Microsoft Project. Each line shows an activity (a task) to be done. To the left we have the name of the activity, and to the right a bar that shows when the activity is to be

---

Fig 3.7 B Data model, room allocation

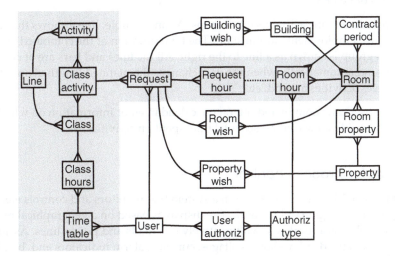

Fig 3.7 C Gantt chart for project plan

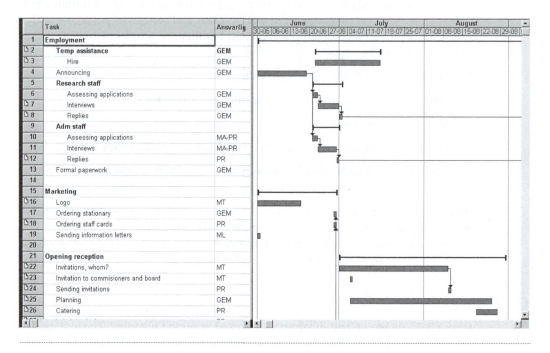

	Task	Ansvarlig	June	July	August
			30-05 | 06-06 | 13-06 | 20-06 | 27-06	04-07 | 11-07 | 18-07 | 25-07	01-08 | 08-08 | 15-08 | 22-08 | 29-08
1	Employment				
2	Temp assistance	GEM			
3	Hire	GEM			
4	Announcing	GEM			
5	Research staff				
6	Assessing applications	GEM			
7	Interviews	GEM			
8	Replies	GEM			
9	Adm staff				
10	Assessing applications	MA-PR			
11	Interviews	MA-PR			
12	Replies	PR			
13	Formal paperwork	GEM			
14					
15	Marketing				
16	Logo	MT			
17	Ordering stationary	GEM			
18	Ordering staff cards	PR			
19	Sending information letters	ML			
20					
21	Opening reception				
22	Invitations, whom?	MT			
23	Invitation to commisioners and board	MT			
24	Sending invitations	PR			
25	Planning	GEM			
26	Catering	PR			

done. The small arrows show that one activity is to be done before another one. As an example, line 11 shows the activity 'Admin staff, interviews'. It is scheduled to be done at the end of June, and it assumes that 'assessing applications' (line 10) has been done first.

We can combine activities into groups. As an example, line 9 shows the activity group 'Employment, admin staff'. The total duration of the combined activities in this group is shown as a line to the right. All the lines and bars are of course moved around automatically when the user changes the planned length of an activity, moves activities around, etc.

The user can zoom in and out on the calendar, enter information on who is responsible for activities, see total time spent on activities, etc.

Map format for process control

Figure 3.7D shows a screen from a system that monitors and controls electrical power in a region of Denmark. The display is based on a geographical map. In the example it is a rural area with relatively few roads and power lines. As additions to the map, the display shows voltages, currents, alarm indicators and 'breakers' that can cut or connect power. Data is sent on communication lines between the control

Fig 3.7 D Map format, power distribution.

Courtesy: ABB Network Control

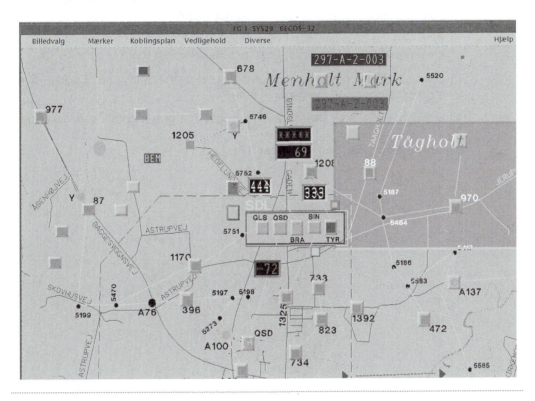

room and equipment in the field (sensors, breakers, etc.) As a result, a few people can monitor and control a large geographical area.

Test yourself

a) What is a gestalt law?

b) Mention four gestalt laws.

c) How can the gestalt laws explain some usability problems?

d) Why is it a bad habit to write long lines with 10-point letters?

e) What are the pros and cons of flashing texts, and how can brain activities explain it?

f) Why may it be a good idea to show the same data as a list and as a classical form?

g) Mention some different ways to show a hierarchy.

h) Mention some different ways to show numbers in analog form. Does a parallel coordinate plot show analog numbers?

i) What are the pros and cons of analog presentations versus digital presentations, and how can brain activities explain them?

j) Does a parallel coordinate plot give a good overview of data? Does a list of records give a good overview of data?

k) Mention some other presentation formats that give a good overview of data.

Design exercises. See Chapter 17.

4

Mental models and interface design

Highlights

- Mental model: The user's understanding of how the system works.

- Design so that user's mental model matches what the system really does.

- Different mental models for system data, system functions, domain, and 'how to do it'.

- Avoid the extremes: Data-focused systems and step-by-step focused systems.

- Key exercises: Reveal someone's mental model. Make extreme designs.

A mental model of an IT system is the user's understanding of what the system is and how it works. It is something in the head of the user, and we can only indirectly see what his mental model is.

The user develops a mental model unconsciously, but often the model doesn't match what the system actually does. This is the cause of many usability problems. A good user interface helps the user develop the right mental model. In this chapter we look at mental models and at ways to design the system so that it induces the right models.

4.1   Hidden data and mental models

Object permanence. The psychologist and mathematician, Piaget, showed around year 1920 that children at the age of 3–6 months develop the ability that he called *object permanence*. When they see an object disappear or being hidden, they believe that it is still there. Before the age of 3 months, they believe that an object doesn't exist when they don't see it. The law of object permanence becomes so deep-rooted that we are not conscious about it. We believe in it even when there is no reason to do so. (Illusionists build heavily on this belief.)

Apparently, object permanence also influences our understanding of IT systems. When we start using a new IT system, we gradually build an understanding of what the system stores 'behind the screen' and how it changes the stored things. We unconsciously build up this understanding – our mental model.

Probably something like this takes place: We see some data on the screen or enter it ourselves. When the system changes to another screen, the data disappears from the screen, and according to the law of object permanence we reckon that it hasn't disappeared from the system. We build up a mental model of where it is and how it relates to other data the system stores.

4.1.1   Example: page format

Unfortunately, our mental model often doesn't match what the system actually does. Figure 4.1A shows an example about the page format in text documents. In all text processors we can set the page format, e.g. the margins and the paper format, in some kind of dialogue box. Once set, we only see the page format indirectly, but we assume it is stored somewhere – more or less like the dialogue box we filled in.

But where is this page format stored? The figure shows three different models the user can build.

Model A. In model A there is only one page format in the computer. It works whenever the user prints out a document. In the figure we have shown it by putting the page format F on the connection between the computer and the printer. Whenever the user retrieves a document from the disk and prints it, it will get the page format F.

Computer novices tend to build this mental model of the page format. Modern text processors don't work like this, but the first ones actually did.

Model B. In model B each document has an attached page format, which follows the document to and from the disk. Whenever a document is printed, it is printed with its own page format. More modern text processors used this model.

Now let us see what happens when a novice user believes in model A, but the system behaves according to model B. Assume that the user types a document, sets

Fig 4.1 A Mental model for page format

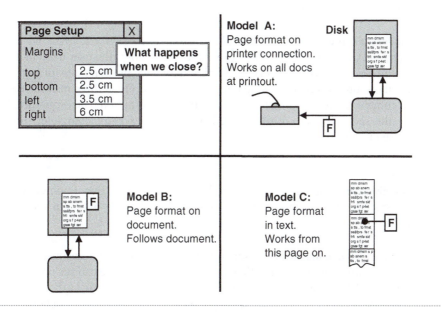

the page format and then prints out the document. Everything works fine. Now he opens another document and prints it, but it doesn't get the same page format. *That stupid computer has forgotten what I told it*, he may say. But it hasn't – it just filed the information in another way than the user thought.

It may take the novice user a long time to learn how the system actually handles the page format. He must rebuild his mental model, and that is hard. The longer he has lived with his wrong model, the harder it is to rebuild.

Model C. In model C the page format is attached at a certain point in the document and is valid from there and on. Modern text processors work in ways much like this.

What happens when a user who believes in model B uses the modern system? As long as he has the cursor on the first page when setting the page format, everything works as he expects. But one day he happens to have the cursor on a later page when setting the page format. Suddenly the system 'forgets the new page format' when printing the first pages. He may try again, and this time he happens to have the cursor on the first page – and see, the system gets it right this time. *That stupid system makes mistakes sometimes*, he concludes.

What happens if we tell the user that the system works according to model C? Most users will be very surprised, and some of them may say: *Does this really mean that I can have some pages with one format and other pages with another one?* Yes, you can. *That is really clever*, they say.

Modern text processors. For the sake of completeness, WordPerfect works according to model C. Microsoft Word is more complex: it allows the user to break the document into sections, and each section may have its own page format. Furthermore, when you set the page format, Word offers three models: the entire document (corresponding to model B); from this point on (corresponding to model C); this section only (a fourth model). Most Word users are completely unaware of these mechanisms.

Lessons

Creative use. When users understand the correct model, they find new ways of using the system. They do this on their own – we don't have to tell them about these new tasks.

Models built unconsciously. Users build their mental model unconsciously, and most of them cannot explain what their model is. However, we can see on their reactions what model they use. If we explain the model to users, some of them will be completely confused, but others respond by telling us how they believe the system works.

User's present model may be unsuited. Many HCI specialists say that the user interface should follow the user's present model. Generally, this is a good idea, but it might also result in an inefficient system. As an example, model A for the page format is the most intuitive model, but it will be very cumbersome when documents have different page layouts or when we exchange documents with other people. As another example, the classroom allocation system in section 3.7 first tried to mirror the present planning tools. However, these tools turned out to be the very source of the planning problems. A novel model successfully solved the problems.

Sometimes non-intuitive or new models may be needed. In these cases, it is very important that the user interface correctly indicates this model. The crucial point is to indicate where data is and what happens to it. It may be done through proper wording on the screens, small examples, pop-up help, or – in case this doesn't work – on-line help, paper documentation or courses (see Chapter 12).

4.1.2 Example: on-line ordering system

This example is from an ordering system that retailers use when ordering goods from their wholesaler. The retailer uses a PC that connects to the wholesaler's system. The PC system has a short user manual that explains how to order, as outlined in Figure 4.1B. It seems simple, just select 'Ordering' from the main menu, fill in the form and click OK.

Fig 4.1 B Mental model for on-line ordering

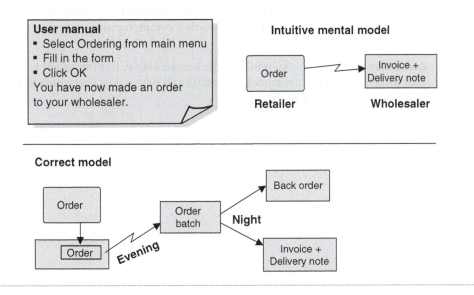

The typical user knows that some cables connect the PC to the telephone network, and in that way the PC is connected to the wholesaler's system. Most users imagine that it works according to the intuitive model shown in the figure. When the user clicks OK, the order will be sent to the wholesaler where it will become delivery notes, invoices, etc., and the next day he will receive his goods.

In reality something different happens, as shown on the second model. In order to provide fast response and save telephone lines, the system only connects to the wholesaler's system at the end of the day. Most of the retailer's work is done off-line on his PC where he has a copy of the inventory and where his daily orders are stored. At the end of the day, the orders are transferred to a batch queue in the wholesaler's system. Over night, orders from all the retailers are processed and become delivery notes, back orders and invoices. If the goods are on stock, they are packed, and early in the morning they are sent by truck.

Is it important for the user to understand this? No – as long as everything works as planned, the user doesn't need to know. Now assume that the user wants to cancel or modify an order. The way to do this depends on where the order is in the system. If it is still in the local PC, he can correct it on-line. If it is in the batch queue at the wholesaler's site, he has to send a correction order. And if it has been processed and packed, he may have to phone the wholesaler's nightline.

The actual system provided means for on-line correction and for sending correction orders, but didn't explain the difference. The result was often chaos, orders being processed twice, conflicts about who made the error, etc. Once users learned how the system worked (got the right mental model), they had no problems.

Large IT systems (mainframe systems) often have similar problems with transactions being sent from one sub-system to several other sub-systems. Correcting a mistake requires considerable insight, in other words a comprehensive and correct mental model.

Conclusion. These examples reinforce the lessons above. It is important to help the user form a correct mental model of the data and where it is. Use words that give the right association of where data goes.

4.2 Models for data, functions and domain

The mental models above were primarily about data, how it was stored and what happened to it. In general, the mental models must cover many aspects of IT systems. Figure 4.2 gives an overview of different mental models. The example is a traditional system used by a company for handling customer orders.

Mental models for data. The user sees some data on the screen or enters some data. When the system removes the window or changes to another window, the user does not assume that the data disappears, but that it is stored somehow (Piaget's law of object permanence). The figure shows the data stored behind the screen – at the back of the system. The user hence forms a mental model of what is stored and how it relates to other stored data, based on the way the data is shown on the screen. In the example, the user might imagine that the system files order forms and customer forms, because there is a screen that shows orders and another screen that shows customers.

Mental models for system functions. A system function is something the computer can do, for instance show some data, change the data or send it over the Internet to another system. The figure suggests that the user understands the system functions in terms of the stored data and its relation to what is on the screen. As an example, when the user selects *Get customer* from a menu, the system somehow finds the customer form and shows it on the screen. When the user sees an order on the screen and pushes *Cancel*, the system not only clears the screen, but also removes the order form from the files. (A more advanced user might have a model that says that the system doesn't remove the order form, but moves it to a file of cancelled orders.)

It is hard to know how correctly this picture reflects everybody's mental model, but many users readily comment that it quite well reflects how they imagine the system. My own experience is that most users imagine the filed forms behind the screen, while their model of functions is fuzzier and less visual. Many users can see that the bubbles illustrate the system functions, but few of them initially imagined the functions as bubbles.

As we saw with the page-format example, a user with a correct mental model can master the system, while a user with a model that deviates from the real system gets into trouble or doesn't utilize the system fully.

Mental models for the domain. Users also have mental models about the real world outside the computer – in the application *domain*. In Figure 4.2 we have illustrated the application domain as the sales desk where the orders are delivered.

A person with domain expertise knows about the objects and data out there, for instance what an order is, what an item number is and how it relates to the stock level. He also knows the procedures used for various tasks, for instance how goods are actually delivered, what happens with discounts, damaged goods, etc. In other words, he has a comprehensive mental model for the domain.

A user with little domain experience has weak or even wrong mental models of what goes on in the domain. He may have to ask the domain expert about damaged goods and other special situations.

Mapping model. It is one thing to know about the domain, and another thing to know how the computer system works. To make things work in practice, you also need to know how to map one to the other. For instance the user has to know which system functions to use to carry out a domain task. He needs a mental model for mapping tasks to functions. A good user interface helps the user form a correct mental model for the mapping.

The user's mental model should also tell him that the computer system records what is delivered and what is on stock, but that the records don't fully reflect what goes on in practice. For instance someone might have forgotten to record the damaged goods, so the computer believes that there are more items on stock than there actually are.

Users of business systems are normally aware that there is a difference between what the computer stores and what happens in the real world outside the computer. The stored data reflects the application domain, but doesn't match it automatically.

For other kinds of systems the difference between the application domain and the computer records is less clear, because the computer directly controls its environment without human intervention. As an example, the embedded computer that controls a video recorder (VCR) seems to be an integral piece of the application domain – the video recording. We are not even aware that a computer is involved, and if we are, we expect that it directly controls the motors and gears in the video and correctly displays whether the video is playing, recording or rewinding.

Terminology. Unfortunately there is much confusion about mental model terminology, particularly because HCI people and software people use terms slightly differently. Here are some of the HCI terms and their meaning in the terminology above:

■ **Structural model.** The model of how the system works. Corresponds to the model of data plus the model of system functions (Preece *et al.* 1994; Shneiderman 1998).

■ **Functional model.** A model of how to use the system. Corresponds to the mapping model above.

■ **Task-action model.** Another term for the mapping model. Explicitly says that it is a mapping from the task to the *actions* to be performed with the computer (Young 1983).

■ **Function.** A very confusing term which in the IT and HCI world may mean something the computer does (a system function), something a user does,

Fig 4.2   Mental models for data, functions and domain

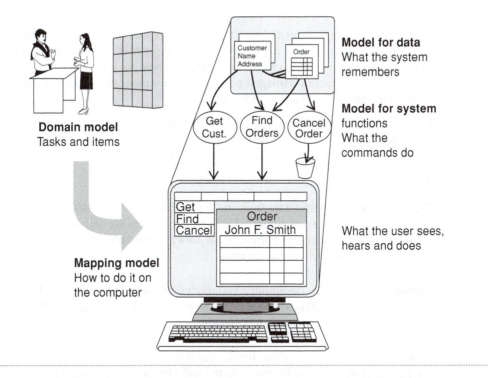

something an organization does, somebody's duty, a cause–effect relationship. When we say *function* in this book, we mean a system function – something the computer does.

4.3   Dialogue levels and virtual window method

HCI experts also talk about *dialogue levels*. There are low-level aspects of the human–computer dialogue, for instance whether you click an icon, a menu point or a function key to carry out a certain function. And there are high-level aspects, for instance how you record damaged goods. There are many definitions of dialogue levels, and experts don't agree on the levels.

Figure 4.3 is similar to Figure 4.2, but now illustrates the dialogue levels we will talk about in this book. The figure also outlines the approach we will use for systematic design of user interfaces – the virtual window method.

Domain level

This level is the tasks and data from the application domain – what goes on in the real world outside the computer. Examples: How orders are delivered, how invoicing and payment are handled, what data to record about a customer, how order numbers and delivery notes relate.

Domain analysis. When designing a system, we first deal with this level. We carry out a *domain analysis*. Domain analysis is part of most development approaches, and not something special for user interface design.

Task description. As part of the domain analysis, we study what the users do and identify their major tasks. We describe the tasks in some detail, but not too much since the tasks will be done differently with the new system.

Data model. In most cases it is important to make some kind of data model. The data model specifies the data people use in the application domain. It describes data in a way that is entirely independent of how it will be shown on the screen and how it will be stored in the computer.

Data level

This level is the data the computer system stores. Examples: Orders, customers and inventory.

Virtual window design. The systematic design method in this book covers the data level with a very important step, design of the *virtual windows*. Virtual windows are the screens that the user should imagine being behind the physical screen – at the back of the system. Usually we draw the screens on paper, but they resemble finished computer screens and have graphical details with realistic data contents. At this stage, however, they have no functions such as buttons, menus or links to other screens.

Fig 4.3 Dialogue levels and virtual window method

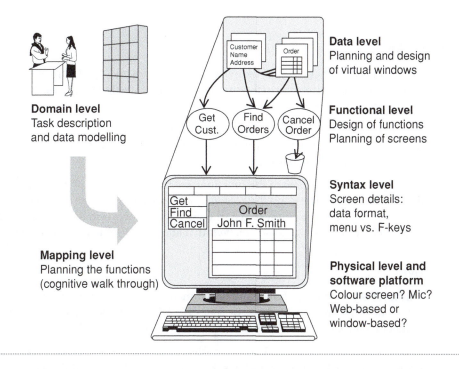

Domain level
Task description
and data modelling

Data level
Planning and design
of virtual windows

Functional level
Design of functions
Planning of screens

Syntax level
Screen details:
data format,
menu vs. F-keys

Mapping level
Planning the functions
(cognitive walk through)

**Physical level and
software platform**
Colour screen? Mic?
Web-based or
window-based?

The virtual windows are closely related to the objects that Piaget talks about in his law of object permanence. They are also closely related to the objects that software people talk about when they say object-oriented design.

Mapping level

This level is how the user maps the task he wants to carry out into the functions that the system can carry out.

Planning the functions. With the virtual window method, we handle this level by looking at each user task and plan the necessary system functions to carry it out. Example: The user task *Receive Order* needs several functions in the system, e.g. *Search Customer* and *Create Order*. The way we walk through the user tasks to identify the necessary functions is sometimes called a *cognitive walk-through*.

Contrary to most design approaches, the virtual window method plans the functions *after* having designed the data presentations (the virtual windows). Experience has shown that this sequence gives much better results for complex systems.

Usually, each function naturally belongs to one of the virtual windows. This is closely related to object-oriented design where developers first define the objects (virtual windows in our case), and then the operations or *methods* for each object (system functions in our case).

Functional level

This level is the functions that the system can perform and what happens when it performs them. With the virtual window method, we design two things on this level: the screens and the system functions.

Planning of screens. The user will not be able to see all the virtual windows at the same time on the physical computer screen. In this step we plan how to fit the virtual windows into the limited screen.

Design of functions. Some of the functions are the result of the planning we did at the mapping level. These are the *semantic functions* and the *search functions*. Other functions are the result of how we fit the virtual windows into the physical computer screen. These are the *navigation functions* that allow the user to move between screens.

Syntax level

This level is how data is shown and how functions are activated. Examples: How to enter a date (24-12-02 or 12/24-02 or 2002/12/24)? What does a red customer number mean? How to activate *Cancel Order* (icon, menu or F4)?

With the virtual window method, we design the syntax for data presentation already when we design the virtual windows. Experience has shown that this is crucial for good designs. In contrast, we delay the syntax for the functions until we have a list of all the functions needed.

Physical level and software platform

The physical level is about the hardware used for the interface. Examples: Colour screen or special display? Keyboard, mouse or wrist keys? Microphone? Built-in loudspeaker or 3-D surround? The software platform is about the operating system and development tools to be used. Examples: Web-based, Linux or Microsoft Access?

In most projects, we usually know the hardware right from the beginning. However, we may, to some extent, choose the software platform during the design. With the virtual window method, we are largely able to abstract from the software platform until very late in the process. We first need it when we design the navigation functions and the function syntax.

4.4   Data and system functions in practice

The virtual window method builds heavily on designing the data presentation before looking at the functions. Distinguishing between data and functions may sound easy, but in practice it is difficult for the novice designer. For this reason we will study an existing user interface to see what is what.

Figure 4.4 shows three windows from Microsoft Word: The main window with the document we edit, the option window where we can change various settings and the search window for finding texts in the document. We will analyse this interface closely.

Data

Persistent data. Data is something that the computer remembers for some time. Persistent data are what the computer remembers for a long time – even when we have closed the program and turned off the power.

In the example, the most important persistent data is the text we have typed. (We must ask Word to save it on the disk to ensure that the latest changes also survive when we turn off the power.) However, Word stores other persistent data, for instance the options we set and the name of the document. Some options are stored as part of the document and may vary from one document to another, for instance *Hide spelling errors*. They are document attributes. However, most options relate to Word as a whole, for instance whether drawings are shown on the screen. They are attributes for the entire Word application. Unfortunately, Word doesn't show what is saved where, so the user's mental model easily becomes wrong, unless he painfully tries out what the system does.

Dialogue data. Some data live only as long as we work with the program. We call them dialogue data. One example is the search criteria we specify when we search for something in the document. Another example is the position of the cursor and the mouse pointer. These positions are data shown in analog form.

Help information. The interface shows a lot of information for helping the user, for instance labels on the various fields, help messages, etc. This information is static – built into the system, and the user cannot change it. Usually we don't talk of this information as data.

The distinction between persistent data, dialogue data and help information is not always clear. As an example, the Word designers might decide to store also the cursor position as part of the document, so that you start in the old place whenever you open a document. The cursor position will become persistent data.

Functions

A function is something the computer can do for us, for instance change some data, bring up another window, print out something, send something over the Internet to another system or activate an external device such as a valve in a factory.

Below we will look at different types of functions, e.g. functions to enter data, functions that do something to the surroundings and functions that let us navigate around in the system. The reason we want to distinguish between these kinds of functions is that we design them into the user interface at different steps of the systematic design process.

Data entry functions. Changing data is one kind of function. In the example, the most important data entry function is to type some text into the document. The cursor shows that *here is the data entry function for text*.

We can change data in other ways. If we click on a check box in the options window, we change some persistent data. If we drag the scroll bar with the mouse, we change the position of the document (dialogue data). If we drag the margin indicator at the top of the document, we change the margin in the document (persistent data). If we select a font from the combo box (e.g. *Times New Roman*), we change the font attribute of some text.

Notice that some of these functions show data at the same time. The check box, for instance, allows us to click on it (a function), and at the same time it shows the data resulting from the latest click. Some HCI people call this *direct manipulation*. Another example of direct manipulation is dragging a file icon from one file folder to another.

Semantic functions. Some functions do something serious, for instance changing persistent data or sending something to the surroundings. We call them *semantic functions*.

In the example, the most important semantic function is the *Save* function, which Word provides in many variants: as an icon, as a menu point (under *File*), as a short cut (Ctrl+S), in connection with *Close document* and in connection with *Close Word*. We can even ask Word to auto-save the document at regular intervals. In all these cases, the Save function changes the most important persistent data – the document.

Also saving of options and printing the document are semantic functions.

In process control systems, for instance for a chemical plant, there are really interesting semantic functions, for instance the button that opens the chlorine intake, or the button that closes the entire plant.

Composite functions. Often a semantic function consists of two or more subfunctions, and in that case it may be somewhat ambiguous which of the subfunctions we call semantic. As an example, think of the function *Create document*. From a logical viewpoint it is a single semantic function, but in practice we have to go through many steps to complete it. One way is to click the *New document* icon,

Fig 4.4   Data versus functions

Screen shots reprinted by permission from Microsoft Corporation

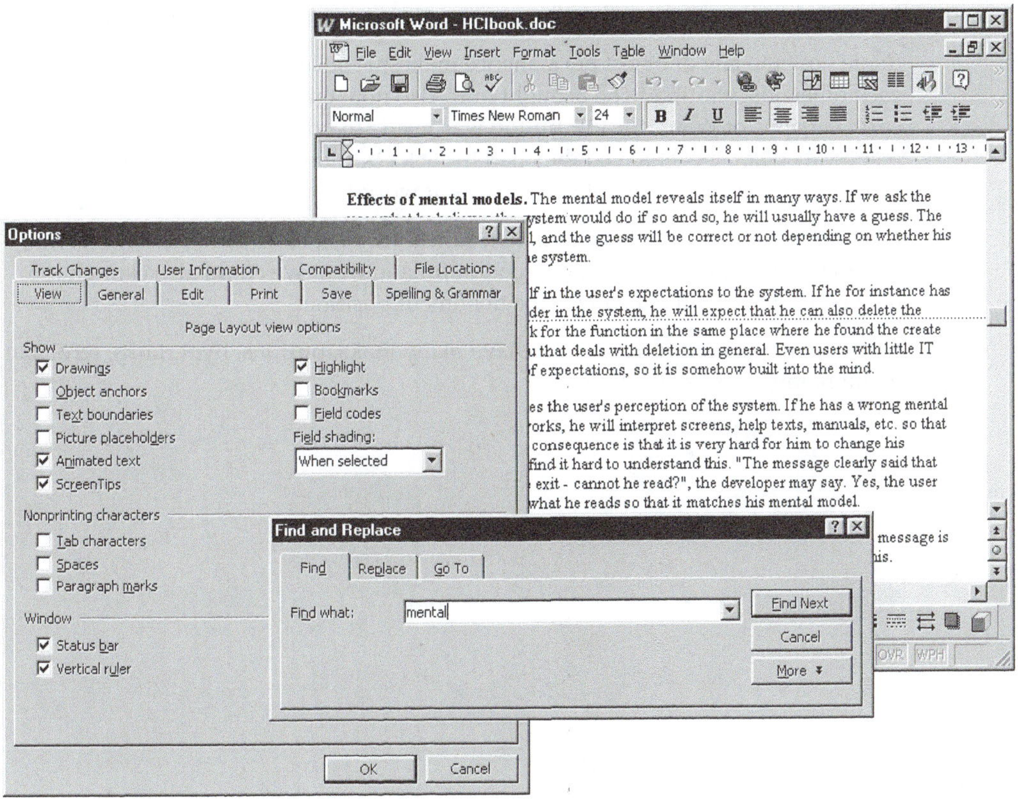

then enter the text and finally *Save* the document. Are all three functions semantic? Yes, we may say so. *Save* is definitely semantic since it changes persistent data. *New document* and enter text are not semantic in isolation, but they are intended to be the first part of the composite semantic function, *Create document*.

Search functions. Search functions don't do something serious, but they help us find data among lots of other data. Search functions often use search criteria, which specify something about the thing we want to find. The search criteria themselves are usually dialogue data. Figure 4.4 shows an example from Word. In large systems and many Web sites, search functions are highly important.

A search function may also be composite and consist of several subfunctions. In case of Word, we have to open the *Find and Replace* dialogue box, enter the criteria and click *Find Next* one or more times. Like the semantic functions, it is a matter of choice which of the subfunctions we call search functions.

Navigation functions. Some functions just help us moving data around on the screen, opening windows or move to another page. These are the navigation functions. In the Word example, the tab pages in the option box are a good example. Each tab page has a navigation function, the area you can click on to bring the page forward.

(Note how the law of object permanence makes us believe that the pages are behind each other, just waiting to be brought out. Also note the position of the OK button. In early versions of Word, the OK button was inside the page to save screen space. The result was that users believed they had to click OK for each page where they changed something. The gestalt law of closure was at work.)

Links in Web pages are also navigation functions, of course. The scroll bar for moving around in the text is a navigation function, but we could also claim it is a data entry function that changes the document position.

Note that navigation functions can have many looks. Buttons, hyperlinks, scroll bars, menu points, short-cut keys, etc.

4.5   Bad screens – database extreme

Let us see what can happen if developers don't design virtual windows at an early stage. In this case, developers tend to take one of two courses: they closely mirror the database on the screens; or they break down each task into small steps and provide a window for each step.

We will first look at designs where the screens are too close to the database.

Patient monitoring

The first example is from a hospital system where nurses recorded temperature and pulse of the patients (Figure 4.5A). Temperature and pulse were in two different tables of the database, and as a consequence the system had a window for each.

Now, what is wrong with this? The user can enter and see all the data, and even correct it if needed.

The problem is that these windows don't support the user's tasks. Obviously, the developers hadn't imagined that a nurse records a lot of data at the same time at the patient's bed, often including temperature and pulse. She wants to record and see all the data at the same time. She cannot keep several windows in her head, and her mental model becomes too complex. Furthermore, it is too laborious to change between several windows to record one observation of the patient.

Surgeons and nurses also use the data to check that the patient recovers properly. In order to do this, they have to compare the development over time of pulse and temperature. If the pulse rises before the temperature, it is a sign of internal haemorrhage, for instance after surgery. If it rises later than the temperature, it is a sign of bacterial infection (somewhat simplified). The difference is impossible to see when the figures are in two different windows.

The conclusion is that the user interface should support two tasks, data recording at the bedside and diagnosis of trouble. But it is not suited for any of them.

Work-hour registration

The second example is from a system that records employee's use of time on different projects and activities. The system shows the records in a long list (Figure 4.5B). The user can add records and edit them through this screen.

In principle, the list is adequate, but it is hard to get a visual overview of the data. There are no patterns or gestalts for automatic perception. When I show this example to professionals who record their time for billing purposes (e.g. auditors, consultants and software developers), most of them say: *Yes, this is how it looks, and it is cumbersome to work with, but are there better ways?*

At the bottom of the figure we show a better way. What would be 14 records (lines) in the first version, is now a single matrix that covers a week's work.

We can now see patterns, for instance that Thursday was something special and that MBH worked almost every day on activity 715. The system also shows total work hours per day and per activity, so we can easily check that a full day has been recorded and we can see which activities take most time. The employee can not only get an overview this way, but also enter his work hours through this screen.

While the list version is quite easy to program, the matrix version is harder – at least with typical standard tools.

The horror story explained

In the horror story from the real-estate company (section 2.3) the main problem was that the user interface was database extreme. The user would see data about a single plot of land in one window, data about a single building on the plot in another window, the street in a third, the sales record in a fourth, the client in a fifth and so on. To create data for a property to be sold, the user would have to create all these pieces of data in separate windows.

In the database, these pieces of data were in separate tables, but in the user's mind they were one single thing.

Fig 4.5 A Bad screens – patient monitoring

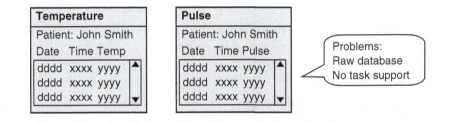

Fig 4.5 B Bad screen – work-hour registration

Time registration		Employee: MBH	
Activity		Date	Hours
102	Lunch	23-09-02	0.5
715	Design DXP	23-09-02	4.0
812	Cust. meeting	23-09-02	3.0
102	Lunch	24-09-02	0.5

Problems:
No patterns
No gestalts
No visual check

Improvement

Time registration		Employee: MBH			Week: 39	Year: 02		
Activity		Mo	Tu	We	Th	Fr	Sa	Su	Tot
102	Lunch	0.5	0.5	0.5		0.5			2.0
715	Design DXP	4.0	3.0	5.0		3.0	4.5		19.5
808	Review SPA		4.5	2.5					7.0
812	Cust. meeting	3.0			7.5	3.5			14.0
Total		7.5	8.0	8.0	7.5	7.0	4.5	0.0	42.5

4.6   Bad screens – step-by-step extreme

Now we will look at the other extreme: the designer breaks down each task into small steps and provides a window for each step.

Web-based order system

Figure 4.6 shows a simplified example from a Web site where customers can shop. The designer had described the user tasks as shown on the top left. Next he designed Web pages for each step. The figure outlines the Web pages for the first task – *create an order*.

Notice that the user first has to choose the task he wants to perform. Does he want to create an order, review an existing one, etc.? Here the designer has forced the user to a very early decision. Although users perform a lot of tasks, they rarely have names for them. The task names – and maybe even the task concept itself – are invented by the designers. For this reason, the users find it hard to choose the right task from the list.

Next the user has to fill in his name and address. When this is done, he has to specify his pay method, and so on. In the last screen he can choose between entering more items for the order and confirming the entire order. Notice the headings on the screens. They are instructions to the user – the screens are only for data entry. If the user wants to look at an earlier order (review it), some other Web pages are needed, and the user may not recognize the order he entered. The different formats make it harder for the law of object permanence to work.

With this interface, the user can complete his task, so what is wrong? First, it is very annoying that the computer controls the input sequence. Although the user has to do all the steps, it is not sure that the sequence is convenient. For instance, in some cases the user would want to see something about the items before ordering anything. If – after entering all his personal data – he doesn't like the goods sold or they are not on stock, he will be quite annoyed.

Furthermore, the user has no overview of the data he enters. He cannot check his delivery address against his own address, he cannot get an overview of the things he has ordered, etc. It is like reading a drivers map through a 'soda straw'.

In addition, he has no overview of the number of steps ahead. Some Web sites have a large number of pages to go through to complete a rather simple task, and many users lose their patience on the way and give up. Some Web sites try to amend the problem by showing a list of the steps to be performed. The list may be shown at the top of the screen or at the left border. However, many users don't understand this list or don't notice it.

In our example, there are also too many pages to go through. One should be enough.

Fig 4.6 Bad screens – step-by-step extreme

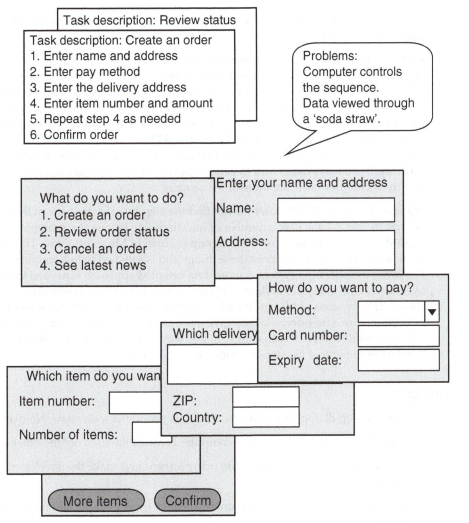

To make things worse, many interfaces with this structure have different pages for different tasks. As we explained above, create order and review order would, for instance, use different screens. This not only confuses the user, but also makes the developer's work much harder.

Mainframe systems. Interfaces with this step-by-step structure also exist for non-Web systems. Traditional mainframe systems often require the user to choose a task up front, and then complete a number of screens one by one.

Successful step-by-step dialogues

For very simple tasks, the step-by-step dialogue may work well. Some users even prefer it. Here are two examples.

ATM. The user dialogue for Automatic Teller Machines (ATMs) is an extreme step-by-step dialogue, and yet we all live happily with it. Why? The reason is that from a user interface viewpoint it is an extremely simple interface. One peculiar thing is that it doesn't show data at all. The data of interest would be the account balance and the PIN code, but for security reasons both are carefully hidden. Many textbooks on software design and HCI use the ATM as a major example. This is very unfortunate since the authors suggest that user interfaces in general should work in this way. It is always dangerous to generalize from a very simple example and claim that more complex ones 'are more of the same'.

Wizards. In Microsoft Windows we can find the step-by-step dialogue in the form of *Wizards* that ask the user a number of questions one by one. An example is the Wizard that helps the user create a diagram (a *chart*) in Microsoft Excel. This may work well if the user rarely does these things and is satisfied with a simple result. However, to master the system, a more data-oriented approach is needed to give overview of the many possibilities and their interaction. When I compare consecutive versions of Microsoft Office, it seems that the Wizards have become more and more data-oriented. They give more choices for each step and illustrate what the result will be of each choice. In this way, the Wizards try to balance between the data-oriented and the step-by-step-oriented extremes.

Conclusions

- Step-by-step dialogues are like reading data through a soda straw. No overview.

- With step-by-step dialogues the computer controls the user, not the other way.

- Step-by-step dialogues require too many screens and make the developer's work harder.

- Avoid the step-by-step extreme unless the task is very simple and needs little data.

4.7 More on mental models

Above we have used the term *mental model* in a broad sense as something in the user's mind or something we can draw and show to others. In the HCI area we distinguish between three related models (illustrated in Figure 4.7A):

Mental model. The model in the user's mind. We cannot see it, and often the user is not aware of his own model. Even if he is aware of it, he may not be able to describe it. From observing the user, we can try to infer what his mental model is.

Cognitive model. The observer's explanation of the user's mental model. It might be a psychologist who observes the user and describes his apparent mental model.

The first model for page format (Figure 4.1A) was a cognitive model. It showed how novice users imagine the page format. The last two models were cognitive models that showed how more advanced users imagined the page formats. Our model for dialogue levels (Figure 4.2) was also a cognitive model. It described how users imagine an IT system.

Conceptual model. The designer's explanation of how the system works. He can use it for two purposes:

- As the plan for designing the details of the system

- As an explanation to the user of how the system works

All three models for page formats were also conceptual models that explained how different text processors worked.

Hey! How can the model for a page format be both a cognitive model and a conceptual model? It *can* be – the model can show how the user believes the system works, and it can show how the system actually works. If the system is easy to understand, the conceptual model for how it works is also a cognitive model for what the user believes.

The nature of mental models

HCI people are not sure what our mental models really are. (See Staggers and Norcio, 1993, for a discussion.) Are they like pictures, or a kind of logic, or step-by-step procedures for what to do? Probably all of these are involved, but in different mixes for different people. It is not so strange if you remember our multi-sensory memory (Figure 3.6B). We remember pictures in one part of the brain, and words and logic in another. I have not heard about a memory for step-by-step procedures, but it might be there too – maybe in some of the motoric brain areas that are less well examined. Or maybe we don't remember the sequence of steps as such but remember a response for each situation that occurs during the task. The sequence is then the result of the alternate computer and human actions. This would also explain why we don't always do things in the same sequence.

The very term *model* suggests that it is something we can experiment with in our mind – as if the brain had a kind of copy of the system. There are some studies of brain signals that suggest that such models physically exist in the brain. For instance, if we imagine a picture or imagine a movement of the hand, some of the same brain signals develop as if we actually saw the picture or moved the hand (see for instance Finke 1986).

Prediction ability. If we ask the user what he believes the system would do if so and so, he will usually have a guess. The guess is based on the mental model. Users with a correct mental model are able to predict what the system will do.

Other effects of mental models. The model also reveals itself in the user's expectations to the system. If he, for instance, has learned how to create an order in the system, he will expect that he can also delete the order. He will typically look for the function in the same place where he found the create function, or look for a menu that deals with deletion in general. Even users with little IT experience have this kind of expectations, so it is somehow built into the mind.

The mental model dominates the user's perception of the system. If he has a wrong mental model of how the system works, he will interpret screens, help texts, manuals, etc., so that they match his model. One consequence is that it is very hard for him to change his model. System developers find it hard to understand this. *The message clearly said that the user should save before exit – cannot he read?*, the developer may say. Yes, the user *can* read, but he interprets what he reads so that it matches his mental model.

On the other hand, if the user has a correct mental model, he doesn't notice if a message is badly phrased or even outright wrong. Many developers should be happy for this.

Developing mental models. We know only little about how mental models develop. Apparently the user develops the model from earlier experience, experience with the new system and explicit guidance or manuals. These factors cannot account for everything in the models, and it is likely that much of the models are innate – built into our brain (Figure 4.7B).

We know that users gradually develop a mental model of the system, more or less consciously. Most of the model develops very fast during the first hours of using the system. Later it gradually becomes more precise.

Fading models. As the user gradually becomes proficient, he uses his mental model of the system only in unusual situations, where he has to think hard and find a solution. During routine tasks he doesn't think about how it works or why. His mapping model helps him choose the right system functions.

Fig 4.7 A Mental, conceptual and cognitive models

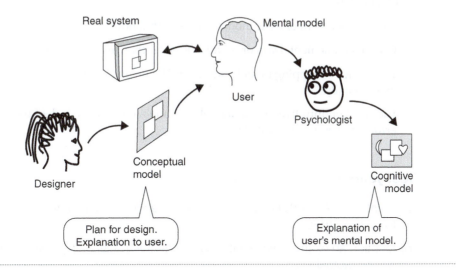

Over the years, he may even forget the correct mental models, particularly if they are non-intuitive or hard to understand. The result can be that he chooses the wrong solutions in unusual situations. This phenomenon has explained many flight accidents and accidents in industrial plants (Rasmussen 1979, 1986).

Fig 4.7 B What are mental models?

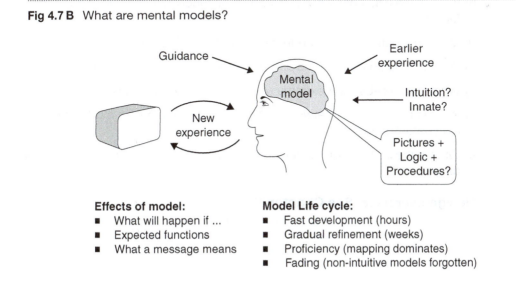

Effects of model:
- What will happen if ...
- Expected functions
- What a message means

Model Life cycle:
- Fast development (hours)
- Gradual refinement (weeks)
- Proficiency (mapping dominates)
- Fading (non-intuitive models forgotten)

Life cycle of mental models. We can summarize these observations as the life cycle of mental models:

▪ Fast development of basic model parts – within hours.

▪ Gradual refinement. Days or months. Radical changes of the model are hard.

▪ Proficiency – mapping model takes over. The mental models are used only exceptionally.

▪ Fading. Non-intuitive mental models become wrong due to lack of use. Serious errors may occur in unusual situations.

Test yourself

a) What does Piaget's law of object permanence say and why is it important for user interface design?

b) Mention an example where the user's mental model didn't match what the system actually did.

c) What is a mapping model?

d) Mention some other kinds of mental models.

e) What is the syntax level of the dialogue?

f) How does the virtual window method resemble the mental models?

g) What is persistent data and dialogue data?

h) What is the difference between a semantic function and a navigation function?

i) Mention a data presentation that is a function at the same time.

j) What is a database-extreme user interface? Mention an example.

k) What is a step-by-step-extreme user interface? Mention an example.

l) What is the difference between a mental model, a cognitive model and a conceptual model?

m) What is the life cycle of mental models? Why is the last stage of the life cycle dangerous?

Design exercises. See Chapter 17.

Part B

Systematic interface design

In part B of the book we look at a systematic approach to user interface design:

- How to analyse and describe the users, their tasks and the data they use (Chapter 5).

- How to plan the necessary screens and the way they present data (Chapter 6).

- How to define the necessary functions for doing the real work and for navigating between screens. And how to find out whether the functions are to be implemented as buttons, menus, function keys, etc. (Chapter 7).

- How to combine it all into a prototype, find the usability problems, and correct them (Chapter 8).

- How all of this relates to traditional systems development and to object-oriented design, what is most important and what doesn't work (Chapter 9).

Most of the analysis stuff in Chapter 5 is classical, although with a new twist. The rest of Part B is novel. Together with some of my colleagues, I have tried the systematic approach in these chapters for several years in larger systems. Gradually we improved the method, and now find it well suited as a routine approach.

5

Analysis, visions and domain description

Highlights

- How to describe the visions – why the system is needed and the large-scale solution.

- How to describe data and user tasks in the domain.

- Dealing with the past and the future.

- Tasks versus scenarios and use cases.

- Key exercise: Describe data and user tasks for the design project.

Before we can design a good user interface, we have to understand the application domain – what goes on in the real world outside the computer system. Why is a new system needed – what are the goals? Who are the present users and what are they doing? Which data is involved? Finding out about this is called *systems analysis* – a study of the existing human and computer system. HCI people tend to call the process *task analysis*, and requirements specialists call it *requirements elicitation*.

We also need a *vision* of what the new system will do. How will the goals be met? Who will use the new system and which tasks will they carry out? What is the *large-scale solution* in terms of technology? We may also define the *requirements* to the new system – what precisely is required to make the system good enough?

Ideally, these findings are documented as vision descriptions, requirements, data models, task descriptions, etc. This is the ideal, but often essential documentation is lacking. For the purpose of designing the user interface, the two most important documents are the *data model* and the *task descriptions*. If they don't exist, the design team should make them.

In the old days, getting a new IT system meant developing it from scratch. Today, many IT systems are bought as commercial products (COTS products – Commercial-Off-The-Shelf). Or the system is assembled from several COTS products. In these cases the user interface largely exists already. Although the user interface exists, it is still a good idea to document visions, tasks, etc., for the new system, for instance to check that the planned solution meets the real needs and have sufficient usability.

In this section we will show task descriptions in detail, and we will outline other techniques that are important for designing the user interface. Some of these other techniques are described in detail in supplementary parts of the book.

We will use the hotel system as an example. Figure 5.1 gives an overview of the visions. Section 2.2 explains more on the background for the hotel case, the simplifications we have made, how we designed the user interface, etc.

Fig 5.1   Visions for the hotel system

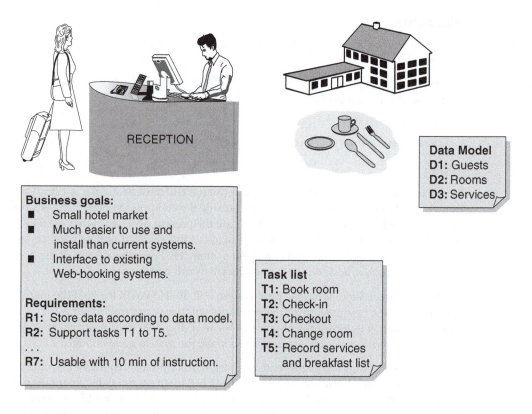

RECEPTION

Data Model
D1: Guests
D2: Rooms
D3: Services

Business goals:
■ Small hotel market
■ Much easier to use and install than current systems.
■ Interface to existing Web-booking systems.

Requirements:
R1: Store data according to data model.
R2: Support tasks T1 to T5.
. . .
R7: Usable with 10 min of instruction.

Task list
T1: Book room
T2: Check-in
T3: Checkout
T4: Change room
T5: Record services and breakfast list

5.1 Visions for the hotel system

5.1.1 Business goals

Many commercial hotel systems exist already. However, they are typically very complex and receptionists have to take a course before they are allowed to work with them. Some systems can be learned in two days, others require more than a week. This means that only larger hotels can use these systems. Small hotels tend to use a lot of temporary staff, for instance students on vacation jobs, and the receptionists cannot get several days of training. As a result, there is a market for a hotel system that is easy to learn.

Small hotels strive to make themselves visible on the Web, but it is difficult. Usually they have someone set up a Web site or they enlist on one of the existing hotel Web sites. Booking, however, is still handled in the old way by phone or fax.

Business goals are the customer's reasons for getting the system. Why would he pay for it? In the hotel case, we can define these business goals for the hotel owner:

a) The hotel wants efficient support of the basic tasks in the reception such as booking, checking in and checking out. (Note: This is the purpose of all hotel systems.)

b) It is much too expensive to send staff on courses. Even temporary staff should be able to handle the basic tasks on their own after a few minutes of instruction. They should only need to ask the boss or experienced colleagues in more complex cases.

c) Installation of the system should be easy. The hotel cannot afford expensive consultants who set up the whole thing.

d) The hotel wants to be seen on the Internet and provide on-line booking. This will attract more customers and save the staff being disturbed all day and night by overseas inquiries.

Note: In this book we only look at goals a and b. Goals c and d are important too for a first release, but we ignore them here.

The developers of the system may have their own business goals. This is particularly true for a supplier who develops products for a wider market. In our case we can define these goals for the supplier:

e) Catch the small-hotel market early. Don't waste time supporting a lot of things in the beginning.

f) The system may over time expand to handle other hotel tasks too, for instance room maintenance and staff scheduling, but there is a significant market without these features.

There will be additional business goals that we don't consider here, for instance about geographical markets, expected sales, marketing and distribution of the system. Some people would call these goals part of a business plan or a product-marketing plan.

5.1.2 Large-scale solution

How do we meet the business goals above? Here is the large-scale plan:

A) Study existing hotel systems in detail, interview receptionists that use such systems, interview receptionists and owners of small hotels. Conduct focus groups with them about the ideal hotel system. Find out what is sufficient for a first release. (The purpose of these activities is to meet business goals a and e.)

B) Develop the user interface of the new system early. Run usability tests to ensure that it is sufficiently easy to use. (The purpose of these activities is to meet business goal b.)

C) Make it possible for a person with only general IT skills to install the system, for instance a person from the local computer store. Base the system on a widely available platform in order that people in the local computer store can install the system and give some support (business goal c). Microsoft Access might be a reasonable choice.

D) The first release may be only for hotels that are so small that a single-user system is sufficient. This makes installation and operation much simpler (business goal c). However, plan for a later multi-user version. (Note: Changing to a multi-user platform is not just an 'add-on' feature. Without planning for it, we may have to scrap most of the first-release programs. Management may not know about this, but developers do.)

Note: In order to fully meet business goals c and d, we have to do more. For instance we have to interview and brainstorm with people in 'local computer stores' and run usability tests of the installation procedure. We also have to study existing Web-booking systems that might serve as portals to 'our' hotels.

Step B on the plan above is the focus of this book. Step A is about elicitation of the requirements. It mentions a few elicitation techniques: study competitive systems, interviews and focus groups. However, there are many other elicitation techniques. Section 15.5 explains some of them. See S. Robertson (2001) or Lauesen (2002) for longer lists.

5.1.3 Requirements

The business goals and large-scale solution above are intentionally somewhat open-ended. On the basis of these it would not be clear what to design and develop. However, when we have done the elicitation in step A, we should be able to make more precise decisions and state them as requirements. Here is an outline of the requirements for the first release.

Functional requirements

Requirement 1 Data to be stored: The system must store the data described in section ... [we show it in section 5.2]

Requirement 2 Tasks to be supported: The system must support the users and tasks described in section ... [we show them in sections 5.3 and 5.4]

Technical interfaces

Requirement 3 Platform: The system must be based on Access. The first release is a single-user system but later releases must be multi-user.

Requirement 4 Screens: Some hotels use small screens (800 * 600 pixels), others use larger ones (1024 * 768 or more) set up with bigger letters to be visible at a 2-meter distance. The system must support all of these. (Note: With Access this needs careful planning.)

Requirement 5 Web portals: The system must interface to the following portals ...

Requirement 6 Accounting: The system must interface to the following accounting systems ...

Quality requirements

Usability: A novice user is a temporary receptionist without previous hotel-system experience. It is assumed that the user has IT knowledge corresponding to simple text processing. The requirements below assume that a support person has set up the system.

Requirement 7 After 10 minutes of instruction, 90% of novice users must be able to carry out tasks T1 to T5, including variants.

Requirement 8 Without any instruction, 50% of novice users must be able to carry out tasks T1 to T5, without variants.

Installability: A support person is ...

Requirement 9 A support person must be able to set up the hotel system on the hotel owner's computer within 30 minutes ...

...

Note: This is the first version of the requirements. During design and development, requirements are usually changed as developers learn about the domain, the technical difficulties and the costs.

In this book we discuss user interface design. We don't discuss requirements and other parts of domain analysis. It is a huge area in itself (see for instance Davis 1982; Beyer and Holtzblatt 1998; Constantine and Lockwood 1999; S. Robertson 2001; Lauesen 2002). When we design the user interface, we assume that management has decided to make the system, that it is reasonably clear what the system is supposed to do and that our project team will develop the system.

5.2 Data model and data description

A very important part of user interface design is to figure out how to show data on the screen. However, we need to talk about data in a way that is independent of how we show it. This is what data modelling is about – a presentation-independent map of the data stored in the computer system. The term *data model* is an old one. As many other terms in the IT world it has been through waves of inflation. Some years ago it became an *information model* and currently it is even called a *knowledge model*. In object-oriented development it is called a *static class model*. Being anti-hype and striving for simplicity, I prefer to keep the term *data model*.

A data model specifies the persistent data to be stored in the system and the relationships between the data. Figure 5.2 is a data model for the hotel system. Each box corresponds to a collection of records of the same type. The *Guest* box, for instance, contains a record for each guest that the hotel system must keep track of. The *Stay* box contains a record for each stay. You may think of the records as *objects* of a certain type or as small index cards.

The connectors between the boxes show *one-to-many relationships*. For instance, the connector between the Guest box and the Stay box shows that one guest may have one or more stays at the hotel. Reading the same connector the other way, it shows that each stay is connected to exactly one guest. In simple terms, this means that each guest may stay a number of times at the hotel.

We have shown the connectors as *crow's feet*, but there are many other ways to show them. The one in the example is an *Entity/Relationship model*, also called an *E/R model* or a Bachman diagram.

A data model is not intuitively understandable, and it is not intended for typical users. However, it is an excellent tool for the designer and the developer. Below we will shortly explain the data model for the hotel system. If you want to learn how to *structure* data models, you should study Chapter 16. If you need to gather the information to be structured, you should study section 15.5.

Guest. The model shows the data we must keep track of for each guest: his name, several address fields and passport number (for foreigners only). These pieces of data are called *fields* or *attributes*. In practice, there will be many more guest attributes, such as a phone number, e-mail address or contact person.

On purpose, we have not split up the name into first, middle, last name; or the address into street, zip, state, etc. The reason is that the hotels we aim at have guests from many countries. The concepts of first, middle, etc., are confusing in many cultures, and so are the zip and state. So we simply ask the receptionist to record name and address as the customer states them. The computer can easily find a zip-like code in the address, no matter where it is in the text.

Stay. According to the model, we have to keep track of the following information for each stay: the stay identification (also called a booking number), the pay method (whether the customer pays by cash or credit card, or has a company account) and the state of the stay (whether it is booked, checked in, checked out or cancelled).

ServiceType. The system also needs a list of various types of services, e.g. different kinds of breakfast. The *ServiceType* box has a record for each type of service, stating its name and price. In simple terms, it is a price list, and each record corresponds to a line on the list.

ServiceReceived. For each stay, the guest may receive several of these services, and the *ServiceReceived* box keeps track of them. Each service-received record relates to exactly one stay and one type of service, as shown by the crow's feet. The record has fields for the day the service was received and how many items were received (quantity). Each service-received record will appear as a separate line on the customer's invoice.

Room. The *Room* box corresponds to the list of rooms. For each room there is a record with room identification (corresponding to the room number on the door), the number of beds in the room, the type of room (whether it has bath, toilet, etc.) and prices.

RoomState. We need some information about the room for each day, e.g. whether it is free, booked, occupied or being repaired at that date. The records in *RoomState* keep track of this. In principle, each room has a RoomState record for each date, showing the actual or planned state that date. If the room is occupied or booked that day, we also record the number of persons staying in it (some hotels give discount for a single person staying in a double room). Notice that a stay may relate to more than one RoomState, for instance if the guest stays more than one night, or if the guest has more than one room.

Data description

The experienced analyst can understand much of the data model just from the model as it is shown in Figure 5.2. However, less experienced people will also need a verbal *data description* as the one we just gave. Furthermore, there are many details to be described too, for instance what is the relation between the state of a stay and the state of the related room states? If one is booked, will the other have to be booked too? In section 16.6 we explain more on what to include in a data description.

Fig 5.2   Data model for the hotel system

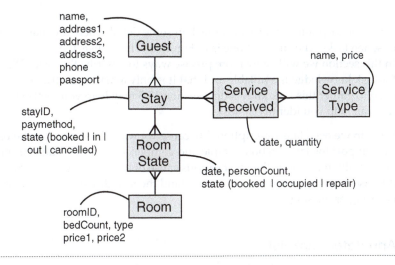

name,
address1,
address2,
address3,
phone
passport

name, price

stayID,
paymethod,
state (booked | in |
out | cancelled)

date, quantity

date, personCount,
state (booked | occupied | repair)

roomID,
bedCount, type
price1, price2

5.3 Task descriptions

A task description explains a user task in some detail. There are many ways to describe tasks. The simplest one is in Figure 5.1. It just lists the tasks by their name. In this section we will show more precise ways to describe the tasks. We assume that the task knowledge is available and that it is only a matter of structuring it. If you need to gather this task knowledge, section 15.5 may help you. It also has techniques that can help you identify all tasks.

Why do we need task descriptions? Because we want to ensure that the user interface can support the tasks in both simple and complex cases. Misunderstanding what the users really try to do is the most serious cause of bad user interfaces. For this reason it is also essential that users can understand the task descriptions and point out what is wrong or missing.

5.3.1 Annotated task list

For most tasks we need a bit more explanation than just the name of the task. Figure 5.3A shows an *annotated task list*. We have divided the tasks into several work areas: the reception, staff scheduling and so on. In our part of the project, we deal only with the reception.

In the reception we have identified five tasks: booking, checking in and so on. Notice the numbering of the tasks: T for *Task*, a number for the work area and a number for the task within the work area. For each task we have added notes about special situations to deal with, for instance that a guest may book more than one room; that the receptionist often reviews the bill with the guest before printing the invoice.

Domain level. We have tried to keep the description on a true *domain level*, meaning that we only describe what the user and the computer do together. We don't talk about what the computer shows on the screen, which functions the user clicks, what paper notes he may use, etc. Why not? Because this division of labour will change when our new system takes over.

To hide who is doing what, we use imperative language, for instance:

> **Correct:** Book room (Imperative)

rather than:

> **Wrong:** User books room   or   Receptionist books the guest

Now and future. We also try to hide whether this is how it is done today or how it will be done in the future. Details of how it is done today are not interesting since things will be done differently with the new system. Details of the future are not known until we have designed the user interface.

Fig 5.3 A Annotated task list for the hotel system

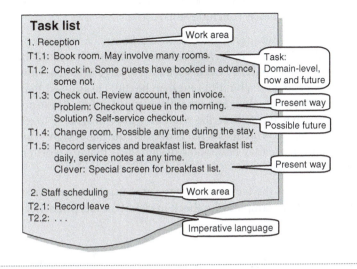

However, sometimes it *is* interesting how the tasks are carried out today. It is interesting in two cases:

- If there is a problem in the way it is done today.

- If there is a particularly clever way of doing it today.

In our new design we should try to eliminate the problems, but we also have to make a system that is at least as good as the present clever ways.

In Figure 5.3A we have shown that there is a problem with checkout: In the morning, there is often a long queue of guests that want to check out. We have also mentioned a possible solution: that the guests can somehow check out themselves without having to see someone in the reception. (Most of them have already presented their credit card.) Here we have described something about the *future*, but take care: we haven't yet decided that it will be that way.

In the example we have also mentioned that the present system has a clever screen for entering who got which breakfast. It is important that our new system is at least as good in this area.

5.3.2 Task description template

The annotated task list works quite well in many cases, but much is left to the intuition of the developer. It is also hard to decide what to include – what level of detail? For many years I thought that it was unrealistic to describe larger tasks in any detail. There were too many variations and special situations to deal with, and different users carried out the same task differently. They did not seem to follow a procedure in the computer-sense of the word. HCI specialists tried to model tasks for many years, but now seem to conclude that it is unrealistic for large tasks (Preece et al., 2002, for instance, concludes this).

Fortunately I was wrong. In 1997, I saw Cockburn's template for *use cases* (Cockburn 1997, 2000) and the examples he used, and suddenly I realized that task descriptions were possible and that they even scaled up to large systems. However, it was advantageous to do it a bit different than he did: He stressed that it was necessary to specify what the user does and what the computer does (these are *use cases*). It turned out to be much better to describe what they have to achieve together (these are *domain-level tasks*). Who does what is decided during design – not during analysis. During analysis we may have some design ideas that are worth recording, but they are not yet decisions.

Figure 5.3B shows the template we have now used for many years (very close to Cockburn's). The example is the check-in task at the reception. Let us look at the details.

Task header

Number and name. Each task has a number and a name, similar to the tasks in the annotated list.

Start. When does the task start? In our case the check-in task starts when a guest arrives and wants one or more rooms. Many developers talk about a *trigger* – what initiates the task. It is roughly the same as our *Start*.

End. When does the task end? In our case, it ends when the guest has got a room and the key, and the accounting has started. (Accounting means that the guest will get an invoice for rooms and services during his stay). Tasks may also *fail*, meaning that they cannot be completed. The result should as far as possible be as if the task had never started. The check-in may fail for several reasons, for instance that there is no free room or that the guest doesn't like the room. In these cases the system should not start accounting or allocate the room.

Notice that our task comprises everything that happens from start to end. The receptionist and the guest will try to finish the task without breaks.

Frequency shows how often the task is carried out. The example says about 0.5 check-ins per room per day. This is the number of check-ins for the entire hotel. In a large hotel we may have 500 rooms, meaning that there are approximately 250 check-ins per day, with most guests arriving in peak hours. We need more than one receptionist to deal with this, so a multi-user system is needed. For small hotels, there may be around 20 check-ins per day, and a single-user system is sufficient.

We also need the frequency per user. In this case it might be up to 60 per day. The frequency per user shows how important efficient task support is. The total for the system shows what kind of computer system we need. Often it will be important to specify the frequencies for peak hours, where the work is most demanding.

Fig 5.3 B Task description template

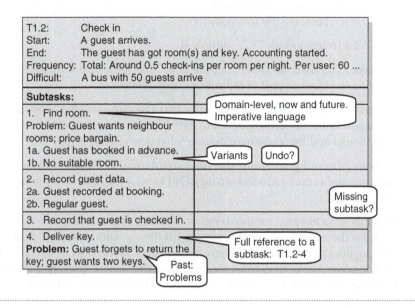

Difficult shows when the task is hard, for instance because it has to be performed fast, is stressing or demands high accuracy. In the example we have mentioned a difficult situation: a bus with 50 guests arrives.

Why are the 50 guests difficult? Imagine them arriving by bus and being checked in individually. Imagine that each guest reports at the reception desk, the receptionist finds the guest, prints out a sheet for the guest to sign and then completes the check-in of that guest. This could easily take over a minute per guest. The last guest will be extremely annoyed at having to wait an hour! Maybe we should provide some way of printing out a sheet for each guest in advance with his room number on it? This will also be a problem for small hotels.

Subtasks

The central part of the template is a list of subtasks. In our case there are four subtasks:

1 Someone (for instance the receptionist) must find a suitable room for the guest.

2 Someone must record the data for the guest, name, address, etc.

3 Someone must record that the guest is checked in and the room occupied.

4 The guest must get the room key.

Notice that we use imperative language to hide who does what – just as for the name of the entire task.

Subtasks are numbered from one and on. This is mainly for reference purposes; they may be performed in other sequences. When referring to a subtask from some piece of text elsewhere, we use this notation:

T1.2-4 [refers to task T1.2, subtask 4]

Variants. The subtasks show the basic flow of a check-in, but there are many *variants*. We describe them as part of the subtask they relate to.

Subtask 1 (find room) has two variants: (1a) The guest may have booked in advance, so a room is already assigned to him. (1b) There is no suitable room, so the receptionist and the guest may discuss what is available, prices, etc.

Subtask 2 (record guest data) also has variants: (2a) The guest may have booked in advance and is thus recorded already. (2b) He is a regular customer with a record in the database.

Variants are a blessing for the designer. You don't have to describe rules or specify logic for the many special cases; simply list the variants to be dealt with. Experienced developers say that as long as there are less than 20 variants in the task, this is manageable. Above that, consider redefining the task or splitting it into several tasks. Cockburn writes all the variants at the end of the use cases. When designing user interfaces we have found it more convenient to write them where the subtask is.

We usually have two columns for the subtasks. The right-hand column is empty in the example, but we will later show how to use it for outlining the solution, specifying the data to be used, etc.

Undo. There is a special variant that we must always consider: *Undo*. The user should at any time be able to cancel what he has done. In many cases he should also have easy ways of undoing the task after having completed it. In our example, the receptionist must be able to undo the check-in during the task, but he also needs a way to undo it afterwards, for instance because he made a mistake or because the guest comes down from his room, saying that he doesn't want the room at all – it is not what he expected.

Usually, we don't specify the undo variant in each task description, because it must be always supported anyway. The risk, however, is that we forget it in the design. In section 7.3, one step of the virtual window method is to look at *Undo* and other standard variants to be dealt with.

Other task headers

Developers wildly disagree on what a task (or use-case) template should contain. Particularly, the task header causes much debate. Here are some popular items that appear in many templates:

Trigger. An external signal or event that initiates the task. This is almost the same as our *Start*. Quite often the trigger is vague, for instance when we decide to look at our e-mail. There may not be any external signal that makes us do this. In this case the starting point is clear, but the trigger is vague.

Goal or purpose. This can mean many things. One is what must be done before the task is complete. It is similar to our *End*. Another is the business purpose of the task. For check-in it might be 'to make sure that guests pay for what they get'. This is correct, but not relevant when designing the user interface.

User. Which kind of users will carry out the task? This information is important to make sure that the user interface is suited for the users. However, the same users carry out many tasks and it will be too cumbersome to describe the users for each task. Instead, we group the tasks according to *work area* and give a separate description of the work area and the users (section 5.4).

Critical. For many years I used the term *critical* to mean the same as *difficult* or *hard*. In practice, however, the concept was often misunderstood. Some analysts would, for instance, write:

Check-in, Critical: It must be easy to learn the check-in procedure. (**Wrong**)

Check-in, Critical: There must be a good overview of today's arrivals. (**Wrong**)

These statements are not situations where the task is difficult to carry out. The first one is a requirement for ease of learning. Okay, it is critical for the success of the product, but not particularly check-in relevant. The second is a suggested solution to a problem. The analyst believed this was an important solution.

Precondition. This is something that must be fulfilled before the task can start. The concept is borrowed from the programming world where a subroutine can assume something in order to work properly. For instance a subroutine that deletes a customer record can assume that the record actually is in the database. If not, the subroutine may do absurd things and the system may crash. The program that calls the subroutine must thus ensure that the customer record exists. The assumption *customer record exists* is called a precondition.

For tasks, however, preconditions rarely make sense. It is always part of the task to check that the necessary conditions are met. Assume, for instance, that we had defined two tasks: (1) *check in a non-booked guest* and (2) *check in a booked guest*. The latter might have this precondition:

Precondition: The guest must have booked in advance.

This would mean that the receptionist had to ask the guest whether he has booked or not. From a domain viewpoint this question *is* part of the task. Often the guest knows, but sometimes he doesn't – or he believes he has but he hasn't. If the receptionist starts on the wrong task, the task fails and it may be cumbersome to back out and do the other task. The only sensible thing to do is to have only one task, and during this find out whether there is a booking for the guest. We handle this as a variant, as explained above.

Many task templates are made by programmers and contain a precondition field. Most analysts look bewildered at this field asking 'what should I write here?' Instead of leaving the field empty – as the only reasonable thing to do – they come up with something like this:

> **Precondition:** The system must be started and the user must be logged on. (**Meaningless**)

These conditions are not domain-oriented, but reflect a specific solution. For instance, they don't make sense for a fully manual reception. The first condition is trivial for a computer-based system, and the second reflects a security requirement that should be specified somewhere else, rather than for each task.

Post-condition. This too is something borrowed from the programming world. A subroutine promises that if its precondition is met, a certain post-condition is true when the subroutine ends. In case of the DeleteCustomer subroutine, the post-condition might be *customer record does not exist*. Post-conditions actually make sense for tasks. However, they are the same as a *goal* or our *End*.

Review with expert users

One of the advantages of task descriptions is that expert users readily understand them. If we review the description of check-in with an experienced receptionist, he will immediately notice that something important is missing: *In our hotel, we don't check guests in until we know they can pay. Usually we check their credit card, and sometimes we ask for a cash deposit. Where is that in your task description?*

'Oops', said the designer and added this line between subtasks 2 and 3:

> 3   Check credit card or get deposit

We should also review the task-header stuff with the expert users. It is particularly important to ask about difficult situations. Only receptionists can tell us about the 50 guests arriving at the same time. They might also tell us about the nightmare when the computer is down and they cannot check guests in because they don't know which rooms are free, who has booked, etc.

Problem description. The task description is basically on the domain level – what human and computer do together, now and in the future. Just as for the annotated task list, we can add information about the present way things are done (problems and clever things). As designers we cannot guess the problems, but during reviews with expert users we can ask about them. There are many other ways to elicit the problems, for instance observing the users. See section 15.5 for elicitation, identifying all tasks, etc.

In the example, subtask 1 has two problems: Some guests, for instance parents with children, want two neighbour rooms. Some guests try to bargain the price and the novice receptionist doesn't know what to offer. Subtask 4 has two other problems:

Many guests forget to return the key when they leave. Some guests, for instance husband and wife, want two keys for the same room so that they can come and go independently without disturbing the reception.

Clever things. While users can explain about the present problems, they rarely know when they have a clever solution. As designers we can look at their present system and identify clever solutions – that is solutions we wouldn't have come up with on our own. (We haven't noted any clever things for the check-in task.)

Task sequence

Although the subtasks are enumerated for reference purpose, no sequence is prescribed. In practice, users often vary the sequence. It is a good idea to show a typical sequence, but it doesn't mean that it is the only one. In our case the sequence may depend on whether the guest has booked or not. If he has booked, there is a free room and the receptionist will most likely record the guest first, and find the room later. If he hasn't booked, the receptionist will most likely look for a free room first.

In a small hotel you may even see subtask 4 being carried out first: A regular guest arrives, and since the receptionist knows him and knows that his favourite room is available, he hands him the key and later records that he has checked in. The system should allow any sequence as long as it makes sense.

Optional and repeatable subtasks. Sometimes one or more subtasks are optional. Usually this is clear from the context, or you may specify it in the subtask. You may also specify it as a variant of that subtask, but this is cumbersome. As an example, let us look at the case where a guest phones to change his booking. Here we have a clear event that triggers a task, but it is not clear what kind of change we end up with. Maybe the guest just wants to inform us of his new address; maybe he wants to book an additional room; maybe he wants to bargain since he has found a cheaper alternative; maybe he ends up cancelling the booking.

Some analysts attempt to define separate tasks for each of these possibilities, but this is cumbersome and doesn't reflect the true user situation. Figure 5.3C shows how to solve the problem by using optional subtasks. See section 5.5 for a discussion of good and bad tasks.

Sometimes the subtasks may be repeated as part of one task, for instance if we describe that a whole group of guests are checked in one by one. We may then simply write that the subtasks are repeatable.

5.3.3 Task & Support approach

In the task template, we have a right-hand column for the subtasks. One use of it is to describe possible ways to support the subtasks. Figure 5.3D shows how it might look for the check-in task. Now the left-hand side shows the domain-level description and the past problems. The right-hand side shows example solutions – the potential computer part in the future. Notice how we explicitly write '*The system shows . . .*' rather than a neutral imperative.

For subtask 1 there was a problem with guests wanting neighbour rooms. The example solution is to provide a floor map with colour indications of rooms to show whether they are free, booked, etc. It may turn out that this solution is too expensive or cannot be ready for the first release. As a result, the example solution may change as we design the user interface.

Another problem with subtask 1 was that guests wanted to bargain the price, for instance in vacation areas with backpackers. A closer study showed that the right discount to offer depended on the time of the day and the free capacity of the hotel. An almost full hotel late in the day shouldn't offer any discounts. The neighbour hotels are probably full too and the backpackers won't risk trying them.

The problem with the keys in subtask 4 could be handled with electronic keys. Each guest gets a new key card and the door code is changed electronically. This too is expensive, and many small hotels would not spend the money – an issue for a later release, maybe.

For subtask 2 we don't suggest any interesting solution. It should be a simple data entry task. We give a reference to the data model where the necessary fields are described. Variants 2a and 2b require a search for the guest. We note that there may be many criteria, for instance name, booking number, phone number.

In general, we write very little about the data used by the task. The same data is used in many other tasks, so it would be too hard for the developer to extract the information from the tasks. The data model is a better place to keep track of all data.

The *Task & Support* approach was developed for use in tender projects. In these projects, the customer writes his requirements to a system, sends out the requirements to several vendors, asks for proposals and selects the best one. A major problem when buying software in this way is to define the requirements without being so specific that the solution becomes too expensive, yet making sure that the system meets the real demands. With Task & Support the customer defines his demands as tasks and outlines possible solutions in the right-hand column.

The vendors modify the right-hand side to show their own solution. As an example, a vendor might write in the right-hand column for subtask 1, that he knows that the weather has an influence on the bargain price. In rainy weather travellers don't shop around that much. So his system has a rain-button, and when set, the system doesn't offer a discount. The customer will find this solution attractive – better than what he imagined. The customer compares the proposed solutions to see how well they support the tasks, and then selects the winner of the tender.

Fig 5.3 C Optional subtasks

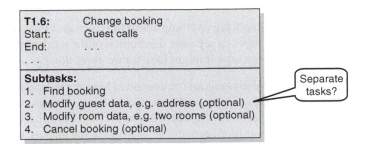

```
T1.6:        Change booking
Start:       Guest calls
End:         . . .
. . .

Subtasks:                               ┌──────────┐
1.  Find booking                        │ Separate │
2.  Modify guest data, e.g. address (optional) │ tasks?   │
3.  Modify room data, e.g. two rooms (optional) └──────────┘
4.  Cancel booking (optional)
```

The Task & Support approach worked amazingly well in practice, and later it turned out to work equally well for product development and other kinds of development projects (see Lauesen 2002).

Fig 5.3 D Task & Support approach

T1.2:	Check in
Start:	A guest arrives.
End:	The guest has got room(s) and key. Accounting started.
Frequency:	Total: Around 0.5 check-ins per room per night. Per user: 60 ...
Difficult:	A bus with 50 guests arrive

Subtasks:	Example solution:
1. Find room. **Problem:** Guest wants neighbour rooms; price bargain. 1a. Guest has booked in advance. 1b. No suitable room.	System shows free rooms on floor maps. System shows bargain prices, time and capacity dependent.
2. Record guest data. 2a. Guest recorded at booking. 2b. Regular guest.	(Simple data entry, see data model) (Search with many criteria, e.g. name, booking number, phone)
3. Record that guest is checked in.	
4. Deliver key. **Problem:** Guest forgets to return the key; guest wants two keys.	System prints electronic keys. New key for each customer.

Past: Problems   Explicit actor   Future: Computer part

5.4 Work area and user profile

The task descriptions don't say anything about the users and the general conditions of the work. We write this as a separate description of the work area and the user profiles. Figure 5.4 shows how it might look for the reception.

Work area. The example gives us an impression of how the reception tasks are carried out: standing, with frequent interrupts, etc. Notice how it improves our intuition. We can imagine the reception with impatient guests who want to check out, while others want to know when their room is ready, how to get to the airport, etc.

We can use this background information for several design decisions. The system should, for instance, support several concurrent tasks because there are frequent interruptions; a mouse might not be ideal when standing at a reception desk; allowing computer games or Web access during night shifts might be an advantage to keep the receptionist awake, etc.

User profile. In the example we have distinguished two types of users: the novice in the temporary job, for instance in the summer vacation; and the experienced user who has spent years in the reception, for instance the owner.

For each type of user we describe their IT knowledge – what they know about IT and what they have used; their IT attitude – is it something they like, want to learn, are scared of, etc.; their domain knowledge – what they know about the tasks in the reception; their domain attitude – do they like their job, just something to be done, etc.

Sometimes it is important to know whether the users have to use the system (mandatory) or whether it is their own choice (optional or discretionary use). In the hotel case it is of course mandatory for the receptionists. Often we also describe the physical abilities of the users – sight, hearing, size, etc. In the hotel case this is not particularly important, but for some applications it is, for instance when designing a system for home care.

Usually users are much more different than what the profiles say. We might have a temporary receptionist who also studies computer science and knows a lot about IT. However, when we write the profile, we try to describe the most difficult level that we need to care about during development.

Basis for usability testing. The user profiles tell us what kind of users we need for usability test and expert reviews during user interface design. The work area description tells us what kind of environment we should try to mimic. The task descriptions tell us which tasks to use for the tests.

Basis for design. The profiles also tell us what we can take for granted and what we need to explain somehow through the interface or the supporting documentation

Fig 5.4 Work area and user profile

> **Work area:** 1. Reception
>   Service guests – small and large issues.
>   Normally standing, for instance facing the guest. Frequent interrupts.
>   Often alone, e.g. during night.
>
> **User profile:** Novice. Often a temporary job.
> **IT knowledge:** Simple text processing. Younger persons have surfed a
>   bit on the Web.
> **IT attitude:** Part of the job, but not fascinating in itself.
> **Domain knowledge:** Knows only the very basics, for instance what
>   check-in is in the simplest case.
> **Domain attitude:** OK but not the career of life. It is just a temporary job.
> **Discretionary use:** Mandatory.
> **Physical abilities:** Normal sight, hearing, size, etc.
>
> **User profile:** Experienced. Often a lifetime job.
> **IT knowledge:** Simple text processing. Some know more, of course.
> **IT attitude:** Curious about how it works in the job.
> **Domain knowledge:** Knows all the procedures and the special cases.
> **Domain attitude:** Likes the job. Likes to be an expert.

or courses. Which terms do the users understand? Which kind of interactions are the users accustomed to, for instance a graphical interface or a push button machine?

5.5　Good, bad and vague tasks

The task concept sounds simple. In practice, however, developers often define tasks poorly, choosing tasks that are too vague or too small. Here are some rules for selecting good user tasks:

Closure rule. Each user task must be 'closed', i.e. finish with a meaningful goal. A true task should run *from trigger to closure*, preferably without breaks. At closure the user 'deserves a coffee break'.

A closed task has a goal that is meaningful to the user. Completing the task gives the user a pleasant feeling – he feels he has achieved something. Psychologists say that most of us love closed tasks so much that we prefer to do the small things that we can complete now, rather than the large things that may take days.

Sometimes we cannot achieve the goal. As an example, we may not be able to book the guest because we have no free rooms. In these cases we close the task without having met the goal. (Unfortunately, this doesn't give the same good feeling.)

While a task has to be closed, the subtasks in the description are usually so small that they are not closed, and consequently they are not real tasks. When designing the user interface, we should care about supporting the entire task – not just each subtask in isolation.

Session rule. Small, related tasks performed in the same work session without breaks should be grouped together under a single task description.

Some tasks are closed when looked upon individually, but they belong together and are carried out in a single session, so they should be described as a single task. The reason is that we want efficient support for the group of tasks rather than the individual, small tasks.

Domain level. Describe what user and computer do together. Hide who does what with imperative language.

We have talked a lot about hiding who does what in the previous sections. If you find this difficult, it is probably because you either describe in too much detail how it is done today, or in too much detail how it will be done in the future. Too many details about today are not interesting since things will be done differently. Too many details about the future are premature – we haven't designed the user interface yet.

Don't program. Don't go into detail with how the task is performed, the exact sequence of steps involved, under which conditions something is done, etc.

Some developers specify too many details of the task, e.g. what to do if the booking number is not correct, which conditions trigger alternative paths among the subtasks, etc. This is the programmer's way of thinking and it must be done at some time, but at analysis time it just clutters the picture and our precious expert users will be lost. Use variants instead to capture alternative conditions to deal with in some way.

Fig 5.5 A Good and bad tasks

Good tasks:
- Closed: From trigger to closure – 'coffee break deserved'
- Session: Small, related tasks without breaks in one description
- Domain level: Hide who does what with imperative language
- Don't program – 'if the customer has booked then ...'

Examples:
1. Manage rooms?
2. Enter guest name and address?
3. Book a guest?
4. Check in a bus of tourists?
5. Change the guest's address etc.?
6. Change booking?
7. Cancel entire booking?
8. Stay at the hotel?

More examples:
9. Arrange a meeting?
10. Monitor a power plant?
11. Wonderland Web site?
12. Computer game?

Examples

Let us try to apply the rules to the examples in Figure 5.5A. Which of the examples are good user tasks?

Manage rooms is an important activity, but it is not closed. You cannot say that now you have finished managing the rooms. It is an ongoing activity and thus not a good task.

Enter guest name and address is not a good task. There is no closure. Receptionists would not feel that they have achieved something after entering this. Entering the guest name and address is part of a larger, more meaningful activity, e.g. booking the guest. Surprisingly, often I see developers describe such small user activities separately. They can spend weeks describing hundreds of them and feel very productive. However, it doesn't help us designing a good user interface.

Book a guest is a good task. It is closed and when the receptionist has done it, something meaningful has been done. It may also be the time for a break – unless other guests need attention.

Check in a bus of tourists is a good task. Although checking in one of them may be considered a closed task, the receptionist would feel that there is no time for a break until all guests are dealt with. The small tasks form a single session to be supported efficiently.

Change the guest's address, etc., can be a closed task, for instance if a booked guest phones and says that he has moved and wants the confirmation to be sent to the new address. *Change the booking* and *cancel the booking* can also be separate closed tasks. However, the three tasks are often done in the same session and should be grouped into a single task description with optional subtasks. Figure 5.3C shows such a task description.

If we handle these actions as individual tasks, we easily end up designing an inconvenient dialogue. First the receptionist has to select the menu item *Change address*, and then find the guest information, correct it, and close the window and the task. If the guest also wants to change his booking, the receptionist then has to select *Change booking*, once more find the guest and then correct his booking. This is obviously inconvenient. It is an example of the extreme step-by-step dialogue explained in section 4.6.

High-level tasks

A stay at the hotel is a long activity with the aim of having the guest leave with a smile on his face. To the receptionist it consists of several smaller, closed tasks such as booking, checking in and checking out. There is a break between each of these. As long as we talk about a system for supporting the reception, *staying at the hotel* is too large a task.

However, if we consider the guest a user of the hotel, we might say that *staying at the hotel* is a **high-level task** for the guest. The guest is the *actor* who carries out the high-level task. When the stay is over and the bill settled, the guest feels a kind of closure. This is not an ordinary task because there are long breaks between the parts. Nevertheless, it is often a good idea to look at the high-level task with a Task & Support template. This allows us to consider better ways of supporting the guest, for instance allowing him to book over the Internet. The result is a kind of *business process reengineering*.

Arranging a meeting may be a long activity with the aim of having the right people meet at the same time in a free meeting room. Here we have tasks in several levels (Figure 5.5B). The top-level is *arrange meeting*. We might call this a *business case*. The meeting coordinator and each participant have a high-level task of their own. The coordinator, for instance, has to figure out who will participate, when and where. Coordinator and participants jointly carry out 'arrange meeting'. They carry out these high-level tasks through a number of e-mail sessions, phone calls, etc. An e-mail session is an ordinary task that runs from trigger to closure. The trigger might be the arrival of a bunch of e-mails. Closure is that this bunch had been dealt with for now. For the sake of completeness, we have also shown some subtasks of the e-mail session in Figure 5.5B. Remember that subtasks are not true tasks. They have no closure.

To make things even more complex, each e-mail session will usually deal with other business cases than this meeting, for instance writing a marketing report, arranging other meetings, carrying out a project.

For the purpose of designing the user interface for an e-mail system, the system should support e-mail *sessions*. Each session comprises a whole bunch of received

Fig 5.5 B High-level tasks and business cases

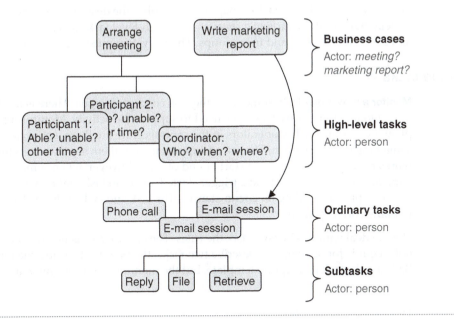

e-mails. The system should support that the user during the session deals with several business cases, several participants, etc.

How might we support the meeting coordinator's high-level task – who, when and where? We would need a system that could keep track of each participant's commitment to the meeting, free dates and free rooms. This would be a kind of database. The user would update the database during e-mail sessions, phone calls, etc.

Who are the actors? In this case, participants and coordinator are actors of the high-level tasks as well as the ordinary tasks. Who is the actor of the business case? No single person. We might say that the *meeting* is the actor. This may sound strange, but it often helps us thinking in this way. The 'meeting' has a life of its own. It somehow needs to be planned, carried out and reported to the participants. The database keeps track of the life cycle of the meeting. In this way we might realize that an IT system for supporting meetings might do more than just the planning. It might also support the meeting itself, the writing and distribution of minutes after the meeting, and sign-off of the minutes by the participants.

In summary, we may have high-level tasks that run over several ordinary tasks. And we may have high-level tasks (business cases) that reflect the life cycle of some abstract entity such as a meeting. Such a high-level task may run across several departments and users.

Chapter 11 describes the design of an e-mail system and how it handles high-level tasks as well as ordinary tasks. Chapter 10 describes the design of a course evaluation system that monitors *teaching a semester*. This high-level task runs over many days and across many users and user groups. The IT system must support all of them.

Vague tasks

Monitor a power plant. In some cases the task concept is vague. There is no clear start or end to the user's activity, yet we need to support the activity. Monitoring a power plant is an example. The operators in the control centre are there just in case something should happen. They need support to help them see that everything works properly, but there is no start or end of this. However, when something happens, we have a clear task: a trigger started an alarm task that may be simple or very complex depending on circumstances. The task ends when the system is working correctly again.

How to deal with this? Easy, break the rules. The closure rule is no law of nature – only a guide for developers. Describe two tasks: the monitor task and the repair task. Both use the task description template, but the monitor task uses only part of it:

T1: Monitor power plant

Start, End, Frequency: N/A, the task goes on forever.

Difficult: When the power is gone.

Subtasks:

1. Check that everything is fine.

   Problem: Hard to get an overview of hundred meters and twenty logs.

2. Operator notices something abnormal. Triggers task T2.

3. An alarm indication arrives from a substation. Triggers task T2.

4. Power is gone. The system switches to back-up power.

T2: Alarm

Start: An alarm indication arrives or the operator notices something abnormal.

. . .

Web sites. Using a public Web site is often a mixture of many vague tasks because users can have many expectations and reasons for visiting the site. As a result, we cannot structure the site to support a few well-defined tasks. This makes Web site designs different from traditional task-oriented designs such as a hotel system.

However, we can distinguish some broad classes of tasks:

a) Explore the site. The user may more or less accidentally enter the site and wants to find out what the site can offer.

b) Look for specific information. The user may be looking for answers to specific questions such as *What are the prices? Where is the closest shop? Why is my bill so large?*

c) Use a product on a trial basis. The user may consider buying a product, but feels uncertain whether the product meets his expectations. He wants a free trial.

d) Buy a product. The user may have decided to buy a product or service from the site.

e) Use the product on a routine basis. The user has got access to the product or service and uses it on a routine basis.

Are these classes good tasks? Not quite, because they are often mixed in one session. The user may, for instance, start exploring the site; then decide to try one of the services offered and then buy it. From the site-owner's point of view, this is a very desirable course of events. It is important to support it efficiently and not treat it as separate tasks. Using the session principle and optional subtasks, we can describe the entire situation as two tasks:

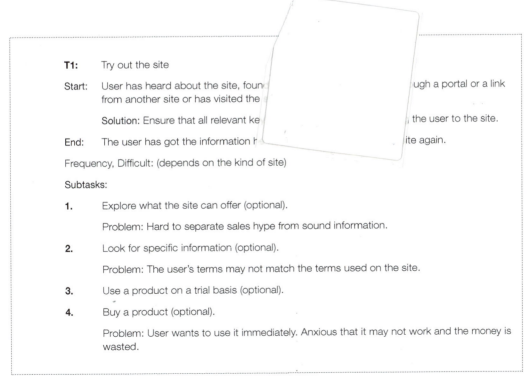

T1: Try out the site

Start: User has heard about the site, foun⌐ ⌐ugh a portal or a link from another site or has visited the ⌐

Solution: Ensure that all relevant ke⌐ ⌐ the user to the site.

End: The user has got the information h⌐ ⌐ite again.

Frequency, Difficult: (depends on the kind of site)

Subtasks:

1. Explore what the site can offer (optional).

Problem: Hard to separate sales hype from sound information.

2. Look for specific information (optional).

Problem: The user's terms may not match the terms used on the site.

3. Use a product on a trial basis (optional).

4. Buy a product (optional).

Problem: User wants to use it immediately. Anxious that it may not work and the money is wasted.

T2: Use product on a routine basis

Start: User has a need for the service.

. . .   (The rest depends on the kind of product. The task is closed in the traditional sense.)

Section 13.5 gives hints on how to define test tasks for Web sites. Section 15.5.8 shows ways to invent tasks that don't exist at present. Section 15.5.9 shows ways to check that you have identified all tasks.

Game programs. Some IT systems don't really have closed tasks because their purpose is hard to specify. Game programs are examples. Their main purpose is to be entertaining – not to complete tasks.

For story-type games, Mallon and Webb (2000) observed an analogy to task closure, however. These games are based on an artificial world where the balance of things has been disrupted. The goal of the game is to close the disruption and restore the balance. During usability tests, it is important to see whether users find out what the goal is (in some games they don't and soon lose interest in the game).

5.6   Scenarios and use cases

The term *task* is closely related to two other terms often used in software development: *scenario* and *use case*. We will explain both of these.

Scenario

The term *scenario* has many meanings. In connection with interface design it has two main meanings: a small story with a vivid illustration of the work area; or a specific case of a task.

Vivid scenarios

Figure 5.6A shows an example of a vivid scenario, a description of an evening in a small hotel reception. Note how we can derive several things from this scenario: the difficult task variant with the bus full of tourists; the problem with adjoining rooms; the need for night entertainment for reception staff.

Scenarios are attractive and give us a good intuition about the work area. However, they don't pretend to cover all tasks, and they are difficult to use in a systematic fashion during interface design. One thing you *can* do is to check that all parts of the scenarios are covered by the different parts of the task descriptions.

Fig 5.6 A Vivid scenario

Reproduced with permission from Pearson education

> **Scenario: The evening duty**
>
> Doug Larsson had studied all afternoon and was a bit exhausted when arriving 6 p.m. to start his turn in the reception. The first task was to prepare the arrival of the bus of tourists expected 7 p.m. He printed out all the check-in sheets and put them on the desk with the appropriate room key on each sheet.
>
> In the middle of that a family arrived asking for rooms. They tried to bargain and Doug always felt uneasy about that. Should he give them a discount? Fortunately, Jane came out from the back office and told them with her persuading smile that she could offer 10% discount on the kid's room. They accepted, and Doug was left to assign them their rooms. They wanted a neighbour room for the kids, and as usual he couldn't remember which rooms were neighbours.
>
> Around 10 p.m., everything was quiet, and he tried to do some of his homework, but immediately became sleepy. Too bad – he wasn't allowed to sleep at work until 1 a.m. Fortunately, the office computer allowed him to surf the net. That kept him awake and even helped him with some of his homework.

Case scenarios

UML (Unified Modeling Language) is a standard notation introduced by one of the object-oriented schools (Booch *et al.* 1999). UML defines scenarios in another way:

A scenario is an instantiation of a use case.

This means that a task description (use case) is the general pattern for doing certain things, while a scenario is how it is done in one particular case. We call this kind of scenarios *case scenarios*. Case scenarios are not quite the same as vivid scenarios. Vivid scenarios may comprise several case scenarios and they give a more stimulating description of the situation. Here are some simple examples:

■ *Checking in a guest* is a task (the general case – any guest).

■ *Checking in John Simpson who has booking number 2533* is a case scenario.

■ The *evening duty* (Figure 5.6A) is a vivid scenario.

Case scenarios are useful as test cases when testing for usability. In contrast, the vivid scenario in Figure 5.6A is not suitable as a test case.

Use case

A use case is a kind of task description, but it is made explicit what the computer does and what the human does. The work has thus been split between the two. There are many ways of describing use cases, and most of them focus on what the computer shall do. Use cases were introduced by Jacobson *et al.* (1994) as a literal translation from Swedish, and the term is now used extensively in connection with object-oriented software development. We will illustrate some of the many kinds of use cases. For a longer discussion, see Constantine and Lockwood (2001) and Lauesen (2002).

Use case diagrams. We will first look at the UML version of use cases. UML comprises several types of diagrams, the use case diagram being one of them. The top diagram in Figure 5.6B shows four UML use cases. The box represents the computerized hotel system and the diagram shows that the receptionist can carry out (be the *actor* of) the use cases *booking, check-in* and *checkout*. These use cases are handled by the hotel system, as illustrated by the bubbles inside the box. Each use case bubble might involve several functions on the user interface, for instance listing free rooms and recording guest information. The same functions may be used in many other use cases.

The fourth bubble is a use case between the hotel system and another computer system, the accounting system. This use case is about the automatic transfer of accounting data from the hotel system to the account system, and the bubble shows the hotel system part of this transfer.

Fig 5.6 B Use cases versus tasks

Reproduced with permission from Pearson education

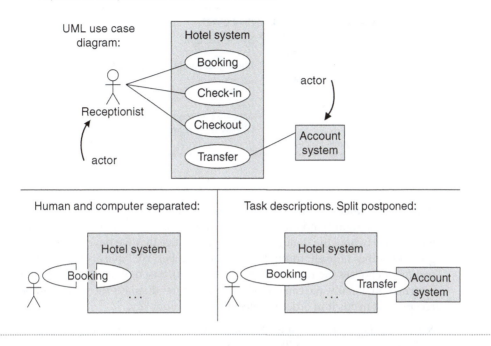

The diagram in the example simply lists the use cases. It adds a graphical hint of the actor who initiates the use case, but otherwise it doesn't really explain how the task is done. In more elaborate use case diagrams, use cases may be connected to each other by means of lines that show that one use case uses another one, for instance as a kind of subroutine.

However, there are other types of use cases than the one defined in UML. In the lower left diagram of Figure 5.6B, we have illustrated a kind of use case where we can see user actions as well as computer actions. The diagram shows that the entire booking task consists of two parts, one carried out by the user and one carried out by the product.

The last diagram in Figure 5.6B illustrates the task concept. The bubble represents the entire task. It floats over the computer boundary, illustrating that the task is carried out by human and computer together, but the division of work is not yet determined.

Human and computer separated

We will now look at a text-oriented version of use cases where we split the work between human and computer. Figure 5.6C shows how it works for the check-in procedure. To keep it short, we only look at an example where the guest has booked in advance. The example and the formats were inspired by Cockburn (2000) and Constantine and Lockwood (2001).

Fig 5.6 C Human and computer separated

Use case: Check in a booked guest	
User action	**System action**
Enter booking number	
	Show guest and booking details
Edit details (optional)	
	Store modifications
Push check-in	
	Allocate free room(s)
	Display room number(s)
Give guest key(s)	

In this figure, there are two columns. The left-hand one specifies what the human does, and the right-hand one what the computer does. Time runs down the page, so we see clearly how the dialogue progresses. Notice that we have specified how the guest identifies himself: through a booking number. We have also specified that the computer chooses the rooms (allocate free room), based on the guest's booking information. Finally, we can see why the computer displays the room number: the receptionist needs it in order to select the right room key.

Now, what is wrong with this? Nothing if what we describe is the way the final dialogue works, and we will in section 7.1 do something similar. However, many developers already describe the user tasks in this way during domain analysis. This means that they design the detailed dialogue already at this stage. Later, the programmers may implement the dialogue exactly the same way, and the result is a step-by-step-oriented user interface with low usability (see section 4.6).

Even in this simple example, we can see that the dialogue has low usability. For instance, the receptionist has no say in which room is allocated to the guest. The computer decides based solely on room type (single, double, etc.). This dialogue will be inadequate if the guest wants two adjoining rooms, for instance. Compared to the task descriptions, we have prematurely decided on too much. It is better to work on the task description level, where we haven't split the work between human and computer, and where we test for usability before we decide for the final dialogue.

Test yourself

a) Mention five things to be done in domain analysis.

b) What is a data model and why is it useful when designing the user interface?

c) What is the difference between an annotated task list and template-based task descriptions?

d) Does a task description explain what users do at present or what they will do in the future?

e) What is the difference between a task description and a work area description?

f) Why is it important to describe *frequency* and *difficult* for a task?

g) Mention some good and some bad tasks.

h) How do we describe a task where subtask 2 sometimes is performed before subtask 3, sometimes after?

i) What is the difference between a task and a use case?

j) What is the difference between a task and a scenario?

Design exercises. See Chapter 17.

6

Virtual windows design

Highlights

■ Virtual windows: Detailed screens for presenting data and for searching. No system functions yet.

■ Few screens to ease learning and support tasks efficiently.

■ Graphical design now to prevent disasters later.

■ Check the screens and keep track of the defects.

■ Key exercise: Design virtual windows for the design project.

Definition

A virtual window is a user-oriented presentation of persistent data. Early during design, the virtual windows may be on paper. They show data, but have no buttons, menus or other functions. Later we allocate functions to them, and finally they become computer screens, Web pages, etc. A complex application will need several virtual windows.

The basic idea when composing a set of virtual windows is this: Create as few virtual windows as possible while ensuring that (1) all data is visible somewhere and (2) important tasks need only a few windows. First we make a plan for what should be in each window (section 6.1), and next we make a detailed graphical design of the windows (section 6.2). Finally we check with users that they understand the windows, and we check against the task descriptions and the data model that everything is covered (sections 6.4 to 6.6). Usually there is a great deal of iterative design at this stage.

The way we design the virtual windows will help us balance between the two extremes: the database-oriented and the step-by-step-oriented user interfaces.

Although we present the design below in a step-by-step fashion, design is not an automatic procedure where you start in one end and end up with a good result. A good design always includes some magic points. The step-by-step procedure is good support for the magic – not a replacement for it.

6.1 Plan the virtual windows

First we make a plan for the virtual windows – which windows do we need and what data should they show. Here is the step-by-step procedure for how to make the plan.

Design procedure

a) Look at an important and frequent task. Imagine the data the user would like to see to accomplish this task.

b) Group the data into a few virtual windows and outline the contents of each window.

c) Look at the next task and imagine the data the user would like to see to accomplish it.

d) If this task reuses data that are in the already planned virtual windows, consider reusing these windows.

e) If the task uses additional data that logically relates to a planned virtual window, consider expanding this window. If not, define new virtual windows with the additional data.

f) Continue from step d with the next task until all tasks are properly supported by data.

g) **Variant:** When outlining the contents of a virtual window, some designers just list the fields to be seen, others make more or less finished graphical outlines. Both are okay – designers are different.

h) **Variant:** For tasks with many steps and many kinds of data, treat the steps one by one as if they were separate tasks.

i) **Variant:** If the result seems messy or too complex, redo the planning, starting with another task.

Below we will show how the procedure worked for the hotel system. Some of the steps in the procedure are very much a matter of judgement. For instance, how do we group data into a few virtual windows? Why is one window not enough? Why not have many small windows? Why reuse windows across tasks rather than making a special one for each task?

To help the designer make these judgements, we use *guidelines* or *rules*. In order to explain them, we have to distinguish between a *window template* and a *window instance*. You may think of the window instance as a window template filled in with data. As an example, a guest window with data for John Simpson is a window instance. All the guest windows use the same window template. A window template is also called a *window type*.

Design rules

1 **Few window templates.** Keep the total number of window templates small. Try to reuse window templates across tasks. (It is easier to grasp few window templates as a mental model.)

2 **Few window instances per task.** For each task, the user should access few window instances. (This improves task support.)

3 **Data in one window instance only.** Avoid that the user can see the same data item in several window instances. Example: John Simpson's address is shown in many windows. In particular, avoid that the user can edit it through several windows. (Seeing the same data item in several windows makes the mental model more complex. Being able to edit it at several places causes confusion about the effect of the change.)

4 **Rooted in one thing.** A virtual window will often be rooted in a single object. It shows data about this object and objects related to the object. Example: Data about John Simpson and all his stays at the hotel. It may also show data about several objects of the same class and objects related to them. Example: A list of guests and their stays. (The entire window gestalt now reflects what is logically related in the data model.)

5 **Virtual windows close to final screen size.** A virtual window may be somewhat larger than the physical screen available, but not vastly larger. At a later stage of the design we can cut the virtual window into a few smaller screens or use scroll bars to give the illusion that this is one big screen. If the virtual window is vastly larger than the physical screen, we lose this illusion.

6 **Necessary overview of data.** The virtual windows must provide overviews of many data, even though the user may need only part of these data. (People understand best when things are in a context. The overview provides the context for the detail.)

7 **Things – not actions.** It is fine to call a window *Breakfast list*, but wrong to call it *Enter breakfast list*. The first suggests that we look at persistent data or things, the latter that this is a function with some dialogue data to support a user action. If a task involves reviewing the breakfast list, the designer would not reuse *Enter breakfast list*, but design another virtual window, *Review breakfast list*.

8 **All data accessible.** Usually all data from the data model must be visible and modifiable through some virtual window. Otherwise we probably lack a virtual window and probably also a task.

These rules are guidelines only. In many cases they conflict, and then we have to strike a balance, for instance between task efficiency and ease of understanding. We will show examples below. The rules cover only the high-level composition of screens. They do not pretend to cover graphical design of the individual windows.

Example: windows for booking

We will now use the design procedure and rules on the hotel system. Let us start with an important and frequent task, the booking task. Which data should the user see to book a guest? He has to see which rooms are vacant in the period concerned, what their prices are, etc. He also has to record the booking and the name, address, etc., of the guest.

Figure 6.1 shows how we have allocated these data to two virtual windows, *Stay* and *Rooms*. The Rooms window gives an overview of when rooms are occupied, their prices, etc. The Stay window will show name, address and stay period for a single guest. It also shows the booked rooms (there may be more than one).

Plural form. Notice the careful use of the plural form for the booked rooms. It suggests that some kind of list or advanced graphical representation is to be used on the screen. The English language distinguishes between singular and plural, but many languages don't. If you work in such a language, we recommend that you add a star to the name to denote zero, one or more. You might also do it in English for clarity. (The star is also the way computer scientists denote zero, one or more.)

During the booking, the receptionist and the computer will somehow have to fill in the Stay window and mark in the Rooms window that the room is no longer free. Notice the pile of completed Stay windows, suggesting that we have recorded several stays. We have only one Rooms window instance, since all rooms are shown there with their occupation status for a period of days. This is also the place where the user selects a free room for a guest.

Checking against the design rules

Let us check this first design decision against the design rules. We will see that the rules have been violated several times already. But don't despair – there will be fewer violations in the rest of the design.

Rule 1. Do we have too many window templates? We have only two, but could we do with just one? Yes, we might show the status of all rooms in every Stay window. Then we would have only one window template. However, we now violate rule 3, *data in one window instance only*. The user might wonder whether the booking of a room has been properly marked in all the Stay windows. We would also violate rule 4, *rooted in one thing*. Data about free rooms doesn't belong to a single stay, but applies across all stays.

In this case, rule 1 conflicts with rules 3 and 4. We have chosen to make the system a bit harder to remember (two window templates rather than one), but prevented some misunderstandings about filling in the windows.

Rule 2. Does the receptionist have to use too many window instances for the booking task? Well, he has to use two windows, so it once more seems tempting to

Fig 6.1 Virtual windows, plan

Reproduced with permission from Pearson education

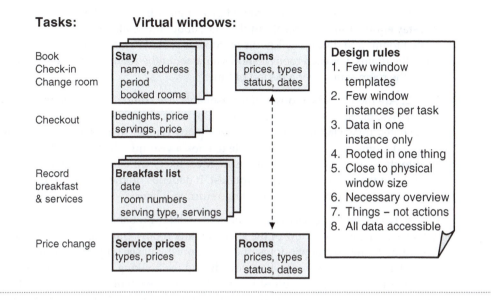

Tasks: Virtual windows:

Book   **Stay**
Check-in   name, address
Change room   period
                booked rooms

Checkout   bednights, price
                servings, price

Record   **Breakfast list**
breakfast   date
& services   room numbers
                serving type, servings

Price change   **Service prices**
                types, prices

Rooms
prices, types
status, dates

Rooms
prices, types
status, dates

Design rules
1. Few window
   templates
2. Few window
   instances per task
3. Data in one
   instance only
4. Rooted in one thing
5. Close to physical
   window size
6. Necessary overview
7. Things – not actions
8. All data accessible

combine them into one. However, this is easy to deal with. Although we need two *virtual windows* for the booking task, we may later choose to show them together on the same physical *screen*, for instance as two real windows or two frames within a single page. We just have to utilize the gestalt laws to indicate that there are two independent gestalts – not one.

Rule 3. Are there places where we show the same data in more than one window instance? Yes, if we have a regular guest with many stays, we will see his name and address in all his stays. What happens if the receptionist changes the address in a stay? Will the guest's other stays change too?

According to the data model in Figure 5.2, the guest's address is stored only once in the database. As a result, the other stay windows will change the address too, but this may not be obvious to the receptionist. (We might change the data model so that the system remembers the address for each stay, but we will not pursue this possibility here.) We could solve the understandability problem by having guest windows separate from the stay windows, but this new window template makes the system more complex.

We have chosen to keep the combined guest and stay window. At this stage we believe that it is not so important whether the receptionist believes that the address is changed in only one stay or in all the related stays. The receptionist will rarely look into the related stays anyway, and if he does, he will see that the address has been changed correctly. However, it is an issue to check during usability tests. We make a note of this for the debriefing after usability tests.

Rule 4. Are the virtual windows rooted in a single thing? The Stay window is rooted in a stay entity. It shows data about this stay, about the related guest and about the related rooms and dates. The Rooms window is rooted in several objects of the same class: the rooms. For each room it shows data about the room (price, etc.) and data about the room states over a period of time.

Rule 5. Are the virtual windows of a reasonable size compared against the physical screen? Yes, the Stay window seems okay. But what about the Rooms window? How many dates are we talking about? and how many rooms? In a large hotel we may have 500 rooms, and it may be possible to book a year into the future. This will be hard to show on even a very large screen. Most likely we will need some way to zoom in on the dates and rooms of interest. It depends on the graphical design, however, so let us make a note on it and return to it later.

Rule 6. Do we have the necessary overview of data? Probably the Rooms window will give us a good overview of the state of many rooms. But what about the stays? According to the virtual windows, the receptionist will see only one stay at a time. Most likely he will need some overview during the booking, for instance to find the right guest in case a regular guest books. Most likely we will need some search window for this. For the time being, we will pretend that we have forgotten about it. Later our checking techniques should reveal the problem.

Rule 7. Are the window names nouns (things)? Yes, both *Rooms* and *Stay* are perfect window names. Some designers might call the *Stay* window *Create Stay*. This shows a function-oriented way of thinking, easily leading to a different window template for changing a stay, and yet another template for checking in. Don't do this.

Rule 8. Is all data visible and modifiable? This is too early to tell. The rule only makes sense when we have all the virtual windows. We will look at the rule once more below, when we have the outline for all the virtual windows.

Check in and Change room

This long discussion was about the first task, booking. Let us look at the next task, check in. Fortunately, the same two virtual windows suffice. If the guest hasn't booked in advance, the procedure is much the same as for booking, except that the room becomes occupied rather than booked. If the guest *has* booked, we just need to find the stay in the pile of Stay forms. We need some search criteria to support that, but we will ignore it for the time being.

Change of rooms uses the same two windows, one for the stay to be modified and one to see free rooms. Again we need a search criteria to find the stay, but this time it is most likely the room number.

Check out

When checking out, the receptionist needs the Stay window, but also some more data. He has to see how many nights the guest stayed, what services he received, the prices and the total. It is useful to verify the data with the guest before printing the invoice.

Where do we put these data? Put it in a new virtual window? No, that would violate few window templates. Instead, we extend the Stay window as shown on Figure 6.1. Whether we want to always show the extensions on the screens too, is a matter of later dialogue design. But when we show them, the graphical look should clearly indicate that this is an extension of the Stay data. For instance, it might be shown inside the same frame as the other stay data.

The extension causes no conflicts with the other design rules. There might be a small problem with rule 5, size of virtual window, since we now have to add service lines to the Stay window. However, it seems to be within what we can handle with scroll bars, tab sheets, etc.

Record services

The last task on our list is recording of services such as breakfast servings. In principle, we don't need a new virtual window for that. The receptionist could simply find the stay window and somehow record the service there. This approach is needed in some cases, for instance when the receptionist records breakfast in connection with the guest checking out early in the morning.

However, in many hotels, breakfast servings are recorded in the restaurant on a list with preprinted room numbers. A waiter brings it to the reception where the receptionist enters the data. It would be laborious to look up each stay by means of the room number, record the breakfast, and then look up the next room. We could improve the procedure with a special interface function that could bring up the Stay windows one by one in room number sequence. However, the receptionist would still have to look at a virtual window instance for almost each room. This would violate rule 2 of few window instances per task.

In Figure 6.1 we have shown another solution, a virtual window that holds a *breakfast list*. There would be a pile of them with one completed window per day. This solution is important for task support, although it violates rule 3 of data in one window only, since breakfast servings are also shown in the Stay windows. The system is now conceptually more complex since the user has to understand the relation between the breakfast window and the Stay windows. For instance, the user may worry whether the system keeps both of them updated or whether he has to do something to have the latest breakfast list transferred to the Stay windows.

This is a quite serious design conflict between task efficiency and ease of understanding. It is important to test whether users understand the suggested solution properly, and if necessary supply adequate guidance in the windows. (Another note for the usability test.)

Got all windows?

We have now handled all the user tasks, and it is time to check the last design rule:

Rule 8. Is all data visible and modifiable? In order to answer that question, we have to go through all attributes of the data model and ask the question for each attribute. We will do this in detail in section 6.5.

However, if we make a simple check now, we may notice that there is no window for changing the service prices, e.g. the breakfast prices. The receptionist can only see the breakfast prices through the charges on the Stay windows, and this place would be a strange place to change the prices. We talk about changing the future prices – prices for something that nobody has ordered yet.

For this reason, we have added a task called *Price Change* (see Figure 6.1). It requires a new virtual window, *Service prices*. There is also a need to change the room prices, but the Rooms window might be used for this since it has the prices already. As shown in the figure, the Price Change task uses these two windows.

Note that Figure 6.1 shows all virtual windows and lists all tasks. It also shows which windows the individual task uses. When the system has many tasks and many virtual windows, we need a better overview. Section 6.8 shows a better approach, based on a matrix. We also use this approach in the design of two larger systems in Chapters 10 and 11.

Are the rules useful?

Since we have so many problems with the design rules, aren't they just plain wrong? Or is the virtual window idea wrong? It is hard to prove either way, and as far as I know there are no competing rules to compare against.

Personally I believe that the rules are correct to a large extent and they reflect common usability problems. When they conflict it is because of inherent conflicts in what we want to achieve. We cannot get everything. For instance ease-of-understanding calls for data not being shown in different ways, while task efficiency calls for different views. The role of the designer is to find solutions that provide a good balance between our conflicting dreams. The design rules help him discuss the conflicts. Our discussions above were examples of this.

The situation is similar to when engineers design a bridge. It has to carry the cars safely, it has to look good, it must be cheap and it must be environmental. All of these requirements conflict, and the good engineer knows how to strike a balance. For a user interface we have similar conflicts. It must be easy to understand, efficient for daily use, cheap to implement and look good.

Exceptions from rule 3: data in one place only

The design rule that causes most problems in practice is rule 3: *data in one window instance only*. We have observed some cases where a violation of the rule doesn't seem to cause usability problems:

a) Assume that the same piece of data is shown in several places and all places are visually updated at the same time. Users intuitively understand that it is the same data in all the places. An example is a measurement that is shown in analog form in one window and as digits in another window. If changes are shown immediately at both places, the user perceives it as the same data. It is the immediate visual feedback that helps the user form the right mental model.

b) Assume that data is shown as a list of items in one window, and as a detail window for one selected item. Then the selected item on the list and the details are perceived as belonging together. Figure 3.5A shows an example: a list of room states and a detail window showing all the data about a selected room. If the user changes some detail data about the room, he expects that the list will reflect the change. It is probably the temporal and spatial closeness of the two presentations that makes the user form this mental model.

6.2 Virtual windows, graphical version

The virtual windows plan can look quite convincing, and developers may conclude that they can come up with the graphical presentation when they design the final screens. When they later do so and try to fill in some realistic data, they realize that the outline doesn't work. There may not be sufficient space for realistic data, the user doesn't understand what the windows show, or the user doesn't get the necessary overview. Consequence: go back and redesign a lot – or ignore usability. For this reason it is important to make a careful graphical design in connection with the plan.

Design procedure

a) For each virtual window in the plan, make a detailed graphical design. Design only the data presentation. (Don't add buttons, menus or other functions. It is too early to fight against these complexities.)

b) Fill in the windows with realistic data. (They may need more space than you expect.)

c) Fill in the windows with extreme, but realistic data. (Extreme data must also be easy to see.)

d) If the windows don't look right, you may have to change the plan for the windows.

Figure 6.2 shows the result for the hotel system. It is not the designer's first version, but number two or three (sometimes hard to tell how many you have made). To give an overview of all the virtual windows in one figure, we have omitted some trivial fields, e.g. phone number, and we have shortened many others.

In the figure we have indicated the tasks that use each window. This is often convenient during design to check that all tasks are adequately covered and that some windows have multiple purposes. Let us give a few comments on the design.

Stay window. The Stay window has a top section about the guest and a bottom section with the rooms he has used and the services he has received. The dotted line separates the past from the future. Above the dotted line we have the nights he has stayed and the services he has received. Below the line we have the bookings – the nights he hasn't stayed yet.

We have indicated which fields the user can modify with a light border, resembling what the fields would look like on the final screen. We have also indicated that the user can choose the pay method with a combo box (drop-down list). Finally, we have used a scroll bar to indicate that the item list may be much longer.

This virtual window may appear almost as it is in the final computer screens. The window may also guide what the invoice should look like, making it easy for the receptionist to compare the two.

Fig 6.2 Virtual windows, graphical version

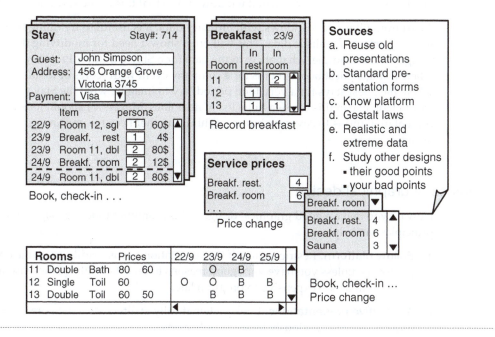

Breakfast. This window shows the breakfast servings for a single day. It has a line for each room and space for two kinds of servings: breakfasts in the restaurant and breakfasts served in the room. In practice, there might be some more columns for other frequent services. The window may appear in almost the same form on the computer screen, and it may also appear as a paper form filled in by the waiters.

Service prices. This window is a simple list of the different services including their current price. It will typically appear in two forms on the computer: as a separate window for changing prices and as a drop-down list when entering or editing service lines on the Stay window (see Figure 6.2). Conceptually it is the same virtual window, but it will look a bit different in the two forms.

Rooms. The rooms window uses a matrix form (like a spreadsheet). There is a line for each room and a column for each date. The letters O and B stand for Occupied and Booked. There may be a long list of room numbers and a long list of dates covering the past as well as the future. Scroll bars indicate this.

Try realistic and extreme data
It is important to test the design by filling in the windows with realistic data, as shown in Figure 6.2. (For space reasons, we have shown address and name fields that are much too short; also the Rooms window is much too small.) We have also shown a complex, but slightly unusual situation: a guest checks into a single room and gets

breakfast in the restaurant. The next day he moves into a double room and gets two breakfasts in the room. The virtual window shows that this is one stay and one guest.

Apart from filling the windows with ordinary data, it is useful to try filling them with extreme, but realistic data. This will often show a need for modifying the design. In the example, what are extreme data for a Stay window? Probably cases where a single guest books rooms for a company event with scores of rooms, or cases where the guest stays for a very long period. Try to imagine what the Stay window would look like in this case – a huge list of item lines. Maybe we should look at other presentation forms to cover such cases. (This is another note for improving the design.)

Sources of graphical design

How do you make a good graphical design? This is another touch of magic, but these principles can help:

1   **Follow platform.** Restrict yourself to presentation forms readily available on the platform – unless you have very good reasons to do differently. (Otherwise the design will be too expensive to program later.)

2   **Alternative presentations.** Look systematically at alternative data presentation formats (we unconsciously focus on only a few).

3   **Reuse old data presentations** – if suited.

4   **Use gestalt laws** to make the user see how things relate to each other.

5   **Study other people's designs.** Look for the good things in their design – and the bad things in your own.

Follow the platform

A thing that often annoys software developers is an enthusiastic designer who comes up with fancy designs that are unrealistic to implement. Now, what is unrealistic and what is not? It depends on the *platform* to be used.

If we develop a system to run on the Microsoft Windows platform, screens will have a certain look unless we spend fortunes adding new features to Microsoft Windows (which is possible, in fact). If we develop a system to run on Macintosh computers, the screens will look much the same, but there are significant differences in the detail. It will be very costly to give the screens the same look as Windows screens.

If we develop a Web-based system, the rules are different since the Web pages must be displayable on all kinds of systems. If we develop a user interface for a special device such as a mobile phone or a hi-fi player, the screen gives heavy limitations. We cannot show things in colour, or things with many details.

If you are a designer and you don't know the platform well, we highly recommend that you design the virtual windows in cooperation with a programmer who knows the platform.

Platform choices

In case of the hotel system, the virtual windows are intended for a GUI platform such as Microsoft Windows or Macintosh. We haven't shown so much detail that it matters which of these to use. What about showing them on the Web? The traditional Web platform is HTML, which basically is aimed at text presentations with embedded pictures for illustration. With some minor changes, we could show the virtual windows in HTML. The main problem would be to replace the scroll bars with up/down buttons. There are other Web platforms, however, and with, for instance, Swing, we could show the virtual windows in the same way as on the Microsoft Windows platform.

No matter which of these platforms we choose, there is one detail in the virtual windows that would be very expensive to program: the dotted line in the Stay window. A platform expert could have told us immediately.

On the Microsoft Windows platform there are many sub-platforms. Two of the most widely used are Visual Basic and Microsoft Access. Access windows connect easily to the database and can show large amounts of data, but there are many limitations in the way data can be shown. Visual Basic can show data in more ways, but is somewhat harder to connect to the database and have troubles showing lots of data fields on the screen.

In case of the hotel system, a fast way to implement it would be by means of Access. The Breakfast window and the Service price window are straightforward to implement with Access. The Stay window is a bit harder, but easy for an Access developer. The Rooms window, however, seems very hard because we want to scroll horizontally over large time spans. Even skilled Access developers find it difficult, but once they find the right trick, it is easy. If we imagined more advanced data presentations, such as graphical curves or floor maps, Access would be a dubious tool. Visual Basic would be feasible, but not straightforward.

Combining platforms. Many business applications these days are made by combining platforms. Users may, for instance, handle data entry and data retrieval with Access screens, present complex data by means of an Excel spreadsheet, and print reports and customer letters by means of Word. Developers use Visual Basic to glue these things together and transfer data automatically between the platforms.

This combination of widely used tools also helps the more experienced users to modify what the system provides, for instance to look at complex data in non-planned ways by means of the Excel spreadsheet, modify the customer letters, or cut-and-paste things into e-mails. All of this makes the task easier for the designer and the developer, since they don't have to deal with all the task variations that users can handle themselves.

However, a system created by combining platforms in this way will usually be somewhat slow to use. The switch between for instance data entry and overview of complex data will not be instantaneous and is not suited for time-consuming tasks or tasks under time pressure.

Apart from such limitations, the designer still has a major influence on the usability of the combined system, and the techniques we describe here can still be used. There is just less freedom to come up with unusual screen designs.

Look at alternative data presentation formats

When finding good ways to present complex data, you need inspiration. We tend to look only at the solutions that immediately come to mind. Looking at the selection of data presentations in Chapter 3 may help you discover other solutions. Books dedicated to data presentation may of course help even more (see Tufte 1983, 1990; Spence 2001). In the hotel system, the Rooms window is inspired by the general matrix presentation and by spreadsheets. Looking at the alternatives, we realize that it might be a good idea to have an additional virtual window showing the rooms on a floor map.

Reuse old data presentations?

If the old system uses some forms or screens already, we may use them in the new system. It will ease learning the new system, but it may also block designs that give better task support. In the hotel system, for instance, the virtual stay window resembles an invoice, thus helping the novice. However, if we want a good overview for a guest who books a few rooms for a long period, the traditional invoice-like presentation is not good.

In section 3.7 we discussed a system for classroom allocation. The old, manual way of presenting data was actually the main reason the system performed so poorly that there appeared to be a constant shortage of rooms, although lots of rooms were free. The designer first copied the old presentation to the computer system, but found out during usability tests that it was a disaster. Many experiments were needed to come up with a better computer-supported presentation.

Use gestalt laws

The gestalt laws help us show data in meaningful groups and in ways that users perceive automatically. In the Stay window, the designer has grouped the guest data into one gestalt and the room and service items into another gestalt. He has separated the gestalts by means of a horizontal line (not the best way, actually).

This is not just to make it look nice. He tried to suggest to the user that the two gestalts belong to different objects, one to the guest and one to the stay. Remember the discussion about whether guest data and stay data should be in the same window? and the issue of what happened when we change the address of the guest? The designer hoped that the gestalts helped the user understand that a change of guest address would influence the guest's other stays as well. Usability tests showed that he succeeded to a large extent. You may notice a detail; the graphical design incorrectly suggests to the user that the payment method also belongs to the guest. It does not – it may vary from one stay to another since the payment relates to the stay. This doesn't confuse users. Their understanding of the domain seems to tell them that the payment method may vary from one stay to another.

The user should also perceive each item line on the Stay window as a single gestalt. This is not clear at all in our design. On the contrary, the laws of proximity and similarity suggest that the columns are the gestalts.

Fortunately, if we make the Stay window with a tool such as Access, some of the gestalt problems disappear. Access automatically makes a frame around the entire list of items, and can separate the list items by a horizontal line. A designer knowing Access well might have made similar lines in the hand-drawn mock-up also.

The designer has also tried to separate the items on the list by means of a dotted line. What does it mean? It separates the items the guest has got already, from the items he has booked. Experiments showed that the users didn't grasp this intuitively. As a coincidence, the dotted line is impossible to make on an Access screen, so a different presentation might solve the usability problem as well as the technical problem.

Study other people's designs

Professional architects and designers of furniture, hi-fi equipment, etc., don't just invent things themselves. They consciously study other people's designs to learn from them. The top designers have learned to look at the good things in the other designs and the bad things in their own.

For some reason this is not so widely used in the IT world. Developers mostly cling to a standard. If they compare their own design with someone else's, they find the bad points in the other design and enjoy the good points in their own.

6.3　Virtual windows in development

Work product. A work product is the developer term for an intermediate result during system development. Figure 6.3 shows four important work products in user interface design:

a) The data model and the associated data description (data dictionary).

b) The task descriptions (in one of the many forms).

c) The virtual windows.

d) A list of design defects or things to find out.

They document different views of the final system, and they duplicate information to some extent.

Design sequence. In which sequence should we make these work products? Until now we have pretended that we first make data models and task descriptions, and then virtual windows. In many cases this sequence is okay, but some designers do it differently. They make virtual windows before the data model. This is because they can better imagine data when they see them as screens. They make the data model later to get a consistent overview of all the data.

Concurrent design. Personally I develop data model, tasks and virtual windows concurrently. Each of these work products tells me something about the other ones. When they are all okay, I feel that the design can move on to the next stage.

Need for early graphical design

In early versions of the technique, we didn't split virtual window design into a planning step and a detail step. We observed that some design teams produced excellent user interfaces, which scored high during usability tests, while other teams produced bad designs. Furthermore, *excellent designs were produced much faster than bad designs*. Why was that?

Gradually we realized that the main difference between good and bad teams was the amount of detail they put into the virtual windows. Both groups could quite fast produce the outline version. The bad teams then continued with dialogue design, but when designing the final screens, everything collapsed. The outline could not become useful screens; fields could not contain what they were supposed to; it was impossible to get an overview of data, etc. The teams had to redesign everything, resulting in a mess.

The good teams took some more effort designing the graphical details of the virtual windows, filling them with realistic data, etc. As part of that, they often went back to modify the window plan, grouping data in other ways. These changes were easy to handle at that time. From then on, things went smoothly. Dialogue functions were

Fig 6.3 Work products to maintain

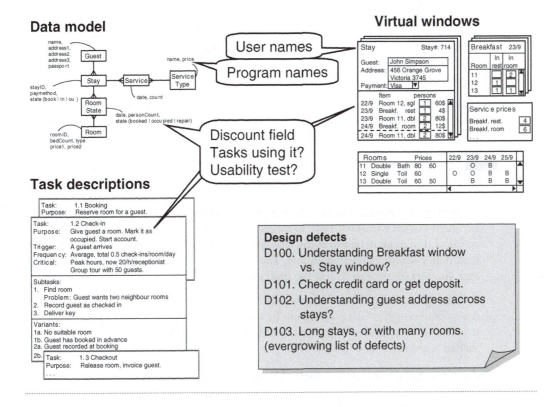

added, and the screen design was largely a matter of cutting and pasting parts of the virtual windows. These interfaces also scored high in usability tests.

For this reason, we have since put much emphasis on a very early graphical design of the data presentation.

Typical problems

Adding functions too early. We have observed that designers tend to add some buttons to the virtual windows from the very beginning. This is against the idea of dealing with only data at this stage, delaying functions to later steps. The designers cannot, however, resist the temptation to put that *Check-in* button on the Stay window.

Why is it bad to add buttons at this stage? Because it easily makes you focus on the windows as function-oriented, for instance one window for data entry, another for data editing, a third for deletion. The result is too many windows, which makes the system harder to understand and also more costly to program. Focusing on the data presentation aspect helps you avoid this.

Another reason it is bad to add buttons at this stage is that the proper planning of buttons requires a good overview of the windows. There may be several choices for which window to put a button on, and you cannot make a good decision until you are sure which windows are available. It turns out that you also need to know how many buttons each window needs, in order to figure out whether there is space for the buttons at all or whether you need to put the functions in menus. Chapter 7 explains how to deal with all of this.

On the other hand, when you review the virtual windows with users, a few functions may help the users understand the window. This is particularly true for data entry and scrolling functions. For instance, we have noticed that users better understand that a field is for data entry if it is a box or a drop-down list. Users also better understand that something is a long list if it has a scroll bar. We have used these tricks in the virtual hotel windows.

Forgetting the virtual windows.   We have observed many cases where designers made excellent virtual windows, only to forget them when designing the final screens. The physical design switched to being driven by available GUI controls and beliefs that traditional windows were adequate. The concern for understandability and efficient task support disappeared, and the final user interface became a disaster.

Two things can help in overcoming this: (1) Make sure that the virtual-window designers know the GUI platform to be used, in order that they don't propose unrealistic designs. (2) Ensure that quality assurance includes tracing from the virtual windows to the final screens.

Forgetting to update work products. The work products shown in Figure 6.3 give different views of the final system, and they duplicate information to some extent. As an example, the stay number field may be mentioned in all these documents.

This duplication of information is in one way a disadvantage because things may become inconsistent. We may, for instance, change the concept *stay number* to *booking number*, but change it only in some places – to the confusion of other developers. In other ways the different views are an advantage, because they help us find design defects. In the forthcoming sections we will see several ways to check things against each other, revealing serious design defects in the hotel system.

However, we often see that designers forget to keep the design results updated during the design process. The result is problems later. As an example, we may find out that the user interface needs a discount field when offering some guests a discount. We add it to the appropriate virtual window, but forget to put it into the data model, so the database will not have this field. Further, there should also be a task or task variant that deals with it, but we forget to update the task descriptions. What are the results? During programming a lot of time is wasted changing the database structure to include the discount stuff. And since the task description isn't changed, we forgot to test whether the user can figure out how to use the discount field.

List of design defects. We also see that designers observe a problem, but later forget about it. For this reason it is important to maintain a list of *design defects* (or design problems). Good developers do this no matter how they design the system. In the hotel case, we noted that at debriefing after usability tests we should check whether the user understands how the breakfast window cooperates with the stay window. We might ask questions such as:

When you have recorded breakfasts with this window, what would you expect that this Stay window should show?

When you have recorded breakfast directly in the Stay window, what would you expect that the breakfast window should show?

Here is a summary of the problems we have noted earlier during the hotel system design.

D1–D35: Problems noted during the first usability test of a hand-drawn mock-up (see Figure 2.3B).

D100: Do users understand that data in the Breakfast list window automatically end up in the stay windows – and vice versa? (from section 6.1, Record services).

D101: Receptionist should check credit card or get deposit before check-in (from section 5.3.2, Review with expert users).

D102: Do users understand that guest name and address is repeated in all the guest's stay windows – while pay method is individual for each stay? (from section 6.1, Checking against design rules).

D103: How to show long stays or stays with many rooms? (from section 6.2, Try extreme data).

Some developers use more space to record and describe each defect, also leaving space for describing possible solutions. They may even use a full paper page per problem. It may be based on a template where the developers also record time found, way found, evidence for the problem, seriousness of the problem, possible solutions, etc. Other developers record the problems in a database, which allows both the full-page printout, and various summaries and overviews.

User names and program names. Names of data fields, etc., will appear in several places in the final system, for instance in screens, prints, help texts, and maybe course material. To avoid confusing users, we should ensure consistency, so it is important that we early on define the names to be used in the user's language.

A good place to do it is in the virtual windows. This means that we have to carefully choose field names and other names, as they will become the standard on the user interface. (Our example in Figure 6.2 is not good, because we have abbreviated names in order to give an overview.) We can review the virtual windows with users and in that way check that the names make sense to them.

The programmers want other names for fields, records, etc., because the user-oriented names may be too long and may have spaces and other characters that are inconvenient in the programming language. To the programmers consistency is even more important, and they often maintain a data dictionary that explains what the names mean (see section 16.6). We may also put the user-oriented names into the data dictionary. Here are some examples:

Program name	User name	Description
stayID	Booking No.	System-generated identification of a stay . . .
bedCount	Beds	The number of beds in the room.
vwServiceList	Service prices	Virtual window showing service prices.

6.4   Checking against task descriptions

When combining data into virtual windows, we have used a rather intuitive understanding of the tasks and their information need. This may be fine in many cases, but we risk overlooking important needs. These missing things have to be added to the growing list of *design defects*. Even good designs always have defects at the beginning. However, one difference between good and bad designers is that the good designers know how to detect the defects. In this section and the next ones, we will look at techniques for finding defects.

Tasks with data

If we have detailed task descriptions, we can check against them. Figure 6.4 shows such a check by means of an extended task description (*tasks with data*). The starting point is the task description for check-in (from Figure 5.3B). We have two right-hand columns: (1) a list of the data that the user has to see during a subtask, and (2) the virtual windows that are supposed to show that information.

Checking procedure

a) For each task, go through its steps one by one imagining that you are the user.

b) Note down in column 2 which data the user would need to see to carry out the subtask.

c) Note in column 3 the virtual windows that hold these data.

d) Note down what is missing, for instance necessary search criteria or other forms of overview.

e) Put the missing things on the *defect list*.

Search criteria. As an example, look at subtask 1, Find room. Column 2 shows that the receptionist has to see the free rooms available of the kind wanted by the customer, and see the prices in case the customer asks. Column 3 shows that the Rooms window provides this data, but some search criteria are needed for large hotels: the kind of room wanted and the period the guest wants to stay. Where could we put these search criteria? There is no need for an additional virtual window; we can put the search criteria on the Rooms window. We have shown it in bold in the figure, but we also have to note it on the defect list.

On-line room map. In the original task description, we had also stated that there was a problem in the present way of doing things: sometimes guests wanted two adjacent rooms, but the receptionist couldn't see which rooms met that criterion. He dreamt of an on-line floor map with room occupation.

This is a situation where the enthusiastic designer may include such a map, without knowing whether it is feasible. It depends on the platform for the system, and also on whether the customer in practice can get the necessary drawings and have them set up with electronic indications of occupation. We will put the floor map on the defect list and later decide what to do about it.

New window for guest search. For variant 1a, the guest has booked in advance and we assume that the reception allocated a room for him at that time. What remains now is to find the guest's booking (*guest and stay details*). Once found, the Stay window shows what we need, but we have no window that allows us to search for the guest. In this case, it is not a good idea to put the search criteria on the Stay window. It doesn't relate to the single stay on that window, but to the entire collection of stays. The user's mental model would be strange. We need a new virtual window. Let us call it *FindStay*.

There was a problem with this variant. It was often hard to find the guest, because the receptionist who booked, spelled the name wrong; or the guest was supposed to bring his booking number, but forgot. We need criteria to support these situations. In the figure we have just shown a need for *soundex* criteria, that is a way to find names that sound alike although they are spelled differently. We will discuss design of the search window in section 6.7.

Other tasks. We will not explain the rest of the check-in task. Figure 6.4 should by now speak for itself. In the same manner, we can go through the other tasks to reveal missing things. Actually, we have identified most of the defects already. We only find additional missing search criteria for stays, e.g. room number in case we want to find the stay details from the room number. Our scrutiny has revealed these additional design defects.

Additional design defects

D104: Search criteria in Rooms window: room type, period free and room number.

D105: Rooms window: allow user to see possible discounts.

D106: New virtual window: FindStay. Criteria: guest name (soundex), phone number, zip code, room number, arrival date, stay number (booking number).

D107: New virtual window: FloorMap. An alternative way to show free rooms. Criteria: as for the Rooms window.

Do it before virtual windows?

We can use tasks-with-data in another way. Before we have designed the virtual windows, we can set up tasks-with-data, leaving the virtual window column blank. We now get an overview of which tasks use which data, and this helps us come up with an outline of the virtual windows.

In this way tasks-with-data become a work product that we make early and update while we make the virtual windows.

Fig 6.4   Tasks with data

T1.2: Check-in Start: A guest arrives . . .		
Subtasks:	Visible data:	Virtual windows:
1. Find room. Problem: neighbour rooms.	Free rooms of type x, price. Map.	Rooms. Crit : type, period. Map?
1a. Guest booked in advance. Problem: Fuzzy guest ID	Guest and stay details.	FindGuest, Stay. Crit: soundex, ...
1b. No suitable room.	All free rooms, price, discount.	Rooms. Crit: period.
2. Record guest data.	Guest detail.	Stay.
2a. Guest recorded at booking.	Guest detail.	FindGuest, Stay. Crit: soundex, ...
2b. Regular customer.	Guest detail.	FindGuest, ...
3. Record that guest is checked in.	Guest and stay details.	Stay.
4. Deliver key.	Room numbers.	Stay.

6.5   CREDO check

Above we checked the virtual windows against the detailed task descriptions – one of the important things coming out of the domain analysis. Now we will check against the other important result of the domain analysis: the data model.

Figure 6.5A gives an overview of how the data model relates to the virtual windows for the hotel system. The Stay window shows data from Guest and Stay, ServiceReceived that relates to the stay, and RoomStates that relate to the stay. Actually, the Stay window also shows some attributes from ServiceType and Room.

Similarly, the Rooms window shows data from Rooms and RoomState. We haven't shown the Breakfast window on the diagram. It would become very messy, because the Breakfast window contains data from ServiceReceived, ServiceType and Room. This window even finds the connection between ServiceReceived and Room by going through Stay and RoomState, without showing data about these entities.

Usually each virtual window contains data from many classes in the data model. In the hotel system, only the Service Price window uses a single class (ServiceType). You may contrast this with the database-extreme user interfaces where each window shows only one class (see section 4.5).

CREDO matrix: data model versus virtual windows

It is important to check that all data in the data model actually can be handled through one of the virtual windows – and that all data in the virtual windows can be retrieved from the database. Our graph in Figure 6.5A cannot help much. We need a more systematic approach. Figure 6.5B shows a way to do it by means of CREDO matrices. In the first matrix we have compared the data model against virtual windows.

Each column of the matrix corresponds to a data model entity and each line corresponds to a virtual window. There is a bottom line showing missing functions – something that cannot be done to this entity. There is a rightmost column showing missing window data – data to be shown, but not available. Each cell in the matrix shows which functions the user might perform on the entity through the virtual window. We use the letters CREDO as follows:

C: Creation of the entity might be done through the virtual window.

R: Reading (seeing) all attributes of the entity is possible through the window. Write a small r and make a footnote if it is possible for some attributes, but not for all.

E: Editing all attributes of the entity is possible through the window, including seeing the old value. Write a small e and make a footnote if it is possible for some attributes, but not for all.

Fig 6.5 A Data model vs. virtual windows

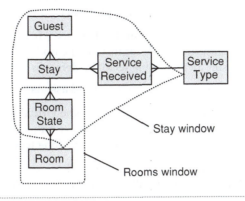

D: Deleting the entity might be done through the window.

O: Overviewing several entities or somehow searching for them is possible through the window.

(Traditionally, this kind of check is called a CRUD check, where U stands for Update. The overview function is not traditionally considered in CRUD checks, but we have found it extremely useful when designing user interfaces. Thanks to Lorraine Johnston for suggesting the nice abbreviation CREDO rather than CRUDO.)

Checking procedure, data model versus virtual windows

a) For each entity class in the data model, ask yourself: Would some of the virtual windows allow the user to create such an entity? Mark these windows with a C in the matrix. If none of the windows are suitable, put the C in the bottom line, *Missing functions*.

b) Can some of the virtual windows show existing data from this entity? Mark these windows with an R for *Read* if they can show (read) all data from the entity. Mark it with a small r if they show only part of the data, and make a footnote on what they show or not show. If some data is not shown in any window, put a C or c in the bottom line.

c) Can some of the virtual windows allow the user to edit existing data from this entity? Mark them with E or e, similar to step b.

d) Can some of the virtual windows allow the user to delete such an entity? Mark them with a D similar to step a.

e) Can some of the virtual windows give a good overview of the entities of this class? Mark them with an O. If no window provides overview or if the overview seems insufficient, put an O in the bottom line.

f) **Checking for missing window data.** Now look at each virtual window and each piece of data in it. Can the data be extracted from the data model? If it cannot, put a note about it in the rightmost column.

g) Review the missing functions and data to see whether there is a good reason they are missing. (Some data may for instance be updated or created by another system.) Transfer all the problems to the defect list.

Let us look at the first entity class (Guest) and ask about C, R, etc.

C: Can we create a guest record through some virtual window? Yes, it may be done through the Stay window, so we write a C for this window. It cannot be done through other virtual windows, so we are done with the C.

R: Which virtual windows show data from the guest record? Only the Stay window does, but it shows all of the data, so we put an R here.

E: Through which virtual windows can the user edit data in the guest record? Only through the Stay window where everything can be edited, so we put an E there.

D: Can we delete the guest through some virtual window? No, not really. It makes sense to delete the stay from the Stay window, but not the guest because the guest may have other stays too. So we put a D at the bottom line.

O: Can we get an overview of the guests through some virtual window? No, so we put an O in the bottom line.

Now look at the second entity class (Stay) and ask the same questions. Through the Stay window, we can read and edit all the attributes, and we can create and delete the stay record. Hey, can we also delete it? In principle, yes. We just have to add a delete button to the final screen. Deletion may be needed when the guest cancels his stay. However, we cannot get an overview of the stays, so we put an O in the bottom line.

For the third entity class (Room) we can do everything from the Rooms window, so there will be no marks in the bottom line. We can even create new rooms or delete them if we provide the necessary buttons. This is not a daily task, however, but happens when we rebuild the hotel. We also have a good overview of rooms. For the sake of completeness, we have shown that some room data is visible through the Stay window (room number, type and one of the prices) and the Breakfast window (only the room number).

The fourth entity class (RoomState) is more subtle. The user can neither create nor delete room states. They seem to exist all by themselves, although the user can change the states. The user can implicitly see some room states in the Stay window (days where a room is occupied), so we have marked it with an r. For these room states, the user can also see the attribute *personCount* (the number of persons staying in the room). The user can see all room states in the Rooms window, but not the attribute personCount. So it has also got an r. What is the conclusion about the bottom

Fig 6.5 B CREDO check

CREDO = Create, Read, Edit, Delete, Overview

Data model versus virtual windows:

Entity Virt. window	Guest	Stay	Room	RoomState	ServiceRec.	ServiceType	Missing window data
Stay	CRE	CRED	r	re O	CREDO	R	
Rooms			CREDO	re O			
Breakfast			r		CReDO	R	roomID
Service charges						CREDO	
Missing fncts	DO	O		(C) D			

Notes: RoomState: personCount editable through Stay, all states through Rooms.
Breakfast: roomID . . .

Data model versus tasks:

Entity Task	Guest	Stay	Room	RoomState	ServiceRec.	ServiceType	Missing task data
Book	CRE O	C		O	Re O		neighbour
CheckinBooked	RE	E O		O	Re		
CheckinNonbkd	CRE O	C		O	Re O		neighbour
Checkout	RE	E O	R		e	R	
ChangeRoom		R		O	Re O		
RecordService				O		C O	R
PriceChange			C EDO			CREDO	statistics
Missing tasks	D	D		(C) e D	ED		

line? The user can see everything through some window, except personCount for rooms that are not occupied. There is no problem, so there is no r in the bottom line.

Edit for the RoomState is similar to Read. What the user can see, he can edit. Overview is provided through the Stay window (overview of rooms occupied by this guest) and the Rooms window (all rooms free, occupied and under repair).

There is nothing interesting about the last two entity classes, ServiceRecord and ServiceType.

Missing window data

Step f of the checking procedure asks us to go through each virtual window, checking that every field in it can be retrieved from the data model.

If we do it carefully, we will notice that the Breakfast window needs to show the room number, but the data is not in the ServiceReceived record according to the planned data model (Figure 5.2). Somehow the designers assumed that the system could find the room number from the stay that the service was connected to, but this doesn't work for stays with more than one room. A room number is necessary in the ServiceReceived record, so we have to change the data model.

Missing functions

While filling in the matrix, we put some marks in the bottom line. Let us review what we found and what to do about it.

Guest: Missing D. Why can't we just delete the guest from the Stay window? Because that would delete the stay too. For reasons of accounting and statistics we need to keep the stay records long after the actual stay. The guest records will have to be deleted at some time, typically after five years, but this is probably not part of the user interface we design. Better to check with the other developers, however.

Guest: Missing O. There is no window to give us an overview of the guests, for instance when we search for a guest with an incomplete criterion. We somehow need a list of guests that match our criterion. (The FindStay window we recognized in section 6.4 will help us.)

Stay: Missing O. There is no window to give us an overview of the stays, and we need it for the same reason as for the guests. Maybe the FindStay window will help us again.

RoomState: Missing C and D. The system should automatically create the necessary RoomState records as the years pass. (The developers solved this problem by omitting room state records for rooms that are free a particular day. The room state record will only be created when the room is booked, etc.) The system should also delete the old room state records after some time.

New design defects

Here are the new defects we found:

D108: Talk to developers about automatic deletion of old data, or a possible user interface for this.

D019: The database has no room number for ServiceReceived.

CREDO matrix: data model versus tasks

Figure 6.5B also shows another CREDO check: data model versus tasks. It works in much the same way. Now we look for what each task can do to each entity and what kind of retrieval and overview it needs.

Checking procedure, data model versus tasks

a) For each entity class in the data model, ask yourself: Are there tasks that create such an entity? Mark these tasks with a C in the matrix. If none of the tasks handle it, put the C in the bottom line, *Missing tasks*.

b) Are there tasks that use existing data from this entity? Mark these tasks with an R for *Read* if they use (read) all data from the entity. Mark them with a small r if they use only part of the data, and make a footnote on what they use. If some data is not used in any task, put a C or c in the bottom line.

c) Are there tasks that edit existing data from this entity? Mark the results with E or e, similar to step b.

d) Are there tasks that delete such an entity? Mark the results with a D similar to step a.

e) Are there tasks that need an overview of the entities of this class? Mark these tasks with an O. If no tasks need an overview, put an O in the bottom line.

f) **Checking for missing task data.** Now look at each task description in detail. Can the data needed for the task be extracted from the data model? If it cannot, put a note about it in the rightmost column.

g) Review the missing functions and data to see whether there is a good reason they are missing. (Some data may, for instance, be updated or created by users of another system.) Transfer all the problems to the defect list.

You may believe that this time we just find the old design defects once more. Let us see.

First you may notice that we have separated the check-in task into two variants: checking in someone who has booked and someone who hasn't. Different things take place in the database in the two cases, so we have split them to get a better understanding.

Let us look at the first entity class (Guest) and ask about C, R, etc.

C: Are there tasks that create guest records? Yes, both Book and CheckinNonBooked do, so we write a C for them.

R: Are there tasks that use (Read) existing guest data? Yes, several: Book, Checkout, etc.

E: Are there tasks that edit existing guest data? Yes, those that also read the data, for instance if the guest has changed address.

D: Are there tasks that delete a guest? No. We put a D at the bottom line.

O: Are there tasks that need an overview of the guests? Yes, both Book and CheckinNonBooked do, for instance to find regular guests. So we write an O for them.

The Stay and Room columns are straightforward. Notice that there is no task to delete a stay. RoomState is more complex. Let us look at it:

C: Are there tasks that create RoomState records? No, this is the same problem we had when checking entities against virtual windows.

R: Are there tasks that use (Read) existing RoomStates? Yes, several: Book, ChangeRoom, etc.

E: Are there tasks that edit existing RoomStates? Yes, Book can change the state to booked, Check-in to occupied, Checkout and ChangeRoom to free. However, none of the tasks can change the state to *repair*. Also, no task mentions changing the *personCount* and in general there is no task that can change an existing booking.

D: Are there tasks that delete RoomState records? No, this is the problem we had earlier.

O: Are there tasks that need an overview of the RoomStates? Yes, both Book, CheckinNonBooked and ChangeRoom do in order to find free rooms. So we write an O for them.

ServiceRecord and ServiceType are straightforward. Notice that there is no task to change or delete a service record.

Missing task data

Step f of the checking task asks us to look for missing task data. If we walk through the detailed task descriptions – including the known problems in the present way of doing the tasks – we notice some missing data.

Book and Check in: The user may need support for selecting neighbour rooms. (Our map view of the rooms might solve it.) We will ignore the problem in the following.

Price change: In order to change the room prices, the manager will need room statistics. In which periods are rooms in short supply, etc. Some of these data may be extracted from saved room state records, others are not available with the planned data model. For instance it would be nice to know how many guests couldn't book because the hotel was full. These data might be collected, but we will ignore it in the following.

Missing tasks

Let us review the missing tasks in the bottom line.

Guest: Missing D. We need to define when guests disappear from the database. We found this problem above too.

Stay: Missing D. Stay records should be kept for some time, but there is also a need for deleting them immediately, for instance when a guest phones and cancels a booking. We don't have a task for this! None of the task descriptions mention it.

RoomState: Missing C and D, partially missing E. We have discussed the missing C and D above. Edit, however, is more of a problem. None of the listed tasks can bring the room to the Repair state or back again. So a task or a subtask is missing. Further, several state changes are not sufficiently covered. For instance the customer may change the booking, but there is no task for this. Also, there is no task that sets the personCount, the number of persons staying in the room.

ServiceReceived: Missing E and D. There is no task to correct wrong recordings of service. A new task or subtask is needed.

New design defects

Here are the new defects we found with this check:

D110: New task or subtask: changing or deleting a booking, before or after check-in.

D111: New subtask for setting the number of persons in the room. This is related to handling the discounts (defect D105).

D112: New task or subtask: changing or deleting service records. (Important during checkout when the receptionist reviews the invoice with the guest.)

D113: New task: Setting or clearing the repair state for rooms.

Notice that we might have done this CREDO check as part of domain analysis. The virtual windows are not needed for it. The result would have been a more complete task list right from the beginning.

Security permissions

In many systems there are different user groups. They have different security permissions so that some users are allowed to do certain things, others are allowed to do other things. In this case it is useful to make a separate CREDO check for each group.

In the hotel case, for instance, the ordinary receptionist will not be allowed to change prices or add and delete rooms. In some hotels they may not even be allowed to change or delete service records.

6.6   Review and understandability test

Above we saw how to check the virtual windows, task descriptions and data models against each other. These are typical developer checks – we can do it by means of logic and our general knowledge. However, we have to check that it also matches the user – is understandable and corresponds to the real tasks. We will now look at this.

Review with users

It is rarely possible to make an in-depth review of a data model with even expert users. They may accept the model, but rarely understand it fully. With the virtual windows, reviews are fruitful because of the detailed graphics and the realistic data.

Review procedure

a) Arrange a meeting with one or a few expert users of the system. Plan for one to two hours depending on the number of virtual windows to review.

b) Either give the experts the virtual windows before the meeting or present them at the meeting. Explain briefly what the windows are supposed to show.

c) Listen to the expert user's comments. (This should take most of the time.)

d) Ask whether the windows show realistic situations, whether data is missing, whether there are more complex situations that may be difficult to show, whether the tasks can be supported with these windows.

e) If you have alternative solutions, show them too and ask for comments.

f) Extract the essential usability defects and write them in the defect list.

g) You may invite the experts to outline alternative solutions, but make sure you check them carefully later.

At the review meeting, make sure you don't explain too much. You are not going to make a sales talk, but to learn about defects in the design. Listen to the user. You may ask questions about issues the users don't comment on themselves.

As a designer, you may show several solutions. Often the immediate reactions from the users give clues about which solution to develop further. Sometimes the users suggest alternative solutions. These suggestions may not be perfect, but often contain ideas to work on. Remember the golden design rule: Find the good points in the other solution – and the bad ones in your own.

It is important to review with expert users. They have good knowledge about the domain and special situations to deal with. As an example, in the hotel case, reviews with experts revealed that seasonal prices were missing (more defects). The user also raised the issue about what a guest really is. Is it one guest although he starts out with one room, and moves to two other rooms the next day? The conclusion was that the term *guest* is ambiguous. It means a physical person, for instance when we say that there are three guests in this room. But it also means the person who pays the bill for the stay – even if it includes many people, and this is the meaning to be used in the screens.

We could not have revealed these problems by reviewing the data model or the window plan with the expert user. The graphical design of the windows and the realistic data did the trick.

Understandability test

An understandability test is entirely different from a review. The understandability test is a kind of usability test. We want to see what the user can figure out on his own.

Test procedure

a) Arrange a meeting with one or two ordinary users of the system. Plan for one to two hours depending on the number of virtual windows to review. Don't give them the virtual windows in advance.

b) At the meeting show the virtual windows one by one. You may explain what the system is about, but not what the windows show.

c) Ask the users: What do you think this window shows? Is it a situation you recognize? If they cannot understand what it is, give them a clue and see what they then can guess. Write down the problems and misunderstandings.

d) Next you may ask about things you are not certain that the users understand correctly.

e) If the user has a reasonable understanding of the windows, put several windows at the desk and ask the user to show how he would use them to carry out some task.

f) Extract the essential usability defects and write them in the defect list.

Treat the understandability test much like a usability test (Figure 6.6). Don't explain more than you would do during a usability test. It is all right to explain what kind of system and what kind of tasks we talk about. But *don't* explain anything about what the windows show. In the case of the hotel system we might, for instance, say:

> We have made drafts of some screens for a new system that can help the reception. The system can keep track of bookings, free rooms, etc. Here is one of the screens. What do you think it shows?

Understandability tests of the hotel windows revealed that the mnemonic marking of room state was not obvious. Some users believed that O (occupied) meant zero – meaning that the room was free! A bad mistake to make in a reception. The tests also revealed that only few users understood that the dotted line on the Stay window showed the border between past and future.

Since we had noted the potential problems about understanding the relation between Breakfast window and Stay window, we asked about it. Users were uncertain what would happen. They guessed that the system automatically transferred the data – or that there was a button labelled *Update*. We also asked about the relation between guest address and stay:

> *If you change the address for one of the regular guests, what do you think would happen to his address on his other stays, for instance a later one that he has booked already?*

(Most users guessed that it would change too, but a few became confused. We have already put it on the defect list – D102.)

Task understanding. If the users have a reasonable understanding of the windows, we can put several windows on the desk at the same time. Then we ask them what windows they would use to carry out a task, for instance booking for John Simpson who wants a room on the 17th October.

> *Which screens would you use to make this booking? Which screens do you expect that the system updates for you?*

We may try out as many tasks as the users and we can overcome. The whole exercise can get quite close to a real usability test, although the windows contain no functions (menus, buttons, etc.) at this stage. Although the users have a much better overview of the screens than they would have on the real system (where they might see just one screen at a time), we still get a good impression of whether they can find out which screens to use, and in what sequence.

During the reviews and understandability tests we noted down the usability problems, thus adding to our list of design defects. According to the discussion above, we have found yet another three:

Design defects

D114: Seasonal prices missing.

D115: Mnemonic for occupied and booked cause misunderstandings.

D116: Distinction between past items and booked items in the Stay window not clear.

Iterative design

As for the real usability test, the purpose is to repair the defects. Again, don't think of ways to repair while you run the tests – it blocks you from recognizing the problem.

Fig 6.6 Review and understandability test

Review:
 Discuss virtual windows with expert user
 Show and outline alternatives
Understandability test:
 Show virtual windows one by one to ordinary users
 Ask what they believe they show
 You may explain and discuss *after* hearing their belief

Have at least one good night's sleep before attempting a repair (or a redesign). Then repair and test again, preferably with some other typical user.

Test early. It is a good idea to test with just the first one or two central screens. This way you learn a lot about the users and how to design the next screens, so that they become better right from the beginning.

Usually the users don't understand your first design at all. Don't despair. Find out why they didn't understand, and what they had expected. Redesign everything or outline several versions, and then test again. This is your last chance to do it so easily.

6.7　Searching

Basic search techniques

A recurring problem in most IT applications is how the user can find the right item in a large volume of data. Figure 6.7A shows six basic search techniques.

1　**Exact keys.** When searching with an exact key, the user has to specify the unique identification of the item he wants. In the hotel, the key for finding a stay might be the stay number (booking number) or the room number for a certain date. If the user knows the correct key, he gets the answer right away. In many cases he doesn't know the key and then we have a problem.

2　**Choice list.** The system shows a list of all the items of a certain kind, and the user picks the right one. In our example, the system might show a list of all the stays. On the screen, such a list can appear in many ways (many syntactical versions of the list):

   a)　**List box.** The list stays on the screen for a long time. This version is good if the list can be on one screen. The maximum length of the list will thus be around 30 items. If the list is longer than one screen, we might use a scroll bar, but the result is that the user loses the overview. The scroll-bar version works only if the list is ordered according to something that the user knows, for instance alphabetically according to the name of the guest. Even in this case, the list shouldn't be longer than around 200 items. Many systems allow the user to click on one of the column headings in the list. The system then sorts the records in the list according to this column.

   b)　**Combo box.** The list unfolds when the user selects it and disappears when the user selects something else. If the list is unsorted, the maximum length should not exceed 30 items. When the list is sorted, the user may type the first characters of the key, and the system scrolls down to that part of the list. Here a maximum length of 200 is acceptable.

   c)　**Hierarchical menus.** The lists roll out on demand. The user selects an item in the first list, which causes the second list to roll out. Then he selects an item in the second list, and so on. None of the lists should be more than 30 items. This technique is good for searching data that are hierarchically organized, for instance computer folders or library classification schemes. The technique is also used for structuring computer menus of functions. This will cause usability problems when the menu hierarchy is not obvious to the user.

In a large hotel there may be 500 stays a day, and if we search among all stays, previous as well as future, there are several hundred thousands. As a result, we cannot use lists of choices alone.

3　**Flicking.** Searching by flicking means that the system shows the first item as a screen or window, and when the user pushes *Next*, it shows the next item. This

Fig 6.7 A Search techniques

1. **Exact keys**
   Enter stay number. Click *Search*.
   Enter room no. + date. Click *Search*.

2. **Choice list**
   a. List box of records
   b. Combo box
   c. Hierarchical menus

3. **Flicking**
   Show first Stay window, *Next, Next . . .*

4. **Approximate key**
   a. Enter part of name. Click *Search*.
      Then choice-list or flicking.
   b. Phonetic search: Cathy = Kathie.
   c. Live search: System updates choice-list
      as user types.

5. **Composite criteria**
   Enter arrival date + zip. Click *Search*.

6. **Overview and zoom**
   Show floor map. Click to see details.

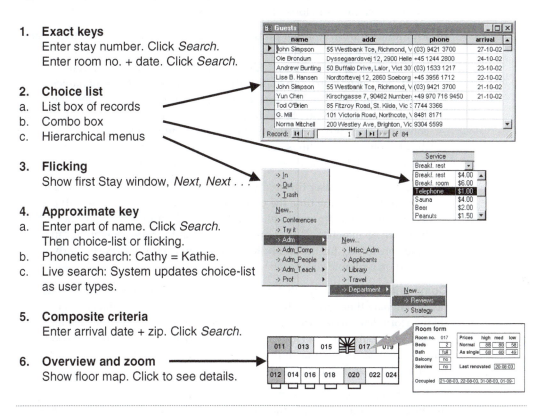

approach may be adequate if there are only a few items to choose from (around 5–10). It is of course completely inadequate for finding a stay in a large hotel.

4 **Approximate key.** With this approach, the user enters something that partially matches an item attribute. There are several ways to do this.

a) **Part of an attribute.** As an example, the user may enter part of the guest name. The system then finds all matching stays, that is stays with guest names that contain this part. The system can show the resulting stays as a list or it can let the user flick through them.

This approach corresponds well to the way humans perceive, but it may be hard to program such a mechanism. As an example, if the user enters the first part of the name, it is fairly easy to make a program that finds the corresponding guests very fast – even among millions of names. The system may use an alphabetic index (like a telephone index) to find the name, and like a human, it doesn't have to look at all the names but may gradually narrow down its search.

But if the name part may be anywhere in the name, the index doesn't help and the system has to look at all the names. This may take a long time.

b) **Phonetic search.** Another problem is that the user may not spell the name the way it is spelled in the database. The result will be *no match*. As an example, the name in the database may be Kathy, but the user tries Cathy and Cathie. To some extent a *phonetic search* can handle this. The computer stores all names in two forms: as the fully spelled name and as a simplified, phonetic spelling where for instance K and C are both stored as K. When the user looks for Cathy, the computer finds the corresponding phonetic spelling and compares it against the filed phonetic spellings. A standard way to do this is called *soundex*. It is used in electronic telephone directories and for passenger identification on flights.

c) **Live search.** The user fills in the criterion character by character, and the system shows all the time the corresponding matches. As the user types, the list becomes smaller and smaller, and when it is empty, the user knows that there are no matches. This approach is excellent for the user, but it can be very time-consuming for the computer if the database is huge, particularly if it is stored on a remote computer.

5 **Composite criteria.** Very often, no single criterion can give us what the user needs. We may then work with composite criteria, where several criteria – each of them incomplete alone – can specify the item we want. In the hotel example, we might, for instance, use two criteria fields: the arrival date and the zip code. There may be a few stays that match these criteria, but the system can show them as a list or let the user flick through them.

Each of the composite criteria may use any of the other techniques. One may, for instance, be a combo box, another uses phonetic search and a third one uses live search.

6 **Overview and zoom.** Any of the diagrams for giving overview of data (section 3.5) can also be used for searching. The user sees the overview, selects the point of interest, and somehow zooms in to see details. Many geographical information systems show a map where the user can click on any point. The system then zooms in to show the area around that point. In the hotel system we could use a floor map. The user may click on any room to see the details of it. We could also use the matrix in the rooms window, which gives an overview in time. If the user clicks on a cell in the matrix, the system shows the stay that occupies the room at this date.

Design rules for searching

Users often have many problems when searching. The system may come out with too many matches, and the user doesn't know which one to choose or how to narrow down the search. Or it may come out with no matches, which can confuse the user even more. Here are some rules for designing good search screens.

1 Consider the criteria the users might know, how many results the search will give and what kind of overview is possible. Based on this, choose a search technique.

2 When showing a list of search results, show the search criteria inside the same gestalt as the results. Otherwise users may misinterpret the list. This is particularly likely if the users look at other things before returning to the list.

3 When the system cannot find any matches, don't use a message such as *Nothing found* or *The system cannot find what you ask for*. Users erroneously conclude that they have to give additional data to help the system find what they want. This only makes things worse. Instead, use a message such as *Nothing matches what you ask for* (see the discussion below). If a live search is possible, it can help users understand when they narrow down the search so much that nothing matches.

4 When showing a list of search results, show additional data for each item on the list. This will help the user guess whether it is worthwhile to click on the list item to see the full details. (Google is a good example. It shows the pieces of text where the keywords are located.)

5 Provide additional criteria that can help the user narrow down the search. It could, for instance, be the dates of interest or the subject area (from a list of possible areas).

6 Allow the user to work on the search results. The user might, for instance, want to build up a list of interesting items by combining several searches and manually selecting or adding items. One solution is to allow the user to mark and transfer search results to his own list. To most users this is far easier to understand than specifying logical criteria with *and* and *or*.

7 Let the system collect search criteria that users actually used, particularly words that gave no match. Review these criteria when the system has been in use for some time to learn how to improve the search technique.

Virtual windows for searching

As an example, we will design the search screens for the hotel system. Our checks in the preceding sections showed a need for finding stays and for finding rooms. Figure 6.7B shows the two virtual windows we proposed initially.

The first search window is a new virtual window. It offers composite criteria for finding guests: the guest name (using soundex), phone number (approximate criterion because it only uses the last four digits) and the date for the stay. It also offers exact criteria through the stay number, or through the room number combined with a date.

The second search window is not new. It is just an extension of the existing Rooms window. It shows the rooms–date matrix, but only the parts selected through the composite criteria *range of dates* and *type of room*. There is also an exact criterion: the room number. Notice a detail: The user may specify the range of dates in two ways, as *Free from + Departure* or as *Free from + Nights*. If the user fills in *Departure*, the system computes *Nights*, and vice versa. Observations of receptionist showed that they sometimes talked about the number of nights, sometimes about the departure date. The system allows them to do both and helps them check both.

Are they virtual windows? Both of these screens are virtual windows because they are user-oriented presentations of persistent data (with the addition of some dialogue data for the criteria). However, we have violated some of the design rules: There is a button – labelled *Search*. (Forgive the designer, he couldn't stand the temptation.) The button signals the purpose of the window and that it shows only a selected part of the persistent data. In the final screens there will be more buttons.

Another violation of the design rules is the name of the first search window – *Find guest*. It doesn't signal a thing, but an action, and this would make it harder to imagine it being used for other purposes. We could have called it, for instance, *Guest list*, but on the other hand we could see only one purpose of the window – finding guests.

Checking against search rules

Let us briefly check against the design rules for searching:

a) We have done our best to select the search techniques, combining several of them.

b) We have shown the search criteria inside the same gestalt as the list of matches. The gestalt is the entire virtual window.

c) When the system couldn't find any matches, the Find guest window originally had a message saying *Couldn't find the guest*. For the rooms window, the list just became empty. During usability tests, we learned to say *Nothing matches what you ask for*.

d) For the Find guest window, we show additional data for each item on the list: arrival date and room number. For the Rooms window, we show the type of room, the prices and also the dates surrounding what the user asks for (helps filling gaps or allowing flexible departure dates).

e) We have provided additional criteria of various kinds, but could imagine more, for instance a range of arrival dates when finding guests.

f) Allow the user to work on the search results, e.g. combining lists. We have not seen a need for this with the tasks we support. There might be a need if we want the system to create mail lists, for instance to regular guests.

g) The rule says: collect search criteria actually used, particularly words that gave no match. We have not planned this, but might do if usability tests showed a need for it.

Later, usability tests of the windows showed two typical problems:

Problem 1: Nothing found. When the user had entered some criteria, clicked the Search button and the system responded *Couldn't find the guest*, then the user

Fig 6.7 B Virtual windows for searching

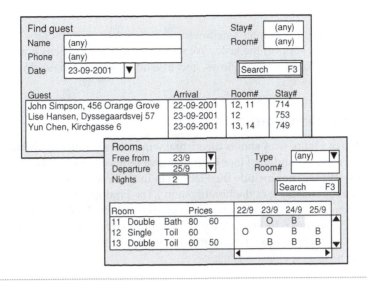

tried to add more criteria. Unfortunately, this didn't help. The system still couldn't find the stay because no stay met all the criteria. Adding more criteria only made it worse. This is a typical usability problem for searches. The users have a mental model derived from fellow humans. If you ask me to find, for instance, a book, and I try but cannot find it, then you will give me more information. You might say *it has a blue cover* or *it is on one of the lower shelves*. This may actually help me locate it, but a computer search is different: the computer has looked carefully at every item in its database, but nothing matches what the user asks for.

Problem 2: Date for what? The date field was ambiguous to the user. Did it mean the arrival date for the guest or what? Unfortunately, it depended on what the user searched for. If he searched for an arriving guest (the most frequent case), he wanted to see only stays where the arrival day was the current day. However, there were also *ad hoc* queries such as *who stays in room 513, there is a message for him*; or who *stayed in room 513 yesterday, he has forgotten a camera*. In these cases we looked for a stay that included the current day (or the previous day), and it didn't matter when the guest arrived. This problem was specific for the hotel case, but similar problems exist in many other search designs.

In section 8.1 we have a longer discussion of the usability problems in this Find guest screen, and the kinds of prototypes we made to eliminate them. Usability-wise this screen was the hardest to make, and in the first usability tests (section 2.3) we already saw lots of problems with it.

6.8 Virtual windows and alternative designs

We will finish this chapter by showing the complete version of the virtual windows and how they support the tasks. We will also see what happens if we don't follow the design rules for virtual windows, and instead make a database-driven or a task-driven design.

Virtual windows versus tasks

The top of Figure 6.8A shows the virtual windows after all our checking. We have the Rooms window and the Floor map that give temporal and spatial overviews of the rooms. (We will not include the Floor map in the rest of the design, but plan to include it in release 2 of the hotel system.) The Find guest window gives us overview of guests and stays. The Stay window gives us all the details of the guest and his stay. The Service price window is the price list for breakfast and other services (it may also appear as a combo box). Finally, the Breakfast window gives the receptionist a fast way to record breakfast servings.

The bottom of Figure 6.8A shows the task list after all our checking. For each task the crosses show the virtual windows used by the task. Note that we have changed task T1.4 from dealing with change of room to dealing with any kind of change of the stay, including cancelling the stay. Similarly, task T1.5 deals with recording and changing of services recorded directly on the guest's account. We have added T1.7 about room repair. Finally, we have added a new work area, Management, which handles two tasks: price changes and adding or changing rooms.

In Figure 6.1 we illustrated the relation between tasks and virtual windows in a way suited for explaining how we came up with the plan. However, the notation is not suited for larger systems with many tasks and windows. The matrix presentation in Figure 6.8A is better. As an example, see how T1.1 (Book) uses the Rooms window to find a free room, Find guest to check whether the guest is a regular and Stay to record the booking. Depending on circumstances, T1.1 may also use the floor map to find neighbour rooms, rooms with balcony, etc.

Notice that most tasks use two to four of the six windows and most windows are reused across several tasks. It is also clearly visible that the Breakfast window is very special. It is dedicated to one single task.

Database-driven design

We will now look at a set of windows derived in another way – driven by the database. If users can see and change everything in the database, they can in principle do everything – apart from printing and other communication with the surroundings.

Fig 6.8 A Virtual windows, complete version

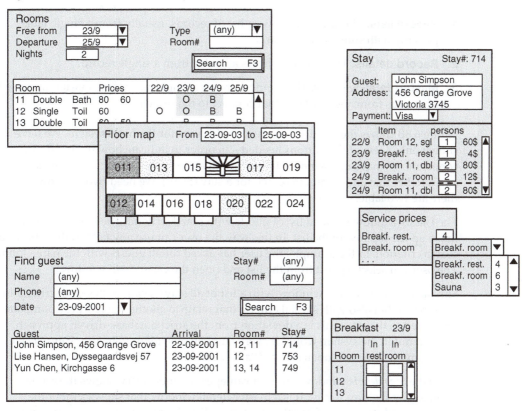

Complete version: Virtual windows used	Rooms	Floor map	Find guest	Stay	Service prices	(Combo box)	Breakfast
Reception							
T1.1: Book guest	X	x	X	X			
T1.2: Check-in	x	x	X	X			
T1.3: Checkout			X	X		x	
T1.4: Change stay	x	x	X	X			
T1.5: Record/change services			X	X		X	
T1.6: Breakfast list							X
T1.7: Room repair	X		x	x			
Management							
T2.1: Price changes	X				X		
T2.2: Add/change rooms	X	x					

Legend: X = Window always used during this task. x = Window sometimes used.

With the database-driven design we basically work with three kinds of windows:

1 **Record lists.** The window shows a list of records, usually from a single table, possibly with some search criteria.

2 **Record details.** The window shows all fields from a single record.

3 **Master-detail window.** The window shows a single record (the master) and a list of records from another table that connect to the master.

Figure 6.8B shows the windows derived in this way for the hotel system. We have shown only a few of the buttons needed – in order to indicate how the windows cooperate. We have one window that allows the user to search for a guest (*Guests*) and another that allows him to search for a stay (*Stays*). We need two windows since there are two tables.

The *Guests* window shows a list of guests with search criteria. The search criteria make up the top row of the list. In this way the user can use any field in the table as a search criterion. In the example, the user has asked for all guests with the name John. The user can select a guest from the list and open the *Guest detail* window.

Similarly, there is a *Stays* window with a list of all stays, again with search criteria in the top row, but also with special criteria that relate to another table – the RoomStates connected to the stay. This is a deviation from the strict database-driven approach, but without it, the system would be very cumbersome to use. The user can select a stay from the table and open a *Stay details* window.

From the *Stay details* window, the user can open a window that shows the rooms occupied by the stay, *Rooms*. It is a master-detail window that shows a bit of the master record (two fields from the stay) and a list of RoomState records connected to this stay. From the *Stay details* window, the user can open another master-detail window that shows the services connected to this stay.

There is also a *Room availability* window where the user can find rooms that are free in a certain period of days, or rooms that are in other states. It is similar to the virtual window *Rooms*, but uses a list presentation rather than a matrix.

There is a special window for entering breakfast lists or other services by room number. It is similar to the virtual window *Breakfast*, but uses a list presentation that requires more typing. There is an empty line at the bottom of the list, and here the receptionist can enter a new service. Finally there is a simple window with a list of service prices – exactly as the virtual window with the same name.

What is the difference?
We have checked the design of these windows by walking through the tasks and by CREDO checks – exactly as we did for the virtual windows. So we are rather sure they can support the user.

Fig 6.8 B Database-driven design

Guests
Criteria:

	john		
GuestID	Name	Address	Phone
745	John Simpson	55 Westbank Tce	3700 ▲
752	John Brondum	Dyssegaardsve	
810	John Ewes	Kirschgasse	

[Search]

Guest details GuestID 745

Name	John Simpson
Address1	55 Westbank Tce
Address2	Richmond, Victoria3121
Phone	(03) 9421 3700
Passport	

[See stays]

Stays
Criteria:
Room [12] Date [22/9]

[Search]

	745	
StayID	GuestID	Payform
1274	745	Visa ▲
1283	745	Master
1390	745	▼

Stay details StayID 1274 GuestID 745

State checked in
Payform [Visa ▼]

[See rooms] [See services]

Rooms StayID 1274 GuestID 745

Date	Room	Persons	Price
22/9	12, single	[1]	60$ ▲
23/9	11, double	[2]	80$
24/9	11, double	[2]	80$ ▼

Services StayID 1274 GuestID 745

Date	Item	Qty.	Price
23/9	Breakfast, rest ▼	[1]	4$ ▲
24/9	Breakfast, room▼	[2]	12$
24/9	Telephone ▼	[12]	2$ ▼

Room availability
From [24/9] to [26/9] Type [(any) ▼]

Room	Type	Prices	Status
11	double, bath	80 60	occ ▲
12	single, toil	60	free
13	double, toil	60 50	booked
14	deluxe	99 79	repair ▼

Service list Date [24/9]

Room	Item	Qty.
11	Breakfast, room▼	[2] ▲
12	Breakfast, rest ▼	[1]
15	Breakfast, rest ▼	[1]
	▼	[ ] ▼

Service prices

Breakf. rest. [4]
Breakf. room [6]
. . .

One difference is that there are more window templates in the database-driven design – 9 windows. With virtual windows there were only 5 if we exclude the floor map that doesn't have a counterpart in the database version. More important is that there is much less overview of data. As an example, while a single virtual window *Stay* showed all data relating to a stay, the same data are split up in four database-oriented windows. The reason is that at least four tables are involved in a stay. As another example, availability of rooms is only shown as a list of rooms, not as a matrix with temporal overview.

The difference also shows up in the number of windows needed to perform a task, as shown in Figure 6.8C. Tasks typically need 4–6 windows, while the virtual window version used 2–4. The consequence to usability is that the solution much less efficiently supports the tasks. It is also much harder for the user to learn the system and understand it.

Design rules?

Which of the design rules could have prevented this inconvenient set of windows? During database-driven design we didn't use the design rule of *few window templates*. We used the rule of *overview of data*, but only in the simplest manner, where we just gave overviews as lists of records. We basically just looked at ways to present the contents of the database in an easy way from the programmer's point of view.

We should notice that the database-driven solution is not intentionally ugly or cumbersome to use. It corresponds quite well to many professional systems in the business area.

Task-driven design

We will now look at another solution – a set of screens derived from a close study of the task steps. We took the first task and looked at its subtasks. For each subtask we defined a screen that supported it. By means of *Next* buttons, the user was taken by the hand from screen to screen through the task.

Figure 6.8D outlines a part of the solution. The user always starts in the main menu and selects the task to carry out. In the example, the user selected *Book a guest*. According to the task description he first selects a free room. As a result, the first window asks him to specify the period and the room type, the next shows the rooms available in this period. This window also shows the room types and prices to support discussions with the guest.

The next subtask is to record the guest, and here the procedure depends on whether it is a regular guest or not. So the next screen asks the user about it. In the example, the user selected *regular* and is then asked to specify some criteria to find the guest. The next window shows the guests that match the criteria and the user chooses one – or uses the *Back* button to search again.

Fig 6.8 C Database-driven task support

Database-driven design: Windows used	Room availability	Guests	Stays	Guest details	Stay details	Rooms	Services	Service list	Service prices
Reception									
T1.1: Book guest	X	X		x	X	X			
T1.2: Check-in	x	x	X	X	X	X			
T1.3: Checkout			X		X		x	X	
T1.4: Change stay	X		X	x	X	X			
T1.5: Record/change services			X		X		X	x	
T1.6: Breakfast list								x	
T1.7: Room repair	X		x		x	X			
Management									
T2.1: Price changes	X								X
T2.2: Add/change rooms	X								

The next subtask is to record the booking. The user sees the guest details and may decide to book the selected rooms. The system also suggests that he reviews the details with the guest. The system then shows the booking with a list of the days and rooms booked. The user may use the *More rooms* button to book additional rooms for the guest. This brings the user to the screen *Enter desired period . . .* and then to *Select among these rooms*. However, when the user now clicks *Next*, the system should not go to the screen that asks whether it is a regular guest, but back to the *Booking* screen. (This little detail may cause the programmer much pain. The result may be that he makes two screens that look the same, but behave differently.)

We have not shown the screens needed to support all the other tasks. It may be possible to reuse some of the screens from booking, but in large projects developers tend to split the design work so that one developer handles task 1, another task 2, etc. The result is that screens will look very different and we easily end up with 20 more screens than the 7 we needed for the booking task. Some professional hotel systems actually have a design like this. A booking looks different from a checked-in stay, and different from a checkout screen. Receptionists find them cumbersome to learn and to use.

What is the difference?
There are some good things about this approach: The user is taken by the hand and guided through the tasks step by step. Actually, many users like this approach if they only use the system for simple things and not all the day.

The disadvantages are many, however:

- The user gets little understanding of what the system does and what data it stores. The user only sees data through a 'soda straw' and doesn't get the great overview.

- The computer controls the sequence. The user is, for instance, unable to find the guest before he selects a room. This may be important in some cases.

- The user is unable to handle exceptional situations. The system must be designed with a path for each of them.

- Although it seems nice to start with a list of tasks, tasks are not as well defined and intuitive to users as the designers assume. Users rarely have a name for their tasks and may not even be able to identify the tasks they do.

- The development work is much larger, partly because there are many more screens, and partly because it is hard to plan all the paths through the screens, particularly if developers try to reuse screens.

Design rules?

Which of the design rules could have prevented this inconvenient set of windows? Actually, the solution violates several of the design rules for virtual windows:

Rule 1. Few window templates ... reuse across tasks. The violation of this rule is obvious. We may even end up with a design where each screen is dedicated to one single task.

Rule 6. Necessary overview of data. This is violated because data are split into many screens. Furthermore, the screens use only simple overviews in the form of lists.

Rule 7. Things – not actions. This rule is primarily about the name of the screens/ windows. The rule is violated in many of the task-oriented screens. The name of the screen is an instruction to the user such as *Enter desired period* or a question such as *Is this a regular guest?* In other places screens tell the users what to do. This is necessary to guide the user, but leaves the user without alternative ways of accomplishing the task.

The solution also violates a design rule for searching:

Rule 2 (searching). When showing a list of search results, show the criteria inside the same gestalt as the results. This is violated for both searches in the example, with the consequence that users may be in doubt about what the list actually shows. The problem is easy to correct, however.

It should be noted that many user interface design methodologies use an approach that leads to this kind of user interface. Some methodologies make a detailed task analysis first and then 'automate' it as above. Other methodologies create detailed use cases at an early stage, and at a much later point they design screens for each step of the use case, with a result similar to the one above.

Platform dependence?

Is the choice of database-driven versus task-driven dependent on the system platform? Some people believe that database-driven is more appropriate for

Fig 6.8 D Task-driven design

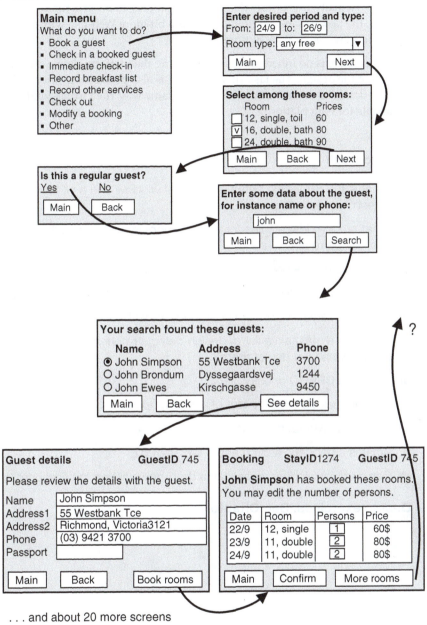

. . . and about 20 more screens

Microsoft Windows or Mac-based systems, while task-driven is more appropriate for the Web. Actually, this is how many systems appear to be structured. In our example designs, the task-driven solution also looks a bit more Web-like with underlined hyperlinks and Next/Back buttons.

However, there is no inherent reason for letting the platform define the large-scale aspects of the design. The task-driven design is also possible for Microsoft Windows and the database-driven for the Web. In the same way, the virtual window approach is suitable for both platforms.

Test yourself

a) What is the difference between a virtual window and a window on the screen?

b) What are the design rules for virtual windows and what is the purpose of each of the rules?

c) Mention a case where two of the design rules conflict.

d) Why is it crucial to make a graphical design of the virtual windows?

e) Is it necessary to fill in the virtual windows with data? Why or why not?

f) Why do we maintain a list of design defects rather than correcting the defects when we detect them?

g) What is a CREDO check?

h) Can we make a usability test of virtual windows?

i) Are search windows virtual windows?

j) What is a phonetic search and a live search?

k) Can a virtual window appear as a drop-down list on the final user interface?

Design exercises. See Chapter 17.

7

Function design

Highlights

■ Attach semantic and search functions to the virtual windows.

■ Define undo mechanisms.

■ Know the platform and transform virtual windows to real screens.

■ Add navigation functions to screens.

■ Choose presentation formats for functions.

■ Support transition from novice to expert.

■ Key exercise: Design functions for the design project.

In this chapter we add functions to the virtual windows and end up very close to the full prototype. We do it in four steps:

■ First we identify the necessary *semantic functions* and *search* functions (see section 4.4 if you need a reminder of what these functions are). We also design the details of any non-trivial data entry functions.

■ Next we turn the virtual windows into final *screens*.

■ Then we identify the necessary functions to *navigate* between the screens.

■ Finally we design the presentation of the functions: push buttons, menus, icons, drag-and-drop or function keys? This is the *syntactic design* of the functions.

We have designed most of the data entry functions as part of the virtual windows. We only need to deal with the unusual ones during function design.

7.1   Semantic functions and searching

In order to identify the system functions, we take the tasks one by one and manually carry them out by means of the virtual windows. During this, we note down which functions we would need in each virtual window. Some usability specialists call this a *cognitive walk-through* of the tasks. Here is the procedure.

Design procedure

a) Place the virtual windows on a desk. Imagine that they are on a huge computer screen.

b) Look at an important and frequent task. You might place the task description in the corner of the desk.

c) Look at the first subtask and imagine how you would carry it out. Which virtual windows would you have to look at, and which fields would you have to fill in? Which system functions (buttons) would be needed to make the system do something, for instance search, create items, save data, delete items, print or send something? You may also need 'buttons' that change data in special ways – other than simple data entry.

The system functions you identify in this way are semantic functions, search functions and non-trivial data entry functions. Don't care about navigation functions that take you from one virtual window to another. The 'screen' is so large that it has space for at least one copy of each virtual window. At this stage you can navigate between virtual windows simply by pointing at them.

d) When you have identified a 'button', give it a name and write it down besides the virtual window where it was needed. Often the button has to do something complex. Write a short description of what it should do (a *mini-spec*).

Don't worry that we call the functions 'buttons'. Later they may become menu items, drag-and-drop or real buttons.

e) Look at the next subtask and imagine how you would carry it out. Again you identify system functions (buttons), but try to reuse the buttons you have defined already. When you reuse a button, it may happen that it should work a bit differently than before. Amend the mini-spec to explain about it.

f) When you are through all subtasks and variants, the system should be able to support the entire task. Review what you have defined. Check to see that you can carry out the task in other reasonable ways, for instance performing the subtasks in other sequences. Sometimes you may have to make minor changes to buttons and mini-specs to achieve this.

g) Now look at the remaining tasks one by one in the same way. Try to reuse the earlier buttons as far as possible. You will normally experience that tasks need fewer and fewer new buttons as design progresses.

h) Review the entire set of functions. Check whether it is possible for the user to switch between two or more tasks at the same time. Check that standard functions are provided, such as Undo, Print and Data exchange.

Is it necessary to make some kind of CREDO check to see that all records in the database can be created, deleted and updated? In principle not, because if we made the CREDO check for tasks against data model, all the necessary tasks and subtasks should be there. So if the system can support all the tasks, it can also create, delete and update what is needed. However, systems development is so complex that designers easily overlook things. So checking once more might be a good idea.

Booking task

Below we will show how the design procedure worked for the hotel system. We start with the booking task.

Figure 7.1A shows our desk with some of the virtual windows. At the bottom right we have placed the task description for the booking task.

Subtask 1, Find rooms. How do we carry out the first subtask? Well, we need the virtual window *Rooms* with the search criteria (vwRooms). We fill in the search criteria for the booking: the type of room the guest wants, and the period of the stay.

Then we somehow activate a button *FindRooms*, and the system shows a list of the appropriate rooms. We have now identified the first 'button' – a search function. We write this function besides vwRooms as shown. Most likely it will become a button or a menu point in that window, but we delay the decision. (Maybe it will be the button we have already put on the virtual window.) For now it suffices to know that it is a function associated with this virtual window.

If one of the rooms suits the guest, we select this room. This gives us another function, *ChooseRoom*. To illustrate the approach, we have written the subtask number besides the function to show when we use the function. Both functions were used for subtask 1.

Subtask 2, Record guest. We continue with the next subtask. It has a variant *Regular guest* for guests that already are in our files. Often guests don't know whether they are in our files, and the standard hotel procedure is to always check whether they are. So it is a good idea to use the window vwFindGuest. We enter part of the guest name and activate a new function *FindGuest*, which shows a list of the guests that match. If one of the guests is the right one, we select the guest (*SelectLine*) and activate *NewStay*. Up comes a window for a new stay (*vwStay*), and the system pre-fills the guest data. We can now check with the guest that his data is still correct, and edit it as needed.

If many guests have names that match, how do we know which of them is the right one? As the virtual search window is designed, we may not have enough data, but if we somehow show the details for each guest as we point down the list, we can determine the right person. We will leave this as a note for SelectLine.

This was variant 2a. If it is not a guest in our files, we don't select anything but just use *NewGuest*. Up comes an empty stay window where we enter the guest data. Whether we have a new guest or retrieved a regular guest, we now have the necessary guest data.

Could we avoid *NewGuest* and reuse *NewStay* instead? If we point at a guest, *NewStay* should show this guest for the new stay, but if we don't point at anything, *NewStay* should show blank guest data – just what we need. However, the problem is whether the user can tell the subtle difference between pointing at nothing and pointing at an incorrect guest. We want to be sure, so we define a separate function for a new guest.

In order to carry out step 2 or 2a we thus needed four functions on vwFindGuest, as shown in the figure. For the sake of completeness, we have also indicated that we enter persistent data in the Stay window (EditData). This is a trivial data entry function.

Special data entry. Most of the data entry functions are trivial, and we have implicitly defined them as part of the virtual window design. However, there are a few special data entry functions in the virtual windows. For instance, the user should be able to fill some of the fields by choosing from a list rather than typing – using a combo box or something similar. In vwRooms, this includes the fields *Type*, *FreeFrom* and *Departure*.

There is a tricky thing with the fields *Departure* and *Nights*. Sometimes the receptionist prefers to specify the departure date, and at other times the number of nights stayed. And he likes to check the two things against each other. We want the system to calculate the field he hasn't specified. To keep track of these details we write them in a mini-spec, as explained below.

We have added a special data entry function in vwRooms: *ResetSearch*. It sets the search criteria to their default value: *(any)* for most fields and the current date for the FreeFrom field. This function is, strictly speaking, unnecessary because the user can set the fields one by one, but it is annoying to do. We have added a similar function to vwFindGuest.

Subtask 3, RecordBooking. At this stage we have a Stay window with guest data and we have selected a room. What we need to do is somehow activate a Book function. It seems natural to activate it through vwStay, so this is where we put the Book function. The function will store the guest and stay data into the database.

We have a variant of subtask 3. The guest may want more than one room, maybe of another kind and for another period. We can again handle this through vwRooms by means of FindRooms and ChooseRoom, as shown in the figure. When we have selected the room, we use Book once more. This time it may be convenient to have the Book function on vwRooms, and we have shown it there with a question mark.

Fig 7.1 A Booking: semantic functions and search

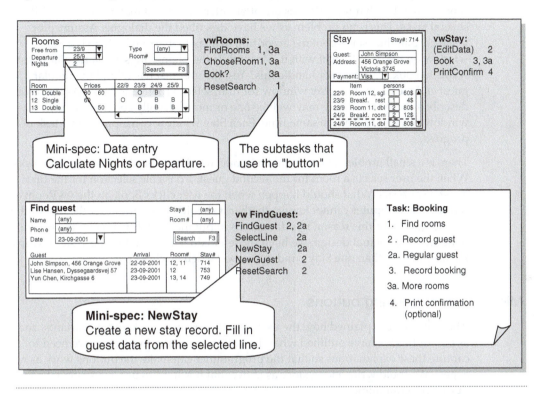

Mini-spec: Data entry
Calculate Nights or Departure.

The subtasks that use the "button"

Mini-spec: NewStay
Create a new stay record. Fill in guest data from the selected line.

Task: Booking

1. Find rooms
2. Record guest
2a. Regular guest
3. Record booking
3a. More rooms
4. Print confirmation (optional)

Can we have the Book function in more than one window? Yes, why not. The Book function requires two things (two *parameters* or *preconditions*) : rooms selected and guest data properly filled out. This suggests that the function could be on either vwRooms or vwStay, or in both places. Actually, we cannot make the decision now. It depends on the platform and the navigation functions, which we haven't looked at yet.

Subtask 4, PrintConfirmation. Finally, we may have to confirm the booking by printing a confirmation and sending it to the guest. This is easy. We just need a PrintConfirm function. A convenient place would be at the Stay window, since it is this stay we confirm.

Task sequence. We have earlier stressed that the user should be allowed to vary the sequence of subtasks (sections 4.6 and 5.3.2). Above we have only looked at one particular sequence. Could we choose another sequence? Yes, we could very well do subtask 2 first, finding or recording the guest. Next we could do subtask 1, finding a suitable room. The only restriction is that we cannot use Book until we have done both subtasks 1 and 2. This is not a restriction caused by the user interface, but a rule in the application area (a *business rule*).

Task switching. Another issue is whether the user can do many tasks at the same time. Remember that receptionists are often interrupted and may be in the middle of several tasks. This is no problem as we have described the dialogue. Assume, for instance, that the user is booking according to a fax that arrived. There is a Stay window on the desk to deal with it. Meanwhile the phone rings and a regular guest wants to book. Can the user handle this? Yes, the user just has to find the regular guest and create another Stay window for him, select a room and book. As we have described the system, there may well be one or more partially completed Stay windows on the desk at the same time. Each Stay window corresponds to a task in progress.

There is a small problem, however. The Rooms window is hard to share by two tasks. When the user selects a room for the second guest, a possible selection for the first guest disappears. What should happen when the user clicks Book on the vwRooms screen? The computer cannot know whether it should book a room for the first or the second guest. For this reason it is dangerous to put the Book function on the Rooms window. In the actual design, we have chosen to do it anyway, but the system warns the user if more than one Stay window is open when he clicks the button.

Mini-specs for booking buttons

Above we have explained how the user would carry out a task and its variants, and as part of this we have outlined what the buttons must do. In practice, we need to capture these explanations so that the programmer can make the buttons work as we expect. We could write a long story as above, but it is hard to use in a systematic way during programming.

In practice, we write a mini-spec for each function. A mini-spec says what the *computer* must do when the user clicks the button. The mini-spec is an outline of the program behind the button.

Figure 7.1A shows part of the mini-spec for NewStay. It captures what we said about NewStay in the long story above. We also describe special data entry functions with mini-specs. Figure 7.1A outlines the mini-spec for the fields Night and Departure. Figure 7.1C shows the full mini-specs. We will comment on them in a moment.

The mini-spec idea was introduced by Tom DeMarco in the 1970s (DeMarco 1979). A mini-spec is written in a more or less formal programming language. Other authors used the same idea, but called the mini-spec a process specification or pseudo-code. Below we have used a very informal language in the mini-specs – in the hope that it will scare usability specialists less.

The other tasks

When we have walked through the booking task, we do the same with the other tasks. The result is shown in Figure 7.1B. Now we have all the virtual windows on

Fig 7.1 B All tasks: semantic functions and search

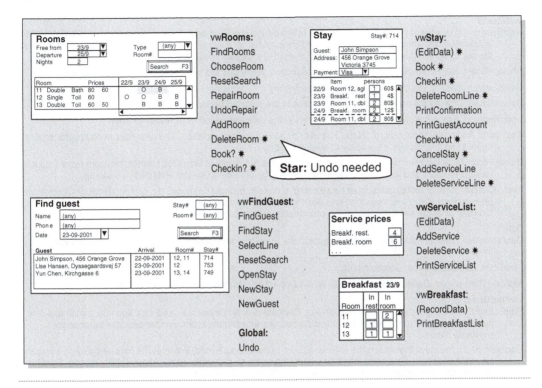

the desk, and each window has a list of functions (buttons). We have not shown in which task each function is used, but many of them are used in several tasks. In total there are about 30 'buttons'. We identified about 11 of them in the booking task.

All mini-specs

In Figure 7.1C we have shown the mini-specs for all the functions (buttons). They are organized with one section for each virtual window. Have a look at the vwRooms section of the mini-specs. It explains all the functions we have assigned to vwRooms. It also has a mini-spec of the non-trivial data fields, explaining the default values of the fields, whether fields are combo boxes or other special presentations, and any special calculations to be performed on the data. As an example, we have specified the calculation of the Nights field and the Departure field.

Global functions and data. Most of the functions and data relate naturally to a specific virtual window, but some do not. These are *global* functions and data. We describe them at the end of the mini-spec. In the hotel example, we have mentioned a global

Fig 7.1 C Mini-specs, hotel system

vwRooms

FindRooms: Show a list of the rooms that are free in the period specified and of the type specified. If a room number is specified, show this room for the specified period whether it is free or not. Set RoomsSelected to the first on the list, to *none* if the list is empty (RoomsSelected is a global variable).

ChooseRoom: Set RoomsSelected and show the selection. Allow multiple selections if possible on the platform.

ResetSearch: Set the search criteria to default (see below).

RepairRoom: Change the state of the selected rooms in the selected period to *Repair*.

UndoRepair: Change the state of the selected rooms in the selected period from *Repair* to *Free*.

AddRoom: Add a new room record. (Note: The user must fill it in for completion. The user may need special access rights to do this. Similar rules apply to other functions.)

DeleteRoom: Mark the selected room as deleted, so that it is not visible in lists. Don't delete the room record, as it is needed for undo and for showing old bookings. Will be physically deleted at database clean up.

Book, Checkin: One or more rooms must be selected. If there is a single open vwStay, perform Book or Checkin on it (see vwStay). If there is more than one open vwStay, ask the user which stay to book or check in. (Note: It is too risky to let the system guess at the proper stay. See details under vwStay.)

Data:
Default values: The search criteria are *(any)*, except the FreeFrom and Departure dates, which are today and tomorrow.

FreeFrom, Departure, Type: Combo boxes.

Nights: When edited, *Departure* is computed. When *Departure* is edited, *Nights* are computed.

vwFindGuest

FindGuest: Show the guests that match the criteria. Only name and number are used. Use soundex match and only the last four digits. In the result list, stay data such as arrival date, room number and stay number are shown as blanks.

FindStay: Show the stays that match the criteria. If room number is specified, interpret the date as the date someone stayed in this room. Otherwise interpret a non-blank date as the arrival date. [After usability testing, FindGuest and FindStay were combined into one, and more criteria fields were added.]

SelectLine: Show a detail window with more guest information: full name, address, zip, phone number. [During programming, the detail window was abandoned. Usability test showed no need for it.]

ResetSearch: Set the search criteria to default (see below).

OpenStay: A stay must be selected. Open a vwStay with the guest and stay information.

NewStay: Create a new vwStay. Fill in the guest part with guest data in case a line is selected. When no line is selected, NewStay works exactly as NewGuest. Might insist that NewGuest is used, but why give the user that trouble.

NewGuest: Create a new, blank vwStay.

Data:
Default values: The search criteria are *(any)*, except the Date field, which is set to *today*.

Date: Combo box.

Continued

Fig 7.1 C Mini-specs, hotel system (*continued*)

vwStay

Book: The function can be used in two situations:
1   vwStay is a new stay (unrecorded) and one or more rooms are selected:
     Create a Stay record and RoomStates for the selected rooms in the selected period with RoomState=booked.
2   vwStay is a booked stay. (Note: The user wants to add further bookings.) Record RoomStates for the selected rooms in the selected period with RoomState=booked.

In all cases the guest data must be filled out (see data description for required fields). Create a Guest record in case this is a new guest, update the Guest record otherwise.

Checkin: The function can be used in three situations:
1   vwStay is a booked stay: Record all its RoomStates as checked in.
2   vwStay is a new stay (unrecorded) and one or more rooms are selected: Create a Stay record and RoomStates for the selected rooms in the selected period with RoomState=checked in.
3   vwStay is a checked-in stay and one or more rooms are selected. (Note: The user wants to use more rooms.) Create RoomState records for the selected rooms in the selected period.

In all cases the guest data must be filled out (see data description for required fields). Create a Guest record in case this is a new guest; update the Guest record otherwise.

DeleteRoomLine: (Note: A stay may comprise several rooms, each with a separate line.) Delete the selected room lines and free the rooms. Leave data for undo.

PrintConfirmation: vwStay must be a booked stay. Print the booking as a confirmation letter.

PrintGuestAccount: Print the stay information as a draft invoice.

Checkout: vwStay must be checked-in. Delete RoomStates for possible remaining days of the stay. Print the stay information as an invoice. Record the stay as checked out. Leave data for undo.

CancelStay: vwStay must be booked or new. Delete the Stay record and all associated RoomStates. Leave data for undo.

AddServiceLine: vwStay must be checked-in. Create a ServiceReceived record for the stay. (Note: The user must fill it in for completion.)

DeleteServiceLine: A service line must be selected. Delete the ServiceReceived record. Leave data for undo.

Data: Payment, ServiceType (in ServiceLine): Combo box.

vwServiceList

AddService: Create a ServiceType record. (Note: The user must fill it in for completion.)

DeleteService: A service type must be selected. Mark the ServiceType record as deleted so that it is not visible in lists. (Note: It may still be in some Service records for old stays and should be shown correctly there. Also needed for undo.)

PrintServiceList: Print all ServiceType records as a price list.

Data: Simple data entry.

vwBreakfast

PrintBreakfastList: Print an empty breakfast list to be filled in by the waiter. Indicate the rooms where nobody is checked in (to avoid recording breakfast there).

Data: Appears to the user as data entry. When opening vwBreakfast, the system shows all breakfasts recorded for all stays the current date. When the user enters anything, it goes right back to the appropriate stay. If there is no stay for the room, the user gets a warning.

Global functions and data

Undo: Reverse the latest semantic function (of those marked with a star on the overview). (To be defined later)

RoomsSelected: For each room selected: Room number, first date, number of days.

function, *Undo*. We have also specified a global variable, *RoomsSelected*. It is dialogue data that keeps track of the rooms selected for the moment. Functions in more than one window need to know which rooms are selected.

When you write mini-specs, it is important to remember that they specify what the *computer* must do. It is an instruction to the computer – a program. As an example, the mini-spec for the first function says this:

> FindRooms: Show the rooms that are free in the period specified and of the type specified. If a room number is specified, show this room for the specified period whether it is free or not. Set RoomsSelected to *none*.

This means that the computer must show the rooms that are free. The computer must also check whether the user has put something in the *room number* field, and in that case show the room – no matter whether it is free or not. Finally, the computer must record that no rooms are selected yet. We often see novice designers write something like this:

Wrong:

> FindRooms: The user enters Period and Type, then clicks FindRooms to see the free rooms.

This is not a mini-spec, but more like a task description or a use case, where we also explain what the user does. In a good mini-spec we sometimes put a comment that explains about the user. The comments are not instructions to the computer, but explanations to the reader of the mini-spec. The AddRoom function provides an example. The user clicks this function to tell the system that a new room has been added to the hotel. The mini-spec says:

> AddRoom: Add a new room record. (Note: The user must fill it in for completion. The user may need special access rights to do this. Similar rules apply to other functions.)

The computer must add a new room record to the database. However, the user must fill it in properly with room number, room type, etc., before the computer can save the new room record. We have written this as a comment in a parenthesis to give a brief explanation. Technically, it is a bit tricky. AddRoom consists of two parts: The first part creates a temporary record for the user to type into. The second part stores the record, but first checks that the user has filled it in properly. In the mini-spec we have also explained about a security issue: Only users with special access rights may add rooms.

Sometimes the function must check that certain preconditions are met. Book and Checkin provide an example:

> Book, Checkin: One or more rooms must be selected. If there is a single open vwStay …

The precondition is that one or more rooms must be selected. If the precondition is not met, the system should somehow tell the user. It can be in many ways, for instance making the button grey to show that it is not active at present, or giving a beep, or showing an error message such as 'You must select a free room'. Error messages and other error indications have a large influence on usability and we discuss them in section 7.9.

Even in this simple system, the mini-specs are surprisingly complex, dealing with what has to be changed in the database and what has to be shown on the windows. The most complex functions are Book and Checkin because they have different effects depending on whether the stay is booked, newly created or checked in. To the user it seems logical to say *Checkin* in all three situations, but inside the system different things have to take place.

At the beginning of the functional design, the mini-specs were more sketchy than Figure 7.1C. Gradually we added more detail. When we had planned the functions, we combined them with virtual windows into mock-up screens that we tested for usability. After the first usability test we found several usability defects and revised the mini-specs as well as the screens. Figure 7.1C shows the mini-specs at that stage. We had not yet described the undo function in detail.

As a result of more usability tests and prototyping, the mini-specs changed further. In Figure 7.1C we have indicated some of the major changes in square brackets (see FindStay and SelectLine). Figure 8.2B shows the final mini-spec for the Book function.

Standard functions

Usually there are some task variants that we don't catch in the domain analysis. Here is a list of some common variants:

- **Undo.** The user should be able to undo all semantic functions, preferably also after having completed the task.

- **Print.** Often there is a need for printing various things.

- **Data exchange.** Often there is a need for exchanging data with other programs, for instance text processors and spreadsheets.

In Figure 7.1B we have put a star on all the functions that must be undo-able. Not all functions have got a star. For instance the user doesn't need to be able to undo search functions. The print functions cannot be undone at all – the sheet has been printed and the user will have to 'undo' by means of the waste-paper basket. You may notice that Figure 7.1B shows a global function (not attached to any particular window) – the Undo function. It can rewind time for the latest star-marked functions. Undo is a complex affair and we have dedicated section 7.3 to it.

It is hard to identify the need for print and data exchange functions without asking reception experts. In Figure 7.1B we have included the PrintConfirmation function, which is an obvious part of the booking task. We have also included a PrintGuestAccount function, because the task description for Checkout says that the receptionist often prints a draft invoice for the guest to review.

We have added a function for printing the service list with prices, since it is handy to have it in the reception. We have also added a function for printing an empty breakfast list for the restaurant to fill in.

We know that in some hotels there is a need for printing check-in forms for the guest to sign, for printing a list of the current day's expected arrivals in case the computer breaks down, and so on. There is also a need to transfer data to spreadsheets for statistical analysis of room occupation. Finally, there is a need to transfer data to an account system for management, billing of company guests and legal purposes. We will not go into detail with these things here.

7.2 Actions and feedback (use cases)

If we want to document more precisely how each task is carried out, we can write *use cases* for each task. In section 5.6 we explained that a use case describes how the work is split between user and computer system. Our design effort has found a way to make this split.

It may be important to check how this split of work relates to the original task – the unsplit work. Figure 7.2 shows a way to do it, *actions and feedback*. This description is a combination of a task description and a use case. We see how the original subtasks are split into user actions and system actions.

Within each subtask, time runs down the page. In the user-action column we see what the user does, and in the system-action column we see what the system does as a response to each user action. From a usability point of view, it is essential that the system gives a visual feedback on its actions, and the system-action column should specify this.

Let us look closer at the booking task. The first subtask is *FindRooms* and according to the figure, it starts with the user entering the search criteria in vwRooms. Next he

Fig 7.2 Actions and feedback (use cases)

Task	User action	System-action & Feedback
1.1 Booking		
1. Find rooms	Enters search criteria in vwRooms. Clicks Find Rooms. Selects a room(ChooseRoom).	Shows free rooms. Shows selection.
1a. No suitable room	Enters new search criteria. Clicks FindRoms. Selects a room.	Shows free rooms. Shows selection.
2. Record guest	Clicks NewStay. Enters guest data in Stay window.	Shows new, empty Stay window.
2a. Regular guest	Enters search criteria in vwFindGuest. Clicks FindGuest. Looks down the list for the right person. Selects the guest if one matches. Clicks NewStay. Edits guest data in Stay window.	Shows guests that match. Shows more details for each guest. Shows new Stay window. Fills it with data about selected guest or data from the search criteria.
3. Record booking	Clicks Book.	Records guest data, stay data, room states. Updates vwRooms and vwStay. Visible feedback to user in vwStay?
3a. More rooms	Uses vwRooms as in subtask 1 or 1a. Clicks Book.	Records additional room states. Updates vwRooms.
4. Confirm (option)	Clicks PrintConfirm	Prints confirmation letter.

pushes *FindRooms*. To the right of *FindRooms* we see the system's response: it shows the free rooms. Next the user selects a room, and the system responds by showing what is selected. If we want to see in more detail what the system does, we have to consult the mini-spec for the function.

The other subtasks are described in a similar way. The user may still choose his own sequence through the task, as long as each system action has the necessary data to work with.

What we have done in Figure 7.2 is simply to write the long story about the dialogue in a more structured way. The more rigid structure helps us find design defects. As an example, in subtask 3, *Record booking*, we have to specify the system feedback. What is it in this case? The virtual windows will be updated, and this means that the Stay window will get a line with the booking, and the Rooms window will show that the rooms are now booked. But is this sufficient confirmation to the user that the booking has been done and recorded? Many users expect that they have to close the window or click an update button, but it is not necessary with our dialogue (usability tests confirmed this problem).

The problem is even worse after check-in because little change is visible in the Stay window as it is designed. We should clearly indicate the state of the stay in both vwStay and vwFindGuest (another design defect). Actually, many test users had already experienced this problem with the first prototype (Figure 2.3A).

Traditional use cases

Traditionally, developers make use cases very early in development, sometimes even as part of requirements. Screens are designed much later. The virtual window approach does it the other way around. The reason is that it is hard to define the detailed dialogue before you know what kind of screens the user will have to look at (Chapter 9 discusses this in more detail).

Early definition of use cases tend to define a dialogue based on what users do at present. There is no opportunity to invent new and better ways of carrying out tasks. As a result, the computer system just automates bits of the tasks – without real innovation (Robertson 2002).

7.3 Undo – to do or not to do

'Undo' means to rewind time so that things done seem not to have been done. If the user has asked the system to perform some function, 'undo' means that the system reverts to the state before it performed the function. All HCI specialists agree that the user should be able to undo everything, preferably several steps back. To undo sounds easy, but as we shall see it is not that simple.

Why undo?

Let us first look at why undo is needed. There seem to be three situations where the user wants to undo:

1 **Slips.** The user by mistake hit the wrong key. As an example, he wanted to check a guest in, but hit Delete instead of Enter. As a result, the system cancelled the booking. An *Undo* button is an easy way out if the user realizes his mistake immediately.

2 **Explore the system.** Exploring the system is a good way to learn how to use it. However, exploring means that the user often chooses functions that turn out not to have the desired effect. The *Undo* button is an easy way out here too, and it should preferably be able to go several steps back. The novice hotel receptionist may want to explore the many check-in variants, but should only do it if undo is available. You explore a Web site by clicking on various links that bring you to other Web pages. You can undo these navigation functions with the *Back* button in the browser.

3 **Domain mistake.** The user did what he intended to do, but much later realizes that he shouldn't have done it. As a simple example, he may decide to delete an old file from the system, but much later realizes that he actually needs it once more. As another example, a receptionist checks a guest out, but later it turns out that it was the wrong guest he checked out. The guest he checked out in the system is still staying in his room. When the receptionist realizes this later, he would very much like to undo what he did. He may have used the system for many other things in between, so he doesn't want to rewind time for the entire system. He wants to rewind it only for the guest he checked out.

It sounds easy to rewind time for only part of the system, for instance for a single guest. Unfortunately, it only works if this part has not interfered with other system parts. If it has, you may have to rewind time for those parts too. Even in the simple hotel system this may happen because guests in some cases compete for the same rooms. We will see examples of this below.

When we talk about the *system*, we usually mean the computer system, but often it is part of a surrounding system, for instance when the computer controls a factory. The computer interacts heavily with the surroundings, so rewinding time for the computer system is of little use. You also have to rewind time for the surroundings. We will discuss this too below.

Which functions to undo?

Which functions would the user like to undo? Not all, in fact. As an example, you may have encountered Web sites that undo too small steps. You may, for instance, have started at the top of a page and then clicked on an internal link that moved you down the same page. When you use *Back*, the system just scrolls back to the top of the page – annoying – you wanted to go back to the previous page. Moving down the page was a navigation function, so it seems that we don't need to undo navigation functions. However, when you click on a link to another Web page, it is also a navigation function, and this one you would like to undo with *Back*.

Let us look at the different kinds of functions more systematically:

Semantic functions. The semantic functions have an effect on the persistent data in the system or on the system surroundings. The user wants ways to undo them. As an example, deleting a document or cancelling a booking are semantic functions that we may want to undo – also after having used the system for other things. Sending an e-mail to someone is a semantic function, and sometimes you really wish you had not sent it. Opening a valve in a computer-controlled chemical factory is also a semantic function and the user may want to undo it.

Data entry functions. If we talk about editing simple data fields, there is not much need for a separate undo function. The user can simply enter the old value. We might say that the undo feature is built into the usual edit functions.

However, if the user edits complex data or cannot remember what was in the field before, he needs an undo feature. As an example, you need an undo feature when you edit a complex document (fortunately most text processors have such features). As another example, you may try to set a lot of options for your system, but suddenly you realize that the settings are much more complex than you thought. However, you cannot remember the original settings. Here too you want to undo the changes, and the system usually provides it as a *Cancel* function.

Navigation functions. In most cases you don't need a separate undo function to undo a navigation function. One of the existing navigation functions can undo the first navigation. As an example, when you use a function that opens a window, you know how to undo it – you simply close the window or use *Cancel*. When you click on a link to a new Web site, you expect the *Back* button to undo your choice. Actually, the *Back* button is the equivalent of closing a window. When you scroll down a long page, you can use the same scroll feature to scroll up again. It would be annoying if the Back button reversed your scrolls.

Search functions. A search function is a kind of navigation function, often controlled by some data entry fields (the search criteria). Usually, the necessary 'undo' is built into the navigation already. Since typical search criteria are simple and easy to remember, there is no need for undoing the edit of them. However, if the criteria are complex, for instance long Web addresses (URLs), there may be a need for undoing the edit.

What is possible to undo?

Let us look at what we can undo from a technical point of view. Some functions are easy to undo, others are hard, and some are impossible.

Navigation and search functions are easy to undo, and usually the necessary undo features are part of the navigation, for instance as a *Close* button, a *Cancel* button, a *Back* button, or a scroll bar.

Data entry functions are also pretty easy to undo, but only as long as the data hasn't been saved and made available to other users. Saving and making it available to others is a semantic function that we discuss below.

Here is how we can handle the simple undo of data edits. When the user starts editing some data, the system first saves the old data contents. Undo is then a matter of retrieving the saved data. The system may save only the latest changed data. This allows one level of undo. The system may also create a list of saved data as a history record of what has happened. This allows several levels of undo, as you find it in many text processors. Keeping this list of changes also allows the system to redo what was undone.

If we want to undo something that was not the previous edit (a domain mistake), the simple approach doesn't work. It is not a matter of just rewinding time. We need to rewind time for only a part of the data. Some text processors keep track of all changes and can make them visible to the user. In Microsoft Word, the Track Changes tool can do this. The user may then point to a single change and undo it.

Semantic functions

Semantic functions may be hard or impossible to undo. In general, when the user has changed some data and saved it in the database, other users may change it or act on the data. If this has happened, undo can be hard or even impossible. Similarly, if the system has influenced the surroundings, it may be hard or impossible to undo these influences.

Simple semantic undo. Let us start with an example where undo is simple. A receptionist cancels a booking by mistake, and before anything else happens, he wants to undo. The cancellation has already been recorded in the database, but if the system saved the old booking data, it can undo the change. This is quite similar to undoing a simple data entry.

Domain-specific undo. In many cases, we may also be able to undo a much earlier cancellation (a domain mistake). If the system saves the old data for the booking, the user may point to this booking and try to undo its changes. Let us look at an example.

Fig 7.3   Undo

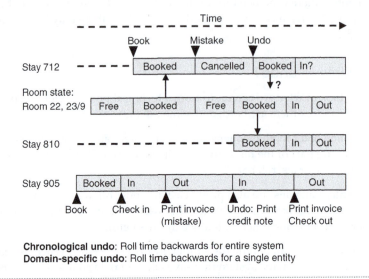

Chronological undo: Roll time backwards for entire system
Domain-specific undo: Roll time backwards for a single entity

Figure 7.3 shows how various entities in the hotel system change state. Time flows from left to right. Look at stay 712. At a certain point in time, the guest books and the system creates a stay record – stay 712. The stay is now in the state *booked*. After some days, the receptionist by mistake cancels the booking. The system doesn't delete the booking, but simply changes its state to *cancelled*.

Some time later, the receptionist becomes aware of the mistake. The receptionist finds the cancelled stay through the FindGuest window and asks the system to undo the cancellation. The system changes the state back to *booked*. If the rooms are still free, everything is fine.

Hard to undo.   Unfortunately, bookings may interact with each other, and then undo can be hard. Figure 7.3 illustrates the problem. When stay 712 was cancelled, the system freed the room that the guest had booked. Assume that it was room 22 on the date 23/9. Before the receptionist realizes the mistake, another stay – stay 810 – books the same room for the same date. As a result, the cancellation cannot be undone completely, because room 22 is not free any more. The receptionist will have to book another room for the cancelled guest – or give stay 810 another room.

Figure 7.3 shows what happens in the database. In the database, there is a RoomState record that keeps track of the *planned* state of room 22 on the 23/9. (Another RoomState record keeps track of room 22 on the 24/9, and so on.) Initially, room 22 was free on the 23/9. However, at the moment where stay 712 was booked, the room state became booked too and the room state record was linked to stay 712. When stay 712 was cancelled, the room state became free (this is the main purpose of cancelling a stay).

A short time later, stay 810 booked room 22 for the 23/9. The room state record became booked once more, but this time linked to stay 810. When guest 810 turned up in the reception and was checked in, stay 810 and the room state changed state to *in*. When guest 810 checked out the next morning, stay 810 and the room state changed state to *out*.

Undo impossible. The example also shows that undo may be impossible. Assume that the hotel is full when the receptionist cancels booking 712, thereby freeing a room. Before the receptionist realizes the mistake, another receptionist books the free room for stay 810. Result: the cancellation of booking 712 cannot be undone – there is no free room on the 23/9. Such things happen in practice, and although the computer system cannot do anything about it, the users have to. They may phone one of the two guests and explain that the hotel has had an accident and the room is not available anymore. Or they may keep the cancelled booking on a waiting list (overbooking), hoping that some other guest doesn't turn up. Or they may book the guest into another hotel in the neighbourhood. And so on.

Compensating transactions. As a different example, assume that the receptionist by mistake has checked out a guest (stay 905 in Figure 7.3). As part of this, the system prints an invoice, which is a legal document. The auditor, for instance, will check all the consecutively enumerated invoices to see that they are all paid and that the money ends up in the hotel's bank account. Now how could we undo? The system might change the necessary things in the database (assuming that nobody else took the apparently free room) and then compensate the legal document with another legal document – a credit note. (A credit note looks like an invoice, but has a Credit Note heading. It tells the auditor that the amount on the credit note should not go into the bank account.)

When controlling a chemical plant, some functions such as opening a valve to let out a chemical compound are also hard to undo. It may involve feeding compensating chemicals into the compound, etc.

In both of these cases, we can rewind time in the computer system, and by means of a compensating transaction 'rewind time' in the surroundings too.

Irreversible changes to the surroundings. Some semantic functions are impossible for the system to compensate. A simple example is printing a short document. Before the system can stop the printing, the printer has printed the few pages. The pain is usually small – the user can just dump the paper into the waste.

With long print jobs, a lot of paper and printer time may be saved if the user can ask the system to undo the print as far as possible. But it should be easy to do so. In Word, for instance, you have to click in strange places and know what you are doing to cancel a print job. It doesn't look like an 'undo' at all.

Sending an e-mail is a semantic function that influences the surroundings. Have you ever written a naughty e-mail? Most people have. Assume that you by mistake have sent it to the wrong person, for instance to the one you tell naughty things about. You would very much like to undo it, but you cannot. A compensating e-mail is not possible.

When the computer system controls a physical system, some functions may be impossible for the system to compensate. As an example, if the operator of the chemical plant asks the system to open the valve to the sewer, thereby letting poison into the river, the system can close the valve, but not undo the damage. As another example, think of the commander who by mistake pushes 'fire missile'. The system cannot undo it. Both of these things have happened in real life with severe damage to the surroundings.

7.3.1 Undo strategy for the user interface

I hope that you at this point realize that undo is not easy. How do we deal with it on the user interface? Here is a design strategy for undo.

A) **Identify the functions to undo.** Look at all the planned functions and identify the ones that need to be reversible. (You may, for instance, mark them with a star as we have done in Figure 7.1B.)

B) **Support slips.** Provide a **chronological Undo** button that as far as possible can undo the latest function, preferably several steps backwards. The purpose is that whenever users make a slip, they can use Undo. In multi-user systems, the button must of course undo only what this user has done.

C) **Support exploration.** A good way to learn a system is to explore it – try various things and see what happens. The chronological undo button helps the user getting out of the mess. If there are dangerous, non-reversible functions, it may be necessary to have a *training mode* where the user can do anything, but dangerous functions don't have any effect on the surroundings.

D) **Support domain mistakes.** Provide a **domain-specific Undo** function. Allow the user to select an entity and undo changes to it – also much later than the change. In multi-user systems, the person who undoes the change may be someone else than the person who made it.

E) **Prevent slips and domain mistakes for non-reversible functions.** There are several approaches to this: separate dangerous functions from harmless functions; ask for confirmation; warn of consequences; use security procedures; reconsider whether the function is really non-reversible (see examples below).

Examples

A) Identify functions to undo

Figure 7.1B shows the functions to undo in the hotel system. We have marked them with a star. Here are the arguments behind our choice.

1 The semantic functions Book and Checkin must be reversible, both after slips and domain mistakes. DeleteRoomLine, Checkout and CancelStay must be reversible

as far as possible, but since the functions release rooms, there are cases where the system cannot undo them. In these cases, the system must tell the user why it cannot undo the function and suggest what he can do. When Checkout is undone, the system must deal with the credit note.

2   Data entry in vwStay must be reversible (EditData), both after slips and domain mistakes. Names and addresses may be so complex that the user cannot remember the old data. There is no need to undo the other data entry functions (in vwServiceList and vwBreakfast). Data here is not complex or hard to remember.

3   Setting a room in Repair state and back to normal (RepairRoom and UndoRepair) needs no undo. The functions provide undo for each other – even in case of a slip.

4   Adding a room to the hotel needs no undo. DeleteRoom can do the job even in case of slips. However, DeleteRoom needs an undo, since it is no easy matter to add a room. It should suffice to provide it only for slips and exploration, and not for domain mistakes. The same reasoning is behind the other add–delete pairs (AddServiceLine/DeleteServiceLine, AddService/DeleteService).

5   There is no need to undo PrintConfirmation and the other print functions. Only a sheet or two are printed, so a mistake is not serious.

6   There is no need to undo the search functions (FindRooms, FindGuest, SelectLine, etc.). The same search functions provide undo. The search criteria are simple and need no undo. For convenience we have already provided a function for resetting them.

7   There is no need to undo OpenStay, NewStay and NewGuest. The user may simply close the windows coming up. We may consider these functions a kind of navigation functions. We plan the rest of the navigation functions later, and they too need no undo.

B) Support slips
We provide a chronological Undo button that as far as possible can undo the latest functions, several steps backwards. Some functions need not be undone this way, as mentioned under (a) above. The Undo button works only on the functions that the user has made recently. It doesn't undo functions that other users have made.

C) Support exploration
We assume that the Undo button is sufficient for harmless exploration. No training mode seems necessary.

D) Support domain mistakes
In the hotel system, the only entities of interest are the stays. The receptionist must be able to select a stay – even if cancelled – and undo changes to it. The Undo button cannot be used for this since it undoes only what the user has made recently. We

allow the receptionist to select any stay and use the ordinary functions Book, Checkin, etc., for correcting the domain mistakes. For instance we will allow him to use Book on a checked-in stay, meaning that he undoes the check-in to a booking.

E) Prevent slips and domain mistakes for non-reversible functions

Some functions are hard or impossible to undo, so it is important that the user doesn't activate them by mistake. Here are some ways to prevent it:

1 **Separate dangerous functions from harmless functions.** Place the non-reversible function away from other functions. It becomes less likely that the user hits it by coincidence. As an example, don't place the CancelStay button besides the Checkin button. And don't place the FireMissile button besides the TrainingMode button.

2 **Ask for confirmation.** As an example, deleting a file may bring up this message:

> *Delete the file?*

This will at least prevent the user deleting the file by a slip or when exploring the system.

3 **Warn of the consequences.** When you delete a file in some systems, you get a message like this:

> *This will permanently delete the file. Do you really want to continue?*

This message will of course prevent the user deleting the file by a slip, but the message is long and scaring, and for everyday use it becomes a nuisance and people just say yes without reading the message. In the hotel system, cancelling a stay might bring a similar message up:

> *When you cancel the stay, the rooms may become booked by others. Cancel anyway?*

This makes more sense, particularly since deleting a booking is not a frequent action. What about this message when the commander pushes FireMissile:

> *Firing the missile may severely harm the environment and kill people. Do you want to fire anyway?*

No, it is too stupid in the context, and it counteracts the need for fast action.

4 **Security procedures.** Request that the user goes through several steps. In the hotel system, CheckOut could bring up this dialogue:

> *Have you checked that breakfast is recorded for the guest? Yes/no*
>
> *Have you checked that this is the guest in room 22? Yes/no*
>
> *Have you checked that the guest leaves one day earlier than planned? Yes/no*

This not only prevents slips, but also helps the receptionist avoid the frequent reasons for having to undo a checkout. However, to the trained receptionist, it is a nuisance.

5   **Really non-reversible?** The best way to handle slips and mistakes is to allow undo of the function. Then there is no reason for warning or confirmation. Are you as a designer really sure that the function cannot be reversible? Most e-mail systems, for instance, have a good solution to deleting messages by mistake. They simply transfer the message to Trash, and then it is easy for the user to undo the deletion at any time (at least until the Trash bin has been emptied).

Most operating systems today have a similar trash bin for deleted files, but it is not quite as visible and easy to control. Microsoft Windows, for instance, keeps asking users whether they want to delete the file – it should be superfluous if the trash bin was easy to use. (The confirm message can be turned off, but this too is not easy.)

In case of the naughty e-mail to the wrong person, present e-mail systems cannot undo the Send. However, the e-mail often resides some time on the recipient's mail server before he sees it. In principle, it would be possible to delete it during this period. It wouldn't save the user in all cases, but in many.

7.3.2   How to implement undo

History log

There are many ways to implement undo. Let us first look at history logs, which are well suited for chronological undo.

The basic idea is to let the system keep a log of all functions done. For each function, the log specifies what was changed, the old value and the new value. The old value allows the system to undo the functions, and the new value allows it to redo. The log might look like this for the hotel system:

Time	Function	Item changed	Old value	New value	Status
12:15	Book	Stay 912	(none)	Guest 102, rooms . . .	done
12:17	Edit	Guest 102 phone	(03) 3718 5353	+45 3917 2300	done
12:23	Checkout	Stay 906	in, rooms . . .	out, rooms . . .	done (later: undone)

This log records that the receptionist at 12:15 made a booking of stay 912. The stay did not exist before. The new value is that it is a stay for guest 102, and the rooms booked are this and that. The status of this function is *done*.

At 12:17, the receptionist edited the phone number field for guest 102 (the regular guest who booked stay 912). The old contents of the phone number field was (03) 3718 5353, and the new is +45 3917 2300. It tagged the function as *done*.

At 12:23, the receptionist checked out stay 906. This included printing the final invoice. The old state of the stay was *in* with certain room states involved. The new state was *out* with different room states. It tagged the function as *done*.

On seeing the invoice, the guest said, 'This is not me'. Oops, said the receptionist and clicked Undo. The system looked into the history log and found the latest function that was done: Checkout. To undo this function, it had to change the state to the previous value, *in*, and change some room states too. Further it had to print a credit note. Finally, it changed the status tag to *undone*.

Assume that the receptionist at this point in time clicks Undo once more. Now the latest function done is Edit. The system would find Guest 102 and change the phone number to the previous value, (03) 3718 5353. The Edit function would be marked *undone*.

Redo. We may also provide a Redo button. It would find the earliest function marked *undone* and perform it once more. For this, the system needs the new value stored the first time the function was done. The Redo button will also once more tag the function as *done*.

Undo impossible. In a multi-user system, it may not be possible to undo certain functions because other users have taken the resources, for instance free rooms. Although the system can suggest ways around it, some human intervention will be required.

Selective undo. Undo may not be entirely chronological. It may be possible for the user to go back to much earlier functions and undo them explicitly. The risk of this being impossible is higher, however, since more changes in the rest of the system have happened since then.

Range of history. A history log could, in principle, keep the log for several years. This may in some systems be desirable for legal reasons to prove what happened. However, for chronological undo it is unnecessary. Users only undo things done recently. Usually the history log for undo holds only functions done by the user since he logged on. In multi-user systems, each user logs his own actions on his own computer.

Complex old and new values. Sometimes a function involves changes in many pieces of data. Examples from the hotel system are booking, check-in, etc. Not only the stay record may be changed, but also the guest record and room states. Describing the entire set of values in the log field *old value* may be a problem. One solution is to log every change of a record in the database – also changes to room state records.

Temporal database

Most database systems contain logs similar to the history log above. Every change of a database record is logged. The log allows the system to recover after power breaks and other disasters, by rolling the database back to a consistent state. The old value is often called a *before image*, the new an *after image*.

In database technology, an alternative to the history log is to keep old versions of all records in the database. Each record is marked with its creation date and time. A record is never changed, but a new record with the new data is added. This is called a temporal database, because the system may go back in time by ignoring all records younger than a certain date. The technique may be used to handle chronological undo, but supplementary techniques are needed to deal with compensating transactions such as the credit note. Handling domain mistakes, where selected functions have to be undone, is also hard.

Mark old data

A temporal database may be costly in performance because the system always has to find the youngest version of any record. A variation of the technique is to keep old records but mark them as *cancelled*. This also provides a good basis for undoing domain mistakes.

As an example, assume that the receptionist changes the phone number of a guest. The system then creates a new guest record with the new phone number and all other guest details. It keeps the old guest record but marks it *cancelled*. When the system finds guests or prints confirmation letters, it will ignore the cancelled records. The receptionist may use a special function to see the history of a guest, and as part of this see the cancelled record with the old phone number.

We may use the creation date and time to uniquely identify the versions of the guest record. The database might then contain these two records:

GuestID	Name	address1 ...	phone ...	creation time	Cancelled
102	John ...	55 Westbank	(03) 3718 5353	2/3 8:55	yes
102	John ...	55 Westbank	+45 3917 2300	23/9 12:17	no

As another example, let us see what happens when the receptionist deletes a stay. The system doesn't erase the stay record, but just marks it *cancelled*. Although the rooms became free, the system doesn't erase the room state records, but mark them *cancelled*. When the system shows free rooms, it ignores the *cancelled* room state records. The receptionist may use the special function to see cancelled stays, and may ask the system to change a cancelled stay into a booking. At this point, the system will try to revive the cancelled room state records, and if the room is still free, it can book it. Otherwise, it may show the stay window with room lines marked as *not valid* and let the receptionist choose an alternative room.

We can combine the history log with marking of old data in the database. Instead of storing the old and new data in the log itself, we store a reference to the cancelled and the new record in the database. Based on this principle, edit of the guest record might be logged like this:

Time	Function	Item changed	Old version	New version	Status
12:17	Edit	Guest 102	2/3 8:55	23/9 12:17	done

7.4　From virtual windows to screens

Until now we have assumed that we had a large screen (the 'desk') where we could see all the virtual windows at the same time. At the next stage of the design we have to pack everything into the limited physical screen. This has two consequences: (1) we have to figure out how to pack each virtual window into the physical screen, (2) we have to come up with navigation functions that allow the user to bring up the screens he needs.

If we have followed the design rule of keeping the virtual windows close to what is physically possible on the screen, we only need to do some 'trimming' of each virtual window. However, we may try to keep several virtual windows on the screen at the same time to support the tasks better. This can be done in different ways depending on which platform our system runs.

Platforms available

The largest gestalts on the user interface are **pages** (sometimes called *windows* or *screens*). Depending on the computer platform, the user interface may show a single page or several, possibly overlapping pages. Let us look at the two possibilities.

Single-page platform, sometimes called a single-document interface (SDI). The application shows only one page at a time on the screen. The standard Web browser is a typical example. If the designer wants to show several virtual windows at the same time, he has to split the page into two or more **frames**, each holding a virtual window (Figure 7.4, screen A).

Multi-page platform, sometimes called a multiple-document interface (MDI). The application may show several pages at the same time. The pages may overlap and the user may drag them around. Such pages are often called **windows**. Examples of multi-page platforms are Macintosh, Microsoft Windows and X-Windows. When the designer wants to show several virtual windows at the same time, he can use a separate page for each of them (Figure 7.4, screen C).

The two types of platform will often reflect two different metaphors for what the user sees on the screen:

Book metaphor.　A single-page platform will often use a book metaphor. The user sees a single book and can turn pages forwards, backwards, and with hyperlinks to an arbitrary page.

Desktop metaphor.　A multi-page platform will often use a desktop metaphor. The user sees several documents on a desk. He can move the documents around and put one on top of the others. (He can often enlarge or minimize them too, what you cannot do on a real desk.)

The choice of platform is often made very early in the project, determined by other factors than sheer usability. The user interface designer may have no influence on the platform choice. For many applications, the choice of platform has little influence on usability, but when supporting complex tasks, particularly when dealing with concurrent tasks, it is harder to use a single-page platform.

Full-screen or part-screen workspaces

To the user interface designer, the basic issue is whether he has a single-page platform or a multi-page platform available. However, the platform may either occupy the full physical screen or part of the physical screen. The user interface designer need not worry so much about this, since he is only working inside the **workspace** allocated to the application.

For the sake of completeness, we will look at the combinations of workspaces and platforms. There are four combinations, numbered A, B, C and D in Figure 7.4. Let us look at each of them.

A. Single-page platform, full-screen workspace
Here the system can show only one page at a time. A page may contain two or more frames, dividing the page in a rather static manner. In the example the designer has packed two virtual windows – vwRooms and vwStay – into a single page. The user cannot change the way the virtual windows are packed.

Navigation functions can lead the user to other pages, and the old page disappears completely. The user can only see one page at a time. Examples of this platform are old character-oriented screens (e.g. mainframe systems with 24 lines of 80 characters), mobile phones, photocopiers and Web sites (with a standard browser).

B. Single-page platform, part-screen workspace
Here the system can show several applications at a time. Our hotel application still shows only one page at a time, but the page occupies just part of the screen. We say that the workspace of the application is a part of the screen. Other applications have other workspaces on the screen.

From the designer's point of view, this platform is similar to platform A. He has to fit the virtual windows into the pages and arrange for navigation functions between pages. Examples of this platform are Web sites running in a part-screen window; e-mail systems with mail in one frame, folder lists in another frame.

C. Multi-page platform, full screen workspace
Here the application can show several pages at the same time, with more or less overlap of the pages. Our hotel system might show each virtual window as a separate page. Pages of this kind are called windows.

Fig 7.4   Various platforms

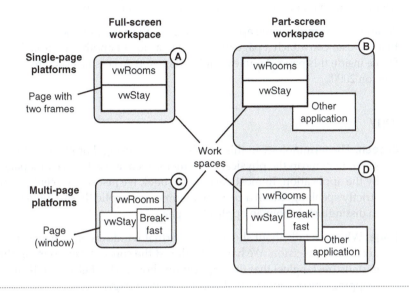

The user can drag the pages around, bring them to the top of the pile and resize them. This means that a lot of the navigation functions are built into the platform, so the designer doesn't have to care about them. If you, for instance, run Word in full-screen mode, it works this way. You may have several documents open at the same time, each of them occupying a page (window) of their own inside the common Word boundary. In general, most applications running in full-screen mode behave in this way on Macintosh, Microsoft Windows and X-Windows. Some applications always run this way and won't restrict themselves to a smaller workspace, for instance Visual Basic.

D. Multi-page platform, part-screen workspace
Here our application also shows several pages at the same time, but they are restricted to part of the physical screen. The operating system may run other applications in other workspaces. From the designer's point of view, this platform is similar to platform C.

Most applications that can run in full-screen mode can also run in part-screen mode. For instance, you can run Word in this way. You may still have several documents open at the same time inside the workspace occupied by Word.

Mixed platforms
Some applications use a mix of the possibilities above. You may, for instance, see a platform D system with most of its pages nicely residing inside a part-screen

workspace. But some of its pages always stay on top of all the workspaces, and the user can move them around on the entire computer screen.

As another example, some applications allow their pages to be *docked*. This means that the user can attach a page (window) to a side of another page so it becomes a frame inside this page. As an example, Microsoft Access has such features from version 2000.

Terminology

Screen. The terminology in this area is very confusing. For instance the word *screen* may mean the physical computer screen, a workspace or a page shown by the application. In most parts of the book we just say 'screen' when we, strictly speaking, mean a page. Sometimes we explicitly say 'physical screen' to distinguish it from an application page.

Page. When we talk about showing the virtual windows on a physical screen, we need more precision. We have introduced the concept *page* to mean the largest gestalts (rectangles) that the application shows. This helps us talk about mapping one or more virtual windows into a page.

Window. The word *window* also has many meanings. On a multi-page platform we often call the pages 'windows'. However, a part-screen workspace is also called a 'window'. In this case we have a large window (the work space) with small windows inside (the pages).

Frame. We use the word *frame* to denote a rectangle within a page. The frame is a rather static thing. Frames cannot overlap, but the user may on some platforms drag the borders between frames.

From a theoretical point of view, we are dealing with nested structures – 'screens' on many levels. The outermost screen is the physical screen. The level below is a workspace – the 'screen' where the application works. The level below is the pages – the 'screens' that the application shows. The lowest level is the frames inside a page. Depending on the platform, some of these levels may collapse into one. Since our natural language is not good at dealing with such levels in general, we try to introduce separate words for each level.

Various authors and companies have introduced other terms to describe these levels, such as *Canvas* for a page or workspace; *Tiled window* or *Panel* for a frame. They may also use the words 'page', 'screen' and 'frame' to mean other things than we do in this book.

Platform trends

From around year 2000, we have seen a trend in the PC world to make single-page applications rather than multi-page. An example is Microsoft's Explorer tool for looking at the file and folder hierarchy. It used to have a separate Find window for searching files by name. Since Windows 2000, this has become a frame inside the Explorer page. By clicking buttons placed some distance from the frame, the user can see either the Find frame or the usual Folder frame. Users take some time to learn this – even if they have no experience with previous versions of Explorer. The law of object permanence suggests why: The folder frame seems to disappear and be overwritten by something different, and the user cannot immediately see how to get it back since the buttons involved are not close to the frame gestalt. The old approach clearly showed that there were two overlapping windows – the Folder window and the Find window.

The change from multi-page to single-page often reflects a change in metaphor from the desktop metaphor to the book metaphor. The user sees a single book and can turn pages in it. For instance, instead of the close button, you now see a Back button. This easily leads to a strongly task-oriented user interface.

In general, with the single-page approach users have much less control of what they want to see at the same time, and they have no support for doing several things at the same time. I don't know the reasons for these changes, but can see two possible explanations:

1   From a pure performance perspective, frames use a bit less screen space than overlapping windows, as pointed out by Cooper (1995), one of the designers of Visual Basic.

2   Due to the e-trade movement at that time, marketing people said: go the Web-way, it is the future. Designers then tried to change the classic applications to a Web-look with a single-page platform.

From a usability viewpoint, the standard Web browser is horrible, and I would much prefer seeing the Web going in the multi-page direction than the opposite. This is not a question of promoting one operating system over another. The multi-page concept exists in much the same form under Unix/Linux, Macintosh and MS-Windows.

We see some trends in this direction. Classical Web pages are HTML-based and have a distinct HTML view very different from traditional graphical user interfaces. Newer Web technologies such as Swing and AWT allow Web sites to look exactly like graphical user interfaces with overlapping windows.

7.5   Single-page dialogue

If we have a single-page platform for the user interface, we have to pack virtual windows into single pages and provide navigation functions between them. Here is the procedure.

Design procedure

a) Look at the tasks one by one and see which virtual windows they use at the same time. (A matrix showing the relation between virtual windows and tasks may be useful. See the example in Figure 6.8A.)

b) Define the pages: Combine virtual windows into pages to minimize page changes during the tasks. Each virtual window should be shown as a separate frame within the page. Also make sure that the pages can fit on the physical screens available.

c) Draw a state diagram for all the pages. On the diagram, show all transitions caused by the semantic functions and search functions defined at present.

d) Review the transitions to check that the user can navigate between all pages. Add any missing navigation functions to the diagram.

e) Write a final list of functions for each page (see the example in Figure 7.8B). Additionally, you may modify the mini-specs (Figure 7.1C) to reflect the page structure rather than the virtual window structure.

Below, we will use the design procedure for the hotel system. The platform might for instance be a Web-based one (using HTML). As good Web designers we want to ensure that also people with small screens can use the system. This means that we should restrict ourselves to pages of around 30 lines of 120 characters (800 * 600 pixels).

If we look carefully at the task–virtual window pattern (Figure 6.8A or 7.2), we notice that the tasks often use two virtual windows at the same time. As an example, the booking task has this pattern:

▨ Subtask 1 and the start of subtask 2 use vwRooms and vwFindGuest.

▨ The end of subtask 2 and subtask 3 use vwRooms and vwStay.

Checkin and Change room have the same pattern. But we can have only one page on the screen at a time. What to do? Let the user flick back and forth between two pages during these subtasks? No, it would be a better idea to combine two virtual windows into one page. Figure 7.5A illustrates how Book and Checkin first use the page containing vwRooms+vwFindGuest, and later vwRooms+vwStay. In total, we end up with four final *pages*.

Fig 7.5 A Page plan, single-page platform

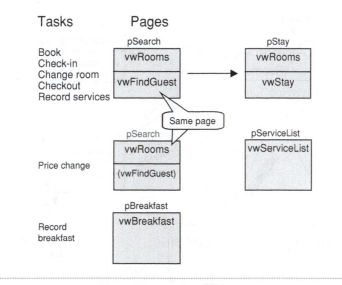

Page plan (single-page platform)

pSearch: Contains vwRooms and vwFindGuest as two frames.
pStay: Contains vwRooms and vwStay as two frames.
pBreakfast: Contains vwBreakfast.
pServiceList: Contains vwServiceList.

Figure 7.5A shows how these pages are used by the tasks. The figure resembles our original plan for the virtual windows (Figure 6.1), but now we talk about final pages, not virtual windows.

Note that vwRooms appears in two pages. This makes it harder for the user to form a mental model where vwRooms is one single gestalt. The graphical design is critical to convey this model. The Rooms part of the two screens should be completely identical, with the same colour, same frame and same position on the screen. The Rooms part should also be a clear gestalt set off from the rest of the screen through colour or frames. (Because of the cramped space on the screen, we cannot use the laws of proximity and good continuation.)

Now, is it realistic to pack two complex virtual windows into one small screen? Surprisingly, yes. We have to pack the fields a bit closer and make the lists a bit shorter, but we can still get space for typical work situations and convey the virtual windows as a mental model. For instance we might set off the top 15 lines for the Rooms part, leaving space for about 10 rooms. More rooms will be visible through some kind of scrolling. The bottom 15 lines are available for searching guests or for a stay, leaving space for around 10 guests or 10 item lines.

Fig 7.5 B State diagram, single-page platform

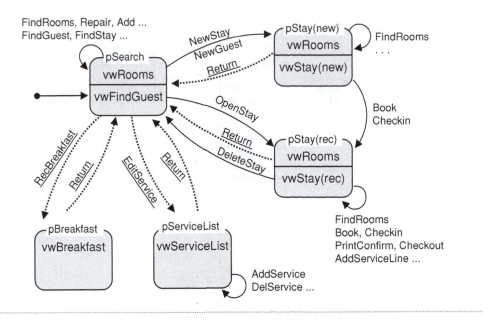

State diagram

At this stage we have four pages that make up the hotel system. The system shows only one of them at a time. How can the user navigate between them? To answer this question we make a *state diagram* of how the screen changes from showing one page to showing another one. Figure 7.5B shows the state diagram for the hotel system.

Each rounded box is a possible state of the physical screen. Basically, we have four states corresponding to the four pages. However, the pStay page can show two different things: (1) A *new stay* that the system hasn't yet recorded because the user is in the middle of a task. (2) A *recorded stay*, corresponding to a booked stay or a checked-in stay. The system behaves quite differently in the two situations, and for this reason we consider each of them a separate state.

As a result we end up with five states. (Yes, you are right, we could split *recorded stay* into *booked* and *checked-in*, thus having six states in total. We don't because the two states are only slightly different – and there is too little space in the figure ☺).

An arrow shows that the screen goes from one state to another as a result of the user activating a certain function. We have written the name of the function on the arrow.

As an example assume that the user is making a booking. He has started in the pSearch page to find the guest and then pushes *NewStay*. The arrow shows that the page now changes to show pStay(new). In this state the user may edit the guest data and push *Book*, and as shown by the arrow, the page changes to show a recorded stay, pStay(rec). The *Book* function must of course check that the guest has got a name and that the user has selected one or more rooms. Otherwise the function refuses to change the state. We might try to show this as further screen states, but it soon becomes too complex. In our case, the mini-spec for *Book* shows what the function must check.

A function may only be used in states where an arrow shows that it can be used. According to the diagram, we can only use *Book* in pStay(new) and in pStay(rec). The latter case is relevant when the guest has booked one room and wants to book another one. It does not make sense to use *Book* when searching for a guest (pSearch) or when recording breakfast (pBreakfast).

Notice the little curly arrow in most of the states. It shows that some functions are permitted in this state, but don't change to another state. As an example, in the pStay(new) state we can use *FindRooms* without changing the state. In the pStay(rec) state we can use *FindRooms* plus *Book*, *Checkin*, and many other functions without changing state. In Figure 7.5B, we have shown most of the functions except a few that don't change state. In principle, we should show all the earlier semantic and search functions (from Figure 7.1B).

Navigation functions

Above we have mentioned only the semantic and search functions that we knew already. Some of them make the user move from one state to another. To navigate between the pages we need additional functions. They are shown as dotted lines and with underscored function names. As an example, we have added the function *RecBreakfast*. It brings the user from the search page to the breakfast page. The function *Return* brings him back to the search page.

In total, we have added six navigation functions to be able to move between the pages. Notice the *Return* function that we have added to pStay(new). Without it, we could return only to the search page after having booked or checked in. We also need a return without doing anything – somehow deleting the uncompleted stay. We have also allowed the *Return* function from pStay(rec), but in this case it doesn't delete anything. It just closes the stay window. If we want to delete the recorded stay, we have to use *CancelStay*.

Start page. In many systems, there is a start page (or a main menu) where the user selects what to do. We could have made such a page in the hotel system also, adding another state to the system. However, we have no such page. Instead, we use the search page. In many tasks it will be the first page to use, so why not save the user a keystroke – and simplify the system too. Our state diagram shows a black dot with an arrow leading to pSearch. This is the standard way to show the initial state of the system. The system is born out of the black dot and enters the pSearch state.

Do you remember the discussion from section 7.1 about the proper place to put *Book* and *Checkin* – on the rooms window or the stay window? In our page-based design the problem disappeared because *Book* and *Checkin* are available only in pages that show rooms and stay at the same time.

7.6 Multi-page dialogue

On a multi-page platform the workspace may contain several pages at the same time (the pages are often called *windows*). The page design is much easier for the multi-page platform. We can usually make each virtual window a separate page. Before we look at the design procedure, we will see how a multi-page system can support the receptionist.

The left-hand side of Figure 7.6A shows a situation where the receptionist is booking a stay. He uses vwFindGuest to look for regular guests, vwRooms to look for free rooms and vwStay to enter information for the new stay. At the bottom of the physical screen we have shown two icons: breakfast (a plate with knife and fork) and rooms (a bed seen from the end – hard to design icons ☺). These icons are miniature versions of vwBreakfast and vwRooms.

The right-hand side of Figure 7.6A shows a more complex situation where the receptionist is handling several tasks. He was recording breakfast – *vwBreakfast*, but switched to handling a booking arriving by fax – *vwStay(new)*. Then a waiter asked whether someone stayed in room 512 – *vwStay(rec)*. And suddenly a guest arrived and wanted to be checked in – *vwStay(rec)*.

As the example suggests, each page has its own 'life', and there may even be several instances of a page. The user can freely change between them when switching between tasks. As we will see, this means that each page has its own state diagram.

One advantage of the multi-page design is that the user can work concurrently on many tasks. In a reception with many interruptions, this will be very useful. With the single-page design, it is hard to work on many concurrent tasks. If the receptionist is making a complex booking and a guest arrives to check in, the receptionist will have to either complete the booking first, or cancel the booking and redo it later.

Design procedure

a) Make a separate page for each virtual window. If the page is too large to fit on the physical screen, consider using scroll bars or tab forms to reduce the page size. Avoid breaking the page into two; it may make the user believe it is two different objects.

b) If two or more virtual windows are small and normally used together, you may consider making them frames within a single page.

c) Draw a separate state diagram for each page. (There may be several page instances open at the same time. The diagram covers all of them). On the diagram, show all transitions caused by the semantic functions and search functions defined at present. Note that a function may cause state transitions on more than one state diagram at the same time. (See the example in Figure 7.6B.)

d) Review the transitions to check that the user can open and close all pages. Add any missing navigation functions (open and close) to the diagram.

e) Write a final list of functions for each page (see the example in Figure 7.8B). Additionally, you may include the navigation functions in the mini-specs (Figure 7.1C).

Page plan

We will now use the design procedure on the hotel system. Each virtual window becomes a separate page as shown in Figure 7.6B. Notice that some of the pages have several instances (vwStay and vwBreakfast). In the hotel system there is no reason to combine several virtual windows into a single page. For simplicity, we have simply labelled the pages with the name of the virtual window.

State diagrams

Since each page has its own life, it also has its own state diagram. At the top left we have the diagram for vwFindGuest. The black dot with an arrow shows that the page opens when the application starts. We can use various functions in this page, but the state of the page doesn't change. It remains on the screen until the application terminates.

The diagram to the right is more interesting. It shows that vwStay may be in two states, a new stay and a recorded stay. The arrows show that *NewStay* creates a stay page (opens it). The arrow comes out of nothing (the dot) and creates a page in the state vwStay(new). The pile of stay pages shows that there may be more pages of this type. In other words, each activation of *NewStay* will open one more stay page.

Note also that *NewStay* appears in two different diagrams, the one for vwStay and the one for vwFindGuest. The rule is that it works in both pages and changes their state according to their own diagram. Thus vwFindGuest does something – ending up in the same state – and vwStay does something else – creating a new stay page.

The *Book* and *Checkin* functions work in the state vwStay(new) and changes the state to vwStay(rec). In other words, the stay is recorded in the database. *Book* and *Checkin* also work in the state vwStay(rec), but leave the stay in the same state. In this case, the functions add another room to the stay. These details are similar to the behaviour of the pStay page in the single-page solution.

OpenStay works much like *NewStay*. In vwFindGuest it ends up in the same state, in vwStay it creates a new stay page in the state vwStay(recorded).

Navigation functions

Looking at the diagram for vwStay we can see that we need a way to close the pages – a navigation function. We have added a *CloseS* function to vwStay. It makes

Fig 7.6 A Multi-page dialogue

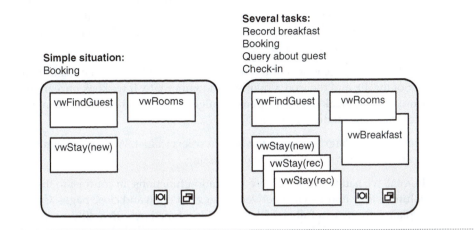

Simple situation:
Booking

Several tasks:
Record breakfast
Booking
Query about guest
Check-in

the page disappear as shown by the bull's eye. It works in state *new* as well as in state *rec*.

At the bottom left we have the state diagram for vwRooms. It can be in two states: as an icon or as a page. We need navigation functions to open and close the page. When

Fig 7.6 B State diagram, multi-page platform

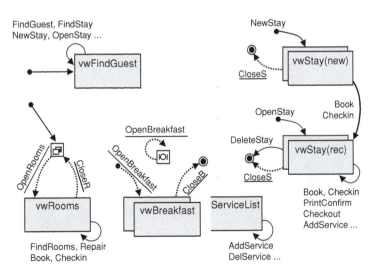

it is an icon and we activate *OpenRooms* (click on the icon), the vwRooms page appears. When we activate *Close* (click on the cross in the corner of the window), it becomes an icon again. Strictly speaking, the diagram says that the icon disappears when the page opens and appears again when it closes. The diagram also shows that the page is iconized when the system starts.

The breakfast page works differently. If we click on the icon, a breakfast page pops out of the air, and the icon remains in the same state. If we click once more on the icon, another breakfast page opens (it might be for another day). When we close a breakfast page, it disappears.

The last state diagram shows the life of vwServiceList. We have shown only part of it, and leave it to you to add what is missing.

In total, we had to introduce five navigation functions. In contrast to the single-page solution, they don't switch between pages but open and close pages. Can you explain why we carefully labelled each *Close* function with a different name in the multi-page design? (In the single-page design we called all returns *Return* no matter which state it returned from.)

Function list. At this point in time we have identified all the functions in the hotel system – semantic, search and navigation. We have listed them in Figure 7.8B. We might also update the mini-specs in Figure 7.1C to include the navigation functions.

Now, what happened to the old discussion about the proper place to put *Book* and *Checkin* – on the rooms page or the stay page? In the single-page design it didn't matter because there was only one page at any time. Now there are several. We have allowed these functions in both pages, but according to the mini-specs, the system warns the user if he uses them from vwRooms while there are several open stays. Actually, usability tests show that users expect the function to be available in both pages.

7.7　More about state diagrams

State diagrams are classical diagrams in the IT world and they are part of UML (Unified Modeling Language). Web developers use similar diagrams to show the transition from page to page, but call them *flow charts*. Most Web developers would be very confused if you talked about state diagrams.

In the standard notation for state diagrams you show each state as a rounded box with the state name inside, but in our figures we have also indicated the page content. We don't always show the page states as rounded boxes, for instance when the page is the same as a virtual window (multi-page designs).

We can define the states in more or less detail. We might for instance distinguish between stay pages in the states new, booked, checked in, checked out, cancelled. For the rooms screen, we might distinguish between room selected and no room selected. In this way our diagram could express many of the rules we now have in the mini-specs, but it would become much larger. The level we have chosen in Figures 7.5B and 7.6B is reasonable for our goal – to identify the necessary navigation functions.

A state diagram gives an excellent overview of pages and functions. When making the diagram, we force ourselves to consider many special situations we didn't cover when walking through the tasks. We also get a good overview of the paths through the system, whether everything can be reached, and whether we can return back home.

State diagrams can grow quite large, for instance the flow chart for a large Web site. In that case we have to split it into several pages of paper.

Modal dialogue – call/return

In our multi-page example, the user could freely move to any page or open it at any time. However, some parts of the user dialogue may be more restricted: When the user opens a page, he has to close it before he can work in other pages. This is called a *modal dialogue* because the user enters a restricted mode of working. A page behaving in this way is often called a *dialogue box*.

Figure 7.7A shows an example. Assume we make a calendar page from which the user can choose a date. The calendar page is a dialogue box. It may be useful from the FindGuest page as well as the Rooms page. The figure shows this dialogue as a state diagram to the left. From the vwFindGuest page, the user can open the calendar box and move to the calendar state. In this state vwFindGuest is still visible, but not accessible. From the calendar state he can move back only to vwFindGuest – thereby closing the dialogue box. From the vwRooms page, the user can move to the calendar box in the same way. Actually, the two calendar boxes on the diagram are the same page, but in two different states. There is no way to move directly from the first calendar state to the second.

This dialogue-box pattern is so frequent that we use a short-hand notation for it, as shown to the right. We show the dialogue box only once. The box can be 'called' from vwFindGuest or vwRooms through the double arrow. The calendar box remembers where to return. We don't show the return as a separate arrow.

You can consider this pattern a modal open-close, a call-return or a hyperlink-back pattern.

Modelling domain entities

The state diagrams we have used above describe the screen states, but we can describe the states of many other things, for instance entities in the application domain. As an example, we might describe the possible states of a hotel stay and how the functions change the state. Figure 7.7B shows this as a state diagram.

A stay is created by the Book function and is then in the *Booked* state. The Checkin function transforms it to the *In* state and the Checkout function to the *Out* state. When a guest turns up at the reception and asks for a free room, the receptionist may check him in without booking, thereby creating a new stay in the *In* state. The guest may also cancel a booking. This might be handled as deletion of the stay, but receptions like to keep track also of cancelled bookings. As a result, the Cancel function transforms the booked stay to the *Cancelled* state.

In the figure all of this is shown as black arrows. They describe what can happen to the domain entity a 'stay'. Notice that everything progresses nicely in one direction from birth to cancellation or checkout. However, in practice, things are not always recorded correctly. Receptionists may by mistake cancel a booking or checkout a wrong guest. This is why we need Undo functions. When we add them, the receptionist can move back and forth in the diagram.

Another issue is what happens to cancelled or checked-out stays. Should they remain in the computer forever? In principle yes, but in practice we run clean-up procedures every now and then, for instance once a year. The clean-up procedure will, for instance, remove all stays older than five years. We have shown this too on the diagram. (Clean-up will also remove RoomState records, guests that haven't been at the hotel for five years, etc.)

Fig 7.7 A   Modal dialogue – call/return

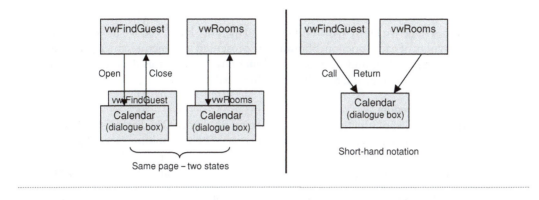

Same page – two states

Short-hand notation

Fig 7.7 B   Domain entity: state diagram for a Stay

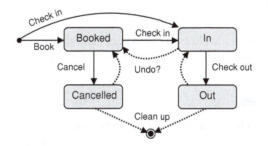

7.8　Function presentation

At this stage we know which functions to include. However, we haven't yet decided the syntax of each function. Should it be presented as a menu item, a push button, a function key, drag-and-drop or a combination? We need this decision in order to finish the prototype. Here is the procedure to deal with it.

Design procedure

a) Write a list of functions for each page on the screen. The list must include all semantic, search and navigation functions. The information is available from the state diagram and the mini-specs. Some functions may be 'global', meaning that they don't belong to any specific page. (See the example list in Figure 7.8B.)

b) For each function decide its presentation form, for instance push button, menu item, drag-and-drop. (See the possibilities below.) Write the decision and maybe a short justification in the list. (It is necessary to know the platform on which the system will be running.)

c) Decide how to handle functions that cannot be activated at present, for instance greying them, hiding them, giving error messages. (See the discussion below.)

d) If the system is also to support experienced users, decide how to handle the gradual transition from using mouse to using keyboard.

Presentation choices

Figure 7.8A is a tentative list of the possible ways we can activate a function. There are probably several more. I have never seen a systematic investigation of advantages and disadvantages of these forms, so the following is based on my own casual observations of users over the years.

Push buttons look a bit different on the different platforms. A button is, for instance, rounded on the Mac, rectangular on Microsoft Windows, a fancy design on the Web. This has little influence on our choice, however. The important thing is that the button is labelled with a text suggesting what the button does. We can also show the short-cut key that activates the function. Users see Mac and Microsoft Windows buttons immediately. The Web buttons are more or less clear, depending on the fancy design. Main weakness: Buttons take precious screen space.

Icons take much less space than push buttons, and many users love their nice look. Weaknesses: Users can rarely guess what an icon means unless they have learned the icon in another context. There is no space for showing the equivalent short-cut key, and as a result users tend to become mouse-dependent. Aware of these problems, some developers make pop-up help (control tips) that pops up when the mouse rests a while on the icon, and

Fig 7.8A Function presentation

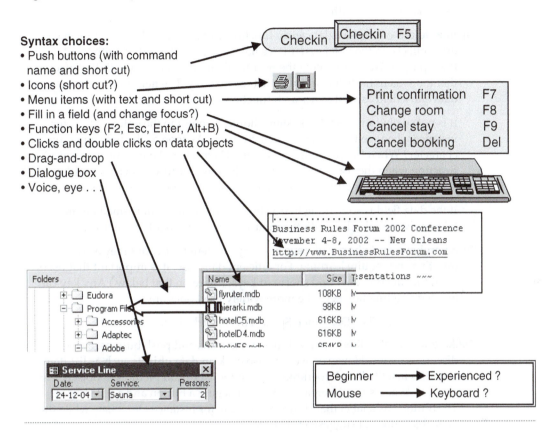

Syntax choices:
- Push buttons (with command name and short cut)
- Icons (short cut?)
- Menu items (with text and short cut)
- Fill in a field (and change focus?)
- Function keys (F2, Esc, Enter, Alt+B)
- Clicks and double clicks on data objects
- Drag-and-drop
- Dialogue box
- Voice, eye . . .

explain what the icon does. The tips are annoying to wait for and the user gets only a single explanation at a time – no overview. Some developers let a help line at the bottom of the screen explain the icon, a habit inherited from old text-based mainframe screens. Most users don't notice these bottom-line texts at all.

Menu items allow a lot of functions within little space. When the menu unfolds, the texts give a good overview of what the entire menu does. We don't just see a soda-straw text for one point at a time. We can also show the short-cut key that activates the function. Weakness: There is no overview when the menu is collapsed. When the menu is at the top line of the window, it is far away from the object it works on, so many users don't notice that the menu items are available.

Pop-up menus appear when the user clicks on the object he wants to do something with. This helps the user mentally connect the functions with the object. However, many users never figure out that they can click here. In the

Microsoft Windows world you have to click the right mouse button – what many users have trouble with.

Fill in a field is of course a data entry function, but it may at the same time have other effects. In the hotel system, we have a breakfast window with the date at the top right. We might allow the user to fill in this date field with the effect that the system finds the breakfast list for that day. The field is in this way a data entry field as well as a search function.

It is not so obvious *when* the system should respond to the entered data, for instance when we type a long search criterion. As soon as the user types any character? When the cursor leaves the field? Or when the user presses *Enter*? Reacting when the user presses *Enter* is dubious because in many cases *Enter* will activate the default button on the screen, often to the surprise of the user.

If the data field is something like a check box, the problem is small because it takes only a single click with the mouse or the space bar to fill in the field.

Function keys and short-cut keys are very efficient to use, but they are not intuitive and require learning. For efficient daily use, it is important that users learn the function keys and short-cut keys. (More on that below.) Any key can be used as a function key. The more widely used ones are

F1, F2, . . . , Esc, Del, Enter, Space, Alt+B, Ctrl+B, etc.

Clicks and double clicks are used to activate icons and push buttons, as we discussed above. However, we can also click on **data objects** such as list items (e.g. files in a file list), hyperlinks (e.g. on the Web) and pictures of objects (e.g. a valve). What is the difference between clicking a button and a data object? The button has a label that shows a function, for instance *Open Stay*, while the data object doesn't suggest a function.

The items in the file list, for instance, illustrate files as icons with their name, size and other attributes (Figure 7.8A). An item such as *hotelC5.mdb* doesn't indicate a function called *hotelC5*. It indicates an object and clicking on it might mean 'Open this object'. Similarly, a hyperlink on the Web should indicate an object, for instance another Web page such as Latest news. Clicking on it will bring us to this Web page. Sometimes you see Web designers use the hyperlink format for a function such as Send. If this was a true hyperlink, clicking on it would bring us to the 'Send page'. The designer intended that clicking would send some data to the Web server.

Weaknesses of clicking on data objects: It can be hard to see where it is possible to click. If you, for instance, click on the *Name* heading in the Explorer file list, the system sorts the files by name. If you click on the *Size* heading it sorts them by size. Few users figure this out on their own. In the Microsoft Windows world it is a frequent problem whether to click or double-click. In contrast, the Web works with single clicks. Finally, there is no way to show the short-cut key, thus making the user a mouse addict.

Drag-and-drop is excellent for drawing where you move shapes around on the screen. It also seems clever for functions with two arguments, for instance booking a room. The booking function has two arguments, a room and a guest. The user could drag the guest to the room – or is it more polite to drag the room to the guest? Weaknesses: In many cases drag-and-drop is not so intuitive as some designers believe. It seems most intuitive in cases where the function means a physical move of an object, for instance moving a file from one folder to another. But if the move is not really a move, but a copy, it is no longer intuitive. An example is the metaphor of dragging the document to the printer to have it printed. Users tend to be afraid that it now disappears from the folder – how to get it back? As with clicking, it is not easy to see what you can drag, and there is no way to show the short-cut key.

Dialogue boxes are small windows that allow the user to specify parameters for a function. The function is activated through a menu item, a push button or some other function presentation, and the dialogue box pops up. The user specifies how the function is to be made, and when he clicks OK or closes the dialogue box, the function is carried out. The figure shows a dialogue box for adding a service line to the hotel guest's account. The receptionist will select the function 'Add Service Line', and the box pops up.

Dialogue boxes may be necessary for complex functions, for instance setting a page format very accurately. However, they are often used for entering some persistent data that could just as well be entered into a virtual window. The *ServiceLine* box is an example of this. The user might just as well enter the service line in the stay window. According to the law of object permanence, the user creates a mental model of where the data is stored. If the user sees the data only in the dialogue box, he easily creates an incorrect mental model of where it is really stored.

Voice, eye, etc. For all the functions above, you use your hands to carry it out. There are alternatives, however. You may speak to the system. This is still a difficult technology, but it has been applied in factories for many years where users have both hands busy with other things while they speak a command or a code number to the computer. The set of commands is very limited and not like natural speech at all.

The technique is maturing, however, and today you can get a good text processor where you speak the sentences you want to enter. You may also encounter public voice-response systems where you can choose options by saying them.

Eye-movement sensors are another alternative input medium. The computer senses where the user is looking and reacts to a wink or a stare of a certain duration. It is a very slow input medium, but has some use for severely handicapped people.

There are other input media too, for instance gloves that can feel the movement of your hand. They are for instance used for manipulating dangerous substances inside a glass box. The user moves his hands as if he was gripping and moving the substances. A robot inside the box moves its 'hands' in the same way. Another example is a 3-D mouse where you move a pencil suspended in six wires, and the computer senses where in 3-D space you are pointing.

Beginners versus experienced

When a user gets a new IT system, he is a novice with this system. If he spends much time with it, he gradually becomes experienced and wants higher efficiency.

What can the user do to become more efficient? One important rule is to use the keyboard rather than the mouse. The keyboard is much faster – and it stresses the arm and shoulder far less.

The transition from novice to experienced is gradual. Typically, the novice is finding his way by means of the mouse. Gradually he gets experience with some functions of the system and starts using the keyboard there. Later he uses the keyboard for all daily tasks, but when he every now and then gets into unknown territory, he reverts to a novice and starts using the mouse again.

It is very important to support this gradual transition. We can of course write a manual or provide on-line help that explains the short-cut keys, but users rarely learn it that way. The best is to show the short cut on the screen where the mouse-based functions are. The user is then reminded all the time, particularly with things he often uses.

Figure 7.8A shows the two best ways to do it: as a push button or a menu point labelled with the short-cut key. Microsoft Windows uses a convention of underlining a letter in the function name, for instance Checkout, and then using Alt+o as the short-cut key.

As mentioned above, icons don't support this gradual transition and locks the user into a semi-experienced role. (Constantine and Lockwood, 1999, has an excellent section about going from novice to expert.)

Function presentation, hotel system

Armed with all this theory, it is time to continue the design of the hotel system. First we make a function list for each of the windows (pages) we had in the state diagram. The final list is shown in Figure 7.8B and it includes semantic, search and navigation functions.

We have to know the platform to use. We assume that it will be Microsoft Windows, and more precisely the sub-platform provided by Access. This sub-platform is used in practice by many developers. It is multi-page and works inside a workspace consisting of the Access master window. It has one peculiarity: only the master window can have menus. Menus are not available in the individual pages.

Next we go through the list and determine how each function should be presented. We also consider the transition from mouse to keyboard. The result is shown in Figure 7.8B. Let us look at some examples.

The first function is *FindRooms*. Novices will use it and we want them to become experienced gradually. Conclusion: Use a button and a short-cut key. The button would probably be labelled *F̲ind Room*, with the underscored *F* showing that Alt+F will be the short-cut key. But the figure doesn't say it explicitly. The wording is difficult to determine without seeing the real prototype and trying it out with users. We could have chosen a short-cut key such as F3 and labelled the button *Find Room – F3*, but we have in most cases chosen the standard way to do it in Microsoft Windows. (More on this below.)

The next function is *ChooseRoom*. In an Access world it involves clicking on the proper line. If the user wants to select several rooms, he can do so only if they follow each other on the list. Then he clicks on the first line, holds Shift down and clicks at the last line. All this is fine and users with some Windows experience can do it. However, what about the experienced users? They shouldn't use the mouse. We suggest that *FindRooms* selects the first room on the list, and then the user can move the selection with the cursor keys (up and down) with or without Shift down. The user may also switch to the list using the standard Windows approach for switching between page sections: F6.

The fourth function is *RepairRoom*. It is used only when a room is out of order or has to be renovated. This is not a beginner's function, and we have put the function in a menu on the main window heading. This menu is to be labelled *Rooms* or something similar. There is no need for a special short-cut key. The function is rarely used so that a short-cut saves little time. Still the experienced receptionist can access it with the keyboard – just following the Windows standard of using Alt+R to get to the R̲ooms menu.

The Rooms menu will contain other functions relating to rooms, for instance AddRoom, DeleteRoom, OpenRooms window. We have designed a similar menu for stays, for breakfast and for service prices.

Figure 7.8B shows a couple of lines labelled *Goto field*. They explain how the user will move from one field to another. The novice user will click on the field he wants to edit, but what about the experienced user? He should use the keyboard only, and Microsoft Windows offers a built-in solution – the Tab key. The user can go to the next field with Tab and to the previous one with Shift+Tab. The designer can easily specify the Tab sequence. The user can switch between screen sections with F6, and between Forms (pages) with Ctrl+F6. Although a standard in Windows, this is not intuitive. Some kind of on-line help or documentation is needed. Chapter 12 discusses this in detail.

Tab keys are fine for routine data entry where the user fills in a form field by field, but for the hotel system he needs to jump among the fields. Experienced users hate to Tab many times, so we have decided to use another built-in method: Underline a letter in the field label in the same way as for buttons. The user can then use Alt+P to go to the _Phone_ field.

You may look at the other functions to see what kind of design arguments we have used to arrive at the presentation.

Alternative short-cut keys

In the design above, we have as far as possible used the built-in methods in Access for short-cut keys. When a letter is underscored, the user can activate that item with Alt+letter. However, there are a couple of problems with this method:

a) Novices don't figure out on their own that the underscored letters can be used this way.

b) You need two hands to type, for instance Alt+P.

c) The actual short-cut letters are very unstable over time.

When the labels change as a result of usability tests or when a new field or button is added later, two items may need the same letter. The designer either has to reassign the letters for several items (expert users hate to relearn all these short cuts) or may have to use strange labels and short cuts such as

| Print confirm | or even | Print confirmx |

All other letters in Print confirm have another meaning already. These short-cut keys are also very inconvenient if the product is to be translated into several languages.

For the hotel system, we considered a more stable approach. Buttons would be activated with a function key and labelled like this:

| Print confirm........F5 |

This avoids all three problems above. Text fields would still be activated with Alt+letter, but be labelled like this:

A. Last name
B. Street

The solution is not perfect, but it avoids problem c, and partially problem a. In the first prototype (the hand-drawn mock-up) we used function keys.

To illustrate this approach, we have used the alternative short-cut keys for the vwStay page in Figure 7.8B.

Fig 7.8 B Function presentation, hotel system

vwRooms	Syntax	Reason
FindRooms	Button+std.shortcut	Used also by novices. Gradual transition to experienced. Std.shortcut uses underlined letter.
ChooseRoom	FindRooms chooses first+Cursor keys	Follow Microsoft Access standard for selecting a range of rooms.
ResetSearch	Button+std.shortcut	Used also by novices. Transition to . . .
RepairRoom	Menu: Rooms+std	Rarely used. Specialists.
UndoRepair	Menu: Rooms+std	Rarely used. Specialists.
AddRoom	Menu: Rooms+std	Rarely used. Specialists.
DeleteRoom	Menu: Rooms+Del	Rarely used. Specialists.
Book	Button+std.shortcut	Used also by novices. Transition to . . .
Checkin	Button+std.shortcut	Used also by novices. Transition to . . .
OpenRooms	Menu: Rooms+std	Microsoft Windows standard would say View menu. Usability test!
CloseR	CloseIcon, Alt+F4	Follow Microsoft Windows standard.
Goto field	Shortcut on label	Standard short cut uses underlined letter in label. F6 switches between screen sections.

vwFindGuest		
FindGuest	Button+std.shortcut	Used also by novices. Transition to . . .
FindStay	Button+std.shortcut	Used also by novices. Transition to . . .
SelectLine	Find chooses first + Cursor keys	Follow Microsoft Access standard for selecting a record.
ResetSearch	Button+std.shortcut	Used also by novices. Transition to . . .
OpenStay	Button+std.shortcut+ Enter	Used also by novices. Transition to . . .
NewStay	Button+std.shortcut	Used also by novices. Transition to . . .
NewGuest	Button+std.shortcut	Used also by novices. Transition to . . .
Goto field	Shortcut on label	Standard short cut uses underlined letter in label. F6 switches between screen sections.

vwStay	(Alternative shortcut keys)	
Book	Button+F3	Used also by novices. Transition to . . .
Checkin	Button+F4	(same)
PrintConfirm	Button+F5	(same)
PrintGuestAcct	Button+F7	(same)
Checkout	Button+F8	(same)
CancelStay	Menu: Stay	Desirable as button, but too many of them already.
DeleteRoomLine	Menu: Stay + Del	Follow Microsoft Access standard
AddServiceLine	Menu: Stay Type in empty line	Follow Microsoft Access standard
DelServiceLine	Menu: Stay + Del	Follow Microsoft Access standard
CloseStay	CloseIcon, Alt+F4	Follow Microsoft Windows standard
Goto field	Shortcut bullet	E.g.: A. Last name

vwServiceList		
AddService	Menu: ServPrices Type in empty line	Rarely used. Specialists.
DeleteService	Menu: ServPrices+Del	Rarely used. Specialists.
PrintServiceList	Menu: ServPrices	Rarely used. Specialists.
OpenServiceList	Menu: ServPrices	Microsoft Windows standard? Usability test!
CloseServiceList	CloseIcon, Alt+F4	Follow Microsoft Windows standard.

vwBreakfast		
OpenBreakfast	Menu: Breakfast+std	Microsoft Windows standard? Usability test!
PrintBreakfList	Menu: Breakfast+std	Might be button, but visible in menu when opening list.
CloseB	CloseIcon, Alt+F4	Follow Microsoft Windows standard.

Global		
Undo	Menu: Undo button	Might be button in vwStay too for visibility. Try without.

7.9 Error messages and inactive functions

At any given time, the user may only activate some of the functions. The remaining functions are *inactive*. How can we tell the user about it? Here are some possibilities:

Greying. We may make inactive functions grey. This applies to push buttons and menu points, as well as data entry fields. The rule is that things must always be visible in order that the user doesn't get confused because things suddenly disappear (the law of object permanence). However, the inactive things must be grey.

What is grey and what is not reflects the current state of the dialogue. As an example, in the hotel system the stay window has a lot of functions, *Book, Checkin, Checkout*, etc. Some of them work only when the stay is new, some when it is booked, etc. The greying might reflect this.

Greying is fine to remind the user of what is allowed, but not always helpful. I often experience users looking at a grey menu point saying, *Yes I am not allowed to use this one, but why not?* They may even try to click the menu point anyway in order to get an explanation. A nice solution would be to allow users to click on grey functions and then through an error message explain what is wrong and what to do.

Hiding. We may hide inactive functions completely. This can be very confusing to the user because he cannot see the familiar functions anymore. It may also be confusing to the user who hasn't seen the functions before. He gets no indication that these functions exist and that he may activate them in some way.

Hiding functions may be necessary if there are many functions. The ordinary hierarchical menus are the standard way to do it. The functions don't take screen space until the user tries to use them.

Error messages. We may show the inactive function without greying or other indications that it is inactive. When the user activates the function, he will get an error message. This is an excellent possibility to tell the user what is wrong and how to correct it. Error messages are also much easier to program than greying. If a time-consuming check is needed for the computer to decide whether a function is active, greying the right menu items will take a long time because the computer has to check all menu items to see which ones to grey. Error messages are much simpler since only the chosen function has to be checked.

The disadvantage of error messages rather than greying is that the user doesn't get an overview of what is possible. He has to use trial and error if he doesn't know what to do. A combination of greying and error messages would be the ideal.

Beep. We may let the computer beep when the user tries to activate an inactive function. This is very common but by far the worst solution. The user cannot see in advance what is possible, and the beep doesn't tell him what is wrong and what to do. Many people turn the sound off completely in office environments to avoid disturbing others – and to avoid being ridiculed for their mistakes. In this case, the user doesn't even get an indication that 'you cannot do this now'.

Guidelines for error messages

Although error messages have many advantages, they are hard to phrase. Many error messages are impossible for the user to understand. Some may even be insulting to the user. Here are some traditional rules for good error messages (see also the heuristic rules and the example in section 14.2).

Good error messages
The good error messages are

1 Friendly. They don't blame the user. They might even place the responsibility with the system.

2 Precise. They explain what is wrong, why the system cannot carry out the function.

3 Constructive. They explain what the user might do to solve the problem.

4 Prevented. They cannot occur, for instance because the user has to choose a value from a list rather than typing in the value as a text. Or because the menu item was grey and couldn't be activated at all. In the latter case, prevention is not that good because the user cannot get an explanation why the function is inactive.

Figure 7.9 shows examples of error messages. Imagine that a guest arrives at the reception and asks for a room. The guest is satisfied with the price and wants to be checked in. The receptionist opens a fresh Stay window, records the name and address of the guest and then clicks *Checkin*. In this situation the computer will check that the receptionist has selected a free room and a reasonable period of days. If this is not the case, the system will show an error message. From the programmer's point of view, a simple way out is to cover all of this with the error message:

```
Illegal room selection
```

From the user's point of view this is not friendly. The message suggests that the user has done something illegal. Nor is it precise – what is wrong?

In order to give a more precise error message, the computer has to distinguish the different causes of the problem. Figure 7.9 shows the relevant messages in three cases:

A) If the user hasn't selected a room at all:

```
No room is selected
```

B) If the user has selected a room and a period, but it is not free in the period:

```
The room is not free in that period
```

C) If the user has selected a room and a period, but the period doesn't start today:

```
You can only check guests in today
```

These messages are much more precise, and the user gets some idea what he might do to solve the problem. Message B and C would be even more precise if they also said which dates the user had selected. What about friendliness? The messages are not truly friendly, but neutral. Should we make them more friendly, for instance

```
Sorry, but the room is not free in the period you have
selected
```

A decade ago, HCI specialists suggested such wording, but today it sounds a bit silly. People know they are talking to an unintelligent computer. They don't expect a human behaviour and prefer a brief statement rather than a long story.

However, the messages are not constructive. They don't suggest a solution. In case A, the user hasn't selected a room at all. Maybe the user doesn't know how to do it. The figure shows a message that briefly explains what to do:

```
No room is selected. Select it from the Rooms window
```

A novice user would think, *Aha, that is how*. A seasoned user might think, *Yes I know, it was a slip*. For message C, it is harder to be constructive, because the computer cannot guess what the user intended. He might have selected tomorrow rather than today, or he might have clicked *Checkin* rather than *Book*. The message tries to help the novice out with this message:

```
You can only check guests in today. Book instead? (Yes/No)
```

In this case the suggestion might give the novice a good idea, but in general such questions can be quite hard to answer for a typical user. It may then be better to just explain what is wrong and leave the solution to the user. What is the best? As always in user interface design there is only one safe answer: *Make a usability test!*

Do you think we are through with the possible messages in this case? Oh, no. What if the user has selected a period that starts earlier than today? In this case the message `'Book instead?'` would be meaningless since the user cannot book a room yesterday. And what if both cases B and C apply: The room isn't free in the period and furthermore the period doesn't start today. Should the system complain about one or the other? It all depends on what the user had in mind, but the computer cannot know. And what about all the other cases where *Checkin* is used? For instance a booked stay or a checked-in stay? We leave this as an exercise (see Chapter 17).

Fig 7.9   Good and bad error messages

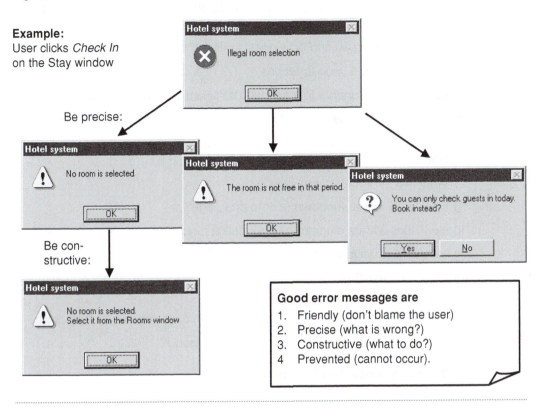

Example:
User clicks *Check In*
on the Stay window

Be precise:

Be con-
structive:

Good error messages are
1. Friendly (don't blame the user)
2. Precise (what is wrong?)
3. Constructive (what to do?)
4 Prevented (cannot occur).

Conclusion

- The four rules above are guidelines only. In specific cases, there may be good reasons for deviating from a rule.

- Only a usability test (or an understandability test) can reveal whether an error message is good.

- It is hard to show precise, constructive error messages. Errors can have many technical causes that we have to distinguish in the message. Further, the computer can rarely guess what the user really intended to do.

Test yourself

a) How do we find out which semantic functions are needed?

b) How do we handle the situation where the user wants to do things in different sequences depending on circumstances?

c) If we had chosen virtual windows differently, for instance split the Stay window into a Guest detail window and a Stay detail window, would we still end up with the same functions?

d) What is a mini-spec and how does it differ from a program?

e) Why do we need undo functions?

f) Can we always undo a function with sufficient programming effort?

g) Why do we need navigation functions?

h) What is the difference between a single-page platform and a multi-page platform?

i) What is a part-screen workspace?

j) How many virtual windows go into one page?

k) How does a state diagram help us define functions?

l) Mention five ways to present functions.

m) What are the issues when supporting beginners and experienced users at the same time?

n) Mention four ways to indicate that a function cannot be used right now.

o) What is needed for an error message to be good?

Design exercises. See Chapter 17.

8

Prototypes and defect correction

Highlights

- Put the pieces together into a prototype.

- Usability tests and defect correction. How to cure the defects.

- Transition to programming and testing.

- Defect tracking.

- Key exercise: Finish the design prototype, test it and suggest cures of the defects.

In this chapter we compose the prototype from virtual windows, functions and page plan. We show how it worked in the hotel case, what usability tests revealed, and how we dealt with the defects.

We also discuss the real system based on the prototype. Finally we explain a systematic way to handle defects.

8.1   The systematic prototype

At this stage we have all the parts for making a good prototype: The virtual windows show the graphical appearance of the pages. The function presentation list gives the functions for each page and the graphical appearance of them. The mini-specs show what each function must do. Here is the procedure to make the prototype.

Design procedure

a) Decide which kind of prototype to use (hand-drawn mock-up, tool-drawn mock-up, screen prototype, functional prototype). Usually, a hand-drawn mock-up is the best (see the discussion in section 2.4).

b) Make a full graphical version of each page (application screen). The input to this is:

   ■ the graphical version of the virtual windows

   ■ the page plan (section 7.5 or 7.6)

   ■ the function presentations (section 7.8)

   ■ the list of defects collected during the systematic design

c) If the prototype is some kind of mock-up, draw the pages with empty data fields. Copy the pages and fill in the data needed for usability testing. If the prototype is functional, fill in the necessary data in the database.

d) Make the necessary menus. For a mock-up, the menus will be on paper slips. The input to this is the function presentations (section 7.8).

e) Make message boxes for all error messages. The input to this is the mini-specs for the functions. They should tell you the errors that might occur. (It is hard to foresee all error situations at this stage. Make also empty message boxes that you might fill in during usability testing.)

f) Make drop-down lists for combo boxes, dialogue boxes, help texts and other pieces that the user may see.

According to the virtual window method, we have only made understandability tests of the *virtual windows* at this stage. Now it is time for usability tests of the prototype.

Evaluation and usability testing

g) You may make heuristic evaluation of the prototype to find potential problems (see section 1.5). Remember that many of these problems will be false – they may not hamper real users. So use your own judgement to decide what to correct at this point. (In contrast, the problems found at usability tests are not debatable.)

h) Run usability tests of the prototype (see the short version in section 1.4 or the long one in Chapter 13).

If the virtual windows have been tested for understandability and revised accordingly, most usability problems at this stage should be function names, error messages and other details. Some problems may be harder, however.

i) Try to find the cause of each usability defect (see the discussion in section 8.4). Consider various solutions and revise the prototype. In special cases it may be necessary to make functional prototypes of some parts of the user interface (see example below).

j) Run usability tests again until the result meets the usability requirements or is deemed acceptable.

k) Add the remaining usability defects to the 'official' defect list.

Example

Let us see how these procedures worked for the hotel system.

Choice of prototype. Which kind of prototype should we use? We decided to use a tool-based mock-up with Microsoft Access as the 'drawing tool'. If this had been the first prototype, it would be dubious to invest the effort of making it with a tool. Even after the systematic design, too many radical changes might be needed. A hand-drawn mock-up would be faster to make and easier to throw away.

In the hotel case, however, we had already made a hand-drawn mock-up at an early stage (section 2.3) and usability tested it. We judged that we were so close to a good prototype that it would pay to make a tool-based mock-up. This would also help us become more familiar with Access, which would be the platform for the final system.

Graphical version. Figure 8.1 shows how we have combined virtual windows and function presentation into a tool-based mock-up. (The version shown is number 2 – revised after a usability test.) The mock-up had empty data fields. We used paper copies of the pages and filled them in by hand for the usability tests. Notice that we also had menus and drop-down lists available, and we had a number of empty message boxes ready for *ad hoc* use during the usability tests. The test team filled in an empty message box whenever an unforeseen situation arose. They saved these *ad hoc* boxes to guide the later programming.

Dealing with earlier defects

While making the prototype, we also tried to deal with the usability defects we had found during the early usability test and the later systematic design. Let us have a look at the major differences between the early hand-drawn mock-up and the tool-based one:

■ There are no menus on the individual pages, but a single main menu. This main menu has a drop-down menu for each of the screens. In Access, it is impossible to have a menu in each application screen (called 'Form' in Access language).

Fig 8.1 Tool-based mock-up

Continued

- We don't use function keys (F2, etc.) as in the first prototype. This is possible in Access, but quite cumbersome. We decided to give the built-in mechanism a try: an underlined letter on a button denotes a short cut. For instance, the F in *Find* means that Alt+F activates that button. You can use the same mechanism for field labels. For instance, the Y in *Stay No.* means that Alt+Y will move the cursor to that field. One problem with this is that novice users rarely find out about it by themselves, but once they are told, the path to proficiency is easy. Pop-up help on the central screens will tell the user about it. (This actually helped most users after some time.)

- We tried new names for the criteria fields on the *Find Guest* window: *Name part* and *Address part*, to suggest to the user that they shouldn't enter the entire name or address. (This turned out not to help at all. Most users still entered the entire name.) We ended up with the version on the figure, *Last name* and *Street*, and it helped some users.

Fig 8.1   Tool-based mock-up *(Continued)*

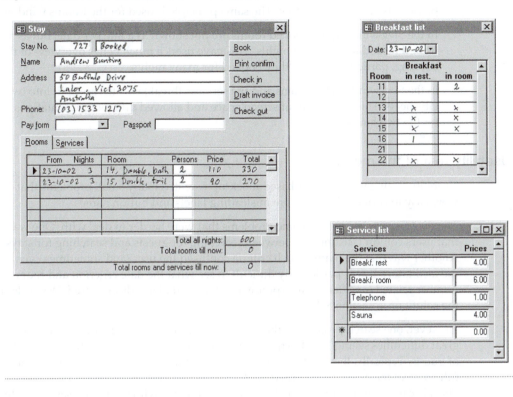

- The *Find Guest* window now has a simpler title than the old *Find Guest/Stay*. However, it has two search buttons: one for finding a stay (for instance when a guest checks in after having booked) and one for finding a guest (e.g. when a regular guest calls to make a new booking). (This turned out not to help at all. Users still couldn't see the difference.)

- The *Rooms* window had two date fields – *From* and *To* – but the *To* field was ambiguous. Was it the last night the guest stayed or the departure date? When listening to receptionists, we noticed that they talked about the departure date and the number of nights. They also often checked with the guest whether these dates were Saturday, Sunday, etc. To support this, the window allows the user to enter either the departure date or the number of nights. The system would then compute the other field and also show the corresponding days of the week.

- The *New Stay* window and the *Stay* window are combined into one. This makes the user's mental model simpler. Actually, design rule 1 for virtual windows could have told us so much earlier. The system gives feedback on the state of the stay through a heading field and through the list of booked rooms on the Stay window.

- The *Stay* window has the most used functions as buttons rather than as menu points. This helped users a lot. The same principle is used for the Rooms window.

- In the *Stay* window, the booked rooms are not shown as a line per date, but as a from-date and a number of nights. This gave users a much better overview of the booking, particularly when they booked for many nights.

- In the *Stay* window, the rooms and the services (breakfast, etc.) are split into two tab-sheets. This saved a lot of screen space and allowed different presentations for the two kinds of things.

Usability test of the mock-up

Usability testing with the tool-based mock-up revealed many small problems that were easy to correct. Examples are misleading labels and button names.

The *Find Guest* window had some problems that were harder to deal with. One was that users couldn't distinguish between searching for guests and searching for stays. Another was that the many search criteria confused the user (and sometimes even the facilitator). It was particularly difficult to see what the date criterion and room number related to. After a few experiments, these problems disappeared. We explain the solutions in section 8.2.

However, one search problem in the *Find Guest* window didn't go away. Users had great difficulties seeing how the name and address criteria related to the resulting list of guests. Typically, they looked at the first field – the name field – and entered the full name of the guest, then clicked *Find*. Usually the 'system' wouldn't find the guest because the spelling in the database didn't match with what the user typed. In one version, the 'system' looked for a partial match, so that for instance *smi* would match *Smiles Johnston, P. Smith* and *Peter Smidt*. Yet the users entered the full name even though the screen text said *Name part*.

Functional prototype. I had almost given up making the search screen intuitive, but decided to give it a last try with a live search where users got immediate feedback on the criteria they entered. You cannot really try this out on a paper mock-up, so I transformed the tool-based version of the *Find Guest* window into a functional prototype of this single window. I also filled in a substantial number of guests, which took some time. After a few experiments with the functional prototype, I felt I had a solution. What would the usability tests show? Suddenly all users could find the guests without being told how. It felt great.

We recorded all of these problems in a temporary list of usability defects. Most of them disappeared and we only transferred the unresolved defects to the defect list (see Figure 8.3B).

8.2   Programming and testing the system

After usability tests and revisions of the prototype, it is time for the technical implementation: programming and testing of the system.

Technical implementation procedure

a) Program the system. The prototype and the mini-specs are the basis for this. If you have a tool-based mock-up or a partially functional prototype, you may expand it into the final system. However, don't try to reuse the program itself. It was experimental and will probably not be suited for a robust and well-structured professional version.

The programming we talk about here is primarily the part that deals with the user interface. In most systems, a large part of the system will deal with technical matters, for instance interaction with other computer systems. Development of those parts can often progress concurrently with the user interface design.

b) Test the system. The purpose is to find and repair bugs and other defects in the program. Usually, the system is tested part by part. Then integration of parts is tested.

c) When the system is reasonably stable, make one more usability test. The purpose is to find any remaining usability defects – not bugs.

Experience shows that developers often make the user interface slightly different from the one we tested for usability. It may unintentionally cause serious usability problems. As an example, the programmer found an easier way to make some part of the user interface, without seeing the possible consequences for usability. As another example, the creative art designer used colours that looked nice, but spoiled usability. We have even seen cases where the boss started interfering with the design and insisted that it should look in the way he believed would be right.

In all of these cases, only a new usability test can reveal whether critical usability problems crept in.

d) Many things happen after this point: Acceptance testing, user documentation, courses and organizational implementation. Chapter 12 explains about user documentation and a bit about courses, but the other issues are not treated in this book.

The hotel case

After prototyping and usability testing, I programmed the system myself – or rather the demo part that dealt with the user interface. Programming would have been rather straightforward if I had known Access much better, but I encountered many surprising technical problems and problems at the detailed dialogue level.

One problem on the detailed dialogue level was that record lists could be presented in two ways in Access: (1) as subforms (we had used this presentation for the *Find Guest* window in the tool-based mock-up) and (2) as a datasheet (I used this presentation in the final system – Figure 8.2A). The subform presentation allowed more freedom in the presentation, for instance with two or more lines per record. However, it was not suited for easy navigation with the keyboard. It took a long time to find out about these differences and modify the program accordingly.

Figure 8.2A shows the final system in a fully functional demo version. Let us look at the main changes from the tool-based mock-up.

Fig 8.2 A Real system

Continued

Fig 8.2 A Real system (*Continued*)

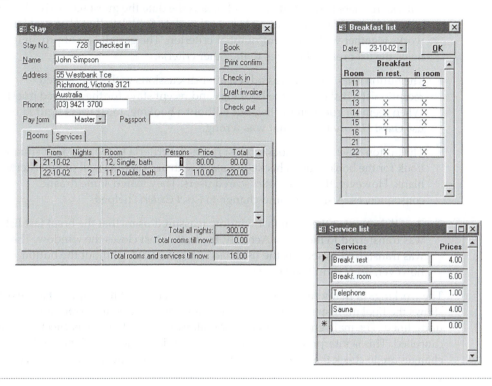

- The *Find Guest* window doesn't ask the user to distinguish between searching for guests and searching for stays. Whatever criteria the user enters, the window shows the stays that match the criteria, followed by other guests that match. In the figure, you see the stays with a stay number and arrival date. Below that you see the guests who have no matching stay.

- The criteria fields on the *Find Guest* window have the labels *Last name* and *Street*. This helped users enter the right kind of information, but actually the system matched whatever they entered against the full name and the full address. A pop-up help (control tip) told them this, and after a while users found out to utilize this feature. For instance, they searched for the zip code by entering it into the street field. And they didn't care whether the name they entered was the first or the last name.

- The *Find Guest* search is live. The figure shows the situation when the user has entered an 's' for the name. As a result the list shows all stays and guests with an 's' somewhere in the name. If the user entered one more letter, the list would immediately shrink, and finally just show the message 'No guests match what you ask for'. This immediate feedback was the main breakthrough in making this screen intuitive.

- The *Find Guest* window has got a date field that works together with the name criteria. It is labelled *Arrival date* and means the date the guest has arrived or is expected to arrive. The window has another date field, labelled *Night*, which works together with the room-number criterion. The gestalt law of proximity helps the user relate the dates to the other criteria.

- The button *Guest History* was added after discussions with experienced receptionists. It shows all the bookings and recent stays for the selected guest. When seeing a guest on the list, but without a booking, most users figured out to use *Guest History* to see what was wrong.

- The button *Reset* on the mock-up just resets the criteria to the standard situation: Look for the booked and checked-in stays with arrival today, all other criteria blank. However, the name *Reset* scared users. They feared some drastic consequences. A simple name-change to *Reset Criteria* helped.

- An *OK* button on the Breakfast window reassured users that the breakfast list was transferred to the stays. Actually, the button just closes the window. The data was transferred as soon as the user had entered a field. Without the button, however, users didn't feel too sure.

The workings of many functions had changed from the first mini-specs. Figure 8.2B shows the final mini-spec for *Book*. The changes from the first mini-spec are underlined. The main change is that *Book* is allowed when the stay is checked in or cancelled. This is interpreted as undoing the check-in or the cancellation. Other changes are to check that the period makes sense; to warn the user when his action is

Fig 8.2 B Mini-spec for the Book function, final version

vwStay (changes are underlined)

Book: The function can be used in <u>these</u> situations:

1   vwStay is a new stay (unrecorded), one or more <u>free</u> rooms are selected, <u>the period starts not earlier than today</u>:
Record Stay record and RoomStates for the selected rooms in the selected period with RoomState=booked.

2   vwStay is a booked stay, <u>one or more free rooms are selected, the period overlaps the present stay period:</u>
<u>Check that the user wants to add further rooms and it is not a mistake.</u> Record RoomStates for the selected rooms in the selected period with RoomState=booked.

3   <u>vwStay is checked in. Check that the user wants to undo the check-in. Make stay booked.</u>

4   <u>vwStay is a cancelled stay. Check that the user wants to undo the cancel. Make the stay booked with the same rooms as originally. Where this is not possible, still show the room numbers but with *unallocated* indication and warn the user of why.</u>

In all cases the guest data must be filled out (see data description for required fields). Create a Guest record in case this is a new guest, update the Guest record otherwise.

unusual, in order to guard against mistakes we had observed during the usability tests.

Usability test of the real system

We usability tested the fully functional demo version with novice users, and the results were very satisfactory. With the old hand-drawn mock-up, novice users had spent 30 minutes completing a single task, and they encountered around 4 task failures during this.

With the demo version, they spent around 35 minutes completing six tasks, covering most of the system functionality. They encountered around 0.3 task failures per task, but these were caused by insufficient understanding of general hotel procedures, for instance that they should check whether a new guest was a regular before recording him as a new guest.

The usability test of the demo version also revealed some obvious program defects, for instance that the feature for undoing a checkout had been forgotten.

8.3   Defects and their cure

When you keep track of defects during development, you should also keep track of their status. Which of them are removed, which ones are pending, etc. It is also interesting to review them at the end of the project to see how they were detected and how they were removed. Here is a suggested procedure to deal with the defects.

Defect handling

a) Create a list or a database for recording defects. Do it early during design. Make room for at least these data:

 ■ Defect identification (usually a sequential number)

 ■ Description of the defect

 ■ How the defect was found

 ■ The cure – or reason for other decisions

 ■ The status of the defect (see example below)

 Some teams record also these data:

 ■ Date the defect was found

 ■ Who found it and who reported it

 ■ Date the status was changed and by whom

 ■ The number of work hours it took to deal with the defect, for instance to cure it.

b) Record all defects (problems) during design, usability testing, programming and system testing. Some teams record defects as soon as they are detected, others record only defects that were not repaired immediately.

c) When a defect is repaired, record the cure and change the status to *Done*.

d) Periodically, review the list of defects and decide what to do with the unresolved ones. Record the decision in the status, and explain the decision in *cure*.

Defect status

There are many ways to classify the defect status. Here is an example:

1 **Pending.** The defect is recorded, but it has not been decided what to do about it.

2 **Rejected.** It has been decided not to do anything about the defect, for instance because it was a false problem.

3 **Ignore.** Although there is a problem, it has been decided not to do anything about it. The problem is small compared to the cost of dealing with it.

4 **Training.** The problem is significant, but it is hard to deal with in the system itself. Users should be trained to avoid the problem, or the user documentation should help the user out.

5 **Done.** The problem has been removed – the defect is repaired.

6 **Release x.** It has been decided to deal with the problem in release *x* of the system.

7 **Duplicate (See . . .).** The defect is reported somewhere else too.

Example

Let us review how the defects were handled in the hotel system. Figure 8.3A is the complete list of defects reported during design of the hotel system. Most of the usability problems that were detected during usability test of the systematic prototype were removed immediately and never entered the official defect list.

The list is divided into sections according to how the defects were found. The first part until D35 stems from the early usability test of the hand-drawn mock-up. Defects D100 to D116 were found during the systematic design and checking process. Defects D117 to D123 were found during usability test of the systematic prototype and the fully functional demo version. Finally, defects D200 and on were planned changes for the first and second releases. They were detected in other ways, for instance studies of the hotel domain and competitor's products.

(In a large project, we would not divide the list according to where the defect was found, but for each defect record how it was found.)

For each defect we describe the problem, the cure or decision and the status. Figure 8.3B gives a bit of statistics. At that point in time we had 70 defect reports. Defect D119 had two statuses: It had to be dealt with through training of staff and also through warnings from the system. So when we count the statuses, we get 71, but only 70 defects were reported. Of these, 49 were dealt with because they were done, rejected or ignored.

We have to deal with the remaining 21 defects before the first release. Two of them are pending – we don't yet know what to do about them. Five require training or user documentation. Many of them (D200–D208) require a significant amount of design and programming. Many of these defects were actually missing features that had been known all the time, but on purpose the functional demo version had not included them.

Let us look at some of the defects in detail. Notice that some of them were easy to deal with, others required significant work and some we didn't know about yet.

D1: **Status: Training.** Some novice users still had initial troubles understanding the stay concept. We judged that it would not help changing the term from *Stay* to *Booking* since it would cause other confusion when talking about a guest that was checked in. The conclusion was to leave the user interface as it was, but make sure that basic instruction or tutorials for the system would explain this concept.

D4: **Status: Done.** The user couldn't see whether the guest was checked in or booked. A *simple design change* helped: The necessary information was simply added to the windows.

Fig 8.3 A Defects and their cure

Defects from early usability test			
ID	**In Find Guest window**	**Cure**	**Status**
D1	The *Stay* concept is not understood by some users	Pop-up texts helped somewhat. Training needed in hotel procedures.	**Training**
D2	Doesn't notice the *Find* button	Live search finally cured the problem.	Done
D3	When you select a certain date, why does the list show earlier dates too?	Three changes: Two dates – one for arrival date and one for room search. Better labels. List all stays and all guests that match.	Done
D4	Not visible whether the guests have been checked in or not	The status is now shown on the guest list as well as in the Stay window.	Done
D5	How do you open the Stay window from the Find guest/Stay window?	Button placed earlier – not after the 'strange' buttons. Live search also helped.	Done
D6	Tries *Enter* to search, but it opens a Stay window. Then tries F2	Live search doesn't need the search button. Enter also searches and then selects the first list item.	Done
D7	Doesn't see that the guest is on the list already	Live search helped.	Done
D8	Doesn't understand why the list becomes empty (made a spelling error)	Live search helped.	Done
D9	Believes the task is complete when she sees the guest on the list	Two changes: Show the state. Show less information on the guest list so that it is more obvious that stay must be opened. Still a problem for some users. Training needed in hotel procedures.	**Training**
D10	Doesn't understand that the Stay screen must be opened	Same cure as D9. Problem not observed later.	Done
D11	Fills in all search criteria, believing they are data fields	Live search helped.	Done
D12	Cannot figure out how to create a new booking	Users now learn it fast (minor problem only). May be due to the ease of experimenting with the real system.	Ignore
D13	Bad window title – avoid the slash	New title is simply Find Guest. System finds stays as well as guests.	Done
D14	What to write in the address field? Street name and zip?	Label changed to *Street*, but system looks for anything. Problem never observed only specialist advice.	Done
D15	Where do you enter zip code or city?	As for D14.	Done
D16	'Date' is insufficient, should be arrival date	As for D3.	Done
D17	The # sign is not understood by ordinary users	Problem never observed, but label changed anyway.	Done
D18	Obscure what *Find* will give (may cover D3 and D8?)	Live search removed the problem.	Done
D19	Search based on passport number is needed	False problem.	Rejected
D20	A guest number is needed in addition to the stay number	False problem.	Rejected
D21	Which of the guests are on the list?	False problem – maybe the other changes prevent it.	Rejected
D22	Not visible how the guest pays the bill?	False problem.	Rejected

ID	**In Rooms window**	**Cure**	**Status**
D23	Doesn't look for functions on the menu	Menu names now hotel-oriented. Now only a minor problem.	Ignore
D24	Believes O means nobody there – room is free	Longer state indications now used.	Done
D25	Doesn't understand the two room prices	A better heading solved the problem.	Done
D26	Does *To* mean last night or departure date?	Label changed to *Departure*. Also *nights* and *weekdays* helped.	Done
D27	Why is there a File menu? *Tools* is better	Same as D23.	Done

ID	**In Stay and NewStay window**	**Cure**	**Status**
D28	Expects that the room can be marked *Occupied* on the Stay screen.	Buttons instead of menus helped.	Done
D29	Uncertain whether check-in has been recorded correctly	Clear state indication helped, but still a minor problem.	Ignore
D30	Cannot see how many rooms the guest has booked	New presentation of room bookings gave the necessary overview.	Done
D31	Hard to find function for printing a booking confirmation	Buttons instead of menus helped.	Done
D32	Are blank fields allowed?	False problem.	Rejected
D33	Why are date fields not editable?	False problem.	Rejected
D34	How to undo data entry?	Problem not yet observed, but likely.	**Release 1**
D35	Where do you change the room prices or give discounts?	Problem not yet observed. Related to discounts in general.	(See D201)

Continued

Fig 8.3 A Defects and their cure (*Continued*)

Defects detected during systematic design

ID		Cure	Status
D100	Do users understand that data in the Breakfast window automatically end up in the Stay windows?	An OK button helped. Automatic update of any open Stay window also gives some feedback.	Done
D101	Receptionist should check credit card or get deposit before check-in	Check-in insists on paymethod to be filled in. The rest of the credit checking is presently manual.	**Release 1**
D102	Do users understand that guest name and address is repeated in all his Stay windows – while pay method is individual for each stay?	Mostly yes. No serious problem.	Done
D103	How to show long stays or stays with many rooms?	New presentation of room bookings gave the necessary overview.	Done
D104	Search criteria in Rooms window: room kind, period free, room number	Made already in first mock-up.	Done
D105	Rooms window to show possible discounts	Presently only discount for *as single*.	(see D201)
D106	New Virtual Window: FindStay. Criteria: . . .	Made already in first mock-up. Revised often since.	Done
D107	New Virtual Window: FloorMap		(see D300)
D108	Talk to developers about automatic deletion of old data, or a possible user interface for this	Not in this demo version.	**Release 1**
D109	The database has no room number for ServiceReceived	Data model changed. Optional field, set by breakfast list entry.	Done
D110	New task or subtask: changing or deleting a booking, before or after check-in	Necessary functions added.	Done
D111	New subtask for setting the number of persons in the room. This is related to handling the discounts	Necessary edit functions added.	Done
D112	New task or subtask: changing or deleting service records	Necessary edit functions added.	Done
D113	New task: Setting or clearing the repair state for rooms	Necessary menu functions added.	Done
D114	Seasonal prices missing	Part of full discount handling.	(see D201)
D115	Mnemonic for the occupied and booked state causes misunderstandings	Same as D24.	Done
D116	Distinction between past items and booked items in the Stay window not clear	New presentation of room bookings gave the necessary overview. See also D117.	Done

Defects from usability test of functional version

ID		Cure	Status
D117	What do the two totals for rooms mean?	Only observed once – medium problem. Training in hotel procedures may help.	**Training**
D118	User doesn't check whether guest is a regular	Training in hotel procedures.	**Training**
D119	Checks out without asking the guest about unrecorded services, e.g. early breakfast.	Checkout should warn. Training in hotel procedures also needed.	**Training** **Release 1**
D120	Cannot undo the checkout	Missing function.	**Release 1**
D121	User expects room grid to reflect the open stay	Seems a good idea since users frequently try to match the Stay window with the room grid.	**Pending**
D122	Users confused about the line for adding a service to the stay. A new line pops up as soon as they start filling in the line for a new service.	Minor and medium problem. This is a general Access usability problem. Try to find Event procedures that can avoid it.	**Pending**
D123	Error message when extending the stay one day is confusing. First system says 'Rooms not free'. Later 'Do you want to add one more room'.	Medium problem. The system doesn't see that some of the days selected are already occupied by the user. Typical example of error message not reflecting the current context.	**Release 1**

Other sources

ID	Additional features for release 1		Status
D200	Book room by type		**Release 1**
D201	Discounts and seasonal prices		**Release 1**
D202	Awareness of time before or after checkout deadline		**Release 1**
D203	Additional room states: becoming free today, maintenance, ready		**Release 1**
D204	Warning about guests not checking out		**Release 1**
D205	Larger fonts than demo version. (Work is done standing)		**Release 1**
D206	Keep cancelled stays with room data. For supporting undo and for statistics.		**Release 1**
D207	Speed up guest search with word index		**Release 1**
D208	Transfer data automatically to accounting system		**Release 1**

ID	Additional features for release 2		Status
D300	Floor map with room states		**Release 2**
D301	Automatic data transfer from telephone exchange		**Release 2**

D8: **Status: Done.** The user didn't understand why the list of stays became empty (he had made a spelling error). *Many experiments were needed.* The problem was cured through many rounds of redesign. It was even necessary to make a functional prototype of part of the system.

D12: **Status: Ignore.** Some users couldn't figure out how to create a new booking – was it a new guest or a new stay? In the mock-up, this was a task failure for many users, but in the demo version, it was only a minor problem that the user soon solved on his own. The user tried one of the buttons, but saw that the resulting Stay window was wrong. He then closed the window and tried another button. The defect was partly the *effect of the mock-up.* It became a minor problem in the functional system. We have often observed that users are more likely to experiment with a real system than with a mock-up. As a result, the problem may change from a task failure to a less serious problem.

D121: **Status: Pending.** When the user was handling a complex booking, for instance with several rooms or an extension of the stay period, he tended to compare the Stay window with the room allocation on the Rooms window. He wanted some indication in the Rooms window for the rooms used by the stay, but the demo version didn't show it. (He could complete his task anyway, but there was a higher risk that the result became wrong.) This change seemed simple, but might be hard to make in the program. The conclusion was to investigate it more closely and then decide.

D201: **Status: Release 1.** The system only supports the discount for single guests who stay in a double room. The discount system in real hotels is more complex, but must be supported before release 1 of the product.

Additional features for the production version

Some of the defects were not detected by the systematic design or usability tests. They are shown as D200 and on. Some of these we have mentioned in the book already, for instance D200 about booking rooms by type. Others we haven't mentioned before, but a study of the hotel domain revealed them.

As an example, the hotel may have other computer systems that the reception system must cooperate with, for instance an account system, or a telephone exchange that automatically records call charges per room.

As another example, the state of a hotel room is more complex than we have assumed in the book. When a guest is leaving, he checks out, but the room is not yet ready for the next guest. It first has to be cleaned and made up. In small hotels they just ask the maintenance staff whether the room is ready, but in large hotels they have computers on each floor for entering the information, or the maintenance staff use a mobile phone to call to the computer.

As a final example, we knew that the demo version had technical deficiencies to be corrected before release. D207 reminds developers of one such problem. The live

Fig 8.3 B Number of defects

Status	Number of defects	To deal with now
Pending	2	2
Rejected	6	
Ignore	3	
Training	5	5
Done	34	
Release 1	15	15
Release 2	2	
Duplicates	4	
Total	71	22
Total number of defects	70	21

search in the Stay window works all right for around 1000 guests, but with a file of 100,000 guests, which larger hotels have, the search will take much too long time with the simple solution used in the demo version. The demo version goes through all guest records looking for character sequences that match the user's criterion. This takes too long when there are many guests. Technically it can be done much, much faster.

We have shown the list of additional features to give you an impression of how things would be handled in a real project. The actual list would be much longer – and growing from year to year as the product is being used and new demands turn up. As you may notice, these lists include usability issues as well as technical issues. In real projects there is no sharp division between these areas.

Defects versus requests for change

Some developers distinguish between defects and requests for change. A *defect* is something where the system doesn't meet the stated requirements. A *request for change* (RFC) is a new wish that a user or customer comes up with. In practice it is often hard to distinguish the two. Does the system violate the stated requirements or is it a new wish? Issues of this kind can end up in court. Ease-of-use defects are often in the gray area.

Our defect list contains real defects, ease-of-use problems and RFCs. Some developers may strongly object to the list being called a defect list. They may better accept the term RFC list, problem list or issue list. Don't fight about the name of the list, but ensure that there is just one list. If you try to work with different lists, you will have to fight many times about whether to put a problem on one list or the other.

In practice the list of defects is very important for planning the next releases of the system. It is one of the sources for figuring out what to include in the next release.

8.4   Problems, causes and solutions

It sounds easy: When you have found the usability problems, you must correct them. Unfortunately, it is not that easy. As we have seen above, some usability problems were easy to correct, others seemed easy, but the solution didn't work. Sometimes several experiments were required, and even a partially functional prototype was needed.

The HCI literature is depressingly silent about this issue. There are lots of writing about how to find the usability problems, but nothing about how to correct them.

Finding the cause of the problem

Personally I believe that the jump from problem to solution is too large. It is like correcting a program bug. The novice programmer just adds something to the program – hoping that it will help. The seasoned programmer first finds the *cause* of the problem – why did the program produce the wrong result – or why did it crash exactly when I clicked the scroll bar? Finding the cause can be a big task in itself, but once found, the solution is usually simple.

Usability problems are a bit harder, for what are the causes? Why didn't the user notice the menu? Why did he misunderstand what the function did? We cannot look into the brain of the user in the same manner as we can scrutinize a program text. We have to use indirect sources to find the cause:

a) Let the user think aloud.

b) Ask the user why he did this, what he expected, etc.

c) Use an eye-movement detector to see what the user actually looked at.

d) Use experience from other user interfaces about what users typically do.

A confusing factor is that users are different. Some encounter problems that other users don't, so in some sense their 'programs' are different.

Problem – cause – solution

In order to at least clarify the concepts, I have tried to make a data model of the concepts involved (Figure 8.4).

Our basic data are the observations of user problems. This corresponds to the class *Observation* on the figure. We cluster observations that reflect the same problem. As a result, each observation relates to exactly one problem, and each problem may be observed several times. Each observation relates to a specific user. We may observe several problems for the same user, so there is a 1:m relationship between user and observation. We may observe the same problem many times, possibly with different users and with different severity. For this reason, the severity is an attribute of the observation – not of the problem.

Fig 8.4   Problem – cause – solution

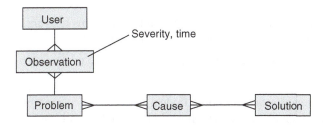

ID	Problem	Observation	Likely causes	Potential cures
	Task: Check-in			
D7	Doesn't see that the guest is on the list already.	B: Annoying M: Annoying	Reads top-down and stops at first seemingly relevant thing: name. Doesn't understand that they are search criteria.	Put list on top, criteria below. Signal that it is a criterion, e.g. with (*any*). Live search to give immediate feedback.
D8	Doesn't understand why the list becomes empty (made a spelling error).	B: Medium problem	Doesn't understand the match principle.	Don't just make it empty – say why. Live search to catch the error immediately.
D9	Believes the task is complete when she sees the guest on the list.	M: Task failure	Lacks domain knowledge.	Guidance on the screen? Tutorial or mini-course?
D10	Doesn't understand that the stay screen must be opened.	B: Task failure M: Task failure	Lacks domain knowledge. No signal that it is possible.	As D8. Show the state and an inviting button on the line.
D11	Fills in search criteria, believing they are data fields.	B: Minor problem M:Task failure	Doesn't relate it to the heading. The two things look alike.	As D7. Redesign so that search criteria also are data fields.

A problem may have several causes and the same cause can result in many problems. We thus have an m:m relationship between problem and cause. Finally, a cause may be cured by several solutions, and a solution may cure several causes. Also here we have an m:m relationship.

An example

In order to see whether the data model actually helps, I have used it to describe some of the observations from the first usability test of the hotel system. Figure 8.4 shows the result.

As an example, D7 occurs when Andrew Bunting arrives and wants to check in. The user looks at the Find Guest window but doesn't notice that he is there already (the list automatically shows guests who are expected to arrive today).

The problem is observed with two users, B and M. For both of them the severity was 'annoying' because they entered the search criteria in vain.

On the basis of thinking aloud and general experience from other systems, we can guess at two causes.

1 Users tend to read top–down and stop with the first thing that seems relevant. In this case it is the field *Name*. Here they enter the name of the guest.

2 They are not aware that the field is a search criterion. They believe it is a data entry field.

For each cause, we can find one or more solutions. To deal with cause 1, we might put the list at the top of the screen and have the criteria below. To deal with cause 2, we could signal to the user that this was a search criterion, for instance by showing (*any*) in the field. We might also use a live search so that the list is updated immediately as the user enters the name. This will make the user pay attention to the list and how it relates to the field he fills in.

Notice that some solutions might solve several problems. For instance, the better signal for the search criterion might also solve problem D11.

A hope for the future
From a practitioner's point of view it would be wonderful if someone could create a list of causes across many systems. And even more wonderful if someone could create a matching list of possible cures. However, this is research for the future.

Test yourself

a) Why did the hotel-system designer make a tool-based mock-up rather than a hand-drawn one?

b) Mention an example where a mock-up is insufficient to test the usability.

c) If you cannot remove all usability problems, what can you do about the rest?

d) Why is it difficult to cure a usability problem?

Design exercises. See Chapter 17.

9

Reflections on user interface design

Highlights

▪ Overview of design activities, the work products and the associated techniques.

▪ Agile versions of the method.

▪ How it all relates to object-oriented design and other design methods.

▪ History of the virtual window method.

We have now painfully gone through a long design process and used many techniques. In this chapter we review how it all relates together and how it relates to other design approaches.

9.1   Overview of the virtual window method

Let us first summarize the systematic design method in this book – the virtual window method. Figure 9.1 gives an overview of all the techniques in the form of a modified waterfall model for systems development.

Domain analysis

In this step we study the application domain to identify the user tasks to be supported and the data to be handled. The result of this step is task descriptions and a data model. It is also a good idea to specify system visions and the usability requirements, including the user profiles.

In order to get these results, we use techniques such as interviews, observation of users, study of existing documents and computer screens. We also need knowledge of various ways to specify tasks, usability requirements, etc.

Virtual window design

In this step we design the screens that the user should imagine being behind the physical screen – at the back of the system. These screens are the virtual windows. They resemble finished windows and have graphical details with realistic data contents, but they have no 'buttons' at this stage.

In order to design the screens, we build on what we got from the domain analysis: the data model and the task descriptions. We also use knowledge of gestalt laws, mental models and different ways of presenting data. We test the design in many ways, for instance by an understandability test (a simplified usability test), CREDO checks and checks of the data demands to carry out each task. This often results in changes to the task descriptions and the data model.

Function design

In this step we plan which buttons the user will need in order to carry out the tasks. We add these buttons to the virtual windows. Next we plan how the virtual windows combine into screens and we allocate navigation functions to the screens. We also make mini-specs: short descriptions of what the various functions must do. Finally, we decide how the functions will be presented: as buttons, menu points, drag-and-drop, etc.

In order to do this, we need the virtual windows and once more the task descriptions. We also use knowledge of semantic functions versus navigation functions, and knowledge of advantages and disadvantages of the various ways to present functions. We use state diagrams to find the necessary navigation functions.

Fig 9.1 The virtual window method

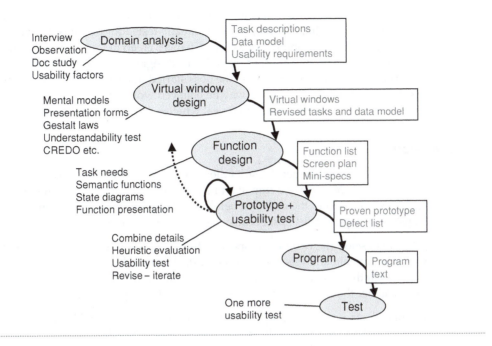

Prototyping and usability test

In this step we combine the screens and the functions into a prototype. We add help texts and error messages. Then we run usability tests of the prototype, notice problems and correct them as far as possible. We may also use heuristic evaluation to point to potential problems. However, the potential problems should be considered good advice, not defects that we necessarily have to correct. During the entire development we maintain a list of defects – problems to be dealt with. At this stage some problems will remain and we plan what to do about them.

If we have done a good design job in the previous steps, the usability problems tend to be easy to correct – without major restructuring of screens. Notice that the difficulty of correcting a problem is unrelated to how serious the problem is to the user. For instance, some task failures may be easy to correct, others may be real hard.

The result of this step is a proven prototype including mini-specs, plus a list of defects to be dealt with later.

Programming

Programming takes place as usual, apart from the fact that the user interface is much better defined than usual. Experience shows that this causes programming to proceed much smoother than in traditional projects.

Test

The test is primarily about finding program bugs and interaction problems between different programs. In principle, we have already tested for usability. However, it is a good idea to test for usability once more. Changes creep in for many reasons: It may be easier to program it in another way; the art designer came up with fancy colours that were not part of the prototype; the boss started interfering with the design and insisted that it should look in the way he believed would be right. In all of these cases, only a new usability test can reveal whether critical problems crept in.

Agile versions

The experienced developer doesn't follow the systematic approach rigidly. First of all, he doesn't complete one step at a time, but often iterates between them, or he completes one part of the interface before designing another part. Second, he often skips some steps or substeps, because they are less important in the actual project.

If I were to select the two most important things in user interface development, it would be domain analysis and usability tests. Without domain analysis we wouldn't know what the system was supposed to do. Without usability test we would have no idea whether the system was easy to use and could support the tasks.

Fortunately, these two techniques are the ones mentioned in all HCI books, and they *are* the most important ones. In small projects they suffice, but in larger projects you will find it hard to correct all the usability problems detected in the usability test. You lose your way in the maze of possible designs.

Virtual windows are the technique to guide you in the maze. Here we ensure that the system will be easy to understand and will support the tasks efficiently. This step gives the master plan for the user interface.

The function design is less critical and can be radically shortened in simple systems, where the designer more intuitively can plan the necessary functions. Yet, even in a simple system such as the hotel system, our systematic function design made the prototype very much better than our first intuitive design of the functions.

9.2 Data design versus function design

In order to compare the virtual window method with other design methods, we will look at the design as three parallel design streams (see Figure 9.2A). One stream is the gradual design of data presentation from the abstract data model to the prototype. Another stream is the gradual design of the system functions, the 'buttons' on the user interface. The third stream is the gradual design of the user's activities – how to carry out the tasks. At the end of the design, the data stream and the system function stream have been integrated on the user interface – the prototype. Design methods vary a lot in how they treat these three streams. (This model was developed in cooperation with Barbara Paech and her colleagues at Fraunhofer Institute, Germany.)

Data design stream. The data design starts with an abstract model of the data in the application domain. During design, this model is transformed into presentations that the user can see on the screen. In the virtual window method, there are two intermediate steps: the virtual windows and the page plan (part of function design). The last step that shows data is the prototype. In the figure, the virtual windows and the prototype have double borders to indicate that they are visible to the user – not some abstract diagram or text. In contrast, the page plan has a single border to indicate that it is an abstract diagram. Note how design of the virtual windows builds on the data model as well as the task descriptions.

In some design methods there are more intermediate data design steps, for instance abstract specifications of the data to be shown in each screen. In other design methods there are no intermediate steps.

Function design. The design of what the system and the users do, may start out as an analysis of what they do together. In the virtual window method the result is the task descriptions. Soon this stream of design splits into two: what the system does (the system functions) and what the users do (the user actions).

System functions. The system functions are gradually refined from high-level functions to more detailed and visible functions. In the virtual window method, there are three intermediate steps in designing the system functions: defining the semantic and search functions, defining the navigation functions and defining the function presentation. Gradually, these steps get closer and closer to what the user will see. At the end of system function design, the functions are visible to the user in the prototype.

The figure shows how the function design builds on the virtual windows as well as the task descriptions. However, the tasks will usually not be visible in the prototype. If we for some reason want to have a task-oriented dialogue, we must explicitly structure the navigation functions accordingly.

User actions. The user actions are, in principle, refined in the same manner as the system functions. As designers define the system functions, they implicitly define what the users will do. Some design approaches pay a great deal of attention to this. Sutcliffe, for instance, talks about designing the work units for users (see below).

The virtual window method pays little attention to explicitly designing the user actions. As part of system function design, it suggests an optional step: writing down the detailed use cases for the user–computer interaction. This is considered a checking activity. The method also recommends to write down the usability requirements together with the user profiles. The user action design is primarily dealt with through the usability tests, which are a very important step of the method. Essentially, the usability tests check that users themselves can select the right actions – in that way designing their own detailed work procedures. This approach is in line with the basic philosophy behind the method: Give users the freedom to do what is convenient at any time – don't try to program them.

9.2.1   A task-oriented design method

As a contrast we will look at a more task-oriented design method, a classic published by Alistair Sutcliffe (1988). The three streams are shown in Figure 9.2B, using Sutcliffe's terms. To better understand the design method, we first look at the function design.

Function design. The function design starts out very much like the virtual window method – with an analysis of what the user and the computer do together. Sutcliffe uses the traditional HCI concepts of task analysis and describes the results as high-level tasks broken down to lower-level tasks. He uses two alternative diagram forms: dataflow diagrams (example in Figure 9.3) and hierarchy diagrams (example in Figure 5.5B). Conceptually, they are similar to our textual task descriptions. He also works explicitly with user descriptions – the experience, motivation, etc., of the users.

User actions. The tasks are split into a computer part and a user part. Users should get the part that *requires initiative, judgement and heuristic reasoning*. Computers should get *repetitive checking, calculations and data handling*. Sutcliffe treats the human part of the functions as a separate design stream. For instance he talks about clustering the user actions into meaningful work units (task closure in our terminology), and organizing the work so that there are natural breaks.

System functions. The system functions are defined in several steps. During *task design*, the system part of the tasks is broken down into smaller and smaller units. We might, for instance, have a high-level system function called *book guest*. Programmers might think of it as a long subroutine that carries out several things and asks the user for input on the way. (At the end of the design, this function might appear to the user as a menu point on the start screen.) This high-level system function is broken down into *find rooms* and *record guest*. (They might, for instance, appear to the user as two

Fig 9.2 A Data and functions: virtual window method

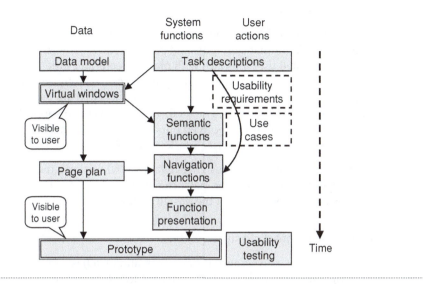

screens with buttons.) The *find rooms* function might again be broken down into a search criterion for room type and a *FindRooms* button.

Selecting the interaction style is a separate step. Should the user dialogue use question/answer, form filling, or typed commands? According to Sutcliffe, the user descriptions are an important input to this choice. Graphical user interfaces are not really considered at this point, and they would also fit badly into the way tasks are designed. Graphical user interfaces were new in 1988 and rarely used for the business applications that make up Sutcliffe's main examples. He treats graphical user interfaces in a separate chapter, Computer Control Interfaces, at the end of his book.

The next steps are dialogue design and module definition. Here the dialogue is broken down into the actual steps at the computer and the screens (modules) to be shown. State diagrams are used to specify the dialogue steps (Sutcliffe also uses the term *network diagram*). Each module is thought of as something that a programmer could make as a unit. Sutcliffe suggests that modules are either data entry modules or data display/retrieval modules. Combining them into one would confuse the user, he suggests. (The virtual window method suggest the opposite, based on Piaget's law of object permanence.)

Data design stream. A data model is the starting point for the data presentation, just as in the virtual window method. Sutcliffe doesn't discuss data modelling in his user interface design book, because it is a part of systems analysis. The presentation of data has a single intermediate step, the module definition. It is an abstract definition of which program modules and associated screens the system should have. The first visual presentation of data takes place during *presentation design* – roughly the same as making a prototype.

Conclusion. Sutcliffe's method has a strong emphasis on designing the user tasks with respect for human strengths and weaknesses. However, the method also leads to a task-oriented user interface with many screens and little user control of the sequence. (Section 6.8 shows an example of such a step-by-step interface). It is also clear that there are no intermediate work products that are visible and immediately understandable to the users. The method seems to aim at supporting traditional clerical work, where users received bunches of paper forms filled in by other staff, for instance sales staff. The user's tasks were to enter these data into the computer.

Sutcliffe recommends that designers evaluate the final product and possible prototypes with the users, for instance with usability tests. However, this doesn't seem to be an integral part of the design method.

9.2.2   Object-oriented design

Object-oriented analysis and design (OOA and OOD) is a recent trend in systems development, although the ideas date back to the programming language Simula around 1968. The basic idea is to focus on the objects in the system, rather than the user tasks. In principle, this promises a different kind of user interface where the user manipulates visible objects on the screen without being guided through a sequence of steps. After some years, object-oriented schools realized that user tasks played a role anyway, and the concept of use cases became popular. Use cases are the object-world equivalents of tasks.

In OOD we compose a system out of objects. An object holds some data, for instance a single record, and it offers various operations (often called *methods*) that work on the object. Some operations may read or update the data in the object, some may create and delete objects, and others may communicate with other objects, for instance a printer or an e-mail system. In the hotel example, a stay would be a good example of an object. The object offers operations such as book, check-in and check-out. The check-out operation, for instance, would also take care of printing the invoice.

Let us see how OOA and OOD deal with the three design streams (Figure 9.2C). As you can see, most of the work products span several streams, so we will explain the work products one by one.

Analysis model. Object-oriented analysis starts with a model of the domain. Which objects exist in the domain outside the computer system and which operations do they have? Some object-oriented schools start with what they call a *static class model*, which is the objects without operations. A static class model is almost the same as an E/R model. Other object-oriented schools start with *responsibilities*, which are the functions to be carried out. Next, they define the objects and their operations. As shown in the figure, they all end up with an analysis model that spans the three streams.

Fig 9.2 B Data and functions: Sutcliffe (1988)

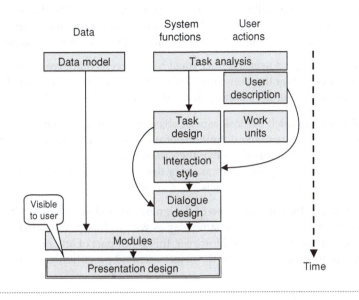

Design model. The next step is to define the objects that should be inside the computer. As shown in the figure, these objects span the data and system function streams. Classical object-oriented schools suggest that the design model is a 'seamless transformation' of the analysis model. This may work all right for the data part of the system, just as a data model for the domain transfers rather seamlessly to a database. However, the function part doesn't transform so easily except for trivial functionality. The reason is, of course, that we have cut away the user action part. Somehow, the designers assumed that what the user and computer do together is similar to what the computer will do alone. This is true only if we fully automate the tasks. (For a longer discussion about when the transformation is seamless, see Lauesen, 2002, section 4.7.)

Screen objects. When we say that the design model defines the objects inside the computer, what are we really talking about? The data stores and program modules? Yes, here object-oriented modelling works all right. But the user doesn't see these objects directly, but through screens. We may consider each screen an object.

How do these screen objects derive from the design objects? The figure shows the transformation with a question mark. Object-oriented schools are rather silent about this transformation. They are not even sure that the screens are objects. They assume that there is a seamless transformation from the design model, but they rarely give examples of what it means when designing the user interface. There are some attempts, for instance that each object must have operations that make it show itself on the computer screen. These approaches produce rather naïve screens that show a single object at a time or a list of objects. The horror story in section 2.3 was about a user interface that followed the naïve approach closely. The database-extreme example in section 6.8 follows the same idea, but is more user-friendly than the naïve solutions since it includes data from many object classes in the same list.

In real life, a good user interface must have screens that give overview and show bits of many objects at the same time. This cannot be derived from the design model without a good understanding of the user tasks.

Use cases. To catch the task aspect, object-oriented schools introduced the use case concept. There are many definitions of use cases, but the dominant ones consider a use case the set of functions that the *system* must perform to support a user task. As indicated in the figure, a use case may describe a bit of what the user does, but the focus is on the system functions.

In principle, the combined use of design model and use cases might produce good user interfaces, much in the same way as we produce good virtual windows by following the design rules. However, this is not part of any object-oriented method, nor is it done consciously by the object-oriented practitioners I have met.

9.2.3   Virtual windows and objects

Is the virtual window method object-oriented? Not in the traditional sense where you are supposed to first analyse the objects in the application domain, including defining the operations for each object. Then you transform these objects in a seamless way into design objects and screen objects.

Although the virtual window method doesn't work according to the object-oriented ideal, we may describe the work products in an object-oriented way. Here is a discussion of the object-oriented concepts we deal with:

Data model = static class model. It is crucial to define the persistent data to be stored in the system, and we do that very early in the form of a static class model (similar to a traditional E/R data model). However, the operations on the classes have little use in the final result and we don't waste time on them. We have the necessary information about 'operations' in the task descriptions.

Virtual windows = user-oriented objects. The virtual windows are good objects and could belong to the object-oriented design model. In a sense, they are the missing link between the analysis model and the screen objects. A virtual window contains data – the data shown to the user. A virtual window template is a class, which may have many instantiations – many objects. There may, for instance, be several Stay windows open at a time. At a later stage, the virtual windows get operations – the semantic functions.

A major difference between the traditional objects in an object-oriented design model and virtual windows is that virtual windows include a detailed graphical

Fig 9.2 C Data and functions: object-oriented methods

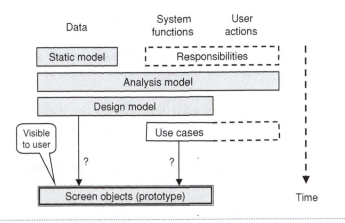

presentation of the data. We also arrive at the proper set of virtual windows from a close study of both the user tasks and the static class model (the data model). This is definitely not a seamless transformation. A lot of imagination and balancing of conflicting demands enter the design process at this point.

Semantic functions = object operations. When we have defined the virtual windows, we add semantic and search functions to each window. This is similar to how designers add operations (methods) to the objects.

While other user interface design methods look at functions first and data presentation later, we say that it does not make sense to define the functions until we know the data presentation, i.e. the virtual windows. In object-oriented terms it should not be a surprise – of course, we cannot define the object operations until we know the objects.

Pages = objects with multiple inheritance. When we transform the virtual windows into final pages (application screens), we essentially define new objects – the pages. They inherit data, functions and visual appearance from the virtual windows they show. We also add some new operations to the pages – the navigation functions that allow the user to move between pages. (Maybe the pages are aggregations of virtual window objects rather than multiple inheritance? I am not sure.)

User interface objects = program objects? In the final user interface, the pages, data fields and functions may appear more or less directly in the program as objects with operations. It depends heavily on the platform used. In some cases, each page, each field and each button becomes a visible *control* or *widget* object in the program. In other cases, only the pages are true objects.

As an example, in Microsoft Access, each page is a program object (a Form in Access terminology). Fields and buttons are in some ways small objects of their own – with their own set of micro-level functions that respond to actions such as clicking, entering a character, etc. However, in other ways they are operations in the Form object, because they share data with the Form where they appear. Much of the mini-specs become program pieces in the micro-level functions.

Some complex program parts may become classes without direct connection to any virtual window. This is where traditional object-oriented programming plays an important role.

Use cases = tasks? Object-oriented designers talk about a use case as the interaction between a system and its users to reach some goal. In principle, it is similar to the user tasks we talk about.

However, in practice the typical use case describes the detailed interaction, and primarily the computer's part of it. If you try to define such use cases early on (and many developers do so), you have defined the user dialogue and the user functions much too early. The result is a poor user interface. Only after designing the screens (or at least the virtual windows) does it make sense to define the interaction and the functions of the system.

When we talk about tasks, we look at user and computer as one single actor and see what they have to do together. Only late in the design do we split the work between user and computer. In this way we can use the tasks as guides for defining the virtual windows, and later as guides for defining the system functions.

UML diagrams? There are other things from object tradition that we don't find useful in designing the user interface. We don't use a lot of UML diagrams. Static class models (without operations) and state diagrams have proven useful. In early versions of the design method, we also used diagrams similar to activity diagrams, collaboration diagrams, etc., but although they could illustrate small system parts, they didn't scale up to full systems.

9.3　History of the virtual window method

Around 1990 Morten Borup Harning and I jointly developed the first version of the virtual window method. We developed the idea of virtual windows, which we at that time called a User Data Model because we mainly looked at it as a visualization of the data in the database. We also showed how to define the functions after having defined the virtual windows, how to transform the virtual windows into screens, and how to use state diagrams for defining navigation functions. We published the method at two conferences in 1993 (Lauesen and Harning 1993) and a more mature version in IEEE Software (Lauesen and Harning 2001).

At that time we used dataflow diagrams to specify the semantic functions. Figure 9.3 shows an example from the hotel system. In a dataflow diagram, each bubble is a function that receives some data and produces some data. As an example, the NewStay function takes a temporary Stay (dotted) and creates a filed Stay (in the pile of stays). FindStay uses search criteria from the temporary Stay, retrieves a matching Stay from the pile and puts it on the top of the pile where the user can see it. Traditional dataflow diagrams don't visualize data, but the designer writes a data expression on the flow arrows. In our version we found it useful to show data as window outlines (the rectangles on the figure).

Dataflow diagrams were state-of-the-art at that time. In UML they appear again as part of activity diagrams, but activity diagrams also show the transfer of control – much like old-fashioned flow charts. Dataflow diagrams are good for describing the large-scale aspects of functionality, for instance tasks. They also allow you to break down a large piece of functionality into smaller pieces.

We found that the dataflow diagrams were nice for illustrating what a few 'buttons' did, but they didn't work well in large examples such as screens with many buttons.

Fig 9.3　Old version of function design

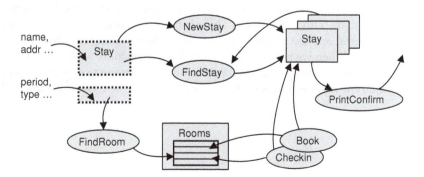

Also, the step to actually deciding where the button was to be shown was too large. Maintaining the diagram when you, for instance, decided that the search criteria were not part of the temporary Stay, but of a separate search window, was also too cumbersome.

In the following years we taught the method at professional developer courses and later at university courses. Gradually, we learned what worked in practice and what didn't, and the method slowly matured. Here are some highlights on the way:

a) We realized that a detailed graphical design of the virtual windows was crucial. Our examples used detailed graphics, but some designers just made outlines – and for this reason their designs failed later in the process.

b) We realized that the virtual windows had to be derived not only from the data model, but from data model plus tasks. On the basis of observations of bad designs, we gradually developed the design guidelines for virtual windows.

c) Around 1994, Harning developed a version of the method where he first designed a user data model – a visualization of the traditional data model. Redmond-Pyle and Moore (1995) used a similar approach. While Redmond-Pyle and Moore jumped from the user data model to the final screens, Harning first designed virtual windows based on the user data model, next the final screens. Lauesen insisted that a user data model was an unnecessary step, and the method in this book goes straight from traditional data model plus tasks to the virtual windows.

d) During all these years, the specification of the functions had been a weak point. The author (Lauesen) tried many alternative ways, for instance using different diagrams or text-based use cases. They were either too complex to be useful, or they didn't scale up. A main breakthrough was a better understanding that there were three kinds of functions – semantic, search and navigation – and that they should be designed in different steps.

e) Another breakthrough was that the semantic functions should be attached to the virtual windows in much the same way as operations are attached to objects in object-oriented analysis and design. In the present version of the method, we walk through the user tasks, identify the necessary semantic functions and attach them to the virtual windows. There is no extra work; it gives an excellent overview; and the result is easy to use in programming and detailed screen design. When we need to specify details of a function, we do it as a mini-spec – an outline of the program behind the function. Trying to express such details with dataflow diagrams or activity diagrams seems to be a waste of time and paper.

Part C

Supplementary design issues

In part C of the book, we present various subjects that are not needed to learn the basic design method, but may be consulted as the need arises.

- Applying the virtual window method in other projects: a Web-system for course assessment and an advanced e-mail system (Chapters 10 and 11).

- Writing user documentation for instance on-line help, introductory courses and reference documents (Chapter 12).

- A comprehensive guide to usability testing with practical advice for finding test users, planning the time, logging and reporting, etc. (Chapter 13).

- Heuristic evaluation and how it compares to usability testing (Chapter 14).

- Systems development, user involvement, task analysis and elicitation of requirements (Chapter 15).

- Data modelling (Chapter 16).

10

Web-based course rating

Highlights

- The virtual-windows method applied on a Web-based system.

- Several user groups with different needs and different rights.

- High-level tasks and low-level tasks in action.

- Overview of complex data in a novel way.

In this chapter we will design a Web application where university students evaluate the courses and the teachers. In the previous chapters we carefully explained how we produced the various work products. In this chapter we explain very little about the production process. We primarily show the work products with comments – in much the same way as a design team would document their results.

This particular university runs around 10 *study lines* (course programmes) and each study line has a *line manager*. A student is enrolled on at most one study line, but may select some courses from other lines. There are around 2000 students, 200 courses and 300 teachers and tutors.

10.1 Visions for the rating system

Business goals

The overall purposes of a system are called the business goals. This term is used also for non-profit organizations, such as this university. The business goals explain why we want to spend money on a new IT system. The course-rating system has these business goals:

a) Teachers should get an early warning about good and bad things in their courses. This will allow them to adjust the course before it is too late.

b) Teachers and management should get final evaluations of the courses. They will use it for improving the courses and for training teachers.

c) Students should get a better basis for choosing courses.

d) Teachers and management should get a financial status for each teacher and each course. This will allow them to allocate teaching load and plan the course selection in a better way.

A simplified version of the course-rating system had operated for a year. Figure 10.1 shows part of the rating screen that the students used. Note that there are 11 questions with a numerical rating on a scale from 1 to 6 (*Overall conclusion*, *There is clear progression*, etc.). There are three text boxes for remarks about *good things* about the course and three for remarks about things that *should be improved*.

The system was developed by the general manager of the university, Mads Tofte. Generally, the results had been good, but there were some problems that a new system should deal with. Some of them were related to the very long Web pages that the students had to fill in. Others were related to teachers not being able to get an overview of the evaluations.

Design aspects

Compared to the hotel system, the course-rating system has several interesting aspects:

▪ Most readers can more easily relate to it since they know the university world much better than the hotel world.

▪ The system is entirely Web based.

▪ It has to integrate with other existing administrative systems.

▪ It has several user groups with different needs.

▪ Giving an overview of data is much harder and requires creative visualization.

Before starting on the design, we will look at the large-scale solution: How do we achieve the business goals listed above? Part of this is to plan what will happen

Fig 10.1 Old course rating page

Guidelines

Your answers on the multiple choice questions are used for computing numerical scores based on this conversion table: I agree completely = 6, I largely agree = 5, I rather agree = 4, I rather disagree = 3, I largely disagree = 2, I completely disagree = 1.

The course Java Basic, overall

To what extent do you agree with the following statements?	Choose
Overall conclusion: I am happy about this course	I largely agree ▾
There is clear progression and cohorence in the contents of the course	I largely agree ▾
I think this course is highly relevant for my future job profile	I rather agree ▾
The contents are very practical	I largely agree ▾
I would like to see more emphasis on practice	I agree completely ▾
I think the theoretical level of the course is high	I rather disagree ▾
I would like the theoretical level of the course to be increased	I completely disagree ▾
I feel that the course gives me good knowledge of relevant literature	I rather agree ▾
I feel I satisfy the specified requirements for the course	I largely agree ▾
I spend a great deal of time on this course, compared to the 15 hours a week it is supposed to take	I rather agree ▾
I think a lot is expected compared to the 15 hours that are the norm	I rather disagree ▾

Write up to three good things about the course

Avoid commenting on specific teachers here.

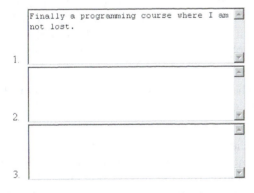

1. `Finally a programming course where I am not lost.`

2.

3.

Write up to three things that should be improved

Avoid commenting on specific teachers here.

`The examples are too mathematical. I would like to see programs that ordinary people could use.`

during the semester. After defining the large-scale solution, we define the requirements to the new system by means of usability requirements, task descriptions, the data the system must deal with, etc. Finally, we design the user interface by means of virtual windows, systematic function design and prototyping.

10.1.1 The large-scale solution

Based on discussions with students, teachers and management, we defined what should happen during a semester to meet the business goals. We recognized that the business goal essentially asked us to support one single high-level task:

High-level task: Manage and monitor teaching of a semester.

The large-scale solution was to break this high-level task into a list of ordinary tasks to be carried out in the future:

Task list for a semester

T1: Planning. During the months before the semester starts, managers plan the courses to be offered during the next semester. Managers include line managers and elected student representatives. They also allocate teachers to the courses. Ratings from the current semester are used as input, but many other factors are also taken into account.

T2: Enrol. Students enrol on the courses. They look at earlier course ratings before they choose their courses. (Most courses are optional for the students.)

T3: Early rating. Around one third into the semester, the students get an e-mail asking them to state three good things and three problematic things for each of the courses they follow. They do it on the Web. The result is visible to the teachers on the course. In their reply, the students may state who they are, but as a default they are anonymous.

T4: Share teaching. If multiple teachers share a course, they make an agreement on how to share the credit for the course. They do so with the same Web application.

T5: Late rating. Close to the end of the course, the students are asked to rate various course factors with a numeric rating. They are allowed to edit the earlier statements they made about the course. They are also asked to rate each teacher on the course. Here too they give numeric ratings as well as comments about good and problematic things about the teacher. They have to do this within a period of around a week and in this period their rating is secret.

T6: Review. After each rating period, teachers review the results for the courses they have been teaching. After early rating, the teachers don't take any action through the system, but after late rating they do. They may decide to hide any inappropriate comment about the courses, or they may write replies to comments. After late rating they can also see the ratings and comments about themselves. Another week is allocated for the review.

T7: Use results. The course ratings are made publicly available to everyone at the university and are studied by students, teachers and management. The teacher ratings and the hidden remarks are made available only to the teacher and to management.

T8: Monitoring. During the semester, management controls the process. They initiate the first rating and the late rating, they follow the number of votes given and they may decide to send out reminders to students who have not voted. They decide when rating stops and when results are made publicly available.

T9: Record marks. When students have got their exam marks, statistics about them are added to the public evaluation results. The identity of the students is kept secret, of course. At this time, management can also see the final financial status of each teacher and each course.

Parts of these tasks are supported by traditional administrative systems. These systems take care of recording students, courses, teachers allocated to courses, students participating in each course and exam marks. However, a separate system handles the course ratings. It is this system we will deal with here.

The old course-rating system could not adequately support all of the tasks above. For instance there was no early evaluation, so teachers had little basis for correcting problems; too few students evaluated their courses, etc. So another part of the solution was to get rid of the major problems with the present system:

Present problems

P1: Only about 50% of the students replied. One reason was that there were too many questions to answer and the system insisted on all of them being answered. Another reason was that there was little overview of the entire questionnaire. It looked like one huge Web page. A typical student would follow three courses per semester and had to answer 11 numerical questions for each of them. The student would have to answer almost the same number of questions for each of the teachers and tutors on the course.

P2: The teachers and tutors were identified by their name, but often the students couldn't remember the name of the teacher/tutor. This might cause them to either not comment about this person or address their comments to the wrong person.

P3: Evaluation was done only at the end of the semester. The result was that problems were revealed too late for the teacher to do anything about them.

P4: It was hard for management to get an overview of the course ratings. Although the system showed averages of the numerical ratings, there were too many numbers to look at.

P5: The system was not integrated with other administrative IT systems. Lists of course participants were often completely out of date and exam marks couldn't be transferred to the rating system and compared against course ratings.

When writing the requirements, we transferred these problems to the proper place in the task descriptions. This made the designer aware of the problem at the right point during design. But just to make sure, we also put them on the list of defects. We could then follow up on them at any time.

10.1.2 Requirements

Functional requirements

Requirement 1   Data to be stored: The system must store the data described in section 10.3.

Requirement 2   Tasks to be supported: The system must support the users and tasks described in section 10.2.

Technical interfaces

Requirement 3   Platform: Like the old system, the new system must operate entirely on the Web with screens made in straightforward HTML (because of the tools used by developers).

Requirement 4   Screens: The system must be designed for small screens of 800 * 600 pixels.

Requirement 5   Data integration: The system must integrate its data with data found in other administrative systems, such as course tables, student tables and employee tables.

Quality requirements

Requirement 6   Response time: When using the system from the local university network, response times for changing to another page in the system must be at most 3 seconds on average. For pages that give overview of many courses, 10 seconds on average is acceptable.

Requirement 7   Data volume: The system must be able to handle 30 study lines, 8000 students, 600 courses and 900 teachers. (These figures allow for a growth factor of 3 to 4.) Each student rates an average of three courses per semester. History data must be kept for at least five years.

Usability, students:

Requirement 8   90% of all students must be able to rate the courses for a semester without task failures the first time they try.

Requirement 9   80% of all students must be able to rate three courses with an average of three teachers in at most 30 minutes the first time they try.

Requirement 10   80% of all students must be able to review the course ratings and understand the results correctly.

Requirement 11   80% of all students must find it easy to review the ratings.

Usability, teachers:

Requirement 12   90% of all teachers must be able to record the teacher sharing without task failures the first time they try.

Requirement 13   80% of all teachers must be able to review the course ratings and understand the results correctly.

Requirement 14   80% of all teachers must find it easy to review the ratings.

Usability, managers:

Requirement 15   After a one-hour course, 80% of managers must be able to use earlier ratings for planning without task failures; identify courses and teachers that need improvement; monitor the rating process without task failures; find it easy to do these things.

We have used a mixture of problem counts (absence of task failures), task–time measurements, understandability measurements and opinion measurements. We have not attempted to define details of how to measure this, how many test persons to use and how to ask about the opinions. We leave these details to the project team.

Note that we have handled the problems with the old system as a special kind of usability requirement: Avoid the present usability problems (requirement 8).

The system is developed as an in-house project. This means that the requirements need not be contractually precise. There should be room for changes during the project as stakeholders and developers learn more about the needs. However, the goals of the system should be kept in view at all times – unless explicitly changed for good reasons.

10.2 Task descriptions and user profiles

Above we listed the tasks to be done through a semester. We considered this task list a single high-level task that is performed jointly by students, teachers and managers. We will now look closer at the individual tasks on the list and the user profiles.

Below we have divided the tasks according to the user roles (student, teacher, manager or public). The user role corresponds roughly to the work-area concept we used for the hotel system. Task T7 (*Use results*) may be carried out by any user, and we have accordingly shown it for each user role. Figure 10.2 gives an overview of the tasks and their users.

Most of the tasks are rather simple, and we describe them as *annotated tasks* with present problems and ideas for solution. Task T8 (*Monitoring* the rating) is more complex and is shown with subtasks. Some of the tasks are partly supported by existing administrative systems, and we will not consider these aspects in the course-rating system.

Student

Domain knowledge: Students know about the courses they rate, but may be uncertain about confidentiality and the consequences of their rating. They know about other courses from rumours and course descriptions outside this system.

Domain attitude: Students are curious about the results of the ratings. Most of them are willing to rate their own courses, but they are also very busy and not willing to spend more than an hour on the rating. Around 20 minutes for the entire rating would be great. Even when they decide to do the rating, they may be interrupted, often many times.

IT knowledge: All students have a basic understanding of the Web and use it every now and then. (Some students are intense users, of course.)

IT attitude: Most students are positive towards IT, but also critical. Some students are older than 50 years and may find IT annoying.

Discretionary usage: Participation in the rating is entirely optional. The only thing that makes students rate their courses is a moral obligation – much like the obligation to vote at an election.

Physical abilities: There are some students with physical disabilities. However, they are all able to use a PC. Some may have problems with small text fonts.

Tasks

T2: **Enroll** on courses. Most of this is presently done with other systems. However, students want to see course ratings before enrolling.

■ Problems: Hard to get overview of course ratings.

Fig 10.2   Teaching one semester – tasks involved

Tasks:	Students	Teachers	Management	Public
T1: **Planning** the teaching			x	
T2: **Enroll** on courses	x			
T3: **Early rating** ■ remarks about courses	x			
T4: **Share teaching** (fractions)		x		
T5: **Late rating** ■ scores for courses ■ revise remarks ■ scores and remarks for teachers	x			
T6: **Review** the results		x		
T7: **Use results**	x	x	x	x
T8: **Monitoring** ■ Start and stop activities ■ Follow progress ■ Send reminders			x	
T9: **Record marks**	(automatic transfer)			

T3:   Early rating. Students get an e-mail asking them to rate and comment on the courses.

■ Problems: Presently this is part of the late rating.

■ Solutions: Record only course remarks at the early stage. (This is all the teacher needs now to improve the course.) Allow recording a bit at a time.

T5:   Late rating. Students get an e-mail asking them to rate courses and teachers.

■ Problems: Too many questions. Impossible to do a bit at a time. Little overview of the questionnaire. Students cannot remember teacher and tutor names. Participant and teacher data are not properly updated.

■ Solutions: Better overview of screens. Reuse remarks from early rating. Allow recording a bit at a time. Allow students to skip the tutors they don't know about. Show picture of teachers. Better data sharing between systems (this is not a user interface issue).

T7:   Use results. Students look at the course ratings and the remarks about each course.

■ Problems: It would be nice to know when the ratings are available.

Teacher

Domain knowledge: Most teachers know about course rating from the earlier system. New teachers may get a short introduction to the system, but ideally they should be able to find out on their own from e-mails they get with links to the Web application.

Domain attitude: Teachers are curious about the results of the ratings and how they fare compared to other teachers. However, they are also scared about the possible consequences for themselves. Given the right atmosphere and support, most teachers are willing to try improving their own performance.

IT knowledge: All teachers have a good understanding of the Web and use it for other administrative procedures too.

IT attitude: Most teachers are positive towards IT, but are becoming more and more critical about the growing number of administrative procedures they have to do through bad user interfaces.

Discretionary usage: Being rated is compulsory.

Physical abilities: All teachers are able to use a PC. Some may have problems with small text fonts.

Tasks

T4: Share teaching. Teachers record the fraction of the credits they will earn. Done on an *ad hoc* basis.

■ Problems: They tend to forget.

■ Solutions: Remind them when they review the ratings.

T6: Review ratings. Teachers review ratings and remarks for their courses and themselves. They may decide to hide inappropriate comments about the courses. They may add a reply to the student's remarks.

■ Problems: There are many remarks to review when courses have many participants. Teachers also have a suspicion that only a few students comment on the course, but each of these students writes many comments. This is hard to see since many comments are anonymous.

T7: Use results. Teachers look at the course ratings and the remarks.

■ Problems: Hard to get overview of data and compare one's own courses against the other courses.

Manager

Domain knowledge: Managers and student representatives have domain knowledge as teachers or students.

Domain attitude: Managers find the ratings very important, but are concerned that too few students rate the courses and teachers don't use the results. They want to monitor what is going on and send reminders to those who haven't done what is expected.

IT knowledge: As for teachers and students.

IT attitude: As for teachers and students.

Discretionary usage: Managing the course rating is compulsory for at least one manager, but for the others it is optional.

Physical abilities: As for teachers and students.

Tasks

T1: Planning. Managers plan courses for the next semester. Among other things, they draw on ratings from the current and previous semesters.

- Problems: Hard to get overview of data. Marks from exam not available (see T9).

T7: Use results. Management looks at the course ratings and remarks, and may also look at the teacher ratings and remarks.

- Problems: Although the ratings for each course presently are counted and averaged, it is hard to get an overview of the data, compare courses, see trends since last semester, etc.

T8: Monitoring. Managers start and stop each stage of the rating process, remind students, etc.

- Subtasks:

    1 Start early rating. Send warning messages to all students.

    2 Start late rating. Send warning messages to all students.

    3 Keep an eye on the number of students that have replied. Send reminders as needed.

    4 Close late rating and start teacher's review. Send warning message to teachers.

    5 Close review period and publish the results. Inform all students and teachers that the results are available.

- Problems: Remember to do it. Remember how far we are in the process.

T9: Record marks. After exams, administration records the marks and managers review the financial status of teachers and courses.

- Subtasks:

    1 As soon as possible after exams and markings, record the marks in the system and make them available for the course-rating system.

    - Problems: Presently not done because marks are recorded in another system and it is too laborious to enter data manually twice.

- Solution: Ensure data sharing (this is not a user interface issue).

2 Management reviews the financial status of each teacher and each course. (This is presently done through another system.)

The public

The 'public' means anybody with a relation to the university: students from any study line, teachers, management (and administrative staff). The user profiles are as described for the user groups above.

Discretionary usage: Entirely optional.

Tasks

T7: Use results. Look at the course ratings and remarks to learn about the courses.

- Problems: Hard to get overview of data.

10.3 Data model for course rating

Figure 10.3 shows the data model for the new system. Most of the boxes have double-line borders. They correspond to entities created and maintained by the existing administrative systems. Some fields in these entities are used only by the rating system and they have to be added to the existing system in some way. There are two boxes that are used only by the rating system, *TeacherRating* and *Action*.

From a user interface viewpoint, it is not important how data are shared between the systems. From a technical viewpoint it can be handled in several ways. The simplest one is to have a university-wide database. The database manager will add the new fields and the two new tables to this database. Another solution is to replicate parts of the central database into a new one reserved for the rating system. Periodically, changes in the central database will be transferred to the rating system database.

Data dictionary

Class: Study line
Each record describes a study line (course programme) offered by the university. In the rating system we need only the name attribute of the study line.

Class: Course
Each record describes a course offered by the university. The course has a code (e.g. JP-1), a name (e.g. Java Basic) and a semester (e.g. S2003 – S means Spring). The field *credits* gives the amount of student credits for completing the course (e.g. 15 ECTS). There are other course fields, but we don't need them here. The course belongs to a study line as shown by the connector. (Technically this will be handled by a foreign key.)

Normalization rules suggest that *Course* is split into two tables: one for the data that doesn't change from semester to semester (e.g. code, course name and credits) and one for the course instance (e.g. S2003). This issue is not important here. However, we assume that we can get data from previous instances of the course by means of the course code.

Class: Person
Each record describes a person that the university keeps track of. A person may be a teacher, a student, administrative staff, etc. Some persons may have several of these roles at the same time, so the role is not an attribute of the person. The system keeps track of the teacher role and the student role through the role entities *Teacher* and *Participant*. Persons are identified by their e-mail address. They also have a name attribute, a picture of themselves – plus other attributes that we don't need here. A person may be enrolled on a study line as shown by the connector.

Class: Teacher

Each record describes that a person serves as a teacher (or tutor) on a course, as shown by the connectors. There are two attributes of interest here: *Role* indicates whether the teacher is the course manager, an ordinary teacher or a tutor. *Fraction* (e.g. 60%) shows how many of the student credits the teacher will 'earn' for carrying out this course. As an example, one teacher may earn 60% of the credits for students on his course, while another teacher earns the remaining 40%. The plan is that the teachers on the course decide and record this fraction themselves. The system will check that the total is 100%.

Class: Participant

Each record describes that a person is enrolled as participant on a course. The participant's ratings of this course are fields in the record.

q1	Integer 1..5. The rating for the first numerical question. (For reasons explained below, we changed the rating from a 6-point scale to a 5-point scale.)
q2...q8	The rating for the other numerical questions. (We changed the number of questions from 11 to 8.)
hours	The total number of hours this student spent weekly on the course.
rem1...	Six text fields, each at most 1000 characters. The student's remarks about the course.
hide1 ...	Six Yes/No fields corresponding to the six remarks. *Yes* indicates that one of the course teachers has decided to hide the remark from the public.
reply1...	Six text fields where the teachers on the course can reply to the student's six remarks.
status	An enumeration field that indicates whether the student is enrolled on the course, has dropped out of the course, is on a waiting list, etc. Inherited from the administrative system. Used for statistics in the rating system.
marks	The final exam marks for the student on this course (e.g. A+, A, A−, B+ in the American system or 0, 1, 2... in some European systems).
anonymous	A Yes/No field. *No* indicates that the student has decided not to be anonymous. (In practice many students decide this because they would like to discuss their concerns with the teacher.)

You may wonder whether q1 ... q8 and rem1 ... rem6 are violations of the first normal form. The number of fields seems to be rather arbitrarily chosen. In fact you might put the data in separate tables, but there is little gain in doing so. The main advantage would be that managers might be able to add new questions or delete existing ones, without having to involve the IT people. In practice, such changes will

Fig 10.3 Data model, new course rating

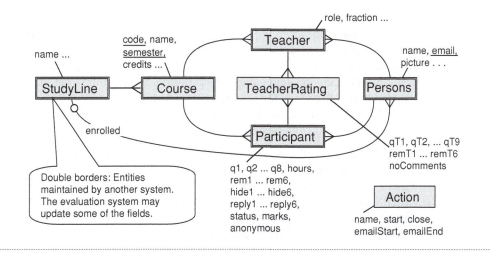

often involve changes to the user interface, to statistical programs, etc., and an IT person has to be involved anyway.

Class: TeacherRating

Each record describes one participant's rating of one teacher on the course. Notice that the class is connected to the teacher as a role, not to the person. The students don't evaluate the person but the teacher in his role on this course. As an example, assume that a student follows two courses where the same person serves as a teacher/tutor. The student will then evaluate the teacher twice – once in each of his roles.

qT1 . . . qT9	Integer 1..5. The nine numerical ratings of the teacher.
remT1 . . . remT6	Text fields, each at most 1000 characters. The student's remarks about the teacher.
noComments	The student didn't know the teacher or didn't want to comment for some other reason.

There is no need for replies from the teachers or indications about *hidden*. Ratings of the teacher are visible only to the teacher himself and to management.

Class: Action

These records describe the various actions that management takes during the semester, for instance starting and closing the early rating. Each record shows when the action starts and ends and which e-mail texts are sent to teachers and students when the action starts and ends.

The Action class is not connected to the rest of the database. We might connect each action to the persons that got an e-mail, but it seems unnecessary to keep track of this.

10.4　Virtual windows for course rating

I made the virtual windows in the usual way (Chapter 6). First I made a plan for the windows. The plan ensured that there were few screens and that each task needed access to only a few windows. I also tried to avoid duplication of data in several windows. Next I made the detailed graphical design. During this some surprises came up, and I had to change the window plan. During CREDO check and understandability test more problems turned up, and I corrected most of them before continuing with the function design.

Figure 10.4A shows the plan for the virtual windows. The plan outlines the virtual windows and their contents at the top. The relationship between virtual windows and tasks is shown as a matrix. In the next figures we show the graphical version of the virtual windows. I might have made the windows with paper and pencil, but since screen space was crucial for many of the windows and I had little HTML experience, I made them in HTML directly. This was the easiest way to ensure that the design was realistic for a simple HTML solution on a small screen. Unfortunately, it was also very time-consuming compared to a paper and pencil version.

Student's rating windows

The most critical tasks for success are the student's early and late rating (T3 and T5). Two windows are planned for this, the course-rating window (details in Figure 10.4B) and the teacher-rating window (Figure 10.4C). In principle, these might have been combined into one large virtual window with everything the student had to do. The virtual window would then consist of space for rating around three courses and 3 to 20 teachers. This was the user interface in the old course-rating system, but students lost the overview and gave up.

In the old system, each course used about $2\frac{1}{2}$ screens as shown in Figure 10.1. In the new system, each of the rating windows was fully visible on an 800 * 600 pixel screen – the minimum screen size that Web designers usually plan for. In order to achieve this, I used a couple of tricks:

- The good things and bad things about each course are shown in separate columns. This utilizes the otherwise empty screen space at the right.

- The number of questions is reduced from 11 to 9. The old system used two questions to find out whether students thought that the practice level was too high or too low. It used another two questions to find out about the theoretical level. This was necessary to ensure that 'Fully agree' was always something good. In the new system, I reduced these four questions to two by using 'Neutral' as the 'good' answer. Three questions were of this kind and appear last on the list. I made several understandability tests to confirm that students understood these unorthodox questions in the intended way. At the same time, I reduced the rating

Fig 10.4 A Virtual windows plan, course rating

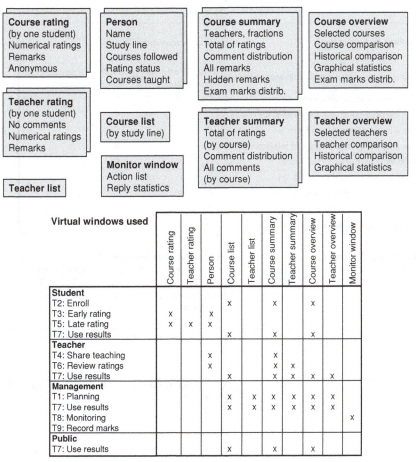

Virtual windows used	Course rating	Teacher rating	Person	Course list	Teacher list	Course summary	Teacher summary	Course overview	Teacher overview	Monitor window
Student										
T2: Enroll				x		x		x		
T3: Early rating	x		x							
T5: Late rating	x	x	x							
T7: Use results				x		x		x		
Teacher										
T4: Share teaching			x			x				
T6: Review ratings			x			x	x			
T7: Use results				x		x	x	x	x	
Management										
T1: Planning				x	x	x	x	x	x	
T7: Use results				x	x	x	x	x	x	
T8: Monitoring										x
T9: Record marks										
Public										
T7: Use results				x		x		x		

choices from 6 to 5 and used a radio button approach for the scores rather than text selection.

■ I dropped the introductory guidelines and moved the bottom items (*Anonymous* and *Save*) to the top. This saved several more lines and utilized the empty space at the right. (Strictly speaking *Save* is a function, and it doesn't belong to the virtual window. Anyway, to an HTML novice, it was nice to know that there would be space for it.)

To make it even simpler for the students, I omitted the radio button part during the early rating. At that time the primary aim is to allow the teacher to adjust the course. The textual remarks are the best vehicle for this. Notice that we still talk about only one virtual window. Conceptually it shows many details, but some of them are only visible at certain stages.

Fig 10.4 B   Virtual window, Course rating

| Course rating: JP-1, Java Basic | I want to be anonymous ☑ | | | | Save |

To what extent do you agree with the following statements?	Fully agree	Partly agree	Neutral	Partly disagree	Completely disagree
Overall conclusion: I am happy about this course	○	⦿	○	○	○
There is a clear progression and coherence in the course	○	○	⦿	○	○
The course is highly relevant for my future jobs	⦿	○	○	○	○
The course gives me good knowledge of relevant literature	○	○	○	⦿	○
I meet the entry requirements for the course	○	⦿	○	○	○
The contents are too practical (neutral if ok)	○	○	⦿	○	○
The contents are too theoretical (neutral if ok)	○	⦿	○	○	○
The course requires too much of my time (neutral if ok)	○	○	○	⦿	○
Total number of hours I spend weekly on the course	12				

Only present during Late Rating

Good things about the course
For publication - don't comment on teachers here

> Finally a programming course where I am not lost

Things that could be improved
For publication - don't comment on teachers here

> The examples are too mathematical. I would like to see examples that real people could use

> Some of the material is completely irrelevant

> Sometimes theory and exercises are out of synch.

Although each window gives a good overview, we now have a problem with navigating between them. Here we need overview too. At first I imagined that later I would add navigation buttons (hyperlinks) from the course window to the teacher windows. However, some courses had many tutors, and although each student would rate only a few, they all had to be visible in the course window. To make things worse, we had the problem of students not being sure about the teacher's names. This called for a picture of each teacher.

As a result, I decided to use a special overview window for each student (Figure 10.4D). It lists all the courses and teachers the student is expected to rate at this stage. It also indicates how much of this the student has done at present.

During late rating the student also sees the teachers with a picture. To utilize the empty space at the right, I show four teachers' pictures in a row. This is important to preserve the overview for courses with many tutors. Notice the unusual combination

Fig 10.4 C Virtual window, Teacher rating

Teacher rating: John Smith
Course: JP-1, Java Basic
I cannot comment on this teacher ☐

To what extent do you agree with the following statements?	Fully agree	Partly agree	Neutral	Partly disagree	Completely disagree
Overall conclusion: I am happy to have this teacher	○	◉	○	○	○
The teacher uses good examples	○	○	○	◉	○
The teacher gives a good overview of the subjects	◉	○	○	○	○
The teacher shows good practical experience	○	○	◉	○	○
The teacher shows deep theoretical insight	◉	○	○	○	○
The teacher provides good help and feedback	○	◉	○	○	○
The teacher is open to new ideas and problems	○	◉	○	○	○
The teacher is enthusiastic	◉	○	○	○	○
The teacher is always well prepared for classes	◉	○	○	○	○

Good things about the teacher
(Only the teacher and management will see it)

> John is always in good mood.

> He helps you just the right amount.

Things the teacher could improve
(Only the teacher and management will see it)

> His examples are sometimes too academic.

of the teacher's names as a vertical list to the left and the teachers' portraits as a horizontal row. The list to the left is part of the checklist of things to rate. 'Confusing' says the heuristic evaluator. Fortunately, with the final prototype users hesitated only a second. Then they correctly chose the correct teacher. (The system also gives them feedback on the Teacher Rating screen, which shows the teacher's portrait as well as the name.)

Teacher's review windows

After the rating, teachers have to look at the results. Two virtual windows are used for this: Course summary (Figure 10.4E) and Teacher summary (not shown, but is

Fig 10.4 D   Virtual window, Person (student and/or teacher)

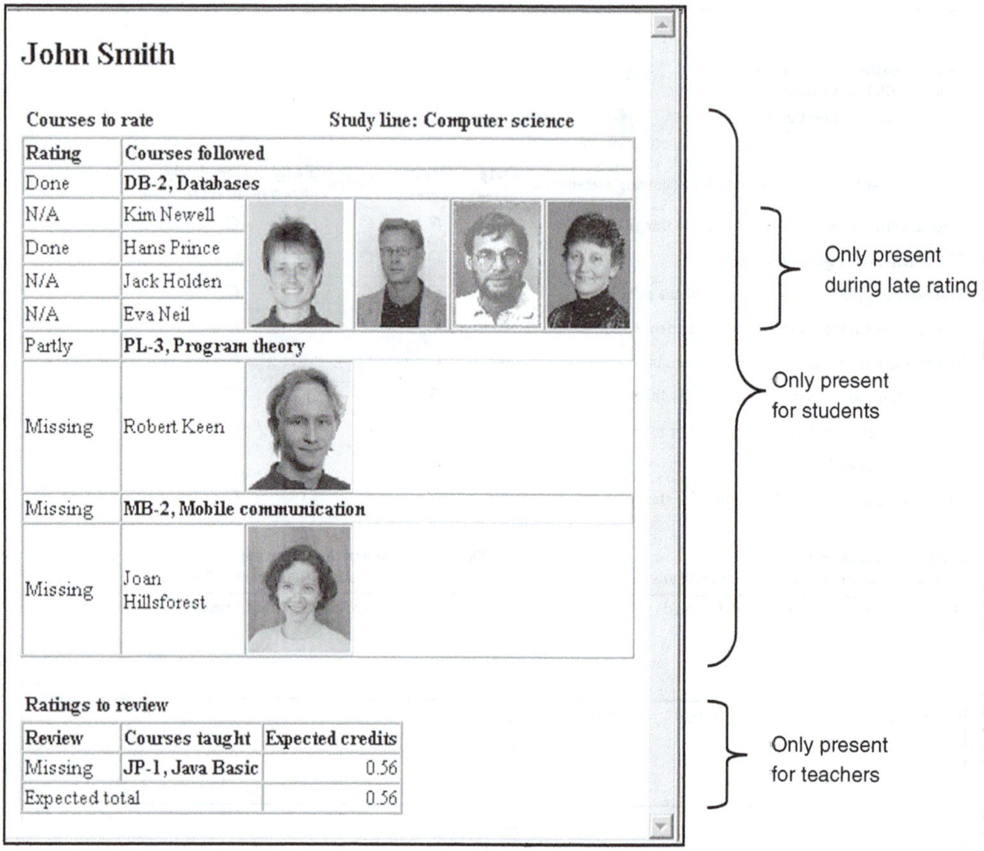

John Smith

Courses to rate   Study line: Computer science

Rating	Courses followed
Done	DB-2, Databases
N/A	Kim Newell
Done	Hans Prince
N/A	Jack Holden
N/A	Eva Neil
Partly	PL-3, Program theory
Missing	Robert Keen
Missing	MB-2, Mobile communication
Missing	Joan Hillsforest

Ratings to review

Review	Courses taught	Expected credits
Missing	JP-1, Java Basic	0.56
Expected total		0.56

Only present during late rating

Only present for students

Only present for teachers

similar to the Course summary). In principle, we don't need additional virtual windows for this. The teacher could go through all the students' rating windows (made anonymous, of course). However, this would violate the design rule about few window instances for important tasks, and it also gives a bad overview of data.

After the late rating, the Course summary window shows the numerical ratings in the same form as the student's rating window, but with totals in each field. The average is also shown. (This is very similar to the way course summaries were shown in the old system.)

After early and late rating, the window shows the student's remarks as a long list. The first part of the list shows the good points, the last part the bad points. The teacher can hide remarks from publication by means of a check box. This is very similar to the old system. For courses with many students, the list may be very long, but it is hard to get an overview. To help a bit, I have added a few things in the new system:

Fig 10.4 E   Virtual window, Course summary

Course summary: JP-1, Java Basic   Semester: S2003

Teachers	Fraction	Estimated credits
Ann Nelson	75%	1.69
John Smith	25%	0.56

Students	
Enrolled:	23
Cancelled later:	5
Replies, total:	20

Number of students	Fully agree 5	Partly agree 4	Neutral 3	Partly disagree 2	Completely disagree 1	Average
Overall conclusion: I am happy about this course	9	4	1	3	3	3.7
There is a clear progression and coherence in the course	9	4	7	0	0	4.1
The course is highly relevant for my future jobs	12	2	6	0	0	4.3
The course gives me good knowledge of relevant literature	5	7	4	4	0	3.7
I meet the entry requirements for the course	11	6	2	1	0	4.4
The contents are too practical (neutral if ok)	4	8	8	0	0	3.8
The contents are too theoretical (neutral if ok)	2	5	10	3	0	3.3
The course requires too much of my time (neutral if ok)	9	4	0	4	3	3.6

Hours:	<5	5-9	10-14	15-19	>19	
Number of hours I spend weekly on the course	2	3	10	3	2	11.8

Number of students with 0, 1, 2, 3 comments	0	1	2	3	Average
Good comments		3	5	12	2	1.8
Bad comments		15	0	2	3	0.6

Exam marks	A+	A	A-	B+	B	B-	C	D
Number of students	2	5	4	3	2	2	1	1

Good things about the course	Student ID	Hide
It is a good idea to have exercises right after lectures. In this way you try it out as soon as possible.	188	☐
Not too much lecturing	188	☐
Finally a programming course where I am not lost	212	☐

Only present during Late Rating

■ The remarks are ordered according to their author. To preserve confidentiality, each student gets an anonymous number for this course, and the number is shown besides the remark. This allows the teacher to get an impression of whether a lot of students made this kind of remark or only a few who repeated it in various ways. (With the old system, teachers complained about not having this information). The name behind the number is kept secret, of course, unless the student wants to be known. In the latter case, the student number is not shown, but the student *name* is shown in the remark box. There is no need to store the anonymous number in the database. The system can generate the number when it generates the screen picture.

■ A three-line section of the window gives an overview of how many students made good comments and bad comments. This also helps the teacher get a feeling for how big the problems are.

Apart from reviewing ratings and using the results, the teachers also have to specify how they share the course credits. According to the principle of keeping the number of virtual windows low, I have handled these data in the Course summary window. This causes no conflicts with other design rules. It also gives a nice overview of the teachers on the course, and it reminds the teachers to specify the sharing when they review the ratings.

A teacher also needs an overview of the courses he has to review. Where should we put this? As usual we should try to reuse the virtual windows we have already. It might be a bit surprising that the planned student window is a good place to put it (Figure 10.4D). What does this mean? It means that the window shows the roles of a specific person. The person may have one or more student roles (course participation) and one or more teaching roles. The window ought to be called a *Person* window. It should of course show only the roles relevant for the person in question. Few people are students as well as teachers and only they will see both kinds of roles.

This solution also helps us provide easy access to the system. Teachers as well as students will by e-mail be asked to log into the Web system with their e-mail address and password. They will then see their own Person window for the rating. From there they can navigate to the windows relevant at this stage. Details of the navigation will be planned later as part of function design.

Manager's windows

Managers will look at the results of the rating, but they also have to monitor the entire process. They must tell the system to give the various user groups access to the right windows, to send e-mails about the start of the various stages, etc. They also need to check how the rating is progressing. The Monitor window (Figure 10.4F) is intended for this. It shows the various activities to carry out, the number of participants who have to reply in each stage and the number of them who have replied.

The stages of the rating are shown in advance, but the manager may add further lines for reminders sent out. Since many of the actions involve sending out an e-mail to some students, the Monitor window also shows the e-mail text to be used as a standard in each case.

Using the results

Course List. When the parties are going to use the results, they have to look at the Course summary windows. In order to do this, they need to search for the course of interest. None of the virtual windows above are suited for this. We need a new one for instance the Course list shown in Figure 10.4F. There is nothing surprising about this virtual window.

Course Overview. A more difficult issue is a better overview of many courses and how they compare. The Course summary window is not suited for this and

Fig 10.4 F   Virtual windows, monitoring and course list

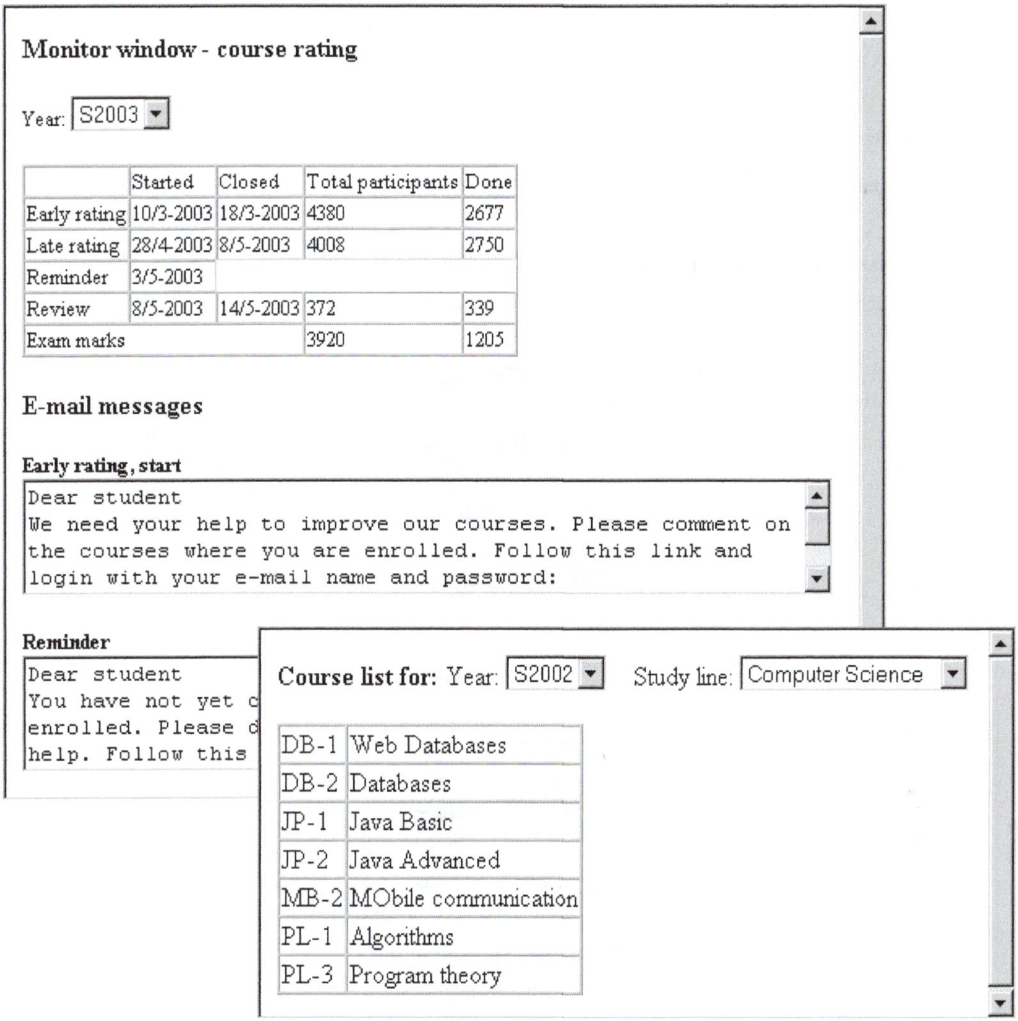

Monitor window - course rating

Year: S2003 ▼

	Started	Closed	Total participants	Done
Early rating	10/3-2003	18/3-2003	4380	2677
Late rating	28/4-2003	8/5-2003	4008	2750
Reminder	3/5-2003			
Review	8/5-2003	14/5-2003	372	339
Exam marks			3920	1205

E-mail messages

Early rating, start

```
Dear student
We need your help to improve our courses. Please comment on
the courses where you are enrolled. Follow this link and
login with your e-mail name and password:
```

Reminder

```
Dear student
You have not yet e
enrolled. Please c
help. Follow this
```

Course list for: Year: S2002 ▼   Study line: Computer Science ▼

DB-1	Web Databases
DB-2	Databases
JP-1	Java Basic
JP-2	Java Advanced
MB-2	MObile communication
PL-1	Algorithms
PL-3	Program theory

managers and teachers complained about it with the old system. Giving a better overview was the most difficult part of the new design. I made several experiments and sought inspiration in the various data presentation techniques, student's attempts at solving the problem, etc.

My best solution is inspired by stock exchange presentations where you can see the closing price, the high and the low, as a single tiny line with sidebars. My version is shown in Figure 10.4G. It looks better in colour, but you should get the idea in black/white too. You see the questions from the student's rating window. For each

Fig 10.4 G Virtual window, Course overview

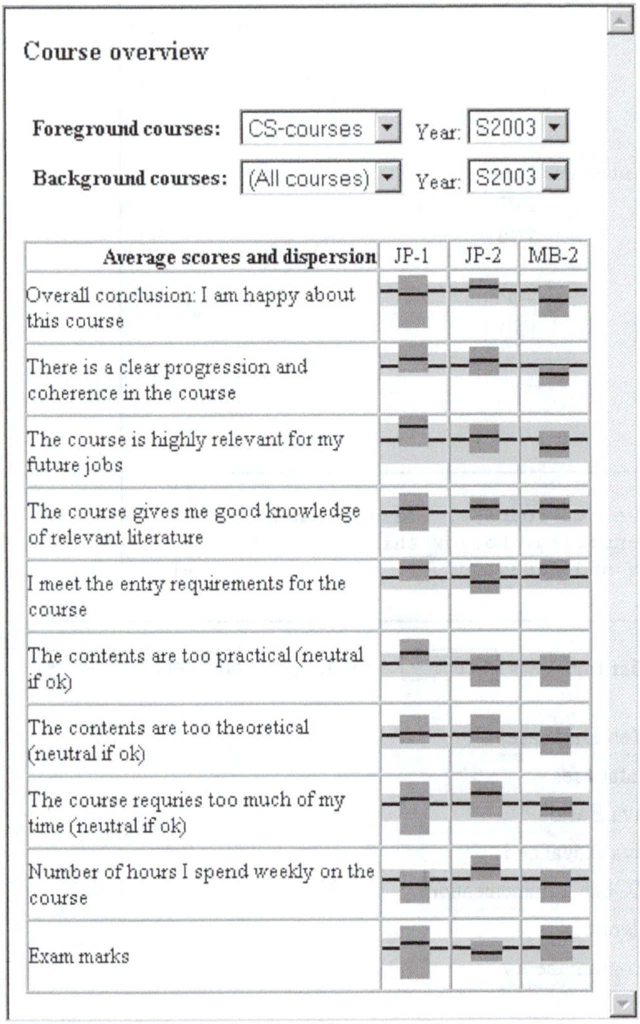

Experimental mini-graphs to show actual distribution against distribution of the background courses

question you see the rating for the courses JP-1, JP-2 and MB-2 as three mini-graphs. You see the ratings on a background, which is the rating for some other course or courses. For the foreground course, you see the average rating, the standard deviation for ratings above the average, and the standard deviation for ratings below the average. For the background course (or courses), you see the same but in a weaker shade.

Now, what are the foreground and background courses? You select them at the top of the virtual window. In the example, the foreground courses are all the courses offered by the Computer Science line. Each of them will have a column of its own (only three of the courses are shown in the example). The background courses are all the courses at the university. You can choose various kinds of background courses. For instance you may choose the courses from the previous semester, thus getting the development for each course.

As an example, look at the top-left mini-graph. It shows that participants on the JP-1 course on average are slightly less happy with the course than the average for all courses. More important, there is a much larger spread of the opinions. Most students are actually very happy with the course, but a significant fraction of the students are more dissatisfied than on average courses. This should tell course management that there seem to be two groups of participants, and it might be a solution to teach them in different ways. (The actual figures are those from the Course summary window shown in Figure 10.4E).

Teacher List. Management needs to search for teachers and branch to the Teacher summary or Teacher overview. It is a straightforward search window and we have not shown it in graphical form here.

Teacher Overview. Teachers and management need an overview window for teachers. It looks very similar to the Course overview, but is not shown here.

Understandability test

At this stage, I made several understandability tests with students, line managers and fellow teachers. There were several problems and I recorded those that I couldn't deal with right away. The defect list already had five problems (P1 to P5) inherited from the present system. Now I added these new problems to the list:

P6: Foreground/background courses. Most course managers and students understood the basic idea about average and deviation without any explanation. However, they had some difficulty relating the foreground/background selection to the mini-graphs.

Colour coding of the data removed this problem to a large extent. The foreground mini-graph became green and the drop-down selection of the foreground became green too, suggesting the relationship between the two. The background graph and drop-down selection became light brown.

P7: Graph dispersion. Many users had difficulty understanding what exactly the dispersion meant on the mini-graphs. Was it the worst opinions and the best opinions? Or weighted somehow? (Actually it was the square root of the variance for ratings above the average and below the average. Admittedly, this is very hard to explain in simple terms.)

A student suggested to remedy the problem with a mini-histogram for the foreground and background courses. This would show the actual distribution of replies. I tried to make a couple of versions using this idea. Some of them are shown in Figure 10.4G for the top-left cell. It should be obvious that although the idea was great, it didn't look great in practice. You didn't get the desired overview this way. I didn't find a good solution, but fortunately the problem is not serious. The final system has an 'explain' button that gives the full story, but very few users try it. (This is the typical pattern for help information. It is not as bad as it sounds, because the users that actually try the help explain to other users what they found out.)

P8: Neutral value. Users spent a few seconds finding out about the 'neutral' value for the rating. They didn't make mistakes, but spent some time to reconfirm their understanding of which questions worked which way.

A colleague suggested a colour coding for the 'ideal' values in the questionnaire. I tried a light yellow background and an explanation in the same yellow colour on the summary screen. This improved the understanding immensely.

P9: Anonymous? Users noticed that on the course-rating screen, they could decide whether to be anonymous. On the teacher-rating screen there was no such indication, and users became uneasy about the issue.

I tried to solve the problem by stating on the teacher-rating screen that teacher rating was always anonymous. However, during the later usability tests, some students complained about this. They wanted to reveal their identity.

P10: Rating state. On the Person screen, the system indicates what the student has rated. Some of the indications are confusing, however.

P11: Link to course description. When looking at courses to take the next semester, students want an easy way to look at the existing course descriptions (the home pages for the courses) and at the same time the course rating.

As a result, the prototype got a link from the course list to the course description.

P12: Screen names. The names on the summary screens were confusing. I had used the name *summary* for the screen with totals and averages and *overview* for the screen with the mini-graphs. The users couldn't remember the difference.

In the prototype, I changed the screen names to *course results* and *course graphics*. This helped.

10.5   Function design

Semantic functions

The virtual windows were now reasonably complete and tested for understandability. Next I walked through the tasks to identify the necessary semantic and search functions.

At this stage we assume that all the virtual windows are visible on a huge screen – like an entire desk – as shown in Figure 10.5A. Notice that some virtual windows have got a new name in light of problem P12.

As an example, for the early rating task, the student just has to fill in the data in the Course Rating window. Since we are in the Internet world, the student needs an explicit *Save* function to store the data in the database. (In the figure the function is called *Save&Return* because later navigation analysis shows that it should also return to the previous screen.)

Figure 10.5A shows all the semantic and search functions in bold. The non-bold functions are navigation functions, which we will explain below.

The task walk-through revealed only a few semantic functions. In order for a teacher to review and reply to the course rating, the teacher needs these functions on the Course Result window: *AddReply* to make space for recording a reply, *Hide* to indicate that a remark is to be hidden to the public and *Save* to store the changes.

The manager needs the Monitor window to start and close the various activities. When an activity starts, the system allows users to do various things, and it sends e-mails about what to do now. Four semantic functions are needed for this: *StartActivity*, *CloseActivity*, *SendReminder* and *SaveText* (to save changes made to e-mail texts).

Search functions

There are also a few search functions. When a user looks for a specific course, he will enter some criteria in the Course List window, then ask for a *Refresh* of the course list. This is a search function. Next the user will go to one of the courses on the list. We may call this a search function too or a navigation function. Similar functions are needed for the teacher list.

The Course Graphics window also has a kind of search criteria, the foreground and the background courses. When the user has filled them in, he must tell the system to refresh the screen.

What about the Person window where the user can select a course he has followed, and then go to the Course Rating window. Is it a search function? Not really, there are only a few courses shown in the Person window so it is more a kind of navigation function.

Navigation functions

Now comes the point where we have to face reality. The screen is not a desk but an 800 * 600 pixel screen. First we have to figure out how the virtual windows map into screens (Web pages). In the rating system it is easy. We have planned each virtual window so that it fits well into a screen. So the screens are simply the virtual windows.

We need navigation functions to go from one screen to another. The technique to plan this is a state diagram. When I first made up the state diagram for the rating system, it was one big mess with arrows going across the entire diagram. It was confusing to the designer and would probably confuse users too. Was this really necessary? A closer study of the diagram showed that there were two problems:

1 **Security.** Depending on the user role, some screen transitions were allowed, others not.

2 **Random browsing.** If a user wanted to browse randomly around in the results, the arrows seemed to cross everywhere.

The regular tasks without random browsing followed a much simpler pattern, so I decided to analyse them first.

Regular tasks

Figure 10.5B shows the state transitions (the navigation links) for the regular tasks. The diagram only shows the links we have to build into the screens. The user can additionally use the Browser's built-in Back button to go backwards. Many of the transition arrows are labelled with S, T or M. This shows whether Students, Teachers or Management are allowed to use this link. If there is no label, anybody can use the link. Also notice that there are three ways a user can enter the system, as shown by the three initial state arrows.

Person. For the rating and review tasks, the user will log in with his own e-mail and password, and start in the Person screen. From here he can branch out to Teacher Rating or Course Rating. From there he can return with Save as shown by the double-line call-return arrow. He may also return with the Browser's Back button without saving anything. If the user is a teacher, he may branch out to see his own course and teacher results, review remarks and specify the sharing fractions. For convenience, he may also branch from the course results to the teacher results.

Course list. Any user of the university intranet may look at the course ratings. To do so, the user enters the system through a link to the course list. He may select a course and see the course description, the Course Results and the Graphics. Although there is an arrow from Course Results to the Teacher Results, an ordinary user cannot use it. Only teachers and management can use this link.

Monitor. A manager will start in the Monitor window. Here he can do the monitor task. He may also review the results and plan courses and staffing. To do this, he can

Fig 10.5 A   Functions per virtual window

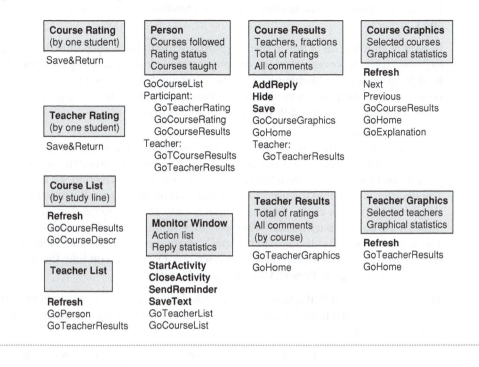

| **Course Rating**
(by one student)

Save&Return | **Person**
Courses followed
Rating status
Courses taught
GoCourseList
Participant:
  GoTeacherRating
  GoCourseRating
  GoCourseResults
Teacher:
  GoTCourseResults
  GoTeacherResults | **Course Results**
Teachers, fractions
Total of ratings
All comments

AddReply
Hide
Save
GoCourseGraphics
GoHome
Teacher:
  GoTeacherResults | **Course Graphics**
Selected courses
Graphical statistics

Refresh
Next
Previous
GoCourseResults
GoHome
GoExplanation |

| **Teacher Rating**
(by one student)

Save&Return | | | |

| **Course List**
(by study line)

Refresh
GoCourseResults
GoCourseDescr | **Monitor Window**
Action list
Reply statistics

StartActivity
CloseActivity
SendReminder
SaveText
GoTeacherList
GoCourseList | **Teacher Results**
Total of ratings
All comments
(by course)

GoTeacherGraphics
GoHome | **Teacher Graphics**
Selected teachers
Graphical statistics

Refresh
GoTeacherResults
GoHome |

| **Teacher List**

Refresh
GoPerson
GoTeacherResults | | | |

Fig 10.5 B   State diagram

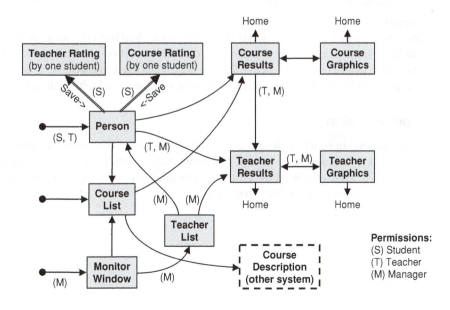

Permissions:
(S) Student
(T) Teacher
(M) Manager

branch to the course list, select a course, and then see Course Results and Graphics. He may also branch to the teacher list, select a teacher and then see Teacher Results and Graphics.

Instead of showing all of this in one diagram, we might have a separate diagram for each user role. However, many screens are accessible from multiple user roles. In the final program we would either have a screen version for each user role or a single version with some programmed way of sorting out who is allowed to go where. I chose the latter solution and thus have only one diagram.

Random browsing

When users look at the ratings, they may browse around in courses through the Course Graphics screen. The graphs may show a course with an interesting reply pattern, and the user may then branch to the Course Result screen to see the details. The diagram shows that the user may go back and forth between Results and Graphics. After a few clicks, the user cannot readily get back to his starting point through the built-in Back button. Managers may similarly browse between teachers. The solution is to provide a link to the user's starting point. This is the Home arrow shown from the Result screens and Graph screens. Depending on how the user logged in, he will go to Person, Course List or Monitor.

The analysis showed that it was these Home links that spoilt the picture in my first state diagram. In the final diagram, the arrow just says *Home* and the mini-specs describe what goes on.

Traditionally, we should put function names on all the transition arrows on the state diagram. In this case most navigation functions have a trivial name such as *GoCourseResult*, so I have not shown the name on the diagram. However, Figure 10.5A shows the full name of the function.

Security

We have expanded the traditional state diagram to deal with the security rules too. We have simply shown the required role on each transition arrow. As an example, a transition from Person to Teacher Results is only allowed to teachers (T) and managers (M). Arrows without any role indication are available to all users.

Function presentation

The final step in function design is to define the way the functions are to be presented to the user. In the rating system we have to utilize the existing traditions on the Web. Figure 10.5C shows the presentation plan for 7 of the 10 screens. The remaining screens follow the same idea.

Fig 10.5 C   Function presentation, rating system (seven windows only)

Course rating	Syntax	Reason
Save&Return	Button, top right	Easy to see.
Teacher rating		
Save&Return	Button, top right	Easy to see.
Person		
GoCourseList	Hyperlink, top right	Standard way. Space available.
GoTeacherRating	Hyperlink on teacher	Standard way. No space used.
GoCourseRating	Hyperlink on course	Standard way. No space used.
GoCourseResults	Hyperlink besides course	Standard way. Empty space used.
GoTCourseResults	Hyperlink on teacher's course	Standard way. No space used.
GoTeacherResults	Hyperlink besides teacher's course	Standard way. Space available.
Course results		
AddReply	Checkbox besides remark	Easy to see. Uses some space.
Hide	Checkbox	Planned already as data entry.
Save	Button, top right	Easy to see.
GoCourseGraphics	Hyperlink, top middle	Should pre-select the course as foreground.
GoHome	Hyperlink, top middle	
GoTeacherResults	Hyperlink on teacher	Standard way. No space used.
Course graphics		
Refresh	Button besides criteria	
GoCourseResults	Hyperlink on course header	
Next	Button above table	Scrolls to next foreground courses
Previous	Button above table	Scrolls to previous foreground courses
GoHome	Hyperlink, top right	
Course list		
Refresh	Button besides criteria	
GoCourseDescription	Hyperlink on course	
GoCourseResults	Hyperlink on course	
Monitor window		
StartActivity	Button on activity line	Indicates action. Takes available space.
CloseActivity	Button on activity line	Indicates action.
SendReminder	Button on top line	
SaveText	Button on e-mail line	
GoTeacherList	Hyperlink, top right	
GoCourseList	Hyperlink, top right	

10.6 Prototype and usability test

At this stage it was quite easy to make a tool-based mock-up of the rating system. The virtual windows were very close to the final screens. Actually, the course-rating screen had got the Save function already when it was a virtual window (ahead of time, admittedly). In order to signal what it did, I renamed it to *Save&Return*. No other functions were needed on this screen.

Figure 10.6 shows three of the more interesting screens. The course graphics screen now shows a more realistic number of courses – nine of them. Problem P6

Fig 10.6 Tool-based mock-up

Continued

Fig 10.6 Tool-based mock-up (*Continued*)

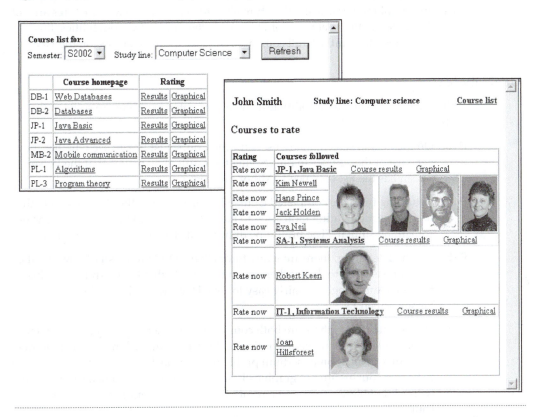

(foreground/background courses) has been corrected so that the foreground-selection field has the same colour (green) as the foreground boxes in the matrix. Similarly, the background field and the background boxes are light brown. The gestalt law of similarity now made users perceive the relationship automatically.

The screen has got *Next* and *Previous* buttons to allow the user to look at more than nine foreground courses. It has got a Refresh button close to the foreground/background criteria. Finally, it has a link from each course to the course results.

The course list screen has links to the course description (the course home page), the course results and the graphics.

The person screen has got hyperlinks to the rating screens for courses and teachers. It also provides links to course results and graphics. For unstructured browsing, there is also a link to the course list.

While I inserted the functions on the virtual windows, I modified the layout a bit here and there. However, I kept the original goal to use simple HTML 3.2 in all the screens. Images (pictures) are used to show pictures of teachers. Each mini-graph in the course graphics is also a small picture (40 * 40 pixels). Otherwise pictures are not used. Combined with the absence of Flash and other advanced possibilities, this makes the screen look rather dull compared to what we typically see on the Web.

Usability test

At this stage I ran several usability tests with the prototype. Here are some of the problems they revealed:

P13: On the Person screen, many users try the CourseList link to see whether they get a list of the courses to rate. Seeing the result, they realize that the Person screen has the list they need. (Minor problem.)

P14: Returning from the completed Course Rating screen to the Person screen, the users expect the rating indication to have changed from RateNow to Done or something similar. (The prototype didn't do it. The final system should.)

P15: During late rating, there are many tutors that a student doesn't know. Yet the student has to go to the teacher screen to indicate that he doesn't know this teacher. (Annoying. It is fairly easy to set a Don't Know indication on the Person screen.)

P16: During late rating, there are both courses and teachers on the Person screen. Some students mix up course rating and teacher rating. Some even fail to rate the course at all. (Some medium problems, some task failures. The cause seems to be that courses are not graphically separated from each other, for instance with a bit of blank screen. As a result, the list of teachers blends with the courses.)

P17: On the Course Result screen, many students have difficulties understanding the statistics about *hours spent on the course*. The reason is the use of the math symbols < and >, which often denote arrows on Web pages.

P18: Managers didn't like the StartActivity and CloseActivity buttons in the monitor window. They would easily forget to press the buttons. They preferred to set up the schedule initially, and then have the system start and stop activities automatically.

At the time of writing, the user interface has been handed over to the IT department, waiting for inclusion in the next release of the rating system.

11

Designing an e-mail system

Highlights

- The virtual windows method applied to tool design.
- Handling multiple purposes and vague tasks.
- Inventing a data model rather than modelling the domain.
- Design to match technical surroundings and standards.

To illustrate the virtual windows approach for a different kind of system, I redesigned an application that most of us know: an e-mail system. An e-mail system consists of a client part and a server part. What we see on our PC is the client. It runs only when we explicitly start it. The server part is running 24 hours a day and collects and sends the mails over the Internet. We will only design the client part. Many e-mail clients exist at present, for instance Microsoft Outlook, Outlook Express, Mozilla, Opera, Eudora.

Designing an e-mail system is very different from designing a business application, such as a hotel system. With the hotel system, we have to support user tasks and data that exist in the domain. With an e-mail system, we are less bound by the domain. Instead we are limited by the technical surroundings for instance the standard e-mail communication protocol, the file systems in the computers, etc. The user tasks are also more varied and we can provide only tools that allow users to *invent* ways to manage their specific tasks.

Before starting on the design, we will look at the business goals and large-scale solution for the new e-mail system. Part of this is an understanding of the high-level tasks where e-mail is involved. After looking at the goals and design ideas, we define the requirements to the new system by means of ordinary task descriptions, the data the system must deal with and the usability requirements. Finally, we design the user interface by means of virtual windows, systematic function design and prototyping.

11.1   Visions for an e-mail system

People use e-mail in many ways, and we want to support all of them. Here are two very general classes of e-mail use:

Simple use. Some people receive few e-mails and can finish with most of them when they receive them. They may file the e-mails for reference, but rarely look into their files. When they occasionally cannot deal with a received mail immediately, they leave it in the Inbox.

Case management. Other people use e-mail as part of more complex tasks. They may for instance be arranging a meeting. This includes finding out who should participate, when they can meet, sending out documents for the participants, booking meeting facilities and sending out the minutes after the meeting. As another example, people may be writing professional reports, and as part of this gather information from several other people or from their own files.

In both cases, the entire task will extend over many e-mail sessions and comprise many sent and received mails. Filing the mails and keeping notes for themselves become essential issues to the users.

English has no precise term for this kind of activity. We might call it a *business case*, but it covers many more things than business. We might call it a *project*, but it might be too small to warrant that term. We will simply call it a *case* and the user activity is *case management*. Typical case managers will have many cases in progress at the same time.

Some kinds of cases are so frequent that companies have special IT systems to deal with them. Examples are order management (each order being a case) and project management (each project being a case). The e-mail system we design is not supposed to handle what these specialized systems can do, but to handle cases of a more general nature.

Mixed use. In practice people are not either simple users or case managers. Many of the e-mails they receive can be handled as *simple use*. Some of them are part of a larger case. It is essential that the system supports a gradual transition between the two kinds.

Business goals

Our goals with the system are:

a) Make an e-mail system that can support simple use as well as case management in an efficient way.

b) Make it easy for users of existing e-mail systems to migrate to the new system.

11.1.1 The large-scale solution

In order to reach these goals we will describe simple usage and case management as high-level tasks that span several sessions at the computer. From this analysis, we will gather design ideas, high-level technical solutions. In contrast, the large-scale solution for course rating was a set of tasks that users had to carry out in the future.

High-level tasks and ordinary tasks

How do we describe e-mail usage as tasks? Is each e-mail session at the computer a task? Or, is the entire management of a case a task? Both are! The session at the computer is an *ordinary task*. Managing the case is a *high-level task*.

In what sense is an e-mail session an ordinary task? It is a working situation where the user focuses on his e-mail for a period of time, preferably without being interrupted. It closes when the user starts doing something else. At this point the user should feel that he has produced something and can leave the e-mail system for now. The session contains many small pieces of work relating to different cases. We might consider each piece of work a separate task, but we don't because we want to ensure that the system supports the entire session well. In conclusion, we want to treat the entire session as a single, ordinary task.

The main requirement to the system is to support the sessions (tasks) well. This should allow the user to manage the business cases well and close them at some point in time. However, the system provides only the potential to do so. It cannot manage the cases for the user.

In order to describe the ordinary tasks (the sessions), we need a better understanding of the high-level tasks that users work with. This understanding will also give us the major design ideas that influence how users in the future could carry out the ordinary tasks.

One class of high-level tasks is management of a case. The case manager will typically allocate a mail folder to the case, possibly with sub-folders. He files messages in the folder, uses them to make decisions, sends other messages, etc.

The other class of e-mail use is filing e-mails for future reference, independent of any current cases. Typically, the user will create a number of folders for different subjects and file the e-mail in the proper folder. We can describe the life cycle of such e-mails as another high-level task.

Figure 11.1A gives an overview of these two high-level tasks and Figure 11.1B gives a detailed description. Task H1 is the management of a case, and task H2 is the life cycle of e-mails for general reference. In the figures I have described the problems that users encounter with present mail systems and also clever ways of supporting certain things. The descriptions are based on my observations of many users, plus interviews and task demos with expert case managers. I have shown the high-level tasks in the Task & Support style, with a right-hand column for suggested solutions.

Fig 11.1 A High-level e-mail tasks, overview

H1	Manage a case
Start:	Case often started before the user is aware of it.
End:	Case completed to the satisfaction of the stakeholders.
Frequency:	A few cases concurrently . . .

Subtasks:	Solutions:
1 Before case is recognized. Problem: Mails scattered in Inbox and Outbox.	S0, S1: Folder hierarchy. S2: Mirror copy in Inbox – reminder.
2 Define the case. Problem: Mails may belong to many cases.	S5: Restructure without the mouse. S2: Mirror copies.
3 Handle received mails. Problems: 3p Hard to see what mail is about. 3q Hard to get overview for decisions. 3r Would like to annotate mails. 3s File hierarchy <> mail hierarchy. 3t Attached files invisible space eaters. 3u File mail and/or attachments	 S4: Auto-relate to sent mail. S2: Mirror copies. S6: Allow edits – visible changes. S3: Integrated file-mail folders. S7: Attached files as mirror copies. S8: Switch from linked to embedded.
4 Handle non–e-mail input. Problem: Notes for private use.	S9: Notes as special messages.
5 Follow up on outgoing mails. Problem: Keeping notes, review Outbox.	S10: Automatic warnings, automatic delete from Outbox.
6 Terminate the case. Problem: Stop filing, archive.	S11: Closed indication for folders. S16: Archiving on other disks.

H2	File mails for general reference
Start:	Reviewing incoming mail or side effect of H1.
End:	Mails discarded.
Frequency:	Rarely above 50 a day.

Subtasks:	Solutions:
1 File Clever: File contact data from mail. Problem: Mail relates to many subjects.	S13: Assign folder to a contact. S12: Extract contact from mail. S2 : Mirror copies.
2 Retrieve. Clever: Searching for contact, date, etc.	S14: Standard search with mirror copy of selected items.
3 Discard Problem: When and what to delete?	S15: Keep track of lastOpened. . . S16: Archiving and retrieval from other disks.

Design ideas

After studying the high-level tasks and the problems, I came up with several design ideas as shown in the right-hand column of the high-level use cases. Most of these design ideas are solutions to one of the problems. Later I found out that most of these solutions existed in some e-mail system, but none seemed to have them all.

Some developers would say that these design ideas become requirements to the new system. This is a subtle issue. It is a bit early to decide that the ideas are requirements. They may sound all right, but we haven't yet tested that they also

Fig 11.1 B High-level e-mail tasks, detailed version

H1	**High-level task: Manage a case.**
Start:	A case often starts before the user is aware of it. At a certain point, it has got so much momentum that he makes it a case and gives it its own case folder.
End:	The case is completed to the satisfaction of all stakeholders.
Users:	Several people are involved in a case, but we will look at the high-level task from a single user's view. It could of course be the manager of the case, but other people involved may also handle it as a case according to their own definition. Messages will typically be stored in a folder for this case (maybe with sub-folders).
Frequency:	Some users are involved in a few cases concurrently, others may be involved in more than 100. Many users deal with around 50 messages a day, and a few deal with more than 100.

Subtasks:	Suggested solution:
1 **Before the case is recognized.** Collect e-mails and other documents that may need action, but are not yet part of a case. It may be mails the user has received or mails he has sent. **Problem:** Many users keep these vague-action mails in their Inbox or Outbox. If there are many of them, they clutter the view.	S0: Use a hierarchical folder system. S1: Use higher level folders for vague cases. S2: Leave a mirror copy of one of the mails in the Inbox for action indication.
2 **Define the case.** At a certain point, the user decides to create a case. Several documents about the case may have accumulated at this point. The name and scope of the case may change, particularly at the beginning. **Clever:** The Explorer-style folder hierarchy is great for restructuring folders. **Problem:** Some of the mails and documents may belong to more than one case, or are also to be kept for general reference.	S5: Move mails and create new folders without the mouse – only the keyboard. And don't disturb the present folder view. S3: Integrated file-mail folders. S2: Mirror copies of mails.
3 **Handle received e-mails.** E-mails are received in batches. Handle those of them relating to this case. Handling an e-mail may involve one or more of this: filing it in the proper case folder, deciding to start some action and reply later, reply or forward to others, trash it (see more details in the ordinary task descriptions later)	
Problems: 3p It is hard to see at a glance what a mail relates to. Many users send out mails with a subject that is their own name of the case, but the receiver may send a reply with another subject. The user may need to see the original message he sent out.	S4: Relate a received reply to the original request using the standard e-mail header *in-reply-to* (invisible in most e-mail systems). Help the user get the original subject and folders this way.
3q It is often hard to get an overview of the other mails and documents needed to make the decision and take the action. One problem is the typical use of out- or sent-folders for messages queued and sent, and the in-folder for messages to be handled. Users cannot remember where the case-relevant messages are and have to search for them in multiple folders.	S2: Mirror copies in the case folder and the Inbox/Outbox folders.
3r The user would like to annotate the received mails, but most e-mail systems don't allow you to do it.	S6: Allow user to edit the message body, but in such a way that the original contents can be shown, for instance with corrections indicated.

Continued

Fig 11.1 B High-level e-mail tasks, detailed version (*Continued*)

3s The system for filing e-mails doesn't correlate with the file system that files other documents. When users create an e-mail folder, they need a strong discipline to create a matching document folder. And when they change folder names, they have to do it in the e-mail system as well as in the file system.	S3: Integrated file-mail folders.
3t Attached files create a huge mess, because they may not be visible through the file system, only through the mail where it was attached. Further, attached files often occupy much space, but in places not visible to the user. As an example, some users keep their mails on the mail server for easy access from everywhere and for automatic backup. However, the mail-server gives them only a small amount of disk storage and it is eaten up by attachments – often pictures – most of which are irrelevant to the user.	S7: Show attached files in the folders where the message is filed.
3u Often the user wants to file the mail, but discard the attachment. Or opposite.	S8: Allow changing embedded attachments to linked, etc.
4 Handle non-e-mail input to the case. Input to the case may come from phone calls, talks with colleagues, something the user reads, or just ideas coming up in the user's mind. They should be handled in exactly the same way as arriving e-mails, being filed, replied to, forwarded to others. **Problem:** It is difficult to file these things if they are not sent to others. Most e-mail systems don't allow you to enter a note and treat it like a mail. Instead, some users send a mail to themselves, others maintain a separate text document with these notes.	S9: Allow notes to be handled in the same way as e-mails.
5 Follow up on outgoing mails. The user may send mails to other people involved in the case, asking them to do something for him. **Problem:** Most e-mail systems don't remind the user of missing replies, so he has to keep separate notes or regularly review the folder of sent mails.	S10: Automatic warning with user-determined delay. For instance warning of missing reply to a message (best if combined with S4).
6 Terminate the case. Some cases close, others are going on forever. For those that close, it is usually necessary to archive many things relating to the case. **Problem:** When a case is closed, the user may want to retrieve things from it, but doesn't want to file things in it by mistake. Present e-mail systems often cause miss-filings because the user happened to select the wrong folder. The user also wants to file the case somewhere with abundant space.	S11: Provide a *closed* indication for folders and possibly hide them. S16: Provide archiving and retrieval somewhere with abundant space.

H2	**High-level task: File e-mails for general reference.**
Start:	Reviewing incoming mail or side effect of H1.
End:	Mails discarded.
Users:	Any e-mail user. Filing will typically be in a folder per subject.
Frequency:	Rarely more than 50 a day.

Continued

Fig 11.1 B High-level e-mail tasks, detailed version (*Continued*)

Subtasks:	Suggested solution:
1 File. When reviewing incoming mails, some may be judged worthy of filing for general use. They may or may not relate to a current case. Examples are general rules prescribed by someone, funny pictures that may come in handy one day, references to documents, references to a potential contact person. Users often maintain folders according to subjects and according to the person they communicate with. **Clever:** Many e-mail systems allow you to file contact information based on the incoming mail. **Problem:** Often a mail may relate to more than one subject, and further relate to a case.	S13: Attach a folder to a contact. S12: Extract contact data from e-mail. S2: Mirror copies.
2 Retrieve. When handling cases or looking for general information, the user may want to retrieve some reference messages. **Clever:** Most e-mail systems have good facilities for searching filed mails according to sender, date, keywords, etc.	S14: Provide standard search features and allow retrieved items to be mirror-copied.
3 Discard. In the long run, there may be a need for discarding messages once thought to be for general use. If they just accumulate, it gets harder to find the relevant ones, and disk space is consumed, particularly by attachments. **Problem:** It is hard to decide when and what to delete. Discarding all mails older than, for instance, five years may cause important reference mails to disappear.	S15: Keep track of last opened and places referenced. Use them as guides for deletion. S16: Provide archiving and retrieval somewhere with abundant space.

work in the use context. At this point they are suggested solutions, not true requirements. Let us have a look at the suggested solutions.

Solution S0: Folder hierarchy. Messages will be saved in a hierarchical folder system as in many existing mail systems. To help users migrate from present e-mail systems, the folder hierarchy should be shown as the familiar Explorer tree in the left-hand part of the e-mail screen.

Birth of a business case. Early in the life of a business case, the case is not recognized as a business case. The user has just sent and received a few messages about the matter. They may be scattered in the Inbox, Outbox or a 'Miscellaneous' folder. At a certain point in time, the user realizes that a new business case has started. He should then create a folder for it and file the scattered messages there.

Often the user knows early on that these messages might turn into a business case of a certain kind. They might for instance relate to arranging a meeting, but the nature of this potential meeting is still unclear and the user doesn't care to invent a separate folder for it. He might create a miscellaneous meetings folder and keep the messages there. In this way it will be easier to extract them later, if the meeting becomes a separate case. The following solution helps handling the early life of a business case:

Solution S1: Allow filing in higher-level points of the hierarchy. Assume that the user has a meetings folder with sub-folders for specific meetings. He should then be able to use the meetings folder for miscellaneous meetings. If the meeting later turns into a business case with a separate meeting folder, the messages are presorted to some extent. (Some e-mail systems, for instance Eudora, don't allow filing in higher-level points of the hierarchy. The user has to create a separate Miscellaneous folder.)

Solution S2: Mirror copies of mails. Some messages relate to more subjects, but can only be filed in one folder. There are several ways around this. Some mail systems allow several keywords to be attached to the message so that it relates to the corresponding subjects. However, users rarely use the keywords. Keeping track of the folder hierarchy and also defining keywords becomes confusing and requires a lot of discipline. What to use when?

Keyword approach. Another solution is to file the mail in an anonymous place, but allow it to be retrieved by any of its keywords. Each keyword is then like a folder of messages having this keyword. Messages with multiple keywords seem to be in several folders. I have tried to make understandability tests of such a design, but users were very confused. 'Where is the message?', they asked. (Piaget's law of object permanence.)

Mirror copy approach. The design idea I try below is to allow mails to be filed in multiple folders as *mirror copies*. Whenever one of the copies is changed, all of them change in exactly the same way. So instead of having keywords, the message now has multiple folders where it is filed. Understandability tests show that this is much easier to grasp, although some expert users are scared that the message will use too much space on their disk.

You may tell the expert user that the mail is filed only once. All the other places are just mirrors (links) that show it. In reality, from a technical point of view, there is no difference between the multiple-keyword approach and the mirror copy approach. It is only the way we explain it that makes the difference.

In practice we expect users to mirror-file most mails in just one or two folders. A mail will only rarely relate to many subjects and cases.

The mirror copy approach also helps us solve other e-mail problems. As an example, when a message is sent in present systems, it first goes into a folder for outgoing mail (queue of messages to be sent), and then into a folder for sent mails. The user later has to delete it or file it, but few do it regularly. As a result it can be hard to remember where the sent mail is – among other sent mails or filed under the proper case? With mirror copying, the user may file the mail before sending it! Outgoing mail is then a mirror copy, and this copy may just disappear when the mail has been sent. Users may keep all the sent mirror copies in a common folder for a few days, because they like to review what they have sent recently. However, the 'original' has already been filed in the proper place.

Solution S3: Integrated file and mail folders. With present systems, users file their messages in a hierarchy of mail folders, and they file other documents in the file hierarchy (formatted text, spreadsheets, pictures, etc.). Since each case or subject often has a mail folder as well as a file folder, it is desirable that the names and structure of the two hierarchies match. Expert users know that this is desirable, but admit that they never take the time to do it properly.

The design idea is to use the file hierarchy directly as the mail folder hierarchy. This has been tried before with each message being a separate file (for instance OS/2 had such an e-mail system). However, these systems were slow since it takes a relatively long time to open a file. The problem was particularly big when searching for mails according to their content. Below I suggest another solution where all messages are physically stored in the same file. We will discuss the details in connection with the data model.

Solution S4: Relate reply to original request. When the case manager sends out a mail, he has written his own subject identification in it, for instance the name of the case and other identification. If the receiver replies with the same subject heading, everything is fine – the case manager can immediately see where it belongs. However, the receiver may want to give the reply message the subject identification that he uses, and as a result the case manager may not easily relate the reply to the proper case.

In general, e-mails should have two subject fields: *my subject* and *your subject*, exactly as current practice for business correspondence. However, the e-mail standard doesn't provide this, but it prescribes that a reply must give a reference to the original request in the form of a unique message identification. The e-mail system should use this for supporting the case manager, for instance to bring up the original request message and suggest the same folder for the new message. The mail system should also allow the case manager to change the subject heading for a received mail, what many e-mail systems don't.

Solution S5: Support filing with keyboard only. The user should be able to file or move messages without using the mouse. It should also be possible to create a new folder as part of the move operation. Since the Explorer tree at the left side of the screen serves as the user's current view of the entire task, the move operation should preferably be done without changing the appearance of the Explorer tree.

Many mail systems do a poor job here, but some (for instance Eudora) provide an excellent solution. When the user starts moving a message, a nested menu pops up. It is structured as the folder hierarchy, and at the top of each menu there is a 'New...' choice. If the user cannot find a suitable folder in the menu at this level, he can simply create a new one on the spot. (See an example of such a menu in Figure 11.5D.)

Solution S6: Allow users to edit and annotate a received message. The receiver may want to add his own comments, correct errors in the mail, etc. Some mail systems don't allow it, probably in order to ensure evidence for what was received. The solution is of course to allow changes but in such a way that the original contents can still be seen if the user asks for it.

Solution S7: Show attached files in the file folders. Some mail systems handle the attachments as embedded into the message. With these systems, the user may be looking for an attached file through the file system, but can only see it through the message where it is attached. One solution is to insert a link to the file (a *short cut*) in the folders where the message is filed. In this way the attached files are visible in the message folders. (This assumes that we implement S3 – *integrated mail and file folders*.)

Solution S8: Allow changing embedded attachments to linked, etc. Some mail systems treat attached files as embedded in the message, others file them in a separate folder and show a link to them in the message. Give the user a function for changing a file from embedded to linked or vice versa, or to delete the file.

Solution S9: Allow notes to be handled as messages. The user may want to write a note for himself and file it in the folders. Apart from not being sent, such a note might be treated as a message.

Solution S10: Automatic warnings. There are several cases where the user wants a warning if something doesn't happen within a certain time. One example is that the user has sent a message to someone, and wants a warning if he hasn't got a reply within a certain time. Another example is that he may have left a message in the Inbox because he doesn't have to look at it until some days later. He may then give himself a deadline. If he forgets the deadline, he wants a warning. He might also want to sort the Inbox according to the deadline of messages.

In general, people seem to use the Inbox for reminders. If reminders are somewhere else (for instance in the box of sent mails), users tend to forget them. However, some disciplined users have separate reminder folders for larger cases.

Solution S11: Provide a *closed* indication for folders. A user may want to close a case so that he can still retrieve the contents, but not inadvertently change something in it. To avoid cluttering the view, he may want to hide the closed folders.

Solution S12: Extract contact data from e-mail. Users maintain a list of their contacts (people or companies), and often their first encounter with a contact is through e-mail. It is obvious to provide a feature that files the sender details in the list of contacts.

Solution S13: Attach a folder to a contact. For some contacts, the user keeps a folder for correspondence with this person. The correspondence with this person may relate to many cases. Provide a feature that creates a folder for a contact or attaches an existing folder to the contact. This will allow the e-mail system to suggest one of the folders where a message will be filed.

Solution S14: Standard search features combined with mirror copying. Provide the usual successful search criteria based on contact, subject, a word in the text, dates, keywords (in our case, a keyword is a folder), etc. Show the result as a list of messages and allow selected ones to be mirror-filed somewhere else too.

Solution S15: Support cleaning up by keeping track of LastOpened and WhereReferenced. Users find it hard to discard hundreds of old messages because some of them might still be valuable. Support the process by showing when the message was last opened for more than 3 seconds (and presumably used) and in which other folders the message is mirror-filed (mirror-filing suggests that it has several uses).

Solution S16: Provide archiving and retrieval somewhere with abundant space. Make it easy to transfer folders to some other storage medium. This is particularly important when users keep their mails and folders on a common mail server with limited space.

11.1.2 Requirements

Functional requirements

Requirement 1	Data to be stored: The system must store the data described in section 11.3.
Requirement 2	Tasks to be supported: The system must support the tasks described in 11.2.

Technical interfaces

Requirement 3	Platform: The system must run on Unix, Microsoft Windows, …
Requirement 4	Screens: Case managers usually have large screens that allow a couple of full messages to be shown at the same time. Other users may work from small screens (800 * 600 pixels).
Requirement 5	E-mail servers: The system must support the protocols …

Quality requirements

Usability:	The requirements below assume that a support person has set up the system.
Requirement 6	Users from other e-mail systems: Without instruction, 90% of users of other mail systems (Eudora, Outlook, …) must be able to use the new system without critical problems for simple mail handling (receiving, filing, sending and replying).
Requirement 7	Novice users: After 10 minutes of instruction, 90% of users without previous e-mail experience must be able to use the system for simple mail handling without task failures.

Requirement 8   Complex mail handling: After a few exercises in simple mail handling and 10 minutes of additional instruction, 90% of experienced users of other mail systems must be able to do the following with a good utilization of the system functionality:

a) File messages in the relevant folders (and explain how the mirror-filing works).

b) Retrieve relevant messages and files, and then compose a message from them.

c) Record notes and annotations in a relevant way.

d) Save relevant attachments from incoming mail and discard irrelevant attachments.

e) Attach files to outgoing mail.

f) Use warnings and retention periods in a meaningful way.

g) Find out how much space the filed mails occupy, including attachments.

Maintainability ...

These requirements are intended for product development and are intentionally loosely defined. It is not sure how far it is possible to get within the budget. However, it is important to conceive realistic mail collections that allow the users to do relevant things with the system during usability tests – as prescribed in the requirements.

11.2 Task descriptions for e-mail

We now have a good picture of the high-level tasks and the solutions. To get a better idea of the necessary functions and the context in which they are used, we describe the ordinary tasks – the true work situations. Figure 11.2A gives an overview of these tasks and Figure 11.2B the details.

Notice that the design ideas are not requirements. They are just a way to support subtasks, variants and problems. The design idea is just one way to do it. We have indicated where the solutions (S0 to S16) enter as a way to support a subtask or a variant.

It was not easy to divide e-mail work into ordinary tasks. Observations showed that users switched between cases all the time. Anyway, I came up with the five tasks shown in the figures. The main distinction between the tasks is the trigger. Here are some comments about the choice of tasks:

T1: Simple handling of received messages or warnings. This is what the user typically does in the morning to handle a bunch of messages or later during the day when the system plays the e-mail sound. The user can handle most of the messages right away (for instance deleting or filing them), others he may have to return to later (we all hate those ☺). The task description shows that there are quite many possible subtasks, even for the simple handling of received mail. All of these are optional for each message received. For some messages the user may send a reply, file the message, print it and delete the attachments. For others he virtually does nothing – just leaves them in the Inbox for later treatment.

You may note that some of the subtasks are not justified by the high-level tasks as described, but are necessary for technical reasons in present e-mail technology. One example is to skip transfer of long attachments if the user works away from the office.

T2: Non-e-mail triggers. These are simple things that the user does on his own initiative for instance sending a message or writing a note for himself.

T3: Complex message handling. These are cases where the user has to review many messages and documents to arrive at a decision, restructure folders, send complex messages, etc. There is no sharp boundary between this task and T1 or T2. Sometimes complex message handling starts while processing the received mails. At other times the user starts the complex message handling on his own initiative.

T4: Clean-up. This task deals with reviewing or deleting old messages. The user will normally do this at times where he is not stressed and has some time available. Many users are always stressed and never make the clean-up.

Fig 11.2 A Task descriptions, overview

T1 — **Simple handling of received mails**

Start:	Morning, beep, I have sent you a mail.
End:	Messages dealt with for now.
Frequency:	Once daily (5–50 messages) . . .
Difficult:	After vacation: 500 mails.

Subtasks: All subtasks optional and repeatable.

1	Transfer incoming mail.	
1a	Skip attachments.	
2	Read a mail. Find related sent message.	S4
3	Delete the mail.	
3a	File attachments anyway.	S8
4	Send reply. Mirror-file in final folder.	S2
4a	Add deadline for reply. : .	S10
5	Forward message . . .	
6	Annotate message, change subject.	S6
7	Write and file note. Add deadline.	S9
8	Mirror-file mail. Delete or file attachments.	S0 . . .
9	Leave mail in Inbox with deadline.	S10
10	Record sender as contact.	S12
11	Resend related message – with changes.	S10
12	Print message with/without annotations.	
13	Start complex task	

T2 — **Non-email triggers – user's initiative**

Start:	Phone call, got an idea, . . .
End:	Message sent, note filed, information found.
Frequency:	A few times daily.
Difficult:	Deadlines – many kinds.

Subtasks: All subtasks optional and repeatable.

1	Review folders.	
2	Compose message – cut and paste, resend.	
3	Define recipients.	
4	Attach files.	
5	Mirror-file and send. Add deadline . . .	S2 . . .
6	Write and file note. Add deadline.	S9
7	Print message.	
8	Start complex task.	

T3 — **Complex message handling**

Start:	Side effect of T1 or T2.
End:	Case created, message or reply sent . . .
Frequency:	A few times daily.
Difficult:	Deadlines – many kinds.

Subtasks: All subtasks optional and repeatable.

1	Search for messages b
1a	Include closed and arch
2	Mirror-file selected mail
2a	Transfer message
. . .	
3	Annotate, write notes .

T4 — **Clean up**

Start:	User's initiative.
End:	Order in growing mess.
Frequency:	Rarely.
Difficult:	Never.

Subtasks: All subtasks optional and repeatable.

1	Review a folder.	
2	Sort by created, lastOpened, size . . .	S15
3	Read, delete, write notes . . .	
	archive.	S11 . . .

T5 — **System set-up**

Start:	Change in technical surroundings ...
. . .	

(Usually system specialist. Not ordinary user.)

T5: System set-up. This task is not justified by the high-level tasks, but is needed for technical reasons. It may involve setting up the Internet connection, choosing the right options, etc. Most users don't carry out this themselves, but have support people help them. We will not discuss screens and functions for these tasks.

Checking ideas against tasks

We have noticed above that some tasks or subtasks are not justified by the high-level tasks, for instance, because they are needed for technical reasons, not for a domain-specific purpose. However, we should check the other way too: are all high-level tasks and solution ideas handled by some ordinary task? When I checked this for the first version of the tasks, there were two kinds of problems:

- According to the task descriptions, some solutions were not needed at all. The reason was that I had forgotten some important task variant. To ease this kind of tracing, the task descriptions now indicate where the solutions are needed.

- Some solutions turned out to be wrong when seen in the task context. Another solution was needed. (In the book, we have shown only the revised solutions.) This is an example why it isn't a good idea to announce the solutions as requirements. The solutions may also change later when user interface design and the cost of implementation is considered. To see whether a proposed new solution is adequate, we can check against the true requirement – the subtask or variant must be supported.

Fig 11.2 B Task descriptions, detailed version

T1	**Simple handling of received messages.**	Solutions
	This task covers only the relatively simple handling of received messages.	
Start:	Several triggers, e.g. arriving in the morning; the sound from the mail system; someone says he has sent a mail; returning from a meeting.	
End:	The received messages have been dealt with for now.	
Frequency:	Once daily (typically morning): 5–50 messages.	
	A few other times daily: 1–5 messages.	
Difficult:	After vacation: 500 mails waiting.	
Subtasks: The following subtasks are all optional and repeatable.		Solutions
1	Ask the system to transfer mail from the mail server.	
1a	The mail always remains on the server.	
1b	Transfer is very slow due to attachments, so skip them temporarily. (Common problem when working away from the office.)	
2	Read a message.	
2a	The message may be a reply to another message or a warning about another message. See this source message too.	S4
3	Delete the message. Typically more than 50% of messages are deleted.	
3a	File the attachments anyway.	S8
3b	Untransferred attachments to be deleted from the server.	

Continued

Fig 11.2 B Task descriptions, detailed version (*Continued*)

4	Send a reply. Mirror-file it in the proper folders. Attach files.	S2
4a	Add a deadline for reply or a retention time in the Outbox.	S10
5	Forward the message to someone else, with or without attachments.	
5a	Add a deadline for reply and/or a retention time in the Outbox.	S10
6	Annotate the message, including changing the subject.	S6
7	Write a related note and file it. Add deadline.	S9
8	Mirror-file the message in one or more folders (rarely more than two folders).	S0, S2, S5
8a	Transfer the message, i.e. delete the mirror copy from the Inbox.	
8b	Create a new folder or rename one.	
8c	Mirror-file the message according to the sender or receiver.	S13
8d	For vague business cases, file the mail in a higher level point of the folder hierarchy.	S1
8e	Look into existing folders to see whether they are relevant.	
8f	Delete attachments or file them as linked attachments (see data model).	S8
8g	The attachments may not yet be transferred from the mail server.	
9	Leave the message in the Inbox for later action.	
9a	Add a deadline.	S10
10	Record sender as a contact.	S12
11	Resend an earlier message, possibly with some changes, for instance to remind the receiver.	
11a	Add a deadline for reply and/or a retention time in the Outbox.	S10
12	Print a message. May be the original version or the annotated one.	
13	Start a complex message task (T3) in order to review several messages in context, restructure folders, etc.	

T2	**Non–e-mail triggers.**	
	This task covers situations where the user for some external reason takes the initiative to send messages, etc.	
Start:	Several triggers, e.g. phone calls, talks with colleagues, ideas coming up in the user's mind.	
End:	The action is done for now, e.g. message sent, note filed, information looked up.	
Frequency:	A few times daily.	
Difficult:	Deadlines of many kinds.	
Subtasks: The following subtasks are all optional and repeatable.		**Solutions**
1	Review a few folders.	
1a	Include closed and archived folders.	
2	Compose message, often using cut and paste of other messages and documents. The pieces copied may be the original version or the annotated one.	
2a	Resend an old message and modify it as needed.	
3	Define recipients.	
4	Attach files.	
5	Send the message. Mirror-file it in the proper folder.	S2
5a	Add a deadline for reply or a retention time in the Outbox.	S10
6	Write a note and file it. Add deadline.	S9
7	Print the message.	
8	Start a complex message task (T3) in order to review several messages in context, restructure folders, etc.	

Continued

Fig 11.2 B Task descriptions, detailed version (*Continued*)

T3	**Complex message handling.**	Solutions
	This task covers cases where many messages have to be reviewed in context.	
Start:	Often a side effect of T1 or T2.	
End:	Handling of the messages are done for now, often resulting in a new case folder, reordered files, some sent messages, reply to some messages.	
Frequency:	A few times daily.	
Difficult:	Deadlines of many kinds.	

Subtasks: The following subtasks are all optional and repeatable.		Solutions
1	Search for messages according to folders (sometimes restricting messages to those that are in two or more folders at the same time), date, deadline, status, contact, subject, pieces of body text.	S14
1a	Include closed and archived folders.	
2	Mirror-file selected messages from the search into another folder.	S2
2a	Transfer the message, i.e. delete the mirror-copy from the old folder.	S5
2b	Create a new folder or rename one.	S5
2c	Delete attachments or file them as linked attachments (see data model).	S8
3	Annotate messages, write notes, send replies, etc., as described in T1 and T2.	

T4	**Clean-up, for instance when a case is closed or folders have become too messy.**	
Start:	The user's own initiative.	
End:	Order has been created in a growing mess.	
Frequency:	Rarely. For the Outbox maybe once a week, for more specialized clean-up, maybe a few times a year.	
Difficult:	Never under stress.	

Subtasks: The following subtasks are all optional and repeatable.		Solutions
1	Review a folder. May be any folder, but reviewing the Outbox is common even if the user has mirror-filed the messages and assigned deadlines/retention time.	
2	Sort messages according to created, lastOpened, number of mirror copies, contact, or size of message including attachments.	S15
3	Read messages.	
4	Delete messages.	
5	Annotate messages.	S6
6	Write notes.	S9
7	Delete attachments or make them linked attachments (see data model). (S8)	S8
8	Close the case, i.e. mark the folder so that the contents are not changed by mistake. (If a message is mirror-filed in at least one closed case folder, it cannot be changed without confirmation.)	S11
9	Archive the folder, i.e. transfer it to another medium. Mirror-filed messages and attachments will have to be physically copied.	S16

T5	**System set-up.**	
	This task is often carried out by specialists, not by the ordinary user.	
Start:	Changes in the technical surroundings, e.g. the user starts using the system, the user moves to another place, the file and message servers change.	
End:	Set up complete, technical problems resolved, etc.	
Frequency:	Rarely, maybe a few times a year. Will be more frequent when moving with a portable computer.	
Difficult:	Any move of location. Stressing until the mail system is operating again. A specialist may not be available.	

Subtasks:		Solutions
Not discussed here.		

11.3 Data model for e-mail

In business applications we can analyse the domain and extract a data model, but the e-mail design is different. The e-mail system is a tool where we to a large extent *design* the entities based partly on entities from the domain, partly on technical entities in the surrounding software system and partly on design ideas. Our suggestion for a data model is shown in Figure 11.3. It describes the 'world' for a user of the e-mail system.

Data dictionary

Class: Folder. The Folders are the existing file folders in the file system. They have a hierarchy as shown by the self-referential 1:m connector, *tree*. Each folder contains *Files* and *FileRefs*. The FileRefs refer to other files. In the e-mail system they refer to embedded e-mail attachments (see below). The figure shows that Folders, Files and FileRefs are parts of the existing file system.

Class: Message. The Message class contains all the e-mail messages for this user. Some messages are replies to other messages, as shown by the 1:m relationship from Message to Message. Messages also comprise *notes* that the user keeps for his own purposes (S9 above). A *note* is a message in a special state.

One way to implement the message class is as a single large file handled only by the e-mail system. This file could have a special format with variable length records, indexes, etc., for optimizing handling of the variable-length mails. Only the e-mail system needs to know about the format. It will not be like a relational database at all. The message file will of course be a file somewhere in the file system, for instance in the folder where the e-mail system is, but from the user's point of view, the file is anonymous.

Class: MirrorCopy. We want each file folder to be also a message folder (S3 above). Furthermore, we want each message to be mirror-filed in several folders (S2). We thus have an m:m connector between Folder and Message. Each message can be filed in several folders, and each folder can contain several messages. We resolve this connector with the connection entity *MirrorCopy*. Each MirrorCopy object represents one message mirror-filed in one folder. A MirrorCopy has no attributes except for the references to Folder and Message.

How can we implement the mirror copies? One way is to have a variable-length field in each message: a list of the folders where the message is mirror-filed (this is how the user will see it). This would work fine except for an annoying detail: When the user renames his file folders or moves them around in the hierarchy, the e-mail system will lose track of which mirror copies moved where.

One way to avoid this is that the e-mail system uses an invariant identification of the file folders, *folderID*, for instance a sequential number. In the messages, it stores the

Fig 11.3   Data model, e-mail

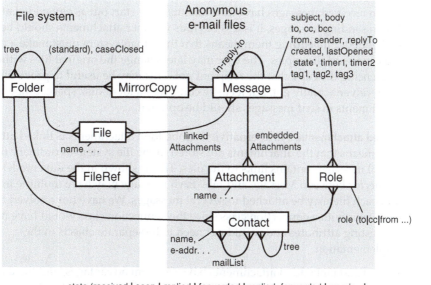

state (received | seen | replied | forwarded | replied+forwarded | warning |
note | composed | queued | sent | reply Received)

folderID. It also stores the folderID in a special file in each folder. Figure 11.3 shows this as MirrorCopy being stored in both the file system and the anonymous e-mail files. The e-mail system also keeps track of the current name and location for each folder. When the user has renamed or moved folders, the e-mail system will find out that the folders are not where they used to be. By scanning all folders, it can update its records of where folders are.

There is no need to have a special file with a folderID in all folders – only in those where mirror copies have been filed. The special file could also contain an index of all messages having a mirror copy in this folder. It depends on implementation details of the e-mail system.

Class: Attachment. A message may have embedded attachments. Each attachment is a file for instance a picture or a spreadsheet. The data model shows this as a 1:m connector from Message to Attachment. Embedded attachments are anonymous files inside the e-mail system.

Class: FileRef. Traditionally, the user can only see the embedded attachments when he opens the message, but we should also make the files visible trough the file system (S7). When the user mirror-files a message in folder X, the e-mail system creates a FileRef in folder X for each embedded attachment in the message. As a result, when a user opens a file folder, he will see the attachments for all messages mirror-filed in the folder. If the user deletes the message, but keeps the attachments, he will still see the attached files.

When received messages have attachments, they start out as embedded attachments. When sending messages, it is less obvious whether attachments should be embedded. Embedding them means that the e-mail system must make a copy of the files and send the copies. The user may later change the original files without influencing the copy that the recipient got. This may be useful to prove which copy the receiver actually got, but it easily consumes a lot of disk space. Embedding attachments in sent messages should be optional.

Linked attachments. An alternative to embedded attachments is linked attachments. This means that the attachments are stored in the file system as ordinary files and the e-mail message contains links to the files. This is shown in the data model as an m:m connector between Message and File. Each message may have multiple linked files and each file may be attached to several messages. We have not resolved the m:m connector with a connection class since the connection class would have no interesting attributes and would not need to be separate objects in the implementation.

Linked and embedded attachments have different advantages, and the user should have means to change any attachment from one form to the other. However, when changing from embedded to linked, the user must select the folder where he wants to physically store the file.

Class: Contact. Contacts are the recipients or senders of e-mails – persons as well as companies. They comprise the user's private contact lists and often company-wide lists of customers, employees, etc. A contact object contains name, e-mail address, postal address, etc., of the recipient. The data model shows that there may be a hierarchy of contacts, similar to the folder hierarchy (the self-referential 1:m connector, *tree*).

Some contacts are not single recipients, but lists of recipients. This is shown as an m:m connector from Contact to Contact. There is no need to resolve the m:m in the model since the connection class has no interesting attributes.

Users may want to assign a folder to a contact. The e-mail system may then automatically mirror-file messages to or from this contact in the assigned folder. We have modelled this as a 1:m connector between Folder and Contact. A contact may have one assigned folder and a folder may be assigned to several contacts.

The contacts are shown as anonymous files within the e-mail system. Depending on the software platform, there might be an existing contact management system that the e-mail system should use.

Class: Role. There is an m:m relationship between messages and contacts. A message may have several contacts for instance several receivers, several cc's, etc.

And one contact may relate to many messages. In the model we have resolved this m:m connector with a connection class, *Role*. A Role object has a single attribute showing whether the recipient was a receiver, a cc person, a sender, etc., for this message.

Attributes

Most of the classes have rather simple attributes. File and Folder for instance, have the usual name, creation date, size, etc., as defined by the file system. Folder has an additional attribute, *caseClosed*, defined by the e-mail system. When *caseClosed* is true, the user cannot change the contents of the folder (S11). The *caseClosed* attribute could for instance be stored together with the invariant *folderID* in the special file of the folder. (Archiving the folder on another medium is a related issue, which we ignore here.)

Message. The message class has a lot of attributes, but most of them are given by the standard e-mail format (see RFC 2822, http://www.faqs.org/rfcs/rfc2822.html). Here is a summary of some of them:

subject: The subject text as the user sees it.

body: The body text that usually comprises most of the mail. May be empty, however.

to, cc, bcc: E-mail addresses of the receivers of the message. Receivers in the bcc list are not revealed to the other receivers. A receiver may be a contact in the Contact class and in this case a Role objects exists.

from, sender, replyTo: E-mail addresses of the senders of the message. If *sender* is different from *from, sender* made the physical send on behalf of *from*. As an example, *sender* could be a secretary sending on behalf of *from*. *ReplyTo* is where a reply message should go (may be a list). A sender may be a contact in the Contact class and in this case a Role object exists.

created: For a received or sent message, *created* is the date and time where the sender ordered the message to be sent. For an unsent message or note, *created* is the date and time where the user created the message.

lastOpened: The date and time when the user last opened the message for more than 3 seconds (and supposedly read it). *LastOpened* is empty for a received message that the user hasn't read. This attribute is not a standard attribute, but gives overview and supports S15.

state: The state of the message. See details below.

timer1: For a sent message, the time at which the mirror copy will be deleted from the Outbox (S2).

timer2: For a sent message, the time at which the user will be warned if a reply has not been received (S10). For a received message, the time at which the user will be warned if the message is still in the Inbox (S10).

tag1, tag2, tag3: User defined tags for a message. They may for instance denote a priority or an action that the user wants to take. (We will not deal with the tags in the rest of the design.)

Message states and special mail folders

The following mail folders have special roles in the system:

Inbox: Here the system files received mails and warnings initially. The user may use the Inbox for anything he has to take action on.

Outbox: Here the system files outgoing mails initially. Whether the message is queued for sending or actually sent is shown as a state indication.

Trash: Here the system files a message when it is not mirror-filed anywhere else. The user may physically delete the message from *Trash*.

A message can be in one of the following main states. In general, the state is independent of where the message is filed. The user may for instance file a sent message in the Inbox, but its state will show that it is a sent message.

received: A message received from the mail server.

seen: A received message that the user has seen. The system may for instance record the state *seen* when the message has been open for more than 3 seconds.

replied, forwarded, replied+forwarded: The message is received and the user has sent a reply and/or forwarded it to someone.

warning: A message generated by the user's own mail system because one of the timers has expired.

note: A message generated by the user for his own local use.

composed: A message generated by the user but not yet queued for sending.

queued: A message to be sent but not yet physically transmitted.

sent: A message physically sent, but no reply has been received yet.

replyReceived: The message has been sent and a reply received.

11.4 Virtual windows for e-mail

Planning

The virtual windows are fairly straightforward to plan because existing e-mail systems are good sources of inspiration. Figure 11.4A shows the virtual windows. In total we need eight window templates:

a) FolderTree: The folder hierarchy window, which has three frames. One is the hierarchy shown as an Explorer tree view. When a folder is selected in the tree, the second frame lists all mails in this folder and the third frame lists all files in the folder. This reflects the integrated mail and file folders. It is an example of an overview presentation combined with two detail presentations.

b) MessageSearch: A window with search criteria and a list of matching messages. As a special case, this window can show a second message folder that the user works on.

c) FileSearch: A window with search criteria and a list of matching files.

d) Message: A window showing a message with body text, subject, senders, date created, state, timers, folders where filed, attachments. Conceptually, each message has its own virtual window instance. Users frequently use two message windows at the same time, for instance to compare messages or copy and paste between them.

e) FileView: A window showing the contents of an attachment or some other file, for instance, with one of the viewer programs that can show the contents in small size. Conceptually, each file has its own FileView window.

f) ProgressIndicator: A small window showing the progress of mail transfer, printing, etc.

g) ContactList: A window listing all contacts in a tree view, much as the Explorer window lists files.

h) Contact: A window showing all the details of a contact. Conceptually, each contact has its own window, and the user may want to see two or more at the same time.

I planned the virtual windows with the matrix shown at the bottom of Figure 11.4A. It has one line for each subtask (with some of them combined to save space in the figure). The line shows which of the virtual windows this subtask needs. For many subtasks the user needs to deal with two messages. To illustrate this, the matrix has two message columns: Message 1 and Message 2. To further show which messages a window deals with, I used this coding scheme:

m: A newly received message.

s: A possible source of this message, for instance the message it was a reply to or the message for which the user wanted a warning after some time.

o: An old message or note that the user looks into.

n: A new message or note that the user composes.

As an example, look at T1.1, *mail transfer*. In the FolderTree, the user will usually see the list of received messages (the Inbox folder). The user will also see a progress indicator. It should for instance indicate whether some messages have attachments that take a long time to transfer.

For T1.2, *read mail*, the user will again see the list of received messages in the FolderTree (the Inbox folder). In Message 1 he will see the specific message and in Message 2 any source message (s).

For T1.8, *mirror-file the message*, the user needs to see the FolderTree to select the proper target folder. If the user wants to file the attachments as linked files, he may need the FileView of the attachment (m).

T2.2, *compose message* during complex message handling, uses a lot of windows at the same time. The user needs to build up a new message (the 'n' in Message 1). He needs access to old messages through Message 2 either from other folders through the FolderTree or through message searches. He may also need access to old files, for instance, through the FolderTree or FileSearch.

There are similar reasoning behind all the other subtasks.

Graphical version

The graphical version could be quite close to existing mail systems. There was no reason to change the graphical form when users knew a good one already. Figure 11.4B shows most of the virtual windows in a graphical version.

FolderTree. The FolderTree window looks like most e-mail systems. The leftmost frame is the tree of folders. The the top-right frame is a list of messages, in this case for the Inbox folder. The new thing is that the bottom-right frame is a list of files in the same folder – attached to mails or independent. The FolderTree window was made as a mock-up, cut from existing mail screens and file system screens.

FileView. The FileView window shows an attachment to the message *Vienna trip*.

Message. The Message window is a handmade mock-up. It is different from existing mail windows because it has some new, important attributes. Figure 11.4B shows two examples of message windows, one for a received message and one for a sent message. They have exactly the same fields, but the contents differ.

Received message. Let us first look at the received message. *To, From, Subject, Attachment*, etc., are as in other mail systems. *Sent* is the time when the sender ordered it to be sent (according to the e-mail standard). The message is in the state

Fig 11.4 A Virtual windows plan, e-mail

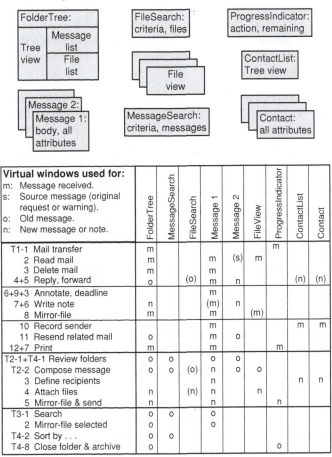

FolderTree: Tree view | Message list / File list

FileSearch: criteria, files

ProgressIndicator: action, remaining

File view

ContactList: Tree view

Message 2 | Message 1: body, all attributes

MessageSearch: criteria, messages

Contact: all attributes

Virtual windows used for: m: Message received. s: Source message (original request or warning). o: Old message. n: New message or note.	FolderTree	MessageSearch	FileSearch	Message 1	Message 2	FileView	ProgressIndicator	ContactList	Contact
T1-1 Mail transfer	m						m		
2 Read mail	m			m	(s)	m			
3 Delete mail	m			m					
4+5 Reply, forward	o		(o)	m	n			(n)	(n)
6+9+3 Annotate, deadline				m					
7+6 Write note	n			(m)	n				
8 Mirror-file	m			m		(m)			
10 Record sender				m				m	m
11 Resend related mail	o			m	o				
12+7 Print	m			m			m		
T2-1+T4-1 Review folders	o	o		o	o				
T2-2 Compose message	o	o	(o)	n	o	o			
3 Define recipients				n				n	n
4 Attach files	n		(n)	n		n			
5 Mirror-file & send	n			n			n		
T3-1 Search	o	o		o					
2 Mirror-file selected	o			o					
T4-2 Sort by . . .	o	o							
T4-8 Close folder & archive	o						o		

Seen, which means that the user has opened it and looked at it for at least some seconds. The field *InOutbox* is not used in case of a received message. The user might ask for a warning if he hasn't removed the message from the Inbox within some days, but he hasn't. *LastRead* gives the time the user last opened and read the message. In this case it was the day after the message was sent.

Filed in shows the folders where the message is mirror-filed. In the example, the mail is both in the Inbox and in the Vium folder. (The Vium folder collects messages relating to the contact *Vium*.) When the user has dealt with it, he should remove it from the Inbox – his action list. At that time it will still be filed in the Vium folder.

Sent message. Now let us look at the sent message. The *Sent* field shows when the user ordered the system to send it. It might still be queued in the user's computer, but in the example the *State* field shows that it has been sent.

Filed in shows that the message is filed in the Outbox, *ITpains* and *Win2000* folders. The user decided before sending the message that it should be permanently filed in *ITpains* and *Win2000*. The field *In outbox* shows that the user has asked the system to keep the message in the Outbox for 8 days. The *Warning* field shows that the user has asked the system to send him a warning message if he hasn't got a reply to the message within 3 days.

FindMessage. The FindMessage window is similar to many other search windows. The search criteria are roughly the same as the file attributes. However, there is only one field for *Contact*, not separate fields for *To, From*, etc. Users may want to look for all mails to, from or cc a specific contact. Note that it is possible to look for messages that belong to two or more folders at the same time (mirror-filed in all of them). In the example we look for messages that belong to *Positions* as well as *Vium* – and with the text *austr* somewhere in the message body.

Progress indicator. Finally, the figure shows the ProgressIndicator. In the example, the system transfers incoming mail. It is at present transferring a mail from amh@itu.dk. If the transfer takes too long, the user may stop all the transfers or skip only the attachments in this mail. Oh, yes! Once again the designer couldn't resist putting some buttons on the virtual window. But they indicate what it is about.

The figure doesn't show the FileSearch window. It is similar to many other file search windows. Nor does it show the ContactList and Contact windows. They will depend on the existing contact management systems on the platform. There are no surprises here.

Understandability test

At this stage I made understandability tests of the virtual windows with two expert case managers and two less experienced users. After the test I made a review with them to discuss what was missing, what they liked, etc. The session took around half an hour with each of them. Here are some of the observations:

Integrated mail and file system

The first virtual window I showed to the users was the folder tree with the message list and file list. Users were asked to explain what it showed. All users immediately recognized the folder tree and the message list as an e-mail system. They also realized that it was the Inbox with received messages. Then they wondered what the file list was. Within a minute they all figured out that it probably was all the attachments to mails in the Inbox. One user, however, then noticed that it probably wasn't correct since the file dates in the file list didn't match the message dates. (She had actually noticed an error in the mock-up.)

The users also didn't guess that non-attached files were in the file list. However once told, two of them immediately saw the consequences: *Aha! Then I don't need to keep the file explorer open at the same time. This is great! And I don't have to maintain two*

Fig 11.4 B Virtual windows, graphical version

FolderTree

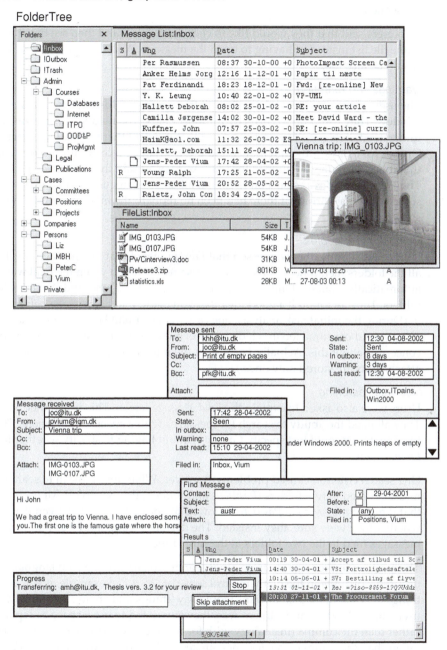

different folder hierarchies! The other two users needed some time to realize these consequences.

Two users said that they would like to click on the mail and then see the attachments in the file list instead of having to open the message. And the other way around would be nice too.

Warnings and retention

The users were asked to explain what all the message fields were for the *Message sent* window. They could do so correctly for most fields. The field *In Outbox* was not understood, however. The users guessed that it meant that the mail had been in the Outbox for 8 days, although they found this a strange piece of information. Once told that it was the retention time in the Outbox, they all said that this was a good idea. The *Warning* field was also a bit hard, but all users soon guessed that they would somehow get a warning if there had been no reply to the message within the 3 days shown.

Multiple mirror copies

Users almost immediately guessed that *Filed in* meant that the message was filed in all the folders mentioned. Three of them also realized that when the mail was deleted automatically from the Outbox, it still remained in the *ITpains* and *Windows2000* folders. They all found it a good idea that you could file the message before sending it. (During the initial task analysis, one case manager had been worried that multiple filing would consume too much disk space, but none of the four users seemed concerned about this. Actually, because of the mirror filing, a message and its attachments are stored only once.)

Message searching

Users were also asked to explain the *Find Message* screen. This was rather painless. They all liked the ability to search for messages with a specific attachment. They also liked that they could just specify *Contact* without having to specify whether it was *To, From, Cc*, etc.

One search criterion caused problems, however: What does it mean to search for messages filed in two folders (*Positions* and *Vium* in the example)? All users thought that it meant messages in *Positions* followed by messages in *Vium*. Even if asked whether they were sure, they insisted. The designer's intention was that it was messages filed in the two folders at the same time.

This problem is well known from other search screens. Our natural language often uses the word *And* in the mathematical sense of *Or*. As an example, if you ask for things in A *and* B, mathematicians would say 'things that are in A *or* in B'. Once the users understood what the intent was, they suggested to use a space as separator rather than the comma (in analogy with for instance a Google search) or a colon rather than the comma. The designer suggested to add an explanation *At the same time* and users said it would definitely help. More experiments are needed.

Conclusion

The tests were rather encouraging, but it was also clear that some kind of introduction or on-line help was needed to help users get the full benefit of the system. We leave this as an exercise about user documentation and support (see Chapter 17, the exercises for Chapter 12).

11.5 Function design and prototype

Semantic and search functions

Once the virtual windows were acceptable, I defined the functions. First I defined the semantic functions and the search functions by walking through the ordinary task descriptions, noting the functions needed for each virtual window. As usual the same functions were used over and over for many tasks and subtasks. Figure 11.5A shows the resulting list of functions. Here are the mini-specs in a 'mini-version':

TreeView. In the TreeView part of the folder tree, the user can of course select, create and delete folders. Deleting a folder means deleting the mirror copies in it. Files that physically are in the folder (e.g. linked files) will be deleted too. When the user has selected a folder, he can open the message and file lists. There are also functions for closing a case (prevent further changes), reopening it and archiving it.

FileList. The file list is a frame in the folder tree, and I have shown its functions as a separate list. In the file list, the user can select files and attach or embed them in the message that is open at this point in time. The system can also do ordinary file management for instance copying, moving and deleting files.

MessageList. The message list is another frame in the folder tree. In the message list, the user can select messages and open them. He may also open the source of the message, for instance if the message is a reply. The user can also delete a message completely (trash it) or just delete the mirror copy he sees in the message list. The user can file a mirror copy of the message in another folder (to be selected as part of the operation) or make a real copy that can be modified independently of the source. The user can also transfer the mirror copy to another folder. Finally, the user can of course do all the usual stuff to the messages: replying, forwarding, sending and resending. Resending means that a real copy is made. The user may then edit it before sending it. Finally the user can print messages and determine which of the many message attributes to show in the list.

Message. From a message window, the user can do many things. He can switch to the next message in the folder or to the previous one by means of *NextMessage* and *Previous*. If he has opened several messages at the same time, they will become a bunch of messages shown in the same window. In this case *NextMessage* and *Previous* will work within this bunch. (The Next/Previous feature was suggested by an expert user during the understandability tests.) The user can record the sender as a contact, and also do all the things he could do to the message through the message list, such as open the source message or trash the message.

The user can edit most of the message attributes. When editing *To*, *Cc* and *Bcc*, the user can of course get the mail addresses from the contact list. The user can also edit the subject and body of a received message, but to ensure evidence of the original message, he can use ShowChanges to see the original version.

Fig 11.5 A Semantic and search functions, e-mail

TreeView	FileList	MessageList	Message
Edit: name	Edit: name	SelectMultiple	Operations on message:
SelectFolder	SelectMultiple	OpenMessage	NextMessage, Previous
NewFolder	AttachFile	OpenSource	RecordSender
DelFolder	EmbedFile	Trash, DelCopy	OpenSource
OpenLists	Delete	FileIn, Copy, Move	Trash, DelCopy
CloseCase	Copy, Move	Reply, ReplyAll, Forward	. . . as MessageList
OpenCase	OpenFile	Send, ReSend	
Archive		SelectAttributes	Edit attributes:
		Print	to, cc, bcc, subject, body

FileSearch	MessageSearch
Edit: criteria	Edit: criteria
Search	Search
Edit: name	SelectMultiple
SelectMultiple	. . . as MessageList
. . . as FileList	

Message (continued):

Edit attributes:
    to, cc, bcc, subject, body
    timer1, timer2
    ShowChanges

Operations on attachments:
    AttachFile, EmbedFile
    MoveTo, Embed
    Detach, Delete
    ViewAttachment
    OpenAttachment

ProgressIndicator		FileView
Stop	Global:	Delete, Detach
SkipAttachment	TransferMail	

Global:
TransferMail
NewMessage
NewNote
Undo
SetUp
Import, Export

ContactList	Contact
Select . . .	Edit: . . .

For an outgoing message, the user can embed files and attach files (link them). The files are selected as part of the function. Notice that there are two dialogs for attaching files: (1) Start in the message and use a function there to select the files. (2) Select files through the FolderTree, and then attach them to the current message.

For any message, the user can change an embedded message to a linked one (MoveTo) or the opposite way (Embed). He may *Detach* a linked file from the message. He may *Delete* an embedded file or a linked one. Finally, the user can view an attachment as a small picture or open it fully as an application.

MessageSearch and FileSearch. In the message search window the user can specify various search criteria and then get a list of matching messages. The user can then do exactly the same to the messages as he could from the message list. The file list works in a similar manner.

FileView. From the attachment viewer window, the user can detach or delete the attachment. It is convenient to be able to do it from here as well as from the message.

ProgressIndicator. Are there any functions in the progress indicator window? Yes, this is the place where the user notices that actions take more time than expected, and this is the natural place to stop the action. In case the action is transfer of an attachment, the user may want to just skip this attachment and continue loading other mails.

ContactList and Contact. From the contact list, the user must be able to select, open, add and delete contacts. In the contact window, the user must be able to edit contact details. We will not go into detail with these parts of the system.

Global. There are a few functions that don't naturally belong to any virtual window, for instance transferring mail, undoing the last function and creating a new message or note. Just as a reminder, I have also listed the set-up functions and import/export functions here.

State diagram and navigation functions

How do we map the virtual windows into screens? The platform in this case is a multi-page platform such as Microsoft Windows or X-Windows. Since there is a need to see several virtual windows at the same time, for instance when composing a complex message from several others, I decided to utilize the multi-page aspect. This also allows the typical case manager to utilize the large screen available. As a result, each virtual window became a page of its own (a real window).

Since the FolderTree is the starting point for everything, I decided to put the global functions there. The result was the pages shown in Figure 11.5B. The *Main Window* holds the global functions, the tree view, the message list and the file list. Note that *Message* and *FileView* have several instances. There are also pages shown with dotted lines. They represent fully open files – the applications that start when the user opens the files. These 'pages' are opened by the mail system, but otherwise not handled by it.

In the figure, I first placed all the semantic and search functions that caused pages to change their visual state. These functions are shown without underlining (using the same notation as in Figure 7.6B). The corresponding state changes are shown with full arrows. In our case, the only state changes were opening and closing of pages.

As an example, the ProgressIndicator opens as a result of Send, Print or TransferMail. It closes when the transfer ends or when the user clicks *Stop*. As another example, a message page opens as a result of *NewMessage*, *Resend*, *OpenMessage* or *OpenSource*. No semantic function could close it at this stage of the design.

After completing the state diagrams, it was obvious that several close functions were missing. In addition, there was no way to open *MessageSearch* and *FileSearch*. As a result I added the underlined functions and the dotted transition arrows.

The design at this stage was best suited for a large screen. However, the system should also be useful on smaller screens. In this case it would be convenient to have the Message window, MessageSearch window, etc., as frames inside the main FolderTree window. This would look exactly as a single-page platform. Some

Fig 11.5 B State diagram, e-mail

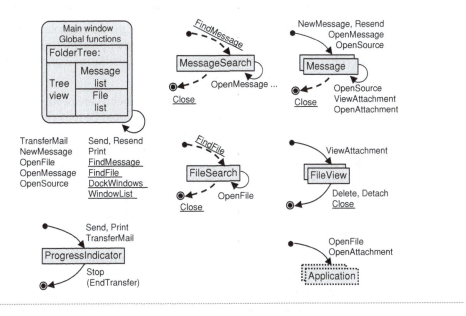

platforms allow the user to drag free-floating pages into a larger window and dock them there as frames, but it is cumbersome having to do this all the time if you work with many messages.

To allow users to switch between multi-page and single-page mode, I added a navigation function *DockWindows*. It makes the system change behaviour: when a window opens, it becomes a frame that replaces the message list and file list. We could describe this changed behaviour as another state diagram. The *DockWindows* function makes a state transition from the multi-page state diagram to a single-page state diagram. We need an *Undock* function to change back to the multi-page diagram. However, it is hardly worth drawing this extended diagram. Mini-specs of the navigation functions can do the job.

When windows are docked, there may be many windows stacked on top of each other in the main screen, for instance if the user has opened a bunch of incoming mail. Some systems support this by means of a *Window* menu that lists the stacked windows and allows the user to jump to any of them. We need such a function too, *WindowList*.

Function presentation

I had now identified the functions associated with each page, including the navigation functions. Next I planned how the functions were to be presented.

Figure 11.5C shows the plan for part of the main window: the TreeView and the Global functions. The figure also shows the plan for the message window.

The plan for a window or frame has three columns: the function name; the menu that shows the function (if any); any buttons, icons or other presentations of the function. I also had columns with short-cut keys and a short justification of my choice, but they are omitted from the figure for space reasons.

There are many functions in the e-mail system, so menus are needed. Buttons would fill too much of the sparse screen space and icons would be too cryptic in most cases. However, the functions used by novices should be clearly visible, for instance as buttons, to help the user getting started. They should also be available in the menus to help the experienced users get a good overview of all the functions. To order the chaos, I spent some hours organizing all the functions into menus. There were two guidelines for me:

1   Menus should be structured according to the objects in the system for instance one menu for files, one for folders, one for messages.

2   Menus should also be structured according to tradition: a file menu, an edit menu, a view menu, etc.

Sometimes this conflicted with the object-oriented structure. As an example, the function *FindMessage* logically belongs to a message menu, but tradition would put it in the edit menu. The result was seven menus: File, Edit, Folder, Message, Attachment, View, Window (see Figure 11.5D).

Knowing the menus, it was easy to decide the function presentation. Let us explain some details of Figure 11.5C.

■   TreeView, Edit name: Editing the folder name would be initiated through a menu point in the Folder menu. The user might also select the folder and then click in the name.

■   TreeView, SelectFolder: Selecting a folder would be done by a click. (Moving the cursor with the arrow keys will work too, of course.)

■   Global, Undo: Would be a menu point in the Edit menu and an icon in the Main window.

■   Message, OpenSource: Opening the source message (for instance the message replied to) would be a menu point in the Message menu and a button in the message window.

■   Message, FileIn: Filing a copy of the current message would be a menu item in the Message menu. It would also be available as a combo box (drop-down menu) on the *FiledIn* field. This combo box would show multi-level lists, structured like the folder tree (see the example in Figure 11.5D).

I made similar plans for the remaining parts: MessageList, FileList, MessageSearch, FileSearch, ProgressIndicator, FileWiew and contact stuff. In total, these buttons and

Fig 11.5 C Function presentation, e-mail

Main Window:		
TreeView	Menu	Button/Icon
Edit: name	Folder	Select+Click
SelectFolder		Click
NewFolder	Folder	Button, Main
DelFolder	Folder	Delete
OpenLists		Double click
CloseCase	Folder	
OpenCase	Folder	
Archive	Folder	
ShowClosed	View	

	Menu	Button/Icon
Global	Menu	Button/Icon
TransferMail	File	Button, Main
NewMessage	Message	Button, Main
NewNote	Message	Button, Main
Undo	Edit	Icon, Main
SetUp	File	
Import, Export	File	
FindMessage	Edit	
FindFile	Edit	
DockWindows	View	
WindowList	Window	

Message list	Menu	Button/Icon
. . .		

Message	Menu	Button/Icon
Operations on message:		
Next, Previous	Message	Icon, Message
RecordSender	Message	
OpenSource	Message	Button, Message
Trash	Message	Button, Message
DelCopy	Message	
FileIn	Message	Combobox
Copy	Message	
Move	Message	
Reply	Message	Button, Message
ReplyAll	Message	Button, Message
Forward	Message	
Send	Message	Button, Message
ReSend	Message	
Edit attributes:		
to, cc, bcc	Message	Combobox
subject, body		(direct)
timer1, timer2		Combobox
ShowChanges	View	
Operations on attachments:		
AttachFile	Attachm.	Combobox
EmbedFile	Attachm.	
MoveTo	Attachm.	
Embed	Attachm.	
. . .		

icons were needed to support the novice users:

- Main window: NewFolder, TransferMail, NewMessage, NewNote (four buttons), Undo (an icon).

- Outgoing message: Trash, Send, ReSend, OpenSource (four buttons), NextMessage, Previous (two icons)

- Received message: Trash, Reply, ReplyAll, OpenSource (four buttons), NextMessage, Previous (two icons)

- FileSearch and MessageSearch: Each of them has a Search button.

- FileView: Delete, Detach (two buttons).

- ProgressIndicator: Stop, SkipAttachment (two buttons).

- Contact, ContactList: Not part of this design.

Prototype

Making the prototype was rather simple at this point. Figure 11.5D shows some pieces of the prototype: all the menus, a multi-level list of folders, the Message window and a dialogue box for the *SelectAttributes* function. Let us explain some of the details:

File, CopyTo. This menu point and several others have an arrow to the right. It indicates that there are sub-menus. In the case of CopyTo, the user would be allowed to select the folder from a multi-level list as shown in the example in the figure. Notice the *New* entry on the lists. It allows the user to create a new folder at this level. Since the user often puts several things into the same folder one by one, each of these menus should remember the last choice and let the user start from there.

View, Select Attributes. This menu point and several others have three dots to the right. They indicate that a dialogue box will open. In this case it is the dialogue box shown at the bottom right. It allows the user to choose the message attributes to show in the message list.

Edit, Font. This menu point and a few others in the edit menu allow the user to do special editing of the message body for instance changing fonts and alignment. (We have not discussed these traditional editing functions previously.)

Message window. The example shows an outgoing message. Notice the buttons for the frequent functions (Trash, Send, Resend, OpenSource). An incoming message will have a Reply and a ReplyAll button instead of the Send and Resend buttons. The two arrow icons are the NextMessage and the Previous functions. Also notice the drop-down arrows that allow the user to add for instance receivers and FiledIn folders.

Usability tests

The usability tests of the prototype revealed several usability problems, of course. As one example, the difference between linked and embedded files was hard to understand. However, only experienced users needed to understand it. Novice users didn't really care, and the available buttons and combo boxes provided an adequate choice. We will not discuss the usability problems further.

At the time of writing, I am still looking for an opportunity to implement the ideas in a real e-mail product.

Fig 11.5 D Pieces of the Prototype, e-mail

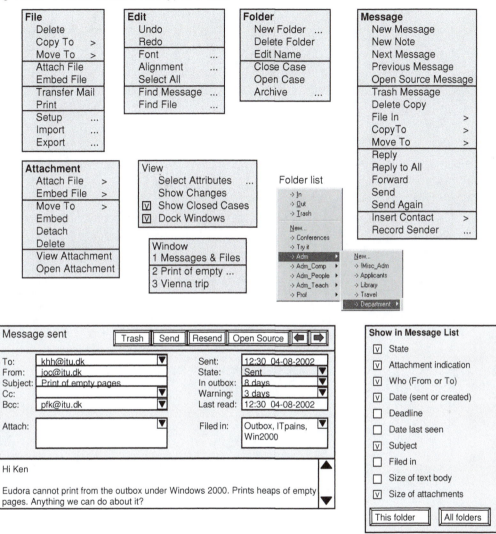

File
Delete
Copy To   >
Move To   >
Attach File
Embed File
Transfer Mail
Print
Setup   ...
Import   ...
Export   ...

Edit
Undo
Redo
Font   ...
Alignment   ...
Select All
Find Message   ...
Find File   ...

Folder
New Folder   ...
Delete Folder
Edit Name
Close Case
Open Case
Archive   ...

Message
New Message
New Note
Next Message
Previous Message
Open Source Message
Trash Message
Delete Copy
File In   >
CopyTo   >
Move To   >
Reply
Reply to All
Forward
Send
Send Again
Insert Contact   >
Record Sender   ...

Attachment
Attach File   >
Embed File   >
Move To   >
Embed
Detach
Delete
View Attachment
Open Attachment

View
    Select Attributes   ...
    Show Changes
[V] Show Closed Cases
[V] Dock Windows

Window
1 Messages & Files
2 Print of empty ...
3 Vienna trip

Folder list
-> In
-> Out
-> Trash

New...
-> Conferences
-> Try it
-> Adm   ▶
-> Adm_Comp   ▶
-> Adm_People ▶
-> Adm_Teach ▶
-> Prof   ▶

New...
-> !Misc_Adm
-> Applicants
-> Library
-> Travel
-> Department ▶

Message sent | Trash | Send | Resend | Open Source | ⬅ | ➡ |

To: khh@itu.dk   ▼   Sent: 12:30 04-08-2002
From: joc@itu.dk   ▼   State: Sent   ▼
Subject: Print of empty pages   In outbox: 8 days   ▼
Cc: ▼   Warning: 3 days   ▼
Bcc: pfk@itu.dk   ▼   Last read: 12:30 04-08-2002

Attach: ▼   Filed in: Outbox, ITpains,   ▼
                                                        Win2000

Hi Ken   ▲

Eudora cannot print from the outbox under Windows 2000. Prints heaps of empty
pages. Anything we can do about it?   ▼

Show in Message List
[v] State
[v] Attachment indication
[v] Who (From or To)
[v] Date (sent or created)
[ ] Deadline
[ ] Date last seen
[v] Subject
[ ] Filed in
[ ] Size of text body
[v] Size of attachments

| This folder | | All folders |

12

User documentation and support

Highlights

- ■ When do users need support?
- ■ What kinds of support are available?
- ■ Planning the support to match the needs.
- ■ How to write support cards, tutorials and manuals.

The ideal IT system doesn't need any user documentation or courses. The user intuitively finds out how to use it. Today this ideal is true for many public systems in the Web area, but more complex systems are far from the ideal. Even a popular productivity system such as Microsoft Word is not quite intuitive – particularly if the user wants to do something a bit advanced, such as writing a two-column text or a table of contents. Tutorial books, courses or good colleagues are needed to learn about the more advanced aspects.

Is the ideal realistic – can the systems become intuitive? I think user interfaces have improved dramatically over the last years. Every now and then I see systems made in the eighties or earlier. Most of them are incredibly hard to use. Courses are needed to use them for even the simplest things. The systems often have a user guide, but it is even harder to use than the system itself. So the IT profession has come a long way since that time. Unfortunately, users also require the systems to do more and more, and the inherent complexity makes them less intuitive.

What about other areas of human activity? Are they more intuitive? Some are. Most children can learn to play a ball, use a hammer or ride a bike on their own – or by imitating others. Even here, they will benefit from an advisor in order to become proficient. However, only extremely gifted children learn to read on their own. Most children take a long time to learn reading, and they need good teachers and tutorials to do so. If it took as long to learn using Word as it took to learn reading, Word would have very few users!

To round off the discussion: Most IT systems need some kind of user documentation, courses or other means of support to make the users benefit fully. In this chapter we will see various ways to do it.

12.1 Support situations

In which situations will users need documentation or support? We can roughly distinguish these situations (Figure 12.1):

1 **Getting started.** Users behave differently the first time they try to use a system. The IT-reluctant user may look at the screen and think *I never figure out about this*. An early success is crucial for this kind of user. Having a supportive colleague at his side may be the best way. The IT-comfortable user behaves differently. *Let me give it a try* the user thinks. If he doesn't succeed, he will try to find an IT-talented user (a 'super user'). The super user looks at the screen and thinks *I should be able to figure this out without reading the manual*. Usually the super user succeeds, but if not, he may be willing to read the manual or the on-line documentation.

This example is quite typical. It shows that very few users try to use the documentation. This doesn't mean that documentation is superfluous. It may be important for super users.

2 **Proficiency.** If users use the system frequently, they need to become proficient, work fast and benefit more from the system. One example is to use the keyboard rather than the mouse. The system may help them make a gradual transition from mouse to keyboard by showing the short-cut key on menus and buttons. (We have discussed this in section 7.8.) However, there are other aspects of proficiency where the system cannot help the user. Super users, courses or documentation are needed.

3 **Lookup – task-related issues.** The user may have a domain-oriented question – one that relates to the task at hand. For instance, a receptionist may wonder *How do I handle a guest who wants to pay part of the bill with credit card and the rest in cash?*. User documentation might address such domain issues, but most user documentation doesn't. Even the local super user may not know the answer, and the result may be that they tell the guest that he cannot pay this way. Later, the super user may experiment with the system to find out how to handle such a case in the future.

In systems for professional use, there are lots of domain issues. The documentation may address them, but it should be in a lookup manner. We cannot expect the user to read the whole book to learn about all the domain issues. The user must be able to look up the issue at hand. However, it is hard to define which terms to look up. Should we provide an entry for 'credit card', 'cash', 'payment', 'split payment' or all of these? The problem is similar to making an index in a book, or finding something on the Internet for which you don't know the right term.

Fig 12.1 Support situations

Getting started:
    IT-reluctant user: 'I'll never figure out about this'.
    IT-comfortable user: 'Let me give it a try' .
    Super user: 'I should be able to figure this out without the manual'.
        (If not: Uses manual and/or on-line help.)

Proficiency: Learning to work fast and master the system.

Lookup – task-related: 'How to pay the bill partly credit card, partly cash?'

Lookup – system-related:
    'If I cancel a stay and then Undo, will the guest get the same room?'

Remember – task-related: 'I handled a split pay once – where did I start?'

Remember – system-related:
    'Which discount code – 03 or 05?'
    'What are the parameters to DLookup?'

---

4   **Lookup – system-related issues.** The user may also have system-related questions – questions about what the system does. For instance, the receptionist may wonder what actually happens when he cancels a booking and then tries to undo the cancellation. Will the system give the guest the same room again? Or he may wonder what this message means: 'Room booked already'. User documentation and on-line help are well suited for system-related issues.

It is fairly easy to help the user look up the system-related issues. The reason is that the issues are well defined: the things that the user can see on the user interface. On-line help is particularly useful here. When seeing the message 'Room booked already', the user might simply click the Help button (e.g. F1) and the system will have a good guess at what the question is. Similarly, the user might point at the Cancel button and ask for help. This doesn't mean that most users will try Help in these situations. But the super users might.

5   **Remember – task-related issues.** The 'task-remember' situation is when the user knows how to handle a certain task, but has forgotten the details. For instance, the receptionist might have tried the split payment situation once, but which menu was the starting point? In principle, the user could find the solution in the lookup way, but it will usually be too cumbersome. In practice we observe users making sticky notes about such issues and then consult the notes as needed.

6   **Remember – system-related issues.** The 'system-remember' situation is when the user knows which function or field to use, but has forgotten the details. For instance, the receptionist may know that he has to fill the discount field, but he has forgotten the discount codes. Older systems used lots of 'codes' and users had to remember them – or consult reference cards provided by IT support. This

is an issue that modern systems have eliminated. Any decent system today provides drop-down lists (combo boxes) or the like. The user doesn't have to remember codes but can look them up on the spot.

Another example is technical systems such as programming tools. The developer may know that he has to write a call of DLookup, but has forgotten the parameters. Modern programming tools tell him as soon as he types the name DLookup.

Creating the mental models

In all of the support situations, the aim is to improve the user's mental models. Using the mental model terms of section 4.2, we can describe the aims in this way:

1 Getting started. We want to establish the first mapping model in the user's mind – how to perform a task by means of the system. Performing a real task is a success criterion for the user. However, in order to help the user learn more, we also want to establish the first mental model for data and system functions. In some cases, the user may not know the domain in advance. Then we also have to establish the first domain model in the user's mind.

2 Proficiency. We want primarily to improve the mapping model so that the user chooses the best and fastest functions. However, we may also want to improve the other mental models so that the user is better able to handle exceptional cases.

3 Lookup – task-related. We want to extend the mapping model to cover another area of the domain. In some cases we may also want to extend the user's domain model.

4 Lookup – system-related. We want to extend the mental model for data and system functions to cover another part of the system.

5 Remember – task-related. Mental models fade over time. We want to refresh the mapping model – or in some cases the domain model.

6 Remember – system-related. We want to refresh the models for data and system functions.

12.2 Types of support

Above we looked at the various situations where users need documentation or support. We will now look at the different kinds of support we can provide. Figure 12.2 gives an overview of the types of support and which situations they best support.

Paper-based support

Books

A paper book can in principle explain everything about an IT system. It may be a *tutorial* that helps the user getting started. It may be a *user manual* (or *reference manual*) where the user can look up various topics about how to carry out tasks or how the system works. Or it may be a technical manual intended for system specialists, for instance the hot-line staff.

Compared to computer-based documentation and help, a book is easy to skim and gives much better overview. It is also easy to write your own comments in the book. Finally, you can look in the book while you work on the screen. Modern computer-based help systems try to compete with books by means of electronic bookmarks, help that stays on the screen while you work, etc. They do not succeed completely, however. One reason is the limited screen space available.

The main problem with books is that most users are unwilling or unable to read this kind of stuff. They may be under time pressure and just want a quick answer, but cannot find it in the book. Or they don't understand what they read because they don't know the strange terms used in the book. Writing a book that overcomes these human problems is difficult – it is not just a matter of giving the author more time to do the job.

Other problems with a book is that it may not be around when the user needs it; it is harder to update in steps with the system updates; it may take precious space on desk, particularly if you work with many systems at the same time.

Figure 12.2 summarizes the situation: Books are best suited for super users. If the book is well written, it may help the super user getting started, becoming proficient and looking up task-related and system-related information. It is not well suited for helping the super user remember details – it is too bulky and too hard to find things.

Card

A card is a small sheet of paper or a folded sheet. It may be a *reference card* with lists of system commands, procedures for various tasks, etc. It may also be a *getting-started card* that helps the user do the first tasks with the system. Sometimes the 'card' grows into a booklet of a few pages.

Due to its size, users are more willing to use a card than a book. It is also easier to carry around.

The limited space on the card is of course a problem. It can only be used for special purposes. Although the space is limited, it can in many cases provide a better overview than a computer-based help system. As an example, the Visual Basic reference card (available at www.booksites.net/lauesen) holds as much text as 3–4 full screens on a standard 800 * 600 computer screen.

Figure 12.2 summarizes the situation: Cards are suited also for ordinary users, although some users may not use it at all. Cards can support getting started and to some extent proficiency (for instance learning the short-cut keys). They are also good for remembering details.

Computer-based support

On-line help

On-line help is the information the computer shows when the user explicitly asks for help. Under Microsoft Windows, the standard way to get help is by means of F1. On-line help can, in principle, cover everything a book can do: tutorial, reference manual, technical manual. In addition, it may provide much better means for searching. Since the system knows what the user is doing – for instance that he is in the Guest screen – it can show help that relates to this situation (*context-dependent help*). The user may also point to something on the screen and ask for help.

Unfortunately, on-line help shares several problems with the book. The user may be unwilling or unable to read the explanations, or he may not know the strange terms used. Writing good on-line help is not just a matter of taking the time to do it. Judging from the on-line help in popular systems, the quality varies immensely even within the same system. Some parts may be excellent and tell you what you need to know, other parts are written by authors who apparently don't know what to write and even don't know the system they write about. As a result, the users may have to search around for a long time, and they don't have a clue whether the information they look for is actually there.

The worst problem with on-line help is that very few users actually use it. I often observe users with good IT experience while they use a new system. When getting stuck, they may try to use the on-line help, but in their first attempt they don't find what they look for or they cannot understand what they read. The result is that they never again try to use the on-line help in this system – even though it might be valuable in other cases. The user's unconscious conclusion seems to be: yet another useless help system. Don't waste time on it.

Figure 12.2 summarizes the situation: On-line help is best suited for super users. It can support proficiency and lookup for task or system-related issues. It may help remember system details – sometimes even for ordinary users. There are some attempts to use it also for getting started, but results are not convincing.

Fig 12.2 Support methods vs. context

Potential use	Support situation					
			Lookup		Remember	
Documentation & support method	Getting started	Proficiency	Task	System	Task	System
Paper						
Book	SU	SU	SU	SU		
Card	U	U			U	U
Computer						
On-line help	?	SU	SU	SU		U
Pop-up, drop-down lists	(U)	U				U
On-screen guides	U				U	
Wizard	?			U		
Assistant	?	?				
Human						
Course	U	U				
Hot-line			U	U		
Super user	U	U	U	U		
Colleague	U	U	U	U	U	U

Legend: SU = suited for super users, U = Suited for other users, (U) = Party Suited, ? = still experimental

Pop-ups, messages and drop-down lists

The computer may provide help on its own initiative when the user tries certain functions. One example is the *pop-up texts* that appear when the mouse rests on an icon or another control. Another example is warning *messages* that appear when the user activates a certain function, for instance the message 'Cancelling the room reservation will allow other receptionists to book the room immediately'. A final example is the *drop-down lists* that allow users to choose from a list rather than remember what to type.

Pop-ups, messages and drop-down lists are very useful for explaining simple things. For instance, a pop-up help is good for explaining to beginners what the various buttons do and what fields mean. An error message with good feedback and instruction can help the beginner out and tell him what the system does. A drop-down list tells the user what kind of choices he has. These are simple things. The techniques are not suited for difficult things such as getting started on a complex application.

The techniques easily become a nuisance for experienced users, who don't want to be warned all the time. Pop-up help avoids this by mean of a one-second delay. This causes another problem: experienced users get annoyed when they actually want to see what the little text has to say. To these users, one second is a long time.

Figure 12.2 shows that pop-ups and drop-down lists are suited for some aspects of proficiency (for instance learning the short-cut keys) and for remembering system details. It has also some use when getting started.

On-screen guide

Some user interfaces are designed in such a way that they guide the user through a sequence of actions. The ATM is a good example. It instructs the user to insert the card, enter the pin code, select an amount and so on. Many Web sites are built on the same principle (Figure 4.6 outlines a typical example). On-screen guides are excellent for systems where the user can carry out only a few straightforward tasks.

With an on-screen guide, the user gets little understanding of what the system stores. The user may not even understand how to retrieve the data again. As a result, the law of object permanence has nothing to work with. For systems where the user needs overview of data and repeated updates of it, this is a problem. Furthermore, the on-screen guide takes precious screen space needed for overview of data. It soon becomes a nuisance to experienced users.

Figure 12.2 shows that on-screen guides are good for getting started and remembering tasks. The assumption is however, that we talk about simple tasks with few variants.

Wizard

A Wizard guides the user through a longer sequence of actions. If the user knew the system well, he could manage without the Wizard. One example is the Wizard that guides users setting up an Internet connection. Another example is the Wizard that guides the Access developer making a drop-down field on a Form. Usually, the user can explicitly control whether he wants to use the Wizard or not.

For carrying out simple versions of a task, a Wizard can be a good help. As the name suggests, the Wizard carries out the task without the user really knowing what goes on. This may be a problem if the situation is not the simple one that the Wizard assumes. The user will then have to explicitly control the many settings, and this requires knowledge of what all these settings mean. The Wizard didn't give any clue to this. Another problem is that the Wizard doesn't help the user becoming more proficient so that he can perform the task without the Wizard.

Figure 12.2 shows that Wizards can support some user tasks ('looking up' the task). There are some attempts to use Wizards also for getting started, but they are not convincing.

Assistant

An Assistant is a computer function that tries to figure out what the user is doing and then breaks in to advise him. A well-known example is the Microsoft Office Assistant (the paper-clip man). Such a computer assistant is an attempt to simulate an experienced colleague who looks over the shoulder of the user. It is a brave attempt, but hard to make successful. Simulating an experienced colleague is not easy.

Some users report that the Assistant sometimes makes a surprising suggestion that they didn't think of themselves. Mostly, however, the Assistant is just a nuisance. All users I know of – experienced as well as novices – soon want to disconnect the

Assistant. The novices have a major problem, however: they cannot figure out how to disconnect the Assistant.

Figure 12.2 shows the Assistant as an experimental technique with potentials for supporting getting-started and proficiency.

Human support

Course

At a typical course, the user gets started using the system. However, courses may cover more than this. They may teach the user about the application domain (for instance hotel procedures), how the system actually works, how to use the system more proficiently, how to use the on-line help, etc. There may be several courses about the same system, for instance one for beginners, one for users with some experience and one for users who are going to teach other users.

A good course is an excellent way to learn. Unfortunately, it is difficult to make a good course. Common problems are that there is too much introduction where the users don't learn to do anything useful; that the users learn to do things step-by-step without understanding what goes on in the system; that the examples are far away from what the users will use the system for; that the course assumes knowledge that the users don't have.

Courses have a special problem that other means of support don't have: timing! The user needs to go on the course at just the right time. If the users get the course long before they start using the system in practice, they will have forgotten what they learnt when they need it. If they get the course after using the system in practice, they will already be experienced and feel bored at a beginner's course. If you introduce a new system company-wide and manage to get the timing right, there will soon be new employees that also need the course. There is rarely a course timed for them.

One way to get around the timing problem is to equip local staff (super users or hot-line staff) to train other users. They may run small local courses at convenient times. The teaching material should be targeted for this situation.

Figure 12.2 shows that courses can support getting started and proficiency (to any level of expertise). Courses are of course useless for *ad hoc* situations such as looking up or remembering.

Hot-line

A hot-line is a phone number the user can call with any questions about the system. Commercial systems normally have hot-lines, and larger companies have their own hot-line as part of IT support. Good supporters at a hot-line are a blessing to users. Users much prefer asking for help rather than struggling for hours with user manuals or on-line help.

Figure 12.2 shows that hot-line can support ordinary users who need help for carrying out a task or finding out what is wrong with the system. Hot-line is not suited for the remember-situations, although some users try to use hot-line for this.

Expert supporters are difficult to find. The real experts are needed for other things, such as developing new systems. To solve the problem, support organizations are often structured in layers. The 'first line of defence' deals with the easy problems: Users who have forgotten their password or who don't know how to deal with the full mailbox that the system talks about. Support people tell that easy problems are more than 90% of the calls. If first-line defence cannot solve the problem immediately, they route the call to a higher level where the expert supporters are. They in turn may now and then have to call the developer or the software vendor to find the solution. All of this works fine except for the expert user who knows that his question is not a first-level issue. He can be quite annoyed having to sort things out with lower level defence before he can get down to business.

Many companies consider IT support too expensive, and IT supporters themselves often feel annoyed about all the stupid users calling them about trivialities. *Have you looked into the user manual* they often ask the users. *No* says the bewildered user. *Okay, try that first, then call again if it doesn't help* replies the supporter. To the supporter this is an efficient solution. It costs him 10 seconds rather than the 5 minutes it might have taken him to resolve the problem. However, he and his management don't consider the time the user now wastes: half an hour – or maybe a visit to a more friendly colleague who spends 15 minutes on the issue. Company-wide, the solution is bad.

Some innovative companies have a different attitude towards support. They try to optimize the entire company operation. As an example, they have realized that some users are so crucial for the business that they cannot join any regular courses (typical examples are sales managers and high-level supporters). A way to help them is by means of *on-demand training*. Whenever such users see they have some time available, they call hot-line (or a local super user). A teacher turns up in a few minutes and gives them as much training as the user's time allows. It sounds like an expensive solution, but it need not be. Users can often learn in ten minutes under personal guidance what they would have spent hours learning at a course.

Super users

A super user is a colleague who knows the system very well. Many super users have a special flair for IT systems and experiment with them. They are also more willing to read the user documentation and use on-line help. Most departments in large companies have a super user – although this person may not be officially recognized as a super user.

As Figure 12.2 shows, super users are very important in practice. They can help the other users getting started, look over their shoulder and help them become more proficient, help them find out about tasks and system functionality. Super users often know something that hot-line doesn't: the application domain. For many systems, the super users may be the most important support resource. IT support could build on them much more than they normally do, for instance give them special training, give them access to the back-office hot-line and listen to their advice.

Colleagues

The ordinary colleagues can help in many cases. They may give the new employees the first training and help them out with simple problems. Colleagues often support each other mutually. *Can anyone tell me how to arrange the text in two columns?* one user may ask at lunch time. *Ask Nancy, she has tried it* replies another user.

Figure 12.2 shows that colleagues can support other users in many matters – as long as the questions are not too hard, of course.

12.3 Support plan for the hotel system

In this section we will use the principles above to make a support plan for the hotel system. Remember that the hotel system is intended for small hotels, often with temporary staff and staff working alone in the night. Staff are expected to have some plain computer experience (such as Word), but little hotel experience. Let us look at the different support situations.

1 Getting started. The hotel system is designed to be intuitively usable, but some users will still be scared initially. *Am I doing the right thing?* Can we support *getting started* better by means of the computer? The system itself has pop-ups, drop-down lists and instructive error messages. They are a good help as usability tests have shown, but not sufficient. However, other computer-based support techniques don't seem right for the small hotel.

What about printed material? A book is not suited – few users would read a book – but a card seems a good choice. What about humans as support for getting started? Courses are unrealistic for temporary staff and hot-line not suited for getting started. A super user may not be available in a small hotel, but sometimes a colleague may give a short instruction. The paper card could support this instruction very well.

The conclusion is recorded in Figure 12.3. We will support getting started with a card and built-in pop-ups and messages. The card should also help colleagues instruct the novice receptionist.

2 Proficiency. Learning to use the keyboard rather than the mouse is possible through a card and via on-line suggestions that pop up. Learning hotel proficiency in general is best done through a course and to some extent through colleagues. We will not plan this as part of the product.

3 Lookup – task-related issues. We can explain some task-related issues through a card, for instance what to remember during checkout. But there are many task-related issues and a card will not suffice. A book would do, but only super users would read it – and there is rarely a super user at night in a small hotel. The best solution is a hot-line, and the system vendor might offer this. A book would be useful for the hot-line staff and potential super users, so we have planned for it.

4 Lookup – system-related issues. The system has some explanation of buttons and fields in the form of pop-up help, but it covers only simple things. More complex issues, such as what happens when the user cancels a booking, cannot be explained this way. On-line help is not suited for ordinary users. Our choice is hot-line and a book for the hot-liners and potential super users.

5 Remember – task-related issues. The 'task-remember' situation is when the user knows how to handle a certain task, but has forgotten the details. A card can

Fig 12.3 Support plan for hotel system

Hotel system	Support situation					
			Lookup		Remember	
Documentation & support method	Getting started	Proficiency	Task	System	Task	System
Paper						
Book			SU	SU		
Card	U	U	(U)		(U)	
Computer						
On-line help						
Pop-up, drop-down lists	(U)	U			(U)	U
On-screen guides						
Wizard						
Assistant						
Human						
Course		U				
Hot-line			U	U	U	
Super user						
Colleguea	U	U	U	U	U	U

Legend: SU = suited for super users, U = suited for other users, (U) = party suited

handle some of these, but hot-line and colleagues seem necessary in many cases. On-line help and on-screen guides are not suited for ordinary users.

6 **Remember – system-related issues.** The 'system-remember' situation is when the user knows which function or field to use, but has forgotten the details. The system helps a lot through the simple screen design, pop-ups and drop-down lists. In some cases it may be necessary to get help from another user.

This analysis leaves us with these things to do:

a) Make a card that helps the user getting started, carry out some key tasks, learn to use the keyboard for efficiency. (Section 12.4 shows and explains the card.)

b) Make a book (a *reference manual*) for support people and potential super users. It should address task issues and system issues in a lookup manner. (Section 12.5 shows sample parts.)

c) Plan a course for general hotel proficiency based on the system. (We will not deal with this in the book.)

d) Offer hot-line support – also in task-oriented matters. (We will not deal with this in the book.)

12.4   Support card

Figure 12.4 shows the support card for the hotel system. It has print on both sides and plastic coating for robust use in the reception.

Getting started

Page 1 helps the user getting started. It shows how to check in a guest, including the many variants of this. The task has to deal with guests who have booked; guests who believe they have booked for today, but haven't; regular guests who haven't booked; non-regular guests who haven't booked; bookings that are wrong; guests who want more than one room.

We also have to deal with the different start-up situations. Usually the system will show the two windows needed for check-in (Find Guest and Room Selection), but someone else may have left it in a state where one or both of these windows are closed. So we have to start explaining how to open these windows. This is also a chance to show the user where the Undo button is. However, we cannot trust that he remembers it, so we also explain Undo at the Check-in button, where the disaster may happen.

The card is not just a step-by-step instruction but also an explanation of the screens. As an example we explain that the list of stays is the stays that match; the room grid shows whether a room is occupied (IN), booked (BOO) or free (blank). Experiments show that this kind of explanation makes the users think about what happens rather than just doing things blind. Understanding is crucial to deal with the many variants.

Showing instructions in bubbles suggest that the procedure is not completely step-by-step, but allows the user to choose the right action depending on circumstances. Notice the many explanations that say why this is done and what the system does. As an example, we explain that *Find Guest* is used to see the guests that match the criteria; *Checkin* tells the system that the guest has arrived and is using the rooms.

We have dealt with a couple of usability problems that remain from the last usability tests. As an example, a few users thought that when the guest was on the stay list, the computer knew about it and there was no need to do anything. Under searching and *Finish check in* we explain how to tell the computer that the guest has arrived. We also give a hint about the terminology problem with *Stay number* versus *Booking number*. In summary, we have tried to follow this advice:

Advice for 'getting started'

1   Take the user through a small but meaningful task (closed task).

2   Make sure this task is harmless or that the user can undo it.

3 Explain what is on the screen.

4 Explain why things are done.

5 Explain what happens – what the system does and what the user can see.

6 Deal with remaining usability problems (found during the last usability tests).

7 When instructions are step-by-step, show the steps with bullets.

8 If possible, use pictures rather than words.

Other basic tasks

Page 2 has two parts. The left part explains how to carry out other important tasks. Now it is more step-by-step, but we still explain why this is done and what the system does. As an example, we explain that the system files a booking as soon as the user presses *Book*. The user doesn't have to close the window or use a Save function.

Notice the many domain-related explanations that haven't anything to do with the computer. As an example, for checkout we ask the user to check with the guest whether he has got breakfast this morning or things from the mini-bar in the room. Usability tests showed this to be a problem, and the decision was to train the users. Here we have an opportunity to do it.

In summary, we have followed much of the advice for 'getting started'. However, we assume that the user knows how to check in, and we have less space available. As a result we don't explain about undo and we don't use space for pictures.

The system supports many other tasks, but we don't have space to explain them on the card. Examples are changing rooms for a guest, changing prices, recording that a room is under repair. Knowing how to perform the basic tasks allows many users to figure out about the remaining tasks on their own (the *accelerator effect*). However, the book for support people should explain it – just to make sure.

Subtask sequences – a philosophical issue

There is a strong similarity between the task descriptions we used for designing the user interface, and the user guide we have on the card. The obvious difference is the language we use. There is a more profound difference, however. During user interface design we stressed that the sequence of task steps was free – unless some subtask needed data produced by other subtasks. The final user interface also allows the user to vary the sequence, for instance record the guest first, then select the room – or the opposite. Unfortunately, we have no good way to explain it in the short user guide. Our language is sequential, and attempts to explain alternative sequences just makes it harder to understand.

On the 'getting started' page, we didn't use ordinary language, but graphics with explanatory bubbles. This better suggests alternative ways to carry out the tasks. It is

Fig 12.4 Support card for hotel system

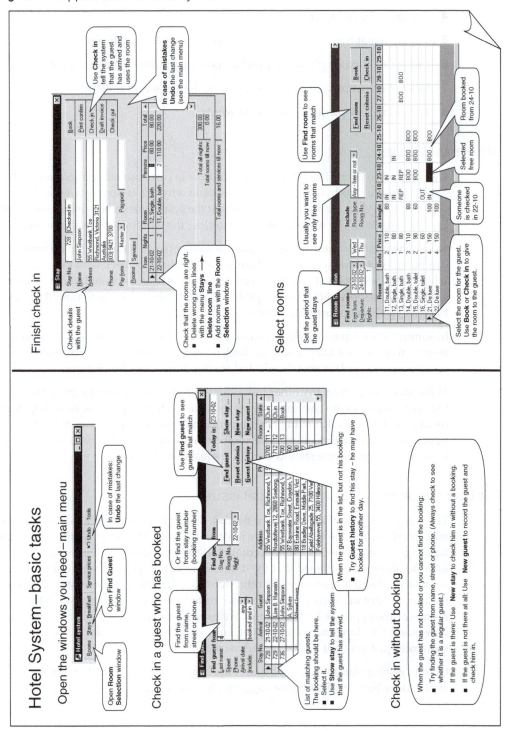

Work fast – use the keyboard – drop the mouse

Field navigation

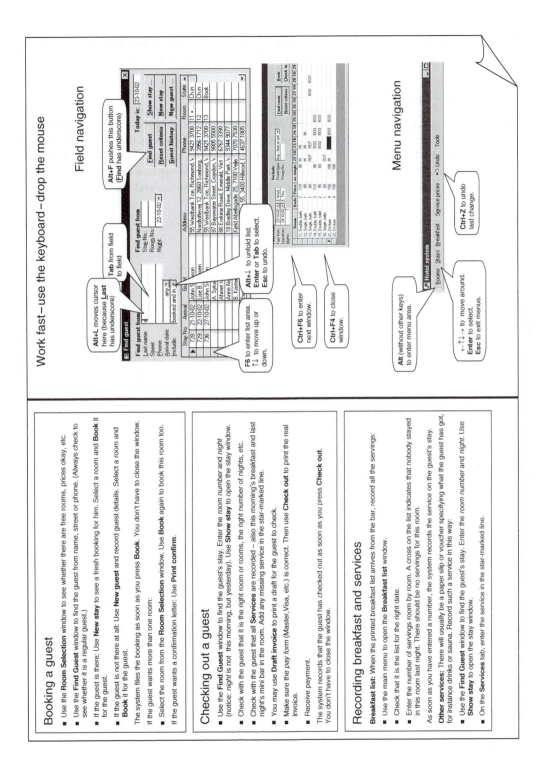

Alt+L moves cursor here (because **L**ast has underscore)

Tab from field to field

Alt+F pushes this button (**F**ind has underscore)

Alt+↓ to unfold list. **Enter** or **Tab** to select. **Esc** to undo.

F6 to enter list area. ↑↓ to move up or down.

Menu navigation

Ctrl+F6 to enter next window.

Ctrl+F4 to close window.

Ctrl+Z to undo last change.

Alt (without other keys) to enter menu area.

←↑↓→ to move around. **Enter** to select. **Esc** to exit menus.

Booking a guest

■ Use the **Room Selection** window to see whether there are free rooms, prices okay, etc.

■ Use the **Find Guest** window to find the guest from name, street or phone. (Always check to see whether it is a regular guest.)

■ If the guest is there: Use **New stay** to see a fresh booking for him. Select a room and **Book** it for the guest.

■ If the guest is not there at all: Use **New guest** and record guest details. Select a room and **Book** it for the guest.

The system files the booking as soon as you press **Book**. You don't have to close the window.

If the guest wants more than one room:

■ Select the room from the **Room Selection** window. Use **Book** again to book this room too.

If the guest wants a confirmation letter: Use **Print confirm**.

Checking out a guest

■ Use the **Find Guest** window to find the guest's stay. Enter the *room number* and *night* (notice: *night* is not this morning, but yesterday). Use **Show stay** to open the stay window.

■ Check with the guest that it is the right room or rooms, the right number of nights, etc.

■ Check with the guest that all **Services** are recorded – also this morning's breakfast and last night's mini bar in the room. Add any missing service in the star-marked line.

■ You may use **Draft invoice** to print a draft for the guest to check.

■ Make sure the *pay form* (Master, Visa, etc.) is correct. Then use **Check out** to print the real invoice.

■ Receive payment.

The system records that the guest has checked out as soon as you press **Check out**. You don't have to close the window.

Recording breakfast and services

Breakfast list: When the printed breakfast list arrives from the bar, record all the servings:

■ Use the main menu to open the **Breakfast list** window.

■ Check that it is the list for the right date.

■ Enter the number of servings room by room. A cross on the list indicates that nobody stayed in this room last night. There should be no servings for this room.

As soon as you have entered a number, the system records the service on the guest's stay.

Other services: There will usually be a paper slip or voucher specifying what the guest has got, for instance drinks or sauna. Record such a service in this way:

■ Use the **Find Guest** window to find the guest's stay. Enter the *room number* and *night*. Use **Show stay** to open the stay window.

■ On the **Services** tab, enter the service in the star-marked line.

also closer to a system-oriented description where we explain what the buttons do, and leave it to the user to use the buttons in a proper sequence.

Proficiency – keyboard use

The right part of page 2 is a summary of how to use the keyboard rather than the mouse. Again we use pictures. There are more short-cut keys than those shown. The user can, for instance, move around in the menus by means of letters rather than the arrow keys. It would clutter the pictures if we tried to explain everything. What we have described is sufficient to let the user drop the mouse and learn the rest on his own.

12.5 Reference manual

The reference manual for the hotel system contains system-related lookups as well as task-related lookups. It may also contain 'getting started' information (a tutorial part), overview lists, indexes and other parts.

12.5.1 System-related lookup

A system-related lookup explains what some part of the system does. It says little about the user tasks and rarely gives step-by-step instructions.

Figure 12.5A shows a system-related lookup for the hotel system. It is section 8 of the reference manual. It describes the *Stay* screen. There is of course a picture of the Stay screen so that the reader can relate the text to the screen. It would be impossible to explain all the many fields in bubbles, but the picture points out some of the less obvious parts.

The text has two parts: field explanations and function explanations (*buttons*). For each field we have tried to follow this advice where it makes sense:

Advice for input fields

1 Explain what the user can write in the field. The *From* field and *Person* field are good examples. For the *From* field, the user can only change the field in a complex manner.

2 Explain from where the user gets the data. *Address* and *Pay form* are good examples.

3 Explain what the system uses the data for. *Name* and *Persons* are good examples.

4 Use active language to show whether the user or the system does something. *Persons* is a good example: 'The system sets *Persons* to the number of beds. You may change it directly.' If we had used passive language, it would be ambiguous: '*Persons* is set to the number of beds and may be changed directly.' The reader couldn't see who does what and easily builds a wrong mental model.

Advice for output fields

5 Explain what the contents mean. *Total rooms till now* is a good example.

6 Explain where the system gets the data from. *Stay no.* and *Persons* are good examples.

7 Explain what the user can use it for. *Passport* and *Total rooms till now* are good examples.

Fig 12.5 A   System-related lookup

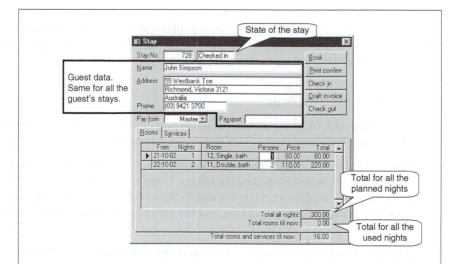

8. Stay screen

This screen shows all data about a stay: the guest's name, address and other details; the rooms he uses during the stay; the services he receives. A *stay* is also called a *booking*.

8.1 Fields

Stay No: The stay number (also called a booking number). The system gives each stay a unique number.

State: The state of the stay (booked, checked in, etc.). The state changes when you check in the guest, checks the guest out, cancels the stay, etc.

Name: The name of the guest. When a guest has many stays, this name appears on all of them. If you change the name, the change will be visible on all these stays. The system uses the name when you search for a guest. It also prints the name on confirmation letters and invoices.

Address, Phone: Other details for the guest. Like the name, changes will be visible for all the guest's stays. The system uses the data to search for the guest and on letters and invoices. Record the data in the way the guest states it. Details such as zip code may be unknown in some countries.

Passport: For foreigners you should record their passport number. It may be used for police reporting in case the guest causes trouble. Like the name, changes will be visible for all the stays.

Pay form: The way the guest pays the bill. The system needs the pay method when you check in the guest. It is a convenient time for you to ask the guest about payment. This field applies to only this stay. The guest may pay in different ways for other stays.

Tab: Rooms

Each line on the *Rooms tab* shows a room that the guest uses during his stay. The fields are:

From: The first day the guest uses the room. You cannot change the date directly. You have to delete the line, select the room again on the Rooms Selection screen with a new *From* date, and book the room. (See section . . . for details).

Continued

Fig 12.5 A System-related lookup (*Continued*)

Nights: The number of nights the guest plans to stay in the room. You cannot change it directly. See *From* for how to do it.

Room: The room number and room type. You cannot change it directly. See *From* for how to do it.

Persons: The number of persons who stay in the room. The system sets it to the number of beds in the room. You may change it directly. If you decrease it to one, the guest will only pay the price for the room as a single room. If you increase it, the guest will pay for an extra bed.

Price and **total:** The system calculates the room price per day and the total for all the planned nights.

Total all nights: The total of all the lines.

Total rooms till now: The total for the nights that the guest has stayed. If he checks out now, he will only pay this amount for the rooms. If the stay is booked only, this field will be zero.

Services tab
. . .

8.2 Buttons

Book: The simple use of the Book button is to book a new stay. The system requires that there is a name for the guest and that you have selected a free room on the *Room selection* screen. The stay becomes *booked* and the system files it immediately.

You may use *Book* in other cases too. When the stay is booked already, you can select an additional room and use *Book* to add it to the stay. When the stay is *checked in*, you may use *Book* to undo the check in to a booking (the system will ask for confirmation before it undoes the check in).

Print confirmation: . . .

Menu: Stays

The main menu *Stays* has these menu items:

Open Find-guest screen: Opens the screen for finding guests and stays. No action if the screen is open already.

Delete room line: You must have selected a line on the *Rooms* tab. The system then deletes it and immediately releases the corresponding room booking or check-in. This allows the room to be used for other purposes.

. . .

If you see similarities between the field descriptions and good *data descriptions*, it is no coincidence. A good data modelling job helps you make a good reference manual. However, you should not copy the data description directly. The reader is usually a different kind of person and the context in which he reads it is different too. Furthermore, on the user interface there will be fields that have no direct counterpart in the data description.

The function part is called *Buttons* because *function* is a fuzzy word to most people. A function could mean a job people have, a task they carry out – or something the computer or a machine does. In the example, the *Button* section covers both the real command buttons and the main menu items that relate to this screen. It is a bit dubious whether to handle the menu items in the screen section or in a separate main-menu section. For menus in the individual screen (*local menus*) it is natural to describe them in the section that explains the screen, but what about the main menu?

In the hotel case, there are no local menus. Due to the limitations in Access, there is only a main menu bar. What would have been local menus on other platforms is in the hotel system a single menu in the main menu bar. This is the justification for describing them under the screen where they logically belong. Since some readers might expect to find the menu item in a separate main-menu section, we have provided such a section too. We have intentionally duplicated some explanations to help the reader.

For each function (button or menu point) we have tried to follow this advice where it makes sense:

Advice for functions

8 Give an example of when the user would use the function. This is to help the user understand the purpose of the function. We should not try to explain all situations. The task-related lookups are better suited for this.

9 Explain what the function does in simple cases. As an example, *Book* records a booking.

10 Explain what the function can also do. *Book* may also be used for booking additional rooms or undo a check-in.

11 Explain any preconditions required. *Book* requires a guest and a free room.

If you see similarities between function descriptions and mini-specs it is no coincidence. They explain the same, but with different emphasis. However, you should not copy the mini-spec directly. The reader and the context will be different. The mini-spec may also explain too many details that shouldn't concern the user.

Cross-references and step-by-step

Notice that the description gives a sketchy step-by-step instruction about changing the *From* date. A full description of this takes about ten lines, and it would be confusing to have it here. Instead we give a sketchy description that will help most readers to remember how to do it. We also give a reference to the full description.

In this way we have made a compromise between two nuisances: spending a lot of space on something that is trivial to most people, and forcing the reader to look somewhere else.

The same procedure is also needed to change *Nights* and *Room*. We could have repeated the same sketchy step-by-step instruction, but since it has been explained a few lines above, we refer to it. The nuisance of a cross-reference is small in this case.

Readers don't read

Many writers assume that readers read from one end to the other. They do for novels, but not for technical stuff. They try to find the right spot and then read there. They will not even read the entire section about the *Stay* screen. We have made an effort so that it is possible to read most pieces in isolation – assuming that the reader has some general idea about the system.

12.5.2 Task-related lookup

A task-related lookup explains how to perform some user task. Usually it will contain a step-by-step instruction. It rarely explains details of what the various system functions can do in other cases.

Figure 12.5B shows a task-related lookup for the hotel system. It is section 14 of the reference manual. It explains how to handle the situation when a room is under repair and cannot be used for guests. This example has a picture of the key screen where the task is done. For other tasks it may be convenient to show several screens corresponding to different steps of the task. For some tasks it may be unnecessary to show any screens at all (the Reference Card has examples of this on page 2).

The example handles a typical situation: The simple version of the task is fairly easy. The user selects the room dates for repair, then sets the state to *Repair*. However, some bookings may block the room these days. This situation requires a lengthy rebooking operation. The programmer approach to describing this would be a structure like this:

> Select the room days
> If some days are blocked then:
>> Find a blocking stay
>> Find another room for the stay
>> Book the room for the stay
>> Delete the old room for the stay
>> Repeat from the beginning
> Set the room state to *Repair*.

Unfortunately, this is very hard to read for ordinary users. Programmers understand immediately, but they have spent a long time learning the principle. Instead, we have used the same approach as in the task descriptions. First describe the simple version, and then describe deviations as a kind of variant. This has proved successful when analysing and describing user tasks in cooperation with users. It also works in reference manuals.

In the example, we have tried to follow this advice where it makes sense:

Advice for task-related lookups

1 Explain the problem. When would this task be needed (the *trigger*). Why is it needed (the *purpose*).

2 Outline the solution. Give a brief overview of the procedure to follow. This prepares the reader for what will follow. Many readers might even say: *Aha, this is how to do it. I don't have to read the rest!*

3 Show the details. Give a step-by-step description of the simple version of the procedure. You may refer to variants, but don't exaggerate.

4 Give a step-by-step description of each variant.

A variant may be complicated and have its own variants. In these cases it is tempting to use sub-variants so that you end up with several levels of variants. Try to avoid it – the reader easily gets confused. Instead you may replace the variant with two or more variants, each dealing with its own combination of situations. Or you may nominate the complicated variant to a task of its own.

5 Clearly mark the steps with bullets or numbers.

6 Explain what the user has to do, what he can see on the screen and what the system does.

7 Use active language to show whether the user or the system does something. Example: 'Select the blocking room line' (the user does something). 'The system asks whether . . . '

8 Use examples to illustrate the procedure and what the screen shows.

9 Use examples to explain non-obvious concepts. In the room repair case, the system measures a stay in nights, but repairs usually deal with working days. An example illustrates the difference.

10 You may use screen shots to illustrate the steps and what the user sees, but don't exaggerate.

12.5.3 Structure of reference manual

The system-related and task-related parts constitute the major part of the reference manual. Depending on the system and the audience, other parts may be necessary. Figure 12.5C shows the contents of the full reference manual for the hotel system.

Table of contents

A table of contents is a must. Most readers who read something in the book will also have a look at the table of contents. Fortunately, modern text processors make it easy to generate a table of contents automatically.

Introduction and installation

Many writers love to write a long introduction, but they don't realize that few readers will ever read it. A reference manual is neither a novel nor a tutorial. People

Fig 12.5 B Task-related lookup

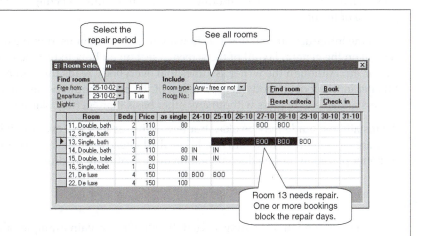

14. Room repair

It may happen that a room needs repair so that it cannot be used meanwhile. In order that receptionists don't check guests into the room, you have to tell the system about the repair.

The solution is to use the *Room Selection* screen. Select the days the repair will take and set the room state to *Repair*. If some bookings use the room on a repair day, rebook them. Here are the details.

How to do it

1. Open the *Room Selection* screen.
2. Select the days for repair: Set *Free from* to the first repair day and *Departure* to the day where the room will be ready. Set *Room type* to "Any - free or not".

You should now see the state of all rooms in these days.

3. Select the room to be repaired.

The figure shows an example where we need to repair room 13 from 25th Oct (after checking out any guests) to 29th Oct (where the room will be ready around noon). Four nights are marked.

4. Check whether there are any bookings that block the room in these days.
5. If nothing blocks, set the room state to repair (use the main menu: *Rooms -> Repair in progress*).

Bookings that block. If there are bookings that block, you have to rebook them. In the example two days are blocked. Rebook them as follows:

6. On the *Find Guest* screen, find the blocking guest by means of *Room No.* and *Night*. In the example, it would be room 13, night 27-10-02.
7. There should be only one stay that matches. Open it (*Show stay*).
8. Use the *Room Selection* screen to find a suitable free room. (Sorry, but the repair selection will disappear from the screen.)
9. Book the room for the guest. The system asks whether it is an additional room. Yes it is - for the moment.
10. Select the blocking room line and delete it (use the main menu: *Stays -> Delete room line*). The old booking has now been replaced by the new one.
11. Now you have to start again from step 2 to select the repair days. If needed, you have to rebook more guests.

will look up things in it and don't care to read a long introduction. It is okay, however, to have a one-page introduction to warn the unsuspecting reader about the purpose of the book.

Often the introduction contains a section about the notation used in the book, a section on the general layout of the screen, a section on how to use the mouse and cursor, etc. Although the writer assumes that everybody reads this and remembers it till later in the book, nobody does. The rest of the book should be intuitively understandable to readers without any other basis than 'getting started'.

An installation guide may be okay, but few of the readers will ever use it because they are working with a system that is installed already. An installation guide might be better placed in on-line documentation on the software medium.

Tutorial

A tutorial is intended for getting started. It will often contain examples and other training material. The intent is that the users will read it from the beginning until they can use the system on their own. Depending on the system and the audience it might be a good idea to have a tutorial as part of the reference manual (maybe it then should be called a user manual, but this is a minor issue). It is convenient to have everything in the same book, but at the same time a large book scares many users: *Will I have to read all of this?*

In the hotel case, the support card serves as a mini-tutorial. A course may be a good idea to make users proficient, but a course will need separate training material with exercises and solutions as handouts. The reference manual seems a bad choice for the tutorial.

System-related lookups

The next sections deal with the screens one by one. The sequence is alphabetical. Each section is for lookup, and even the bits of each section are largely possible to read in isolation. We have also included a section about the main menu, thus intentionally duplicating some information from the screen section.

In a large system, there would of course be many screens, but the principle would remain the same. Based on the name of the screen (visible in the title bar or some other heading), the user will be able to find the right section.

Task-related lookups

The next many sections are task lookups. While there was a natural ordering of the system lookups (alphabetical by screen name), this is not quite as obvious for the tasks. Users don't really have names for tasks although they can recognize a task name as 'this is probably what I look for'. For this reason alphabetical task names

Fig 12.5 C Structure of reference manual

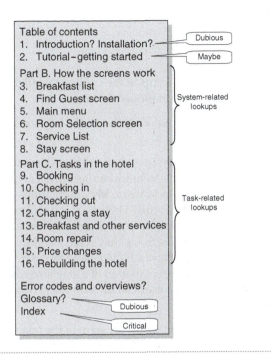

don't really help. We have chosen to order the tasks according to their frequency of use. In a large system, we might arrange the tasks by work area, for instance tasks for the reception, tasks for accounting, tasks for purchase, and within each work area by frequency.

Since we divide the lookup parts into system-related and task-related parts, why don't we divide the parts into two books? For a large system it seems to make sense, but in general, users have difficulties distinguishing system-related issues from task-related ones. For this reason it is essential that the index covers everything. The index directs the user to the proper place, although he doesn't know whether his question was system-related or task-related.

To educate the users a bit (if possible) we have divided the book into two parts, A and B, as shown. The section numbers run across the parts.

Error codes and overviews

In some systems it may be a good idea to have various kinds of overview, for instance lists of error codes with explanations, lists of command names, etc. In the hotel case we have not yet seen any use for it, partly because the user interface seems to provide the necessary help, for instance error messages in plain text with suggestions for what to do.

Glossary

A glossary defines unusual terms in the system. We might for instance define the strange term 'stay' in a typical glossary manner.

Stay. A stay is a guest's booking or actual occupation of some hotel rooms for a period of time.

Although formally correct, this is very hard to understand – particularly if you don't know the term already. Many technical writers insist on glossaries, but don't realize that few readers can understand them. My observations are that glossaries confuse users rather than help. Why is this? I believe it is because humans only understand in context, and with a glossary there is no context. It would be much better to explain what a stay is in connection with the Stay screen, and this is what we have done in the system-related lookup (Figure 12.5A). Now the user has a picture that shows an example of a stay. The short explanation of a stay also continues explaining what a stay consists of and what the user can do with it – giving additional context for understanding.

The conclusion is: Embed each glossary term in the text where it can be explained in context. Include the term in the index so that the reader will find it surrounded by its context.

Index

An index is an alphabetical list of subjects with associated page numbers. It allows the reader to look up any relevant subject and find the place in the text that explains about the subject. Modern text processors have good tools for this. As an example, look at this piece of the reference manual:

8. Stay screen

This screen shows all data about a stay: the guest's name, address and other details; the rooms he uses during the stay; the services he receives. A *stay* is also called a *booking*.

We want two entries in the index that refer to this piece of text:

stay.......................x
booking...............x

The 'x' has of course to be replaced with the proper page number when we print the final version. To make the index, we insert special *index marks* or *target marks* in the source text, something like this XE command in Word:

---

8. Stay screen

{XE "Stay"} This screen shows all data about a stay: the guest's name, address and other details; the rooms he uses during the stay; the services he receives. A *stay* is also called a *booking*. {XE "booking"}

In the last page of the book, we insert another command that tells the text processor to generate the index at this place. The system collects all the XE commands, finds the page numbers and generates the index.

In principle it is easy, but in practice it is awfully difficult to insert all the right index marks. What terms would the reader actually use when looking for this place? And how many places should he be guided to if he looks for *Stay*? From the reader's point of view, there are these problems:

a) Readers often know their problem but cannot give it words, so they don't know which term to look up.

b) The subject they look for is not in the index although it is in the book.

c) When they find the subject in the index, there are references to too many pages.

d) When they look into one of these pages, it doesn't contain what they expected.

Here is some advice to avoid this:

Advice for indexers

1 Include all terms that appear on the user interface. The *Stay screen* section should thus have index marks for *stay, stay no., pay form, draft invoice, total rooms till now* because all of these terms appear on the user interface and are described in the *Stay* section.

2 Include domain terms and system concepts. In the hotel system we should include for instance *regular guest* and *foreigners* (domain concepts) as well as *booking, stay* and *undo* (system concepts).

3 Permute the terms. In the hotel system we should include

       stay, cancel x

   as well as

       cancel, stay x

4 Include synonyms. In the hotel system we should include *booking* as well as *reservation* (a term which is not used in the system), and *modify* as well as *change*.

5 Give a hint on what you find if you follow the reference. In the hotel system, a reference to *room repair* could lead to many things. When the reference goes to the task-oriented description of Room repair, write

> *room repair (recording planned repairs)*..........x

and when the reference is to how you charge the guest for damages, write

> *room repair (charging troublesome guests)*......x

6 Check that each entry in the index refers to at most two pages (preferably only one). Subdivide the entry if all references are useful. As an example, you might have inserted references to a lot of places that deal with *Stay*. The result might be this entry in the index:

> *stay*.................... 5, 13, 25, 30

Which one should the user follow? Upon closer look, it might turn out that page 5 just mentions *Stay* without saying anything substantial about it. Drop this reference. Page 13 is the definition and also the Stay screen. Page 25 is about recording various kinds of stays and page 30 is about what exactly happens when you cancel a stay. The proper references should now be these:

> *stay, cancel*.................. 30
> *stay, definition*........... 13
> *stay, recording*........... 25
> *stay, screen*................. 13

12.5.4 Browsing and language

There are a lot of details that influence the usefulness of the manual. Some of them are related to helping the reader find the right place fast. Amazingly, when looking up something, readers tend to start browsing the book rather than using the table of contents or the index. Instead of fighting this 'bad habit', we can support the readers in what they intuitively do. Here is some advice:

Advice to support browsing

7 Number the sections and use section numbers for cross-referencing. Use at most three-level numbers. Section 2.5 and 2.5.3 are okay, but 2.5.3.2 is not (it is too hard to keep in your mind while turning pages). Some writers insist on using section headings without numbers, but it is much harder for the reader to find a section by its name. Will the reader have to browse forwards or backwards?

8 Use page headers and/or footers that support browsing. They should contain these data: page number, section number and section name. In larger books there may be chapters divided into sections. It may then be convenient to include also the chapter name in the page header. These data should be on the outward side of the book (right for right-hand pages, left for left-hand pages) so that the reader can see it without opening the book fully.

Many technical writers also include a version number and date on each page in order to keep track of what was added when. Okay, but keep it in a corner and use small letters so that the reader doesn't normally notice it.

9 Make the pages look different. When browsing, readers don't see the body text and cannot recognize a page from the words on it. Readers more or less consciously recognize pages from the figures, bullet sections, framed text parts or text parts with a different background. Make sure many of your pages include such elements to make them easy to recognize, but don't exaggerate.

Language

The language also has a huge influence on the usefulness of the manual. Few people have a natural talent for writing a clear language. Most of us need years of practice and feedback from better writers. We can do little about it in this book. There are a few things I would like to warn against, however, since they are very common in user documentation and manuals.

10 Avoid the passive voice. Always make it clear whether the user or the computer does something. We have mentioned it for system-related lookup as well as task-related lookup above, but it applies to all parts of the manual.

11 Avoid acronyms such as TOC for *Table of Contents* or RPC for *Remote Procedure Call*. It doesn't help that you explain the acronym in the introductory section and then use it in the rest of the manual. Remember that the reader doesn't read the introductory section – and even if he does, he cannot remember all of it until he reads the section he is really interested in. You may introduce an acronym if you are very, very sure that 95% of your audience knows it already. The remaining 5% will then have to learn the acronym.

12 Avoid useless 'warnings'. We often see manuals filled with framed text such as this:

> **Warning:** You must select a customer and a free room before using *Book*

There is no need to warn. The hotel system will tell the user what is wrong. The writer might have heard about this precondition for *Book*, but obviously didn't know what would happen. Or maybe the writer just had difficulties structuring his text to include this precondition in a natural way. *If* you warn, also say what would happen, for instance like this:

> **Warning:** You must select a customer and a free room before using *Book*. Otherwise the system will crash due to an error in the current release.

Test yourself

a) Mention six types of situations where support is needed.

b) In which ways can we support users?

c) What is a support plan?

d) What might a reference manual contain?

e) Should a reference manual contain a glossary? Are there alternatives to a glossary?

f) What should be mentioned in the index?

g) System X had an 800-page user manual, split into 10 chapters. Chapters had different authors and each author had made an index at the end of his own chapter. Comment on this approach.

Writing exercises. See Chapter 17.

13

More on usability testing

Highlights

- Planning the tests: where, who, how and how much time?

- How to find test users.

- How to find test tasks.

- Test log (for log-keeper only) and test report (for use inside the project).

In section 1.4 we gave the basics of usability testing. In this chapter, we give an in-depth guide. If you want to know even more, there are books on the subject, for instance, Dumas and Redish (1993).

During a usability test, we let a user (the test subject) try to carry out realistic tasks using the system or a mock-up of it. During the test, we observe which problems the user encounters. The facilitator or the log keeper notes down what happens, in particular the problems.

13.1 Common misunderstandings

There are many misunderstandings about usability tests:

- It is *not* necessary to have a functional system. Even a paper and pencil version of the screens can reveal most problems.

- It is *not* a demonstration of the system where a developer or a marketing person shows how to perform various tasks with the system. The users and customers may be very excited about the system, yet be completely unable to use it on their own.

- It is *not* a test where a colleague is the test user. Most likely he knows so much about computers that he will not encounter certain kinds of problems. And he may know so little about the application area that he encounters problems that real users don't. It is essential to find test users that correspond to the intended audience for the final product.

- The test does *not* have to take place in a special usability lab with video, electronic log and semi-transparent glass walls. A desk with a PC, a facilitator, a log keeper and preferably a motivated developer is sufficient in most cases. When you test with paper mock-ups, you may even do without the PC.

Purpose of usability testing

What is the purpose of usability testing? Why do we test? Figure 13.1 shows some possible answers.

Usability testing during development. Let us first look at the purposes during system development.

The purpose is *not* to find bugs in the system. Developers have more cost-effective ways to do that. Of course it may happen that we encounter bugs during a usability test. For instance, the early version of the system that we use for usability testing might crash every now and then, or the mock-up hasn't got all the necessary message boxes. We note down these problems to help the developers correct them, but this is not the purpose of the usability test.

The main purpose is *not* to prove that the system is easy to use. Developers without usability experience believe that their system is easy to use, and want to prove it just before delivery. They find a scaring number of problems, but are not able to correct them at this stage. However, if we have made usability tests early during design, it is a good idea to make a check also at the end, to catch problems that have sneaked in after design.

At first sight the prime purpose is to find usability problems, but it is only part of why we really make the test: We want to correct the problems. If we don't plan for

Fig 13.1 Usability test – misunderstandings

```
Not demo of system
Not a test with colleague as user
Functional system not necessary
Usability lab not necessary
```

```
Purpose of usability testing during development?
1.  Find program bugs?
2.  Prove that system is easy to use?
3.  Find problems?
4.  Correct problems?
5.  Experience the users?

Purpose of usability testing with final system?
```

changes too, there will be no improvement of the final product, and testing will be a waste of time. This is why it is so important to run usability tests early during design, preferably before anything has been programmed.

An important side effect of early usability testing is that developers experience the users, their domain knowledge and attitudes and their IT knowledge and attitudes. This can strongly improve the intuition that developers use when they design the interface.

Usability testing in other cases. Usability testing can be used in other cases too. For instance we may want to measure the usability of a product we want to buy. Or measure usability of an old system we plan to improve.

13.2　Planning the test

Figure 13.2 shows the important things to consider when you plan a usability test. You can use the figure as a template when you plan your own usability tests. In the figure we have filled in the template corresponding to a usability test of a hotel system we develop.

How many users?

How many test users do we need? Some HCI experts claim that we need at least 10 users to get statistical significance otherwise testing is of no use. Unfortunately, this is often used as an argument for not even trying, since fellow developers can clearly see that 10 users would require a huge amount of work.

Experience shows that at the beginning of development, we should test with only one user! We find so many serious problems with just one user that it would be foolish to test with another user before the worst problems have been corrected. Not all of the problems are usability problems. Some of them are problems in the experimental set-up, for instance that the prototype set-up and the test tasks don't match.

In the next round of testing, we can use 2–4 users. It gives a lot of observational data to keep track of. Of course we may miss some problems that relatively few users encounter, and by coincidence none of our test users. From a practical point of view, this is the kind of risks we have to run in most projects. In practice, we cannot make everybody happy. (See section 13.4 for a detailed discussion.)

When I help developers make usability tests for the first time, the following usually happens: The first user arrives to the test and soon runs into a lot of serious problems. Developers look at each other, thinking: what an idiot – he cannot be a typical user. Then the next user arrives and soon runs into much the same problems. Now developers become uneasy – maybe there are some problems with the user interface. And when the third user encounters the problems, developers are convinced. In most cases this achieves the prime purpose – developers become motivated to improve the user interface.

So with developers who are unfamiliar with usability tests, three users seem a good choice for the first test. For usability-experienced developers, one user for the first test is the right choice.

Which users?

It is important to find out what kind of test users we need. Their knowledge should correspond to those users we expect in practice. We need not care so much for the ideal users who understand fast and know many IT systems already, but should look for those in the weaker end of the user group.

Fig 13.2   Planning the test

Which users:	One + revision. Then 2–4 (lots of data).
Domain knowledge:	E.g. know reception work.
IT knowledge:	E.g. text processing.
Finding test users:	Actual users; on the street; marketing agent, . . .
Test site:	E.g. our meeting room, customer's site, public area, usability lab.
Facilitator:	Main contact with user.
'Computer':	Designer – make sure he doesn't interfere.
Log keeper:	Notes down – particularly the problems.
Test tasks:	E.g. book guest A based on a letter. Receive guest B who has booked. Change room for guest C who is checked in.
Presenting tasks:	E.g. written, acting, explain. Don't give hints!
Start-up state:	E.g. system started, guest B booked, guest C checked in.
User instruction:	As in real life. E.g. short written user's guide? Colleague's intro? Course?
Test method:	E.g. observe one user at a time, think aloud one at a time, two users discussing.
Data collection:	E.g. written notes (log), tape, video, computer log, usability lab.
Debriefing:	Good things about the system? Bad things? Do you think the system could . . . ?
Planning the time:	Welcome and intro: 10 min Test tasks 60 min Debriefing 10 min Reporting the problems 100 min Total, one user 3 hours Time for three users ??

We can specify the *user profile* in two dimensions: The user's domain knowledge (their professional knowledge in the application area) and the user's IT knowledge. (See more on user profiles in section 5.4.)

In case of the hotel system, can we assume that our hotel users have reception experience? Or, should we also cater for temporary assistants on the night duty? Can we assume that they know IT on the text processing level? Or that they have tried another reception system before?

Sometimes we need the help of other people to find test users. These people must know the answer to these questions in order to select the right users. Section 13.3 explains more about finding test users.

Where to test?

Where should we run the test? There are several possibilities:

1 In our own meeting room. This is fine because we have easy access to the prototype and other equipment, and we can avoid interruptions. The problem is to have the user travel to our place. Further, the test environment may not reflect the real working conditions.

2 At the user's site. This would normally be at the user's workplace. The advantage is that the user doesn't need to travel and the environment is the right one. The disadvantage is that we have more trouble setting up the prototype and we cannot control interruptions. Further, the user may feel uneasy because his colleagues may watch him during the test.

3 In a public place. This is useful for public systems, such as library systems and travel information systems. The environment is the real one, and we may even be lucky to find our test users on the spot. The disadvantage is the trouble of setting up the prototype and other equipment in this place.

4 In a usability lab. We may have one in our own company or we may rent one from another company. As we explain below under *data collection* this is much more cumbersome and only worth the effort for systems where we have a functional prototype and want to study fast user actions.

Roles in the test team

The test team consists of designers and/or HCI specialists. The team must handle three roles:

- The **facilitator** who has the main contact with the test user, gives him the test tasks, asks him to think aloud, asks him what he is looking for, etc. The facilitator is also the leader of the test.

- The '**computer**'. Unless we use a fully functional prototype, we need a person who simulates what the computer does, changes screens, writes the computer's replies, etc. Some people call him *The Wizard of Oz*. This person will usually be a designer, since he knows best what the computer should do.

- The **log keeper** writes down what happens, where the user encountered problems, what the user believes about the system, etc. The log keeper may cautiously interfere with the user, for instance to clarify a problem or to hold the user back while the log keeper writes his notes. However, the log keeper must respect the facilitator's leading role during the test, otherwise it may end up in a mess.

We can allocate a person to each of these roles, but often we let two persons share them. As an example, one person can be facilitator and computer at the same time; the other person is the log keeper. Sometimes I have played all the roles alone, but that is hard, particularly with long tests. I soon get a feeling that I miss too many problems or let the 'computer' do the wrong thing.

Some HCI specialists say that developers should not be present during the test. Developers may observe what is going on through a remote TV screen or from a neighbouring, glass-separated observation room. The argument is that developers cannot refrain from interfering with the users, giving them help and advice – or commenting on what they do.

My own experience is that many developers are really good on the test team as soon as they get the idea of what it is all about. Soon they can run usability tests on their own. I have only a few times observed developers interfering inappropriately, for instance, in utter frustration shouting to the user from the back of the room *look at the bottom of the screen* (error messages appeared there, but the user hadn't noticed). A good facilitator can handle this in a joking fashion and the developer won't do it again.

Test tasks

We have to plan the tasks that the user should try. It is not sufficient to mention the tasks, we need to plan the specific data to be used. In Figure 13.2 we have indicated the specific guest to book. We need his name, address, when he arrives, etc., for instance in the form of a letter or fax.

Many developers have some difficulty stating the test tasks in a good way. They tend to give the user a recipe for carrying out the task, rather than giving them a problem to solve. We return to this in section 13.5.

Finding the important problems depends crucially on the tasks we include in the test. It should be obvious that we cannot find problems that occur when carrying out task X if we don't try out task X. On the other hand, a test session with a single user cannot last more than 1–2 hours. Longer tests are exhausting for the user as well as the test team. This puts a limit to the number of tasks we can try out.

Fortunately, the accelerator effect helps us. When the central screens are right – so that users understand them – developers are better able to make the remaining screens right too. Furthermore, when the users understand the central screens of the system, they find it easier to understand the rest. For this reason, start testing with the tasks that use only the central screens. (Section 2.4.3 explains more on the accelerator effect.)

Presenting the tasks

We can present the tasks to the user in different ways. One way is to write them on a slip of paper. This ensures that all test users get them in the same way and that we don't unintentionally give them additional hints. We can also act the work situation more vividly for instance with a 'guest' who arrives with his luggage and asks for a room.

However, the most common way is simply to tell the user what task he should carry out. Make sure that you don't give him hints on how to do it.

Start-up state

We must plan the initial state of the system when we start the test. Which windows are visible, which data do they show and what does the 'database' contain? In the example we want to show the start-up window of the hotel system. The database and the windows must show that guest B has booked and guest C is checked-in. These data are necessary to carry out the planned tasks.

User instruction

How much instruction and training should we give the users before they start on the tasks? The answer is: as close as possible to what they would get in real life. If we are designing a Web site for public use, there will be no user training at all, so we shouldn't give any during the test.

If we have planned a written instruction, we can let the user read an outline of it. (In this way we also test the written instruction.) A variant is to tell the user roughly the same as we would have written. (This is actually a good way to plan what to write in the real version.) If we plan an introductory course, we can try out a first version of it in connection with the usability test.

In the hotel case, we might plan courses for new users, but in practice people are often exposed to the new system without taking the course. The most realistic situation for new users is that another receptionist gives them a five-minute introduction to the system. We can easily do the same as an introduction to the usability test, but we should take care not to deal too explicitly with the actual test tasks.

In the hotel case, we might also be ambitious and go for making the system easy to use without any introduction. Actually, even the five-minute introduction is ambitious. Many existing hotel systems require that the user follows a one-week course.

Test method

We can carry out the test in many ways:

- **Observe only.** Let the user work on his own while we just observe what he is doing. This is good for measuring task times, but gives little feedback on how to improve usability. It also works best with fully functional prototypes.

- **Think aloud.** Ask the user to think aloud and explain what he does and why. Ask him to explain in case you cannot understand what he is doing or why he gets stuck.

- **Cooperation.** Ask two test users to work together on the task. Encourage them to discuss what they are doing. Some users find it strange to think aloud, but readily discuss the task with a fellow user.

It is generally assumed that users encounter the same problems whether they work silently or think aloud. Although one experiment confirms the assumption (Hoc and Leplat 1983), it is not well tested. Most of us have experienced that we find a solution to a problem as soon as we explain it to others. Thinking aloud might thus help the user finding the solution. My own observation is that the problems are the same, but thinking aloud changes the problem from a task failure to a major or minor problem. It would be interesting to see further investigations of this.

Data collection

We can collect data in many ways: written notes, audiotape, video, computer logging of actions, usability lab. What should we use in practice?

Written notes are usually the most important. The log keeper takes these notes during the test. To follow what is going on, he may have to hold the user back every now and then or ask for clarification of problems. We show an example of written notes in Figure 13.7B. It is useful to have copies of screens available for writing some of the notes. After the test, we go through the notes and extract the problems.

Audiotapes are a good supplement to the notes. Ask for the user's permission before starting the tape recorder. You may listen to all of the tapes after the tests, but usually it takes too much time. In practice it suffices to use the tape only when there is some doubt about the notes.

Video is also a good supplement to the notes, but the technical set-up is much more demanding. Typically you need two cameras, one to show the participants from the front and one to show the screen. Going through the recordings afterwards is time consuming, just as for the audiotapes.

In the classical usability tests, the test team didn't use thinking-aloud. They recorded the experiment on video and later studied the tapes and noted the usability problems. This was very time consuming and 1 hour of usability test might require 4–8 hours post-processing. Furthermore, although they could observe the usability problems, they could only guess about the causes.

Video has advantages, however:

- We can reduce the amount of thinking-aloud and instead study the tape afterwards with the user at our side. If we do it immediately after the test, we get a good explanation of the usability problems. The advantage is that we avoid the potential risk that thinking aloud makes it easier for the user to solve the problem. The procedure is time consuming, however.

- We can record users that work at full speed, typing and clicking their way around. We can later study what happened in slow motion, and with the user at our side we can get good explanations. This works only with fully functional prototypes or with the finished system. Actually, it is an excellent way to study users at their daily work, which is a good source for improving the system.

- With video, a lot of people can follow what is going on during the test. They will usually be in a neighbouring room where they can talk freely without disturbing the user. If marketing people and developers are present here, the debate will be quite vivid: *I told you that . . .* and *maybe we should . . .*

Computer logging is crucial if we want to study fast user actions. You need special software to make the computer record the log. The log shows what exactly the user pushed and how long he took doing it. Of course this works only with a functional prototype or a finished system.

Usability lab. A usability laboratory consists of a room where the user works with his tasks and an adjoining room where the test team observe what the user does. A huge, semi-transparent glass window separates the two rooms so that the user cannot see the test team. There are video cameras that allow the team to see details and record what happens. There is also a remote computer screen so that they can see what is on the user's screen. Computer logging is of course available too, as well as facilities for later reviewing and synchronizing of computer log and videotapes.

The main advantage of usability labs is that they allow a large team to observe the user without disturbing him. However, this can also be achieved with simple video, which doesn't occupy two rooms permanently. All the other features of a usability lab can be handled in simpler ways, as explained above.

Sad to say, but the real purpose of a usability lab has often been to promote usability and show to the rest of the world that *we know how to work with usability*. Often the usability work failed anyway because people thought, *if we get a usability lab, we will get usability*. This is definitely wrong, and a usability lab is at most a small part of producing good user interfaces. Even when the company succeeds with usability, the lab soon becomes empty as developers find simpler ways to run usability tests.

Debriefing

When the test is over, we should take some time to get the user's impression of the system. Plan what to ask, for instance, what the user found easy or difficult, what the user believes the system would do in this and that case. In that way we can get indications of task efficiency and understandability. (More on this in section 13.6.)

Planning the time

A test session with a single user shouldn't take more than 1–2 hours. Longer tests are exhausting for the user as well as the test team. After the test itself, we have to write a test report with a list of the usability problems. A plan for the first test could look like this:

First test, one user	Clock hours
Welcome and intro	10 min
Test tasks	60 min
Debriefing	10 min
Total for the test	80 min
Writing the test report	100 min
Total for test and reporting	3 hours

This is a realistic plan for the first test with a mock-up. Notice that writing the test report takes less than 2 hours. This is because we use the written log from the test and extract the usability problems from it. (More on this in section 13.6). If we have to listen to audiotapes or study videotapes, reporting may take 4–8 hours.

The figures above are the clock hours. Professionals also care about the work hours involved. Assume that we have two developers on the test team: the facilitator and the log keeper. The log keeper also writes the test report. The work hours will be like this:

	Work hours	
Test with one user	Facilitator	Log keeper
The test itself	80 min	80 min
Writing the report		100 min
Total work hours		260 min (4.3 hours)

In these figures for work hours, we have not included the user's time. As explained in section 13.3, test users are usually 'free' from the project's point of view.

In the first test, we usually find so many serious problems that it is a waste of time to try with a second user before the worst problems have been corrected. We should not expect to try more than one or two test tasks, although we may have prepared several more. Often the best way to correct the serious problems is to redesign the user interface radically. In this case, it is wise to try with a single user once more.

If we don't redesign, but only correct the worst problems, we may test with three new users. This will have to take place a few days later to leave time for correcting the mock-up. The plan for such a test could look like this:

Series of three users	Work hours	
	Facilitator	Log keeper
Welcome and intro	10 min	10 min
Test tasks	50 min	50 min
Debriefing	10 min	10 min
Adjustments before next test	10 min	10 min
Total for one test	80 min	80 min
Total for three tests	240 min	240 min
Writing the test report		180 min
Total work hours		660 min (11 hours)

Notice the 10 minutes after each test to handle various unexpected problems before the next user arrives. Also note that the total time to test with three users is not three times the time to test with one. Why? Because reporting for users two and three is faster than for user one since many of the problems are the same.

13.3 Finding test users

A usability test must of course be made with users that correspond to the real users we expect in practice. It may be difficult to find such persons, and as a result developers are tempted to use a colleague as the test user. They may find some usability problems in this way, but not all the relevant ones. Most likely the colleague knows so much about computers that he will not encounter certain kinds of problems. And he may know so little about the application area that he encounters problems that real users don't.

A related mistake is to test the system with users who have been involved with analysis or design of the system. They also know too much to be representative users. However, as pointed out by Carlshamre and Karlsson (1996), expert users are very good at finding missing functionality as part of a usability test.

If we are to test the ease-of-learning aspect of the system, we should use new users for testing each new version. Testing for task efficiency, however, assumes experienced users and the same users may well test several versions if we allow them to gain experience with each version.

So, from where do we get the test users? It depends on the kind of system.

System for internal use. If the system is for internal use in a company, it is rather easy to find real users. We may need some persuasion to make them spend the time for a test, but usually it is possible. Remember that each user will have to spend only 1–2 hours (we would normally not use the same person twice).

Products for a broad audience. If the product is for a broad audience for instance a typical Web site, we can find people on the street and invite them to be test users. For instance once we tested a public library system. We found test users by asking people who visited the library.

You may also ask a marketing agent to find people with the profile you have specified. They use the telephone directory or special databases, phone people and ask them a few questions to see whether they have the right profile. If everything is okay, they invite them to the test. Most people say yes, and receive at most a nominal amount to cover their travel expenses. (The marketing agent, however, will charge you more.)

Niche products. Many companies develop products for a narrow market, for instance welding machines or noise measurement equipment. In these cases, a marketing agent cannot help because phoning around at random will rarely hit a person with the right profile. We have to find users or potential users for the product.

The developers are often responsible for finding such users, but they hesitate and don't know how to go about it. They have few social contacts with users, and their attitude is far from approaching users or customers whom they don't know. In many product-developing companies they are not even allowed to. Sales and marketing staff have much better potential for getting user contact, but someone has to motivate them. We strongly suggest that finding test users is planned early and supported by other departments of the company. Grudin (1991) discusses this issue in detail and many other barriers between developers and users, for instance, mutual disrespect between marketing and development, lack of user motivation and balancing between too many user profiles and too few.

13.4 How many users?

Some HCI experts claim that we need at least 10 users to get statistical significance, otherwise testing is no use. Unfortunately this is often used as an argument for not even trying, since fellow developers can clearly see that 10 users would require a huge amount of work. More modest HCI experts say that 3 users are enough. In this section we will study the problem closer.

First of all users are different. User X may not notice the *Search* button, while user Y notices it immediately. How can this be? There are several reasons:

- Users have different backgrounds and for this reason expect different things on the screen.

- Users scan a screen in different ways. The general belief is that we look at the top left and move our attention towards the bottom right, but this is a very rough approximation. Eye-tracking equipment shows that users have very individual scan habits (Noton and Stark 1972; Pan *et al.* 2004).

- Users have different cognitive abilities. Some users panic if there are too many things on the screen, others soon get an overview. Some are good at getting an overview of pictures, but not of texts. Others are opposite.

Since users are different, usability problems will have different hit-rates. Some problems are encountered by only one user, some by two users, some by three and so on. As an example, let us assume that we have usability tested an early mock-up with 10 users. Figure 13.4 shows part of our problem table. Problem P1 was hit by U1 (user one) as a medium problem, by U2 as a task failure and so on. In total P1 was encountered by seven users – it had a hit-rate of 7. Similarly P2 had a hit-rate of 4. P3 had a hit-rate of 10 – it was encountered by all users.

The middle part of the figure shows a bar graph of the hit-rates. To the far right we see that 14 problems had a hit-rate of 10. In other words, 14 problems were encountered by all the users. Five problems had a hit-rate of 9. By coincidence, no problem had a hit-rate of 6. In total 60 problems were observed.

Singular problems. The most surprising thing is that 16 problems were encountered only once. We call these problems *singular*.

The pattern with a lot of singular problems to the left and a lot of frequent problems to the right is typical for early usability tests. As we improve the user interface, the number of frequent problems drops, but many singular problems tend to remain (section 14.4 shows an example from a mature system).

The first test user. Let us imagine what happened with the first test user. Figure 13.4, bottom part, shows the problems encountered by this user (in dark colour). The user would for sure encounter all problems with hit-rate 10. By definition they are encountered by all 10 users – also the first one. The first user would also encounter around 90% of the problems with a hit-rate of 9, 80% of the problems with a hit-rate of 8 and so on. The first user would only encounter one or two of the singular problems.

The second test user. Now imagine what happens with the second user. This user would also encounter all of the 10-hit problems. He would encounter most of the 9-hit problems once again and around 90% of those 9-hit problems that U1 didn't encounter. These new problems are shown as medium grey in the figure. U2 would encounter half of the 5-hit problems once again and around 50% of the undiscovered 5-hit problems. Finally, U2 would encounter one or two new singular problems.

The remaining users. Which problems are left at this point? Those shown in white in the figure. We see that almost all of the high-hit problems are discovered, while many low-hit problems are left. The remaining users essentially help us reveal these low-hit problems.

Testing with one more user. What would happen if we tested with one more user – U11? We would most likely find one or two additional singular problems and maybe one more low-hit problem.

Discussion

This example shows that it is a good idea to test with just one user the first time. We will detect most of the high-hit problems and several low-hit problems. The only problem is that we don't know for sure which of these problems are high-hit and which are low-hit. If we try to correct all of them, we will waste time on the low-hit ones. However, at this early stage, most of the problems we detect *are* high-hit ones. On the other hand, we don't risk a lot by using our sound judgement to correct only what we consider the most important ones. When we test again, we will see how well we succeeded.

The example also shows the effect of testing with two users. Now our problem list includes nearly all high-hit problems, but also several low-hit ones. Many problems on our list are encountered twice at this point in time. These are good candidates for repair, since most of them are the high-hit ones. Testing with a third user gives us added confidence about which problems are high-hit. The new problems we detect with the third user are mainly low-hit problems.

The next seven users give us mainly additional low-hit problems, but also some added confidence. In addition, they may change several problems that until now appeared singular into low-hit problems.

Which of the 60 problems are worth correcting? Basically we want to correct the high-hit problems. They cause troubles for most of the users. We would most likely ignore the singular problems. They are endless and we will only help 1 out of 10 users when we correct a singular problem. Depending on our quality goals, we may also correct some low-hit problems. If we for instance have a goal that no problem may be encountered by more than 10% of the users, we need to test with at

Fig 13.4 Problems and hit-rates

Problem	Users										Hit-rate
	U1	U2	U3	U4	U5	U6	U7	U8	U9	U10	
P1 Believes ...	med	fail	fail	min		min	fail			fail	7
P2 Doesn't ...	fail		fail		med			med			4
P3 Tries ...	fail	med	med	min	min	med	min	ann	fail	min	10
P4 Asks ...									min		1
P5 Annoying ...				ann		ann					2
. . .											

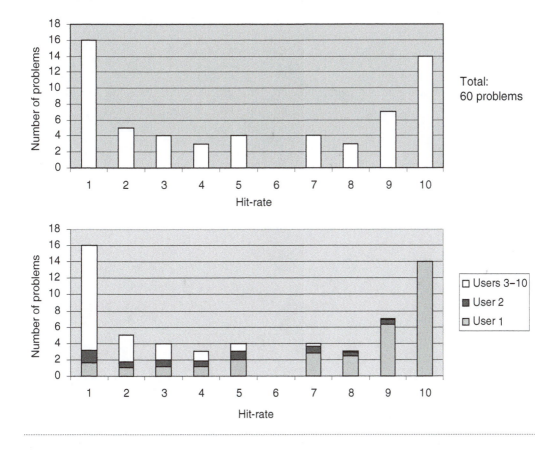

Total:
60 problems

least 10 users. Any problem encountered more than once should then be corrected. (We get better confidence if we test with 20 users. In that case, any problem encountered by two or more users should be corrected.)

Unfortunately, the decision on what to correct is more complex. For instance we should take the seriousness of the problems into account. We might for instance ignore all observations where a problem causes only minor or medium problems. This would drastically shorten the columns in Figure 13.4. We can then use the same reasoning as above to select the serious (*critical*) problems to correct.

We also have to take into consideration the cost of repairing a problem. We will for sure correct low-cost, high-hit problems. And we will for sure ignore high-cost, low-hit problems. It is more dubious whether we also want to ignore high-cost, high-hit problems. Section 13.7 discusses how to use cost/benefit estimates to decide.

13.5 Which test tasks?

It is important to find good test tasks in order to find all usability problems. How to find them depends on the kind of system we talk about.

Systems for professional use. Most IT systems are developed to help users do their tasks better. Our hotel system is an example. Other examples are accounting systems, production control, power distribution, medical scanners and newspaper editing. A text processor such as Microsoft Word is also for professional use, although for many kinds of users and many purposes.

The common characteristic of these systems is that they have to support a set of well-defined tasks. By studying these tasks, we can define what the system shall do and we also get a list of tasks to test.

Web sites. Many Web sites have to attract customers and inform about the company behind the Web site. These purposes don't correspond to well-defined user tasks. At the same time, the site may have to support ordinary tasks, for instance, buying products or allowing customers to review their bills.

When we test a typical Web site, there are many vaguely defined tasks we could test. How do we identify them? Here are some sources for identifying test tasks:

1   **Expectation-oriented.** Identify the different target groups of people to attract to the site. Ask representatives for each of them about their expectations to the site. Ask them before they see the site. The result could be small test tasks like these:

    What would you expect Wonderland to tell you on their Web site? What services can the company offer of interest to you? Assume you want to apply for a job with Wonderland – what is your impression about the company?

2   **Business-oriented.** What is the company's goal with the Web site? What do they expect that the customer/user would do? This could generate these test tasks:

    What are the prices for the services? Where is the closest shop? How to call them on the phone?

3   **System-oriented.** Study the Web site and find the tasks and information that the developers apparently expected the user to look for. This could generate this test task:

    Wonderland offers a possibility for you to order spare parts for their products. Your Wonderland gadget has no light in its display anymore. What spare part would you order and what does it cost?

4   **Label-oriented.** Study the structure of the site and make test tasks that can reveal whether users understand the labelling. (Here it is extremely important to

avoid hidden help.) This could generate this test task:

The site has a link labelled 'staff'. To where would it take you?

5 **Structure-oriented.** Make test tasks or questions that can reveal whether the user has a clear sense of where he is on the site. An example could be this test task:

When the user is in the middle of some of the other tasks, ask: *How many screens do you think are left before you have completed what you do? Where will the system take you afterwards? How could you cancel what you are doing?*

6 **Search-test.** Make test tasks that should cause the user to try the search functionality (if present). For instance,

Find out whether the site explains about hazards when using the product.

Plan a sequence of tasks

When you have identified the tasks to use for testing, plan their sequence carefully. Try to cover as many parts of the system as possible in order to catch as many usability problems as possible. Further, the difficulty of the tasks should gradually increase so that we find the basic problems first and the more subtle ones later. Figure 13.5A shows a wrong way to do it. Let us see why.

Easy tasks first. One important thing is to start with an easy task. The first task cannot be too easy. In the hotel system it would for instance be a bad idea to start with a task where a customer wants to book two rooms, one for 3 days and the other for 2 days. Often developers choose tasks that are difficult for the system and where the developers are proud of their solution. Such tasks are much too hard for the first-time user.

On the other hand, the task may not be so small that it is meaningless to the user. As an example, asking the user to record the name and address of a guest is not a task in itself. It is meaningless unless it is combined with check-in or booking. All tasks must give the user a feeling of having accomplished something – the task must be *closed*. (More on this in section 5.5.)

Independent tasks. The tasks should not be too dependent on each other. Ideally, the user should be able to carry out the tasks in any sequence. This gives you freedom to change the planned task sequence during the test, in case the user has serious problems with some of the tasks. In this way you allow the user to find many problems within the short time available.

In the hotel example, for instance, we planned three tasks: one for guest A, one for B and one for C. We can try out these three tasks in any sequence. In contrast, in Figure 13.5A, the team has planned the same tasks, but for the same guest. The user has to succeed with the first task in order to try the second task, and so on. Not a good idea.

Fig 13.5 A Test tasks – planning

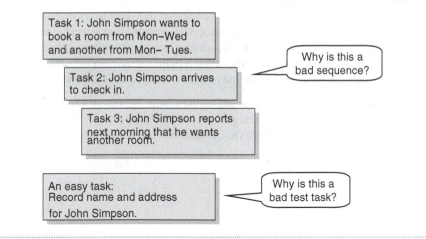

Task 1: John Simpson wants to book a room from Mon–Wed and another from Mon– Tues.

Task 2: John Simpson arrives to check in.

Why is this a bad sequence?

Task 3: John Simpson reports next morning that he wants another room.

An easy task:
Record name and address
for John Simpson.

Why is this a bad test task?

Hidden help

A frequent weakness in usability tests is that the test team provides hidden help, without realizing it themselves. The help can be in the way the test tasks are stated or in the response the facilitator gives the users during the test. Figure 13.5B shows three versions of a test task in the hotel system: a guest wants to check in.

In version A, the user gets a recipe for checking in. The result is that the user may complete the task during the test, but in real life he would not because there is no help in that case. This version looks more like what you would write in a user guide.

Fig 13.5 B Test tasks – hidden help?

Version A:
John Simpson wants to check in. Find him on the FindGuest screen.
Double click to open his Stay screen.

Version B:
John Simpson wants to check in. He has stay number 710.

Version C:
John Simpson arrives 23rd October. He says there should be two rooms for him.
If asked: He cannot remember his booking number (or stay number).
He lives 456 Orange Grove, Victoria Australia (can't remember zip code)
He leaves 26th October.

Version B looks more innocent, but it too has hidden help. First, we have suggested that the user has to make some kind of check-in. (In actual tests with the prototype in Figure 2.3A, some test users didn't realize that they had to check the guest in, because the system seemed to have all the necessary information already from the booking.) Second, we have used the term *stay number*, which directly matches something on the screen. (Actually, it is usually called a booking number or a reservation number in the hotel business and some users were confused about the *stay#* on the screen.)

In version C we have tried to avoid hidden help. We haven't used any of the words on the screen and the guest himself says as little as possible, but is able to answer some questions. (The answers should match what is in the database, of course.)

13.6   Carry out the test

Welcome and intro

When the test user arrives, he is a bit nervous. Users tend to feel that they are in for some kind of exam, and they are scared of looking stupid. Create a relaxed atmosphere for instance with a cup of coffee. Chat about daily matters and the user's background and expectations. Use the opportunity to check that the user has the background required for the test – not more knowledge and not less.

Make sure to explain the purpose of the usability test:

> *We want to find where the system is hard to understand or inconvenient. We know the system too well, so we cannot see it ourselves. We need your help. If you have problems with the system, it is the system's fault – not yours. We are not testing you; we are testing the system.*

Give the user the planned introduction to the system, if any. Explain as a minimum what the purpose of the system is. In the hotel case, we should for instance explain that the system is supposed to help the receptionist with the daily tasks. Don't demonstrate how the system works unless it is part of the introduction that would be given in real life.

Try the tasks

Now give the user the first test task and ask him to carry it out by means of the system. Take care not to give any hidden help (see section 13.5).

If you have planned the test as a think-aloud experiment, then encourage the user to explain what he does and why. Observe and listen to him. Meanwhile, the log keeper jots down notes on what the user does, particularly when he runs into problems. When you cannot understand what the user is doing or why he gets stuck, ask him what he is looking for and why he did as he did. If the log keeper cannot scribble his notes fast enough, it is okay to ask the user to wait a moment.

In early times HCI specialists insisted that the user shouldn't be interrupted or helped if he got stuck. Today we say that if the problem has become obvious and the user has had ample time to resolve it, the facilitator should interrupt and show the user how to get on, so he can encounter other problems. The price for this is to report the event as a task failure.

Some test users criticize the system or propose how it should work. Designers participating in the team can become very upset about this and start explaining to the user why this is not possible, that it is against the standard, etc. Avoid such discussions and receive the critique in a positive spirit. Note it down even if it sounds stupid. Later it may turn out to be the source of a real good solution.

When the user has completed the task, give him the next task. Don't worry whether he will get through all the tasks – he rarely will in practice. When the planned time has expired, stop the test. If you try to continue, everybody will soon be exhausted and stressed and the quality of the results will drop.

Debriefing

When the test is over, take some time to interview the user. Try to find out whether the user likes the system and whether he understands what goes on. The following questions tell us about the user's subjective satisfaction and may also show whether he understood what the system does:

Is there something you like about the system? Something you don't like?

The following questions tell us about the user's understanding of what the system does:

Do you think the system can remember the guest from one visit to another?

Could the system book two rooms for one guest?

What do you think is wrong if the system shows this message?

```
credit card not validated
```

And what would you do about it?

Finally, the following questions may tell us whether the system seems fit for use (necessary functionality) and whether it seems efficient. Unfortunately, we cannot get the full answer in this way, but it is worth getting pieces of the answer:

Do you think the system could support your tasks?

Is there something you doubt it could do?

Are there places where it seems too cumbersome to use it?

Logging what happened

Most log keepers find their job hard at the beginning. What to write and how much? After a few attempts, however, they usually find it easy. Figure 13.7B shows a typical handwritten log from an actual usability test. The system under test was to be used at a university for booking rooms for teaching, meetings, exams, etc.

The entire log for about 1.5 hours of test was about four such pages. The log shows the main points of what the test user did and said. In addition, the log has some other important indications:

- *Task1, task2,* etc., show that here the test user got a new test task.

- We recorded the test on audiotape, and the marks 1A, 1B, etc., indicate where we switched to a new tape or tape side.

- The time is shown when the test user got the task and also for other important points during the test. This helps locate the corresponding part of the audiotapes.

- P6, P7, etc., are added after the test itself. They indicate an occurrence of Problem 6, 7, etc. The test report has a list of all the problems enumerated P1, P2, etc. The indications in the log allow us to check that all observed problems are included in the report and all problems in the report are observed somewhere in the log.

13.7 Test report and analysis

Running the tests is less than half of the work. You have to report the findings so that others can understand them. If you develop a system, the important thing is to decide how to improve the system. The test report is the key information for these decisions.

Reporting the problems

The log from the tests is very cryptic to outsiders and only the test team have a chance to understand it – and only within a few days. After that time it will be incomprehensible, even to the author.

For this reason, the log keeper has to write a list of the problems the user encountered. They must be in such a form that people knowing the system understand the problems. The log keeper must write this list as soon as possible, preferably within 12 hours, while he still can recall what happened during the test (Figure 13.7A).

He reads through the logs and extracts all the usability problems he observed. He numbers the problems P1, P2 and so on. He also marks in the log that this was problem P1, etc. Often the same problem has been encountered several times, for instance for two test users. In these cases he reports the problem only once, but indicates the users who encountered it.

Figure 13.7C shows an example of a test report corresponding to the log in Figure 13.7B and a similar log for another test user. Note how problems P6 and P7 occur in the log and in the test report. Note also that P7 was encountered by HR and SL, but with different severity. In contrast P6 was encountered only by HR.

Ideally the description of each usability problem should specify where in the dialogue the problem occurred and what the problem was (what the user misunderstood, expected or wanted). If the user or developers have proposed a solution, it should be specified too, but don't force solutions at this stage – and don't worry about it.

Some other members of the test team should review the report to make sure that it is understandable. Often they have some additional observations to be included.

In some cases we have been two log keepers on the team. We listed the problems independently and then compared. The overlap was 80–90%. There are two causes of differences: (1) One person observed or logged something that the other person overlooked. They agree on including it. (2) They disagree whether something is worth reporting, for instance because the problem is too small or because it relates to something that is outside the scope of the project.

Fig 13.7 A Test report and analysis

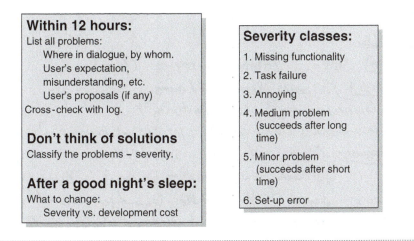

Within 12 hours:
List all problems:
   Where in dialogue, by whom.
   User's expectation,
   misunderstanding, etc.
   User's proposals (if any)
Cross-check with log.

Don't think of solutions
Classify the problems – severity.

After a good night's sleep:
What to change:
   Severity vs. development cost

Severity classes:

1. Missing functionality

2. Task failure

3. Annoying

4. Medium problem
   (succeeds after long
   time)

5. Minor problem
   (succeeds after short
   time)

6. Set-up error

Classifying the problems

The report in Figure 13.7C uses this classification of problems:

- **Missing functionality.** The system cannot support the user's task.

- **Task failure.** The user cannot complete the task on his own or he erroneously believes that it is completed.

- **Annoying.** The user complains that the system is annoying or cumbersome, or we observe that the user doesn't do it in the optimal way.

- **Medium problem.** The user finds the solution after lengthy attempts.

- **Minor problem.** The user finds the solution after a few short attempts.

- **Set-up error.** Something is wrong in the set-up of the test.

This is the classification from section 1.3 with addition of the *set-up error*. In practice, we encounter problems that have nothing to do with the system being tested, but only with the way we conduct the test. As an example, we might have put some wrong data into the database.

At this stage it is important not to care about how to correct the problems. If the team does this, they cannot classify the problems objectively according to their importance to the user. If they have no idea how to correct the problem, they even tend to reject that there is a problem at all.

So don't worry how to solve the problems. Instead try to understand how the user experienced the system. Then sleep on the problems – at least one night. Often

Fig 13.7 B Log from usability test

<u>User: HR</u>   95-01-05

14:35 |1A| Intro. Criteria for rooms: Clever!

14:42 Task 1 ✓ Chooses Requests right away.

P6.   Class/responsible ?? Course/activity ??
       Class overview: Class ~ course? L101 is that Accounting?

P6.   <u>Requests</u>: Course: is it IT&M? Tries IT&M
                 If heading only "Course" — believe it is Accounting.

P7.   <u>Course</u>: Requested ?? With trouble: Demand per class = 60.

P1.   Makes the rest on her own. But wonders "#hours" on Request.

14:55 Task 2
|1B| Start OK. Course: Compute demand/class myself? Fills in <u>OK</u>.
       Different classes, different #hours? No? Aha!
       <u>Requests</u>: Try "Tu", but what about "Th"? I want a new line
                                                      Copy & Paste OK
P5.   Warning: The system is stupid, I correct to Thursday
       (Wonders what a request line really is).
       <u>Team room?</u> Maybe try "Room". Probably doesn't work. Help?
       ⎧ Will try details (because I don't know what it is). Oh, should
       ⎪ choose a Line. Wrong try. Looks for a button with "Rooms".
P8.   ⎨ I have to make a new line. Not happy to copy (because you cannot)
P9.   ⎪ Writes on new line: Additional rooms. Why doesn't it respond? change "type"
       ⎩ Stupid computer.
          I still haven't specified the room size.
          Find Room? Won't try Details because it failed before.
          when she chooses details, all is easy. Details: More inf on
                                                            Request?
       The other team rooms: L101 (lecture) → details. Wrong—ok, but why?
          Writes on new line etc. No, I want to copy!
          OK. Changes to Th → details (wants to check). Guesses
          that it has copied the details too.

Fig 13.7 C Test report

Room allocation system, handdrawn mock-up, version 6.
Usability test 5 Jan 1995. Test users: HR and SL

Observed problems (with severity class)
P1:   (HR, SL: Minor)
     In RoomRequests: Not obvious what #hours means. (It means number of hours per week.)

P2:   (HR, SL: Cumbersome)
     A request line concerns an interval of weeks. There is a need to split it in two or more to reflect several
     intervals of weeks. Possible with cut and paste, but a split-function might be convenient.

P3:   (SL: Minor)
     In RoomRequests: If there are empty lines, you should be able to fill them in without first using NewRequest.

P4:   (SL: Medium)
     RequestDetails: Hard to see the new data, e.g. 'count', because the old data from the request line are here too,
     but in a new way. You cannot see what is new and what is old.

P5:   (HR, SL: Minor)
     When copying a request line: The copy will often conflict with the new line. Important to allow copying and
     then correct the copy. Suggestion from HR: don't warn until you leave the line.

P6:   (HR: Task failure)
     In RoomRequests: The labels Class/Responsible and Course/Activity are not intuitive. Class and Course are
     also easy to mix up.

P7:   (HR: Medium; SL: Minor)
     Course screen: 'Requested' not intuitive.

P8:   (HR: Medium)
     Requesting additional rooms (team exercises) in connection with lectures hard to figure out. Attempts in vain
     through Rooms.

P9:   (HR, SL: Cumbersome)
     When a line has been copied, you should be allowed to change the type, for instance to Additional Rooms.

. . .

P27: (HR: Minor; SL: Medium)
     In search criteria, the word Include doesn't suggest the right meaning. Proposals: Limit to, Select.

Other observations
Many of the problems are related to the basic concepts such as Class, Course, Request and Teaching. These concepts
are used in the manual system, but with context-dependent meanings and varying terms. It is probably unrealistic to
believe that new users can figure out about these concepts on their own. We should try a version with examples on
the screen or examples in a help text.

amazing ways to solve the problems come up during sleep. (More on correcting usability problems in section 8.4.)

What to correct?

The next step – after a good night's sleep – is to prioritize the problems. Top priority problems are to be corrected first. Often the team members fight over the priorities. The usability specialists may give a certain task failure a high priority, while the developers give it a low priority. Who is right? The conflict usually disappears if they instead look at two factors:

- Benefit: the importance of the problem to the user (task failures are usually important).

- Cost: the number of work hours to correct the problem (if no solution is known or we need redesign of many screens, the cost seems high).

The parties can agree on these two factors. Next, comparing the cost against the benefit gives the priority. Critical problems (task failures and 'annoying') will be high on the list if they are easy to correct. Minor problems that are hard to correct will be low on the list. It may happen that the team decides to correct minor problems because it is easy to do so, while leaving some critical problems because they are hard to correct.

14

Heuristic evaluation

Highlights

- Various kinds of heuristic evaluation.

- Cheaper than usability testing? Not necessarily.

- Missed problems and false positives? It depends.

- Users are different and randomness is inevitable.

- A precise statistical comparison of 8 expert teams against 9 usability teams (CUE-4).

Heuristic evaluation and usability testing are two different techniques for finding usability problems. With heuristic evaluation, someone looks at the user interface and identifies the problems. With usability testing, potential users try out the user interface with real tasks. The problems found with usability testing are *true* problems in the sense that at least one user encountered each problem. The problems found with heuristic evaluation are *potential problems* – the evaluator suspects that something may be a problem to users. Early in development, heuristic evaluation has a hit-rate of around 50% and reports around 50% false problems. This is the first 'law' of usability (section 1.5).

In the world of programming there are similar techniques. During a *program review*, someone looks at the program text to identify bugs. This corresponds to heuristic evaluation. During a *program test*, the program is run on the computer and the programmer checks the results. This corresponds to usability testing. Good program reviewers can identify around 90% of the bugs and they report few false bugs.

14.1 Variants of heuristic evaluation

Heuristic evaluation may vary according to the way the system is introduced to the evaluators, the way the evaluators look at the system, the evaluator's background, etc.

Introducing the system

Explain the screens. The designer may explain each of the screens to the evaluator before the evaluation. This of course helps the evaluator so that he may miss some of the problems that real users might encounter. If the designer explains a lot, the exercise may turn into a design review where designer and evaluator discuss problems and alternative designs.

Explain nothing except the purpose of the system. If the designer doesn't explain the screens but only the purpose of the system, the evaluator will be on his own in a way similar to a user. This approach is suited for systems to be used without introduction or training. However, if the system is reasonably complex, the evaluators need some introduction to the system. As a result the evaluator may miss some problems. Experienced developers try to strike a balance by giving only a brief introduction to each screen.

Method

Heuristic rules. The evaluators may use a list of rules (guidelines) for identifying potential problems. They look at the screens one by one, trying to determine where the rules are violated. No doubt, rules help identify potential problems that otherwise would have been overlooked. However, if the list of rules is long, evaluators are unable to check all the rules carefully. We will look at some examples in section 14.2.

Subjective judgement. The evaluators may look at the screens one by one using their subjective judgement and earlier experience. This is the typical approach, particularly if the evaluators are potential users. Even if the evaluators use heuristic rules, they cannot suppress their subjective judgement, so it is hard to isolate the effect of the heuristic rules.

Task-based evaluation. The evaluators may be asked to check how various tasks are carried out – or they may define such tasks on their own initiative. With this approach, the exercise becomes quite similar to a usability test. The main difference is that the test subject (the evaluator) also records the problems. This variant may have a hit-rate close to usability testing as we will see in section 14.4.

Unfortunately, the task-based evaluation assumes that the system is operational. If the system is still a mock-up, the evaluator doesn't know how the system will react (the human 'computer' is not there). As a result, the evaluator may believe it works in one way and he will not realize that it is intended to do something else.

Evaluators

Usability specialist. The evaluator may be a usability specialist – a person with knowledge of usability principles and experience in using them. However, the specialist has no expertise in the application domain. Usability specialists tend to report more potential problems than other kinds of evaluators. However, they still miss around 50% of the true problems when using heuristic rules or subjective evaluation.

Fellow developers. Developers without specific usability expertise can serve as evaluators, but most of the results I have seen are not good. Fellow developers tend to focus on technical details and deviations from the user interfaces they develop themselves. They tend to suggest changes rather than pointing out the usability problems. If they discuss their findings with the designer, they easily end up in technical debates about what is possible and what should be done. (I often hear about usability courses for developers where participants review each other's designs. Usually it ends in a disaster, particularly if they all try to design the same system.)

Potential users. Ordinary users may be so confused about all the screens that they cannot express the problems they have. This doesn't help the designer improve the user interface. Expert users that have been involved in the development tend to look for the system's ability to handle special situations, and they cannot see the problems that novices will encounter.

Number of evaluators

One at a time. Evaluators may work in isolation. Each evaluator writes down his own list of problems. With several evaluators, this gives the designer a heavy job trying to combine all the problem lists.

Combined list. Evaluators may be asked to come up with a combined list where each problem is mentioned only once. Also, problems mentioned by only one evaluator must be on the list. This gives the evaluators a heavy job reviewing each other's lists.

Common list. Evaluators may be asked to come up with a common list of problems – the problems that they all agree on as potential problems. In practice, this means that some evaluators have to realize that they have missed some problems that others detected. Other evaluators have to realize that a problem they pointed out may not be a problem after all. All of this requires time-consuming negotiations, and for this reason it is rarely done in practice.

Early evaluation

Early evaluation is highly important, and at this time only a mock-up is available. The typical heuristic approach will be as follows:

- Introduction: A developer briefly explains the screens.

- Method: Subjective judgement supplemented with heuristic rules. Screens are largely assessed one by one. (Task-based evaluation is not suitable.)

- Evaluators: Usability specialists if available. Sometimes fellow developers with a good sense of usability.

- Number of evaluators: Two. Developers combine the lists into one.

This is the approach we assume in the first law of usability. It has a 50% hit-rate and reports 50% false problems, primarily because developers explain the screens and because evaluation is done screen by screen rather than task-wise.

14.2 Heuristic rules and guidelines

Heuristic rules can serve several purposes:

- Guide the designer during the design process (the design rules for virtual windows are examples).

- Help evaluators identify problems in the user interface (checking that the rules are followed).

- Explain observed usability problems (why did the user make this mistake).

Many authors have published heuristic rules for user interfaces. Already in 1986, Shneiderman published the 'eight golden rules' of dialogue design (also in Shneiderman 1998). The rules are as follows (with shortened explanations).

Eight golden rules of dialogue design (Shneiderman 1986)

1   Strive for consistency. (Use the same terminology and procedures in all parts of the user interface.)

2   Enable frequent users to use short cuts. (Examples are short-cut keys, abbreviations and macros.)

3   Offer informative feedback. (The system should indicate what it is doing and which state it is in.)

4   Design dialogues to yield closure. (A dialogue should give the user the sense of having completed his task.)

5   Offer simple error handling. (The system should detect errors and inform the user of how to handle the situation. As far as possible, the system should prevent the user from making errors.)

6   Permit easy reversal of actions. (Provide *Undo* as far as possible.)

7   Support internal locus of control. (Make the user feel that he is in control – not the system.)

8   Reduce short-term memory load. (Users should not have to remember information from one screen to another, they should choose from lists rather than type commands, etc.)

These rules are still valid today. Shneiderman thought of the rules as design guidelines to be used by the developer while he designs the user interface. They can of course also be used by heuristic evaluators to identify usability problems.

Around 1990, Jakob Nielsen and Rolf Molich developed a list of heuristic rules, specifically aimed at heuristic evaluation (Molich and Nielsen 1990). The authors also used the rules to explain observed problems. The list is rather similar to Shneiderman's golden rules. The list has later been modified, extended to 10 rules and published in other places. Here is the original list, illustrated with problems encountered in the hotel system.

Molich and Nielsen (1990)

1 Simple and natural dialogue. (Avoid irrelevant information and do things in a natural and logical order.) This rule has no counterpart in Shneiderman's golden rules. It is a very broad rule that can vaguely explain many problems. In the hotel system, we might, for instance, claim that the rule explains why many users didn't find the menu that helped them print a booking confirmation: the menu was not in a natural order relative to the fields filled in by the user.

2 Speak the user's language. (Use words familiar to the user. Avoid computer and system jargon.) This rule too has no counterpart in Shneiderman's golden rules. In the hotel system, the term *Stay* was unfamiliar to most users. Yet most users soon guessed what it meant. Surprisingly, hotel people had no term that covered the system concept of a stay, so the problem was not easy to repair. Users sometimes said *guest*, sometimes *booking*, but none of these correctly reflected the stay concept, which users praised once they understood it.

3 Minimize the user's memory load. (Users should not have to remember information from one screen to another, they should choose from lists rather than type commands, etc.) None of the hotel system problems related to this rule, thanks to the use of combo boxes and a minimal set of windows.

4 Be consistent. (Use the same terminology and procedures in all parts of the user interface. Follow platform conventions.) None of the hotel system problems directly relate to this rule. Actually, some problems were caused by an attempt to follow the platform conventions. The Microsoft Windows guidelines said that a window had to have a *File* menu. In the hotel system there was no natural use for a File menu, so the designers twisted their mind to put something in it. The users didn't buy the solution.

5 Provide feedback. (The system should indicate what it is doing and which state it is in.) This rule can explain some of the problems in the hotel system, for instance that users couldn't see whether they had completed the check-in task. There was no visible feedback.

6 Provide clearly marked exits. (Users should always see the way back, for instance when they by mistake have entered a wrong screen.) You have to stress your imagination, however, to make the rule cover undo. The rule partly matches Shneiderman's rule of *Easy reversal of actions*, which clearly covers undo.

7 Provide short cuts. (Intended for experienced users, unseen by the novice.) The hotel system tried to follow this guideline, but in a few places it didn't. However, we couldn't observe the problem because we didn't try with experienced users. This is a good example of a guideline that exceeds what we can easily find with usability tests.

8   Provide good error messages. (Error messages should be friendly, precise and constructive.) The hotel system tried to follow this rule, but sometimes missed. One example is that the user wanted to extend a booking with one more day. In the room grid, the user marked the entire period including the nights booked already and clicked *Book*. The system replied that the room wasn't free in the entire period and suggested that the user choose another room. The user was bewildered because the room was already partially booked by the guest and free the next night. Although the system formally was right in its statement, it should have recognized that the guest had the room already.

9   Error prevention. (Prevent users from starting erroneous actions.) This rule is part of Shneiderman's rule of simple error handling. In the hotel system, the error mentioned under point 8 could have been prevented if the user was only allowed to select free rooms. In general, the use of combo boxes and lists to choose from, prevented a lot of errors. At the same time, it reduced the user's memory load.

Example: an error message from Microsoft Word

Let us try to use the heuristic rules on the situation shown in Figure 14.2. The example is from an old version of Microsoft Word. The user tries to set the line spacing so that there is half a line empty after the text. The system responds as shown in the figure, and even offers help. When the user tries the help, the result is as shown. It should be obvious that the dialogue is ridiculous and almost insulting. The problem is that the user should have typed *0.5 li* rather than *0.5 lines*. Now, what do the Molich–Nielsen rules tell us about it?

1   Simple and natural dialogue? Not quite. It is not obvious what *Before* and *After* mean. Before what?

2   Speak the user's language? Not quite. The user tries to write *lines*, the system insists on *li*.

3   Minimize the user's memory load? Even if the user figures out what to type, it is hard to remember the next time.

4   Be consistent? No problem. Or will the user miss an OK button in the Help box?

5   Provide feedback? No problem. If the user succeeds, the system will give visual feedback in the form of the new line spacing.

6   Provide clearly marked exits? No problem. Or will the user miss an OK button in the Help box?

7   Provide short cuts? No problem. There are shortcuts in the standard way.

8   Provide good error messages? (Error messages should be friendly, precise and constructive.) No, definitely not. Telling the user that he has done something invalid is not friendly. The message is not precise because it doesn't say which

Fig 14.2 Heuristic rules

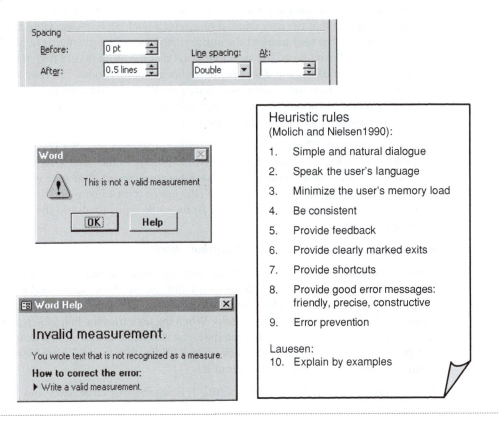

field is wrong. Finally, it is definitely not constructive because it doesn't really tell the user what to do – it only pretends to do so.

9 Error prevention? No, definitely not. A solution would be to allow the user to select the measurement unit from a list.

What is the result of this rule-based evaluation? Several potential problems and suggested solutions, from explaining what *Before* and *After* mean, to adding a Close button on the Help box. As evaluators, we might report all of these problems and suggestions. Imagine that we used the heuristic rules in the same systematic way on every detail of the user interface. It would take a long time and the designer would be flooded by potential problems and suggestions.

If we look for a simple and fast solution to the line-spacing dialogue, I would use an additional heuristic rule of my own.

Lauesen

10 Explain by means of examples.

This rule would tell the designer to change the error message to, for instance:

Write the spacing as 0.5 li, 0.5 pt or 0.5 mm.

How can it happen?

This example from Word is quite scaring, but also very common. In Office 2000, the error message is still the same, except that there is no Help button in the message anymore.

Most of us often see nonsense messages and help texts similar to the one here. How can it happen? The reason is that error messages and help texts are made by technical writers – often at the last moment before release. The technical writer may master the English language but doesn't understand what the system does. Imagine that you were a technical writer. You got this message box to fill in – among a hundred others. You have to write *something* but haven't got the time to find out when the message occurs, what a *measure* is and what the user is allowed to write. Under these circumstances you end up writing something that pretends to give an answer but is sheer nonsense.

14.3   Cost comparison

Is heuristic evaluation cheaper than usability tests? Sometimes – it depends on how the techniques are carried out. Let us look at low-cost approaches early during design – the most critical point in user interface development. At this point in time, it doesn't make sense to test with a lot of users. We know that there will be serious problems that most users encounter, and we want to find them early. We may run a usability test with three users, one by one. We assume that we have developers with some usability background. They will run the tests, one as a facilitator and one as a log keeper. In the low-cost version, this should take a total of 11 work hours, including writing the test report (see details in section 13.2):

Series of three users	Work hours	
	Facilitator	Log keeper
Total for one user	80 min	80 min
Total for three users	240 min	240 min
Writing the test report		180 min
Total work hours		660 min (11 hours)

Let us compare it with a low-cost heuristic evaluation with two independent evaluators. We assume that each evaluator uses his subjective judgement and lists the problems he finds. Then he meets with a developer to explain his findings. (This approach corresponds to inspection techniques used for program reviews. The alternative is to write a detailed report. It will take much longer, and the developers will most likely misunderstand it anyway.)

The time needed for the evaluation depends on the number of screens and their complexity. We assume that the system at this stage has around 8 screens of medium complexity. The total time used will be around this.

Two evaluators, subjective judgement	Work hours		
	Clock hours	Evaluators	Developer
Introduction to the system	0.5	1.0	0.5
Evaluating the system	2.0	4.0	
Listing the problems	1.0	2.0	
Explaining them to developer	1.0	2.0	2.0
Total	4.5	9.0	2.5

In this case, heuristic evaluation is a bit more expensive, 11.5 hours against 11. The figures change of course, if we use fewer or more test persons and evaluators, or if we vary the reporting approach. If evaluators check against heuristic rules, time for heuristic evaluation will rise.

However, there are additional costs that we haven't mentioned. One is the time it takes to prepare a mock-up for early usability testing. Making the basic screens is much the same whether the screens are to be used for usability testing or heuristic evaluation. However, to prepare for usability testing, we have to make screen copies and fill them with realistic data. Depending on the kind of system, this can take several hours.

Another factor is the time it takes to find test persons versus heuristic evaluators. This again depends on the kind of system and the developer environment. Sometimes finding test users takes much time; in other cases it is harder to find the right kind of evaluators.

14.4 Effect comparison (CUE-4)

Early evaluation

Let us ignore the cost for a moment and look only at the effectiveness: the number of problems found. When used early in development with paper mock-ups, heuristic evaluation is less effective. It finds only around 50% of the problems that real users encounter. Also serious task failures may be overlooked by evaluators. The main reason seems to be that evaluators at this point in development cannot experiment with the system. They need a bit of introduction from the developer and tend to evaluate the system screen by screen, rather than task-wise.

Heuristic evaluation also reports a lot of false problems – problems that real users don't encounter, or only very few users. Trying to correct all of these false problems is much more costly than any time saved by using heuristic evaluation rather than usability testing.

Properly used, heuristic evaluation is valuable anyway. The trick is to consider heuristic evaluation a help similar to when you have someone read and comment on a paper you have written. Many of the comments are obvious when you hear them – why did I overlook this, the author wonders. Other comments are more dubious, and you may decide not to deal with them – particularly if it hard to do so. However, the difference between writing a paper and designing a user interface is that if a reader gets stuck, he can most likely just skip a small part of the paper. But if users get stuck, the problem is real.

Effectiveness is not only a matter of precision: finding all the true problems and no false ones. It is also about coverage – how many screens can we deal with. Here, heuristic evaluation is more effective than usability testing. While users get exhausted after about an hour and may have used only a few screens, evaluators can keep going for several hours and can cover a lot of screens in that time.

Late evaluation (CUE-4)

When the system is operational, heuristic evaluation may work more like usability testing. The evaluators can experiment with the system and use themselves as test users. We will look closer at an ambitious comparison project in this area.

At the CHI 2003 Workshop, Rolf Molich and Robin Jeffries had arranged the CUE-4 experiment (Molich 2003). They had persuaded 17 of the world's best usability teams to evaluate the same public Web site, www.hotelpenn.com. This site offers on-line booking on *New York's Hotel Pennsylvania*. It had been used daily for around a year.

Eight of the usability teams were requested to use heuristic evaluation (expert evaluation) and the remaining nine teams to use usability tests. Apart from this, the teams could choose the evaluation approach (variant) they preferred. The result of their evaluation should be a list of the problems they had identified and the degree of seriousness (category) for each problem. They were instructed to report not more than 50 problems per team. The data is available for download (see Molich 2003).

Six teams reported 50 problems: one team 49 problems and the remaining teams between 20 and 36 problems. Apparently, the limit of 50 had an influence on what seven of the teams did. There was no apparent correlation between the number of problems and whether the teams used heuristic evaluation or usability testing.

My Masters student Mimi Pave Musgrove studied all the problem reports to see whether there was any significant difference between *E-teams* (expert/heuristic evaluation) and *U-teams* (usability test). I helped with the statistics.

Making a list of distinct problems

The first task was to make a list of distinct problems, with each problem mentioned only once. This was an immense task. First of all there were around 600 problem reports. For each of these, Musgrove had to see whether the problem was on the distinct list already or whether it had to be added to the list. This was usually quite hard since teams reported in different styles and used different terms to report essentially the same problem.

In many cases it was not clear whether two problem reports were the same problem or two different ones. As an example, when one report pointed out an unreadable black text on dark-green background in screen B, and another report pointed out a similar text in screen C, do we then have one or two distinct problems? In this case Mimi decided that it was the same problem. A careful developer would correct both problems if directed to just one of them.

In some cases a single report contained two essentially distinct problems, and in other cases a team reported essentially the same problem twice. Sometimes the problems were reported as suggestions for change rather than a problem. And sometimes a positive finding was reported, for instance *the user liked the one-screen approach*, together with a negative one from another team, for instance *the one-screen approach is annoying*.

Problem counts

The end of this hard work was a list of 145 distinct problems with an indication of the teams that had reported each problem. Figure 14.4A shows the first problems on this list. The teams were identified as A, B, C ... In the figure they are arranged so that the E-teams are shown first, and the U-teams last. As an example, problem 3 was detected by four E-teams (teams B, D, G and R) and by six U-teams (teams A, H, K, L, N and S). In total, it was detected by 10 teams (hit-rate = 10). Problem 3 was that it was difficult to compare promotion price and normal price. Users had to look at different screens to see the two prices.

The seriousness of the problem is in most cases stated as the code P, Q or R, roughly corresponding to minor problem, medium problem and task failure. Codes A, C and T show good ideas, positive remarks and program errors (bugs). Note that different teams may report the same problem with different degrees of seriousness. Problem 3 is a good example of this. Many teams report that it is a serious problem, and many report that it is a minor problem. Team R, however, doesn't explain the problem, but gives a suggestion for a change in the user interface.

The middle part of Figure 14.4A gives an overview of the hit-rates for all 145 problems. No problem was reported by all 17 teams, but one problem was reported by 16 teams. Two problems were reported by 10 teams, one of them being problem 3 as we explained above. There were 54 singular problems – reported only once.

Compared to the similar statistics for early problems (Figure 13.4), we have few high-hit problems but still a lot of singular problems. Most of the high-hit problems had probably been removed during development.

If we ignore all reports that are not task-failures (degree R), there are only 49 problems left. Their hit-rates are shown on the lower part of Figure 14.4A. The remaining 96 problems never showed up as something serious. The top-hit was problem 25, which nine teams found serious. There are still a surprising number of singular problems among the R-problems. All of them looked serious to the teams that reported them.

The bar graphs only tell us how many times each problem was reported in total. We cannot see how many times it was reported by E-teams versus U-teams. If we look at the raw data in the list, problem 3, for instance, was reported roughly the same number of times by E- and U-teams. In contrast, problem 6 was reported once by E-teams and four times by U-teams. Does this mean that U-teams were better at detecting this particular problem? The short answer is *yes, but it is a coincidence.* We will now look closer at this question.

First, we need a better overview of E- versus U-problems. Figure 14.4B shows a matrix with all problems according to their E- and U-hit-rates. As an example, look at the top row of the matrix. It shows all the problems that were not reported by any E-team. Of these, 24 problems were reported by a single U-team. Seven were reported by two U-teams, another seven by three U-teams, and one problem by four U-teams.

Similarly, the first column shows the problems that were not reported by any U-team. Of these, 30 problems were reported by a single E-team, three by two E-teams and one by four E-teams. All other problems were reported by E-teams as well as U-teams. As an example, three problems were observed by seven U-teams and six E-teams.

Fig 14.4 A Problems reported by 17 top-level HCI teams

CUE-4 hits per distinct problem

ProblemID	B	C	D	E	F	G	P	R	A	H	J	K	L	M	N	O	S	Hit-rate
1	R		R			Q	Q	Q	R	Q		Q	Q	Q	Q	R	R	13
2						Q	Q									R		3
3	Q		Q			R		A	Q	R		P	P		Q		Q	10
4												Q						1
5	Q			Q		R			R							Q		5
6		Q							P	R		P	Q					5
7				C	R		Q	R	Q	P	Q	C	Q	R	P	Q	Q	13
8						R			Q							R		4
9		Q	R	R		R	Q	R	P	Q		Q	Q	R	R		Q	13

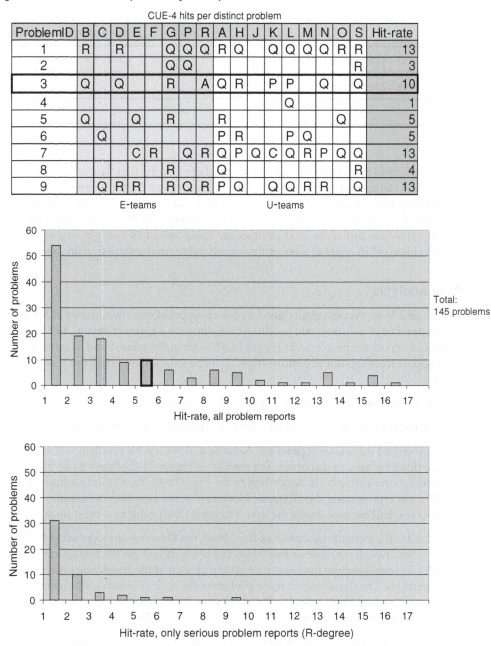

E-teams · U-teams

Total: 145 problems

Hit-rate, all problem reports

Hit-rate, only serious problem reports (R-degree)

In summary, we have these figures:

	Count	Percentage of U-problems
Problems observed by E but not by U	34	31% (false problems)
Problems observed by U but not by E	39	35% (missed problems)
Problems observed by E as well as U	72	
Problems in total	145	

These figures are somewhat better than predicted by the first 'law' of usability. The first law claims that heuristic evaluation misses 50% of the problems detected by usability tests. In our case heuristic evaluation missed only 35%. The first law also claims that heuristic evaluation predicts 50% false problems. In our case it predicted only 31% false problems. And even so, are these 'mistakes' really mistakes or only coincidences? In order to answer this question we need a statistical analysis.

Statistical analysis

If E- and U-teams are equally good at detecting problems, the number of E-hits and the number of U-hits would be almost the same for a given problem. As a result, we would expect the problems in Figure 14.4B to lie in the white band around the diagonal from top-left to bottom-right. To some extent they do so, but it is not too clear.

Let us state our expectation as a statistical hypothesis:

Hypothesis A: E- and U-teams detect a given problem with the same probability

What would this mean in practice? Assume that we have a problem that is observed five times because of its nature. The middle of Figure 14.4B shows these five observations as five balls. According to the hypothesis, they fall at random into the 17 bowls representing the 17 teams. However, in our case each team can receive at most one ball because they were asked to report the problem at most once.

What are the possible outcomes of this? Well, the U-teams can together get either zero, one, two, three, four or five balls. The E-teams will get the remaining of the five balls. We can compute the exact probability of each of these outcomes, given our hypothesis. The figure shows these probabilities. As an example, the chance of four U-teams getting a ball is 16.3%. This is exactly what happened to problem 6 above. It was observed five times, four of them by U-teams. So this outcome is quite probable.

Note that the probabilities are not symmetrical. The chance of zero U-hits is smaller than the chance of zero E-hits. This is because there are more U-teams, so the chance of them getting nothing is smaller.

Fig 14.4 B Problems according to E-hits and U-hits

All problems

E-hits	U-hits 0	1	2	3	4	5	6	7	8	9
0		24	7	7	1					
1	30	9	6	3	2	2				
2	3	5	1	3	2	1				
3		3	4	1	1	3	2		1	
4	1	1	1	1		2	2			1
5				3	1				1	
6								3		2
7								1	2	1
8					1					

Five observations dropped at random

B C D E F G P R A H J K L M N O S

E-teams · U-teams

U-hits:	0	1	2	3	4	5
E-hits	5	4	3	2	1	0
Probability:	0.9%	10.2%	32.6%	38.0%	16.3%	2.0%

Probability of a problem observed N times having
E expert observations and U usability observations

E-hits	U-hits 0	1	2	3	4	5	6	7	8	9
0		52.9%	26.5%	12.4%	5.3%	2.0%	0.7%	0.2%	0.0%	0.0%
1	47.1%	52.9%	42.4%	28.2%	16.3%	8.1%	3.5%	1.2%	0.3%	0.0%
2	20.6%	37.1%	42.4%	38.0%	28.5%	18.1%	9.7%	4.1%	1.3%	0.2%
3	8.2%	21.2%	32.6%	38.0%	36.3%	29.0%	19.4%	10.4%	4.1%	0.9%
4	2.9%	10.2%	20.4%	30.2%	36.3%	36.3%	30.2%	20.4%	10.2%	2.9%
5	0.9%	4.1%	10.4%	19.4%	29.0%	36.3%	38.0%	32.6%	21.2%	8.2%
6	0.2%	1.3%	4.1%	9.7%	18.1%	28.5%	38.0%	42.4%	37.1%	20.6%
7	0.0%	0.3%	1.2%	3.5%	8.1%	16.3%	28.2%	42.4%	52.9%	47.1%
8	0.0%	0.0%	0.2%	0.7%	2.0%	5.3%	12.4%	26.5%	52.9%	100.0%

How do we compute the probabilities? In principle, we compute the total number of ways that five balls can fall into 17 bowls. Then we compute how many of these ways give zero U-balls, one U-ball, etc. The probability is the number of 'good' ways divided by the total number of ways.

Technically speaking, the probabilities are a hypergeometric distribution. In Microsoft Excel, we can compute the probability of getting x out of five balls with this formula:

Probability(x U-hits) = HypGeomDist(x, 9, 5, 9+8)
when there are 9 U-teams, 8 E-teams and 5 hits in total

In the same way, we can compute the probabilities when there are 6, 7 and other hits in total. In the lower part of Figure 14.4B, we have shown these computed probabilities in a matrix. You find our 5-ball probabilities in the skew band of framed cells. The circle shows where problem 6 belongs.

We have coloured all cells that are unlikely as outcome. The colour is dark if there is less than 5% probability of a problem ending up here or in cells further away from the diagonal. The colour is light if there is between 5 and 10% probability of a problem ending up here or further away from the diagonal.

As an example, a 5-hit problem with zero E-hits has a probability of 2% and is thus in dark colour. A 6-hit problem with one E-hit has a probability of 8.1%. With zero E-hits it has a probability of 0.7%. In total, it has an 8.8% probability of being this far away from the diagonal. Thus, it has a light colour.

These light and dark colours are the ones you also see at the top of the figure. Notice that there are a few problems in the unlikely, coloured areas. In the upper right-hand area there are five unlikely problems. In the lower left area there are two unlikely problems. All other problems are in very likely positions.

Can we say that the odd problems are unlikely and that they prove a difference between E- and U-teams? No, because the unlikely, coloured areas cover cells with probabilities below 10%. Some problems should by chance end up there. Our first guess might be that 10% of all problems should end up in the upper right-hand area. We would thus expect 14.5 problems there. There are only five! Something must be wrong. Maybe some teams have made a secret agreement on sharing the problems more evenly than chance?

Fortunately, our guess of 10% was wrong. It would be right if the outcomes had been distributed over a continuous scale, for instance according to a normal distribution, but in our case they are not. Our observations are only yes or no, and we count the yeses.

Figure 14.4C shows a precise calculation of the expected number of 'unlikely' problems. Let us as an example look at the circled cell with four U-hits and one E-hit. A problem observed five times would end up in this cell with a probability of 16.3%.

Fig 14.4 C Observed problems: predicted hits on average

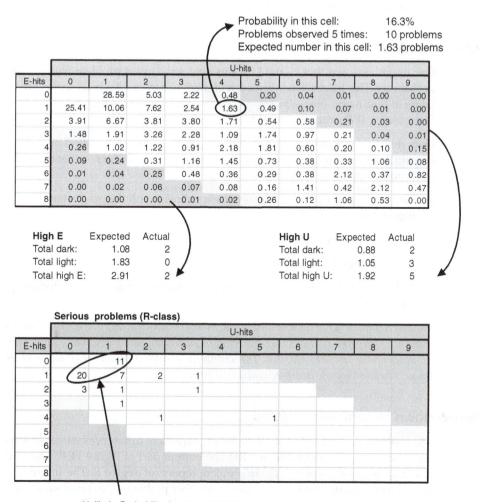

Probability in this cell: 16.3%
Problems observed 5 times: 10 problems
Expected number in this cell: 1.63 problems

E-hits	U-hits 0	1	2	3	4	5	6	7	8	9
0		28.59	5.03	2.22	0.48	0.20	0.04	0.01	0.00	0.00
1	25.41	10.06	7.62	2.54	1.63	0.49	0.10	0.07	0.01	0.00
2	3.91	6.67	3.81	3.80	1.71	0.54	0.58	0.21	0.03	0.00
3	1.48	1.91	3.26	2.28	1.09	1.74	0.97	0.21	0.04	0.01
4	0.26	1.02	1.22	0.91	2.18	1.81	0.60	0.20	0.10	0.15
5	0.09	0.24	0.31	1.16	1.45	0.73	0.38	0.33	1.06	0.08
6	0.01	0.04	0.25	0.48	0.36	0.29	0.38	2.12	0.37	0.82
7	0.00	0.02	0.06	0.07	0.08	0.16	1.41	0.42	2.12	0.47
8	0.00	0.00	0.00	0.01	0.02	0.26	0.12	1.06	0.53	0.00

High E	Expected	Actual
Total dark:	1.08	2
Total light:	1.83	0
Total high E:	2.91	2

High U	Expected	Actual
Total dark:	0.88	2
Total light:	1.05	3
Total high U:	1.92	5

Serious problems (R-class)

E-hits	U-hits 0	1	2	3	4	5	6	7	8	9
0		11								
1	20	7	2	1						
2	3	1		1						
3		1								
4			1			1				
5										
6										
7										
8										

Unlikely. Probability that singular U-hits <= 11 is 3.8%

There are ten 5-hit problems in the data. As a result we would expect 16.3% of the ten problems to end up here, in other words 1.63 problems on 'average'.

The figure shows the expected problems in every cell. We have computed the total expected problems in the unlikely areas. For instance in the dark-coloured high-U area, we would expect 0.88 problems. Actually two problems are observed in this area. In the entire high-U area we would expect 1.92 problems, but actually there are 5. There is a small difference.

Similarly, in the high-E area we would expect 2.91 problems, and 2 are observed. We cannot get much closer.

Conclusion A

Our hypothesis was that E- and U-teams detected a given problem with the same probability. This has been confirmed with high accuracy. Maybe U-teams are slightly better at finding problems, but they have at most done it for two out of the five high U-problems. (We cannot say which of these five.)

Does this disprove the first law of usability, that E-teams should find only 50% of the U-team problems and produce 50% false problems? Yes it does, but only for the conditions that this project dealt with:

- Late evaluations where E-teams can experiment with the product and use themselves as test subjects

- Top-level HCI people

- Very few high-hit problems

- A dedicated effort by U-teams as well as E-teams to find unusual domain situations

The last condition is not documented in the numbers involved, but it is obvious when you read the test reports. It means that creativity in identifying domain situations has a large influence on the problems reported. This creativity is much the same for all top-level HCI teams, whether they use heuristic evaluation or not.

Narrow down to serious problems

The analysis above dealt with all problems. Are there differences when we look at only the serious problems (degree R)? The bottom part of Figure 14.4C shows the E–U matrix when we only include problem reports of degree R. The singular problems dominate and there are very few other problems. No problem at all is in the unlikely areas. There are simply too few problems for any to hit the unlikely cells.

However, there is a suspicious thing in the matrix. The singular problems are wryly distributed: 11 for the U-teams and 20 for the E-teams. In the first matrix they were more evenly distributed: 24 U-reports and 30 E-reports. Are these distributions unlikely?

Let us test this statistical hypothesis:

Hypothesis B: E- and U-teams detect a given singular problem with the same probability

This hypothesis is only slightly different from the first one, but the statistical model is different because each problem is observed only once. We now imagine each singular problem as a ball being dropped at random into one of the bowls – meaning that it is observed by one of the teams. Contrary to our first hypothesis, each bowl may in this case end up with several balls.

Since 9 of the 17 teams are U-teams, a ball will end up in a U-bowl with a probability of 9/17, assuming that our hypothesis is true. We can compute the exact probability that the U-bowls end up with x out of N balls. Technically speaking we have a binary distribution with $p = 9/17$. In Excel, we can compute the probability with this formula:

Probability(x singular U-problems) = BinomDist(x, N, 9/17, False)

when there are N singular problems in total, 9 U-teams and 17 teams in total

In our case, N is 31. The probability of x being 11 comes out as 2.2%. We want to find the probability that $x \leq 11$. We can do this by computing the probabilities for $x = 11, 10, 9, \ldots, 0$ and adding them. Excel can do this for us when we let the last parameter be *True*. The result is

Probability($x \leq 11$) = 3.8% when we look only at serious, singular problems

Or as the statisticians say, this wryness is significant on the 3.8% level. When we compute the same for all problems – not just the serious ones – we get

Probability($x \leq 24$) = 13.3% when we look at all singular problems

According to statistical tradition, this would not be considered a significant wryness.

Conclusion B

E-teams report significantly more serious, singular problems than U-teams. If we look at all the singular problems, there is no significant difference between U and E. The reason seems to be that heuristic evaluators judge the singular problems as more serious.

This is not so surprising after all. It is hard for an expert to judge how serious a usability problem is to an ordinary user. It is more surprising that a similar difference doesn't show up for non-singular problems. Unfortunately, there are much too few serious problems to reveal any difference.

15

Systems development

Highlights

■ Waterfall, iterative and incremental development.

■ Good and bad user roles.

■ Task analysis – interviews, observations, task demonstration, workshops . . .

This chapter is intended for readers with an interest in computing but no prior knowledge of systems development. It will help you understand what is involved in systems development and how user interface design can fit into the rest of development. You also learn how to gather information about user tasks and data.

Systems development starts with someone wanting to improve something, preferably through IT. The development is completed when the new system is installed and the intended users apply it. After this, there will normally be a maintenance phase where the system is improved.

There are many theories and models for how to develop a system. In practice, developers rarely follow a model exactly, but they modify existing models or come up with their own model. This chapter explains what development usually comprises and the terms used in practice.

In spite of all models and theories, less than half of all development projects succeed. There are many reasons for this. Sometimes it turns out that the project becomes too expensive and is too complex technically. At other times demands and technical possibilities change during the project, making it pointless to complete it. In quite a few cases the project is completed from a technical viewpoint, but users or customers reject the result because the system is too hard to use compared to the benefits.

15.1   The waterfall model

First we will look at the traditional model for systems development – the *waterfall model*. It says that systems development is carried out as a predefined sequence of *activities*. Each activity must be completed before developers start on the next activity. Each activity is thus a separate *phase* of the project.

Figure 15.1A shows the traditional phases and their results.

Pre-investigation. During pre-investigation the company identifies possible new systems and assesses whether some of them seem worth developing. This is very much a management-level activity, although with lots of input from technically competent people. According to the traditional model, the next phase starts when a system has been selected for development.

Analysis. During the analysis phase, the project team studies the existing work process more closely, identifies data to be stored by the system and identifies problems to be handled by the new system. Some authors claim that 'analysis' includes designing the major aspects of the new system; others insist that analysis is only about studying what exists.

Sometimes the work processes are significantly different in the new system. As an example, in e-business some of the old work processes may become fully automated and other work processes will be handled by the customer rather than the vendor. In this case the project team designs the new work processes very early and most people would say it is part of analysis. Some people call it *organizational design*.

In practice, people use the terms *pre-investigation*, *analysis* and *design* in slightly different ways, and there are no clear rules for what is done when. In this book we use the term *domain* for what people and the IT system do together. A *domain description* is a document that describes those aspects of the domain that are of interest when developing the new IT system. We say that the developers do *elicitation* and *task analysis* when they gather information for the domain description.

Requirements. The requirements specification is the result of the analysis. It is a document that describes what the new system shall do without saying too much about how it is to be done. It is important that the requirements can be *validated*, meaning that users and customers can determine that the requirements match their needs. It is also important that the requirements are *verifiable*, meaning that it can be determined at the end of development whether the requirements are met.

Design. During design, developers define the major structure of the new system, for instance the way data is to be stored in the system, the program modules to be developed and which existing software packages to use. Some developers distinguish between major design and detailed design. It is basically a question of how small program modules they define and how detailed they do it.

Fig 15.1 A   Systems development, waterfall model

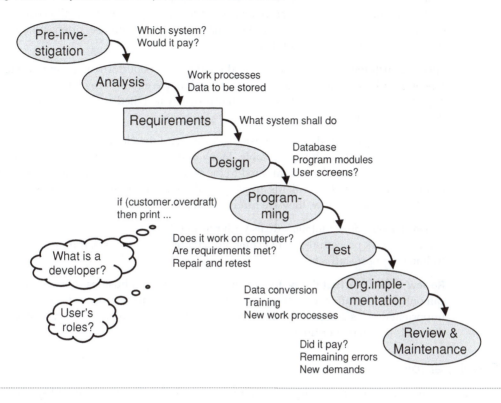

Developers disagree to what extent the user interface is defined during system design. Some say that it is to be done during programming, others that the major aspects should be defined during design. In this book an important message is that it pays to make a detailed design of the new user interface early during system design. In this way it is affordable to revise the user interface design several times to ensure that users can understand the interface. Experience shows that it also makes the later programming much more straightforward.

When the new system uses existing software packages, it makes no sense to redesign their user interfaces, of course. But it may be worthwhile to test how easy the packages are to use before deciding to deploy them.

Programming. During programming, developers produce the new programs to run on the computer. The program is written in some programming language, and Figure 15.1A shows a tiny piece of such a program. A typical middle-sized program, where five programmers have worked a year, may have around 60,000 such program lines. They must all be painfully correct and consistent to make the program function as intended.

Testing will usually consist of at least two different tests. First the programmers test that the program functions correctly, i.e. produces the right results in all possible circumstances and never breaks down. This is called program test, often split into a module test and an integration test.

Next the customer's representatives and the developers perform an acceptance test. It is often split into a system test (testing that all requirements are met) and a deployment test (testing that the system is properly installed and that the necessary data is in the database).

During testing a lot of defects are usually found, and developers correct them and test again until the result is acceptable. Many defects are not corrected because the cost of doing so is too large compared to the benefit. As an important example in our context, most usability problems are very costly to repair at this stage, and since the benefit is considered low, they are rarely corrected.

Organizational implementation deals with putting the system into daily operation, changing work procedures, converting old data files to new ones, training users, training support staff, etc.

Review is to check that the system meets expectations and business objectives. This can only be done after some time of daily operation. **Maintenance** is to correct important defects detected during daily operation, and to enhance the system as new demands develop over time.

Developer roles

A developer (*systems developer*) is a person who carries out major parts of system development. We talk about an analyst, designer, programmer or tester when the person primarily deals with the corresponding development activity. A *software developer* is a person who primarily works with design, programming and test. Some years ago, a developer tended to be either an analyst, a designer or a programmer. Today, most developers are expected to cover a much larger part of development.

Software developers use the term *implementation* for programming and testing. This often causes confusion when they speak with business and organization people, who use the term implementation to mean *organizational implementation*.

Developers are usually IT experts, but users can also play important roles during development, particularly in the initial and final phases. See more about user roles in section 13.4.

Realistic waterfall

The waterfall model for systems development prescribe the phases above, carried out in a strict sequence so that you don't work on a new phase until the previous one has been completed and accepted. This model is unrealistic and probably it has never been carried out with a successful result. There are many reasons for this, for instance that it is hard to anticipate problems that come up in the next phase and wreck what was done earlier. Also demands change as time passes, new technologies become available, developers have been too optimistic, users and developers have misunderstood each other, etc.

Figure 15.1B shows a more realistic version of the waterfall model. The project team still carries out analysis, design, etc., but not in the strict, phased manner. The activities overlap. In the example, the team makes some analysis and states some requirements already during pre-investigation.

During analysis they also design critical parts of the system, and even program and test particularly risky parts.

Instead of the phases, we now have some *decision points* shown by the vertical lines. At these points in time, the team, customer and management decide whether to continue development. In principle, this is a matter of comparing the cost of continuing with the likely benefits. Unfortunately, these decisions are often made on a very superficial basis, and many projects are allowed to continue although the environment and the expected hurdles have changed so much that it would be wiser to stop.

Fig 15.1 B Waterfall model, realistic course

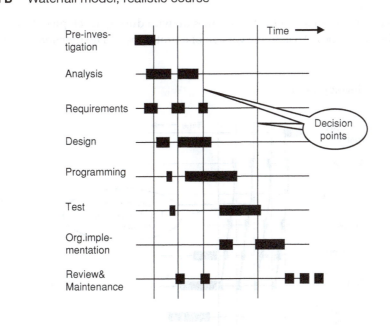

15.2 Iterative development

Figure 15.2 shows a different project model, *iterative development*. The team still carries out analysis, design and so on, but the sequence is different.

Now they carry out analysis–design–programming–test in several rounds to see how the users respond to the result. Usually the users want some changes when they see what they would get, and then developers carry out another round of analysis–design, etc.

At some point in time it is decided that the result is good enough. Programmers now improve the program so that it cannot crash, test it further and put the entire system into operation.

Notice that there is no requirements specification. Instead, the team gradually figures out during the iterations what the system shall do.

This model is quite popular, but it is feasible only if you have a development platform that makes it very easy to make new programs and new user interfaces, or change what you already have. Modern database tools can do this quite well, but they are suitable only for business applications, not for technical applications. Using such a platform also severely limits the user interface to what is easily available with these tools.

The system versions that the team comes up with during development can more or less be prototypes. An extreme version of a prototype has no functionality, only dead

Fig 15.2 Iterative development

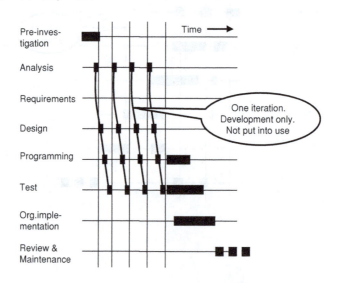

screen pictures. It requires little programming. There are also functional prototypes that have any degree of functionality from a few live screens to an almost finished system. In general, the more programming the team has invested in a prototype, the less they are willing to change it.

In spite of some sound principles in the iterative approach, these projects often fail. The programs may become so messy due to the many changes that they cannot be made robust and reliable. Or, the team may forget what the whole purpose of the system was and be lost in ingenious ideas that turn up on the way. And finally, the first version may have been so costly that the team clings to it rather than making a completely different version.

15.3 Incremental development

Incremental development and iterative development are often confused. The prime difference is that with incremental development you put each version into operation, as shown in Figure 15.3. You then observe how it works and start developing a new version.

You continue in the same way version by version, always guided by experience from earlier versions and changing demands in the environment. As the figure shows, the next version will usually start a bit before the previous version is complete. This is because some problems are noted during the previous version, but the team decides to deal with them in the next version.

Each version may be developed according to a realistic waterfall model with requirements specification, design, etc. Since each version is a much smaller project than the entire system, there is a much larger chance that it succeeds.

One of the great advantages of the method is that it eliminates a large risk in systems development: when users have got a new version, they soon learn to use it in ways nobody anticipated, and as a result new demands turn up. As an example, electronic mail started with a demand for electronically leaving a telephone message. When people had used it for half a year, they had invented e-mail discussions and e-mail management. Now there was a need for filing the e-mails, attach documents, etc. Some researchers call this the *task-artefact cycle*: a task creates needs for artefacts

Fig 15.3   Incremental development

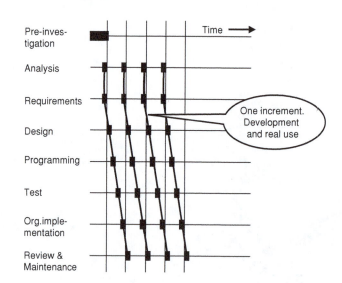

(tools) to support it. Getting the artefacts changes the tasks, which in turn creates needs for new tools, and so on.

In order for a system to remain robust throughout many versions, the design foundation and development tools must be adequate. A critical part of the design foundation is the data model: the plan for the data the system must store. A good long-term result requires that this plan is more ambitious than the first versions put into operation.

15.4   User involvement

Some designers claim that if you involve the users, the project will be a success. Unfortunately, user involvement is no guarantee of success, as we have seen in several failed projects (Redmond-Pyle and Moore, 1995, have a wonderful example). True, it is important to involve users in the development process, but how? Here are some roles they can play:

1   Members of design teams or workshops where the user interface is designed. This is sometimes referred to as participatory design.

2   Reviewers who assess the user interface and discuss it with the developers.

3   Test users in usability tests, where they try to carry out tasks with the new user interface.

4   Test users who exercise the system at delivery time to check that everything works correctly. They primarily help finding bugs in the system.

5   Knowledge sources of how tasks and business procedures are currently carried out.

6   Brainstorm participants who produce ideas and identify problems.

7   Members of the steering committee for the project.

Users can carry out all of these roles, and in roles 3, 5, 6 and 7 they may be instrumental in the project's success. The risky thing is if users in role 1 (designers) also handle roles 2, 3 and 7 where they should represent ordinary users. They are no longer typical users and are so absorbed by their design that they may have a problem in seeing its weaknesses. They may even forget the business goal of the system in their design fascination.

15.5　Elicitation and task analysis

In Chapter 5 we have shown how to describe the data in the system and how to describe the user tasks. From where do we get this information? We get it from various *elicitation* activities such as interviewing users, observing what they do, studying paper forms and other documents. Some developers call these activities *task analysis*.

Elicitation comprises more than task analysis. Other parts are identifying stakeholder interests, creating visions for the new system, finding out whether a new system will pay off, creating commitment for the new system and writing the requirements for it. In this section we will mainly look at ways to gather data for the task descriptions and data models. (See Beyer and Holtzblatt, 1998, S. Robertson, 2001, or Lauesen, 2002, for more on elicitation and requirements.)

Involving users

As an interface designer, you cannot just sit at your desk and write down the user tasks. You have to get the information from real or potential users.

Existing tasks. Often the project is about improving support for a work domain that exists already, either through developing a new system or by improving an existing one. In these cases it is relatively easy to find users and study their tasks. This is the case for the hotel system. Even if no such system existed at present, we could study what receptionists did already.

Invented tasks. In other cases there are no users at present. If we, for instance, were the first team to develop a Web-based shopping system, there would be no tasks to study. Instead we would have to study people's shopping habits, interview them about the demands they might have and try to imagine ways to meet their demands. In that way we would create new tasks that resemble existing tasks only to some extent. See more in section 15.5.8.

15.5.1　Interviewing

Interviewing is good for getting knowledge about the present user tasks and data. Many analysts consider interviews the main elicitation technique, and it can of course be used for many things, depending on whom you ask and what kind of questions you ask.

Whom to interview. Whom should you interview to get information about current work and current problems? Preferably some members from each user group. Make sure that you interview not only the officially nominated representatives of the user group, but ordinary staff members as well. Often management has nominated a representative (typically a middle-level manager) for a group of users, but experience shows that many representatives don't really know what is going on in the daily business, although they believe they know. Getting information from the real end users can be critical.

Usually it is a good idea to interview two kinds of end users, the average user and the expert user. The average user can give us an impression of the typical user profile, what is hard to do at present and how the normal tasks are carried out. The expert user is the person the other users ask when they have a problem. Sometimes the nominated representative may be an expert user, but often he is not. The real expert user will have the larger overview, know about difficult situations and special rules to follow.

What to ask? It depends upon when we ask. Initially, we would ask broad questions about daily work and daily problems in the work area we are going to support. The main purpose is to identify a first task list and the primary problems to get rid of. Later we will ask more detailed questions in order to write task descriptions and data models.

Communication barriers. One of the things we want to end up with is task descriptions. So why not use the task description template as an interview guide? When we have filled in all parts of the template for all the tasks, we are done. However, it is not that easy. If we ask users the literal questions on the template, for instance what tasks they perform, what triggers each task and so on, they will be very confused and may give misleading answers. There are several reasons for this:

a) Users may be uneasy to explain about things, particularly problems, fearing that it may harm them to speak openly.

b) We use the terms *task, trigger, purpose* and so on with a special meaning that most people don't know.

c) Users don't think about their work as a set of tasks, for much the same reason as they are not aware of their mental model for a computer system. The task concept is something we as designers use to model what is going on.

d) Users may not be aware of problems in the current way of doing things.

e) When users don't know the answer, they may try to answer anyway, and come up with answers that sound logical, but don't reflect reality. This is not because they are lying; they actually try to do their best.

Fear of talking. We can to some extent deal with issues of fear (a), by explaining users:

- what the system is about (for instance a system to help you keeping track of the work hours);

- why we interview them (to find out how they do it today and where the problems are);

- what we will do with the answers (make a user interface that is easy to use and remove many of the present annoyances).

If necessary, we must promise the users that everything they say is confidential and we will only use it in ways where it is impossible to see or guess who gave the information. (And then we must fulfil the promise by all means.)

In the old days, users were often scared of losing their job to the computer, and didn't want to cooperate. Although this may still be an issue sometimes, it is much more rare. These days we largely develop systems for people that are stressed and dream of better support for their work, or we develop systems that people can use at their own discretion (e.g. public Web systems).

Users don't know. We have to deal with issues (d) and (e), that users don't know, by other means than interviews. Observations, task demonstrations and workshops can help as explained below.

Strange terms and questions. We can deal with issues (b) and (c) by asking the questions in a different way. Actually, we may use the task description template anyway. We just have to ask the questions differently. The template is for our own use.

Figure 15.5A shows an interview guide for the work place in general. Figure 15.5B is a similar guide for the individual tasks. The figures also show what kind of questions we may ask to get the information. Remember that we don't have to follow the list point by point during the interview. Instead we should try to follow the interviewee. Every now and then we should consult our list to find out what we haven't covered yet. We must be open to new issues that turn up during the interview, and the lower part of the interview guide is set off for this (sometimes it turns out that we need many additional sheets of paper for the unforeseen).

Questions to ask about the work place

Work area. We might ask the user 'Where and when is the work done? Are you standing or sitting at your work?', but it easily sounds naïve to the user. Instead we might ask, 'Could you show me around the place?' This is a good way to chat a bit – and ask questions about what you see. Use your eyes – don't be absorbed by the chat.

User profile. We may ask, 'What is your IT experience', but it easily sounds threatening. Instead, try 'What have you used computers for? Do you use them at home too? Is it something you like or just something you have to?' Ask similar questions about the user's domain expertise.

Tasks. This is the most difficult part. First of all, we must explain to the users what part of the work we want to support (the entire work area, or only secondary activities such as keeping track of work hours). Now, if we ask them to list the tasks they perform in that area, most of them will be very confused. It is better to ask what they are doing now (in that area) or what they last did. Next, we may ask them what other things they do in that area, and whether their colleagues do the same or have other roles in the area. We may also start using our own logic and figure out that

Fig 15.5 A   Interview guide – the work place

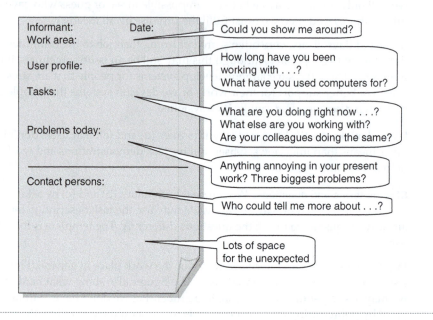

something is missing, for instance in case of the work hour reporting, how to report a long absence. We then ask about this.

What we end up with, will usually not be a good list of tasks, but bits and pieces that we later have to combine into closed, good tasks. 'Later' means when we have interviewed and studied other users, and slept a few nights.

Problems today. This is sometimes easy to deal with because our informant is the kind of person that likes to explain about problems and how things ought to work. We just have to listen and take notes. In other cases we need some prodding, 'Do you sometimes feel stressed about this? Is it difficult in some cases? When? When do you have to ask someone else for help?' This also helps us identify the critical tasks, which are the most important ones to study closer.

Contact persons. Among the many unexpected things that turn up during the interview, contact persons are an important matter. Often we have encountered something strange or complex, but our user couldn't explain it. Then we may ask, 'Who could tell more about this?' Note down the person's name, phone number, e-mail and role.

Questions to ask about a task

Task. At this stage we have some idea what the task is about, and we may have a preliminary name for it. We should try to explain to the user what we believe

Fig 15.5 B Interview guide – task details

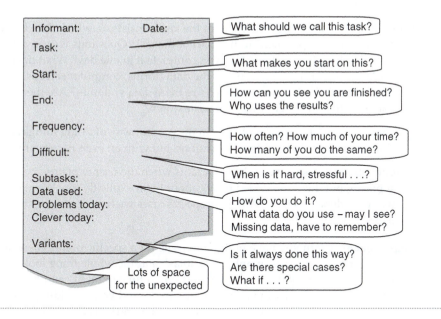

the task is about to test that it makes sense to him too. Ask him what a good name for it would be. Remember that tasks often are unconscious to users and rarely have official names.

Start or trigger. Some tasks start with a trigger – an event. However, 'trigger' is a strange word to users. In the task template in section 5.3.2, we use *start* instead of *trigger*. Simply ask, 'What makes you start on this? Do you sometimes start for other reasons?' If there is a starting event, you may ask more about it.

End or task purpose. We may ask, 'What is the purpose of this task?', but usually users become uneasy, because they cannot really explain properly. If you ask a manager, he may even be directly offensive: 'I am the manager, don't question why I do as I do.' In the task template in section 5.3.2, we use *end* instead of *purpose*. We can then ask questions such as 'How can you tell that you are finished? Who uses the results and for what?'

Frequency. This is usually easy. Ask, 'How often do you do this? How much time a day/week/month do you spend on it? How many of you do the same?' We want to find out not only how much this user is loaded by the task, but also how many other users spend their time on it. The latter gives us an indication of the need for training and also the load the system must deal with.

Difficult. Here we want to learn about situations where good task support is particularly difficult. Ask, 'Is this task sometimes hard to carry out? Needs high precision? Stressing? Why?' To some extent, it is the same questions we asked for *problems* in the work place. Here we have narrowed the focus and may learn more about the specific task.

Subtasks. Here we want to learn what the task consists of, which data is used and any specific problems in this part of the task. Questions we can ask include 'How do you do it? Can you complete it in one day? What data do you use? Could you show me some of the data (forms, computer screens, documents)? Could I have a copy? Are there data you miss? Are there things you have to remember or have to write down?'

The questions about the problems in the present way of doing things are similar to those about difficult situations, but with an even narrower focus.

Variants. Sometimes we hear about variants when the user explains about the subtasks, but it is a good idea to ask about them explicitly too. We may ask, 'Is it always done this way? Are there special cases we have to deal with? What happens if ...'

Empty space? Often you have nothing to write for a specific point. There are no problems, the task consists of only one subtask and the whole thing looks like a simple data-entry thing. Don't despair and spend time to fill the empty space with empty words. Some tasks and subtasks *are* simple, and you shouldn't waste time on them. Just write the facts, for instance 'simple data-entry task'. You might add which data is entered.

In other cases the space is empty because you haven't got the information yet. You feel there is something fishy about it, but the users couldn't explain. Don't try to guess. Write an honest question mark. You may find out later when talking to other users.

Group interviews

Instead of individual interviews, you can conduct group interviews. A group of users from the same work area can tell you more about the present work, the problems and the critical issues than can individual users. The group inspire each other to remember critical issues, describe day-to-day work, etc. An important thing when conducting such interviews is to keep a balance between participants so that nobody can dominate, and all feel safe in giving their opinion.

You can run group interviews in many ways, and the technique blends gradually into brainstorms and the *workshops* explained below.

15.5.2 Observation

Users are not always aware of what they really do and how they do it. If you ask them, they may come up with logical, but wrong explanations; not because they are lying deliberately – they are doing their best.

As an example, consider a simple task. How do you find a section in a cookbook, manual or textbook that you know well? Like most people, you would probably say that you use the list of contents or the index. Observation, however, shows that in 80% of cases where this would be a good approach, people start skimming through the book, believing that they can remember or guess where the section is. Only if that approach doesn't succeed, do they use the logical approach with indexes, etc.

One way around this mental blindness is to observe what is really going on. The analyst can spend some time with the users, observing their daily tasks. In some cases, analysts use video cameras (with the users' permission) to lengthen the period of observation. This has the advantage that you can later review critical parts of the tapes with the users and ask what really happened.

Observation vastly improves your knowledge of the current work and some of the associated work problems. It also serves as a check of other information. Unfortunately, the real critical issues and tasks often escape observation. With a power distribution system, for instance, the critical situation is when something goes wrong once a year. The analyst is rarely around at that moment.

15.5.3 Task demonstration

In many cases the users cannot explain what they do in their daily work. But they are able to show you how they do specific tasks. This may supplement the information we get by observing the users in their daily tasks. However, task demonstration is also a way to observe rare, difficult tasks.

As an example, the experienced receptionist will be able to show how to handle the bus of 50 tourists. This may happen only once a week, so it would be hard to observe. Similarly, the power system operator would love to explain in great detail what happened in the last power-failure disaster, how they handled it and what they would have liked to do.

Usability problems. Sometimes you want to identify usability problems in the present system, for instance in order to document how the new system could improve user performance. Mostly, experienced users are not aware of any usability problems, although there may be serious ones. To identify the problems, you need some kind of task demonstration. You may set it up as a usability test with test tasks you have identified in other ways. We have done this several times and it always turned out that the present system was inconvenient in many ways.

15.5.4 Document studies

Document studies are another way to cross-check the interview information. It is also a fast way to get information about data in the old 'database'.

You have to study existing documents such as forms, letter files, computer logs and documentation of the existing computer system. You may also print screen dumps from the existing system. You may identify the interesting documents or screen dumps during the interviews and observations.

In order to find out what all the data fields mean and what they are used for, you have to interview users. Often much of the data seems to be used by nobody anymore, at least by none of the users you talk to. Here it is important to ask for contact persons. Who might use this? Who knows about such things in the company?

15.5.5 Questionnaires

The above techniques get information from relatively few users. You can use questionnaires to get information from many people. You can use them in two ways: to get statistical evidence for an assumption, or to gather opinions and suggestions.

In the first case, you ask closed questions such as 'How easy is it to get customer statistics with the present system: very difficult, quite difficult, easy, very easy ...' You can use the results to see how important the problem really is.

In the second case, you ask open questions. Essentially, you can ask the same questions as during an interview, e.g. 'What are the three biggest problems in your daily work?' and 'What are your suggestions for better IT support of your daily work?' It can be quite difficult, however, to interpret the results. The respondents might have misunderstood your questions, and you may misunderstand their answers. During an interview, you can check your understanding immediately and ask questions you hadn't thought of before.

It is difficult to classify the results of open questions since you cannot clearly see whether two issues really are the same. For this reason, open questions should be asked of relatively few people.

There is also a high risk of misunderstanding with closed questions. To reduce this risk, it is essential that you know the domain already. Interviews are a good way to start.

Before sending a questionnaire form to many people, always test the form on a few people from the target group. You will be surprised how much they can misunderstand. Revise the form and make another test before you send out the final version.

15.5.6 Brainstorming and focus groups

In a brainstorming session you gather a group of people, create a stimulating and focused atmosphere and let people come up with ideas without risk of being ridiculed. The facilitator notes down all ideas on a whiteboard. Soon each idea spawns new ideas, most of them ordinary ideas, some stupid and some very promising. An important rule of the game is not to criticize any idea. Even seemingly stupid ideas may turn out to have a valuable 'diamond' seed in them. If creativity doesn't come by itself, the analyst may raise a few issues he has noticed during interviews.

Focus groups resemble brainstorming sessions, but are more structured. The term *future workshop* is also used to mean roughly the same. A focus group starts with a phase where participants come up with problems in the current way of doing things. Next comes a phase where participants try to imagine an ideal way of doing things. The group also tries to explain why the ideas are good. This helps formulate goals and requirements for the new system.

Several groups of stakeholders may participate. At the end of the session, each group identifies their high-priority issues – the most important bad things to get rid of or the most important new things to get. When later prioritizing the issues, it is important that each stakeholder group gets solutions to some of their high-priority issues. If a stakeholder group doesn't get anything in return, they are rarely willing to contribute to the system. (See Lauesen, 2002, for detailed advice and examples of focus groups.)

15.5.7 Domain workshops

There are many kinds of workshops and the term blends into brainstorming sessions and prototyping. In a domain workshop, users and developers cooperate to describe the tasks and the data. In a design workshop, they cooperate to design the user interface (sometimes called participatory design).

There are many ways to describe the tasks, and some teams prefer text forms (e.g. task descriptions), others a graphical notation (e.g. dataflow diagrams or activity diagrams; see Lauesen 2002).

We have good experience with using task descriptions directly to structure the workshop. The participants get a short introduction to task descriptions, primarily by seeing and discussing some existing task descriptions. Then they cooperate to make task descriptions for their own work area. At the beginning an experienced designer who knows about task descriptions 'holds the pen'; later, other developers or users may take over while the designer assists from the background.

It is important that expert users participate in domain workshops. They know all the business details in their own domain. Sometimes, however, expert users know only their own narrow work area and lack an overview of the bigger picture. To gain this overview, experts from several work areas may have to participate, and the designer will have a fascinating job in trying to make ends meet. Things are much easier if you can find experts with cross-domain expertise.

Managers may participate, but they rarely know the real details of the procedures and cannot replace the expert users. However, they may be instrumental in defining goals and visions.

15.5.8 Inventing new tasks

In some cases there are no existing users and no existing tasks. As an example, this often happens when you design a Web site. Here are some techniques you can use to invent new tasks:

a) User expectation. Identify the future user groups of the site. Groups might, for instance, include potential customers, potential job applicants, internal users in the company, newspaper reporters. Interview some from each group to find out what they would expect to find on the site.

b) Owner expectation. Identify the owner groups that have an interest in the site (stakeholders). Groups might include management, sales people, support people, personnel department. Interview them to find out what they expect from the site; why the company would spend money on the site; what they expect users to do.

c) Run focus groups with potential users. You may also include company stakeholders in the same focus group. The purpose is to gather ideas for what the site should offer.

d) Role playing. Imagine the user's new tasks. Write down what the users would do in various situations. Inspiration for this comes from the expectation interviews and the focus groups. The result of this is task descriptions for the new tasks. Now make a role play where developers and/or users simulate what users would do. In some cases you can even record the time it would take to carry out the new tasks. Role playing may be done before you have a user interface. If you have a user interface mock-up, role playing becomes a kind of usability test.

The purpose of describing these new tasks is to provide a basis for screen design and a basis for usability test tasks. See section 5.5 for ways to describe vague tasks, for instance those associated with many Web sites. See section 13.5 for ways to define test tasks for Web sites.

15.5.9 Covered all tasks?

In spite of all our interviews, observations and brainstorms, we may fail to reveal all the tasks. How can we ensure that all tasks have been covered? It is impossible to guarantee such completeness, but here are some guidelines for getting close.

All domain events covered? Most tasks start with an event, for instance that the customer calls to book a room, or that the breakfast list arrives at the reception. Conversely, all events must somehow be handled by a task, either manually, or supported by the computer, or fully automated. So if we have a list of events, we can check that each event is handled somewhere.

As an example, we may ask users about the events in a reception. What can happen there? Receptionists may tell about the auditor arriving to check the accounts, guests reporting that the toilet doesn't work, the night watch not turning up, etc. For each event we ought to ask: Should this be supported by the new system? For the auditor arriving, the answer is yes. He will check that rooms occupied are actually covered by a check-in, and the system must help him find out. For the toilet not working, the answer is yes too. The system must be able to record that the room is not available for check-in. For the night watch not turning up, it is probably a matter for human action without support from the system.

The event list is a different way to look at the domain, so although it is no more perfect than the task list, it may catch something that the task list doesn't – and vice versa.

Difficult tasks covered? Difficult tasks are those that are time-consuming, frequent, hard or performed under stress. It is important to identify these because they need careful support. When observing users, you may see the time-consuming and frequent tasks, but rarely the difficult or stressful tasks; you have to ask about them. In the hotel reception, you might only identify the busload of tourists as a difficult task if you asked about stressful and hard situations.

At least as good as before? There is a difficult problem in this area: introducing a new system may turn an easy task into a difficult one. As an example, one manufacturing company replaced their old IT system with a new one based on a commercial one they bought. The old system had a very sophisticated screen picture that gave an excellent overview of pending repair jobs in the factory. However, the users were unaware that they used a sophisticated screen. The new system showed only traditional lists of data records that didn't give the same overview, and it would be very expensive to create new sophisticated screens. The task that used the repair list had not been stressful using the old system, but it was using the new one. Although the analysts had catered for all difficult tasks, they had not realized that the new system would create a new difficult task.

This problem is hard to deal with. Experienced designers may notice that the old system has such an unusual screen – but only if they take the time to observe what the users are doing or ask them to show how to do it in the old system. The designer must be experienced in two things: user interface design, and the tools used to program the interface. Otherwise he will not notice that this screen is unusual and important. Once he notices, we have a good place to record the observation: in the task descriptions. In the examples of section 5.2, we have indicated 'clever things' in several places.

Business goals covered? Most systems are made with a business goal in mind. Why will the system owner spend money on it? Often the system owners can tell you about these goals. In order to meet the goals, some user tasks must be carried out in a new way – or new tasks must be invented. Now check that you have described these tasks in such detail that we can see how the business goals are met. This is a very powerful technique to ensure that the goals are realistic. See Lauesen, 2002, for real-life examples where this had not been done, and as a consequence the business goals were missed although the system worked as intended.

A warning: The analysis of goals versus tasks may be very painful because it often reveals profound inconsistencies in the way the company 'thinks'. Do it very cautiously with understanding managers. Don't do it in large stakeholder groups unless you have tried it in a smaller group first.

CREDO check. CREDO stands for Create–Read–Edit–Delete–Overview. In order to make a CREDO check of the user tasks, we need a description of the data to be stored in the system – data model. We now look at each piece of data and ask ourselves how that piece is created, read, edited and deleted, what kind of overview is used and whether some task description deals with it.

If no task description deals with it, we will probably have to add such a task. Usually you identify some surprising new tasks in this way. In other cases there may be good reasons for not adding the task, for instance because the data is maintained in another system. Section 6.5 explains more about CREDO checks.

Some of the missing user tasks are often small tasks, such as updating the customer's address or deleting the customer. They may be grouped together according to the session principle into larger maintenance tasks (section 5.5).

16

Data modelling

Highlights

- The entity–relationship model for data: classes, entities and relationships.

- Data dictionary: Data descriptions in text form.

- Modelling business data, a word processor, maps, etc.

- How to store the data in the computer.

- Normalization: finding the true objects and storing data in one place only.

This chapter is a short tutorial in data modelling. The purpose of a data model is to describe all the data to be filed in the computer system. Traditionally, data models were primarily used for business applications, but today they are used also in the technical area in the form of static class diagrams.

At the beginning we will use a simple hotel system as an example. Chapters 6 to 8 develop the user interface for this hotel system. Section 5.2 is a summary of the data model for the hotel system.

The purpose of the hotel system is to support the reception staff in their daily tasks: booking rooms, checking guests in and out, etc. We will simplify the system a bit and assume that when the guest books a room, the receptionist will choose a specific room for him. (In most hotels they just book an anonymous room, for instance an anonymous double room or an anonymous single room. Only when the guest arrives will they assign him a specific room.)

The purpose of data modelling is to describe the data the system shall keep track of, for instance rooms, guests and the relation between them. Data models can be shown in many ways, for instance as entity–relationship (E/R) models, UML class models or tables in a relational database. We will look at all these forms in the chapter.

16.1   Entity–relationship model

Figure 16.1 illustrates part of the data in the hotel system. The left-hand part of the figure illustrates the objects we want data about. The right-hand part of the figure shows the corresponding E/R data model.

The objects

The figure shows that the *Guests* box contains a number of index cards. Imagine that the box contains an index card for each guest that the hotel wants to keep track of.

The *Stays* box contains an index card for every stay the guests have had at the hotel. Some guests stay just one night and don't come back for another stay. Other guests stay often at the hotel – they are regular guests, and the hotel wants to keep them in the database. Some guests have several rooms at the same time, or change rooms during their stay. (Some stays involve more than one person, for instance parents with their children. The *guest* is simply the person who pays the bill.)

The figure shows that each guest is tied to his stays with 'strings'. Notice that two guests have three stays each, while two other guests have no recorded stays at present. In general, a guest can have zero or more stays. Reading the figure the other way, each stay has exactly one guest. We cannot have a stay without a related guest, and no stay can be related to two or more guests. We call the relationship between guests and stays a *one-to-many* relationship.

The *Rooms* box contains an index card for each hotel room. There is a relationship between rooms and stays, but as the figure shows, it is more complex than the one-to-many relationship. A single stay may comprise several rooms, for instance in case of the family stay. Reading it the other way, a single room can be used for many stays over time (but not for two stays on the *same* date). We call this a *many-to-many* relationship.

The E/R model

The entity–relationship (E/R) model to the right captures all of this in a compact diagram. The diagram is a simplified version of the boxes and strings to the left. Notice that the connector with a single crow's foot symbolizes a one-to-many relationship (1:m), and the double foot connector symbolizes a many-to-many relationship (m:m).

These simple symbols are a very strong tool. With them we can model all kinds of data that occur in business and technical areas.

Fig 16.1   E/R data model

How objects relate to each other   Entity–relationship data model

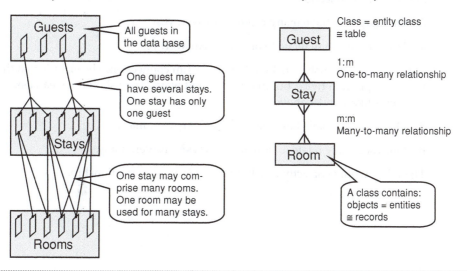

It is important to read the 1:m connector in the right way. Look at the crow's foot that connects Guest with Stay:

Reading from Guest to Stay: One guest object fans out into several stay objects.

Reading from Stay to Guest: Looks like an arrow that for each stay points at exactly one guest.

In data modelling jargon we call the boxes *classes* or *entity classes* and the crow's feet *relationships*. Notice a little detail: In the left-hand diagram we wrote *Guests* (plural) because we thought of the box as containing all the guests. In the E/R diagram we conventionally write *Guest* (singular) because we think of the box as a single guest.

Each box contains **objects** – sometimes called *entities* or *records*.

Asking the right questions

It is important to find out whether a connection is 1:m or m:m. To do this we have to answer two questions, for instance these for the Guest–Stay connection:

1   One guest may have how many stays? Answer: many.

2   One stay may have how many guests? Answer: one.

Conclusion: It is a 1:m connector (a 1:m relationship).

Wrong questions

Quite a few novices make a mistake here and ask these questions, for instance for the Stay–Rooms connection:

3 One stay may have many rooms? Answer: yes.

4 Many rooms may relate to one stay? Answer: yes.

Then they erroneously conclude that it is a 1:m connection. The error is that they ask the same question twice, but in two different ways. They should instead ask questions like 1 and 2 above:

5 One stay may have how many rooms? Answer: many.

6 One room may relate to how many stays? Answer: many.

Then they would correctly conclude that it is an m:m relationship.

16.2 Entities and attributes

For each entity we need to record some data on its 'index card'. These data are called *attributes* or *data fields*. Figure 16.2 shows some attributes for the hotel data model.

For a *guest* we need to record his name, address, phone number and passport number, as shown in the figure. We set off space for these fields for all guests, no matter whether we fill in something or not. For instance, we record passport numbers for foreigners only.

We don't record the guest's stays in his index card because there are 'strings' from the guest index card to his stay index card.

For a *stay* we need its identification number (often called a booking number) and how the guest pays for the stay (cash, Visa, Master, etc.). We also need to know which guest this is about, but according to the 1:m connector, there is a 'string' to exactly one guest. By following the string we can get all necessary data about the guest.

We also have to know which rooms the stay is about, and again the connector helps us. According to the m:m connector there should be a string to each related room.

There is just one nasty problem here: we need to record the dates that the stay uses the rooms. Where should we do this? One way would be to put a date on each of the strings, but E/R modelling doesn't allow this. The figure suggests another solution: that we write a list of room numbers and associated dates as attributes for the stay. But this suggestion violates another rule in data modelling:

> **First normal form:** For each class there must be a fixed number of attributes, each of a fixed length.

What the figure suggests is to make an arbitrarily long list of attributes, so this violates the rule. We might define an upper limit such as 99 rooms for a stay, but it would cause a lot of wasted space in the computer for ordinary stays that only involve a single room. Further, it actually occurs that a single guest, for instance a large company, books several hundred rooms for the yearly sales meeting. In general, it is awkward to define such arbitrary upper limits for data.

The problem occurs for most m:m connections. The solution is to introduce an additional box, as we will explain in the next section.

For a *room* we need its room identification – the number written on the door to the room. We also need to know how many beds there can be in the room – including possible extra beds for children. We need to know the type of room – whether it is single, double, with bath, with Jacuzzi, etc. Finally, we need two prices: the ordinary price and a discount price in case a double room is used as a single room.

Hey, we have introduced two prices! Doesn't it violate the first normal form? Fortunately not, because we only have a fixed number of prices – two. (In some hotels the discounts can be much more complex and then we need additional boxes. We ignore it here.)

Keys

Notice that some attribute names are underscored. They are *keys* – attributes that uniquely identify the entity. A room, for instance, has a unique identification – the number written on the door. There is only one room with this number.

A stay also has a key, the stayID or booking number. Such numbers are traditionally used in the hotel business. They are written, for instance, on the booking confirmation sent to the guest.

The guest has no key according to the diagram, and E/R models don't require a key for every class. However, some database systems require keys for each class, for purely technical reasons (more on that later). If we don't have keys for the guests, how do we find a guest in the database when he turns up at the reception, saying *I have booked a room, but forgotten the booking number*? Well, we have to find him by his name, and if several guests have the same name, then by his address, phone number, etc.

Notation

The right-hand part of Figure 16.2 is a very compact way to describe the classes and their attributes. We simply list the attributes beside each class. It is the main notation we use in this book. There are other ways however, for instance this textual description of the model:

Classes:
Guest (name, address, phone, passport)
Stay (stayID, paymethod)

Relationships:
Guest–Stay: 1:m

In large systems there is often an awful lot of attributes. In commercial business packages such as SAP, BAAN and Navision, there may be for instance more than a hundred attributes for the customer class. As a result we would show only a few important attributes on the E/R model, the rest have to be separate, long lists in text form.

Fig 16.2 Attributes and keys

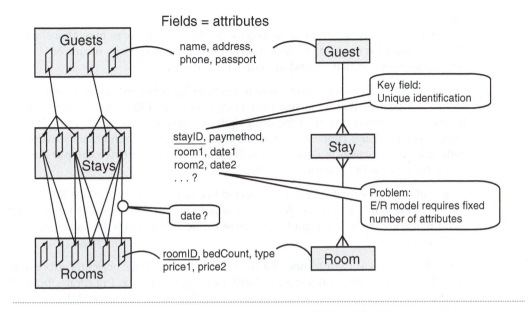

16.3 Resolving m:m relationships

In practice we often start out with a data model that has a lot of m:m relationships. When the model is finished, we have transformed most of these by means of additional classes so that we end up with 1:m relationships.

Let us see how we can transform the m:m relationship between Stay and Room. Figure 16.3A shows that we have added a new class, called *RoomState*. Each *object* in this class corresponds to one of the *strings* between Stay and Room. In Figure 16.2 there are eight strings connecting Stay and Room. They correspond exactly to the eight RoomState objects in Figure 16.3A. These objects are where we will put the attributes we couldn't place in Figure 16.2.

Note that each RoomState object is connected to exactly one Stay and one Room. So instead of the m:m relationship, we have now got a connection class (RoomState) and two 1:m relationships. The right-hand side of Figure 16.3A shows the corresponding E/R model.

Let us have a look at the attributes for RoomState. A RoomState object records that a specific room is occupied at a specific date by a specific stay. The 1:m connectors tell us what room and what stay we are dealing with, but we have to record the date itself in a RoomState attribute.

Once we understand what a RoomState really is, we find other important things to record there. For instance, we could record how many persons would stay in the room on that date. (In case only one person stays in a double room, there is basis for a discount.) We should also record what kind of state the room is in:

▪ booked (reserved for a guest who hasn't yet arrived)

▪ occupied (a guest has actually moved in there)

▪ repair (the room is being repaired so that nobody can stay there this date)

Why haven't we defined a state saying that the room is free? We might do it this way, but the result is that we would have a lot of records specifying free rooms far into the future. Large hotels may have 500 rooms and allow booking two years ahead. This would require 365,000 room state records mostly saying that the room is free. With the solution we have chosen, a room is free at a specific date if there is no room state record for it at this date.

Enumeration type. In Figure 16.3A, we have shown the room state as a single field with *booked, occ, repair* in parentheses:

state (booked | occ | repair)

It means that the field can hold only these values. In database practice, the field would hold a number that is either 1, 2 or 3. We don't show these numbers to the users, but show 1 as *booked*, 2 as *occupied*, etc.

Fig 16.3 A Resolve m:m with connection class

Reproduced with permission from Pearson Education

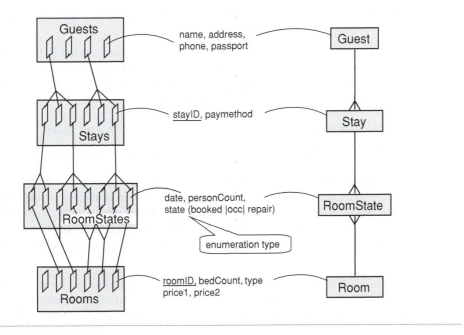

What has happened to the attributes for the other classes? They are the same except for the Stay attributes, which now are completely straightforward.

Naming the connection class

In practical data modelling we introduce many connection classes like RoomState. Technically speaking, it is a simple transformation of the E/R model, but it is usually hard to find a good name for the class. This is because the connection objects aren't physical things we can touch. Who would think of a room state as a separate object? We even have a separate object for each day!

In our case we have been lucky to find a meaningful name. Many developers give up and just construct a composite name from the two classes being connected. In our case they might have come up with this name

Stay_Room

instead of RoomState. We suggest that you try to find a meaningful name. When you find one, it usually gives you an aha-experience: Aha, the connection objects show the state of the room each date!

The full hotel data model

In the hotel model we have now dealt with guests, stays and rooms, but a guest is also charged for services he receives, such as various types of breakfast, phone calls, etc. Let us extend the data model to include this.

The top of Figure 16.3B shows our first attempt. We have added a class for the service types. One of the service type records could, for instance, specify that there is a service called 'Full breakfast' with a price of $6. What is the connection between Stay and ServiceType? Let us try the usual questions:

1   One stay may involve how many service types? Answer: many.

2   One service type may involve how many stays? Answer: many.

Conclusion: It is a m:m relationship, as shown in the figure. We better break it by means of a connection class. Each object of the connection class would correspond to a string connecting a stay with a service type. What would such an object signify? Aha, maybe some *service received* during that stay. What attributes could the received service have? The date it was received and maybe the quantity received (e.g. the number of serves).

The result is shown in the lower part of Figure 16.3B. Here we have a full data model for the hotel system. Apart from adding the service stuff, we have changed a few things that turned up later in systems development and user interface design:

- We have split the address attribute into three attributes. They would correspond to three address lines printed in a letterhead to this guest. On purpose, we haven't split the address into street name, street number, zip code and other things commonly seen on paper forms. Why? These things vary a lot from country to country, and many foreigners have great difficulty figuring out what to write in the zip-code field. We want the system to sell internationally and cater for foreigners everywhere. (There are drawbacks to this solution, for instance that it is harder to make statistics of where guests come from.)

- We have added a *state* attribute for Stay. Why? Because it is important for the receptionist to see whether a particular stay is still booked or whether the guest has arrived; whether the guest has checked out and paid his bill; or whether the guest has cancelled his stay. The state of the stay is related to the room states so that if the room states are occupied, the stay is checked in. However, the relationship may be more complex, for instance if the guest has checked into one room from today and booked another room from tomorrow. For this reason it gives the developer more freedom to have a separate state of the stay.

Why did we stop with these classes and attributes? We could have modelled a lot more, for instance the employees, who is on duty when, suppliers to the hotel (washing service, food supplies and so on) and bank accounts. The list is endless.

Fig 16.3 B Hotel data model

Reproduced with permission from Pearson education

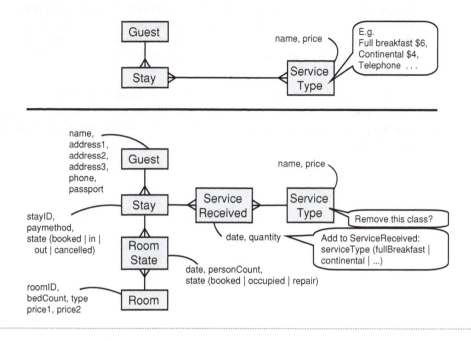

The answer is that we have only modelled what is needed to support the tasks we want to support.

Enumeration type versus class

Figure 16.3B shows a design question: Do we need the ServiceType class? What if we removed it and instead added the service type to ServiceReceived as an enumeration field? ServiceReceived would then have these fields:

ServiceReceived: date, quantity, serviceType(fullBreakfast | continental | ...)

This would correspond to the way we model the state of RoomState. The receptionist can choose the proper value to store in the record. This solution would cause two problems:

ServiceType had two attributes. We don't have the price anymore. Okay, we could put this as another attribute on ServiceReceived – a bit inconvenient now, because the receptionist would have to enter the price. It could easily end up with different guests paying different amounts for the same service. But let us assume that this was okay.

Impossible to add another type of service. How should we handle the situation that the hotel needs another type of service, for instance a charge for sauna? While the user can add, edit and delete records from a class, he cannot add new values to the enumeration list. The enumeration list is built into the system. To change it, we must ask the programmer to do it. If we have the service types in a separate class, we can easily give the user a screen where he can add, edit and delete service types.

Room states are different from service types. The user doesn't need to add another kind of room state. If there should be a need for another state, we would have to involve the programmer anyway to program the rules and checks associated with this new state.

16.4 The relational data model

There are many ways to implement a data model in the computer. It can be done as data objects linked together in main memory, as a network database with records linked together on the disk, as disk files with an application specific format or as a relational database. In this section we will look at the latter possibility.

A relational database consists of a number of tables, and each table contains a list of records. Newer computer databases are structured as relational databases. If we have an E/R model without m:m relationships, it is easy to translate it into a relational database. Each class becomes a table, and we add a few new attributes. Figure 16.4 shows how it works for the hotel system.

Guest. The guest class becomes a table with one record per guest – the example shows three guests. All guests have the same set of attributes: a name, address1 and so on. All the name fields must have the same length, meaning that the computer sets off equal space for all names. The same rule applies for the other attributes, and as a result all guest records have the same length – they have space for the same number of characters. This structure helps the computer find the records very fast.

Note that we have added a new attribute to Guest, *guestID*, which is a unique number for each guest – a key for the guest. Thus two guests in the database may not have the same guestID although they may have exactly the same name and address. The reason we need a guestID is to allow a stay to refer to a guest. We will look at that below.

The guestID does not exist in the work domain outside the computer. People don't have such identifications and even the receptionist need not know about guestID's. For this reason we call guestID an artificial key. It exists only for technical reasons.

Stay. Now look at the Stay table. It has of course the attributes stayID and paymethod. The stayID is a key, similar to an invoice number. It exists in the work domain, so we call it a natural key.

We have added a new attribute to Stay, *guestID*. It serves as a *reference* to the guest who has this stay. This is the way we handle a 1:m connection in a relational database. By means of this reference, the computer can go from the stay to the corresponding guest very fast – typically around 20 milliseconds. It can also go the other way. If it knows a guest, it can find all the guest's stays by going through the stay records looking for stays that refer to this guest. Even if there are thousands of guests and stays, the computer can find the right ones fast – typically around 100 milliseconds. If it really looked at all these thousands of stays, it might take minutes, but various tricks allow it to do it much faster (for instance 'secondary indexes').

RoomState. The RoomState table has two new attributes, one pointing to the stay involved and one to the room. These two references correspond to the two 1:m connections from RoomState.

Room. The Room table has no surprises. It has a roomID attribute, corresponding to the room number on the door. This is a natural key existing in the work domain.

Terminology

Primary key. The unique key in a table is called the *primary key*. We use a full underscore to show the primary key. In the Guest table, the guestID attribute is the primary key. It uniquely identifies the guest.

Foreign key. In database terminology the references are called *foreign keys* because they refer to a primary key in another table. In the Stay table, the guestID attribute is a foreign key that refers to the Guest table. We often put a dotted underscore on the foreign key to help the reader. In Figure 16.4 there are three foreign keys corresponding to the three 1:m connectors.

Why is it called a relational database? It is because in the relational world of data modelling, a table is called a *relation*. So with this terminology, a relational database consists of relations – as simple as this. Notice that we have called our crow's feet *relationships* to distinguish them from relations. Sometimes, however, people call the crow's feet relations – and a lot of confusion may arise. In this book we use the terms table and relationship (or connector) to avoid any confusion.

If you are good at math, you may understand why a table is called a relation. A table specifies a mathematical relation between all the attributes of the table. The table is simply a list of all the valid combinations of attribute values. (In mathematical terminology a *relation* is a subset of the Cartesian product of all the attribute sets.)

Composite keys

Three of the four hotel tables have got a primary key, but RoomState didn't get any. Should it? No other tables refer to it, so in principle it need not have a primary key.

However, there is a special rule for relational databases:

A table may not have two identical records.

We fulfil this rule if we have a key in the table. No two records can have the same key so all records will be different at least for the keys. But there is no need to have a key – all records may be different anyway.

If we want, could we use some of the RoomState fields as a key? We can quickly see that no single field is suited as a key. Several RoomState records will have the same stayID, several will have the same roomID and so on.

However, it is possible to use several fields as a *composite key*. What about using a combination of stayID and roomID? Unfortunately no – a specific room may be booked several days in a row by the same stay. There will be one RoomState record for each day and they will have the same stayID and roomID.

Fig 16.4 Relational data model

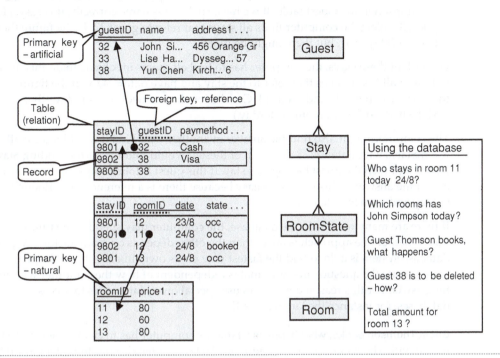

What about a combination of roomID and date as the key? If two RoomState records had the same roomID and the same date, something would be all wrong: We would have booked the same room for two different purposes at the same day. This is called a double booking – a disaster in a booking system.

Conclusion: If we use roomID and date as a composite key, we have guarded against double booking. In Figure 16.4 we have underscored these two fields, showing that they make up the key.

Searching and updating a database

How can the computer use a relational database? Let us look at the questions shown in Figure 16.4:

Who stays in room 11, today 24/8? First the computer has to look through all RoomState records to find one with roomID=11 and date=24/8. There is one in the figure and the corresponding stayID is 9801. Now the computer finds the corresponding Stay record by means of the reference (the arrow). The Stay record shows that the guest has guestID=32, and the computer finds this guest record (again using a reference). The guest is John Simpson.

Which rooms has John Simpson, today 24/8? The computer may begin by finding John Simpson in the Guest table. If we have spelled his name correctly, it is easy. He is guest 32. Next the computer finds all stays that refer to guest 32. In the figure there is just one, stay 9801, but there might be more.

For each of these stays, the computer has to find all rooms involved. To do this, it has to look at all RoomStates that refer to the stay and have date=24/8. In the figure there are two: room 11 and room 13. Conclusion: he has two rooms today. (By the way, he had a different room yesterday.)

The computer might also find the answer in another way. First it would look at all RoomStates with date=24/8. For each of these it would find the corresponding Stay record and then the guest having this stay. If this guest is John Simpson, the room is one of the answers. This method is easy because there is a reference from RoomState to Stay and from Stay to Guest.

If there are many records in the database, the computer may spend some time on this. Whether one approach is faster than the other depends on many factors. A good database system is able to find the fastest way on its own. In order to do this, we have to state the question in a way that is independent of how the computer will find the answer. For this reason developers use special query languages to access databases, for instance the language SQL.

Guest Thomson books, what happens? First the computer has to create a new Guest record with Thomson's name and address. The computer also has to find a guestID for him – a number that isn't used for any guest already. Next it has to create a new Stay record, give it a unique stayID and assign the proper guestID.

Now it has to find a free room. It may do so by scanning all rooms, looking for those that haven't any RoomState records in the period requested by the guest. These are the rooms the receptionist can choose from. When he has chosen one, the computer must create a RoomState record for each day in the period requested by the guest. These RoomState records must get the right roomID, stayID and the state *booked*.

In practice there are some complexities to deal with. If something goes wrong during the process, for instance that there is no suitable room available, everything the computer has done until then must be undone. For instance, it has to delete the guest record and the stay record. We use the term that the entire process must be an *atomic transaction*. This means that either everything is done or nothing is done.

Another complexity in practice is that the system must cater for the situation where the computer or the network breaks down during the process. Also in these cases the transaction must be atomic. Professional database systems are able to ensure atomic transactions – even in case of computer malfunctions.

Guest 38 is to be deleted – how? Assume that we want to delete guest 38 from the database. It seems easy – we just have to remove his Guest record.

However, what if he has booked some stays? We better delete these Stay records too, since they otherwise would refer to a now disappeared guest record. And what about RoomState records connected to these stays? We better delete them too in order to free the rooms. This is an example of a *cascading delete* – all records related to the root record (the guest) have to be deleted too.

Total amount for room 13? The guest in room 13 asks what his bill amounts to at present. What should the computer do to answer this question? First it has to find the RoomState record for room 13, date 24/8. It shows that the room is occupied by stay 9801.

Next the computer has to find all RoomState records relating to stay 9801 and showing the state *occupied*. In the figure there are three such records: room 12 the 23/8, room 11 the 24/8 and room 13 the 24/8. For each of these the computer must find the Room record in the last table, extract the room price and total all of them. (The computer also has to look at ServiceReceived and add their prices too.)

Redundant data – totals in the tables?

Since it is a bit complex to compute the total amount for a stay, we might be tempted to add a *total* field to the Stay table. Here we could accumulate the amounts as the data is entered into the system. In this way the latest total would always be available.

The disadvantage is that we would have to update the *total* field all the time, both when the guest stays another night and when we change something, for instance move the guest from one room to another.

In our hotel system it is hardly worth the effort to maintain a total. The system can easily compute it at demand. But in other systems it may be necessary. Consider your home telephone bill, for instance. The balance on your telephone account consists of thousands of calls since your subscription started, minus all the payments you have made. Here it is convenient for you and the telephone company to record the new balance, for instance whenever a new bill is sent out.

Such a balance field is an example of *redundant data* – data stored in a record, but in principle computable from other data in the database. The general rule in database technology is to avoid redundant data and instead compute the necessary results at demand. This more easily ensures that the database is always *consistent* – that nothing in the database conflicts with other things in the database. However, other concerns, for instance speed and storage space, may dictate otherwise.

16.5   From informal sources to E/R model

From where do we get information about the entities, attributes and relationships that go into the data model? There are many sources, for instance existing forms and screens, written descriptions and business rules, our own common sense and logic, studies of what users do, interviews, etc.

Car registration.   We will look at an example: Registration of cars (motor vehicles) and their owner. Which relation is there between them? Our first guess – based on common sense – is that a car has one owner, and one owner may own several cars. In other words, a 1:m connector between owner and car (see Figure 16.5).

We may start guessing about the attributes. The car has a licence number (on the licence plate) and the owner has a name and an address – and maybe a civil registration number? It all depends on what the model is to be used for. We seem to need more information.

Assume we want to plan the database for the motor vehicle office in Wonderland (rules actually differ a lot from country to country). Figure 16.5 shows part of the official rules in Wonderland. We see that they record the civil registration number of the owner, but in case the owner is a company, they record the company tax file number. They also record the fuel type (the road tax depends on the fuel type). There is also something strange about a *primary* owner or user – what on earth is this and how do we model it?

Finally, as a last comment, they tell us that they may record more than one owner and user. Oops! This was not a 1:m connector, but an m:m connector. Or are there two m:m connectors, one for the owners and one for the users?

Let us try the simple version first – only one m:m connector. We better resolve it with a connection class (make a sketch of your own). Each record in the connection class corresponds to one person owning one car. If the car has many owners, each of them has a connection record to this car.

Role entity.   As usual with a connection class, what should we call it and which attributes does it have? Let us scrutinize the official description once more to find things that could become attributes of the connection class. What about *primary*? Yes, it might be a good idea to have a primary attribute in the connection class. When the attribute is *yes*, it shows that this person is to receive the certificate (and the road tax bill). Any other owners must have *no* for *primary*. What about the owner–user issue? We might have this as another attribute in the connection class. It shows whether this person's role is being an owner or a user.

Now we also found a natural name for the connection class: *Role*. It shows whether the person is an owner or a user, and whether he is the primary person. The trick of using a role entity often helps us in data modelling. The role entity may come out naturally when we resolve an m:m relationship.

Fig 16.5 Data sources

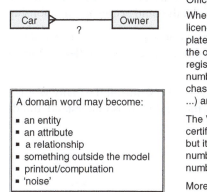

Official source text

When a car is registrated it gets a licence number (shown on the license plate). The Vehicle Office also records the owner's name and address, civil registration number or company tax file number, the make (producer and model), chassis number, fuel type (Petrol, diesel, ...) and the registration date.

The Vehicle Office sends a registration certificate to the primary owner or user, but it doesn't show the civil registration number or the company registration number.

More than one owner and user may be recorded.

A domain word may become:

- an entity
- an attribute
- a relationship
- something outside the model
- printout/computation
- 'noise'

Broad names. We have one small problem left – what should we call the *Owner* class? It covers both owners and users, so let us call it *Person*. Oh, that gives us another problem because it covers persons as well as companies. We will stay with the name *Person*, meaning a legal body, either a person, a company or a public authority. This is a good example of a problem we often encounter in data modelling: the concept we want to model doesn't have a good name in our natural language. Some developers would create names such as *owner/user* or *person/company*. This is okay, but no matter what name we choose in this case, we need an explanation of what it covers. A data dictionary is the place to describe it (see section 16.6).

Solution. In section 16.15 you find two finished models for the car-owner database. One corresponds closely to the discussion above. The other also shows graphically that only one person can be primary. Try to finish your own model before you look at the solution. Also make the table version and fill in an example of cars with multiple owners/users and an example of persons that own/use multiple cars.

Systematic use of informal sources. To check that our data model covers all the rules, we can systematically go through the text to see what has happened to each word. In general, a word used in the domain may end up in these ways:

1 As an entity, e.g. *car, owner, user*. May get new names or be combined with other entities.

2 An attribute, e.g. licence number, make, fuel type. The names may change here too.

3 A relationship, e.g. *owner*, which at first became an m:m *owns* relationship, later an attribute in the Role entity.

4   Something outside the model, e.g. *Vehicle Office, sends*. This seems to be outside the domain we are interested in. However, if there were several Vehicle Offices, we might be interested in keeping track of who sent what. Then we would need a box for Vehicle Offices and model the send action as a relationship.

5   Printout/computation/system action, e.g. *registration certificate; doesn't show the civil registration number*. These things have to be handled by the system, but not as part of the data model.

6   'Noise', e.g. *when, gets, licence plate*. These are all the many words in our spoken language that glue things together and help us understand, but don't go into the data model.

16.6 Data dictionary

We can model a lot of things with an E/R model, but there will always be data aspects it cannot describe, for instance special cases, how the names in the data model relate to what users say in daily life, where data come from in the domain, and where it is used. Some verbal data description is needed.

A data dictionary is a verbal data description structured systematically. You may arrange it alphabetically according to field names, but this can be confusing unless you also have a data model to explain how fields belong to classes. If you have a data model – or an outline of one – structure the data dictionary according to the classes of the model.

Figure 16.6 shows part of a carefully written data dictionary for the hotel system. Each entity (class) has its own description, including a description of each of its attributes. We have numbered the classes D1, D2 and so on. We have numbered the attributes for each class 1, 2 and so on. This is similar to the way we number tasks and subtasks. The numbers are convenient when you refer to classes and attributes from other parts of the design documents.

For each entity, we explain what it means and we mention other names used in practice for the entity. We also give a few examples of the entity, particularly unusual ones.

In our case, we have shown the special example of a company being a guest. When we look at that in detail, we notice that although the company gets the bill (is the *guest* in the formal sense), the company probably wants to know which person stayed there. So we need a new attribute for the stay: the name of the employee staying on behalf of the company. This attribute is missing in our data model, but should be there. We will ignore it in the following.

For each attribute, we explain what it means and specify its type (text, number, etc.) and the length of the field. Often we see trivial descriptions, e.g.

guestName: The name of the guest.

This is hardly worth writing. A good description tells the reader something non-trivial.

The figure may give you some ideas for what to write. For the guest name there is information about where the name comes from and what it is used for; which is not trivial. In order to write it, we need domain knowledge, and that is an essential part of the domain analysis.

We have also made a brave decision: we won't use more than 50 characters for the name. This is not so much to save space, but to help users. Some people have long names, but if the receptionist enters the entire name, it is not easily visible on the screen, and when printed out, the system has to cut it, sometimes into something funny or incomprehensible. It is better to have the receptionist truncate it in a meaningful way in the first place.

Below are some questions that may help you to write better data dictionaries. To illustrate the principles, we have added references such as [a] to the figure to show how the questions have been addressed.

Warning: You don't have to answer all the questions for every entity and attribute. However, if you don't know the answer, there is a good reason to ask expert users.

Check-questions for each entity

a) Which entity name is used in the data model? How does it relate to other names used by people in the domain?

b) How does the entity relate to other entities?

c) Are there cases where it doesn't have the usual relation to other entities?

d) Are there special things to consider when creating or deleting the entity?

e) Give a typical example of the entity. Give also unusual examples of the entity.

Check-questions for each attribute

f) Where in the domain do the values come from?

g) What are the values used for in the domain?

h) Which values are possible for this attribute?

i) Can the attribute have special values, e.g. blanks, and when?

j) Give typical and special examples.

As an example, here is how we have answered the questions for the passport number:

f) Where in the domain does it come from? The description says from guests who obviously are foreigners. The receptionist asks to see their passport. This also means that we don't record it always [question i].

g) What are the values used for in the domain? The description says it is for 'reporting to the police in case the guest doesn't pay'. Could we have guessed this? No, it is knowledge we have to gather from expert users.

h) Which values are possible? The description only says that there are at most 16 characters. Although each country has a standard for its passport numbers, there doesn't seem to be a worldwide one, and anyway it is not essential since the police – in case – will be satisfied with these 16 characters.

i) Can the attribute have special values? No special explanation, but we can see that a blank field is the usual thing.

j) Give typical and special examples. We haven't found it necessary.

Fig 16.6 Data dictionary

D1: Class: Guest [Notes a, b ... refer to guidelines]

The guest is the person or company who has to pay the bill. A person has one or more stay records. A company may have none [b, c]. 'Customer' is a synonym for guest, but in the database we only use 'guest' [a]. The persons staying in the rooms are also called guests, but are not guests in database terms [a].

Examples
a.   A guest who stays one night.
b.   A company with employees staying now and then, each of them with his own stay record where his name is recorded [d].
c.   A guest with several rooms within the same stay.

> Attribute missing in data model

Attributes
1. name: Text, 50 chars [h]
        The name stated by the guest [f]. For companies the official name since the bill is sent there [g]. Longer names exist, but better truncate at registration time than at print out time [g, j].
2. passport: Text, 16 chars [h]
        Recorded for guests who are obviously foreigners [f, i]. Used for police reports in case the guest doesn't pay [g] . . .

16.7 Network model: flight routes

Figure 16.7 shows an example with a more complex connection class. We want to model all flight routes in the world so that we can find connections between any two cities.

As a typical example, we have shown American Airline's route AA331, starting from Chicago, stopping at Columbus and Washington and ending in New York. To simplify the case a bit, we assume that each city has only one airport. The little form shows the data about this route. It operates Monday and Wednesday, both days with the schedule shown.

Our first outline of the data model consists of the cities and the routes. Each route may comprise multiple cities, and each city may host several routes. We thus have an m:m relationship. We resolve it with a connection class, but what does a connection record represent? An obvious solution is to let it represent a stop on the route, corresponding to a line on the form. For AA331 we would thus have four connection records, Chicago, Columbus, Washington and New York. The first one would have a departure time and a blank arrival time, the middle ones would have arrival and departure times and the last one will have arrival time and a blank departure time.

However, database experts don't like having blank fields because they make computations harder. In practice, airlines model the routes differently. Instead of modelling the stops, they model the sections travelled. AA331 consists of three sections: Chicago–Columbus, Columbus–Washington and Washington–New York. A section is usually called a *leg* and it always has a departure time and an arrival time. It also has a departure city and an arrival city, so it connects to two cities.

The figure outlines the final model. Notice that there are two m:1 connections between leg and city, because the leg has a departure city and an arrival city. In such cases it is convenient to label the connections as we have done on the figure. The figure also shows a 1:1 relationship between leg and leg. We have called it *Next*. If we are at one of the legs and follow the Next relationship, we come to the next leg on the route. For the last leg there is no Next, of course.

We have not shown the attributes. Write them yourself without artificial keys or foreign keys. Then add any artificial keys and foreign keys needed to make a relational database, but show them in parentheses. Finally, check that your model covers everything from the schedule form. Compare your solution against the one in section 14.15.

This kind of data model with two 1:m connectors between the same two classes is quite common. We call it a *network model*. The characteristic thing is that objects in one of the classes have to be connected to many other objects in the same class. In the flight route case, the cities are connected to other cities through the many legs of the many flight routes. We find similar models in project planning where one project

Fig 16.7 Network model: flight routes

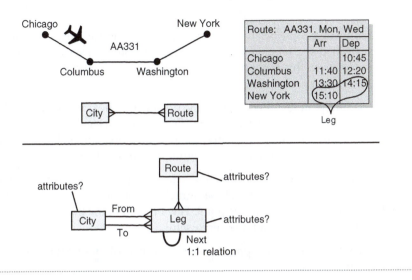

activity has to be finished before certain other activities can start. A network model should not be confused with a *network database*. Network databases are alternatives to relational databases (see section 16.13).

16.8   Example: text processor

Some software people believe that data models are useful only for business administration and relational databases, such as the hotel system and the flight routes. However, this is not true. In this section we will model something completely different – a text processor.

The basic entity in text processing is the document. The document has a lot of data, for instance the text we write, margins, fonts, pictures, etc. How all of this relate to each other varies from one text processing product to another. Here we will use Microsoft Word as an example, and Figure 16.8 shows the model.

We see that a Word document contains one or more *sections*. Each section contains one or more *paragraphs*, and each paragraph one or more *characters*. Most Word users will be surprised already at this point. Few of them know that a document is divided into sections, but it is – and it is very useful.

The strength of the model appears when we put attributes on the classes. The figure shows some examples.

Document.   The document entity has, for instance, a file name attribute (not surprising) and zoom information – the magnification factor and the display form (e.g. normal view, page layout, etc.). Word files these data together with the document, so when you open it again, you start in the same zoom state.

Section.   A section has attributes such as page margins, the paper size, which page headers and footers to use, how many columns the text consists of. This means that if you divide the text into sections, one section may be single column, another three columns. (You can divide it into sections with Insert → Break → Section breaks.)

Paragraph.   A paragraph has attributes about alignment (left-aligned, centered, etc.), indentation for the first line and next lines of the paragraph, line spacing before and after the paragraph, whether it is a heading to go into the table of contents, etc.

Character.   Finally, the individual characters have attributes about the type font (Times, Arial, etc.), font size, font style (bold, italic, etc.). These attributes can thus change not only from one word to the next, but from one character in the word to the next.

Amazingly, Word doesn't have a word entity. As an example, you can define the language for any sequence of characters – not just for words. Thus you may write this word

    ChateauOverflow

and have Chateau checked for French spelling and Overflow for English spelling. The language is an attribute of the character, not of a paragraph or a word.

Fig 16.8 Example: text processor

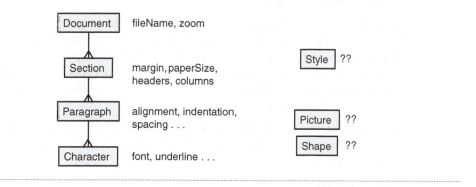

Setting attributes. You can set all of these attributes through icons (e.g. Bold) or menus (e.g. Format or Insert → Break). Usually the writer doesn't set these attributes explicitly for each character and each paragraph. This is because Word sets them automatically in most cases, for instance in these ways:

1 When you type a character, it automatically gets the same attributes as the previous character – same font, size, language, etc.

2 You explicitly select a *style* (a template) for the paragraph. It contains a collection of attributes that as default apply to the paragraph and its characters.

3 When you press Enter, Word creates a new paragraph with the same paragraph attributes as the previous paragraph. (The previous paragraph may however specify that the next paragraph must use a different style. Headings, for instance, do this.)

4 Word tries to guess that here the user seems to type a heading, a numbered list, etc. Then Word sets the style accordingly. Fortunately, you can switch this *AutoFormat* feature off, because Word too often makes a wrong guess, and it is very cumbersome to convince Word that it was wrong.

Is your document in a database? Just to make sure: Word works according to the data model on the figure, but it is *not* implemented with a relational database. It would be thousands of times slower. Your document is stored in a file with a special format, and when you open the document, Word keeps it in working memory, which is why you have to save it before closing the computer.

Investigate Word objects. Figure 16.8 also shows some other entities that are part of Word, for instance *Style* and *Picture* (which is a special kind of *Shape object*). We mentioned *Style* briefly above, but it is a complex concept because some styles are common for all documents, others belong to just this document. We leave it to you to map the attributes of *Style* and *Picture*, as well as their connectors to the other entities in Word. To do this, you have to experiment with Word. Ideally, you should just look up the concept in the on-line help, but it is usually hard to get adequate information about the objects that way.

Actually, all the Word objects are available through the programming language Visual Basic. This means that you can write a program that reads and sets any attribute of your document, paragraph, etc. So one way to get a description of a Word object is through the Visual Basic documentation. (In order to try out the following, you may need to run the Microsoft Office installation program and add the *Visual Basic Help* option.)

Try to find information about the paragraph object. First you must find the way to the Visual Basic documentation. Unfortunately, the procedure varies from one version to another.

From Word 2003 do this:

Help → Microsoft Office Word Help → Table of Contents →
Microsoft Word Visual Basic Reference

From Word 2000 do this:

Help → Microsoft Word Help → Contents →
Programming Information →
Microsoft Word Visual Basic Reference

From Word 97 do this:

Help → Contents and Index → Contents →
Microsoft Word Visual Basic Reference → Visual Basic Reference →
Microsoft Word Visual Basic Reference (yes! once more)

Now you are in the help system for the part of Visual Basic that deals with Word. Look under *Objects* →*P* to find the description of the paragraph object. You now see what is supposed to be an overview of the paragraph object. Judge for yourself.

To get more details, click 'Properties'. Now you get an alphabetical list of all the paragraph attributes (called properties in Visual Basic). Select for instance 'FirstLineIndent' and see the description. Judge for yourself.

Try finding information about the word concept. There is no word object, but a *Words collection object*. It has a more useful documentation than the paragraph object, and shows that although there is no word entity with attributes of its own, you can let your program address individual words.

Fortunately, there is better information about style, picture and shape objects, but it is still hard to learn the system that way.

There are huge problems with this kind of on-line documentation. One of them is that you get no overview. You get tiny pieces of information and have to combine them in your head. It is like trying to read a map through a soda straw. And you are even in completely foreign territory!

16.9 Hierarchies and trees

Figure 16.9 shows a typical organizational hierarchy with the headquarter at the top (D1) and three departments below (D1.1, D1.2 and D1.3). Some of them may be divided into sub-departments. For large organizations, there may be many more levels in the hierarchy. In computer science we call such structures *trees* – means just the same. We find tree structures in a lot of connections, for instance in library classification schemes and in file directories in a computer.

How can we model this company hierarchy? One way is to use three classes – the headquarters (usually with only one object), the departments and the sub-departments. They connect nicely with 1:m connectors as shown on the figure. In the list of attributes, we have shown some of the attributes in parentheses – those that are needed only in a relational database. When the organization grows, we may have to add more levels. Can you feel something is wrong here? We shouldn't have to change the model just because the organization grows. And somehow all these levels are just the same.

Now the organization decides to model their projects too. They also decide that any project must belong to one organizational unit. Some projects belong to the headquarters, some to the departments and some to the sub-departments. How would we model this? Figure 16.9 shows one way. We have one project class with the attributes *projID* and *name* (plus many others). It has three m:1 connectors to headquarters, departments and sub-departments because it potentially may belong to either of them – and it most likely will have to shift from one level to another as time passes. However, at any time only one of these connectors has the actual connection. If we have to make a relational database for the model, the projects would also need three foreign keys, one for each level in the hierarchy (shown in parenthesis). Two of these foreign keys must be nil, because the project belongs to only one level in the hierarchy.

Can you see how the mess grows? When the organization adds another level in the hierarchy, they also have to add another project attribute. And they have to change all their reporting programs, data entry programs and so on. I have actually seen some large organizations that modelled their data this way. The IT department was busy all the time fixing the mess, and users were frustrated because they didn't understand all the rules and reports.

The solution is to have only one organizational class – let us call it *Department*. It contains headquarters, departments and so on. (Headquarters may be a bit upset about now being a 'department', but that is another issue.) Any department may have other departments below it. We can simply model this as a 1:m connector from *Department* to *Department* (Figure 16.9, bottom). When we read this crow's foot from the 1-end, it means *has other departments*. When we read it from the m-end, it means *belongs to one department*.

Fig 16.9 Hierarchies

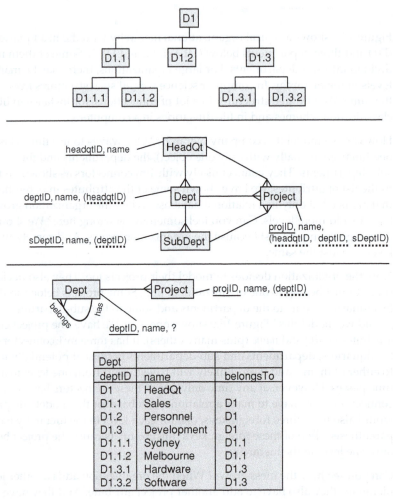

The figure also shows a relational table for this model. We use the general rule that an m:1 relationship is represented as a foreign key pointing from the m-end to the 1-end. In our case it is natural to call the foreign key *belongsTo*. Note that all departments belong to another department, except for headquarters – the top-level department.

It is now trivial to deal with the projects. Each project belongs to just one department, and each department may have many projects. We need a project table, but we don't have to modify anything in the department table.

16.10 Network model: road map

Could we model a geographical map as a data model? Yes, but the model depends on what we want to use the map for.

Finding shortest car routes

Let us first assume that we want to use the model for finding the shortest driving route from one place to another. Figure 16.10 shows an example – a bit of a road map for Melbourne. The map is in a modern style that gives you a lot of overview and a lot of details. Roads are shown as lines of varying thickness according to the size of the road (different colours in the original). Roads with square dots such as Swan Street have trams, which slow down the car traffic.

You can see roundabouts as small circles and one-way streets marked with an arrow besides the road. Notice that there are dead-end streets. You can also see parks, a railroad with two sausage-shaped stations, and the river with bends. Notice that where Swan Street crosses the river, the bridge also crosses a road running along the river bank. If you tried to turn from Swan Street to this road, you would drop down nine metres.

We want to capture only some of these data – those that relate to car driving. We don't need to model rivers, parks and railroads. Which entities do we deal with? The first suggestion could be roads, for instance Swan Street. How do we keep track of the connection between roads? We might make an m:m relationship between the road class and itself as shown in Figure 16.10. This connector would tell us that we, from Swan Street, can get to several other roads. We could resolve the relationship with a connection class in the usual way. However, Swan Street is a very long road, and we would have no information on where it crosses the other roads.

A better suggestion is to divide all roads into road *sections*, where a section goes from one junction to the next. Since Swan street crosses many other roads, it would be divided into many sections. (Most of these crossings happen to be T-junctions.) In the data model, we keep track of the junctions in the class *Point*. A point may be a junction for three, four or even more sections, but it can also represent the end of a dead-end road, or a point in the middle of a straight road where the road happens to change name.

Try to put crow's feet between the three classes in the figure. Hint: It is somewhat similar to the flight routes.

How would you deal with the situation where Swan Street crosses another road on a bridge? Where would you put these attributes?

1 The road name?

2 The length of the road?

3 The geographical coordinates (latitude and longitude)?

4 One-way street – and which direction?

5 Bikes only? Pedestrians only?

6 Street numbers (odd numbers in one side of the street, even at the other)?

Does this give us sufficient information for finding the shortest route (in kilometres or in miles) for a car? And for a bike? Notice that we are not talking about the program needed to compute the result – for a large road map we need an expert programmer to make a sufficiently fast program. We only talk about whether the program has the necessary data in the model.

What further information do we need to find the fastest route for a car (shortest time, not shortest length)? Finish the model on your own before you see the solution in section 16.15.

Drawing the map

By means of the data in the model, we could draw a primitive map. First we mark all the points on the map according to their geographical coordinates in the model. Then we could show each road section as a straight line between its end-points. However, we couldn't draw curves and bends, nor could we show the width of the road.

It would be easy to add information about the width of the road. It is just one more attribute for *Section*. We could deal with the bends by dividing the bending section into tiny sections that could be shown as short lines, but it takes too much space and computation time.

Another solution is to divide roads into sections that are either straight or circles. For a circular section we just need the end-points and the radius. Road engineers plan roads much this way. However, they work with three shapes of the sections: straight, circle and clotoid. The clotoid is a curve that gradually curves more and more. It can thus fit to a line in one end, and to a circle in the other end. In the model we just need to store the end-points, the start radius and the end radius.

Fig 16.10 Network model: road map

Copyright Melway Publishing Pty Ltd. Reproduced from Melway Edition 31 with permission

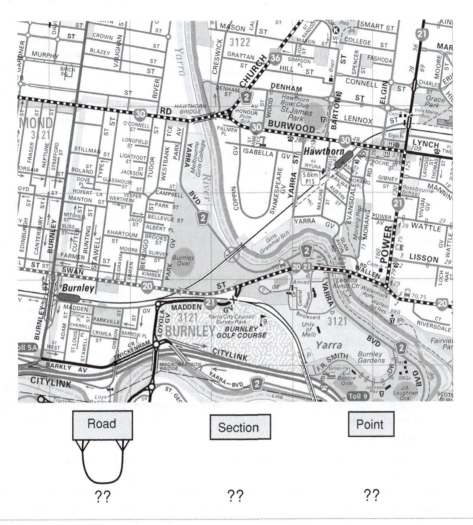

Road	Section	Point

??   ??   ??

16.11 Subclasses

Sometimes a group of entities are similar in many ways, yet different in other ways. As an example some hotel guests are private persons, others travel for companies with special discounts and pay rules. How do we model this – one class for all guests or one class for private guests, another for companies? In object-oriented modelling, this is a big issue and analysts use the concepts of classes and subclasses plus special notation to address it. But in E/R modelling it seems less important and there is hardly a standard notation for it. Furthermore, relational databases don't support subclassing directly.

We will illustrate the issue with an Internet broker for second-hand cars. He helps sellers and buyers find each other, and both private car sellers and professional car dealers can announce their cars on his Web site. They pay a fee for this. The car dealers have a special subscription and get various services that private sellers don't, for instance price statistics. At present the buyers don't pay anything, but in the future – when everybody is craving to buy from the site – they may do so.

Figure 16.11 shows the broker's data model. Each car is announced on the Internet with an advertisement. The advertisement has attributes about the period of dates where the ad is on the Web (the seller pays according to the number of days), information about the car (make, age, etc.), the desired price and a free text (for praising the car).

Attributes in boxes. We have shown the attributes in another way than those of the previous models. In the new notation, the attributes are listed inside the class box. This is the typical way they are shown in object-oriented modelling. Unfortunately, this notation uses much more space and for this reason gives a poor overview of complex models.

The advertisements are announced by a customer, and each customer may of course announce several ads, so we have a 1:m connector. In principle, the system can also keep track of who clicks on each advertisement – at least if the user is logged on as a customer. This would be an m:m connector, however. (Keeping track of this relationship could be useful, but we will not discuss it here.)

Subclass diagram

Now comes the interesting point. There are two kinds of customers, private and dealers. The figure shows how we can model this using a notation borrowed from object-oriented modelling. The triangle-branch shows that *Private* is a subclass of *Customer*. *Dealer* is another subclass. For all customers, the system records their customer ID and two phone numbers as shown in the *Guest* class. For private sellers

Fig 16.11 Subclasses: internet car broker

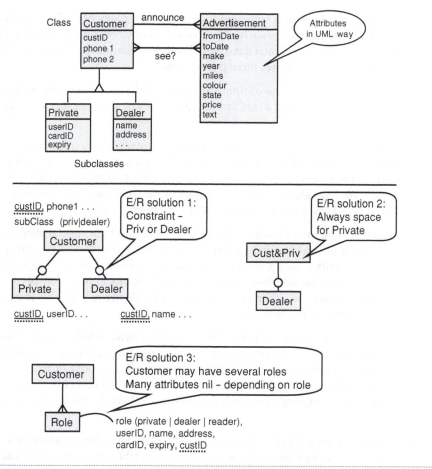

Subclasses

the system also records a userID (for logging on), the pay card number, the expiration month and a few other attributes. For a dealer, the system records his name and address plus several other attributes.

What does this mean? First of all, a customer must be either a private customer or a dealer. He cannot be both at the same time, and in most systems he cannot change subclass once he has been created. Second, a dealer has the common attributes found in Customer plus the special attributes found in Dealer. If you think of this in terms of records, a customer has only one record, but the private record is not the same length as the dealer record. This is one reason relational databases don't deal with subclasses – all records in a class must have the same length in the relational database.

Subclasses in relational databases

The subclass diagram is sufficient if we want to implement the data model in an object-oriented language such as Java or C++. However, what do we do if we want to implement it as a relational database? There is no standard solution, but the bottom part of Figure 16.11 shows three possibilities.

In solution 1 we have the common attributes in the Customer table with custID as the key. We have added a *subClass* attribute to show whether it is a private customer or a dealer.

All the private customers have a table of their own with their special attributes. This table also has a custID attribute, which we may use as a key or as a foreign key that refers to the main Customer table. There is a 1:1 connector between *Customer* and *Private*. We have shown a zero at one end of the connector. It means that a customer record may have a *Private* record, but it need not have one.

All the dealers have a similar table of their own with their special attributes. For each customer there is either a record in *Private* or a record in *Dealer*. We can address each table with custID, thus getting from Customer to Private or vice versa. This solution is very close to the subclass diagram, but the E/R model does not specify that each customer must have either a Private record or a Dealer record. This is a constraint that the program has to ensure.

Solution 2 is quite similar, but we have put the Private attributes into Customer (Cust&Priv). In case the customer is a dealer, we don't use these Private attributes. The solution is more efficient in practice because the majority of accesses are about private customers, and for them we can do with one table access. Furthermore, the space wasted in Cust&Priv is minimal because relatively few records are about dealers.

Solution 3 is more flexible than the other two. We have the common attributes in Customer, but we have combined the other two tables into one – *Role*. Each Role record has all the attributes we find for Private as well as Dealer. It is a matter of proper programming to use the right attributes for the right subClass. This solution allocates space in a very pessimistic way, thus wasting a lot.

Why is solution 3 more flexible? Because the ideal of two subclasses is often too simple. We might for instance have a customer that acts as a private customer as well as a dealer. We can just give him two Role records – one for each of his roles. Or we may have a dealer with several offices and several addresses. We just give him a Role record for each office. Or we may have a customer that in some ways is like a private customer (paying with credit card, for instance) and in other ways is like a dealer (having access to price statistics). We give him just one role and fill in the necessary fields. This last case corresponds to what object-oriented design calls *multiple inheritance* – the customer inherits properties from private customer as well as dealer.

Subclassing in practice

While subclassing is important in object-oriented programming, it is a source of many errors in data modelling. This is not because the E/R notation cannot express subclassing. It is because the real world rarely has clear subclasses. Objects often belong to several subclasses at the same time, or they change subclass every now and then. Even when we believe we have a clear case – for instance the car dealer model – it turns out that the real world has all kinds of mixtures between the subclasses. Here is some advice for apparent subclasses in E/R models:

▪ Don't use subclassing unless very important.

▪ Consider a role pattern instead. It allows a single object to have many roles in relation to other objects. It also allows the object to change roles dynamically. A role corresponds to a subclass, but is more flexible.

▪ Use optional values (null values) to deal with variants. In relational models, all fields of the primary key must be non-null. Other fields may be null.

16.12 Various notations

In the preceding section, we showed a 'modern' notation for the attributes. In this section we will look at alternative notations for the connectors – the crow's feet.

Cardinality

A connector has a *cardinality*, i.e. whether it connects one A record to many B records, or one B record to many A records. Often it is useful to be more specific about the cardinality of a relationship. Does a guest always have at least one stay, or are zero stays allowed? Does a RoomState always relate to one stay or can it be stay-less? Figure 16.12A shows how this can be expressed by means of crow's feet. We use stylized zeroes and ones (circle and bar) at the ends of the connector to show whether it may be zero at that end or always more than zero.

Without a circle or bar, we haven't considered whether zero is possible or not. This is how we have made models in the previous sections.

The first three relationships in the figure are variations of the 1:m relationship. In the second of these, we have labelled the relationship. If we read from A to B, we want this relationship to mean 'owns' (*A owns B*). If we read the other way, the meaning should be 'belongs to' (*B belongs to A*). We used such labels for the organizational hierarchy (Figure 16.9). Sometimes one name suffices, for instance for the flight routes (Figure 16.7).

The fourth relationship is a 1:1 variant. Each B has zero or one A. Each A has a B, but we don't know whether it may have zero B's.

The last relationship is an m:m variant. Each A has one or more B's, and each B has zero or more A's.

Referential integrity

It is often important to ensure that a foreign key in the relational database points to something. In the two top connectors in Figure 16.12A we have *referential integrity*, meaning that each B always refers to an A. The consequence is that we cannot create a B until we have created an A. Opposite, we cannot remove an A until we have removed all Bs that connect to it.

Some database systems (for instance Microsoft Access) can automatically ensure referential integrity and if necessary delete all the connected Bs when we delete an A.

Object-oriented development uses the term *aggregation* of A and several Bs. A is the whole and B the parts. This roughly corresponds to referential integrity – the parts cannot exist without the whole. In the hotel system, a stay must always have a guest. This corresponds to referential integrity between guest and stay – or an aggregation of the guest and his stays.

Fig 16.12 A Notational variations

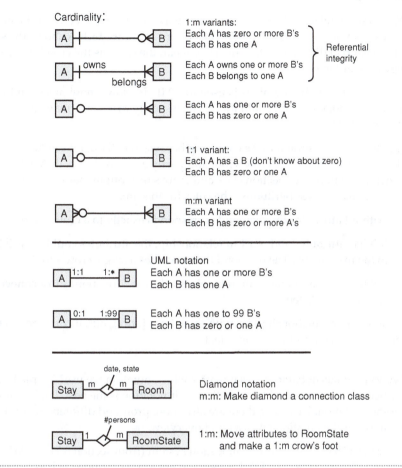

Cardinality:

1:m variants:
Each A has zero or more B's
Each B has one A

Each A owns one or more B's
Each B belongs to one A

Referential integrity

Each A has one or more B's
Each B has zero or one A

1:1 variant:
Each A has a B (don't know about zero)
Each B has zero or one A

m:m variant
Each A has one or more B's
Each B has zero or more A's

UML notation
Each A has one or more B's
Each B has one A

Each A has one to 99 B's
Each B has zero or one A

Diamond notation
m:m: Make diamond a connection class

1:m: Move attributes to RoomState
and make a 1:m crow's foot

When to be precise?

Should we always specify the detailed cardinality, for instance whether zero connections are allowed? As a general rule it is not important for designing user interfaces. Don't waste mental energy on these details. It easily sidetracks you into unimportant special cases.

However, there *are* cases where a precise cardinality helps us understand the model. As an example, when we have a 1:1 connector, there is usually something strange going on. Why do we need two classes connected one-to-one? Couldn't we just combine them into one by putting all the attributes into one of the classes? Very often this is the case. If not, it is usually because they are not always linked one-to-one. There may be a zero in one end. We saw an example of this for the car broker system in the previous section.

Other notations

We can show relationships in many other ways than crow's feet, and the notation varies from one school to another. The bottom of Figure 16.12A shows the same 1:m relationship in different notations. They mean the same as the crow's feet, although they look different.

The notation with the numbers is used in UML. It allows more precision than the crow's feet notation. You could for instance specify that a stay may have a maximum of 99 room states.

The diamond notation may be confusing because the diamond can have attributes. Thus it serves partly as a crow's foot and partly as a box. It can always be transformed into a connection class and crow's feet, but in many cases the connection class is superfluous. The rules for this are:

- Without attributes the diamond corresponds exactly to a crow's foot.

- If it has attributes and is a 1:m relationship, the attributes could as well be added to the m-side box. The diamond then becomes a single crow's foot.

- If it has attributes and is an m:m relationship, it corresponds to a connection class and two crow's feet.

If it is a ternary relationship, i.e. with three lines jutting out, it corresponds to a connection class and three crow's feet.

Overview versus notation. Does it matter which notation we use? People having learned one notation tend to claim that their notation is the best. It takes time to learn another notation. However, there are also more profound differences, for instance to what extent the notation gives a good overview.

Figure 16.12B shows the room allocation system (from section 3.7) in UML notation and in E/R. Try to use the UML version to answer a question such as *How many Request hours belong to a Class activity? One or many?* Even seasoned UML modellers have a hard time here. Try to answer the same question using the E/R version. The answer is obvious. The reason E/R works so much better is that it mobilizes our automatic recognition of patterns, while E/R puts heavy demands on our controlled (focused) attention (see also section 3.6.1). It is a pity that the UML notation has become the prevailing standard rather than the much older E/R notation with the good overview.

Fig 16.12 B Room allocation system in UML and E/R

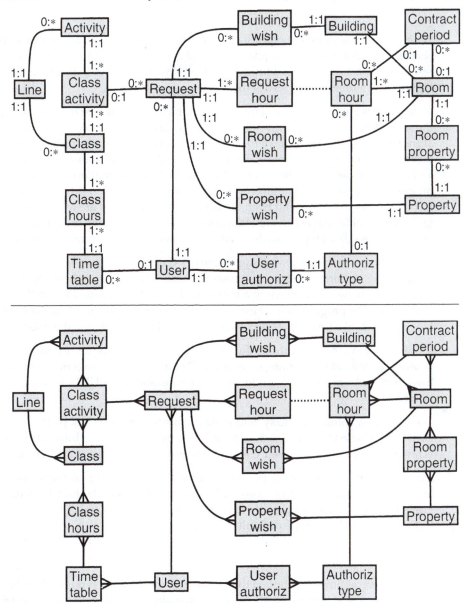

16.13 Ways to implement data models

We have a couple of times emphasized that a data model can be implemented in several ways, for instance as a relational database stored on disk or as objects residing in main memory and linked together. When should you do what? Figure 16.13 summarizes a few of the many possibilities.

A database is good if you have large data volumes that cannot be in main memory at the same time. It is also an easy solution if many users need to access the same data at the same time, or if data have to survive computer or network crashes. Large business applications are typical examples. The data volume is almost unlimited, and even a simple PC can hold around 10 Gb (10 thousand million characters). The program needs around 10 milliseconds (one hundredth of a second) to access a record, because it has to get it from the disk. Newer databases are relational and use foreign keys, older databases are often network databases, which use pointers instead of foreign keys. Both types can deal with computer crashes and multiple users.

Data structures in the programming languages C or C++ are good if we have complex calculations or require fast response time. The data must however be able to fit into main memory, meaning a volume below 100 Mb (around 100 million characters). The program can access the data in a record in around 1 microsecond (one millionth of a second). This is 10,000 times as fast as a relational database.

C or C++ are also good solutions if we need complex graphics, for instance to show geographical maps, things moving, 3-D stuff, etc. Such programs are however hard to move from one platform to another, for instance from UNIX to Microsoft Windows.

Java is an easy solution if the system must be able to run on several platforms, be easy to distribute to lots of users, or be able to cooperate with the Internet. The speed is not quite as high as for C and C++, and the graphics capabilities are very limited.

One thing that software developers spend much time on is to break the limits, for instance make complex calculations on huge data volumes and with advanced graphics. For such applications there is a need to combine several of the technologies, which is quite difficult.

Keys?

We have several times mentioned that in the E/R model there is no need for keys unless they exist as natural attributes in the domain, for instance the room number that is written on the hotel door. When we implement the data model, we may need additional keys, however. Figure 16.13 summarizes when keys are needed:

Invariant ID. We can use an artificial key as an invariant identification. In many cases we may for instance use a person's name as identification, but people

Fig 16.13 Implementing data models

Large data volumes	Database, e.g. relational
Persistency, crash survival	Database, e.g. relational
Complex calculations	C, C++
Fast response	C, C++
Complex graphics	C, C++
Platform-independent	Java or .NET
Access on the Internet	Java or .NET plus database

Ambitious systems:
Large data volumes, fast response, platform-independent, etc. Solution?

Keys – when?
  Ensure uniqueness
  Invariant identification
  Reference for foreign keys – relational database only

change names, and then it becomes hard to keep track of the person's history. A civil registration number or a customer number is the solution here. This issue has nothing to do with whether we use relational databases or not.

Uniqueness. We can use a key to make sure that something occurs only once. We had an example in the hotel system where roomID+date had to be unique for RoomState. If two room states had the same roomID+date, it would mean two guests booked into the same room the same date. In relational databases, all records in a table must be unique, and a key is one way to ensure this.

Target for a foreign key. In a relational database, a 1:m connector must be implemented with a foreign key in the m-side table. The foreign key points to a record in the 1-side table. For this reason, the 1-side table needs a key, and if it hasn't a natural one, we must make an artificial one.

How do programmers handle 1:m connectors if they don't use foreign keys? The programming languages have many other ways. One is to use pointers where the m-side record contains the memory address of the 1-side record. Another is to use arrays of records. The program can address the records by means of their sequential number in the array (their *index*). Arrays are however not suited for adding or deleting arbitrary records.

Finally, some platforms offer a special *container object*, which allows the program to put other objects into the container, retrieve them in many ways and delete them. In this way the container object serves as a 1:m connector.

Older databases are often network databases. Here the records are linked together on the disk in much the same way as objects are linked together in an object-oriented program. Network databases don't need foreign keys.

16.14 Normalization

In the preceding sections we have intuitively come up with the 'right' data model, but how do we know that a data model is good? Normalization is one way to check that a data model is sound, and if it is not, transform it to a better model. Normalization is usually considered a specialist's subject, something very difficult and mathematical. Knowing a bit about normalization is good, however. It helps you model the world – and it helps you communicate with the technical people. In this section we have hidden the math.

There are several purposes of normalization:

- Avoid redundancy, meaning avoiding that data is stored in more than one place.

- Find the 'true' objects, meaning breaking down composite objects into the smallest meaningful objects.

- Ensuring fixed-length records. This is primarily of interest for relational databases, but is a side effect of the normalization.

As an example, assume that we in the hotel system had put the guest's name and address in the stay class. For guests with several stays, this would mean that we stored the name and address in many places. There would be redundancy in the data, and we would have trouble changing the name or address of the guest. We would have to correct it in all his stay records. We might also say that the guest and his stays from a logical point of view are two different things.

Database specialists talk about five normal forms, but we will only look at the first three of them. The normal forms deal only with the internal logical structure of the data model. They cannot say anything about whether the model correctly reflects the real world.

The example

Figure 16.14A shows the example we will work with. It is about a company where the personnel department keeps track of the courses that employees have taken. At present they have a primitive database with one table and one record per employee. The key in this table is *empID*. The table has a long text field called *courses*, and the personnel staff simply write the courses here. The table also records the name and department of the employee. This is the database we want to normalize. We will end up splitting the table into four tables that represent the 'true' objects in this area.

First normal form

We can see immediately that something is wrong: the course field is arbitrarily long, and soon we may have a situation where some employee records have no space for all their courses. The first normal form talks about this.

First normal form: *For each primary key, there must be a fixed number of fields of a fixed length.*

Cure: *Move the variable-length stuff to a separate table.*

The present table suffers from having a field without fixed length. The first attempt to cure the problem was to give each employee a record for each course he has taken. This is shown in the second table of Figure 16.14A. We have added an artificial key for the courses. Now all the fields have fixed length, but we have violated the other rule of the first normal form: An employee has a variable number of records and fields. As an example, Bunting had two courses and now two records, and he might get many more. We also see that empID is not really a key, since it is not unique anymore.

The final cured version is shown at the bottom of Figure 16.14A. We have split the database into two tables: One with a record per employee and one with the repeating stuff – a record per course taken. In E/R terms we now have a 1:m relationship between Employee and CourseTaken. The link between the tables is taken care of by the foreign key *empID* in the CoursesTaken table. Notice that empID+courseID can be used as a key (if we assume that an employee takes a course only once).

Second normal form

We will now look closer at the CoursesTaken table. There is some redundancy here because the combination (courseID=2, courseName=Word) is repeated several times (Figure 16.14B). Whenever courseID is 2, courseName will be 'Word'. We call this a functional dependence.

Functional dependence. CourseName is functionally dependent on courseID because if we know courseID, there is only one possible courseName. Another way to say this is that two different course names will have two different courseIDs.

In principle, we might have two courses with the same name. For this reason the functional dependency doesn't go the other way. CourseID doesn't depend on courseName.

The second normal form talks about functional dependence between attributes. It also requires that the model is on first normal form.

Second normal form: *Must be on first normal form. Furthermore, non-key fields must be functionally dependent on the entire key.*

Cure: *Move fields that depend on a partial key to a separate table.*

In the example, the entire key is (empID, courseID), so courseID is a partial key. The course name is functionally dependent on this partial key. The table is thus not on second normal form.

What about the *year* field? Is it also functionally dependent on courseID? No, it depends on the combination (empID, courseID), so it fulfils the second normal form.

Fig 16.14 A Normalization and first normal form

Purpose:
Avoid redundancy (same data several places)
Find the 'true' objects
Ensure 'table format'

First normal form:
For each primary key, there
must be a fixed number of
fields of fixed length

Employee qualifications				
empID	name	deptID	deptName	Courses
100	Thomson	5	Sales	Windows, Word, Access
101	Smith	7	Accounting	Word
102	Bunting	5	Sales	Word, Access

Variable-length
attribute

Employee qualifications						
empID	name	deptID	deptName	courseID	courseName	year
100	Thomson	5	Sales	1	Windows	1996
100	Thomson	5	Sales	2	Word	1996
100	Thomson	5	Sales	3	Access	1997
101	Smith	7	Accounting	2	Word	1996
102	Bunting	5	Sales	2	Word	2000
102	Bunting	5	Sales	3	Access	2001

Fixed-length
attributes

Variable number of
fields for same key

Key repeated   Redundancy   Course list

Cure:
Move variable-length stuff to a separate table

Employees			
empID	name	deptID	deptName
100	Thomson	5	Sales
101	Smith	7	Accounting
102	Bunting	5	Sales

CoursesTaken			
empID	courseID	courseName	year
100	1	Windows	1996
100	2	Word	1996
100	3	Access	1997
101	2	Word	1996
102	2	Word	2000
102	3	Access	2001

Employee ──────────< CourseTaken

According to the rule, we now move the courseName field to a separate table. And we of course need a key to link the two. This key is courseID. The result is a CoursesTaken table with courseID as a foreign key that points to the course in the Courses table. In E/R terms we have created two tables linked with a 1:m connector.

Fig 16.14 B Second normal form

Second normal form:
First normal form+
non-key fields must depend on *entire* key

Cure:
Move fields depending on a partial key to a
separate table

CoursesTaken		
emplD	courseID	year
100	1	1996
100	2	1996
100	3	1997
101	2	1996
102	2	2000
102	3	2001

Doesn't depend on emplID

CoursesTaken			
emplD	courseID	courseName	year
100	1	Windows	1996
100	2	Word	1996
100	3	Access	1997
101	2	Word	1996
102	2	Word	2000
102	3	Access	2001

Courses	
courseID	courseName
1	Windows
2	Word
3	Access

CourseTaken ⊳——————⊣ Course

Third normal form

Now the normal forms are happy with the course-related tables. But let us look at the Employees table again (Figure 16.14C). It too has redundancy. The combination (deptID=5, deptName=Sales) is repeated and would occur many times in the full database. There is a functional dependency between the two, so whenever deptID is 5, deptName will be 'Sales'.

The third normal form talks about this kind of dependency.

Third normal form. *Must be on second normal form. Furthermore, non-key fields must be functionally independent.*

Cure. *Move the dependent fields to a separate table.*

In our case deptName depends on deptID, but deptID is not part of the key. As a result the table is not on the third normal form. We cure the problem by moving (deptID, deptName) to another table and leave a link to it from the Employees table.

Fig 16.14 C Third normal form and final model

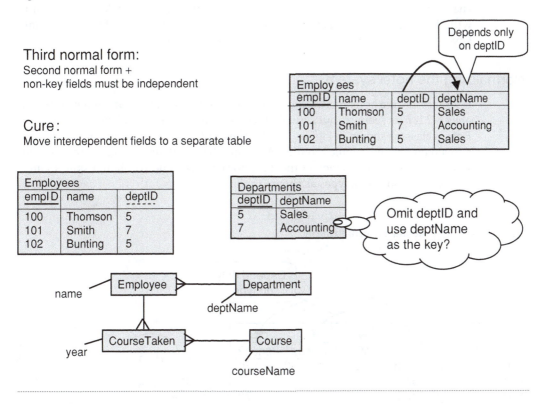

Third normal form:
Second normal form +
non-key fields must be independent

Cure:
Move interdependent fields to a separate table

Depends only on deptID

Employees

emplD	name	deptID	deptName
100	Thomson	5	Sales
101	Smith	7	Accounting
102	Bunting	5	Sales

Employees

emplD	name	deptID
100	Thomson	5
101	Smith	7
102	Bunting	5

Departments

deptID	deptName
5	Sales
7	Accounting

Omit deptID and use deptName as the key?

name — Employee ▷ — Department — deptName

year — CourseTaken ▷ — Course — courseName

Final normal form

In general, we can apply the normalization cures many times and break the tables into simpler and simpler tables, but in our example all the rules are met now. Apart from the foreign keys, each attribute occurs in only one table and all non-key attributes depend on the entire key.

We have shown the final E/R model at the bottom of Figure 16.14C without foreign keys and artificial keys, since they are needed only in the relational model. Now the model looks almost painfully simple. This is a good sign that we have found the true objects. We can look at each of them and say *yes, this is really a basic, simple object*. Only the CoursesTaken class is a bit strange, but it is really a connection class introduced to resolve the m:m connection between Employee and Course.

Invariant keys? Assume that all departments had unique names. Would it then be possible to use deptName as a foreign key from Employee? In principle, yes. We would then have a department table consisting of only the department name. This would not be a good idea, however, since it would be hard to change the name of a department – and departments change name in practice. We would have to create a new department record with the new name, then go through all employees and change their foreign key to the new department name and finally delete the record with the old department name. This is a good example of the need for an invariant key – a key that never needs to be changed (see also section 16.13).

Normalizing the hotel system

If you review the hotel model (Figure 16.3B), would you say we are down at the 'true objects'? It may seem so, but actually there is a functional dependency within the Rooms class, as shown in Figure 16.14D. The attributes price1, price2 and bedCount depend on *type*, not on the roomID. We cannot have different prices for rooms of the same type. This is a violation of the third normal form, and we should split Rooms into Rooms and RoomTypes as shown in the figure.

Fig 16.14 D Hotel system normalization

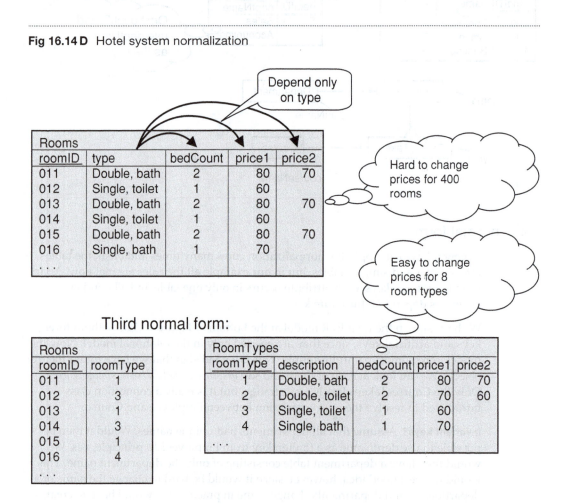

Notice how hard it would be to change room prices for 400 rooms according to the unnormalized model. The user would have to go through the rooms one by one and adjust the prices. In the normalized model, the user would only have to change prices for each of the room types. (Even large hotels have rarely more than six room types.)

If we had structured the address fields more, for instance with separate zip-code fields and city-name fields, there might be functional dependencies here too, because the city-name field depends on the zip code, and not on the guestID.

16.15 Solutions

In this section we present the solutions to the design discussions from the earlier sections.

Cars and owners

Figure 16.15A shows the data model for cars with multiple owners and users. There was an m:m relationship between Car and Person, and we resolved it with the Role class.

Car should be obvious, but notice that we have used *licenceID* as the key. It is a completely natural key – unique and easily visible on the licence plate. Could we have used *chassisID*? At first sight, yes, but it turns out that there exist handmade cars and they have licence plates too, but no chassisID.

The Role class has two attributes, *role* and *primary*. We have not shown the two foreign keys that would be needed in a relational database. The *role* attribute can have the value 'owner' or 'user'. The *primary* attribute is *yes* if the person is the primary owner/user of the car. He will get the certificate and the road tax bill. Only one of the owners/users can be *primary*, but this model cannot specify it. We must write it in the data dictionary.

The Person class is a bit hard because a 'person' can be either a human or a company, and they have different IDs. Strictly speaking, we should consider subclassing (section 16.11), but we have found an easy way out. We have space for both the civID and the compID, but use only one in any given record. The other will be blank or maybe zero. These two fields make up the Person key.

Below the E/R diagram we have shown the relational tables for Cars and Roles. *Cars* should be obvious. *Roles* is more complex since it needs foreign keys to Person. Since Person has a two-field key, we also need a two-field foreign key consisting of civID and compID. One of them will be blank (or zero). The Roles table shows an example where a car has a user and an owner, one of them being a company. It also shows an example where the same person is the user of one car and the owner of another one.

Below the tables, we have shown a slightly different E/R model for cars and owners. We have added a 1:m connector from Person to Car, which shows that each car has one primary person. (Notice that a person can be primary for many cars.) The Role class has now only one attribute – *role* – which may be 'user' or 'owner'. With this model we don't have to write in the data dictionary that there can be only one *primary*.

Flight routes

Figure 16.15B shows the E/R model for the flight routes. City has only a name attribute, which we also use for foreign keys. In the original flight-schedule paper

Fig 16.15 A Solutions, cars and owners

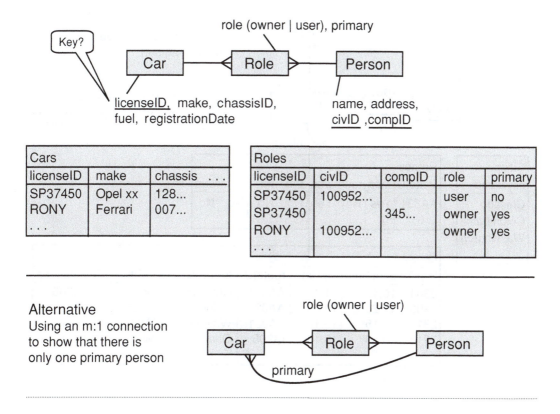

form there was an indication of the days of the week. The rule is that a certain route flies at most once a day of the week. If the airline wants to fly the same legs several times a day, they use separate routeIDs. As a result, we need seven yes/no fields (booleans) in the Route class to show which day of the week the route is operating.

The Leg class has basically just two attributes – deptTime and arrTime. The rest is handled through the connectors. In a relational database we may need an artificial key for the leg, legID. We need a foreign key to the route (routeID) and foreign keys for the From and To relationships (fromCity and toCity). We also need a foreign key for the Next relationship to point to the next leg on the route (nextLeg).

Could we use some existing fields as the key for Leg? Yes, a combination of routeID and fromCity would be unique. A route doesn't land twice in the same city. Then we don't need the legID, but now nextLeg would be two fields, so we don't save anything.

Do we need the Next relationship at all? To find the next leg on the route, we could just look in the database for all legs with the same routeID and sort them according

Fig 16.15 B Solutions, flight routes

Route — routeID, mon, tue, wed, thu, fri, sat, sun

cityName

City — From — Leg — (legID), deptTime, arrTime, (routeID, fromCity, toCity, nextLeg)

To

Next

Cities
cityName
Chicago
Columbus
Washington
. . .

Routes							
routeID	mon	tue	wed	thu	fri	sat	sun
AA331	Yes	No	Yes	No	No	No	No
. . .							

Legs						
legID	deptTime	arrTime	routeID	fromCity	toCity	nextLeg
2304	10:45	11:40	AA331	Chicago	Columbus	2305
2305	12:20	13:30	AA331	Columbus	Washington	2317
2317	14:15	15:10	AA331	Washington	New York	(null)
2318	10:00	19:15	IA905	Orlando	Madrid	(null)
. . .						

to departure time. Works fine except for one little thing: time zones. If we for instance fly the opposite way with American Airlines (route 332), we might actually land in Chicago before we have left Columbus – measured in local time. Chicago is one hour behind Columbus. We can repair this by using Greenwich Mean Time (GMT) for all times in the database, and then deal with the local times through attributes for the cities. A very sensible approach, in fact.

Road map

Figure 16.15C shows the E/R model for the road map. A point has just two attributes, x and y – the longitude and latitude of the point on the globe (or on the map). A road has just a name, but in large maps there are many roads with the same name. So we also need an indication of the township, the state and maybe the country. We would need further classes for these. In the relational model we have used an artificial key *roadID*.

A section has an m:1 connection to the Road it belongs to, and m:1 connections to its start and end point (From and To). The model uses the convention that *up* the road is

Fig 16.15 C Solutions, road map

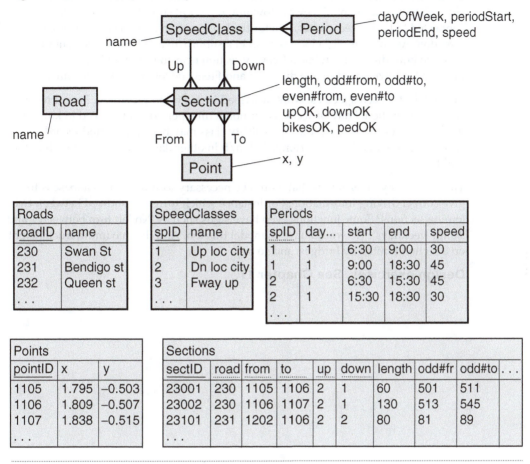

in the direction From–To. The section has many attributes: The length for instance in metres; two intervals of house numbers (odd numbers in the range odd#from – odd#to, and even numbers in the range even#from – even#to); in which directions driving is allowed (upOK and downOK); and whether bikes and pedestrians are allowed (always in both directions if allowed?).

As an example, a freeway section would have upOK and downOK=yes, bikesOK=no and pedOK=no. (Some freeways, for instance in Australia, would have bikesOK=yes.) A bike path in a park would have upOK and downOK=no, bikesOK=yes and pedOK=no.

Travel time may vary with day of the week and time of the day. In theory, each section should have its own records for travel times up and down for the various periods of time. However, in practice, this data would be impossible to get. Instead the model uses a collection of speed classes, for instance 'Up local city', 'Down local city', 'Freeway uptown', 'Freeway downtown', 'Local suburb'. A road section will be connected to two speed classes, one for the Up direction and one for the Down direction. As an example, a local section in a suburb area will have LocalSuburb speed in both directions, while a freeway section near the city will have FreewayUpTown speed in one direction and FreewayDownTown in the other.

The details for each speed class are described in its Period records. A Period record specifies an optional day-of-week, an optional time period, and a speed in km/h for this period. As an example, the UplocalCity class may have one Period record specifying 30 km/h in the morning, 45 km/h in other day times and 55 km/h in the night.

There are many other things that would be necessary to store if the database is to give correct driving information. For instance which turns are allowed between two joining sections? Some junctions even have signs such as 'No left turn between 7 and 9 a.m. weekdays'. We would have to model this too. And the maximum truck height on a section limited by bridges, and so on.

Design exercises. See Chapter 17.

17

Exercises

The exercises below cover all the book chapters, and are arranged with a section for each chapter. In addition there are four design projects, shown as Figures 17.1 to 17.4. Many chapters have exercises that ask you to work out something for one of these design projects, for instance state the usability requirements, design virtual windows, make a prototype, test the prototype for usability. In addition, there are more specialized design exercises for special purposes.

Chapter 1 Exercises: Usability

Exercise 1.1 Usability requirements for an improved system

Choose a Web site that you – or people you know – find a bit hard to use. (It is a good idea to choose a Web site of interest in your local community).

Now imagine that you were asked to redesign the Web site to improve usability. Define measurable usability requirements for the new site. Give a short justification of your choices. (Don't try to redesign it. Just state the usability requirements.)

Exercise 1.2 Carry out a usability test

Choose a Web site (preferably the one you have chosen in exercise 1.1) and carry out a simple usability test of it.

Follow the plan in section 1.4. Be careful when defining the test tasks and choosing the test users. Carry out the test with one user or preferably two.

Your reply should contain:

a) description of the test tasks

b) profile of the test user(s)

c) a list of the problems you found

d) a comment on the adequacy of the usability

Chapter 2 **Exercises:** Prototyping and iterative design

Exercise 2.1 Make a prototype

Design a prototype for work-hour registration (Figure 17.1). Make the prototype as a paper mock-up. Write down a list of the user tasks that the system must support. In addition, use your intuition and sound judgement.

Your reply should contain:

a) list of user tasks

b) the prototype – ready for usability test

Exercise 2.2 Heuristic evaluation of the prototype

Have a colleague who knows about usability, look at the prototype you developed in exercise 2.1. (It may be one of your fellow students on the course). Ask him to find as many usability problems in it as possible. Write a list of them.

Exercise 2.3 Usability test of the prototype

Carry out a usability test of the prototype you developed in exercise 2.1.

a) Plan the test according to section 1.4 (checking with Chapter 13 would be a good idea too).

b) Carry out the test.

c) Write a test report.

d) Compare the problems you found against the heuristic evaluation.

e) Suggest solutions to the *critical* usability problems.

Your reply should contain the plan, the test tasks, the test report, the comparison and the suggested solutions.

Chapter 3 **Exercises:** Data presentation

Exercise 3.1 Gestalts on a Web site

Study the gestalts used on an existing Web site (preferably the one you used in exercise 1.1). Which gestalts are there? Comment on their suitability for the purpose of the site, and on the influence they may have on usability.

Exercise 3.2 Gestalts in the prototype

Study your prototype from exercise 2.1 and identify the gestalts that are clearly visible. To what extent are these gestalts suitable for the user tasks? Could the gestalt laws explain some of the usability problems you detected?

Exercise 3.3 Flight collision

At present, all commercial air traffic takes place on a kind of 'roads' (corridors) that lead from one airport to another. There can be several corridors stacked on top of each other. Before an airplane is allowed to take off, the air traffic controllers have assigned a sequence of corridors to the plane. In many parts of the world, there is so much air traffic that planes have to wait for a long time before they can get a slot all the way to the next stop. However, the advantage of corridor flight is that it is easy for air controllers to check that airplanes don't collide.

To increase the air space capacity, experts discuss whether planes in the future should be allowed to fly in a straight line from the take-off airport to the landing airport. They will be assigned an altitude to use, and the altitude may be reassigned by air traffic controllers on the way. They may also be asked to wait in the airspace for a few minutes (done by turning in a circle).

With the straight-line approach, it becomes essential that flight controllers can see whether some planes are on a colliding course, meaning that they will get too close to each other if they continue in the present direction and altitude. Getting too close might be defined as getting closer than 300 m vertically (1000 ft) and 5 km horizontally within the next 20 minutes. (A typical airplane flies about 300 km in 20 minutes.)

Air traffic controllers see the airplanes as dots on the radar screen with a flight number below, e.g. QA 357. There may be around 100 planes in the area controlled by one traffic control centre. The system behind the whole thing knows the altitude, direction (heading) and speed of each airplane, and in principle it could show these data on the screen. It can also easily compute which planes are currently on colliding courses according to the definition above.

Design a data presentation that gives the air controller a good overview of the situation, particularly of collision risks. He should be able to easily identify the planes that are at risk and see whereabouts the collision might occur.

Exercise 3.4 Project management

This exercise is about designing data presentations that give department managers and project managers in a software house a good overview.

a) Design a data presentation that gives a good overview of projects and all their activities. Particularly, it should be easy to see whether some activity is at risk of using too many work hours. It should also be easy to see whether there are activities where too little work is being done.

b) Design another data presentation that helps management staff projects with people that are free from other duties in the necessary period.

This exercise is part of the larger design project in Figure 17.4, but here the goal is solely to design a good visualization. Read the project description in the figure to get the background.

Chapter 4 **Exercises:** Mental models and interface design

Exercise 4.1 Mental models for e-mail

Find a person who uses e-mail regularly, but is no expert. Find out how he believes his e-mail system works. Where is the e-mail stored, for instance before he receives it, when he has received it, when he has filed it, when he has deleted it? Also find out how he believes the receiver identification works, for instance how his own name for the sender corresponds to the e-mail address, and how the system finds out where the receiver is located. Describe this as a cognitive model.

Now ask an expert about the same (or build on your own knowledge if you are an expert). Describe this as a conceptual model and compare the conceptual and the cognitive model.

Variant. If you are several students working in a group, each of you may try to describe your own mental model of e-mail. Then compare and describe the differences.

Exercise 4.2 Mental models for Microsoft Word styles

Microsoft Word has a concept called *styles*. You can choose a style from a combo box (top left of the screen). The result is that the selected text is formatted according to the style you selected. There are predefined styles, for instance for a heading on level 1, a heading on level 2, a TOC 1 (Table Of Content on level 1) and so on.

The user can change the format for a style, for instance defining that level 1 headings shall be size 14 point and bold. How does this influence the headings the user has made already? And what happens when the user changes the format of one of the headings he has made, without touching the other headings?

Make a precise model of this, if necessary by experimenting with Word. Next find a Word user who has some knowledge of Word and has tried to use styles, without being an expert. Describe his mental model of how the styles work. Compare it with your own model.

Exercise 4.3 Analyse your prototype

Analyse the prototype you made in exercise 2.1 for the work-hour registration. What persistent data and dialogue data does it use? What functions does it have?

Now outline a work-hour registration system that is extremely database oriented, and one that is completely step-by-step driven. Discuss where your design was positioned relative to the two extremes.

Chapter 5 Exercises: Analysis, visions and domain description

Exercise 5.1 Design project, domain analysis

In this exercise and exercises in the next chapters, you will systematically design the user interface for a new system. The size and complexity corresponds roughly to the hotel system.

Choose one of these projects:

- Circulation of periodicals (Figure 17.2)
- Photocopier (Figure 17.3)
- Activity monitoring (17.4)

If in doubt, we recommend *Circulation of periodicals* (Figure 17.2).

In this exercise we ask you to make the following for your chosen design project:

a) A data model

b) Task descriptions (for complex tasks), an annotated task list for simple tasks

c) Usability requirements

In real life, you would have to study the domain, interview users, etc. It is great if you can do this in your design project. However, you may assume that the author has done it already and has written down his observations in the project description. Your role is to structure these observations, but also to use your logic and intuition to complete the descriptions.

Chapter 6 Exercises: virtual windows design

Exercise 6.1 Design project, virtual windows

In this exercise we ask you to make the following for your chosen design project:

a) Virtual windows, the plan version, including any search windows

b) Virtual windows, graphical version

c) Tasks with data

d) CREDO check

e) Understandability test

f) A list of design defects that you found during the process, with an indication of how you found each of them.

Exercise 6.2 Improve hotel system

The project manager for the hotel system comes rushing in and tells you that an understandability test has revealed that the developers completely misunderstood what the hotel system should do. In most hotels you don't book a specific room number, but a room *type*, for instance a *double with bath* or a *single with toilet*. Only when the guest arrives does the receptionist allocate a specific room, for instance room 12.

The reason for this business procedure is that otherwise you may end up in a situation where there is space for a new guest, but if he stays for more than a single day, he has to change room during the stay. Here is an example.

Room	18/8	19/8	20/8	21/8
11 double	O	O	B	B
12 double	O	O		
13 double			B	B

Assume that all other rooms are fully occupied. If a new guest (G) arrives on the 19/8, we may allocate him to room 13, but if he wants to stay more than one night he needs to move from room 13 to room 12 on the 20/8. If we hadn't allocated room 13 to another guest (H), who arrives on 20/8, we could have let guest G stay in room 13 and checked guest H into room 12 when he arrives.

A related point is that hotels often overbook. They promise more rooms than they have, because usually some guests don't turn up. In case of overbooking the room cannot be allocated at booking time, but the hotel keeps track of the number of booked rooms per room type per day.

The project manager wants a proposal for an improved data model and virtual windows that can handle this. He also wants to see how it relates to the tasks.

Exercise 6.3 Seasonal prices

In the hotel system there are more room prices than those shown in the virtual windows. The two shown are the normal price at this time of the year, and a discount price for double rooms used as a single. In addition, there may be up to three sets of seasonal prices: high, medium and low. The hotel manager can decide in which periods the prices are high, medium and low.

Change the virtual windows to deal with this, particularly so that it is easy to overview when a customer is on the phone.

Exercise 6.4 Search screens

The Yellow Page company in country X needs a redesign of their search screens. Customers complain that they cannot find the kind of shops they look for, and if they find some, they are too far away from where they live. Often people cannot spell properly. Sometimes they remember a special shop by its place in town, but cannot remember the name. Make a systematic analysis of the search problem, select suitable search techniques and design the search screens.

Chapter 7 Exercises: Function design

Exercise 7.1 Design project, function design

In this exercise we ask you to make the following for your chosen design project:

a) Semantic and search functions for each virtual window

b) Mini-specs for the three hardest functions

c) Task with Actions and Feedback for the most complex task

d) State diagrams for the dialogue with an indication of the navigation functions

e) The function syntax with a brief justification

f) A plan for dealing with Undo

Exercise 7.2 Follow the state transitions

To improve your understanding of state diagrams, write down the state transitions for these hotel tasks:

a) A guest phones to book a room. He is a regular guest. The receptionist knows that there are lots of rooms available.

b) A guest phones to change his booking so that he gets two rooms rather than one.

c) While the receptionist enters the breakfast list, a guest arrives to check in.

First look at the state diagram for the single-page platform (Figure 7.5B). Follow it when the user carries out the task. The following table records the first steps of task (a). Complete the table for the rest of this task and tasks (b) and (c).

Subtask	Function	New state
Start-up		pSearch
Find guest	Enter name . . .	(same)
	FindGuest	(same)
	NewStay	pStay(new)
Find room	Enter period . . .	(same)
	FindRooms	(same)
	SelectRooms	(same)
	Book	pStay(rec)
Confirm	. . .	

Next do the same for the multi-page platform (Figure 7.6B). In this case you need a state for each of the windows and the diagram will look like this:

Subtask	Function	vwFind Guest	vwStay	vwRooms	vwBreakfast
Start-up		Open	(none)	Open	(closed)
Find guest	Enter name . . .	(same)			
	FindGuest	(same)			
	NewStay	(same)	new		
Find room	Enter period . . .			(same)	

We have written *(same)* when the window reacts to the function but remains in the same state. We have left the cell empty when the window doesn't react.

Exercise 7.3 Add a floor map

The discussion of the hotel system has mentioned the need for a floor map with room occupation. Now assume that we have decided to add it to the system. Outline the virtual windows, and show the corrected lists of semantic and search functions. Finally, show the corrected state diagrams for either the single-page or the multi-page system. Add the necessary navigation functions and suggest a syntax for them.

Exercise 7.4 Error messages

In section 7.9, we discussed some of the error messages that were needed when a user clicked *Checkin* for a new stay. Analyse the possible situations in a systematic way and suggest good error messages. Also analyse the potential errors in other situations where *Checkin* could be used, for instance a booked stay, a stay that is checked in already, a stay that has been cancelled or checked out, and cases where undo is needed. Suggest error messages as needed.

Make an understandability test of some of the error messages with a potential user.

Chapter 8 **Exercises:** Prototypes and defect correction

Exercise 8.1 Design project, finish the prototype

In this exercise we ask you to make the following for your chosen design project:

a) A finished prototype, for instance as a paper mock-up.

b) Heuristic evaluation of it, for instance with another student from the course. List the usability problems he mentions.

c) Make a usability test of the prototype and list the problems found. Comment on the differences from the heuristic evaluation.

d) Try to give an explanation of the usability problems and propose ways to avoid the problems.

Chapter 9 to 11

(There are no exercises for these chapters.)

Chapter 12 **Exercises:** User documentation and support

Exercise 12.1 Design project, user support

In this exercise we ask you to make the following for your chosen design project:

a) Make a support plan for the system.

b) Write sample parts of the documentation or on-line help or whatever you suggest for support.

Exercise 12.2 User documentation for new e-mail system

Chapter 11 describes the design of a new kind of e-mail system. Many of the new features are not intuitive, and users will need documentation and support. Assume that you are in the project team for the e-mail system.

a) Make a support plan for the e-mail system.

b) Write sample parts of the documentation or on-line help or whatever you suggest for support.

Exercise 12.3 User documentation for a development tool

If you have tried to develop a user interface, for instance by means of the free Access booklet www.booksites.net/lauesen, you should have some idea what kind of support you would like.

a) Make an ideal support plan for the development tool.

b) Write sample parts of the documentation or on-line help or whatever you suggest for support.

c) Comment on how this plan could be achieved in practice by the tool supplier.

Chapter 13 to 15

(There are no exercises for these chapters.)

Chapter 16 Exercises: Data modelling

Exercise 16.1 Persons, rooms and phones

Make an E/R data model for how employees, the rooms of the company and the local phone numbers relate to each other. Use your common sense of how these things relate. However, notice some special things that apply in some companies: several persons, for instance staff in the store room, may share a phone number. There are also cases where two rooms share a phone number, so that you may answer the phone in either room. You may assume that each person has only one room number in the database – the room in which his snail-mail will be delivered.

a) Show the model when each person has only one phone number.

b) Next show the model when a person may have many phone numbers where he can be reached.

For each of these questions, show the E/R model without foreign keys or artificial primary keys. Also show the table form with the necessary keys and illustrative examples of data.

Exercise 16.2 Data model for an evening school

Make an E/R model for courses in an evening school. The data to be included are illustrated by this list of participants for a course:

Course: 2305 Greek for beginners		
Teacher: Ted Petrides		**Period: Spring 2004**

Participants:

Civ.reg.no.	Name	Price
100830-0217	Peter Hansen	$42
160950-0128	Susan Ritz	$84
. . .		

a) Show the model when there is no fixed price for participating in the course. Each participant may negotiate his own price depending on his specific situation. Also assume that each course has only one teacher.

b) Modify the model so that there are different groups of participants, for instance normal, students and senior. Participants cannot negotiate a price, but are charged a fixed price according to the group they belong to.

c) Modify the model further so that there are also different groups of courses, for instance short, long and advanced courses. The price for a course now depends on the participant group as well as the course group, for instance according to the table below.

d) Finally, modify the model so that teachers may teach some courses and be participants in other courses. Also allow a course to have more than one teacher.

For each of these questions, show the E/R model without foreign keys or artificial primary keys. For one of the questions, also show the table form with the necessary keys and illustrative examples of data.

Prices	Course type		
Participants	**Short**	**Long**	**Advanced**
Normal	$50	$84	$110
Students	$35	$56	$80
Senior	$25	$42	$60

Exercise 16.3 Data model for a library

A library has books. Some books exist in several versions, for instance

Patrick James: Travelling in Africa, 1996
Patrick James: Travelling in Africa, 2002

There may also be several copies of a book, for instance if a lot of people want to borrow it.

The library has borrowers and it sends out reminders to borrowers who have exceeded the loan period.

The library catalogues list a lot of key words, organized hierarchically. Each book may have several of these keywords. As an example, here is part of the keyword list for an IT research library (using the Computing Reviews classification):

D. Software
. . .
H. Information systems
H.1 Models and principles
H.2 Database management
H.2.1 Logical design

Make a data model that describes these aspects of the library.

a) First assume that we deal only with proper books and that a book has only one volume.

b) Modify the model so that it also covers books in several volumes, periodicals, pieces of art, and music.

c) Write a data dictionary for your model.

Warning: Question (a) is rather straightforward, but there are many ways to model question (b), and libraries do it differently. Librarians even write theses about the concepts involved. If you feel really dedicated, you might interview staff in your local library to find out how they organize things.

Exercise 16.4 Data model for marriages

Make a data model for persons in a country and who is married to whom. The model should reflect that only people of opposite sex can be married (at least in this exercise). Include some sex-related attributes, for instance *done military service* (we assume that only men may do this) and *number of births* (women only – even in these modern days). Use subclassing in this exercise, although we generally advise against it.

a) Assume that we want to record only the present situation.

b) Assume that we also want to keep track of the history, so we can see who was married to whom earlier.

For each of these questions, show the E/R model without foreign keys or artificial primary keys. Also show the table form with the necessary keys and illustrative examples of data.

Exercise 16.5 Time stamps

There is often a need to describe data that varies over time. In the hotel, for instance, the manager may decide that from May 15 to August 31 they use high-season prices, 140 for double rooms and 100 for single rooms. After this period they use the normal prices again.

Show how to extend the hotel data model to cope with this. Explain how the system should find the room price if John Smith books a room for July.

Exercise 16.6 Data model for public transportation

Make a data model that will allow the system to find the fastest public transport from one street address to another in the same city. The model must include data for all streets and data for all bus and train timetables.

Such a database is behind present Web services that allow the public to find the best connection.

Exercise 16.7 Design project, data model

Make a data model for your chosen design project. Show it as an E/R model as well as tables with realistic data.

Exercise 16.8 Data model for Microsoft Word

Section 16.8 outlines a data model for documents in Microsoft Word, but it leaves open how *style*, *picture* and *shape* relate to the rest. Extend the model so that it handles these objects too. Note that it will be necessary to experiment with Word, look into the on-line help, etc., to find out how the objects relate to each other.

Exercise 16.9 Normalization

The following outline of a relational database is far from being normalized. Bring it on third normal form through a series of transformations.

The database describes orders that a company has to deliver. At present there is only one table and it has these attributes:

Order table

1. Order number

2. Order date

3. Delivery form, e.g. by taxi, self–pick-up, postal service, UPS.

4. Customer number

5. Customer name

6. Customer address, e.g. 32 Ringway

7. Zip code (only national addresses)

8. City

9. Item list (a long text field with names of the ordered goods, e.g. 'Box of 10 CDs, Trispect software, Access guidebook')

10. Prices (a long text field with the corresponding prices, e.g. '$3.00, $149.95, $12.30')

11. Number of items (a long text field with the corresponding number of items, e.g. '6, 1, 1')

12. Item group names (a long text field with the group names for the items, e.g. 'stationery, software, books')

Fig 17.1   Design project: work-hour registration

Background

At all entries to the Happy Life insurance company, there are card readers that can read the ID cards for the employees. When an employee swipes his card in the reader, the system checks that he is allowed to pass. If so, it opens the door and records the time he passed. There is a card reader on each side of the door, so the system can record whether the employee arrived or left.

If an employee forgets to use his card, for instance because he passed together with a colleague, the system cannot record anything. If the employee inserts his card several times with in a short time, for instance because he isn't sure that the system recorded him correctly, the system records only one time.

An employee may come and go several times a day, and the system records all arrival and departure times.

Requirements

The personnel department of Happy Life wants a system that can record the work hours of all employees based on the recorded arrival times and departure times. The company wants to introduce flexi time, where employees to a large extent can decide when they want to arrive and leave as long as the weekly total is the required number of hours. If an employee works more hours than required in a week, he may work fewer hours in later weeks. One purpose with the recording is to keep track of this.

The difference between the hours worked and the required hours is called the *flex-status*. All employees are very interested in this status. If they have worked too many hours, they are allowed to take hours off – even single days. If they have worked too few hours, they have to catch up – or they will have troubles with the boss.

The basic idea is that employees do the necessary registration themselves, primarily by means of the card reader, but also manually by means of a PC connected to the internal computer network.

In case an employee has forgotten to use his ID card, he must be able to record his work hours manually. (If he does this too often, his boss may see it in the statistics and want a talk with him.) Many employees also want to check what the system has recorded automatically.

In addition, an employee must be able to manually record special reasons for not being at work: External meetings (for instance with customers), participation in external courses, vacation, leave due to birth, illness. All of these are considered a kind of work hours outside the company premises, and the company wants to keep track of how many hours are spent on each of these things.

It may also happen that employees have leisure activities on the company premises, for instance table tennisor meetings on local community matters. The hours spent on this should be excluded from the automatically recorded work hours, and honest employees will record this manually.

Continued

Fig 17.1 Design project: work-hour registration (*Continued*)

Finally, the employees must be able to see their own flex-status and check that it has been computed correctly.

Although the basic idea is that employees do the recording themselves, there may be situations where this is not possible, for instance in case of prolonged illness or overseas work for a period. For this reason each employee should authorize two other employees to be able to act on his behalf, for instance check his flex-status and record work hours manually.

The system must be used by all employees, including cafeteria staff and guards that have very little IT experience.

Assumptions

There are around 500 employees in Happy Life. They have initials (their abbreviated name) which is also part of their e-mail address, but they don't remember each other's initials. We simplify the project in this way: All employees have a workday of 8 hours (including 30 minutes for lunch) and work five days a week. They may place their work on anyday of the week including Saturdays and Sundays. Nobody will work across midnight. The system knows about holidays, where people are not expected to work.

Your job is to design the user interface seen by the employee. Recording employees, generating statistics, etc., are done by the personnel department, and it is not part of this project.

The system runs under Microsoft Windows. The dialogue starts when the user has been logged on. The system thus knows who the user is, so he will not have to identify himself again. As an alternative, you may design the system for the Web, so that employees can use it from home or when travelling.

Fig 17.2 Design project: circulation of periodicals

The Happy Life insurance company has about 500 employees and subscribes to about 50 periodicals (magazines and journals). The periodicals are circulated in the house and employees can subscribe to the circulation. Few employees subscribe to more than 8 periodicals. Some periodicals have so many readers that the company gets more than one copy.

At present, subscription works in this way: When a periodical arrives to the company, it goes to the library where it is registered. Next, the librarian attaches a list of the subscribers to it, and sends it to the first employee on the list. The internal snail-mail service is used for the physical transport. The employee is supposed to read it within three work days, sign off on the list with name and date, and send it to the next employee on the list. When the last employee on the list has read it, here turns it to the library, where it becomes available for common use.

Continued

Fig 17.2   Design project: circulation of periodicals (*Continued*)

Unfortunately, employees often forget that they have received the periodical and they don't pass it on to the next on the list. There is no way a reader can tell the other readers that he is away for many days, and as a result several periodicals may pile up in his pigeon hole while he is away. When a reader is too busy with other things, there is no way he can pass the periodical on immediately and see it later when other readers have had the chance. After a while nobody knows who is supposed to have the periodical. It is one big mess to keep track of the whole thing, and employees keep accusing each other of being messy, careless, etc. Quite often an employee urgently wants to read an article in one of the periodicals, but not even the librarian knows where it is right now.

It is quite cumbersome for the librarian to enroll and delete people from the circulation, so for this reason it is presently only possible twice a year. Twice a year the library committee also reviews the company's subscriptions in general, and decide which new periodicals to subscribe to and which to cancel. They do this on the basis of cost, number of readers and more subjective information about the importance of the periodical.

The company has an IT department that develops business applications for in-house use. The department suggests to make a computer-supported system that can keep track of the entire periodical circulation. The existing paper lists will disappear, so nothing will be attached to the physical periodical.When an employee has finished reading a copy, he tells the system, and the system tells him where to send the copy with the internal snail-mail system. The next reader has to acknowledge that he has received the copy. The system should of course warn people when they have forgotten to pass the copy on or forgotten to acknowledge that they have received a copy.

The personnel department, where the library belongs, finds it an excellent idea. In particular, they would like to prioritize people on the circulation list according to vacation (people cannot read journals when they are on a three-week vacation) and according to their ability to observe the circulation deadlines (the three work days for passing the journal on).

Assumptions
Employees have initials (their abbreviated name) which are also part of their e-mail address, but they don't remember each other's initials. Each employee has a *mail code* (an internal zip code for their pigeonhole) that tells mail staff where to deliver the snail-mail. The general personnel systems keep track of this, so it is not an issue in the circulation application.

Your job is to design the user interface for the circulation system. Depending on your experience and the time available, you may omit the user interface for the librarian. You may also simplify the system by assuming that there is only one copy of the periodicals.

Assume that the system runs under Microsoft Windows. The dialogue starts when the user has been logged on. The system thus knows who the user is, so he will not have to identify himself again.

Take care with the terminology in this project. We just say 'periodical' but we mean three different things: (1) A specific copy you can hold in your hand, for instance BYTE, February 2002, Happy Life's copy 2; (2) An issue of the periodical, for instance BYTE, February 2002, no matter which copy; (3) The series of issues, for instance BYTE or Scientific American.

Fig 17.3 Design project: photocopier

There are many modern photocopiers that can do a lot of clever things, but few users can figure out how to operate them.

When copying something, these modern wonders first scan the original and stores it on a disk (up to 900 pages). Then they can print copies in several ways, for instance with print on both sides, on different kinds of paper, enarged, or with two original pages per print page, etc. If the user has made a mistake, for instance chosen the wrong paper, there is no need to scan the whole thing in again. The system can also store scans for several people at the same time, limited only by the disk capacity.

Your job is to design the user interface for such a copier, limited only by the existing hardware. This means that you are restricted to the existing display and its resolution, the existing number of scanners and paper trays, etc. You may, however, redesign the physical appearance of the buttons and their labels, but you may not increase the number of buttons.

Select an existing copying machine of this kind and study its hardware. Then design a better user interface. The new design must of course be able to do at least the same kind of things as the existing one.

Fig 17.4 Design project: activity monitoring

The software house OnTimeSoftware develops software on contract, usually at fixed time, fixed price, and with specified functionality and quality. One of the hardest problems is to detect early on that an activity will take longer than expected. If you can detect it early, it is possible to help the developer currently carrying out the activity, for instance by letting a seasoned expert review the work and offer guidance. If you detect the problem late, the activity may have run off the track, be costly to correct, and it will soon hamper many other activities.

Seasoned project managers know that they can get an early warning in this way: The developer responsible for a given activity records every day how many hours he has worked on the activity, and every weekend he gives an estimate of the remaining number of hours. Project management now computes an estimate of the total number of hours for the activity:

total expected = hours spent + hours remaining

In a straightforward activity this figure remains constant from week to week, and when no hours remain, it is finished. If the figure starts increasing, something is wrong, and help is most likely needed. Experience is that the problem in this way can be detected between 60% and 80% into the activity, while it otherwise tends to be detected when more than the total expected time has been used.

Unfortunately, the procedure is cumbersome to manage, and company management wants to support it with an IT system. At the same time they want a better record of the work hours per activity, which many developers at present record many days too late. The recording is at present also used for billing some of the customers, and for collecting experience data of hours used for various sizes of projects.

Continued

Fig 17.4 Design project: activity monitoring (*Continued*)

When staffing a project, department managers and project managers have troubles getting an overview of who will be available in the period where the project is carried out. They expect the system to give them an overview of this too.

Specification

OnTimeSoftware has around 80 developers and around 40 open projects with around 800 planned or running activities. Many projects run for just a few months, but some run for a couple of years. Most developers work on less than 10 activities at a time, but a few may work on more than 20 each week.

Each project consists of a set of activities, usually planned weeks before they start. An activity is primarily carried out by a single developer – responsible for this activity – but sometimes other developers may assist for some hours. OnTimeSoftware has experienced that project management is much harder if more than one person is allocated to an activity. So they take great care dividing projects into activities for a single person. There is also a special 'overhead' project that consists of activities such as vacation, illness, lunch and courses.

Developers must on a daily basis record how much time they have spent on their activities – with an accuracy of half an hour. The system must remind them if they have forgotten. This recording is presently considered annoying, and it is crucial that the system makes it easy. For instance it must be easy to find the proper activity numbers.

Developers must once a week (Friday or Monday) give an estimate of the remaining time for all activities that they are responsible for. Again, the system must remind them if they forget. When the responsible developer reports that the remaining time is zero, the activity is finished and he doesn't have to report remaining time any more.

The project manager (or any other developer) must be able to create projects and activities, and nominate a responsible developer for each activity. To do this, he must be able to see when this developer will be available. He must be able to see how the hours spent and the estimated total develop over time. It is particularly important to identify activities that have a growing estimated total or where little work is done. Finally, he must be able to see who is responsible for this activity and what else this developer is supposed to work on.

Project managers and department managers will typically monitor several projects in this way. It would be convenient if they can get a good overview of the projects they watch particularly closely.

Assumptions

Employees use initials of up to four letters and people usually know each other's initials. The company has already a system that records all employees, invoices customers based on hours used, collects experience data, plans projects with a Gantt diagram, etc. There is no reason to deal with these issues in this project.

Continued

Fig 17.4 Design project: activity monitoring (*Continued*)

Projects have a number and a name, e.g.

9511 DXP version B.

An activity is denoted by the project number and an activity number. Furthermore, it has a name, e.g.

9511-12 Design of communication module.

You may assume that the system is to run on Microsoft Windows in a network. The user has logged on to the PC, so the system knows who he is.

Written exam, January 2000

The following are the original exam questions from a 4-hour written exam. The students had followed a one-semester course according to this book. They had followed two other courses in the same semester. Most of them had a bachelor in non-IT subjects, such as history, health, biology or business. Most of them had only IT knowledge on a user level, typically Microsoft Office. Of the 40 students sitting for the exam, 38 passed. Here is the original text. Notice that the students had no prior knowledge of the library system or the contractor system.

The assignment contains 5 questions. Total time available: 4 hours.

Open book exam: Any books or notes are allowed.

There is a time estimate for each question.

Library System

The figure below shows a screen from an existing, old library system. It doesn't use mouse, but only keyboard and function keys.

Question 1 (estimated time: 15 minutes)

Which functions can you see in the screen?

Indicate for each function whether it is semantic, searching or navigational.

Question 2 (estimated time: 20 minutes)

The library system has been usability tested with 10 users. Among other things, the test showed this:

P1: About half of the users couldn't find out how to start the search.

P2: About half of the users tried to start the search with Enter, but the system didn't react.

Try to explain the cause of these problems.

Question 3 (estimated time: 25 minutes)

The library system is to become Windows-based with mouse. Novice loaners, experienced loaners, as well as librarians will use it. Which presentation (syntactical design) would you recommend for each of the functions on the screen – and why? It is sufficient to describe the presentation. You don't have to draw the entire screen.

```
                        USER SEARCH
 ┌──────────────────────────────────────────────┐
 │ Found: 27, enter more data or show records with F11 │
 └──────────────────────────────────────────────┘
 Fill in two lines at most. Change line by means of the arrow keys.

 ┌────────────────────────────────────────────────────────────────┐
 │                                                                  │
 │  Author      :_____    Enter full name or only │
 │                                           first or last name.    │
 │                                                                  │
 │  Title:      :_____    Enter up to three key words │
 │                                                                  │
 │  Subject     :_____    Enter up to two words   │
 │                                                                  │
 │  Subject code :_____    Find the code in the orange │
 │                                           book. Remember the dot. │
 └────────────────────────────────────────────────────────────────┘

 You may type only the beginning of a word followed by ?. E.g.: "rainb?"

 Start search: f10                              Start from scratch: f16

 You are searching in the collection of this library. Change search area: f15

                 If in doubt: ASK THE LIBRARIAN
```

Contractor System

Imagine that you are to participate in developing a system that supports building contractors who carry out small construction projects.

A contractor employs various types of workmen, e.g. masons, plumbers and carpenters. You may assume that the contractor has no more than 20 workmen of each type, e.g. 20 masons.

A building *project* consists of several *activities*, e.g. digging trenches for the foundation, bricklaying, installing water pipes, tiling. A project in small contractor companies like this has typically 5 activities and rarely more than 20. Each activity is carried out by only one type of workmen. Bricklaying, for instance, is done entirely by masons. Also tiling is done entirely by masons. An activity requires a number of work hours. Tiling may, for instance, require 12 mason hours.

Each activity uses various materials, e.g. concrete, pipes and wash basins. There are more than 20,000 different kinds of materials.

A project starts when the contractor makes a proposal or a quotation. As part of this, he calculates the expected cost, for instance in the way shown in the figure below. Note that the work hours have not yet been split into activities, but are stated as a total for each type of workmen. Similarly, materials are not split into activities.

Typically, there are a hundred open projects, i.e. projects where a proposal has been made or where the work is more or less started.

Project: Renovation of bathroom Client: Peter Hojborg, Sotoften 5, 2860 Gentofte Building location: Granvej 27, Liseleje			Project: 9-56 Date: 1/4-99
Cost calculation, date:	15/4-99		
Labur	Hours	Unit cost	Cost
Mason	30	200	6.000
Plumber	6	200	1.200
Painter	8	200	1.600
Materials, etc.	Count	Unit	
Removal	2	ton	2.000
WC, Caroma 1526	1	pieces	3.500
Pipe, 12 mm copper	15	metre	600
Fittings, various			400
Total			15.300
Profit and risk	30%		4.590
Total quotation			19.890

When the proposal has been accepted, a staff member (typically a workman) is nominated as project manager. The project manager splits the project into a set of activities. For each activity, he plans the start and end date, and he assigns the workmen who will perform the activity. He must select a period where the workmen are available, and somehow he must record that now the workmen are occupied by this activity.

Several workmen may work on the same activity. As an example, the project manager may let two or more masons share the tiling activity. In the course of a single day, a workman may work on several projects.

Generally, each workman has a work plan for the next few months. However, activities don't always proceed as planned, so the project manager must be able to change the plan, for instance by assigning other workmen.

Among other things, the contractor system must be able to support the following tasks:

T1: Create a project, including making the cost calculation and finding prices of various things.

T2: Split a project into activities, including checking that they match the cost calculation. Staff the activities and assign an expected start and end date.

T3: Adjust staffing of the activities while the work progresses, including changing the start and end date, and recording that activities are finished.

Question 4 (estimated time: 60 minutes)

Make an E/R data model for the contractor system. Show the attributes for each entity class.

Question 5 (estimated time: 90 minutes)

Design virtual windows for the contractor system. First, show them in the plan version in such a way that the reader can see which tasks use which windows. Next, show the graphical version.

Written exam, January 2001

The following are the original exam questions from another 4-hour written exam. The students had followed a one-semester course according to this book. They had followed two other courses in the same semester. Most of them had a bachelor in non-IT subjects, such as history, health, biology or business. Most of them had only IT knowledge on a user level, typically Microsoft Office. Of the 43 students sitting for the exam, 41 passed. Here is the original text. Notice that the students had no prior knowledge of the companies BIT and SH, nor about knowledge databases.

The assignment contains 5 questions. Total time available: 4 hours.

Open book exam: Any books or notes are allowed.

There is a time estimate for each question.

Development method in BIT

The software supplier BIT develops and markets IT products for companies that publish newspapers and periodicals. BIT has products that help placing stories and advertisements on the pages, manage the work of the journalists, etc. BIT has around 20 developers and they use a phase-based development method, described in a method manual. Here is a short summary of those parts of the book that relate to the user interface and to usability.

When BIT develops a new product, it is usually the marketing department that comes up with the idea. In cooperation with the development department, marketing writes a requirements specification that states what the system has to do. Here is an example of one of the many requirements for a new product:

> *Requirement 17: It must be possible to use special markings for dividing a newspaper article into several text boxes that have to appear on different pages in the final newspaper. As an example, text box one may end up on the front page and text box 2 on page 8.*

As part of the requirements work, the manual recommends that the developers make a prototype. The manual says:

> *A prototype is a quick draft of some of the screens. The developers explain to the marketing people how the screens are supposed to work. The purpose is to make sure that what the developers imagine, match what marketing expects.*

Developers now write a design document that specifies the data model (using an object-oriented model in UML notation), how the program is to be divided into modules, and how the user will navigate between the screens (a kind of state diagram).

When the design document is ready, developers (and sometimes a marketing person) review the document, checking among other things that the product will meet the requirements and be easy to use.

Next programming starts, then testing of the program modules one by one, and finally a test that they work correctly when combined. (Unfortunately, the resulting products don't quite meet the customer's expectations, and they are not easy to use.)

Question 1. Method improvement (estimated time: 20 minutes)

BIT asks you whether this development method is sufficient to ensure usability, and what they might have to do to improve it. What would you recommend? Remember that a development organization cannot handle too many changes at the same time, so give them a few good recommendations that fit into their present world. Also explain to them why you recommend this.

Knowledge database in the software house SH

The SH software house is growing so large that employees don't any longer know each other. They are now around 100 staff and expect to grow to 500 in a few years. The joint knowledge of the employees is the company's largest asset, but it is now hard for an employee to find those colleagues who, for instance, know something about Microsoft Access, or know about Alka Insurance that just called to get a proposal for design of their Web site, or know the slightly troublesome employee Jacobson from Alka.

It is estimated that each employee on average wastes 20 minutes every work day to find colleagues who can provide such knowledge. For this reason, SH wants to create a knowledge database that all employees can use. In the database they plan to record this:

1. The professional expertise of the employee, for instance IT products they know and other expertise, for instance from the insurance business. It would also be nice to know what degree of expertise they have in these areas, for instance expressed like this: 'Microsoft Access, some developer expertise'.

2. Information about customer companies and the contacts SH has in these companies.

3. Information about SH's projects. (There is about one new project per year per employee.)

The primary need is to be able to identify the colleagues who know about these things. But the system is also intended for simple daily things, such as finding the phone number or home address of a colleague – based on parts of his name.

(There may be a need for getting information about other things than the colleagues. For instance there might be a need for a list of all projects SH has with a particular customer. Ignore such needs in this exam.)

SH realizes that the employees are so busy that they will not record all these things about themselves and the contacts they meet, if it is a separate task to do so. Such a task does not seem sufficiently important to the employee. For this reason, the system must support tasks that seem more important to the employee, and as part of this capture data for the knowledge database.

One of these tasks is a central registration of the projects. At present all projects use a paper form, like the one on the figure. The system must store the data in a database, so that project team members as well as other employees can draw on it. At present, most team members have a copy of the form, and they often annotate it with scribblings about the contact persons, as shown in the figure. These hints are often valuable for other employees, so it is important to capture them too.

Another task is to record the expertise of the employees. The idea is to let it be a standard part of the home page that most employees have already and update regularly. The expertise must be described with keywords taken from an SH-wide list. It is crucial that the list of keywords doesn't grow wildly, but it should also be easy to add new keywords. SH imagines that employees can freely add a keyword if they don't find a suitable one in the list. Each time they do so, SH's librarian gets a message about it, and at a suitable moment the librarian reviews it and determines whether a new one is really needed or whether an existing one could be used. The librarian may change the keyword and inform the employees who have used it already, about the change, and why it was made.

Experience from other companies suggests that the list of keywords easily becomes 1000 to 2000 keywords.

Assumptions to make it simpler

In order that you don't get lost in unimportant details, we assume that only the following is recorded about persons: name, home address, phone at work, phone at home, e-mail. In real life there is also a need for fax and mobile numbers, etc., but there is no reason to mention them in your reply. The same assumption applies to companies. You can also assume that all addresses are in your local country.

Assume that a person cannot be both an SH employee and a contact person in another company. (In real life many important contacts move from a customer company to SH – or opposite. Ignore this.)

Assume that everybody is allowed to see everything and in principle change anything. For remarks about contact persons, it is however important to be able to see who recorded the remark and when. (The system knows who types something, so it can record it automatically.)

```
┌─────────────────────────────────────────────────────────────────────────┐
│  Project      Intranet_____      Project id   01005   │
│                                                     Created      2002-11-22│
│  Client       Alka Insurance                                             │
│               Engelholm boulevard 1                                      │
│               2630 Taastrup                                              │
│               70 12 14 16                                                │
│                                                                          │
│  Contacts for the project      UML-phanatic, Blue cross                  │
│                                                                          │
│           Soren Jacobson, 70 12 24 16, viltrup@alka.dk    IT deptís representative│
│           Ellen Skov, 70 12 12 18, elskov@alka.dk         User representative│
│                   Huge influence, home Friday                            │
│                                                                          │
│  SH project team                                                         │
│           Pia Torbjoern, 1880, piat@sh.com               project manager │
│           Uffe Larsen, 1883, uffeman@sh.com              designer        │
│                                                                          │
└─────────────────────────────────────────────────────────────────────────┘
```

If you encounter problems that you cannot readily solve, then explain the problem in your reply. It is better to explain the problem than to spend so much time on solving it that you don't deal with the other questions.

Question 2. Task list (estimated time: 20 minutes)

Identify the tasks that the system has to support. Describe them as an annotated task list.

Question 3. Data model (estimated time: 45 minutes)

Make an E/R model for the knowledge database. State the attributes for each entity class. If you include artificial keys and foreign keys, show them with appropriate underscores. For non-trivial entities, give a short explanation as in a data dictionary.

Question 4. Virtual windows (estimated time: 45 minutes)

Design virtual windows for the system. First, show them in the plan version in such a way that the reader can see which tasks use which windows. Next, show the graphical version. You may omit any windows that only the librarian will use.

Question 5. Search window (estimated time: 30 minutes)

Design the central search window that supports the system's prime aim: to find employees based on their name, or based on their knowledge about a professional area or a contact person. The design of this window must be sufficiently precise to be used as a mock-up. Briefly explain what the window shows and how the user enters the search criteria.

References

This chapter contains two lists of the same literature: (1) arranged according to subject and (2) arranged according to author. Both lists are annotated. Some references are mentioned under more than one subject.

References according to subject area

Usability evaluation

Bailey, Robert W.; Allan, Robert W. & Raiello, P. (1992) Usability testing vs. heuristic evaluation: a head-to-head comparison. *Proceedings of the Human Factors Society 35th Annual Meeting*, 409–413. Bailey *et al.* studied a very small system where 77 experts had found 31 usability problems by means of heuristic evaluation (Molich and Nielsen 1990). Bailey *et al.* found that only 2 of the problems were worth correcting in the sense that there was no measurable effect of correcting the remaining 29 problems. Lauesen's comment: They would probably have found an effect of correcting a few more of the 31 usability problems if they had used more varied test tasks, but the trend seems clear: Heuristic evaluation finds many false positives.

Carlshamre, Pär & Karlsson, Joachim (1996) A usability-oriented approach to requirements engineering. *Proceedings of ICRE'96*, IEEE Computer Society Press, 145–152. A simple, effective approach to task analysis and usability testing.

Cuomo, Donna L. & Bowen, Charles D. (1994) Understanding usability issues addressed by three user-system interface evaluation techniques. *Interacting with Computers*, **6**(1), 86–108. Compares problems detected by a usability test with those predicted by three evaluation techniques: heuristic evaluation, cognitive walkthrough and guidelines. Heuristic evaluation detects about 60% of the problems detected in usability testing, and reports 50% false positives. Also compares the kinds of problems reported by the three evaluation techniques.

Desurvire, Heather W.; Kondziela, Jim M. & Atwood, Michael E. (1992) What is gained and lost when using evaluation methods other than empirical testing. *Proceedings of HCI'92*, Cambridge University Press, Cambridge, UK, 89–102. Compares heuristic evaluation against usability testing. Reports 44% hit-rate of heuristic evaluation, and 50% false positives, which they call 'potential problems'.

Dumas, Joseph S. & Redish, Janice C. (1993) *A Practical Guide to Usability Testing*, Ablex Publishing. A comprehensive guide to most aspects of usability testing and usability in general.

Frøkjær, Erik; Hertzum, Morten & Hornbæk, Kasper (2000) Measuring usability: are effectiveness, efficiency, and satisfaction really coordinated? In *Conference Proceedings. Conference on Human Factors in Computing Systems (CHI 2000)*, The Hague, 1–6 April 2000 (eds T. Turner, G. Szwillus, M. Czerwinski & F. Paterno), ACM Press, New York, 345–352. Measures three usability factors, effectiveness (error rate and quality of results), efficiency and satisfaction, for 87 users trying 20 difficult tasks over a period of 10 days. Concludes that there is little correlation between the three factors.

Henderson, Ron; Podd, John; Smith, Mike & Varela-Alvarez, Hugo (1995) An examination of four user-based software evaluation methods. *Interacting with Computers*, **7**(4), 412–432. Compares four methods of getting information about usability – all based on real users using the software: think-aloud (while viewing a video of what had happened), questionnaire, interview and logging of computer actions. Conclude that the four approaches reveal rather different issues, but the think-aloud seems to be the strongest, followed by interviews. The questionnaire method seems dubious for interface development.

Hoc, Jean-Michel & Leplat, Jacques (1983) Evaluation of different modalities of verbalization in a sorting task. *International Journal of Man–Machine Studies*, **18**, 283–306. Shows that thinking aloud doesn't disturb the identification of problems.

Jørgensen, Anker Helms (1990) Thinking-aloud in user interface design: a method promoting cognitive ergonomics. *Ergonomics*, **33**(4), 501–507. A short, thorough description of practical experiences with the thinking-aloud version of usability testing. The designers conducted the usability test, and it worked fine. They were surprised at the number of problems detected. This caused them to change attitude, improve the user interface and actually remove many of the problems.

Molich, Rolf (2003) Comparative Usability Evaluation – CUE. Available at: www.dialogdesign.dk/cue.html. Documents and results available for download from CUE-4 (and earlier comparisons of evaluation methods). In CUE-4, 17 top-level usability teams evaluated the same Web site, 8 of them using heuristic evaluation and 9 usability testing.

Molich, Rolf & Nielsen, Jakob (1990) Improving a human–computer dialogue. *Communications of the ACM*, March, 338–348. The authors designed a user interface to a very simple system that allowed users to enter a phone number and get information about the subscriber to this number. The system had two screens. The authors asked 77 designers and programmers to look at the screens and identify as many problems as possible. The result was a list of 31 potential usability problems. The authors judged 8 of these as serious. They recommended nine heuristic rules and compared the problem list against them. Later Bailey *et al.* (1992) tested whether there was a measurable user effect of correcting these problems. They concluded that correcting just two of the problems had the same effect as correcting all of them.

SUMI (Software Usability Measurement Inventory). Available at: *http://www.ucc.ie/hfrg/questionnaires/sumi/*. Accessed 30 June 2004. A questionnaire-based evaluation system for user interfaces, sponsored by the European Union. SUMI has 50 questions you can ask for any system. It has a database of how other systems fare on this scale so that you can compare your own system against other's.

Brain, ergonomics and cognition

Bailey, Robert W. (1996) *Human Performance Engineering*, Prentice-Hall, Englewood, Cliffs, NJ. Excellent description of what humans can do, physically and mentally. User profiles and how to determine them. General discussion of the design process, but no examples of real design results. Good discussion of user interface elements, but mainly on the 'which controls are available'-level. Good advice for user documentation and training. Statistical methods for comparing tests.

Card, Stuart K.; Moran, Thomas P. & Newell, Allen (1980) The keystroke-level model for user performance time with interactive systems. *Communications of the ACM*, **23**(7), 396–410. Breaks down the user part of the task into basic elements and measures the time for each type of element.

Damasio, Antonio R. & Damasio, Hanna (1992) Brain and language. *Scientific American*, September, 63–71. Explains the different language centres of the brain, and how concepts are formed as an association of different sensory memories.

Finke, Ronald A. (1986) Mental imagery and the visual system. *Scientific American*, March, 76–83. Shows experimentally how mental images use the same brain mechanisms as vision, and how they also influence what we believe we see.

Goldman-Rakic, Patricia S. (1992) Working memory and the mind. *Scientific American*, September, 73–79. A detailed explanation of the brain centres involved in memory, and how they relate to object permanence and to motor responses when memories are retrieved.

Livingstone, Margaret S. (1988) Art, illusion and the visual system. *Scientific American*, January, 68–75. An easy overview of the vision centres for form, colour and movement-depth. Also explains how it relates to the illusions used in graphical arts.

Matlin, Margaret W. & Foley, Hugh J. (1997) *Sensation and Perception*, Allyn and Bacon, Boston, 550 pp. A handbook of what our senses can achieve. Includes vision, hearing, touch, smell and taste.

Mishkin, Mortimer & Appenzeller, Tim (1987) The anatomy of memory. *Scientific American*, June, 62–71. A detailed account of the various brain centres involved in associative memory, linking different kinds of sensory memory, for instance vision, touch, smell and emotions. Also shows that the cognitive association areas (insights) are different from habit-learning (learning by repetition without insight).

Norman, Donald A. (1988) *The Psychology of Everyday Things*, Basic Books, New York. A classic about how we intuitively use physical things (affordance) and understand how they work (mental models). The physical things are, for instance, doors, water faucets, VCRs and keyboards. Gives examples of good and bad affordance, and correct and wrong mental models.

Noton, David & Stark, Lawrence (1972) Eye movements and visual perception. *Readings from Scientific American. Perception: Mechanisms and Models*, W. H. Freeman, San Francisco, 218–227. The authors analysed how subjects moved their eyes when they study large pictures (the scan path). Each subject had his own scan path, but the path varied from picture to picture.

Nygren, Else; Lind, Mats; Johnson, Mats & Sandblad, Bengt (1992) The art of the obvious. *Proceedings of CHI'92*, 235–239. Studied a medical application to find out why users didn't use it. The reason was that the computer version had lost a lot of the visual qualities that the old paper forms had. The users were not aware that they had used these qualities, but responded by not using the new system.

Pan, Bing; Hembrooke, Helene A.; Gay, Geri K.; Granka, Laura A.; Feusner, Mathew K. & Newman, Jill K. (2004) The determinants of web page viewing behavior: an eye-tracking study. *Proceedings ETRA 2004*, San Antonio, TX, ACM, New York. The authors studied how 30 subjects looked at 11 popular Web sites. The subjects scanned the pages in different ways depending on their gender, the type of site, the sequence in which they looked at the pages, etc.

Rasmussen, Jens (1979) On the structure of knowledge – a morphology of mental models in a man–machine system context. Report M-2192, Riso National Laboratory, Roskilde, Denmark.

Rasmussen, Jens (1986) *On Information Processing and Human–Machine Interaction: An Approach to Cognitive Engineering*, Elsevier, Amsterdam.

Rock, Irvin & Palmer, Stephen (1990) The legacy of gestalt psychology. *Scientific American*, December, 48–61. The history and findings of the gestalt school, and its conflicts with other schools of psychology. Also shows examples of several gestalt laws.

Staggers, Nancy & Norcio, A.F. (1993) Mental models: concepts for human–computer interaction research. *International Journal of Man–Machine Studies*, **38**, 587–605. Explains the many views on mental models and the known facts about them.

Treisman, Anne (1986) Features and objects in visual processing. *Scientific American*, November, 106–115. Explains what creates contrasts and objects, and how it relates to processing in the brain. Gives many fascinating examples of how the visual brain centres mix up things. Might be considered the neural base for the gestalt laws, although the author doesn't mention 'gestalts'.

Young, R.M. (1983) Surrogates and mappings: two kinds of conceptual models for interactive devices. In *Mental Models* (eds D. Gentner & A.L. Stevens), Lawrence Erlbaum Associates, Hillsdale, NJ, 35–52.

Zeki, Semir (1992) The visual image in mind and brain. *Scientific American*, September, 43–50. A very detailed description of the vision centres in the brain, blind-sight and many other vision defects.

Data visualization

Nygren, Else; Lind, Mats; Johnson, Mats & Sandblad, Bengt (1992) The art of the obvious. *Proceedings of CHI'92*, 235–239. Studied a medical application to find out why users didn't use it. The reason was that the computer version had lost a lot of the visual qualities that the old paper forms had. The users were not aware that they had used these qualities, but responded by not using the new system.

Spence, Robert (2001) *Information Visualization*, Addison-Wesley, Reading, MA. A huge collection of surprising ways to show complex data, illustrated with real-life applications and stories of how the presentation helped solve domain problems. Spence has systematic approaches to the presentation, for instance characterizing it as presentation of univariate, bivariate or trivariate data.

Tufte, Edward R. (1983) *The Visual Display of Quantitative Information*, Graphics Press, Cheshire, CT. A unique, rich collection of creative ways to present complex data. Good source of inspiration for user interfaces, but offers little systematic approach to choosing the right presentation.

Tufte, Edward R. (1990) *Envisioning Information*, Graphics Press, Cheshire, CT. Another rich collection of ways to present data.

Task analysis, specification and requirements

Beyer, Hugh R. & Holtzblatt, Karen (1998) *Contextual Design. Defining Customer Centered Systems*, Morgan Kauffmann, San Francisco. A solid approach to work analysis and redesign of work. Uses affinity diagrams to find the common structures and variants in user tasks. Also shows how to study documents and other artefacts to get ideas for new systems.

Booch, Grady; Rumbaugh, James & Jacobson, Ivar (1999) *The Unified Modeling Language, User Guide*, Addison-Wesley, Reading, MA. A definition and explanation of UML. See later developments at www.rational.com. The Object Management Group (OMG)'s definition of UML is available at http://cgi.omg.org/cgi-bin/doc?ad/99-06-08.

Carlshamre, Pär & Karlsson, Joachim (1996) A usability-oriented approach to requirements engineering. *Proceedings of ICRE'96*, IEEE Computer Society Press, 145–152. A simple, effective approach to task analysis and usability testing.

Cockburn, Alistair (1997) Structuring use cases with goals. *Journal of Object-Oriented Programming*, September/October, 35–40; November/December, 56–62. Also available at: http://members.-aol.com/acockburn/papers/usecases.htm. The now classical paper on various meanings of use cases and good examples of Cockburn's goal-oriented use cases.

Cockburn, Alistair (2000) *Writing Effective Use Cases*, Addison-Wesley, Reading, MA. The full approach of goal-oriented use cases on various levels. Lots of good advice on what to do and what not. Many real-life use cases. Excellent discussion of UML versus text-based use cases. Insists on use cases describing the split between user and product – in that way limiting the solutions at a too early stage.

Constantine, Larry & Lockwood, Lucy A.D. (2001) Structure and style in use cases for user interface design. In *Object Modeling and User Interface Design* (ed. M.V. Harmelen), Addison-Wesley, Reading, MA. A solid discussion of various use case styles and why most of them fail to describe true technology-independent tasks.

Davis, B.G. (1982) Strategies for information requirements determination. *IBM Systems Journal*, **21**(1), 4–30. How to elicit requirements through questionnaires, studies of existing systems, critical success factors, decision studies and prototypes. Also discusses mental limitations that make elicitation difficult.

DeMarco, Tom (1979) *Structured Analysis and Systems Specification*, Prentice-Hall, Englewood Cliffs, NJ.

Grudin, Jonathan (1991) Systematic sources of suboptimal interface design in large product development organizations. *Human–Computer Interaction*, **6**, 147–196. Mainly discusses problems of getting access to real users, particularly in large organizations. Mentions small software houses as the hope.

Jacobson, Ivar; Christerson, Magnus; Johnsson, Patrik & Övergaard, Gunnar (1994) *Object-Oriented Software Engineering – A Use Case Driven Approach*, Addison-Wesley, Reading, MA. Introduced the use case concept and outlined a relation to object-oriented modelling.

Lauesen, Soren (2002) *Software Requirements – Styles and Techniques*, Pearson/Addison-Wesley, London. Covers many aspects of requirements. Treats quality requirements in depth.

Robertson, James (2002) Eureka! Why analysts should invent requirements. *IEEE Software*, July/August, 22–24. Shows why it isn't enough to give the customer what he asks for. Progress is made by exceeding what the customer even dreamt of. Gives some hints on how to do it.

Robertson, Susanne (2001) Requirements trawling: techniques for discovering requirements. *International Journal of Human–Computer Studies*, **55**, 405–421. An introduction to a long list of elicitation techniques, for known as well as undreamed demands.

Rumbaugh, James; Jacobson, Ivar & Booch, Grady (1999) *The Unified Modeling Language Reference Manual*, Addison-Wesley, Reading, MA. (A companion to UML User Guide, see Booch *et al.* 1999).

Spool, Jared M. (1997) Market maturity. *Eye for Design*, January/February. Shows that the key requirements change as a market develops. Functional requirements are important early, and usability and other quality requirements later.

User interface design

Bailey, Robert W. (1996) *Human Performance Engineering*, Prentice-Hall, Englewood Cliffs, NJ. Excellent description of what humans can do, physically and mentally. User profiles and how to determine them. General discussion of the design process, but no examples of real design results. Good discussion of user interface elements, but mainly on the 'which controls are available'-level. Good advice for user documentation and training. Statistical methods for comparing tests.

Beyer, Hugh R. & Holtzblatt, Karen (1998) *Contextual Design. Defining Customer Centered Systems*, Morgan Kauffmann, San Francisco. A solid approach to work analysis and redesign of work. Uses affinity diagrams to find the common structures and variants in user tasks. Also shows how to study documents and other artefacts to get ideas for new systems.

Constantine, Larry & Lockwood, Lucy A.D. (1999) *Software for Use: A Practical Guide to the Models and Methods of Usage-Centered Design*, Addison-Wesley, Reading, MA. Describes a systematic design method for user interfaces, starting with elicitation of essential use cases and ending up with prototypes and usability testing. Also has a good section on helping users to get from novices to experts. As in other usability and design books, the weakest part is how the screen design 'pops out of the air'.

Cooper, Alan (1995) *About Face, The Essentials of User Interface Design*, IDG Books Worldwide. Cooper is one of the designers of Visual Basic. Here he explains the principles of all the low-level user interface things in a graphical interface: mouse, focus, message boxes, help, wizards, file system, etc. He explains about the good as well as the bad aspects of these. Nothing about usability tests or large-scale design.

Cox, Kevin & Walker, David (1993) *User Interface Design*. Simon and Schuster (Asia), Prentice-Hall, New York. Outlines a systematic way of designing user interfaces. Based on dataflow, data models, guidelines and prototypes, but no task descriptions. Doesn't use virtual windows, but more abstract user objects that are close to the data model. Stresses the importance of visualization and overview, but the examples are rather sketchy and deal with small applications. Has a good chapter on user documentation, course development and on-line help.

Dix, Alan; Finlay, Janet; Abowd, Gregory & Beale, Russell (1998) *Human–Computer Interaction*, Prentice-Hall, Europe. Covers many aspects of HCI, for instance human perception and thinking, all kinds of input and output devices, usability factors and ways to measure them, standards, graphical and math-like specifications of dialogues, a bit on programming the user interface, evaluation techniques (including usability testing) and CSCW (Computer Supported Cooperative Work). Also gives a thorough explanation of the keystroke-level model of Card *et al.*

Lauesen, Soren & Harning, Morten Borup (1993) Dialogue design through modified dataflow and data modelling. In *Human–Computer Interaction, VCHCI'93*, Vienna, September 1993 (eds T. Grechenig and M. Tscheligi), Springer-Verlag, New York, 172–183. Explains what is still the core of the virtual window method: How to define the screens and add functionality to them. At this time the function design was based on dataflow diagrams. It took years to develop the present approach. The paper also appeared in a shorter version in: Salvendy, G. & Smith, M.J. (eds) (1993) *Human–Computer Interaction, HCI International'93*, Orlando, August 1993, Elsevier, Amsterdam, 220–225.

Lauesen, Soren & Harning, Morten Borup (2001) Virtual Windows, *IEEE Software*, July/August, 67–75. A short explanation of virtual windows. Uses a slightly simplified version of the hotel system as an example.

Nielsen, Jakob (2000) *Designing Web Usability*, New Riders, Indianapolis. A classic about designing contents and appearance of Web sites. Covers many things, for instance what customers look for on Web sites, how to use the space on a Web page, how to organize the entire site, dealing with an international audience, lots of examples of good and bad design, plus suggestions for improving the bad designs.

Preece, Jennifer; Rogers, Yvonne & Sharp, Helen (2002) *Interaction Design – Beyond Human–Computer Interaction*, John Wiley & Sons, New York, 500 pp. In many ways similar to Preece *et al.* (1994), but more focused on the design process. Shows a few examples of software engineering notations used during design. Still little about the actual design of the user interface.

Preece, Jennifer; Rogers, Yvonne; Sharp, Helen; Benyon, David; Holland, Simon & Carey, Tom (1994) *Human–Computer Interaction*, Addison-Wesley, Reading, MA, 800 pp. Covers many aspects of HCI, for instance the history of HCI and interviews with people who influenced it, human perception, automatic versus controlled activities, mental models and social aspects, all kinds of input and output devices, components of graphical interfaces, development and design processes, usability evaluation and experimental design. Little about the actual design of the user interface.

Redmond-Pyle, David & Moore, Alan (1995) *Graphical User Interface Design and Evaluation*, Prentice-Hall, Europe. One of the few books that actually show a systematic way of designing good user interfaces. Based on usability requirements, task descriptions, data models and evaluation of prototypes. Doesn't use virtual windows, but more abstract *user objects*. The user interface itself is not designed in several steps – even the first screens are complete with functions and navigation. Illustrated with development of a system for supporting a hot-line desk. The main problem with the first prototypes was that there were too many screens (virtual windows might have eliminated this problem). Has a wonderful case story of the previous hot-line system that was developed with participatory design and iterative prototyping, yet failed to provide adequate usability. Only the expert users that had participated in the design were able to use it.

Shneiderman, Ben (1998) *Designing the User Interface*, Addison-Wesley, Reading, MA. Defines the usability factors *Time to learn*, *Speed of performance*, etc. The factors were defined already in the 1986 version. Also stated the *eight golden rules of dialogue design*. Covers usability from many points of view and gives examples of various kinds of interfaces.

Sutcliffe, Alistair (1998) *Human–Computer Interface Design*, MacMillan Education, London, 200 pp. An HCI book with a software engineering focus. Describes practical and more formal ways of specifying interactions. Outlines a design method, and has a few examples of screen design. There is an introductory chapter on human sensation and perception.

Standards

Card, Stuart K.; Moran, Thomas P. & Newell, Allen (1980) The keystroke-level model for user performance time with interactive systems. *Communications of the ACM*, **23**(7), 396–410. Breaks down the user part of the task into basic elements and measures the time for each type of element.

ISO/IEC 9126 (extended version 2001–2002) Information technology, software product evaluation, quality characteristics and guidelines for their use. A standard that covers all aspects of software quality. The extended version has several ways of measuring usability – more than this book covers.

ISO 9241 (1998) Ergonomics requirements for office work with visual display terminals. A standard for measuring usability. Uses usability factors similar to this book. Tends to rely on opinion polls for measurements.

ISO 13407 (1989) Human-centered design process for interactive systems, 26 pp. A standard process for designing user interfaces. Prescribes task analysis, prototyping, evaluation (with expert users), revision of the design and late during implementation – usability testing.

SUMI (Software Usability Measurement Inventory) Available at: http://www.ucc. ie/hfrg/questionnaires/sumi/. A questionnaire-based evaluation system for user interfaces, sponsored by the European Union. SUMI has 50 questions you can ask for any system. It has a database of how other systems fare on this scale so that you can compare your own system against other's.

Other

Lauesen, Soren & Vinter, Otto (2001) Preventing requirement defects. An experiment in process improvement. *Requirements Engineering Journal*, **6**, 37–50. Reports on the process improvement experiment at Bruel & Kjaer, how the existing requirements problems were analysed to arrive at a new requirements approach, and what the results were when using the approach in the next project. About half of the existing product defects were usability problems. Early prototyping and usability testing had a major effect.

Mallon, Bride & Webb, Brian (2000) Structure, causality, visibility and interaction: propositions for evaluating engagement in narrative multimedia. *International Journal of Human–Computer Studies*, **53**, 269–287. Studied and interviewed users who tried many kinds of multimedia production. Identified critical success factors for such products.

Spool, Jared M. (1997): Market maturity. *Eye for Design*, January/February. Shows that the key requirements change as a market develops. Functional requirements are important early, and usability and other quality requirements later.

Rouse, Richard (2001) *Game Design, Theory & Practice*, Wordware Publishing, Texas. Defines the 'usability factors' at work in game programs, what players want and expect. Discusses how game ideas are created and transformed to products, tools for game design, etc. Brings interviews with experts in game design.

References in alphabetical order

Bailey, Robert W. (1996) *Human Performance Engineering*, Prentice-Hall, Englewood Cliffs, NJ. Excellent description of what humans can do, physically and mentally. User profiles and how to determine them. General discussion of the design process, but no examples of real design results. Good discussion of user interface elements, but mainly on the 'which controls are available'-level. Good advice for user documentation and training. Statistical methods for comparing tests.

Bailey, Robert W.; Allan, Robert W. & Raiello, P. (1992) Usability testing vs. heuristic evaluation: a head-to-head comparison. *Proceedings of the Human Factors Society 35th Annual Meeting*, 409–413. Bailey *et al.* studied a very small system where 77 experts had found 31 usability problems by means of heuristic evaluation (Molich and Nielsen 1990). Bailey *et al.* found that only 2 of the problems were worth correcting in the sense that there was no measurable effect of correcting the remaining 29 problems. Lauesen's comment: They would probably have found an effect of correcting a few more of the 31 usability problems if they had used more varied test tasks, but the trend seems clear: Heuristic evaluation finds many false positives.

Beyer, Hugh R. & Holtzblatt, Karen (1998) *Contextual Design. Defining Customer Centered Systems*, Morgan Kauffmann, San Francisco. A solid approach to work analysis and redesign of work. Uses affinity diagrams to find the common structures and variants in user tasks. Also shows how to study documents and other artefacts to get ideas for new systems.

Booch, Grady; Rumbaugh, James & Jacobson, Ivar (1999) *The Unified Modeling Language, User Guide*, Addison-Wesley, Reading, MA. A definition and explanation of UML. See later developments at www.rational.com. The Object Management Group (OMG)'s definition of UML is available at http://cgi.omg.org/cgi-bin/doc?ad/99-06-08.

Card, Stuart K.; Moran, Thomas P. & Newell, Allen (1980) The keystroke-level model for user performance time with interactive systems. *Communications of the ACM*, **23**(7), 396–410. Breaks down the user part of the task into basic elements and measures the time for each type of element.

Carlshamre, Pär & Karlsson, Joachim (1996) A usability-oriented approach to requirements engineering. *Proceedings of ICRE'96*, IEEE Computer Society Press, 145–152. A simple, effective approach to task analysis and usability testing.

Cockburn, Alistair (1997) Structuring use cases with goals. *Journal of Object-Oriented Programming*, September/October, 35–40; November/December, 56–62. Also available at: http://members.-aol.com/acockburn/papers/usecases.htm. The now classical paper on various meanings of use cases and good examples of Cockburn's goal-oriented use cases.

Cockburn, Alistair (2000) *Writing Effective Use Cases*, Addison-Wesley, Reading, MA. The full approach of goal-oriented use cases on various levels. Lots of good advice on what to do and what not. Many real-life use cases. Excellent discussion of UML versus text-based use cases. Insists on use cases describing the split between user and product – in that limiting the solutions at a too early stage.

Constantine, Larry & Lockwood, Lucy A.D. (1999) *Software for Use: A Practical Guide to the Models and Methods of Usage-Centered Design*, Addison-Wesley, Reading, MA. Describes a systematic design method for user interfaces, starting with elicitation of essential use cases and ending up with prototypes and usability testing. Also has a good section on helping users to get from novices to experts. As in other usability and design books, the weakest part is how the screen design 'pops out of the air'.

Constantine, Larry & Lockwood, Lucy A.D. (2001) Structure and style in use cases for user interface design. In *Object Modeling and User Interface Design* (ed. M.V. Harmelen), Addison-Wesley, Reading, MA. A solid discussion of various use case styles and why most of them fail to describe true technology-independent tasks.

Cooper, Alan (1995) *About Face, The Essentials of User Interface Design*, IDG Books Worldwide. Cooper is one of the designers of Visual Basic. Here he explains the principles of all the low-level user interface things in a graphical interface: mouse, focus, message boxes, help, wizards, file system, etc. He explains about the good as well as the bad aspects of these. Nothing about usability tests or large-scale design.

Cox, Kevin & Walker, David (1993) *User Interface Design*. Simon and Schuster (Asia), Prentice-Hall, New York. Outlines a systematic way of designing user interfaces. Based on dataflow, data models, guidelines and prototypes, but no task descriptions. Doesn't use virtual windows, but more abstract user objects that are close to the data model. Stresses the importance of visualization and overview, but the examples are rather sketchy and deal with small applications. Has a good chapter on user documentation, course development and on-line help.

Cuomo, Donna L. & Bowen, Charles D. (1994) Understanding usability issues addressed by three user-system interface evaluation techniques. *Interacting with Computers*, **6**(1), 86–108. Compares problems detected by a usability test with those predicted by three evaluation techniques: heuristic evaluation, cognitive walkthrough and guidelines. Heuristic evaluation detects about 60% of the problems detected in usability testing, and reports 50% false positives. Also compares the kinds of problems reported by the three evaluation techniques.

Damasio, Antonio R. & Damasio, Hanna (1992) Brain and language. *Scientific American*, September, 63–71. Explains the different language centres of the brain, and how concepts are formed as an association of different sensory memories.

Davis, B.G. (1982) Strategies for information requirements determination. *IBM Systems Journal*, **21**(1), 4–30. How to elicit requirements through questionnaires, studies of existing systems, critical success factors, decision studies and prototypes. Also discusses mental limitations that make elicitation difficult.

DeMarco, Tom (1979) *Structured Analysis and Systems Specification*, Prentice-Hall, Englewood Cliffs, NJ.

Desurvire, Heather W.; Kondziela, Jim M. & Atwood, Michael E. (1992) What is gained and lost when using evaluation methods other than empirical testing. *Proceedings of HCI'92*, 89–102. Cambridge University Press, Cambridge, UK. Compares heuristic evaluation against usability testing. Reports 44% hit-rate of heuristic evaluation, and 50% false positives, which they call 'potential problems'.

Dix, Alan; Finlay, Janet; Abowd, Gregory & Beale, Russell (1998) *Human–Computer Interaction*, Prentice-Hall, Europe. Covers many aspects of HCI for instance human perception and thinking, all kinds of input and output devices, usability factors and ways to measure them, standards, graphical and math-like specifications of dialogues, a bit on programming the user interface, evaluation techniques (including usability testing) and CSCW (Computer Supported Cooperative Work). Also gives a thorough explanation of the keystroke-level model of Card *et al*.

Dumas, Joseph S. & Redish, Janice C. (1993) *A Practical Guide to Usability Testing*, Ablex Publishing, Norwood, NJ. A comprehensive guide to most aspects of usability testing and usability in general.

Finke, Ronald A. (1986) Mental imagery and the visual system. *Scientific American*, March, 76–83. Shows experimentally how mental images use the same brain mechanisms as vision, and how they also influence what we believe we see.

Frøkjær, Erik; Hertzum, Morten & Hornbæk, Kasper (2000) Measuring usability: are effectiveness, efficiency, and satisfaction really coordinated? In *Conference Proceedings. Conference on Human Factors in Computing Systems (CHI 2000)*, The Hague, 1–6 April 2000 (eds T. Turner, G. Szwillus, M. Czerwinski & F. Paterno), ACM Press, New York, 345–352. Measures three usability factors, effectiveness (error rate and quality of results), efficiency and satisfaction, for 87 users trying 20 difficult tasks over a period of 10 days. Concludes that there is little correlation between the three factors.

Goldman-Rakic, Patricia S. (1992) Working memory and the mind. *Scientific American*, September, 73–79. A detailed explanation of the brain centres involved in memory, and how they relate to object permanence and to motor responses when memories are retrieved.

Grudin, Jonathan (1991) Systematic sources of suboptimal interface design in large product development organizations. *Human–Computer Interaction*, **6**, 147–196.

Mainly discusses problems of getting access to real users, particularly in large organizations. Mentions small software houses as the hope.

Henderson, Ron; Podd, John; Smith, Mike & Varela-Alvarez, Hugo (1995) An examination of four user-based software evaluation methods. *Interacting with Computers*, **7**(4), 412–432. Compares four methods of getting information about usability – all based on real users using the software: think-aloud (while viewing a video of what had happened), questionnaire, interview and logging of computer actions. Conclude that the four approaches reveal rather different issues, but the think-aloud seems to be the strongest, followed by interviews. The questionnaire method seems dubious for interface development.

Hoc, Jean-Michel & Leplat, Jacques (1983) Evaluation of different modalities of verbalization in a sorting task. *International Journal of Man–Machine Studies*, **18**, 283–306. Shows that thinking aloud doesn't disturb the identification of problems.

ISO/IEC 9126 (extended version 2001–2002) Information technology, software product evaluation, quality characteristics and guidelines for their use. A standard that covers all aspects of software quality. The extended version has several ways of measuring usability – more than this book covers.

ISO 9241 (1998) Ergonomics requirements for office work with visual display terminals. A standard for measuring usability. Uses usability factors similar to this book. Tends to rely on opinion polls for measurements.

ISO 13407 (1989) Human-centered design process for interactive systems, 26 pp. A standard process for designing user interfaces. Prescribes task analysis, prototyping, evaluation (with expert users), revision of the design and late – during implementation – usability testing.

Jacobson, Ivar; Christerson, Magnus; Johnsson, Patrik & Övergaard, Gunnar (1994) *Object-Oriented Software Engineering – A Use Case Driven Approach*, Addison-Wesley, Reading, MA. Introduced the use case concept and outlined a relation to object-oriented modelling.

Jørgensen, Anker Helms (1990) Thinking-aloud in user interface design: a method promoting cognitive ergonomics. *Ergonomics*, **33**(4), 501–507. A short, thorough description of practical experiences with the thinking-aloud version of usability testing. The designers conducted the usability test, and it worked fine. They were surprised at the number of problems detected. This caused them to change attitude, improve the user interface and actually remove many of the problems.

Lauesen, Soren (2002) *Software Requirements – Styles and techniques*, Pearson/Addison-Wesley, London. Covers many aspects of requirements. Treats quality requirements in depth.

Lauesen, Soren & Harning, Morten Borup (1993) Dialogue design through modified dataflow and data modelling. In *Human–Computer Interaction, VCHCI'93*, Vienna,

September 1993 (eds T. Grechenig and M. Tscheligi), Springer-Verlag, New York, 172–183. Explains what is still the core of the virtual window method: How to define the screens and add functionality to them. At this time the function design was based on dataflow diagrams. It took years to develop the present approach. The paper also appeared in a shorter version in: Salvendy, G. and Smith, M.J. (eds) (1993) *Human–Computer Interaction, HCI International'93*, Orlando, August 1993, Elsevier, Amsterdam, 220–225.

Lauesen, Soren & Harning, Morten Borup (2001) Virtual Windows, *IEEE Software*, July/August, 67–75. A short explanation of virtual windows. Uses a slightly simplified version of the hotel system as an example.

Lauesen, Soren & Vinter, Otto (2001) Preventing requirement defects. An experiment in process improvement. *Requirements Engineering Journal*, **6**, 37–50. Reports on the process improvement experiment at Bruel & Kjaer, how the existing requirements problems were analysed to arrive at a new requirements approach and what the results were when using the approach in the next project. About half of the existing product defects were usability problems. Early prototyping and usability testing had a major effect.

Livingstone, Margaret S. (1988) Art, illusion and the visual system. *Scientific American*, January, 68–75. An easy overview of the vision centres for form, colour and movement-depth. Also explains how it relates to the illusions used in graphical arts.

Mallon, Bride & Webb, Brian (2000) Structure, causality, visibility and interaction: propositions for evaluating engagement in narrative multimedia. *International Journal of Human–Computer Studies*, **53**, 269–287. Studied and interviewed users who tried many kinds of multimedia production. Identified critical success factors for such products.

Matlin, Margaret W. & Foley, Hugh J. (1997) *Sensation and Perception*, Allyn and Bacon, Boston, 550 pp. A handbook of what our senses can achieve. Includes vision, hearing, touch, smell and taste.

Mishkin, Mortimer & Appenzeller, Tim (1987) The anatomy of memory. *Scientific American*, June, 62–71. A detailed account of the various brain centres involved in associative memory, linking different kinds of sensory memory, for instance vision, touch, smell and emotions. Also shows that the cognitive association areas (insights) are different from habit-learning (learning by repetition without insight).

Molich, Rolf (2003) Comparative Usability Evaluation – CUE: www.dialogdesign. dk/cue.html. Documents and results available for download from CUE-4 (and earlier comparisons of evaluation methods). In CUE-4, 17 top-level usability teams evaluated the same Web site, 8 of them using heuristic evaluation and 9 usability testing.

Molich, Rolf & Nielsen, Jakob (1990) Improving a human–computer dialogue. *Communications of the ACM*, March, 338–348. The authors designed a user interface to a very simple system that allowed users to enter a phone number and get information about the subscriber to this number. The system had two screens. The authors asked 77 designers and programmers to look at the screens and identify as many problems as possible. The result was a list of 31 potential usability problems. The authors judged 8 of these as serious. They recommended nine heuristic rules and compared the problem list against them. Later Bailey *et al.* (1992) tested whether there was a measurable user effect of correcting these problems. They concluded that correcting just two of the problems had the same effect as correcting all of them.

Nielsen, Jakob (2000) *Designing Web Usability*, New Riders, Indianapolis. A classic about designing contents and appearance of Web sites. Covers many things, for instance what customers look for on Web sites, how to use the space on a Web page, how to organize the entire site, dealing with an international audience, lots of examples of good and bad design, plus suggestions for improving the bad designs.

Norman, Donald A. (1988) *The Psychology of Everyday Things*, Basic Books, New York. A classic about how we intuitively use physical things (affordance) and understand how they work (mental models). The physical things are for instance doors, water faucets, VCRs and keyboards. Gives examples of good and bad affordance, and correct and wrong mental models.

Noton, David & Stark, Lawrence (1972) Eye movements and visual perception. *Readings from Scientific American. Perception: Mechanisms and Models*, W. H. Freeman, San Francisco, 218–227. The authors analysed how subjects moved their eyes when they study large pictures (the scan path). Each subject had his own scan path, but the path varied from picture to picture.

Nygren, Else; Lind, Mats; Johnson, Mats & Sandblad, Bengt (1992) The art of the obvious. *Proceedings of CHI'92*, 235–239. Studied a medical application to find out why users didn't use it. The reason was that the computer version had lost a lot of the visual qualities that the old paper forms had. The users were not aware that they had used these qualities, but responded by not using the new system.

Pan, Bing; Hembrooke, Helene A.; Gay, Geri K.; Granka, Laura A.; Feusner, Mathew K. & Newman, Jill K. (2004) The determinants of web page viewing behavior: an eye-tracking study. *Proceedings ETRA 2004*, San Antonio, TX, ACM, New York. The authors studied how 30 subjects looked at 11 popular Web sites. The subjects scanned the pages in different ways depending on their gender, the type of site, the sequence in which they looked at the pages, etc.

Preece, Jennifer; Rogers, Yvonne & Sharp, Helen (2002) *Interaction Design – Beyond Human–Computer Interaction*, John Wiley & Sons, New York, 500 pp. In many ways similar to Preece *et al.* (1994), but more focused on the design process. Shows a few examples of software engineering notations used during design. Still little about the actual design of the user interface.

Preece, Jennifer; Rogers, Yvonne; Sharp, Helen; Benyon, David; Holland, Simon & Carey, Tom (1994) *Human–Computer Interaction*, Addison-Wesley, Reading, MA, 800 pp. Covers many aspects of HCI, for instance the history of HCI and interviews with people who influenced it, human perception, automatic versus controlled activities, mental models and social aspects, all kinds of input and output devices, components of graphical interfaces, development and design processes, usability evaluation, and experimental design. Little about the actual design of the user interface.

Rasmussen, Jens (1979) On the structure of knowledge – a morphology of mental models in a man–machine system context. Report M-2192, Riso National Laboratory, Roskilde, Denmark.

Rasmussen, Jens (1986) *On Information Processing and Human–Machine Interaction: An Approach to Cognitive Engineering*, Elsevier, Amsterdam.

Redmond-Pyle, David & Moore, Alan (1995) *Graphical User Interface Design and Evaluation*, Prentice-Hall, Europe. One of the few books that actually show a systematic way of designing good user interfaces. Based on usability requirements, task descriptions, data models and evaluation of prototypes. Doesn't use virtual windows, but more abstract *user objects*. The user interface itself is not designed in several steps – even the first screens are complete with functions and navigation. Illustrated with development of a system for supporting a hot-line desk. The main problem with the first prototypes was that there were too many screens (virtual windows might have eliminated this problem). Has a wonderful case story of the previous hot-line system that was developed with participatory design and iterative prototyping, yet failed to provide adequate usability. Only the expert users that had participated in the design were able to use it.

Robertson, James (2002) Eureka! Why analysts should invent requirements. *IEEE Software*, July/August, 22–24. Shows why it isn't enough to give the customer what he asks for. Progress is made by exceeding what the customer even dreamt of. Gives some hints on how to do it.

Robertson, Susanne (2001) Requirements trawling: techniques for discovering requirements. *International Journal of Human–Computer Studies*, **55**, 405–421. An introduction to a long list of elicitation techniques, for known as well as undreamed demands.

Rock, Irvin & Palmer, Stephen (1990) The legacy of gestalt psychology. *Scientific American*, December, 48–61. The history and findings of the gestalt school, and its conflicts with other schools of psychology. Also shows examples of several gestalt laws.

Rousse, Richard (2001) *Game Design, Theory & Practice*, Wordware Publishing, Texas. Defines the 'usability factors' at work in game programs, what players want and expect. Discusses how game ideas are created and transformed to products, tools for game design, etc. Brings interviews with experts in game design.

Rumbaugh, James; Jacobson, Ivar & Booch, Grady (1999) *The Unified Modeling Language Reference Manual*, Addison–Wesley, Reading, MA. (A companion to UML User Guide, see Booch *et al.* 1999).

Shneiderman, Ben (1998) *Designing the User Interface*, Addison-Wesley, Reading, MA. Defines the usability factors *Time to learn*, *Speed of performance*, etc. The factors were defined already in the 1986 version. Also stated the *eight golden rules of dialogue design*. Covers usability from many points of view and gives examples of various kinds of interfaces.

Spence, Robert (2001) *Information Visualization*, Addison-Wesley, Reading, MA. A huge collection of surprising ways to show complex data, illustrated with real-life applications and stories of how the presentation helped solve domain problems. Spence has systematic approaches to the presentation, for instance characterizing it as presentation of univariate, bivariate or trivariate data.

Spool, Jared M. (1997) Market maturity. *Eye for Design*, January/February. Shows that the key requirements change as a market develops. Functional requirements are important early, and usability and other quality requirements later.

Staggers, Nancy & Norcio, A.F. (1993) Mental models: concepts for human–computer interaction research. *International Journal of Man–Machine Studies*, **38**, 587–605. Explains the many views on mental models and the known facts about them.

SUMI (Software Usability Measurement Inventory) Available at: http://www.ucc.ie/hfrg/questionnaires/sumi/. A questionnaire-based evaluation system for user interfaces, sponsored by the European Union. SUMI has 50 questions you can ask for any system. It has a database of how other systems fare on this scale so that you can compare your own system against other's.

Sutcliffe, Alistair (1998) *Human–Computer Interface Design*, MacMillan Education, London, 200 pp. An HCI book with a software engineering focus. Describes practical and more formal ways of specifying interactions. Outlines a design method, and has a few examples of screen design. There is an introductory chapter on human sensation and perception.

Treisman, Anne (1986) Features and objects in visual processing. *Scientific American*, November, 106–115. Explains what creates contrasts and objects, and how it relates to processing in the brain. Gives many fascinating examples of how the visual brain centres mix up things. Might be considered the neural base for the gestalt laws, although the author doesn't mention 'gestalts'.

Tufte, Edward R. (1983) *The Visual Display of Quantitative Information*, Graphics Press, Cheshire, CT. A unique, rich collection of creative ways to present complex data. Good source of inspiration for user interfaces, but offers little systematic approach to choosing the right presentation.

Tufte, Edward R. (1990) *Envisioning Information*, Graphics Press, Cheshire, CT. Another rich collection of ways to present data.

Young, R.M. (1983) Surrogates and mappings: two kinds of conceptual models for interactive devices. In *Mental Models* (eds D. Gentner and A.L. Stevens), Lawrence Erlbaum Associates, Hillsdale, NJ, 35–52.

Zeki, Semir (1992) The visual image in mind and brain. *Scientific American*, September, 43–50. A very detailed description of the vision centres in the brain, blind-sight and many other vision defects.

Index

index (in user documentation) 408
information model *See* data model
innovation (brainstorm) 482
innovation (new tasks) 230, 483
interactive system 4
interface
   – technical 4
   – to user 4
interviewing 475
   – guide (template) 477
ISO (standards) 22
iterative design 44
   – Bruel & Kjaer case 45
   – virtual windows 200
   – weak points 45
iterative development 42, 470

J

Jacobson 162
Jeffries 454
Jeppesen xviii
Jespersen xviii
Johnston xviii
journals, circulation system 558
Jørgensen xviii

K

Karlsson 425
keys (data model) 528
   – primary and foreign keys 500
keys (for searching) 202
keys (function keys and short-cuts) 262
keystroke counts (usability measurement) 29
knowledge management system (case study)
   568

L

lab tests (data presentation) 94
Lauesen 26, 136, 138, 151, 301, 305, 475, 485
laws
   – first usability law (heuristics
   – 50% hit-rate) 19, 458
   – gestalt laws 68–71
   – law of closure 68
   – law of good continuation 68
   – law of lines? 71
   – law of object permanence (Piaget) 106
   – law of parallel movement 70
   – law of proximity 68
   – law of similarity 69
   – second usability law (little correlation …)
     34
   – third usability law (more effort, less …)
     44
learning (transition novice-expert) 264
Leplat 421
library (exercise) 553, 563
life cycle (of mental models) 130
line graph (data presentation) 88
line length (text layout) 76
lines, gestalt law of 71
list format (data presentation) 85
live search 204, 281
Livingstone 83
Lockwood x, 138, 162, 163
log keeper (usability test) 15, 418
logging usability problems, methods 421
logging usability problems, sample log 436

M

magazines, circulation system 558
main menu (start screen) 251
mainframe systems
   – mental model problems 110
   – step-by-step dialogue 125
Mallon 160
manual *See* reference manual
many-to-many relationship 524
map format, data presentation 87
map format, hotel system 187
mapping level (dialogue level) 115
mapping model (mental model) 112
marketing people (finding test users) 425, 426
Matlin 585
matrix format (data presentation) 87, 88
medium problem (usability problem) 13
meeting (arranging one) 156
memory (and concepts) 98
memory (associative) 96

Palmer 68
Pan 427
parallel coordinate plot 90
parallel movement (gestalt law) 70
participatory design 474
patient monitoring 121
perception
    – automatic and controlled 94, 98
    – focus and attention 94
    – multi-sensory association 96, 127
performance measurement (of usability) 22
periodicals, circulation system 558
persistent data 117
phonetic search 204
photocopier (case study) 560
physical level (dialogue level) 116
Piaget 106
planning (classroom allocation) 99
planning (Gantt diagram) 101
platform
    – database driven vs. step-by-step 214
    – for virtual windows 178
    – GUI-based 179
    – page-based 248–53
    – page-based vs. windows-based 244
    – trends 246
    – window-based 253
post conditions for tasks 148
preconditions, for functions 221, 226
preconditions, for tasks 147
prediction ability (mental model) 128
Preece xii, 112, 144
presentation of data *See* data presentation
presentation of functions 260–68
primary key (data model) 500
print functions 227
print functions (undo) 235
probabilities (hit-rates) 458
problems *See also* defects
    – corrections (hotel case) 285
    – corrections and priorities 442
    – counts of (as usability measure) 26
    – CREDO check 190, 194
    – in present user tasks 143

– problem list (test report) 436, 438
– problem list (test reporting) 18
– solutions (theory) 290
– types of 12, 13
– with virtual windows 183
process control (power distribution) xvi, 102
program error (bug) 12
programmer (developer role) 468
programming, hotel system 279
project management system (case study) 560
project planning (Gantt diagram) 101
prototypes 58–64
    – course rating system 340
    – design procedure 274
    – e-mail system 377
    – full contents of 61, 274
    – hotel system, first 50
    – hotel system, last 274
    – large data volumes 62
    – many screens 62
proximity (gestalt law) 68
proximity, law of 71
purpose of a task 147
push buttons 260

Q

quality factor 6
questionnaires 482

R

radar chart (data presentation) 90
Rasmussen 129
real-estate case (abusing usability testing) 56,
    122
realistic data (design rule) 177
records (data model) 139, 489
Redish 413
Redmond-Pyle x, 306, 474
redundant data (data model) 503, 531
reference manual 399
    – contents 404
referential integrity 524
relation (definition) 500